SOCIAL LIFE IN NORTHWEST ALASKA

Men of Kotzebue Sound, 1816. Watercolor by Ludovik Choris. Courtesy of the Beinecke Rare Book and Manuscript Library, Yale University (Western Americana Division, MSS 260, box 2, sketch 28).

SOCIAL LIFE IN NORTHWEST ALASKA

The Structure of Iñupiaq Eskimo Nations

ERNEST S. BURCH, JR.

University of Alaska Press
Fairbanks

© 2006 University of Alaska Press

P.O. Box 756240
Fairbanks, AK 99775-6240
www.uaf.edu/uapress

Printed in the United States.

This publication was printed on paper that meets the minimum
requirements for ANSI/NISO Z39.48–1992 (Permanence of Paper).

Library of Congress Cataloging-in-Publication Data
Burch, Ernest S., 1938–
    Social life in northwest Alaska: the structure of Iñupiaq Eskimo nations / Ernest S. Burch, Jr.
    p. cm.
    Includes bibliographical references and index.
    ISBN 13: 978-1-88963-78-5 (cloth: alk. paper)
    ISBN 10: 1-889963-78-X (cloth: alk. paper)
    ISBN 13: 978-1889963-92-1 (pbk.: alk. paper)
    ISBN 10: 1-889963-92-5 (pbk.: alk. paper)
1. Inupiat—Historiography. 2. Inupiat—Social life and customs. 3. Inupiat—Interviews. 4. First contact
of aboriginal peoples with Westerners—Alaska—History—Sources. 5. Ethnology—Research—Alaska.
6. Alaska—History—Sources. 7. Alaska—Social life and customs. I. Title.

E99.E7B8888 2006
979.8004'9712—dc22   2005051187

Cover and text design by Dixon J. Jones, Rasmuson Library Graphics.

Cover photo: Eunice Sage of Kivalina, wearing a fancy dress parka, early twentieth century. Photo
probably by Ralph Lomen. Courtesy of the Department of Ethnography, National Museum of Denmark,
Copenhagen.

This book is dedicated to Charles Lucier, with thanks
for his generous sharing of information and ideas,
for his frequent challenges to my assumptions and conclusions,
and for his friendship over many years.

Contents

Figures

Maps

Tables

Preface and Acknowledgments

This volume is based on more than forty years of research—in fourteen Alaska Native villages, and in nearly that many libraries and archives. The work was supported financially at various times by the Department of Anthropology, University of Chicago; the Department of Biological Sciences, University of Alaska Fairbanks; the Alaska Historical Commission; NANA Museum of the Arctic; the U.S. National Park Service; the U.S. Minerals Management Service; the Subsistence Division of the Alaska Department of Fish and Game; and the former Canada Council (now the Social Science and Humanities Research Council of Canada). I am grateful to these organizations for their support.

Thanks are due also to the staffs of the Alaska and Polar Regions Department, Rasmuson Library, University of Alaska Fairbanks; the Rare Book, Manuscript, and Special Collections Library of Duke University; the Department of Ethnography, National Museum of Denmark; the Smithsonian Institution; and to Douglas Anderson and Charles Lucier for permission to reproduce illustrations from their collections or reports.

Several individuals have supported my work by sharing information with me, commenting on all or portions of early versions of this volume, or through other kinds of assistance. Specifically, and in alphabetical order, I thank Douglas Anderson, Kelly Anungazuk, the late Laurel Bland, John Bockstoce, Barbara Bodenhorn, Don Callaway, Janet Cohen, Eileen Devinney, Robert Drozda, Ann Fienup-Riordan, William W. Fitzhugh, Robert Fortuine, Lawrence Hamilton, Roger Harritt, Igor Krupnik, Gretchen Lake, Owen Mason, Rachel Mason, Robert McLaughlin, Eileen Norbert, Karen Ongtowasruk, Robyn Russell, Jeanne Schaaf, John Schaeffer, Jack Scott, Tim Sczawinski, Karen Sinnok, Rose Speranza, Julie Sprott, Branson Tungiyan, the late James VanStone, the late Robert Weiser, Clifford and Shirley Weyiouanna, and Peter Whitridge for their help.

Special mention must be made of a few. Charles Lucier has shared with me his field notes and his insights into traditional Iñupiaq life for many years; few colleagues can match his generosity in these respects. Lawrence Kaplan advised me on various linguistic matters, among them being the correct spellings of many Iñupiaq terms; if any of them are rendered properly, it is due to his help. Herbert Anungazuk shared with me his own extensive knowledge of life in Wales, assisted me in some of my fieldwork, and conducted some research himself on my behalf. Finally, Lois Myers provided endless help through research assistance, bibliographic work, and editorial chores.

Finally, I wish to thank the numerous Iñupiaq elders who taught me about the subject matter of this book. They are too numerous to list here, but they are cited throughout the book and listed in the References at the end. I am very grateful for their help.

Iñupiaq Eskimo Orthography

Malimiut Dialect*

CONSONANTS

	Labials	Alveolars	Palatals	Velars	Uvulars	Glottals
Stops	p	t	ch	k	q	'
Voiceless fricatives		s		kh	qh	h
Voiced fricatives	v		y	g	ġ	
Voiceless laterals		ł	ḷ			
Voiced laterals		l	ḷ			
Nasals	m	n	ñ	ŋ		
Voiceless retroflex		sr				
Voiced retroflex		r				

VOWELS

	FRONT	BACK
High	i	u
Low		a

* This is the standard writing system used by Alaskan Iñupiat and by the Alaska Native Language Center, University of Alaska Fairbanks.

Chapter One

Introduction

When they first came to the attention of Westerners in the late 18th and early 19th centuries, the Iñupiaq Eskimos of northwestern Alaska were divided among several social units, which have been variously referred to in English as "societies" (Burch 1980), "nations" (Burch 1998a), and "tribes" (D. J. Ray 1967, 1975b:103–20). In their own language, the Eskimos called them *nunaqatigiich*.[1] But regardless of what label is used, these organizations were the Iñupiaq counterparts of modern nation-states.

This is the third and last of a series of volumes I have written on the early-contact nations of Northwest Alaska. The first, *The Iñupiaq Eskimo Nations of Northwest Alaska* (Burch 1998a), was a social geography in which I (a) identified the nations that used to exist in the region; (b) described their environmental settings; (c) reconstructed the numbers, distribution, and seasonal movements of their members; and (d) described how they met their demise as autonomous social systems. In the second volume, *Alliance and Conflict: The World System of the Iñupiaq Eskimos* (Burch 2005), I described the types of relations obtaining between and among the several nations formerly existing in the region. The purpose of the present volume is to describe how these nations were organized internally and how they functioned.

In addition to presenting a different perspective on Iñupiaq nations than the first two volumes did, this work also focuses on a slightly larger geographic area. It includes not only Northwest Alaska (the NANA Region), but also the Point Hope (Tikiġaq) district immediately to the northwest, and the Shishmaref and Wales districts immediately to the southwest. The change was made because the Tikiġaġmiut of the Point Hope district, and the Kiŋikmiut of the Wales (Kiŋigin) district, were the largest and most complex of all the Iñupiaq nations of northwestern Alaska. Including them expands the range of variation in the phenomena under investigation, which I think makes the study more interesting than it otherwise would have been.

The purpose of this introductory chapter is to set the stage for the analysis that follows. I begin by defining the region and the time period of primary concern. I then briefly describe the early-contact Iñupiaq people and the societies of which they were members. Next, the discussion turns to how I analyze those societies, and how I acquired the information with which to do so. Finally, I present a summary account of the country inhabited by the early-contact Iñupiat (pl.), its climate, and its plant and animal life.

Place and Time

The study region is located in northwestern Alaska between (roughly) Cape Beaufort, on the north, and Cape York, on the south. It includes the entire coastline and all of the drainages reaching the sea between those points (see Map 1). The region is approximately 375 miles (600 km) from east to west, and 240 miles (385 km) from north to south. It was chosen as the focus of my research because Nicholas Gubser (1965), John Murdoch (1892), and Robert Spencer (1959) had published major ethnographies of Iñupiat living farther north, and because E. W. Nelson (1899) and Dorothy Jean Ray (1964, 1967, 1975b, 1984) had published important ethnographic reports on the area just to the south. I thought I could make a greater contribution to knowledge if I focused on the area in between. The geographic extent of my research slightly overlapped the regions covered by the authors mentioned above.

The early-contact period is defined as AD 1800–48. This period was chosen because it is the earliest time on which both oral and documentary sources can shed light, but the latest time in which Iñupiaq societies were essentially free of Western influence. It is thus the only time for which a comprehensive ethnographic account of the structure of Iñupiaq Eskimo nations can be compiled.

The period from 1800 to 1848 was an era in which Western influence, although present, was minimal. Most of the few Westerners who visited the region were interested in exploration rather than exploitation, although some trading vessels did visit it. No doubt a few European genes flowed into the Native population from these strangers, but neither the explorers nor the early traders had much impact on Native ways of life. The worldwide fur trade was just beginning to make its influence felt, but it had not yet led to major changes in the Iñupiaq economy. As of 1848, no European diseases are known to have reached the study region, no Westerners had tried to settle there, and no missionaries or other outsiders had attempted to transform Iñupiaq beliefs or behavior. That situation changed significantly in 1848.

In 1848, two events occurred that initiated an exponential increase in Western influence. One was the arrival of the first American whaling ship in north Alaskan waters (Bockstoce 1984, 1986; Bockstoce and Burns 1993). The number of whalers increased dramatically over the next few years, and by the early 1880s, the whalers had nearly exterminated two pillars of the coastal economies, the bowhead whale and the walrus. From the first, the whalers were accompanied by independent trading vessels whose masters quickly discovered the potential of the Native fur trade.

The second major event, also in 1848, was the arrival of the first of many British Navy ships whose crews were participating in a massive search for the missing expedition led by Sir John Franklin (Bockstoce 1985). The Franklin search lasted seven years, during three of which one ship or another remained in or near the study area over the winter, and during all of which several ships visited the region in summer. These developments initiated Western-Native contacts of unprecedented scale and duration, and led to major changes in Iñupiaq life.

The first attested epidemic struck the region in the late fall of 1851. According to one of John Simpson's sources from Point Barrow,[2] the sickness came from the Asiatic coast, and killed many people in the large villages at Point Hope (Tikiġaq), Icy Cape (Qayaiqsiġvik), Cape Smythe (Utqiaġvik), and Point Barrow (Nuvuk). Forty people died at Point Barrow alone, out of a total population of about 360 (Simpson 1875:237). If the sickness really did

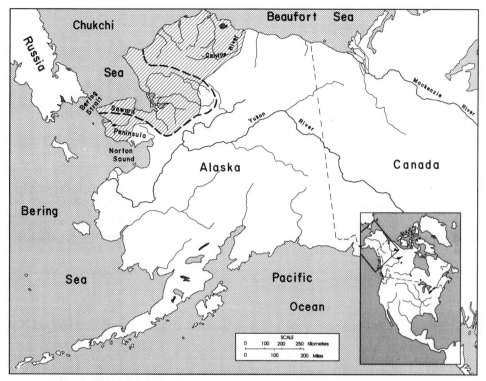

MAP 1. General orientation map. The shading shows the Iñupiaq language area in the early 19th century. The heavy broken line encompasses the portion of it covered by this study.

come from the Asiatic coast, then many others had to have died in the study region as the epidemic swept northward from Bering Strait.

The Iñupiat

The first Westerners to visit Iñupiaq settlements north of Bering Strait arrived there early in the 19th century. They found the country inhabited by a small and widely scattered population of people who depended entirely on hunting and gathering for their existence. These people were the Iñupiaq Eskimos.[3]

In 1816, Otto von Kotzebue (1821), the first Westerner known definitely to have visited the study region, described the Iñupiat as being

> of a middle size, robust make, and healthy appearance; their motions are lively, and they seemed much inclined to sportiveness: their countenances, which have an expression of wantonness, but not of stupidity, are ugly and dirty, character-ized by small eyes and very high cheekbones; they [the men] have holes on each side of the mouth, in which they wear morse [walrus]-bones, ornamented with blue glass beads, which gives them a most frightful appearance. Their hair hangs down long, but is cut quite short on the crown of the head. Their head and ears are also adorned with beads. Their dresses, which are made of skins, are of the same cut as the Parka in Kamtschatka; only that there it reaches to the feet, and here hardly covers the knee; besides this, they wear pantaloons, and small half-boots, of seal-skin (I:209–10).

Ten years later, F. W. Beechey (1831), who spent much more time in the region than Kotzebue did, elaborated:

> Their dress…consisted of a shirt which reached half way down the thigh, with long sleeves and a hood to it, made generally of the skin of the reindeer, and edged with the fur of the gray or white fox, and sometimes with dog's skin. The hood is usually edged with a longer fur than the other parts, either of the wolf or dog.… In wet weather they throw a shirt over their fur dress made of the entrails of the whale, which, while in their possession is quite water tight, as it is then, in common with the rest of their property, tolerably well supplied with oil and grease…(F. W. Beechey 1831, I:340; see also pp. 339, 341, 345, 359, 360).

Beechey (1831, II:300, 303) found the Iñupiat to be "continent, industrious, and provident," but also "warlike, irascible, and uncourteous."[4] In 1838, Aleksandr Kashevarov (VanStone ed. 1977:81, 87–88) found the inhabitants of northwestern Alaska to be "warlike," "well built," and "strong."

Dr. John Simpson (1875), who spent several years in northwestern Alaska in the late 1840s and early 1850s, and who actually measured and weighed several individuals at Point Barrow, described the Iñupiat in greater detail:[5]

> In stature they are not inferior to many other races, and are robust, muscular, and active, inclining rather to spareness than corpulence. The tallest individual was found to be 5 feet 10 inches [180 cm], and the shortest 5 feet 1 inch [155 cm]. The heaviest man weighed 195 lbs. [88.5 kg], and the lightest 125 lbs [57 kg].… Their chief muscular strength is in the back, which is best displayed in their games of wrestling. The shoulders are square, or rather raised, making the neck appear shorter than it really is, and the chest is deep; but in strength of arm they cannot compete with our sailors. The hand is small, short, broad, and rather thick, and the thumb appears short, giving an air of clumsiness in handling anything; and the power of grasping is not great. The lower limbs are in good proportion to the body, and the feet, like the hands, are short and broad, with a high instep (Simpson 1875:238).

Simpson's account applied specifically to people living some distance north of the study region, but it probably applied equally well to the inhabitants of the coastal portions of the region of present concern. However, people living near the head of Kotzebue Sound, and particularly those living in the interior, along the Noatak, Kobuk, Selawik, and Buckland rivers, were described by later observers as being significantly taller, more robust, and more Athapaskan in appearance than their coastal counterparts.[6] The early Iñupiat generally were infested with lice, and many had dark blotches on their faces from frostbite (Hooper 1884:10; Thornton 1931:36–37, 50).

Several early observers commented on Iñupiaq teeth.[7] Simpson (1875) noted that

> the incisors of the lower jaw do not pass behind those of the upper, but meet edge to edge, so that by the time an individual arrives at maturity, the opposing surfaces of the eye and front teeth are perfectly flat, independently of the wear they are subjected to in every possible way to assist the hands (Simpson 1875:239).

With regard to the uses to which teeth were put, John Kelly (Wells and Kelly 1890) claimed that they were

> used for pinchers, vises, and fluting-machines. The teeth are employed in drawing bolts, untying knots, holding the mouth-piece of a drill, shaping boot-soles,

stretching and tanning skins. When they become uneven from hard usage they
are leveled off with a file or whetstone (Wells and Kelly 1890:15).

A more graphic idea of early-19th-century Iñupiaq appearance can be conveyed by
means of some illustrations. These sketches were made by Tim Sczawinski based on early-
19th-century renderings.[8] My analysis of what the sketches show was aided by information
provided by Iñupiaq elders Frieda Larsen (1999), Albert McClellan (1987), Levi Mills (1987),
Thomas Mitchell (1987), and Evans Thomas (1987).

The first illustration (Figure 1) is of a young woman. Her hair has a part (*quppiġñiq*) down
the middle, and the front portion of each side is gathered and bound with a thin strip of
leather (*tugliġun*). She has an ivory amulet (*aanġuaq*) hanging around her neck, and decorative wolverine skin tassels (pl. *niġrat*) on her lightweight summer parka. She also has four
tattoo (sing. *taviuġun*) lines extending from her lower lip to her chin. The second illustration (Figure 2) is of a middle-aged woman who is wearing a rain parka made of walrus or
bearded seal intestine trimmed with bleached and decorated strips of sealskin. Her parka
hood comes to a point, standard for females, and she has one thick and two thin tattoo
lines on her chin. The large hair piece under her chin was probably made from the throat
hair of a bull caribou.

The next two sketches are of men. Both have the characteristic shaved crown, bangs in
front, and longer hair hanging down on the sides and back. Both also have light mustaches,
and some facial hair around the chin. Figure 3 shows a relatively young man wearing a small
labret (*tuutaq*) on each side of his mouth, and goggles (dual *iriġaak*) of the kind worn for
protection against bright sun reflecting off of the snow-covered landscape. A small amulet
is suspended from his parka just below the neck. Figure 4 shows a somewhat older man
wearing a large labret at the right side of his mouth, and a necklace (*quŋusiġun*) consisting
of ivory beads on a sinew string. These accoutrements suggest that he was a man of some
substance. Like the young woman, the men are wearing lightweight summer parkas with
hoods trimmed with short-haired wolf skin.

These four faces hardly represent the full range of variation in early-19th-century Iñupiaq
appearance. However, they do provide a good general idea of how the people whose social
organization is the subject of this book appeared to early Western observers.

Nations

Aleksandr Kashevarov (VanStone ed. 1977:81) was the first Westerner to bring along an
interpreter during his exploration of northwestern Alaska, and he learned a number of
things about Iñupiaq life that his predecessors had missed. Among them was the fact that
the Iñupiat were "divided into several families living in friendly or unfriendly relations with
each other." Kashevarov identified several of these "families" by name, and recorded the
coastal locations of their territorial borders. John Simpson (1875:233), who learned to speak
the Iñupiaq language, characterized Kashevarov's "families" as "sections," which he said were
"named after the portions of land they inhabit or the rivers flowing through them."

The "families" or "sections" noted by Kashevarov and Simpson were mentioned only
sporadically in the ethnographic and historical literature on northwestern Alaska over the following century. Finally, in 1967, Dorothy Jean Ray (1967) wrote an article focusing specifically
on such units. She referred to them as "tribes," characterized them at some length, and identified several whose territories were formerly located on the Seward Peninsula. She said that

FIGURE 1. Sketch of a young woman.

FIGURE 2. Sketch of a middle-aged woman.

FIGURE 3. Sketch of a young man.

FIGURE 4. Sketch of a middle-aged man.

each tribe constituted a "well-ordered society in which a chief and often a council played an important role. The influence of their government extended over a definitely bounded territory within which the inhabitants were directed by a system of rules and laws."

In general, my own research has corroborated Ray's findings. However, instead of referring to these entities as "tribes," I originally denoted them as "societies" (Burch 1980), society being a concept that, if carefully used, is more useful than "tribe" for comparative purposes. More recently, in deference to the wishes of my senior informants, I have taken to referring to them as "nations" (Burch 1998a). "Society" and "nation" are used interchangeably in this volume.

Like the nations we observe and experience in the modern world, those of the early-19th-century Iñupiat were politically autonomous social systems whose members exercised dominion over discrete territories that, for reasons discussed elsewhere,[9] I refer to as their estates. They also generally regarded themselves and acted as separate peoples. In contrast to nations in the modern world, however, those of early-19th-century northwestern Alaska were minute in scale, lacked governments (contra Dorothy Jean Ray), and were supported by an economy based entirely on hunting and gathering. The ages of these nations are unknown, although they were probably reckoned in centuries in most cases by the beginning of the 19th century.[10]

Table 1 lists the nations relevant to this study, identifies the geographic districts in which their estates were located, and indicates both the estimated sizes of the different populations and the approximate areas of the several national estates. Both estimates are for the beginning of the 19th century. The locations of the estates of the specific nations that are the focus of the present study are shown in Map 2.

Table 1. Estates and Populations, ca. AD 1800

Nation	District	Estimated Population	Estimated Estate[a]	
Akuniġmiut	Central Kobuk	700	5,900 mi²	(15,340 km²)[b]
Kaŋiġmiut	Buckland River	300	4,680 mi²	(12,168 km²)[b]
Kiŋikmiut	Wales	800	1,365 mi²	(3,549 km²)[c]
Kiitaaġmiut	Lower Selawik	700	1,860 mi²	(4,836 km²)[b]
Kivalliñiġmiut	Kivalina	365	2,180 mi²	(5,668 km²)[b]
Kuuŋmiut	Kobuk Delta	415	840 mi²	(2,184 km²)[b]
Napaaqtuġmiut	Lower Noatak	300	4,015 mi²	(10,439 km²)[b]
Nuataaġmiut	Upper Noatak	535	5,720 mi²	(14,872 km²)[b]
Pittaġmiut	Goodhope	430	2,725 mi²	(7,085 km2)[b]
Qikiqtaġruŋmiut	Kotzebue	390	2,000 mi²	(5,200 km²)[b]
Siiḷviim Kaŋianiġmiut	Upper Selawik	570	3,175 mi²	(8,255 km²)[b]
Tapqaġmiut	Shishmaref	510	2,550 mi²	(6,630 km²)[c]
Tikiġaġmiut	Point Hope	1,300	4,300 mi²	(11,180 km²)[d]
Totals		7,315	41,310 mi²	(107,406 km²)

[a] = includes the area five miles (8 km) offshore in the case of coastal estates
[b] = Burch (1998a)
[c] = calculated specifically for this volume
[d] = Burch (1981)

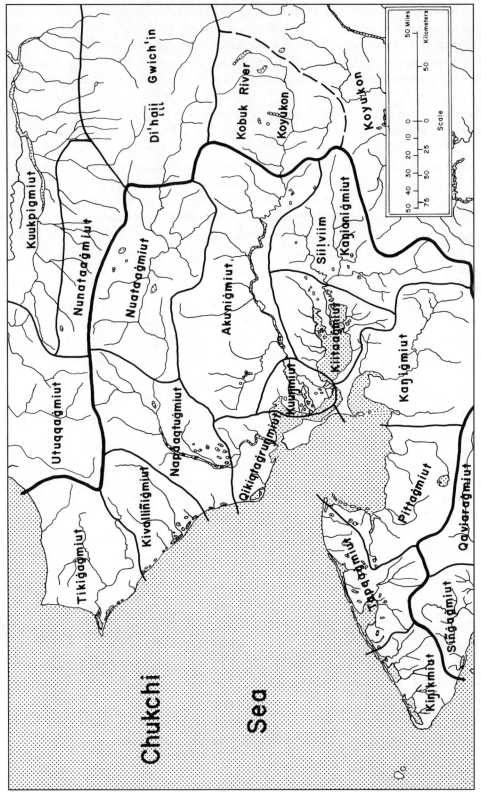

MAP 2. Political map of the study region and adjacent areas, ca. 1800. The nations whose estates are inside the heavy line are the ones covered by the present work.

Iñupiaq Eskimo, or *Iñupiatun,* was the common language throughout most of the study region during the early contact period. Alaskan Iñupiaq was, and still is, divided into two dialect groups (Kaplan 1984:13; 1990:142; 2001:250). One group, North Alaskan Iñupiaq, is divided into two dialects, North Slope and Malimiut. The second dialect group is Seward Peninsula Iñupiaq, which is also divided into two dialects: Qawiaraq and Bering Strait. Each dialect is and was further divided into subdialects. In the early 19th century, each subdialect was associated with a particular nation; nowadays, subdialects are associated with specific villages. The research on which the present study is based was conducted among speakers of all of the dialects except Qawiaraq. However, it was primarily carried out among Malimiut speakers, and most of the Native terms presented in this volume are of Malimiut origin.

During the study period, the headwaters of the Noatak River and the upper portion of the Kobuk River valley, although falling within the study region, were not inhabited by Iñupiat. The Noatak headwaters fell within the estate of the Di'haįį Gwich'in, an Athapaskan people who were driven out of the area by Iñupiat shortly before the mid-19th century (D. Adams 1960.1; Burch 1998b; Burch and Mishler 1995). The upper Kobuk district was inhabited by a Koyukon-Athapaskan-speaking people whose name for themselves is not known with certainty.[11] Over the course of the 19th century, the members of this population were assimilated by Iñupiat (Burch et al. 1999). Virtually nothing is known of the internal organization of these two Athapaskan nations.

Analytic Approach

Contemporary Iñupiat usually like to learn about their ancestors and their ways of life by listening to or reading stories. Unfortunately, however entertaining and informative stories may be, they provide a very inefficient means of telling how Iñupiaq nations operated. For one thing, they usually deal with extraordinary people and events rather than the humdrum of everyday life. This book is concerned with the ordinary as well as the exceptional. In addition, even if stories did contain all the relevant information, tens of thousands of pages would be needed to tell enough of them to cover all the pertinent aspects of Native life. No publisher could afford to produce such a large amount of material, but even if one could, it would take the better part of a lifetime to read.

Like it or not, a more efficient, and more analytical, approach is required. The particular approach I use in this book was developed by Marion J. Levy, Jr. (1952, 1966). Since it is rather different from schemes with which most readers are likely to be familiar, at least some space must be devoted to describing it. In this section I outline its general features; in later chapters I elaborate on the elements most relevant to their particular subject matter.

I introduce the approach by means of an analogy which, although not perfect, may be instructive. I assume that most people who read this book have, from time to time, purchased items requiring assembly before they could be used. The specific analogy is with a snow machine, with one Iñupiaq society being analogous to one snow machine. Because different snow machines are very similar to one another, a description of one serves, at least in general, to describe them all; a few extra comments can deal with variations. Similarly, the Iñupiaq nations were very similar to another, which is why I can describe several of them in roughly the same terms.

Now, assume that you order a snow machine by mail at an enormous cost saving. When it arrives, you find out why it was so cheap: all you get is three large boxes of parts and a set of instructions on how to put them together. Like most such instructions, these are divided into two sections: one listing the machine's individual parts, or components (track, gears, so many nuts and bolts of a certain size, spark plugs, etc.), the other describing how they need to be assembled in order to produce a working snow machine. What you do *not* get is an engineer's analysis of how the machine works once you have it up and running. Topics such as the flow of energy through the system, the stresses to which the different parts are subjected as they grind against one another and the terrain over which the machine travels, how the controls work to start and operate the machine, or the effects of rust and wear on the machine's operation are not discussed.

The analytic approach used in this book is analogous to the instruction book that comes with the snow machine except that it is more complete. In addition to listing the parts and telling how they fit together, I describe how the system works, or, more accurately, used to work. The "system" in this case is not a snow machine, but a traditional Iñupiaq nation. The five basic elements in the approach are outlined in Table 2, along with their mechanical analogs.

Table 2. Basic Elements in Social System Analysis

Social Analysis	Mechanical Analog
Framework	
Role differentiation	Parts, or components
Solidarity	Arrangement of parts
Operation	
Economic process	Energy flow
Political process	Friction, lubrication
Integration process	Information

The basic components of a social system are roles, or positions (e.g., father, female, boss), among which people are allocated. The roles differentiated within an Iñupiaq nation are discussed in Chapter 2.

In order for there to be a social system there has to be more than a set of roles; there must be relationships (e.g., husband-wife, mother-daughter) between and among people filling the various roles. The term used to identify this part of the analysis is "solidarity," which is the subject of Chapter 3. Together, the analytic structures of role differentiation and solidarity constitute the "framework" of a social system, of which a society is one type.

The other three primary aspects of a social system have to do with how it operates; here one speaks of "processes" rather than components and connections. The process that is roughly analogous to the flow of energy through a mechanical system, such as a snow machine, is the economic process, which has to do with the production and consumption of goods and services. The political process concerns the allocation of power and responsibility among the people filling the various roles in the system; this process is roughly analogous to the friction between the moving parts of a snow machine and the ways in which one lubricates them in order to reduce that friction. The final social process, integration, has to do with how people adjust to their life situation. The two major subcategories here are information and motivation; while the former has an analog in some mechanical systems, the latter does not. Separate chapters are devoted to each of these three processes.

All of the primary technical terms employed in the analysis are defined at appropriate places in the text. Since this volume is descriptive rather than theoretical in emphasis, I do not elaborate on their theoretical implications. Readers interested in such a discussion can refer to the sources cited. However, it is appropriate to note at the outset one general attribute of the definitions I use: they almost always denote a broader range of phenomena than those in more common social science usage, not to mention in general discourse. For example, I present in Chapter 5 a definition of "political" denoting what most social scientists refer to as "social control." Given the definition I use, "political" does not require that a government be a subsystem of the nation involved, whereas most definitions do, at least implicitly. My definition facilitates the comparison of the political process in micro-scale societies, such as those of interest here, with those of modern nation-states; most definitions make such a comparison difficult or impossible.

In recent years it has become fashionable to assert that Native science is holistic, whereas Western science is fragmented. The approach I am using might appear at first glance to be an extreme case of fragmentation. Actually it is not. Although the terms I use are likely to be unfamiliar, most Iñupiaq readers should find my approach congenial once they understand it. This is because all I really do in each of the following chapters is look at the same thing—a traditional Iñupiaq nation—from five different points of view. In this approach, one cannot ask whether a given action is *either* economic *or* political *or* integrative, since all human action is characterized by economic, political, *and* integrative features at the same time. The three aspects are discussed separately to avoid confusion, but in every case, one must keep in mind the implications of each for the others.

One of the features of the analytic approach used here is that one cannot argue in general terms about which process or aspect is more (or less) important than any other. They are all equally important because no social system can exist without all of them.[12] In principle, then, an equal amount of space should be devoted to each one. That is impossible, however, because the amount of available information varies considerably from one to another. The relative length of the following chapters is based on the amount of material available to me, not on the relative significance of the subject matter.

The Data

This book is based on two types of data, documentary and oral. The former consist primarily of published and unpublished reports prepared by explorers in the 19th century. The latter consist of accounts about 19th-century phenomena that were obtained from Native oral historians in the 20th century. The two types are discussed separately below.

Documentary Sources

The earliest information we have on Iñupiaq life based on something other than archeological evidence dates from the early 1700s. It was acquired by Russians from the Chukchi (and possibly Asiatic Eskimos), whom they were attempting to subdue by force of arms (Golder 1960:151–62; Majors 1983:98–129). Chukchi knowledge of Alaska was based partly on observations made in the course of intercontinental trade and warfare (Burch 2005:129–32), partly on information acquired from Iñupiaq traders, and partly on conjecture.

In 1732, Mikhail Gvozdev and Ivan Fedorov visited the Diomede Islands, in Bering Strait, the first Westerners known to have communicated directly with Iñupiat (Golder 1960:161). They attempted to collect tribute from the islands' inhabitants, but were forcefully rebuffed. Over the following several decades bits and pieces of information on northwestern Alaska continued to be collected by Russians from Chukchi sources, and by other Westerners during brief visits to the Alaskan coast. The latter include James Cook, who visited Norton Sound, the Seward Peninsula, and Bering Strait in 1778 (Beaglehole 1967:1433–41);[13] Nikolay Daurkin, who visited the Diomede Islands in 1763 (Masterson and Brower 1948:64–67); Ivan Kobelev, who visited the Diomedes in 1779, and the Diomedes, Wales, and King Island in 1791 (Chernenko 1957); and Joseph Billings, whose expedition visited Bering Strait and the Seward Peninsula in 1791 (Merck 1980; Sarychev 1806–7, II:44–42; Sauer 1802:242–48). Most of these expeditions involved contacts just south of the region of primary interest here.

During the early decades of the 19th century occasional Russian and English exploring expeditions visited the study region, and each of them made contact with Iñupiat.[14] The one led by Otto von Kotzebue, in 1816, first brought the region to the world's attention, and left Kotzebue's name etched permanently on the regional map (Chamisso 1986; Choris 1822; Kotzebue 1821). Much more informative, however, were the observations made by Frederick W. Beechey (1831), in 1826 and 1827, and by Aleksandr Kashevarov, in 1838 (VanStone ed. 1977).

After a hiatus in the early and mid-1840s, Europeans returned to northern Alaska in considerable numbers during the Franklin search expeditions of 1848–55. In addition to having a significant impact on Native life, these expeditions also resulted in the collection of a considerable volume of useful information. Of particular importance are the ethnographic data acquired by John Simpson (1875), whose work is cited throughout this book.

The final Franklin search vessels left north Alaskan waters in 1855. The activities of American whalers continued with only occasional interruption for nearly another sixty years, however, and Western traders continued to operate in the region. Unfortunately, none of them recorded much information on Native life.

In 1878, the United States government began to extend its hegemony over northwestern Alaska through annual summer patrols by vessels of the U.S. Revenue Marine. The objectives of these cruises were to establish a U.S. government presence in Alaskan waters, to impose customs duties on traders where necessary and appropriate, and to enforce a ban on the sale of alcohol and firearms to members of the Native population (D. J. Ray 1975b:188–94). During the 1880s, the members of several of these expeditions produced a number of extremely useful reports on Native life.[15] Also traveling in and writing about the area during that decade were Charles Brower (ms), John W. Kelly (Wells and Kelly 1890), George Stoney (1900), and Henry D. Woolfe (1893). Harrison R. Thornton (1931) wrote a highly informative book on Wales based on his personal observations there in 1890–93.

By 1910, the traditional Iñupiaq nations had ceased to exist as autonomous social systems (Burch 1998a). In principle, control of disruptive forms of behavior had been taken over by U.S. commissioners and deputy marshals supported, if necessary, by the U.S. military, although minor matters were still handled at the local level. Foreign policy had been taken over by the U.S. government, and government intervention (usually through local teachers) in the daily life of the Natives was becoming pervasive. Most of the Iñupiat in the study region had been converted to Christianity. The Iñupiat people survived, but they were beginning the long process of assimilation by the United States (Burch 1998a:323–27). It was at this point that oral historians began to replace documents as sources of information on 19th-century Iñupiaq life.

Oral Sources

The threshold between documentary and oral history research was marked by the work of Vilhjalmur Stefansson, Knud Rasmussen, and Edward Curtis. They were the last investigators to meet people who actually lived during or very near the end of the study period, and the first to interview Iñupiat about what life used to be like.

Vilhjalmur Stefansson (1914b, 1944, 1951) was an explorer and ethnographer. As far as I know, he never set foot inside the study region. However, he spent quite a bit of time in northern Alaska, where he learned to speak fluent Iñupiatun. While there, he met and hired as assistants some immigrants from the Kotzebue Sound area, and he lived with them for prolonged periods between 1908 and 1918. From them he acquired a fair amount of information relevant to this volume even when he was living and working in northern Canada.

Knud Rasmussen (Ostermann and Holtved 1952; Rasmussen 1925, 1932, 1933) visited northern Alaska in the spring of 1924, at the end of his epic sled journey across the northern part of the continent. A native of Greenland, he was able to converse with Iñupiat in a dialect comprehensible to them immediately upon his arrival. Although he was in the region for only a few months, his linguistic ability and his keen interest enabled him to acquire considerable useful information about traditional Iñupiaq life.

Edward Curtis (1930) was a photographer who visited western Alaska in the summer of 1927 in the final stage of his monumental effort to photographically record traditional Native American life before it became impossible to do so. Working through an interpreter, he also collected myths and legends, and recorded descriptions of customs and conditions in Native communities. His book on Alaska contains chapters on Wales, Kotzebue, Noatak, Kobuk, and Selawik, all relevant to the present work.

Those of us who came after Curtis have relied for our information entirely on Native historians who learned about traditional ways of life from their parents and grandparents. Many of our sources were raised while storytelling was still the primary means whereby historical information was transmitted from one generation to the next. Others had been reindeer herders who had walked all over the country during the early decades of the 20th century, who found remains of former settlements and other residue of earlier years, and who inquired about what they saw. And finally, a few were simply intellectuals who were fascinated by the history of their people and who made it their business to find out about it from knowledgeable elders.

The investigators whose work contributed most directly to this volume were Froelich Rainey, Don Charles Foote, Albert Heinrich, and Charles Lucier. In each case, I was able to draw not only on their publications but also on their field notes.

Froelich Rainey (1907–92) spent the period January–July 1940 in Point Hope investigating the traditional Iñupiaq way of life (Bockstoce 1993). He published a slender although well-regarded monograph and a few articles based on this work, but they do not reflect the impressive breadth and depth of his research as demonstrated in his field notes.[16]

Don Charles Foote (1932–69) carried out extensive geographical research in Point Hope, Noatak, and the upper Kobuk, during the period 1959–65 (*Tundra Times* 1969). His premature death prevented him from publishing the results of his oral history studies, but he left behind an excellent set of field notes.[17]

Albert Heinrich spent much of the period 1944–55 in the Bering Strait area, during which he became interested in and did considerable research on the kinship system in several villages, including Wales and Shishmaref. His findings were summarized in a few articles and a PhD thesis, but much more useful information (for present purposes) is contained in his MA thesis and field notes.[18] Heinrich was not an historian, but he contributed more than anyone before him to an understanding of how Iñupiat communities operated.

Finally, Charles Lucier did his research primarily in Buckland and in the Kotzebue area in 1951–52. Although he has published several papers based on this work, his field notes contain a considerable amount of as-yet-unpublished data, which he has very generously permitted me to use.[19]

My own field research was carried out in all parts of the study region between 1960 and 1999. In 1960–61, I spent nearly eleven months engaged in a participant-observation study of subsistence in Kivalina (Saario and Kessel 1966). At the time, Kivalina was a conservative community with a population of about 150 people whose houses were built in extended family clusters. Half of the twenty-four dwellings were covered with sod. Travel was by dog team in winter and by skin-covered or wooden boat in summer. The people were overwhelmingly dependent on hunting and fishing for their livelihood. The village had a one-room school over which a single (usually) non-Native teacher presided, two Christian churches under the supervision of Native preachers, and a village store. Government housing programs, surveyed property lines, electricity, television, telephones, the widespread use of snow machines, and the general use of stove oil for heat all lay a decade or more in the future.

In 1964 I returned to Kivalina for seven months with my wife, Deanne, to conduct another participant-observation study. Except for recent births, deaths, and the addition of two families who had moved over from Noatak, the village was unchanged from my earlier visit. The focus of the research this time was family relationships (Burch 1975a). The family study was completed in 1965 with another four-month stay in the village, during which my primary technique of data collection shifted from participant observation to formal interviews.

During all of my research up to this point I was more interested in what was happening while I was in the village than I was in the past. However, through the collection of personal and family histories in conjunction with my study of family life, and through the examination of sixty years' worth of community records stored in the school, I was able to develop a fairly comprehensive understanding of both continuity and change in the Kivalina district from the time of my research back to about 1880.

In 1969 I returned to Alaska, this time with my wife and two daughters, for a nine-month period of intensive research. My objectives were to broaden the geographical scope of my knowledge of Iñupiaq life, and to extend it farther back through time. I was based in Kotzebue, but visited a number of other communities. My primary research technique consisted of formal interviews with elders who the Natives themselves considered to be expert historians.[20] Fortunately, my knowledge of life in Kivalina gave me an invaluable background for this type of investigation. This was because my new sources could readily compare and contrast what I had observed or learned about life in Kivalina with patterns existing in other villages and/or at earlier points in time.

I had not intended to conduct a study of social change in 1969–70, but that is what I ended up doing. I had to because, in order to find out with some degree of reliability what Iñupiaq life had been like in the early 19th century, I had to determine what changes had taken place since then and when and why they had occurred. In the process, of course, I also learned what had remained the same.

Since 1970, I have returned to northwestern Alaska fourteen times on brief (two-to-three-week) research trips during which I have traveled to all of the communities in the study region that I had not visited previously. In addition to investigating other subjects during these trips, I attempted to fill in gaps or reconcile discrepancies in my earlier material. Over this thirty-year period, the number of elders who commanded special knowledge of 19th-century affairs steadily declined to the point where virtually none is left. This development brought the period of fruitful oral history research on Iñupiaq nations to a close.

Methodology

The primary method used in preparing the reconstruction of early-19th-century Iñupiaq life presented in this book is what ethnohistorians call "upstreaming" (Fenton 1962).[21] This involves the interpretation of information about the past in the light of patterns discovered in the present, and "linking these to earlier patterns in a direct sequence, but against the tide of history, going from the known present to the unknown past" (Fenton 1962:12). Upstreaming requires one to do a study of social change, even if, as in this book, it is the initial period that is of primary interest.

Beyond that, there was nothing mysterious about how the work was carried out. Levy's analytic framework posed the questions, and the documentary and oral sources, separately or in combination, provided the answers. For example, the model says that *if* a society is to persist, there must be role differentiation on the basis of absolute age, relative age, generation, sex, economic allocation, political allocation, cognition, the nonhuman environment, and solidarity (Levy 1952:306–7). My job was to go through the data, see what information I could find concerning those topics, organize it, and present it in a comprehensible way. Following that general procedure, I simply worked my way through the model and the data.

The challenging part was to ensure that data required by Levy's demanding model were available. Toward that end, much of my fieldwork was designed to fill gaps in the existing knowledge of Iñupiaq societies. The various requirements of the model, my knowledge of the information contained in the early documentary sources, and my awareness of the research done by others were influential in guiding my own investigations.

In the preparation of this book, and particularly in writing parts of Chapter 4, I relied rather heavily on the work of other investigators in addition to the explorers and researchers mentioned above. My contribution here was to bring together the many scattered bits of information obtained by them and to present the resulting synthesis in terms of a single theoretical framework.

But how, one may ask, can I be sure that the phenomena described in this book did in fact occur during a forty-eight-year period that ended more than a century and a half ago? Before I address that issue, I wish to make clear the fact that I am not claiming that these phenomena were *restricted* to that period. I have little doubt that, at least at the level of detail I am able to employ here, they originated well before 1800, and I know from observations I have made personally since 1960 that many of them still exist today, albeit in modified form.

Returning to the question posed above: the short answer is that I cannot be absolutely certain that all of the phenomena I describe here were in existence during the study period. However, I am reasonably confident of it. Many of the data on which this volume is based were acquired from Native historians long after the fact, and there is no suitable documentary or archeological information against which one may test them. However, much of the oral history material on which I based two other volumes *could* be tested, and it was always cor-roborated. Initially very cautious about the conclusions that could be drawn on the basis of oral history data, I have gradually acquired enormous confidence in the accuracy of what my informants told me (Burch 1991).

Of greater concern to me than the validity of claims of knowledge about the early 19th century is the certainty that an enormous amount of information on traditional Iñupiaq life has been lost. I have attempted to compensate for gaps in my own data by using information obtained by others, and this has helped considerably. But there is no denying the fact that what I present here is a broad outline, and not a thorough description, of early-19th-century Iñupiaq life. A further limitation due to the time gap between now and the study period is a tendency to emphasize ideal patterns of behavior at the expense of actual ones. In other words, I have more information on how people were *supposed* to act than on how they actu-ally did act. This weakness was offset to some extent by the fact that every one of my Native sources was aware of the difference between ideal and actual behavior, and some of them made a point of making sure that I understood the difference myself.

Citations

Since I was privileged to work with so much original material in the preparation of this volume, it seemed appropriate to employ an unusual procedure in identifying my sources. Wherever possible, instead of citing the researcher as the source of my information, I cite the specific informant(s) who provided the researcher with the information in the first place. Thus, with regard to material I collected myself, instead of following the customary procedure of making a general reference to my field notes, I cite both the specific person who gave the information to me and the date on which he or she did so. Similarly, instead of making a vague general reference to Froelich Rainey's field notes, I cite the specific informant who gave him the information.

Information on the Iñupiaq contributors to a number of other useful bodies of information is also available, and, in many such cases, the reference will be to the original source of the information rather than the organization or person who acquired or published it. Included in this category are the unpublished records of the Bureau of Indian Affairs investigations of historic and cemetery sites under the Alaska Native Claims Settlement Act (ANCSA), the NANA Cultural Heritage Project, the NANA Elders Council, the National Park Service, and the Kawerak Eskimo Heritage Project. Published records of this nature include a number of volumes produced by the Northwest Arctic Borough School District[22] and the National Bilingual Materials Development Center,[23] and a single publication of data collected by the Mauneluk Cultural Heritage Program (Gray et al. 1976).

Where their identity is known, individual informant's names are included in the list of sources right along with the authors of books, articles, and manuscripts. The procedure is unwieldy because of the number of people and interviews involved, and because of varia-tions in the way different investigators recorded and organized their material. However, this approach seemed to me to be the best way to establish with precision the authority on which this book rests. It is also an effective way to credit the specific individuals who contributed to what is likely to remain as an enduring record of their ancestors' ways of life. Finally, since all or most of this unpublished material already is, or eventually will be, accessible to the public in archival settings, the approach will assist future investigators in locating data of particular interest to them.

The Geographic Setting

The final task remaining to be accomplished by way of introduction to this volume is to present a summary description of the country in which the Iñupiat lived. To this I now turn.

The study region is located far enough to the north that the Arctic Circle crosses it about seventy-five miles (120 km) north of its southern border. At the circle, the sun is continuously above the horizon for twenty-four hours at the summer solstice, in late June, and below it for twenty-four hours at the winter solstice, in late December. The seasonal variation in the amount of sunlight increases exponentially with distance north of the line, so differences in the amount of light received on any given day at Point Hope, on the north, and Wales, on the south, are obvious to even a casual visitor. Because of refraction, or the bending of light passing through Earth's atmosphere, the total amount of sunlight reaching the region over the course of a year theoretically exceeds the total amount of darkness,[24] although cloud cover often negates this effect. In summer, the potential warming effect of prolonged daylight is offset to a considerable degree by the low angle of the sun, which travels around the horizon rather than across the sky in the course of its daily circuit. It is also often offset by cloud cover. In winter, the inhibiting effect of darkness is reduced by the fact that the country is covered with snow, which reflects the light received from the moon and stars.[25] From about mid-March to late May, when there is both an ample (and a steadily increasing) amount of daylight *and* snow on the ground, the glare is intense.

The Landscape

The major features of the landscape are shown in Map 3. Most conspicuous are several mountain groups of the Brooks Range, on the north, the Chukchi Sea (including Kotzebue Sound), on the west, and three major river systems—the Noatak, Kobuk, and Selawik—crossing the region from east to west near the center. The western sector of the Brooks Range consists of four mountain groups: the Baird, De Long, Endicott, and Schwatka mountains. All were glaciated during the Pleistocene and much of the terrain in and around them today is characterized by postglacial landforms. A few small glaciers remain in the highest and most rugged upland in the study region, the Schwatka Mountains, whose highest point is Mount Igikpak, with an elevation of 8,510 feet (2,594 m).

Outside the mountains, the country features several ranges of low, generally rounded gray hills, and a number of broad, often nearly featureless lowlands covered by thaw lakes, marshes, pingos, and patterned ground. The lowlands generally are underlain by alluvium, and by windblown sand and soil deposited in early postglacial times. In most places, these deposits have become consolidated and covered with vegetation, but a few sand dunes remain active in the Kobuk valley. Baldwin Peninsula, which forms most of the eastern border of Kotzebue Sound, is the terminal moraine of glaciers that pushed gravel and soil out of the Kobuk and Selawik valleys during the early Pleistocene. Most of the largest interior lakes in the region were formed where moraines dammed waterways after the glaciers melted. Portions of the Seward Peninsula are covered by an ancient lava flow, and much of the plain extending southward from Cape Espenberg is covered with a layer of volcanic ash. The entire

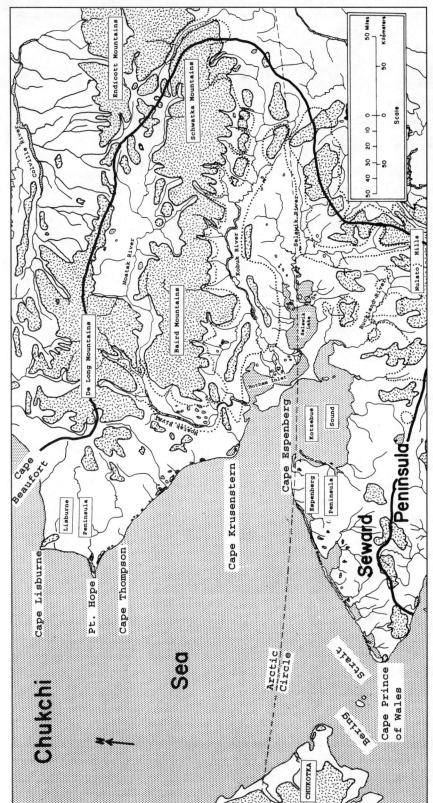

MAP 3. Geographic setting of the study region. The dotted line shows the location of the tree line. The forested zone is toward the east and south of that line.

study region is underlain by permanently frozen soil and rock (permafrost), only the top few inches (ca. 10 cm) of which thaw during the summer.

The southeastern Chukchi Sea (including its innermost arm, Kotzebue Sound) is a relatively shallow body of water whose floor slopes gently downward toward the northwest. Its shore consists primarily of long stretches of gravel beach behind which lagoons have formed in many areas. Prominent capes punctuate the coastline at Cape Lisburne, Cape Thompson, and Cape Prince of Wales, as do smaller ones along the south coast of Kotzebue Sound and along the Chukchi Sea coast north of Point Hope. Capes Krusenstern and Espenberg, which form the northern and southern limits, respectively, of Kotzebue Sound, technically should be called "points." Rather than being the type of eminence usually associated with the word "cape," they, like Point Hope, are cheniers, which are low plains of beach gravel heaped up by current and wave action over the millennia into series of parallel beach ridges.

Tides are minimal in the region, the highest being about four feet (1.22 m) in Eschscholtz Bay, at the extreme southeastern corner of Kotzebue Sound. Tides have so little impact on human affairs in the region that, at many places along the coast, people are only vaguely aware of their existence. Storm surges, on the other hand, can raise the level of the sea by several feet (ca. 2 m). Strong offshore winds have exactly the opposite effect.

The rivers and the seashore were very conducive to travel in the large open boats, called *umiat* (sing. *umiaq*), formerly used by the Iñupiat. Although paddles and sails could be and often were used to power these craft, the most common procedure was to track them along the beach or riverbank with the aid of dogs. When the sea got rough, it was possible in many places to portage the craft and its contents across the barrier beach to the protected waters of a lagoon and proceed. It was necessary to paddle or sail around the capes, however, and rough weather in their vicinity brought coastal travel to a halt. In the rivers, the main obstacle to boat tracking is heavy shrub growth along the banks. However, most downriver movements were made in early summer, when water levels are high and tracking was unnecessary. Later in the summer, when people traveled back upstream, lower water levels often expose long gravel bars in most of the rivers, making tracking relatively easy. (High water, on the other hand, made tracking very difficult.)

Like Alaska in general, northwestern Alaska is regarded by most people as being a set of pristine landscapes virtually unchanged by man. That view is basically correct except in the vicinity of Red Dog mine and its port site, southeast of Kivalina; the Bornite area, in the Kobuk River valley; and areas around the modern settlements (see Map 4). However, humans have had some impact on the landscape in other areas as well. Mining operations at the end of the 19th century and in the first few decades of the 20th led to the silting up of several rivers and streams on the north side of the Seward Peninsula. This resulted in significantly reduced fish runs in several river systems. In the Selawik district, even in the early contact period, the Natives themselves sometimes dug trenches between landlocked lakes and nearby rivers. Water rushing out of the lakes enlarged the trenches into permanent channels linking the two bodies of water. In contrast to mining operations, this type of work frequently had a positive effect on fish populations by opening up new spawning areas and migration routes for them.

Natural geomorphological processes have always been at work, of course, and the landscape is not the same now as it was two hundred years ago despite the modest amount of human intervention. In the interior, the most common changes have been rearrangements of watercourses, as floods eroded bluffs, created new channels and blocked off old ones, and

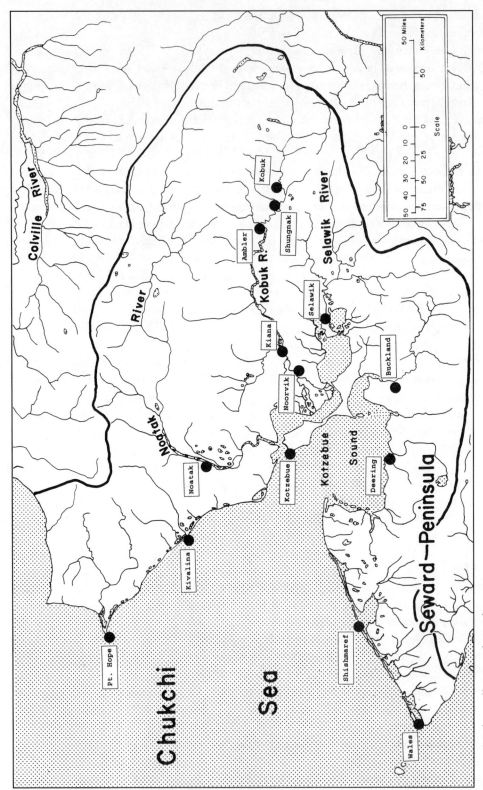

MAP 4. Modern villages in the study region.

altered the structure of gravel bars and fishing holes. Since most interior-dwelling Iñupiat spent (and spend) the winters living on or near riverbanks, these developments have necessitated periodic changes in settlement location, probably since time immemorial. Many early-19th-century sites have washed out, while others have survived at a steadily increasing distance from the water's edge. In the northeastern corner of Selawik Lake, Shoniktok Point, formerly a major hunting area, is reportedly greatly reduced from its early-19th-century size. Many lakes that used to exist, including some that were once considered good places to fish or drive caribou, have silted up and become marshes or grasslands since the beginning of the study period. On the other hand, many thaw lakes formed on permafrost have gradually expanded, while others have changed their location and shape due to wave action and permafrost melting.

On the coast, wind and current have built up shorelines in some places, but have eroded them away in others. Over the last two hundred years there have been major changes in the shoreline at Point Hope, at the sites of the modern communities of Kivalina, Kotzebue, Shishmaref, and Wales, at Capes Krusenstern and Espenberg, and at Sheshalik Spit. Presumably all of these trends originated in ancient times.

Climate

The climate of the study region is a function of its far northern location, the land/sea transition, the generally northward flow of water in the southeastern Chukchi Sea, and the blocking effect of the Brooks Range.[26] The far northern location of course means that the climate generally is cold. However, it is relatively moderate for such a high latitude, partly because of the flow of relatively warm surface water out of the Pacific Ocean into the Chukchi Sea, and partly because the Brooks Range helps shield most of the region from the cold, heavy air of the Arctic Slope.

Winter temperatures typically are much colder inland than they are along the coast, whereas in summer the pattern is just the reverse.[27] During the period 1956–80, average temperatures at the coastal town of Kotzebue in the warmest month, which is usually July, were ordinarily in the 50s F (10° to 15° C), with extremes of 30° and 85° F (–1° and 30° C). At Kobuk village, about 150 miles (240 km) inland, average July temperatures tended to be in the mid- to upper 60s F (13° to 15° C), with extremes of 29° and 92° F (–1.6° and 33° C). In the coldest month, usually February, temperatures at Kotzebue averaged around –3° F (–16° C), with a range of –52° to 40° F (–47° to 4° C). At Kobuk, February temperatures averaged about –10° F (–12° C), with extremes of –65° and 38° F (–54° and 3° C). Since the period covered in this book was during "the little ice age," temperatures may have been significantly cooler than the above figures suggest.[28]

The seasonal contrast between coastal and interior climatic regimes often creates a monsoon effect. In winter, atmospheric pressure over the land is generally higher than it is over the Chukchi Sea, which leads to a prevailing surface flow of easterly wind moving down the major river drainages toward the coast.[29] In summer, the pattern tends to be just the reverse. These normal conditions are altered from time to time by cyclonic storms boiling up from the south, and by pressure systems strong enough to overcome local circulation tendencies.

The impact of the cold winter temperatures on humans is increased by windchill, which significantly raises the chances of frostbite and hypothermia. Wind is nearly constant on the coast, blowing at an annual average speed of 13 mph (21 kph) at Kotzebue. It is generally lighter and more variable inland, although topography has a considerable influence on local wind conditions. Some interior localities are notorious blowholes, while others remain calm even in the midst of violent storms.

Low temperatures resulted in frozen waterways for much of the year. Freshwater freezeup began at higher elevations inland, usually in September. By mid-October, most of the rivers and lakes in the study region were covered with ice. Saltwater freezeup began in the inner reaches of Kotzebue Sound in late October, and along the outer shorelines somewhat later. Kotzebue Sound was usually completely frozen by early December, with the rest of the southeastern Chukchi Sea following a week or two later. The breakup process began near the headwaters of the creeks and rivers in early to mid-May, and usually reached the sea by the end of May or early June. The breakup of the saltwater ice took another month or more to complete, the ocean finally becoming ice-free by early to mid-July.

During the ice-free period cloudy skies generally prevailed, and daily temperatures were relatively uniform. When the ocean and rivers were frozen, the climatic characteristics tended to reverse. For the traditional Iñupiat, freezeup and breakup were major environmental thresholds having a profound effect on the way people moved about. When the waterways were open, journeys were made mostly by boat, whereas during the freezeup period, they were made mostly with sleds.

Precipitation was generally light (Bowling 1985; National Climatic Data Center 1984). Annual amounts ranged between about 5 and 14 inches (13–36 cm) at Kotzebue, with an overall average of about 8 inches (20 cm). In the 20th century, annual precipitation at the interior village of Kobuk was nearly double that received at Kotzebue. In all parts of the study region, precipitation fell mostly as rain during the months of July, August, and September. Because the ground was permanently frozen, runoff approached 100 percent. This greatly magnified the impact of rainfall on water levels. Two or three consecutive days of what might be considered little more than a heavy mist in many other parts of the world can lead to flooding here.[30] In traditional times, a rainy summer made overland travel hazardous because of the danger of fording swollen creeks; fishing was made impossible by the swift current; and ascending the rivers by hand-pulled boats was difficult because of the force of the current and the submergence of gravel bars.[31]

From early October until early May, most precipitation was in the form of snow, although snow could fall in any month of the year. During the 1956–80 period, average annual snowfall at Kotzebue was about 50 inches (130 cm), with a maximum of about 70 inches (175 cm). At the interior village of Kobuk, the average annual snowfall was slightly more than 56 inches (142 cm), with a maximum recorded snowfall of 82 inches (208 cm) in one winter. Although the amount of snowfall did not differ greatly between the interior and the coast, it was differently affected by wind in the two sectors. In coastal areas, where the wind blows more or less constantly, the snow often became packed hard enough after a month or two for a person to walk on it without breaking through. In the interior, particularly in forested areas, the wind was less relentless, and the snow on the ground was often soft and rather deep by mid-winter. In most interior areas, therefore, people had to use snowshoes to get around in winter, and trails had to be broken for dogs or people pulling sleds. In most coastal areas this was unnecessary.

The above description applies to Kotzebue Sound, and to the Noatak, Kobuk, and Selawik drainages. To the northwest, the weather is much more strongly influenced by systems on the north side of the Brooks Range. This sector is generally drier, colder, and windier than Kotzebue throughout the year, but particularly in winter, when northerly winds prevail. The transition between the arctic climate and that of Kotzebue Sound is amazingly abrupt. A coastal traveler going from Cape Lisburne to Kotzebue can experience blizzard conditions the whole way from the cape to a point just south of Kivalina, pass into calm air within the space of a few miles (ca. 10 km), and complete the journey quite comfortably. Inland, the eastern border of the arctic air mass seems to follow the western margin of the De Long Mountains.

In the southwestern sector of the study region, along the northern shore of the Seward Peninsula, the climate is generally a bit warmer and more moist than it is at Kotzebue. The distinguishing feature of the climate in this area is the comparatively high frequency with which it is struck by cyclonic storms coming north out of the Bering Sea. These may occur at any time of year, but they are particularly disruptive in winter, when they can cause sudden thaws and flooding, only to be followed by an abrupt return to subfreezing temperatures.

Vegetation

The most notable feature of the vegetation of the study region is its division into two parts by the latitudinal tree line.[32] As indicated in Map 3, the tree line strikes irregularly westward across the northern side of the Kobuk River valley to Kotzebue Sound, curves northward to encompass much of the lower portion of the Noatak River valley, then angles southward across the eastern portion of the Seward Peninsula. North of, or, more accurately, outside of, the tree line, the country is covered by tundra vegetation. South of, or within, the tree line, the landscape is dominated by northern boreal forest except at higher elevations, where tundra prevails, and on level plains, most of which are covered by marshlands. During the study period, the tree line was a bit farther south than it is now. Since the study period, local changes in vegetation have occurred from time to time due to tundra and forest fires caused by lightning, and to overgrazing by domesticated reindeer.

Tundra is a cold-climate plant community lacking trees (Viereck et al. 1992:276). Instead of trees, the vegetation consists of a variety of mosses, lichens, forbes, grasses, and dwarf shrubs. Even in this seemingly barren region, a wide variety of plants grow whose leaves, fruit, bark, or roots are potentially beneficial to humans for food, medicine, and a number of other important purposes (A. Jones 1983; Viereck 1987). It is also true that, even within the tundra zone, a heavy growth of large shrubs (willows, poplars, alders), punctuated by groves of balsam poplar reaching 10 feet (3 m) or more in height, is frequently found on floodplains, along riverbanks, and in protected, well-drained areas. Finally, one must note that, before the introduction of wood-burning stoves around the beginning of the 20th century, the beaches of northwestern Alaska were littered with enormous quantities of driftwood, most of which came from interior Alaska via the Yukon River and the current flowing north through Bering Strait.[33]

Forest is a plant community made up predominantly of trees and other woody plants, growing more or less closely together (Viereck et al. 1992:263). Common trees in northwestern Alaska are white spruce, black spruce, paper birch, balsam poplar, aspen, and tamarack, all of which occur in various combinations, both with one another and with understory plants. Within the boreal forest, tree growth is greatest along the lower slopes of hills, along riverbanks, and in lowland areas with diminished permafrost influence. Even within the forested zone, there are large expanses of bog and tundra, and tundra vegetation is ubiquitous at higher elevations.

Animal Life

The Iñupiat were dependent primarily on hunting and fishing, and secondarily on gathering, for raw materials. They did not, and for all practical purposes *could* not, grow crops of any kind. Their only domesticated animal was the dog, which was used as a draft animal.

Anthropological works on northwestern Alaska often use phrases like "great herds" to characterize the game populations of the study region (e.g., D. J. Ray 1964:79). This contrasts sharply with the views expressed by some 19th-century observers, however. For example, in July 1885, S. B. McLenegan (1887:69), who was exploring the upper Noatak River, observed that "the almost entire absence of life is one of the characteristic features of this region." Similarly, toward the end of the 19th century, Eugene McElwaine (1901), whose northern experience was on Kotzebue Sound and in the Kobuk River valley, claimed that

> one may travel for weeks along the coast, up the streams, over the tundra and through the woodlands of Arctic Alaska without seeing an animal larger than a muskrat or a ground squirrel, and should the traveler carry a rifle he would probably find it a useless incumbrance [sic], and to lighten his pack, would likely trade off the gun to the first aboriginal he chanced to meet (McElwaine 1901:182).

How does one reconcile these opposing views?

The answer is that most of the animal and fish populations on which the Iñupiat relied are extremely dynamic, undergoing dramatic fluctuations in distribution and numbers, both seasonally and over the longer term. At certain times of year there is, indeed, hardly a bird or mammal to be seen anywhere. As luck would have it, both McLenegan and McElwaine were in the country during precisely such a season, but also during an era when the populations of large game were low. Today, even though most of the game populations have been restored, one can travel over the same country in July and August, and see scarcely any more animals than they did. However, McLenegan and McElwaine ignored fish, which are especially abundant at the time of year when the most conspicuous land animal—caribou—is at its scarcest.[34]

Land Mammals

The barren-ground caribou was the terrestrial mammal of primary importance to the Iñupiat. Caribou hides were the primary clothing material throughout the study region; from them, people also made tent covers, packs, bags, bedding, and other goods. From the meat and organs people acquired food, and from their antlers and bones they made components of tools and weapons.

Nowadays, the study region falls within the range of a single herd, the Western Arctic Caribou Herd (WACH). During the early 19th century, however, the region fell within portions of the ranges of three herds: the WACH,[35] with calving grounds on the north slope of the De Long Mountains, but with a much smaller range than it has now; what I have called the Seward Peninsula Caribou Herd (SPCH) (Burch 1998a:294), with calving grounds apparently in the southern part of Espenberg Peninsula; and what I have called the Nulato Hills Caribou Herd (NHCH) (Burch 1998a:177), with calving grounds apparently in the northernmost sector of the Nulato Hills.[36]

Barren-ground caribou are notable for the length and speed of their seasonal migrations (Burch 1972:344–46). In the early 19th century at least some animals from one herd or another ordinarily were present for at least part of the year in each sector of the study region. Caribou meat is edible at any time of year, but the animals are generally fattest, hence tastiest and most nutritious, in late summer and early fall, before the October rut.[37] Caribou were most eagerly sought for clothing in summer and early fall.

Caribou populations fluctuate in size over time, although whether these changes follow a regular cycle has not been determined. However, in the second half of the 19th century, the three caribou populations of northwestern Alaska experienced catastrophic, noncyclical, and possibly unprecedented declines. By 1910 both the NHCH and the SPCH had become extinct.[38] The WACH had been reduced to a tiny fraction of its former size, and its range restricted to only a small part of its former extent, all of it north of the study region. The NHCH and the SPCH have never been reconstituted. The WACH, which remained very small for more than two human generations, eventually recovered. Its range, and no doubt its size, are much larger now than they were during the study period, although its calving grounds remain in the same general area north of the De Long Mountains where they were before the crash.

The caribou may have been the most important terrestrial animal in the traditional economies of the study region, but it was by no means the only one. Others include brown (grizzly), black, and polar bears; mountain (Dall) sheep; a variety of fur-bearers (beavers, ermines, ground squirrels, marmots, martens, minks, muskrats, otters, red foxes, white foxes, wolves, wolverines); porcupines; and tundra hares. These species are and were distributed unevenly over the region, and they played different parts in the economies of each nation. Their numbers, too, have fluctuated over the past two hundred years. For example, mountain sheep and many of the fur-bearers—especially beaver—were hunted nearly to extinction in the late 19th and early 20th centuries, but have recently recovered.[39] Musk oxen, which may have been exterminated shortly before the beginning of the study period, have been artificially reintroduced. Moose, which were not present at all in the early 19th century, are now found throughout the study region (Coady 1980). The snowshoe hare has moved into the country in recent decades.

Sea Mammals

Sea mammals played an important part in the economies of several of the traditional nations of the study region.[40] This was true primarily of nations whose territories were located on or near the coast, but some people who spent the winter far inland spent two months or more on the coast every summer. Sea mammal products were traded from the coast into the most remote corners of the country.

Bowhead whales are and were the most notable sea mammals harvested in the study region, but seals were probably more important—in the sense that coast dwellers could survive without whales, but they could not get along without seals. Seals were the main source of oil (rendered from blubber); their hides provided material for boat covers, boots, tent covers, rope, and storage containers of various types; and their meat and internal organs were consumed as food.

Three main species of seal visit the study region: the ringed seal, bearded seal, and spotted seal. All are seasonally migratory. Ringed seals appear when the ocean begins to freeze in the fall, and they leave when the ice drifts away the following summer. Their numbers tend to be high when the ice is thoroughly broken up with cracks and leads, and low when the sea is frozen solid. The much larger bearded seals usually arrive off the northwestern Alaskan coast in March and remain until the ice leaves in late June or early July. However, young bearded seals used to be present in very large numbers before freezeup in the northeastern corner of

Kotzebue Sound, in Hotham Inlet, and in Selawik Lake. This is no longer the case. Spotted seals are present during the period of open water, frequenting lagoon outlets and sandbars, and they used to travel long distances up some of the rivers, particularly the Noatak.

The waters of northwestern Alaska are visited every year by bowhead and gray whales, of which the former were the more important by far to the Iñupiat.[41] Even a small bowhead can provide several tons of meat and blubber for food, baleen for snares and nets, and bones large enough to use in house construction. Bowheads moved from the Bering Sea through Bering Strait in April, following leads, or long openings in the ice, toward the north. They headed south again in early fall. Within the study region, they were the focus of major hunts at Wales and Point Hope, a secondary hunt at Cape Lisburne, and occasional forays from a site located between Kivalina and Cape Thompson.

Walruses provided hides for boat covers, ivory tusks for components of tools and weapons, and meat for food. Walruses moved north from the Bering Sea in late spring and early summer, often hauling out on drifting ice pans during breakup. With the onset of autumn, they began returning south. They were hunted primarily in the Wales and Point Hope districts, secondarily by people living in the Shishmaref and Kivalina districts.

Both bowheads and walruses were hunted nearly to extinction by American whalers between 1848 and 1914, with the primary decline coming before 1880.[42] Walruses have recovered over the past several decades, but the size of the modern bowhead population compared to its 1848 level is a matter of dispute.

The final sea mammal of significance in the traditional economies of the study region is the beluga, or white whale.[43] Beluga were harvested primarily for the outer layer of blubber with the skin attached, known as *maktaaq*.[44] This was consumed as human food. The meat was dried and used primarily as dog food.

Beluga began to move into the study region through Bering Strait while the ocean was still ice-covered. Most of these early arrivals continued toward the north, but others arrived shortly after the ice left Kotzebue Sound in June. The main body of this second group made a clockwise circuit around Kotzebue Sound, beginning just east of Cape Krusenstern, and eventually moving to a major calving area in Eschscholtz Bay, in the southeastern corner of the sound. They left the sound by diverse routes later in the season. Dozens of animals in this second group used to split off from the main body and spend some time in Hotham Inlet and Selawik Lake. This splintering reportedly no longer occurs. The population as a whole is greatly reduced in size, and movements are much more irregular than they used to be. This is allegedly due to harassment by motorboats and the influence of the Red Dog port site south of Kivalina, although climatic shifts may also be a factor.

Fish

The third major category of animals is fish. Species harvested by the Iñupiat included several species of salmon, several species of whitefish, sheefish, Dolly Varden char, arctic char, lake trout, blackfish, burbot (ling cod), several species of sculpin, longnose sucker, grayling, saffron cod, arctic cod, herring, flounder, pike, and smelt. All of them except pike, and landlocked lake trout and arctic char, are seasonally migratory, moving either into and out of the region altogether, or between saltwater and freshwater, or up and down river systems, or between main rivers and their tributaries. The relative abundance of the various species differed from one district to another, as did the timing of their movements, but most districts were home to large numbers of fish at one time or another every year.

The significance of fish in the traditional economies of the study region is often overlooked by anthropologists, but was repeatedly mentioned to me by Native informants. In general, the relative importance of fish in a given district was inversely proportional to that of sea mammals. Thus, fish were least crucial to survival in the Point Hope and Wales districts, and most important in the Selawik River drainage and the central Kobuk and lower Noatak districts. But fish were caught and consumed in every part of the region.

The migratory movements of the different fish populations were generally regular in both direction and timing from one year to the next. This made them potentially easy to harvest. All people had to do was set gill nets, construct weirs, or use seines in the rivers, or chop holes in the ice on the frozen river or ocean surface, and catch the fish as they passed through. The greatest impediments to fishing success were high water in the rivers, and rough seas in the unfrozen ocean, both of which made fishing almost impossible. Particularly in those interior districts where fish were the primary source of food, poor fishing conditions in summer often resulted in famine the following winter.

Long-term statistical data are lacking, but elders I interviewed in 1970 told me that the salmon and Dolly Varden char runs into the rivers had declined dramatically during their lifetimes. They attributed this to the recently established commercial fishery at Kotzebue. The downward trend has continued unabated since 1970. Elders also told me that fish runs in many parts of the Seward Peninsula had been disrupted and reduced due to silting caused by mining operations during the early decades of the 20th century. Fish runs in these watersheds have not recovered.

Birds

Birds comprise the final category of animal of importance to the traditional Iñupiat. Along with their eggs, they were valuable sources of food, and their skins were sometimes used to make clothing. Important varieties included several species of goose, duck, crane, swan, and loon, all of which nested in the region in enormous numbers. Most of the capes along the coast were summer homes for sea-cliff-nesting birds, such as the thick-billed and common murre, black-legged kittiwake, glaucous gull, and horned and tufted puffin. Capes Lisburne and Thompson, in particular, were noted for their large colonies of these birds. Rock and willow ptarmigan were another important source of food, especially in winter, as was the snowy owl. Other important birds included golden and bald eagles, whose feathers were important in certain rituals, and also as warrior insignia during raids and battles. The final important bird to the Iñupiat was the raven. These clever birds provided people with feathers and skins for ceremonial performances, and they held a prominent place in Native folklore.

Discussion

Most of the animal species found in the study region occurred to some extent in each nation's estate, but their relative abundance and the timing of their movements differed from one district to another. To the degree that a certain species was unavailable or occurred in small numbers in a given district at a crucial time of year, its human inhabitants had to either rely on stored supplies, harvest alternative resources, trade for the missing goods, or travel to where the animals could be found. In practice, the members of every Iñupiaq nation followed some combination of all of these strategies, the precise mix varying from one nation to another.

Obviously, people had to know the land and its resources, and they had to know how to make and use the weapons and other devices required to harvest and store the resources their country provided. Since many of the resource species were dangerous or otherwise difficult for one person to acquire, the Iñupiat had developed procedures whereby several individuals could cooperate in a hunt and then share in its returns. They also had social mechanisms for congregating peacefully in relatively large numbers at certain times and places where food resources were abundant, then dividing into smaller and more isolated groups during less affluent times.

In concluding this section, it is appropriate to point out that the sizes of many of the animal populations of the study region have undergone dramatic changes since Westerners first arrived there. This is important, because it means that one cannot easily extrapolate from the current situation to earlier periods; one must have specific data regarding those periods. Northwestern Alaska may seem to many people like North America's last wilderness, but its animal populations have fluctuated dramatically in size and distribution over the past two hundred years at least in part due to human influence.

Notes to Chapter One

1. *Nunaqatigiich* (pronounced, roughly, "noo-nuh-kuh-tee-geech") means, in its most literal interpretation, "people who are related to one another through their common possession of land." In practice, the term denoted the members of a particular nation (e.g., Canadians, French), or, more generally, a particular nation as an institution (e.g., Canada, France).

2. The source was "Arkveksina" (Simpson 1852–54: entry for May 25, 1853).

3. For early descriptions of Iñupiat see F. W. Beechey (1831, I:393–94, 405–6), Hooper (1881:56–57; 1884:101, 103), Kotzebue (1821, I:205), Seemann (1853, II:50–52), Simpson (1875:238–42), Thornton (1931:27–28, 30–32, 36), Wells and Kelly (1890:15–16).

4. F. W. Beechey (1831, II:300, 303). The Chukchi lived in easternmost Asia, across the Bering Strait from Alaska.

5. The raw data on his measurements are in Simpson (1852–54: entry for April 21, 1854). For other observations on Iñupiaq appearance, see F. W. Beechey (1831, I:360), Hooper (1881:56–57; 1884:101, 103), Kotzebue (1821, I:205), Seemann (1853, II:50–53), Simpson (1875:239–41), Wells and Kelly (1890:15–16).

6. Cantwell (1889b:81, 82, 88), Hooper (1881:56; 1884:101), McLenegan (1887:75), Nelson (1877–81: notebook 12, entry for July 15, 1881; 1899:26–29), Seemann (1853, II:50), Stoney (1900:829), Thornton (1931:27–32), Wells and Kelly (1890:15–16), Whymper (1869a:167–68; 1869b:159–61), Woolfe (1893:151).

7. Hooper (1884:101), Seemann (1853, II:51), Thornton (1931:28); see also Scott (1991:800–2).

8. F. W. Beechey (1831, I:343, 360), Choris (1822), Kotzebue (1821, I:frontispiece).

9. Burch (1998a:309–10; 2005:26–28). The concept originated with Stanner (1965).

10. Burch (1998a:318).

11. Burch et al. (1999); R. Cleveland (1965.7, 1965.8); cf. Raboff (2001:10–11).

12. Levy (1952:34–55, 62–71).

13. Cook actually got as far north as Icy Cape, which is north of the study region, but he had no contact with Natives north of the Seward Peninsula.

14. This account is not intended to be complete. It is limited to the expeditions that are most relevant to the present work.

15. Cantwell (1887, 1889a, 1889b), Healy (1887, 1889), Hooper (1881, 1884), McLenegan (1887, 1889), Rosse (1883), Townsend (1887).

16. Froelich Rainey (1941a, 1941b, 1947). Some of Rainey's field notes are in the archives of the Alaska and Polar Regions Department, University of Alaska Fairbanks. The rest are in the possession of John Bockstoce. In preparing this book, I had access to both sets of documents.

17. Don Charles Foote's field notes are in the archives of the Alaska and Polar Regions Department, University of Alaska Fairbanks.

18. Albert Heinrich (ms, 1955a, 1955b, 1960, 1963a, 1963b, 1972), Heinrich and Anderson (1968).

19. Charles Lucier (1954, 1958), Lucier and VanStone (1991a, 1991b, 1992, 1995). Some of Lucier's field notes are in the archives of the Alaska and Polar Regions Department, University of Alaska Fairbanks, while the rest are still in his possession. He has generously given me access to many of the latter.

20. For a more complete summary of the research methods used in 1969–70 and subsequently, see Burch (1991; 1998a:12–21; 2005:48–52).

21. Upstreaming is analogous to what archeologists call "the direct historical approach" (Steward 1942).

22. Lee, Sampson, and Tennant (1991, 1992), Lee et al. (1990), Mendenhall, Sampson, and Tennant (1989).

23. Gray, Pulu, Newlin, and Ramoth-Sampson (1981a), Johnston and Pulu (1980), National Bilingual Materials Development Center (1980a, 1980b), Pulu, Gray, Newlin, and Ramoth-Sampson (1981), Pulu, Johnston, Ramoth-Sampson, and Newlin (1979), Pulu, Ramoth-Sampson, and Newlin (1980), Ramoth-Sampson and Newlin (1981).

24. This means that the sun is often visible even when it is below the horizon.

25. The reflection is much greater beyond the tree line than within it.

26. The section on climate is based on personal observation and the following sources: Bernhardt (1970), Bowling (1985), W. A. Brower et al. (1977), Hartman and Johnson (1984), Hopkins, Karlstrom, and others (1955:120), Hopkins and Sigafoos (1951:C57–C58), National Climatic Data Center (1984), Selkregg (1976a:10–24; 1976b:6–33, 40), Walker (1969).

27. Weather data from Kotzebue are from the National Climatic Data Center (1984). Those from Kobuk are from Bowling (1985) and Schoephorster and Bowen (1965:2).

28. Since 1980, surface air temperatures in northern Alaska have become much warmer than they were during the 1956–80 period (Moritz, Bitz, and Steig 2002:1497).

29. According to Nelson Walker (1969a), a bush pilot based in Kotzebue for several decades, the prevailing winter wind at higher elevations in the mountains is from the north, and is usually fairly strong.

30. I have personally seen flooding result from four consecutive days of ¼ inch (6 mm) of daily rainfall in the Kivalina district.

31. See McLenegan (1887), S. Young (1974:11–12, 581–82).

32. The discussion of vegetation is based on personal observation, Bliss and Gustafson (1981:17–18, 32–39 passim), Selkregg (1976b:134–41), Viereck et al. (1992).

33. F. W. Beechey (1831, I:345, 370, 374, 380, 383, 387, 413, 418, 419, 420, 454, 457, 463; II:251, 266, 269, 309, 316, 317), Bertholf (1899b:113), Moore (1851:28), Stefansson (1909:603–4; 1914b:8).

34. McLenegan explored the Noatak during a particularly wet summer. The high water may have prevented him from seeing any of the thousands of salmon that must have been in the river. Why McElwaine failed to take account of the fish resource, which was often enormous on the Kobuk River, is not apparent.

35. The western arctic herd was originally called the "Arctic herd" (Hemming 1971:5–11; Skoog 1968:294–96).

36. My knowledge of the SPCH and the NHCH is based almost entirely on information acquired from oral sources.

37. During and after the rut, in the fall, the meat of caribou bulls is pretty rank. However, people have told me that after a month or two of seasoning in a frozen state, even this meat is very tasty if eaten frozen and raw.

38. Nelson (1898:126; 1899:24, 118, 229), Nelson and True (1887:285), Wells and Kelly (1890:9), Woolfe (1893:146).

39. Campbell (1978), Nelson (1899:119), Tickett (1970.1), Walker (1986).

40. A number of species of sea mammals are found in Northwest Alaskan waters—often as occasional visitors—in addition to those discussed here. They were of little importance in the Native economy, which is why they are not mentioned.

41. Gray whales were not systematically hunted in the study region, hence are not discussed here.

42. Bockstoce (1980; 1986:129–42, 346–47), Bockstoce and Botkin (1982, 1983), Woolfe (1893:146).

43. "Beluga" is a Russian loan word that technically refers to a species of fish, a variety of sturgeon that is an important source of caviar. "Belukha" is the Russian word for the white whale, which is a mammal.

44. *Maktaaq* is the blubber and attached skin of a beluga; *maktak* is the blubber and attached skin of a bowhead or gray whale.

Chapter Two

Role Differentiation

A role is a position differentiated in terms of a social system, whether it be a society as a whole or a relationship involving two friends (Levy 1952:159).[1] Roles are the basic components of every social system, and thus a good subject with which to begin a comprehensive analysis of any society.

We cannot see, touch, smell, or hear roles, but we are all aware of their existence. Indeed, we have names for many of them, such as doctor, wife, murderer, cook, hunter, teenager; each of these terms denotes a particular role. However, many other roles do not have names.

The analysis of role differentiation concerns who does what, when, and where (modified from Levy 1952:299; 1966:178). Levy (1952:299–348) has identified a number of bases on which roles are differentiated in every society: the nonhuman environment, absolute age, relative age, generation, sex, economic allocation, political allocation, religion, and cognition. The relevant data from northwestern Alaska will be presented under these headings.

Nonhuman Environment: The Yearly Cycle

Role differentiation on the basis of the nonhuman environment concerns roles differentiated on the basis of time and space. Role differentiation on the basis of space concerns the different activities people engage in depending on where they live or happen to be; or, in many cases, different types of space are created so that people can engage in particular types of activity more appropriately or effectively. In the modern United States, for example, there are differences in how people act in urban and rural settings, inside a house and outside, in a bathroom and a dining room, in a football stadium and a swimming pool, and so on. The list seems almost endless because, in a highly industrialized society, an enormous number and variety of activities are carried out in spaces created especially for them.

The number and variety of differentiated spaces was very limited in a traditional Iñupiaq nation. Furthermore, within each nation, at any given time of year, what was going on in one location pretty well mirrored, or paralleled, what was happening everywhere else. For example, when people living in the Napaaqtuġmiut settlement of Aġviaq were fishing in late August, that's what their fellow countrymen living at Napaaqtusuġruk were doing as well. When the former shifted to caribou hunting in the fall, the latter did also. For these reasons, it is not particularly useful to include in the present study a separate discussion of role differentiation on the basis of space; most of the relevant information can be conveyed through a discussion of role differentiation in time.

At least two patterns of role differentiation in time occur in all societies. These are usually referred to as the yearly and daily cycles, or rounds. The yearly cycle concerns the extent to which activities are differentiated according to season, or time of year. The daily cycle concerns the extent to which activities are differentiated according to time of day. Other possibilities, such as a weekly cycle, also occur in many societies, but they were not realized in northwestern Alaska during the study period. For convenience, the traditional Iñupiaq yearly and daily cycles are discussed in separate sections of this chapter.

In a land where the temperature and the amount of daylight undergo such dramatic seasonal fluctuations as they do in northwestern Alaska, it may be expected that role differentiation on the basis of season would be pronounced. And, indeed, such was the case. But seasonal variation in human activities was due less to changes in temperature and light, as such, than it was to seasonal variation in the abundance and distribution of the animal and plant species on which Iñupiaq economies were based. These varied from one district to another, with the result that the members of each nation followed a yearly cycle that was more or less distinct from the annual rounds of its neighbors.

The inhabitants of each district divided the year into a number of units. On a general level, there were just four of them, which correspond to our own broad divisions of summer (*upiṅaaq*), fall (*ukiaq*), winter (*ukiuq*), and spring (*upiṅaksraq*) (Ramoth-Sampson 1987). Also in all districts, the middle of winter was considered to be marked by the appearance of two stars, known as *aagruuk* (dual), in the early-morning eastern sky.[2]

On more specific levels, there was a much larger number of units based on certain relatively precise events or developments that recurred annually. These were primarily, but not necessarily exclusively, phenomena in the nonhuman world. These are usually presented, and the information about them was usually solicited, as names for "moons," roughly approximating Western months.[3] However, my own research indicates that during the study period, different times of year were divided not into a rigidly standardized set of units such as our months and weeks, but into a flexible set in which the units were denoted by descriptive terms. For example, Table 3 lists twenty-two seasonal units formerly identified by the Kivalliñiġmiut (A. Hawley 1976.2; Kennedy 1976; M. and M. Swan 1976). For particular purposes, other divisions were made as well. The Kivalliñiġmiut spent the fall and winter months inland, and the spring and summer months on the coast. This is reflected in the list, particularly with respect to changes in the sea ice between mid-May and mid-July, but not in December or January. They could, and probably did, add to this list units such as *amiqtuġvik*, the time to make new boat covers (early July); *nuġġiaqtuġvik*, the time to travel inland to hunt caribou, particularly fawns, for clothing (July); and *tiŋŋivik*, the time when ducks start their southward migration (September).

People who spent all or most of the year on the coast divided the year somewhat differently from those who spent all or most of the year in the interior.[4] In the major whaling villages of Point Hope (Tikiġaq) and Wales (Kiŋigin), for example, many activities were differentiated with regard to the whaling season. Thus, at Point Hope, *nutaqsivik* (ca. January) was the time when crew members scraped the wooden paddle and spear handles in preparation for the whale hunt; *puuġriuġvik* (ca. February) was the time to make sealskin floats; and *utiuġvik* (ca. March) was the time when they turned the floats hair side out (Rainey 1947:257). For the

Table 3. Seasonal Units of the Kivalliñiġmiut

NAME	MEANING	CALENDAR MONTH
siqiññaatchiaq	new sun	late January
siqiññaasugruk	sun starts coming up strong	late February
paniqsiqsiivik	sun is strong enough to dry meat	late March
qiġit tatqiat	moon when the hawks come around	April
upiṅġaġruaq	snow starts to melt	late April
auksalakkaa	snow getting soft; hard to travel	early/mid-May
suppivik/supluġvik	rivers start flowing	late May/early June
siqumitkaa	breakup of sea ice	early to mid-June
tuvaiyaġvik	sea ice broken up but floating around	late June
sikuiġvik	sea ice gone	early to mid-July
uunaġuġaa	sun getting hot	mid-July
tiŋmiat itchaviat/itchavik	moulting time for geese	mid-July
tiŋŋivik	geese flying again	late July/early August
amiġiaqsivik	velvet gone from caribou antlers	early September
ukiagraġaa	early fall	mid-September
milukataiqsivik	willow leaves drop off	late September
qinugaa	ice starts to form	early October
kuugich sikuġai	freshwater freezeup	mid-/late October
ukiuġaa	just after freezeup	late October
nuliaġvik	caribou rutting season	late October/November
siqiñaiḷaq	no sun	December/early January

most part, such distinctions were superimposed on, or used in conjunction with, others. For example, January (or thereabouts) was also known as *irraasugruk,* "the time of severe cold."

In order to simplify the presentation, I have arbitrarily divided the study region into quadrants, each of which contained the estates of two or more nations.

Northwest Sector

The northwest sector of the study region consists of the estates of the Tikiġaġmiut, Kivalliñiġmiut, and Napaaqtuġmiut. These are shown in Map 5, along with portions of the estates of two neighboring peoples. The dots in this map represent settlements that were ordinarily occupied around the time of freshwater freezeup, in October, and often for several months thereafter.

Beginning on the northwest with the Tikiġaġmiut, one can see that the population was distributed in a number of small settlements scattered along almost the entire coastal margin of the estate, one large settlement located at the tip of Point Hope, and a few other small ones located on the lower and middle Kukpuk River.[5] The riverine settlements were situated at good fishing spots, although they were also in areas where one had reasonable expectations of finding caribou during the fall and winter months. The coastal sites, on the other hand, were located at good seal-hunting spots near the mouths of streams where freshwater (or freshwater ice) could be obtained for drinking. Caribou were hunted from these locations as targets of opportunity.

The fall/winter settlements of the Kivalliñiġmiut were all located inland along the banks of the Wulik, Kivalina, and upper Kukpuk rivers or their tributaries.[6] Caribou could be

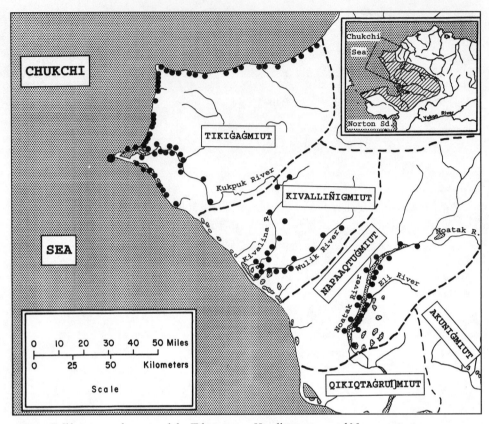

MAP 5. Fall/winter settlements of the Tikiġaġmiut, Kivalliñiġmiut, and Napaaqtuġmiut.

hunted from any one of these places, but the primary criterion in choosing where to settle was access to fish, both before and after freezeup.

Good fishing spots were also the primary consideration in the location of Napaaqtuġmiut fall/winter settlements along the lower Noatak River and its tributaries.[7] However, the main fishing season here was in late summer and early fall, before freezeup. The highest density of settlements, and also the largest settlements, were along sloughs and channels connecting the lower Eli and Noatak rivers. This is where large quantities of salmon were harvested in late summer and stored for winter consumption. The Napaaqtuġmiut continued to fish after salmon season was over, but the emphasis shifted to Dolly Varden char and grayling.

In all three districts, what happened during the winter depended on the extent to which supplies had dwindled during the fall and early winter. If supplies were good, people might stay in the same settlement all winter long, with occasional visits to relatives and friends living elsewhere. Or, desirous of a change in diet from fish or seal meat, people might move for a few weeks to areas known or thought to have lots of caribou. When supplies ran out and could not be replenished locally, the relatively large aggregations of early fall divided into smaller units as people spread out in an effort to find food. Among the Tikiġaġmiut, both the desire for a change and desperate need often drew people into the interior, for caribou and fish, whereas among the Kivalliñiġmiut and Napaaqtuġmiut, those conditions tended to bring them to the coast, for seals.

The advent of spring brought a wholesale rearrangement of the populations of all three nations in this sector. In mid- to late March, Tikiġaġmiut living in outlying settlements began to move into the village of Tikiġaq (at the tip of Point Hope), with a much smaller gathering at Uivvaq (near Cape Lisburne), in preparation for the whaling season. At about the same time, the Kivalliñiġmiut and Napaaqtuġmiut began to move to the coastal sectors of their respective estates. In order to hunt the large bearded seal, they moved right out onto the ocean, living in snow houses built on the sea ice. This situation is depicted in Map 6, which shows the distribution of the population of the three nations during April and May of an ordinary year. Although the Qikiqtaġruŋmiut have been assigned to the southwest sector of the study region for purposes of this exercise, Map 6 shows the locations of their spring settlements as well.

Map 6 indicates a very large concentration of people at Point Hope, a much smaller one at Uivvaq, and a still smaller one at Nuvua, the northernmost spring camp of the Kivalliñiġmiut. Nuvua was the southernmost of the spring settlements in this sector where whaling was carried on with some regularity.

The Kivalliñiġmiut and Napaaqtuġmiut lived on the ice until it began to rot, in mid- to late May, sometimes a bit later. At that point they moved their camps ashore, but continued to hunt seals on the ice. The Tikiġaġmiut remained at the whaling grounds until the whales stopped running, which was usually in late May or early June. After placing the harvest in cold storages dug into the ground, and following the celebration of the whaling festival (see

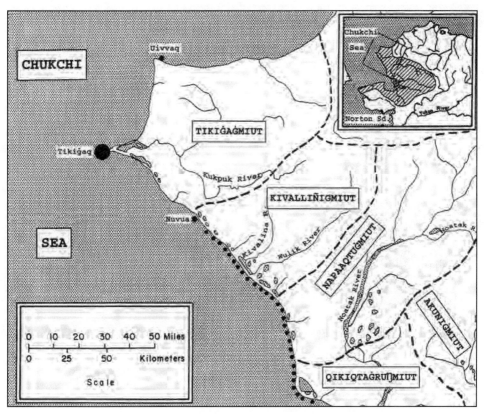

MAP 6. Settlements of the Tikiġaġmiut, Kivalliñiġmiut, Napaaqtuġmiut, and Qikiqtaġruŋmiut in April and May.

Chapter 6), they spread out along the coast to hunt seals (see Map 7). In all three districts, as well as in the Qikiqtaġruŋmiut district immediately to the south, seals (particularly bearded seals) were pursued by men on foot until the sea ice broke up, after which it was conducted by crews traveling in large skin boats (pl. *umiat*). This continued until the ice left the coast, usually in early to mid-July.

After the ice left, the members of the three nations in the northwest sector, as well as the Qikiqtaġruŋmiut just to the south, spent a week or so storing their harvest and generally getting organized. What happened next differed from one nation to another.

The Tikiġaġmiut had a number of options open to them for the summer, and the members of each family decided more or less independently which one they would follow. Some chose to go to the major trading center of Sisualik (about which more later), which is just beyond the lower right-hand border of the sector map; others chose to go to the secondary emporium near the mouth of the Utukok River, which is some distance off the map to the north (see Map 8). The former often stopped off at Cape Thompson on the way to collect the eggs of cliff-nesting birds, while the latter did the same thing at Cape Lisburne. Several families spent the summer living in small coastal camps from which they hunted sea mammals, mostly beluga whales, while others headed into the interior to hunt marmots, ground squirrels, and particularly caribou. Except for a few elders and children left behind to assist them, the major settlement of Point Hope was largely abandoned from mid-July to late August.

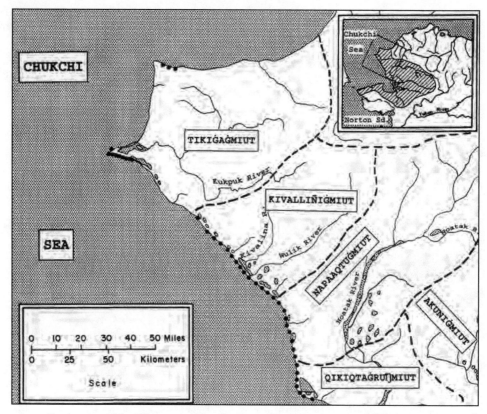

MAP 7. Settlements of the Tikiġaġmiut, Kivalliñiġmiut, Napaaqtuġmiut, and Qikiqtaġruŋmiut, mid-June to mid-July.

The Kivalliñiġmiut had a narrower set of options available to them. The first thing they did after the spring seal hunt was over was gather together at a place called Kivaliik (see Map 8) for a celebration. Then they split up. Most families headed into the interior to hunt caribou. They traveled up the Kivalina or Wulik rivers by boat, taking their spring harvest with them. After storing supplies and boats at their intended wintering places, they headed northeast on foot, looking for caribou, traveling in large family groups. The few families whose members did not go caribou hunting headed south along the coast to participate in the trade fair at Sisualik.

The Napaaqtuġmiut, and the Qikiqtaġruŋmiut to their south, followed yet a different program. After the occupants of the northernmost Napaaqtuġmiut camp had packed their supplies and generally organized themselves, they loaded their boats and headed south along the coast. When they got to the next settlement, they were joined by the people living there. The flotilla moved south along the coast, growing steadily as the people at each successive camp joined it. When they reached Cape Krusenstern, they turned east and followed the northern shore of Kotzebue Sound to Sisualik. The Qikiqtaġruŋmiut to the south followed exactly the same procedure, arriving at Sisualik shortly ahead of the Napaaqtuġmiut. Virtually all of the members of both nations participated in the Sisualik fair.

Movements at the end of the summer, meaning mid-August to mid-September, were essentially the reverse of those made in July. The Napaaqtuġmiut left Sisualik first, and

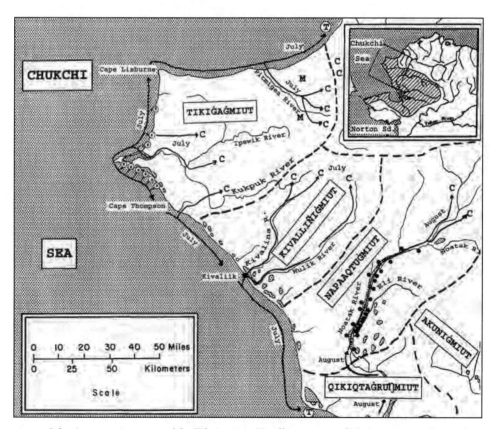

MAP 8. July–August movements of the Tikiġaġmiut, Kivalliñiġmiut, and Napaaqtuġmiut. C = caribou hunting areas; M = marmot hunting areas; S = seal and beluga hunting areas; T = traders.

ascended the lower Noatak to their respective salmon-fishing stations. These were located at or very close to their intended fall/winter settlements. The women, children, and elders stayed there to fish, while the men ventured to the mountains in the northern part of the Napaaqtuġmiut estate to hunt caribou. The Tikiġaġmiut and Kivalliñiġmiut returned home later, and at a somewhat more leisurely pace, from both the trade fairs and the caribou hunt. About the time freshwater freezeup struck in the fall, and barring complications of some kind, people ended up back where they had been the year before.

Northeast Sector

The northeast sector of the study region consists of the estates of the Nuataaġmiut, of the upper Noatak River, and the Akuniġmiut, of the central Kobuk River. In contrast to those discussed in the preceding section, the estates of these people were located a considerable distance inland. The locations of the fall/winter settlements of these two nations are shown in Map 9, which also shows the estates of their Athapaskan neighbors to the east (Burch 1998a, 1998b; Burch et al. 1999), and their Iñupiaq neighbors to the north.

At the time of freshwater freezeup, usually in late September or early October, the Nuataaġmiut tried to be at good fishing stations along the Noatak River and some of its tributaries, and on the shores of some lakes located along the southern edge of the De Long Mountains.[8] The upper Noatak district as a whole was considered to be prime caribou country, particularly in the fall, but most of the settlements were located more precisely at good places for catching fish just after freezeup.

The Akuniġmiut were ordinarily distributed among several settlements located along the Kobuk River, most of them being near the mouths of tributary streams.[9] These villages were situated at good places to catch fish after freezeup, and either at or near prime fishing locations of middle and late summer. The Kobuk valley usually offered good caribou hunting during the fall and winter seasons as well. Because they were able to harvest both summer and fall resources within a fairly restricted area, several of the Akuniġmiut villages were rather large by inland Iñupiaq standards, six of them averaging seventy or more inhabitants each. However, the larger Akuniġmiut settlements did not always consist of a single cluster of houses. Often what appears as a single settlement on the map, and which was usually referred to as one by the people themselves, was actually two or three smaller clusters of houses built at some distance from one another. Since it was the custom of the Akuniġmiut to build new houses each fall, it was fairly easy for people to relocate from one year to the next.

Winter seems usually to have been harder for the Nuataaġmiut than for the Akuniġmiut, primarily because the latter relied more heavily on fish, a more reliable resource than caribou. There is no meaningful way to show the winter movements of either people on a map, since they were rarely the same two years in succession. All one can say is that the Nuataaġmiut tended to divide up into small groups and travel about much more than the Akuniġmiut did, although caribou were important in both districts as winter progressed, and hares and ptarmigan were often crucial resources in March.

The Nuataaġmiut took advantage of the northward migration of caribou toward their calving grounds in March and April, thus ending what was usually a late-winter season of privation. As the caribou moved farther north, the people moved back to their fall/winter settlements, which is where they had stored their boats the previous fall, to await breakup. The Akuniġmiut, in contrast, moved out of their fall/winter villages into relatively small spring camps, where they hunted muskrats and waterfowl, and fished, until early summer.

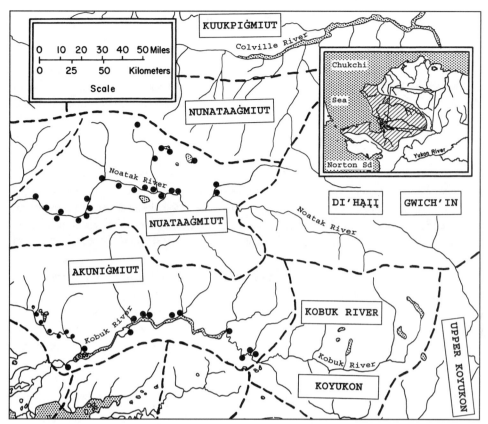

MAP 9. Fall/winter settlements of the Nuataaġmiut and Akuniġmiut.

In May, after breakup, the movements of the two peoples of the northeast sector diverged almost completely. The great majority of the Nuataaġmiut left their homeland altogether, traveling down the Noatak in a flotilla of boats to the delta. They passed right through the estates of the Napaaqtuġmiut and the Qikiqtaġruŋmiut as they did so; however, as shown in Map 7, the inhabitants of those two districts were all out on the Chukchi Sea coast at that time of year. The Nuataaġmiut halted for a few weeks in the delta to sew clothing, then moved to Sisualik, first to hunt beluga, then to participate in the trade fair.

The people who remained behind on the upper Noatak ordinarily spent the summer in the northern portion of the Nuataaġmiut estate or, perhaps, just north of the divide in Nunataaġmiut country. These people were highly mobile during the summer months. Traveling on foot, they went wherever they thought they would find caribou. The primary focus was on obtaining prime summer caribou skins, which they acquired by driving caribou into lakes and spearing them from kayaks, by driving them into corrals, and with snares set along trails through the willows. They also fished in the creeks and lakes, and hunted birds, marmots, and other small game.

The great majority of Akuniġmiut, in contrast, did not leave their homeland for the coast. The few families who did lived in the upper reaches of the Akuniġmiut estate. On their way downriver, they purchased furs and other products on credit from their fellow countrymen, then paid them back with commodities from the coast when they returned home in late August. Those who remained behind moved to summer fishing stations, most of which were inhabited by extended families linked through females, such as a mother and her married daughters.

Once the women, their children, and related elders were settled for the summer, the men and youths headed north through the mountains to the Noatak valley to hunt caribou for their late-summer skins, the very best for clothing. Once there, they generally headed east, so that when they recrossed the mountains on their way home, they would arrive back at the Kobuk at a point upriver from their families. Older men, who could not easily travel as far as the Noatak, went into the hills on the Kobuk side of the divide and hunted marmots.

The late July–early August situation in the northeast sector is depicted in Map 10. For the Nuataaġmiut estate, the main impression I am trying to convey via the map is one of emptiness. At least 80 percent of the Nuataaġmiut were at Sisualik, well outside their estate, at this time of year (Burch 1998a:95). Those who stayed behind usually spent the summer well to the north of the Noatak River; the dots and arrows on the map suggest roughly how they might have been distributed in a typical year.

The other occupants of the main portion of the upper Noatak valley (below the headwaters) in late July and early August were Akuniġmiut men. They, too, generally remained away from the river, since in summer caribou prefer the cooler temperatures and stronger winds of higher elevations. The main routes from the Kobuk valley to the Noatak are shown by lines on the map, and the eastward turn once they got there is shown by arrows. Akuniġmiut fish camps are depicted in Map 10 by a series of dots intended to show that these settlements

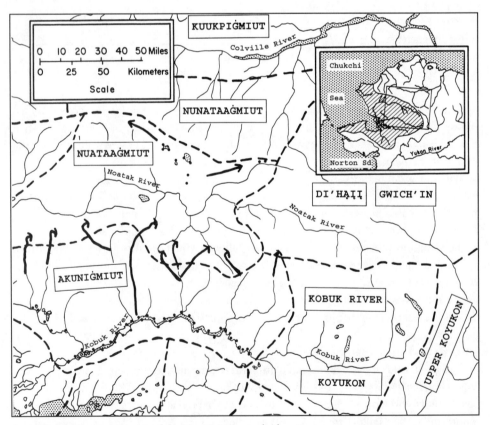

MAP 10. Summer movements of the Nuataaġmiut and Akuniġmiut.

were small, numerous, and widely scattered along the river. The marks do not depict specific sites, however, since fishing-camp locations often varied from one year to the next due to changes in the river's course.

About or just before mid-August, the Nuataaġmiut began the long trip back up the Noatak River to their estate. Under excellent conditions, which meant low water in the river and a following wind, even those intending to winter at the upriver end of their estate could reach their goal in about two weeks. With high water or contrary winds, the trip could take a month or more. If freshwater freezeup came early, they might not complete the journey by boat; they would have to stay where freezeup caught them until the ice was strong enough, then carry on by sled. Depending on just where they were, they might store their *umiaq* for the winter at that point, or else they would carry it forward by sled.

The Akuniġmiut men, meanwhile, headed eastward up the upper Noatak valley, carrying their harvest of caribou hides and fat with them. Eventually, usually sometime in early September, they reached the pass through which they intended to return to the Kobuk valley. They crossed it, descended to the tree line, and built rafts. With these, the hunters floated downriver to rejoin their families at the fish camps after an absence of some six to eight weeks. Then, using canoes, they ferried themselves and their families to their intended fall/winter campsite.

Southeast Sector

The southeast sector of the study region consists of the estates of the Siiḷviim Kaŋianiġmiut and Kiitaaġmiut in the Selawik River drainage, the Kuuŋmiut in the Kobuk River delta, and the Kaŋiġmiut in the Buckland and adjacent river drainages. The locations of their fall/winter settlements are shown in Map 11.

The Kiitaaġmiut lived in a large number of settlements, most of which were very small.[10] Most of the dots on the Kiitaaġmiut portion of the map actually represent what I call "settlement zones." These consisted of perhaps two or three tiny settlements situated within the area encompassed by the dot. Each such zone was referred to by a single name, even if the houses involved extended over two or three miles (3–5 km) of riverbank. All of the houses were located at good fishing places, most of which were near the outlets of streams or sloughs connected to lakes. As these considerations suggest, fishing was the primary subsistence activity of the Kiitaaġmiut during the fall, and to an only slightly reduced extent during the winter months as well. Most families returned to the same fall/winter dwelling every year. Caribou were hunted as targets of opportunity throughout the year, but were systematically sought as a change of diet from time to time during the fall/winter period.

The Siiḷviim Kaŋianiġmiut also spent the fall and winter months living at good fishing places, but their settlements tended to be larger, and the houses less spread out, than was the case among the Kiitaaġmiut.[11] They were somewhat less dependent on fish, but more dependent on caribou and small game, than their downriver neighbors.

The Kuuŋmiut, of the Kobuk River Delta, were yet another people who were heavily dependent on fish during the fall and winter months.[12] However, here there was a major difference between the very large settlement of Kuupaamiut, with fifteen to twenty houses, and all of the others, most of which consisted of only one or two houses. The resource that made possible Kuupaamiut's unusual size was an abundance of young bearded seals in late summer and early fall prior to freshwater freezeup. Caribou were hunted as targets of opportunity, and ptarmigan and hare were taken whenever possible, but apart from surplus

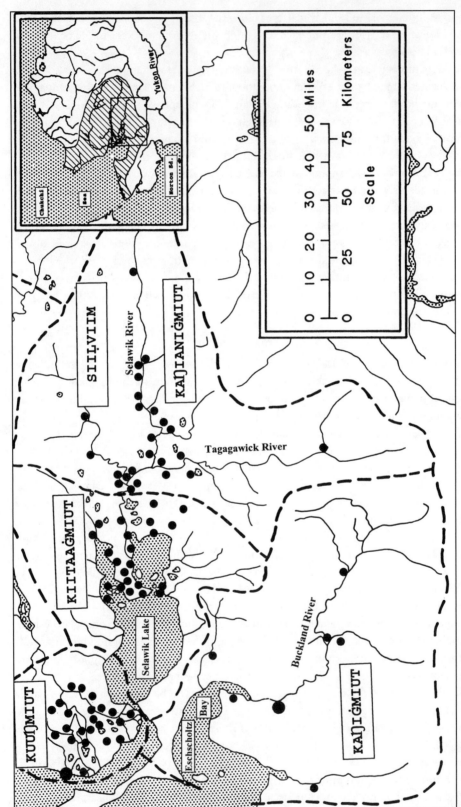

MAP 11. Fall/winter settlements of the Siiḷviim Kaŋ̇ianiġmiut, Kiitaaġmiut, Kuuŋmiut, and Kaŋ̇iġmiut.

seal meat acquired in the fall at Kuupaamiut, fish constituted the staple food throughout the fall and winter months.

The fourth and final estate to fall within the southeast sector was that of the Kaŋiġmiut, whose fall/winter settlements were located primarily along the Buckland River.[13] Here again, one settlement stood out as being much larger than the others, this being Makkaksraq, with some twenty houses. Other settlements were located on the Kiwalik River, to the west, and the Kauk River, to the north. During the early fall, the Kaŋiġmiut occupied themselves with a variety of subsistence activities, including caribou hunting, fishing through the river ice, and seal hunting on Eschscholtz Bay, off the Buckland River mouth. Makkaksraq served as a home base from which people came and went depending on the activities in which they were involved. Fishing fell off considerably during the winter, but caribou hunting, in the interior, and seal hunting, on the coast, acquired greater significance. During a lean winter, the large aggregations of fall split up, as families moved about independently of one another looking for food. During more bountiful times, caribou and seal hunting were undertaken as much for a change of diet as anything else, and often involved relatively brief forays to the mountains or the coast by groups of men rather than by entire families.

Almost all of the Kuuŋmiut moved out of the Kobuk delta onto the frozen surface of Hotham Inlet for a few weeks in late March or early April. During this period they lived in snow houses and supported themselves by catching sheefish through holes in the ice. The Kiitaaġmiut did exactly the same thing, but on the frozen surface of Selawik Lake. The Kaŋiġmiut had a variety of options. Some stayed where they were and fished through the river ice; others ventured into the hills to hunt bears emerging from hibernation and caribou. Still others moved out onto the ice of Kotzebue Sound to hunt seals. The Siiḷviim Kaŋianiġmiut, by contrast, stayed pretty much where they had been throughout the previous fall and winter.

The approximate distribution of people in April is shown in Map 12. The people living on the ice did not necessarily set up camp at the same place every year, nor did the caribou-hunting Kaŋiġmiut necessarily return to the same localities every year. Those portions of the map relating to the Kaŋiġmiut, Kiitaaġmiut, and Kuuŋmiut estates indicate general trends, not a set of definite locations. The portion relating to the Siiḷviim Kaŋianiġmiut does, however, indicate specific places.

The ice began to rot as spring progressed, and those who were living on it were forced to move ashore and return to their fall/winter settlements. Then virtually all of the people whose estates were in the southeast sector of the study region moved to small, one- or two-family camps to await breakup. These were spread widely across low-lying areas, and were too numerous, too frequently changed, and too small for useful depiction on a map. When breakup came, the emphasis turned to hunting muskrats, although waterfowl, fish, and caribou were also pursued when conditions warranted.

Summer brought yet another rearrangement of the population. About half of the Kuuŋmiut went to Sisualik to hunt beluga and for the trade fair, as did a few families from each of the other nations with estates in the southeast sector. These included most importantly the Siiḷviim Kaŋianiġmiut families whose fall/winter settlements were located in the upper reaches of the Tagagawik and Selawik rivers. They were relatively specialized traders, and operated much like the upriver Akuniġmiut traders mentioned previously. In general, however, except for the Kuuŋmiut, the inhabitants of this sector did not participate in the Sisualik fair.

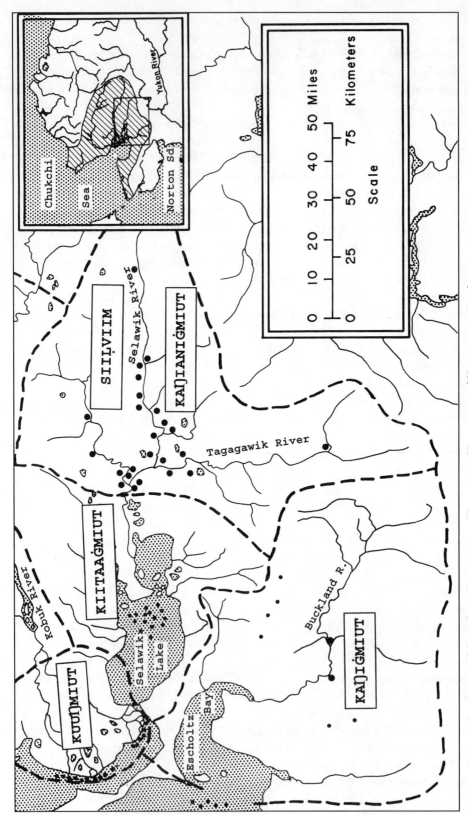

MAP 12. General distribution of the Siiḷviim Kaŋianiġmiut, Kiitaaġmiut, Kuuŋmiut, and Kaŋiġmiut in April.

The Kiitaaġmiut held a large gathering at Sauniqtuq around the end of June, then moved to summer fishing stations. The Siiḷviim Kaŋianiġmiut moved directly to summer fishing camps, most of which were located at or near their fall/winter settlements. Indeed, many of the Siiḷviim Kaŋianiġmiut did not have to relocate very often or over very long distances throughout the year. They were the most sedentary inland population living in all of northwestern Alaska. The Kaŋiġmiut, in contrast to the other three nations in this sector, moved to the shores of the inner reaches of Eschscholtz Bay and hunted beluga during July, and often remained there for the rest of the summer. In late July and August, groups of men left their families from time to time and hunted caribou in the hills in or adjoining this sector.

Map 13 shows the general distribution of the population in mid to late July. At this season, many of the Kuuŋmiut fall/winter settlements were abandoned, their inhabitants having gone to Sisualik. The uppermost fall/winter settlements of the Siiḷviim Kaŋianiġmiut were also abandoned, and for the same reason. Most of the Siiḷviim Kaŋianiġmiut, as well as most of the Kiitaaġmiut, were close to their fall/winter settlements, too much so to be able to show the difference on a map of this scale. The Kaŋiġmiut are shown as being at their beluga-hunting camps on Eschscholtz Bay. Finally, the map shows the locations of the caribou-hunting areas, which could be used almost any time in July and August, but which were always used in August.

Southwest Sector

The fourth and final division of the study region is the southwest sector, which includes the northeastern portion of Kotzebue Sound and the northern portion of the Seward Peninsula. This sector encompasses the estates of the Qikiqtaġruŋmiut, Pittaġmiut, Tapqaġmiut, and Kiŋikmiut. The locations of the fall/winter settlements of the four nations in the sector are shown in Map 14.

Freezeup found the Qikiqtaġruŋmiut distributed among a number of settlements located around the northern perimeter of Baldwin Peninsula, the northern shores of Kotzebue Sound and Hotham Inlet, and the banks of the extreme lower Noatak River.[14] Their largest settlement, Taksruq Saaŋa, was near the northwestern tip of the Baldwin Peninsula, just south of where the modern town of Kotzebue now stands. Just before freshwater freezeup, the major subsistence activity in most of these settlements was hunting spotted and young bearded seals. After freezeup, attention shifted to fishing through holes cut in the ice, caribou hunting, and the pursuit of ptarmigan and small game. The diverse resource base provided by their country enabled the Qikiqtaġruŋmiut to make a living without requiring any of them to leave their estate over the course of an entire yearly cycle.

Pittaġmiut fall/winter settlements were located along the southern and western shores of Kotzebue Sound, and inland along the Goodhope River.[15] Subsistence efforts were devoted to hunting seals along and near the coast, hunting caribou in the interior, and fishing just about everywhere people lived.

The fall/winter settlements of the Tapqaġmiut were located along the coast.[16] Their dominant settlement, Qigiqtaq, was located on the island near where the village of Shishmaref now stands, but a number of outliers extended out along the coast for some distance on either side. The Tapqaġmiut could and did travel by boat along the coast after freshwater freezeup, but many of them devoted their attention to hunting seals with nets along the gradually expanding edge of saltwater ice. Others ventured inland from time to time after the lagoons froze to hunt caribou, and to fish in the interior of their estate.

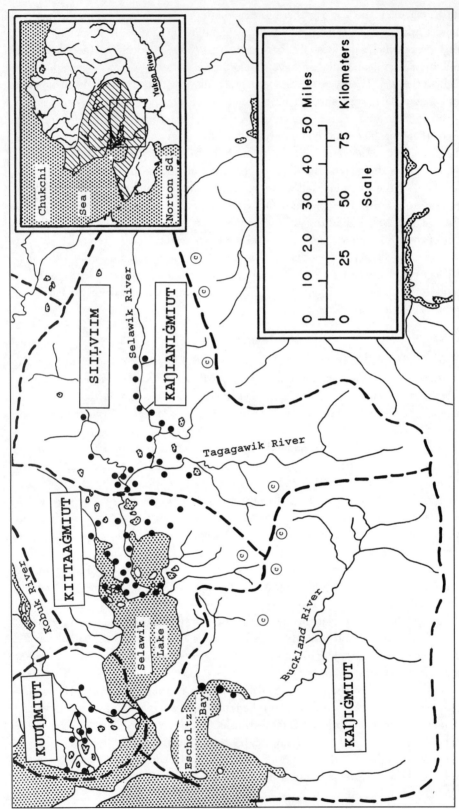

MAP 13. General distribution of the Siilviim Kaŋianigmiut, Kiitaaġmiut, Kuuŋmiut, and Kaŋigmiut in mid- to late July. C = major caribou hunting area.

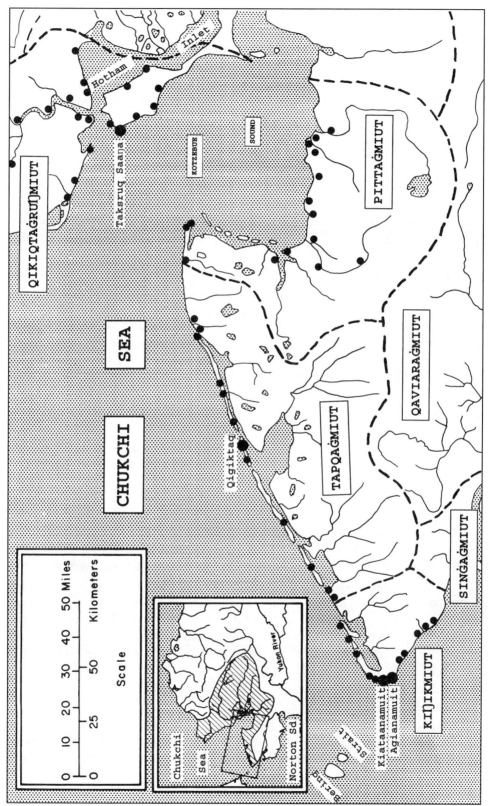

MAP 14. Fall/winter settlements of the Qikiqtaġruŋmiut, Pittaġmiut, Tapqaġmiut, and Kiŋikmiut.

Kiŋikmiut settlements were likewise strung along the coast.[17] The Kiŋikmiut had two major settlements, Kiataanamiut and Agianamiut, which were located about a hundred yards (100 m) apart just north of Cape Prince of Wales, near the westernmost point of the Seward Peninsula; they were known collectively as Kiŋigin. Even more than the Tapqaġmiut, the Kiŋikmiut focused on hunting seals with nets at this time of year. Because of their almost total orientation to the sea, which does not freeze until two months or so after freshwater does, and because of their relatively southern location, the Kiŋikmiut could and did travel by boat later in the season than anyone else covered by this study.

Winter found the people in the southwest sector based more or less where they had been at freezeup because that is where they had the largest stores of food. That is not to say that they were stuck in one place, however. During the winter many Qikiqtaġruŋmiut ventured to the northern part of Hotham Inlet to hook for sheefish through the ice, and they hunted caribou and small game as opportunity arose or necessity dictated. The Pittaġmiut and Tapqaġmiut, although remaining primarily on the coast, also ventured inland from time to time to hunt caribou and to fish.

Mid- to late March brought about a substantial rearrangement of all four populations in the southwest sector (see Map 15). The Qikiqtaġruŋmiut, as noted earlier, moved out onto the sea ice along the coastal border of their territory to hunt seals. The Tapqaġmiut and Pittaġmiut did likewise. However, the Pittaġmiut all moved to the ice off Cape Espenberg, at the northwestern extremity of their estate, whereas the Tapqaġmiut were spread out in tiny settlements scattered all along the coast of their estate; only the largest are shown in Map 15. The Kiŋikmiut, in contrast, all moved to Wales to hunt bowhead whales. This distribution of the four populations remained fairly constant until the ice left in late June or early July, except that people living on the sea ice had to move ashore when the ice grew too rotten to be safe. After the sea ice broke up, the members of all four nations continued to hunt sea mammals by boat, with the emphasis among the Qikiqtaġruŋmiut, Pittaġmiut, and Tapqaġmiut being on bearded seals, while the Kiŋikmiut focused primarily on walrus. Occasionally, the Tapqaġmiut were also able to hunt walrus on the floating ice.

The departure of the sea ice in late June or early July signaled another change in subsistence emphasis and in the distribution of people. After their spring harvest of seals had been dried and stored in pokes, around mid-July, virtually all of the Qikiqtaġruŋmiut moved to Sisualik (see Map 16). At about the same time, the Pittaġmiut took their harvest back to their fall/winter settlements, then spread out. A few Pittaġmiut families went to Sisualik, but most headed inland toward the southern portion of their estate to fish, to pick berries and greens, and especially to hunt caribou and small game. Most Tapqaġmiut headed toward their main village of Qigiqtaq for several days of feasting and games, then spread out widely over the interior of their estate, hunting caribou and small game, fishing, and picking berries and greens. They also conducted a major communal hunt of molting waterfowl near the lower Serpentine River. Map 16 shows only the most regularly visited places of the summer season. A few Tapqaġmiut families went to the Sisualik fair.

The most diverse summer program was followed by the Kiŋikmiut. Some of them went to hunt and fish near the head of Kotzebue Sound and to attend the Sisualik fair, while others headed south to attend the fair at Point Spencer. Still another group headed across Bering Strait to trade in Chukotka. A few people remained behind to hunt caribou in the interior of their estate, while a final group simply stayed at home in their fall/winter villages,

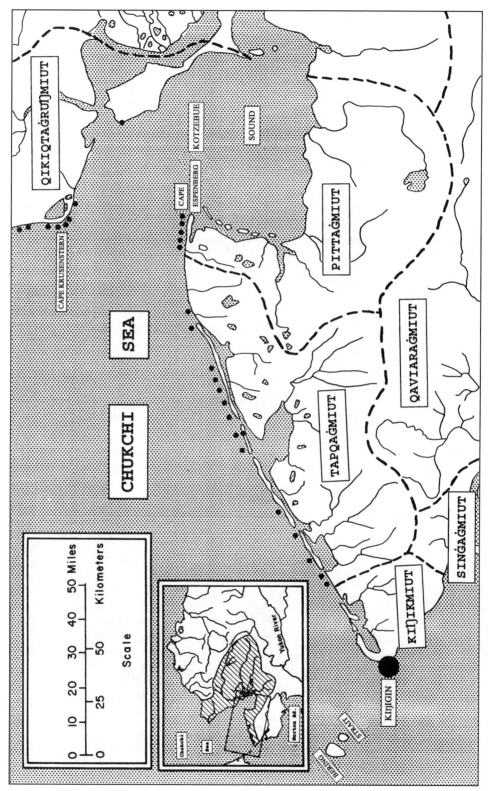

MAP 15. Spring settlements of the Qikiqtaġruŋmiut, Pittaġmiut, Tapqaġmiut, and Kiŋikmiut.

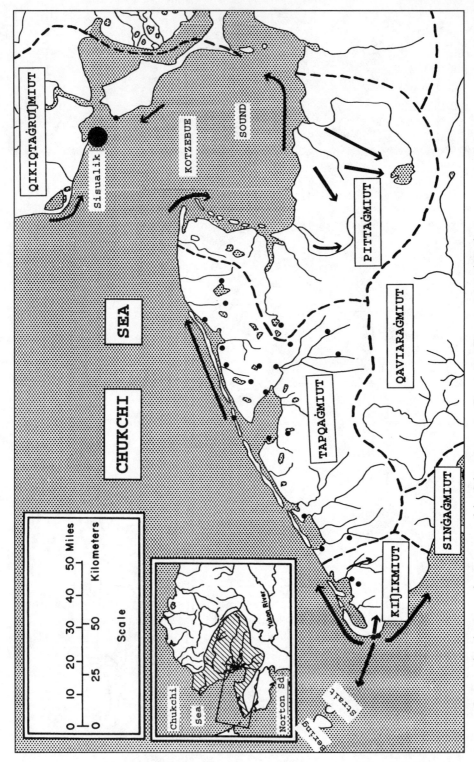

MAP 16. Summer distribution and movements of the Qikiqtaġruŋmiut, Pittaġmiut, Tapqaġmiut, and Kiŋikmiut.

fishing, hunting beluga and waterfowl, and harvesting a wide variety of berries and other vegetable products.

The Qikiqtaġruŋmiut were the second group, after the Napaaqtuġmiut, to depart Sisualik. By the middle of August, most of them were either at their fall/winter settlements or else scattered along the northern shore of Kotzebue Sound harvesting salmon. The other peoples in the southwest sector were much more dilatory in returning home, taking their time for a month or more, depending on the weather and on hunting and fishing conditions. Almost all of them were back in their fall/winter villages by the time of freshwater freezeup, although a few boatloads of Kiŋikmiut did not reach home until late October.

Discussion

Despite the uniqueness of the annual cycle of each nation, there were certain common elements. One was a holiday season, which took place during the short days of late November–early January.[18] John Simpson (1875) described the phenomenon as follows:

> As midwinter approaches, the new dresses are completed, and about ten days at this season are spent in enjoyments, chiefly dancing in the kar-ri-gi [*qargi*], every one appearing in his or her best attire. This time of the year being one in which hunting or fishing cannot well be attended to, and no indoor work remaining to be performed, is perhaps sufficient reason why it should be chosen for festivities in the high latitude of Point Barrow, when the sun is not visible for about seventy days; but it may not equally explain the prevalence of the same custom about the same period in Kotzebue Sound (Simpson 1875:262; see also Simpson 1850a: entry for January 10, 1850; Stoney 1900:569–70; Wells and Kelly 1890:12, 24; Woolfe 1893:140–41).

Several decades later, Vilhjalmur Stefansson (1944) made a similar observation:

> The winter darkness is to the Eskimo about what the hottest period of summer is to the city dweller. The darkness, as such, may not be agreeable to the Eskimo any more than the heat, as such, is agreeable to the man of the city, but to each of them it means the vacation period. The clerk gets his two weeks in which he can go to the seaside or to the mountains. The Eskimo has found it inconvenient to hunt during the periods of extreme darkness and sees to it that he has laid by a sufficient store of food to take him through for a month or two. Having no real work to do, he makes long journeys to visit his friends and, arrived, spends his time in singing, dancing and revelry. For this reason most Eskimos look forward to the winter darkness more than to any other period (Stefansson 1944:24).

A second common element in the several yearly cycles was some sort of involvement in the trade fair at Sisualik. This event drew some two thousand people, representing every nation in the study region, for two to four weeks of trading, feasting, dancing, and socializing each summer.[19] The extent of national involvement varied, however, ranging from virtually 100 percent of the Napaaqtuġmiut and Qikiqtaġruŋmiut populations to only about two or three boatloads of Kiitaaġmiut. Despite these variations, the fair was a major factor in the spread of goods and information throughout the study region, linking the several nations into a particularly well-integrated sector of the North Pacific Interaction Sphere (Burch 2005:242).

Within each district, settlements were concentrated in areas of relative resource abundance during the period of occupation.[20] The locations of these areas changed seasonally as the animals (including fish) on which people relied moved about during the course of their own yearly cycles. On a general level, the most important factors were the distribution and movements of caribou, in the interior, and of sea mammals, on the coast. More specific considerations in settlement location were the following: (1) access to good fishing places; (2) the availability of fuel, house building material, and drinking water; (3) local topography; (4) security against attack; (5) protection from the elements (especially wind and ice push, in winter, and flooding, in late spring); (6) availability of small game, for food; and (7) access to major travel routes (J. Foster 1970; A. Hawley 1970.2; Tickett 1970.2). These considerations led people to spread out in a number of settlements dispersed over the district in which they lived, and, in the great majority of cases, to change their place of residence two or more times each year.

Two seasonal thresholds had a major impact on human movement throughout northwestern Alaska: freshwater freezeup and breakup. The former, which usually occurred in October, brought boat travel on rivers and lakes to an abrupt halt. Saltwater freezeup usually did not take place until December, but subfreezing temperatures and storms made ocean travel unpleasant and often dangerous after about mid-October. Consequently, the shift from boat to sled transport occurred in all districts at about the same time. Freshwater breakup on the rivers normally took place in May, followed by the more protracted breakup of the sea ice some three to six weeks later. During the postbreakup flood it was possible (although sometimes dangerous) to travel downriver by boat, but two-way river travel did not become feasible until nearly a month later.

The most regular distribution of the human population from one year to the next was at the time of freshwater freezeup. There were two major reasons for this. First, it was the end of the season during which food supplies accumulated over the summer and early fall could be transported in bulk by boat in most districts. Second, in most districts there were very specific locations where it was almost always advantageous to live for the month or two following freezeup. In the interior most of these were at or near the mouths of tributaries to major rivers. Fish migrating under the ice out of or into the tributaries could be easily caught there with weirs. On the coast, the best locations were at places frequented by ringed seals soon after the sea ice began to form along the shore. In most years these fall/winter settlements were occupied until supplies ran out, which could be anywhere from three to five months later.

The regularity of human seasonal settlement and movement was based on the long-term consistency of the migratory movements of the fish and game animals on which the people depended for their survival. But this consistency was more of a long-term average than it was a program rigidly adhered to every year by either humans or their prey. In any given year, many factors could alter the patterns described above. An early freezeup, for example, sometimes caught people far from their intended destinations in late fall, and that affected where and how they lived for the next several months. Heavy rain in August and early September sometimes hindered fishing efforts to such an extent that people depending on the late-summer fishery for their well-being during the fall and winter had to live on resources and in places other than the ones they preferred. Bad ice conditions on the coast often complicated, and sometimes even prevented, seal-hunting and whaling operations, and forced people who preferred to live there to move inland. At the level of specific families, the amount of variation could be even greater. Injury, illness, old age, death, damage to sleds or boats, a family head's error in judgment about when and where to move—all these added still greater complexity and variation to the real-world situations in which people lived.

Nonhuman Environment: The Daily Cycle

The daily cycle of the Iñupiat varied radically over the course of a year, depending partly on the amount of available daylight, and partly on whether or not people were "in residence" or traveling.[21] In order to take account of this variation, I divide the material into four sections. Two of them concern seasons in which the difference between night and day is marked, roughly approximating the pattern found in more southerly latitudes. The first extends roughly from late August to mid-November, while the second is from late January to early April. For convenience, I refer to the former as the autumnal equinox period, and to the latter as the vernal equinox period. The time falling between them, from roughly late November to late January, is a third, which I refer to as the winter solstice period. This is the dark time of year, when the sun does not rise above the horizon at all for a few days in the northern portion of the study region, and when it is dark or in twilight most of the time everywhere. The fourth section deals with the spring and summer, the period from mid-April to late August. This is a time when darkness is minimal or nonexistent, and hence imposes no constraint on human activities.[22] For convenience, I designate this time as the summer solstice period. In each section I discuss the differences between the in-residence and traveling patterns, beginning with the former in each case.

The Autumnal Equinox Period

During the autumnal equinox period, as also in the vernal equinox period of late winter and early spring, the difference between night and day is marked, but these are the only times of year when this is so. The Iñupiat divided the twenty-four-hour cycle into two main parts, much as we do: *uvluq*, or day, and *unnuaq*, or night.[23] Day, in turn, was divided into two unequal parts: *uvlaaq* (morning) and *anaqasaaġiaq* (late afternoon). The early part of the night was also divided in two: *tanuġak* (dusk) and *unnuk* (evening). Human activities were differentiated in general accordance with these broad divisions.

The autumnal equinox period was a time of intense activity. In the interior, the major subsistence effort focused on caribou before freezeup, and on fish afterward, although in many districts men focused on caribou while women tended to the fishing. Along the coast it was a somewhat quieter time, although, as ice built up along the shore and seals began to appear beside it, hunters set nets for them or, a bit later, pursued them with harpoons. Coastal people also did some hunting and fishing in the interior sectors of their estates during this period, particularly during its early portion.

Men rose early, usually well before dawn, from late September on.[24] After dressing, and sometimes even before, they went outside, partly to attend to the call of nature, and partly to assess weather conditions. The latter could occupy them for as much as half an hour, but the procedure was crucial to making an informed decision about how and where they would spend the rest of the day. If the weather was bad or about to become so, they prepared to spend the day making or repairing tools, weapons, or utensils, or just loafing. If, on the other hand, the weather forecast was favorable, they returned to the house and prepared to venture forth. In either case, they sometimes had a quick breakfast (*itqutaq*) of seal oil (*uqsruq*), with or without frozen raw fish or meat (*quaq*), before setting out; often they had nothing except a drink of water. Depending on the circumstances, they spent the daylight hours building or tending fish weirs or hunting caribou, in the interior, or hunting seals, along the coast. These activities were undertaken on foot, usually in the company of one or more close male relatives.

Women, meanwhile, roused themselves, lit the lamp, tended to the call of nature in (with chamber pots) or near the house, made sure that food and water were available for anyone who was hungry or thirsty, and perhaps had a bit to eat themselves. (People ate raw frozen or dried food, with oil, as they pleased during the day.) They then busied themselves with a variety of tasks. Depending on just where they lived, they might check their snares for ptarmigan and hare, hook for fish through holes chopped in the river or (later) ocean ice, collect firewood, acquire water or ice (to melt) for drinking purposes, and make sure that the family dogs were tended to. Alternative chores included scraping, softening, and trimming hides, and making and repairing clothes. Most of these endeavors were undertaken in the company of other female members of the community, so that gossip and conversation enlivened the drudgery. Child care was a constant concern, but usually could be undertaken without much difficulty in conjunction with these other activities. Children either played nearby, looked after younger siblings or cousins, or tried to help their mother, aunt, or grandmother with her chores.

As the day progressed into early afternoon, the hunters headed home, whether successful or not, but in any event having surveyed the country for signs of game. The women's morning chores completed, they prepared for the men's return. When a successful hunter arrived home, he told his wife where any kills had been made, and she hitched up the dogs and went to fetch the harvest. Perhaps after a quick snack, he then repaired to the *qargi*, about which more is said below, to share the experiences and observations of the day with the other men and older boys, and to manufacture or repair tools, utensils, or other equipment.

As day progressed into evening, the women arrived home with their husband's harvest, then prepared the one cooked meal of the twenty-four-hour period. This was served to men and older boys in the *qargi*; women and children ate their dinner (*nullautaq*) together at home. Whenever the need arose or opportunity beckoned, women checked the clothing of the various members of their family and made any necessary repairs. They also fed the dogs. Men remained in the *qargi* until they decided to retire for the night. They were sometimes joined there by women and children for storytelling sessions or other evening entertainment, although the peak season for this type of activity seems to have been during the short days of the winter solstice period.

The *qargi*, or community hall, was one of very few specialized man-made spaces in an Iñupiaq village. It was used as a gathering place and workshop by men and older boys during the day, and by everyone during storytelling sessions, seances, rituals, and dances, in the evening or on special occasions (Eliyak 1931; Trollope 1855:873). In a small settlement, the *qargi* was simply the largest house, which functioned as both a dwelling and as a community hall. In years when abundant food supplies indicated that an unusually long period of occupation would be possible, and in settlements containing perhaps five houses or more, a separate building was often erected to serve this purpose. In the largest settlements, where there were several *qargich* (pl.), the buildings were permanent structures (F. Beechey 1831, I:367; II:266, 276, 302). For major occasions, such as a messenger festival, when dozens of people arrived from out of town, a special, temporary building was often erected to house the festivities.

When everyone returned home at the end of the evening's activities, they disrobed and went to bed. The final procedure was for the wife to close the air vent and blow out the lamp.

The house was then pitch-black until someone relit the lamp or the first rays of morning sunlight penetrated the skylight. That does not mean that total silence was maintained throughout the night, however. When the spirit moved them, people chatted, sang, or told stories, while the others participated, listened, or slept, as they preferred.

The travel routine during this period was not much different than the in-residence pattern, except that the major activity of the day for the people involved was working to transport themselves and their possessions from one place to another. Prior to freezeup, this was usually by boat, while afterward it was by sled. Men, women, children, and the one to three dogs owned by most families usually worked together to pull, push, or steer the boat or sled; only infants and the aged rode. A break for lunch seems to have been a regular part of the travel routine. Progress, whether by boat or by sled, was usually slow, perhaps two to three miles (3 to 5 km) per hour, the emphasis being on perseverance rather than speed.

Whether the travelers were proceeding by boat or by sled, a new dwelling was erected each night. In most cases this was constructed of a series of thin poles with the butt ends placed in an oval or circle in the ground, and bent over and tied together in the middle to form a dome-shaped frame. The latter was then covered with a tarpaulin made of caribou hides. The members of some inland nations preferred tipi-shaped tents.

In general, when Iñupiat traveled their evening camps were set up to be rather permanent, even when the intention was to give them only a single night's use. They could never know for certain when a storm, high water, early freezeup, or some other disruption might confront them the next day, and they wanted to be prepared. Alternatively, and on a more positive note, they could not know in advance when a large band of caribou (for example) might pass by early the next morning and relegate travel to a lower priority.

When people were really in a hurry, perhaps trying to beat an early freezeup to their chosen fall/winter settlement location, they just turned the boat over and slept under it for a few hours before setting off again. Men who left their families behind to go off on long caribou-hunting expeditions by boat usually slept under an overturned boat as well. If they hunted on foot, they just took a small tarpaulin along to serve as shelter. No matter what the context, they tried to have one cooked meal every evening, with snacks of dried or frozen (and raw) meat and oil earlier in the day.

The Winter Solstice Period

Toward the end of November, the period of daylight narrows to just a few hours in northwestern Alaska, and the sun's rays strike the earth at a very low angle. Eventually, on December 21 or 22, the sun disappears altogether for at least one day at the Arctic Circle, and for progressively more than that toward the north. It is a time of prolonged darkness everywhere in the study region. It was also the holiday season of the Iñupiat (E. Curtis 1930:164–65; Samms 1900–1: entries for period Nov. 19 to Dec. 28, 1901).

The arrival of the holiday season did not mean that the daily routine of getting up and going to bed was abandoned, but it did have a major impact on what happened in between. The winter solstice period was often a time of extensive travel, when people went, usually by invitation, to visit friends or relatives in other villages, or to participate in a messenger festival (see Chapter 6) in a foreign country. In this connection, it needs to be pointed out for the benefit of readers from more southerly latitudes that night in the Arctic is not as dark as one might expect. Starlight and moonlight are reflected off the snow-covered landscape, especially beyond the tree line, and although hunting might be a bit difficult, visibility in good weather is sufficient to permit setting up and breaking camp, and traveling slowly but safely even at midnight.[25] Those who stayed at home preparing to host such an event did not have to deal with travel problems, but they did have to prepare their facilities and plan the festivities for the crowd about to descend upon them.

The expeditions undertaken during the winter solstice period varied in length from a few dozen to hundreds of miles, and they sometimes took several days or weeks to complete. Travel conditions were often hazardous due to variable ice thickness on the rivers and ocean, overflow on the rivers,[26] avalanches in the mountains, and darkness and cold temperatures everywhere. Sled loads were particularly heavy because most travelers intended to make a significant contribution to the festivities once they arrived at their destination, and because they were usually loaded up with gifts during the return trip. The daily procedure was pretty much the same as in the fall, but greater care was taken to erect a safe, warm dwelling each night.

Just what happened when the outward trip was completed depended on the precise purpose for which people had been invited. If it was for a messenger festival, the daily program consisted of a complicated array of rituals, feasts, dances, ceremonies, games, and athletic contests. If the trip was just to visit relatives or friends, the daily agenda was basically the same, but with fewer rituals, ceremonies, or other formal events. During the daylight hours, such as they were at this time of year, the major activity everywhere seems to have been playing Eskimo football, a kind of mixture of soccer, rugby, and keep away. The trip home closely resembled the trip out, except that the excitement and anticipation were gone.

The Vernal Equinox Period

By early February the sun is high enough, and it shines for a long enough period each day, to have something of a liberating effect on human activities. It is usually bitterly cold at this time of year, however. People whose supplies were still good usually remained in their fall settlements, and followed a daily cycle rather similar to that of the postfreezeup period the previous fall. However, in most districts and in most years, the surplus of food built up over the previous summer and fall was exhausted by the end of the holiday season. This meant that the people living in those districts had to set out in search of food.

The winter search for food involved the division of settlements into smaller units than existed in the fall. It was a time when most households moved about the country looking for caribou and places where they could hook for fish through holes chopped in the river ice. Wherever they found caribou, fish, ptarmigan, or hares, they stopped. When supplies gave out, they moved on. Even many members of the coastal-dwelling Kiŋikmiut, Tapqaġmiut, and Tikiġaġmiut followed this pattern in January and February, although a certain proportion of the population of these nations remained at home for seal hunting as well. The daily routine was pretty much as it had been for travelers during the holiday season, except that the number of daylight hours steadily increased as the season progressed.

Famine, or at least severe hunger, often stalked the land in late winter. As the situation deteriorated and people became weak from hunger, movement became increasingly difficult. Ultimately, it became impossible. The daily routine in such circumstances seems to have been pretty much limited to setting snares for ptarmigan and hares in nearby shrubs and hoping for the best. Otherwise, people stayed in bed to conserve energy. Instead of the routine of breakfast, nibbling during the day, and eating a large dinner in the evening, people were reduced to an occasional snack. In extremis, people ate ptarmigan dung, pieces of boiled clothing, and eventually their dogs, who also would have been starving. Sometimes meals disappeared altogether from the daily agenda.

Late March usually brought better conditions. Fish began moving about in the rivers, ptarmigan began arriving in increasingly large numbers, caribou started their spring migration, and seals began to sun themselves on top of the sea ice. These developments signaled major seasonal changes with regard to subsistence, and to a number of relocations of the human population. Whereas human movements earlier in the winter were largely ad hoc—that is, directed to the solution of immediate problems with regard to food—those of late March and early April were a preplanned part of the yearly cycle. They were made not in response to present conditions, but in anticipation of changes that normally occurred in spring every year. Thus, Tapqaġmiut, Kivalliñiġmiut, Qikiqtaġruŋmiut, Napaaqtuġmiut, Pittaġmiut, and many Kaŋiġmiut families moved en masse to the coastal sector of their respective estates to hunt seals, while Kiŋikmiut and Tikiġaġmiut all moved to the major whaling centers. Others living in the interior repaired to places where fishing and muskratting were usually good just before, during, or after freshwater breakup. During these movements people followed pretty much the same daily routine that they had while traveling during the holiday season. However, the daily travel period was usually much longer, and the amount of time spent in bed was correspondingly less.

The Summer Solstice Period

Darkness is a minor factor in human affairs in the far north between mid-April and mid-August. Hunters and travelers could and did conduct their affairs without having to worry about a daily period of enforced idleness. Since snow begins to melt during the day and freeze at night in late April or early May, many people traveled and hunted at night, and rested during the day. Hunters pursued their prey for three or four days or more at a time, returning home only when their efforts had been successful or when exhaustion or bad weather forced a retreat. After a snack and perhaps a nap, the hunters headed back out again while their wives processed the harvest. Children often played out all night long in good weather, and slept during the day.

People worked more and slept less during the summer solstice season than they did during its winter counterpart. However, except when traveling or engaging in a collective hunt, during which coordinated efforts were necessary, individuals seem to have worked, eaten, and slept pretty much when they wanted to. The daily routines even of members of the same family were not closely synchronized. The main concern was that what needed to be done got done. The notion of a daily cycle, in the sense of a series of activities recurring regularly at certain times during each twenty-four-hour period, had little meaning under these circumstances.

Absolute Age

Role differentiation on the basis of absolute age concerns roles for which people are eligible because they are "conceived as being in a particular age span and that age span is conceived as being such that an individual can be a member of one and only one such span at any one time" (Levy 1952:308). It consists of the patterned changes in an ordinary individual's activities as that person proceeds from birth through death. Role differentiation on the basis of absolute age is more commonly referred to in anthropological studies as the "life cycle."

The Iñupiat did not number years, hence did not know or measure a person's age in years. Instead, they differentiated absolute age roles in terms of categories broader than those marked by years. These characterized a person's changing intellectual and behavioral abilities as he/she moved through the life cycle.[27] Thus, one person might become an adult (*iñuguŋaruq*) when he/she was eighteen years old, while another might be a year older. Adulthood was, nevertheless, an age category through which every normal person passed, and, when doing so, was expected to have certain capabilities, and certain rights and responsibilities.

Birth

Iñupiaq babies entered the world in a tiny parturition hut (*igñivik*) located a short distance away from the main house.[28] In winter it was often made of snow; at other times it was usually a small tent. In some districts the expectant mother was consigned to this hut three or four weeks before the baby was due; in others, the period of isolation lasted just a few days. Regardless of this period's length, prospective mothers had to make their own fires, prepare their own food, and use special utensils throughout. They wore old clothes, since whatever they wore when the baby was born had to be thrown away when leaving the birthing hut. Women whose time came while the family was traveling had to give birth without these preparations, usually in a hastily built shelter or even a hollowed-out snowdrift, but they still had to prepare their own food and use special utensils, both before and after the birth.

The expectant mother was the sole occupant of a birthing hut, although an older, more experienced woman often stood outside to offer advice. In some districts men were forbidden to approach the birthing hut; in others, the woman's husband was in attendance, and even assisted in a difficult birth. In some districts, older women stood nearby singing incantations during the birthing process to keep evil spirits at bay.

A woman had her baby while kneeling on or squatting over a skin, with her legs spread apart. This was reportedly less painful than the supine position used today, and it also enabled the mother to see what was happening and to perform necessary chores without changing position. The mother promptly tied the umbilical cord with sinew and cut it with a sharp knife, then washed the baby in urine.[29] The refuse was burned inside the hut. The mother remained in seclusion with her baby for several days, then emerged to rejoin her family. These procedures had to be modified when people were traveling, but they were adhered to as closely as circumstances allowed.

Infancy and Childhood

A newborn infant was *aniqqamiaq*.[30] It was born with a body (*timi*), a soul (*iñuusriq*), life (breath) (*anigniq*), and a personality (*iḷitqusriq*), all of which would develop during its lifetime (Aġviqsiiña 1941.1; Ramoth-Sampson 1987; Sours 1987; Martha Swan 1984.5). But it lacked a name (*atiq*). Without a name, it was not fully human.[31] One of the first orders of business, therefore, was to give it one. Just who assigned the name apparently varied: it could be the mother, father, one of the grandparents, or some other relative. Usually, a baby was named after a deceased relative. In such cases, the latter's soul was thought to be returned to life through the infant, which, accordingly, was expected to develop a personality and character resembling those of its namesake. Over time, this practice led to a tendency for particular names to be associated with specific nations; a knowledgeable stranger could guess where a person came from just by hearing his/her name (H. Anungazuk 1999.1). All names were gender-free.

If a baby cried excessively or got sick after it was named, it was assumed that a mistake had been made (Martha Swan 1984.5). Other names were tried until its behavior indicated that the name givers had gotten it right. (Presumably, some babies died before this happened.) Some children received more than one name at birth, but it was more common for additional names to be acquired over the course of one's life, rather like nicknames. Although infants ordinarily were named after people, many names had literal meanings denoting a variety of nonhuman objects, such as plant and animal species, as well as locations (Stefansson 1914b:346–47). On some occasions, babies were given names commemorating special events or their own birthplaces; presumably in such cases the infant had to develop its own personality and character without the assistance of an ancestral soul.

Newborns and infants were clothed in soft skins, and wore diapers made of moss or sea-weed held in place with a skin cover. They were carried in the back of the mother's parka, held there by a strap around the mother's waist. A baby could be shifted around to the front for nursing without being exposed to the elements.

A baby became an infant (*ililgauraq*) when it began to crawl or otherwise move about on its own. At some point the youngster began to reach for solid food when its mother was eating. That is when she started chewing tiny bits of meat to soften them, then fed them to her child.

An infant became a child (*ililgaaq*) when it began to walk.[32] It was at the *ililgaaq* stage that boys and girls began to be dressed differently (Simpson 1875:245). As its teeth erupted a child needed progressively less help in eating solid food, but children were not completely weaned until they were four or five years old, sometimes even older.

The care of an infant or young child was primarily the job of the mother, but the father, older siblings, and other relatives helped. Young children were picked up and coddled when-ever they fussed, and, in general, an effort was made to satisfy their every whim. Boys were catered to more than girls, but, as a rule, Iñupiaq children lived in a supportive, nurturing environment. One exception to this was the deliberate toughening of boys between the ages of about two and five; they were made to go outside naked for a time every morning, regardless of the weather (B. Hawley 1982; J. Killigivuk 1960.1; Rainey 1947:243).

During the early part of this phase, perhaps when they were around three or four years of age, sometimes older, children became aware of their surroundings (*qaugri–*) (H. Anungazuk 1999.1; R. Cleveland 1970.1; Stefansson 1914b:282). I am not sure how or if this threshold was recognized by either children or parents when it happened, but it seems to have been associated with a particular event or place that caught the child's attention in a way that nothing ever had before. Later on, people recalled it as an important point in their lives, the time of their earliest memory.

As youngsters developed, they began to follow elder siblings and parents as they performed chores around the house and its vicinity, and eventually they started trying to emulate them (Aġviqsiiña 1940.1:74; H. Anungazuk 1999.1; Hooper 1881:109; S. Obruk 1983.2). As this happened, a child became a little boy (*nukatpialugruaq*) or a little girl (*niviaqsialugruaq*), and began to learn the roles appropriate to its particular sex on reaching adulthood. Boys learned to hunt by stalking small birds and trying to kill them with slingshots or small bows and arrows, and, later, by following their father on short hunting trips. It was toward the end of this phase that boys were first allowed to accompany their fathers to the *qargi*. Girls were taught how to sew, look after younger siblings, collect firewood, set snares for ptarmigan and hares, and carry out the many other duties of an Iñupiaq woman.

Puberty

As children approached puberty, the difference between male and female activities became progressively more evident in their behavior. A boy became *nukatpiaġruk*, and began to follow his father and/or other older male relatives on progressively longer hunting trips (E. Curtis 1930:148; A. Hawley 1964.3; Thornton 1931:93–94, 95, 98–99). A girl was *niviaqsiaġruk*, and began to provide significant help to her mother in such activities as sewing, setting snares for ptarmigan and hares, and preparing food.

It was usually during the *nukatpiaġruk* period that a boy made his first kill of a significant game or fur-bearing animal, although there had to have been a considerable range of variation in precisely when this happened. When it did, the event was recognized in several districts with a feast, and in others with a series of ritual observances.[33] Everywhere, however, the boy was required to divide the meat and skin and give his harvest away, usually to elders.

Puberty was reached by girls at about the age of thirteen, and by males slightly later.[34] The event was ritually recognized only for females. Throughout the study region menarche was surrounded with a variety of taboos and rituals that varied in their severity from one nation to another. The most difficult were found among the Akuniġmiut, of the central Kobuk River valley, and the Kiitaaġmiut and Siiḷviim Kaŋianiġmiut, of the Selawik River valley; in those nations, a girl was required to endure them for an entire year. At least among the Akuniġmiut, and possibly in some other districts, charcoal was used to darken the bridge of a girl's nose and the area around her eyes. Throughout that period, a girl lived in a separate little hut (*aalġuvik*) of her own, some distance apart from the others, and had a minimum of communication with anyone. Her parka had a hood large enough to cover her face. Food was passed in through the doorway by the mother or elder sister, but males were not allowed to approach the hut. She had to eat and drink out of a special bowl, and she could have a small fire in the hut, but no lamp. Her clothes were burned at the end of her period of isolation, and she had to begin wearing new ones.

Similar restrictions existed in other districts, but the period during which they were in force was rarely longer than a month, and usually lasted just a few days. Everywhere, the girl had to wear a parka with a very large hood, the edges of which were weighted down with small stones to keep her face hidden from view. She was not allowed to talk with or look at men or boys. In most areas a black streak was drawn across the girl's face, either just above her eyes or across the bridge of her nose to signify her status. When the family was traveling, it was impossible to adhere strictly to these requirements, but they were followed as closely as possible.

Adulthood

The period between puberty and full adulthood—the "teenage" period—was *nutaġaaluk*. It was marked among males by increasingly aggressive approaches to young women, and the substantial assumption of adult roles in providing for the family's welfare. Among females, it was a period of shyness and withdrawal, but it also was a time in which they, too, began to shoulder fully adult roles in many aspects of life.

During this stage most women had their chins tattooed and most young men began to wear labrets (Niġuwana 1940.1:6; Simpson 1875:239, 241; Wells and Kelly 1890:16). Both events were usually recognized by a feast thrown by the parents. Neither practice seems to have been a definitive indicator of a person's age, but by the time one reached full adulthood, labrets and at least some tattoos were usually already in place.

An adult of either sex was *iñuguŋaruq*; a young woman was *niviaqsiaq*, and a young man was *nukatpiaq*. The first order of business for individuals approaching this age category was to get married. Marriage is discussed at some length in the following chapter, but it can be summarized here as having been a somewhat chaotic process involving the aggressive pursuit of a young woman by one or more suitors (Simpson 1875:252–54; Stoney 1900:830; Wells and Kelly 1890:10; Woolfe 1893:135). Chastity before marriage for either males or females was not expected and probably was rarely achieved, and there was a considerable amount of trial and error before a couple finally settled down together. There was no marriage ceremony or other formal recognition of the creation of a marital bond.

Full adulthood was achieved with marriage and the arrival of offspring. The activities, rights, and responsibilities of people in this age group are discussed in detail in subsequent chapters, and in later sections of the present one. Perhaps the main point to make for present purposes is that full adulthood was attained not through an abrupt behavioral change or ceremonial recognition, but through a relatively smooth development from earlier patterns.

Similarly, one proceeded seamlessly from young adulthood to the next stage of life, *qatqitchuaq*, that of a person in his or her prime. People in this age group were apparently in their late thirties and forties, more experienced and knowledgeable than their juniors, but still strong and active. My impression is that both men and women in this age group generally were physically stronger than they had been during their early adult years, although not necessarily faster or as agile. But they tended to be better hunters, seamstresses, traders, and politicians than they had been earlier, or would be again.

Old Age

Old age began with a visible decline in energy and strength, but not necessarily in abilities related to intelligence, knowledge, and experience, all of which were highly respected qualities (A. Hawley 1973.3; Simpson 1875:245, 249, 250; Stoney 1900:831, 832; see also Stefansson 1958). Flecks of gray in the hair were an indicator of membership in the class. Individuals who were specifically identified to me as being in this category, known as *utuqqanaaq*, ranged from their mid-fifties to their early seventies. Although *utuqqanaaq* is usually translated as "elder," most of the people in this age group probably were individuals 21st-century Westerners would call "middle-aged." Interestingly, some of the oldest people in the category were considered to be still in it because one or more of their parents was still alive. As long as one was still the child of a living person, one was not considered to be in the final age group, that of the truly aged.

In the oldest age category, a male was *aŋayuqaksraq*, and a female was *aaquaksraq*. People in this class were apparently in their seventies or older, of whom there were enough representatives to catch the attention of early explorers (McLenegan 1887:75; Simpson 1875:245–46). These were people who tended to be physically frail, and who consequently had to be looked after to a greater or lesser extent by their children and grandchildren. However, many of them were capable of imparting valuable advice and information, some could provide entertainment in the form of stories and anecdotes, and a few could work powerful magic. Old women who could no longer sew or scrape skins contributed significantly to family welfare by making twine out of sinew or bark, a laborious, time-consuming process (Brower ms:158).

Death

When death came, the survivors had to practice a number of ritual observances in the midst of their grief.[35] The details varied to some extent from one nation to another, but the general pattern was pretty much the same everywhere.

The soul (*iñuusriq*) of a recently deceased person was regarded as being exceptionally dangerous. In many districts, if a person died inside a house, the building had to be abandoned immediately (and permanently) by its other occupants because the angry soul might linger inside. Therefore, people who appeared to be on the verge of death were removed before they passed away, if possible, and placed in a small outhouse constructed for the purpose.

Regardless of where a person died, the eyes were closed and covered with black stones or some other black substance, and a skin was placed over the face. The body was wrapped in skins, removed from the dwelling through the skylight (as necessary), and dragged, not carried, to the grave site. It was installed there along with many of the tools, weapons, and implements that the deceased had used in life. Some informants said these were left to equip the soul of the deceased for life in the spirit world; others claimed it was to keep the soul happy; and still others maintained it was just to get the goods out of the house because no one else would dare use them (Simpson 1852–54: entries for Dec. 17, 1853, Feb. 9, 1854, Feb. 12, 1854).

Graves (*iḷuvġich*) took a variety of forms, varying according to the nation, the season, and the particular circumstances surrounding the death. Among the Tikiġaġmiut, bodies were wrapped in skins or placed in boxes either directly on the ground or on elevated platforms. Among the Kiŋikmiut, they were wrapped in skins, placed on the ground, and covered with rocks. Elsewhere, the prevailing pattern was to place the covered body on the ground or a platform with a tipi-like framework of logs or driftwood erected over it. In areas lacking sufficient wood for such an edifice, the body was covered with willows, and a single pole was stuck in the ground to mark the site. During periods of famine, or during crucial seasonal movements, more hasty arrangements usually had to be made. Graves were placed at some convenient spot near where the person died. The only places with formally designated graveyards were the large settlements of Point Hope and Wales.

The people who removed the body from the house and took it to the burial site had to remain isolated from everyone else for three or four days, obey a number of taboos, and practice several rituals. Grief was expressed through crying and loud moaning by both males and females during this period, and the ordinary activities of daily life were pretty much suspended. When this period had passed, the survivors visited the grave site to make sure that everything was in order, then carried on with their lives. Graves might be visited in later years, but, in general, they were left to the vicissitudes of climate, bacteria, foxes, ground squirrels, and dogs, and usually deteriorated fairly quickly.

Relative Age

Role differentiation on the basis of relative age refers to a distinction of roles among individuals on the basis of their comparative ages (Levy 1952:321–22). It has to do not with how old a person is in absolute terms, but how old a person is relative to some other person (or set of persons). The alternatives are same age, older, and younger.

Role differentiation on the basis of relative age was strongly institutionalized in northwestern Alaska, primarily, but not exclusively, within the family. It was symbolized in the terminological distinction between older brother (*aapiaq*) and older sister (*aakiaq*), on the one hand, and younger sibling (*nukatchiaq*), on the other. Older siblings had authority over younger ones, while younger siblings were expected to defer to their seniors and to do what they were told. At the same time, older siblings were expected to mentor and protect their juniors.

The deference of juniors to seniors was taught early in life. In contrast to modern American parents, who typically encourage young children to "stand up" to authoritative behavior on the part of older siblings, Iñupiaq parents taught them to submit. But even before a child was old enough to have any control over its own actions, its older brothers and sisters were involved in caring for it, and they were taught to be concerned about its welfare.

The differential allocation of power and responsibility on the basis of relative age was most clearly defined within the family, which was one social context in which who was older or younger than whom was absolutely clear. But, to a lesser extent, it pervaded the entire social system. Adults generally were acutely aware of who was older and younger than they were among the members of their own nation. One did not know birth dates, but one did know, and remembered, who was born the same winter or summer as oneself and, by extension, who was older or younger.

It would be overly simplistic, but not totally misleading, to characterize a traditional Iñupiaq society as a pervasively hierarchical system based on relative age. One interesting consequence of this is that friendships were hard to come by except in large villages. In order to be friends, people had to be the same age, certainly born the same year. Since most people spent most of their time in the context of tiny settlements occupied by very close relatives, the chances of having a nonrelative of the same age living nearby was relatively low. Among elders, the age equivalency requirement was gradually relaxed; among people in their seventies or older, people born several years apart often considered themselves to be of the same age.

Generation

Role differentiation based on generation concerns activities associated with a person's position relative to other individuals in the line of direct real, assumed, or fictive biological descent from a common ancestor (Levy 1952:324–25). "Real" biological succession is that which actually occurs. "Assumed" biological succession is what is thought to occur; among the Iñupiat, the only question would have concerned a child's paternity. Finally, "fictive" biological succession concerns adoption, when people act as though a biological connection exists even when they know that it does not.

Role differentiation on the basis of generation is not restricted to the direct line of succession, but includes all of the individuals known to be at a given level in a line of succession. One's siblings and cousins, for example, are of one generation, and one's parents and their siblings and cousins are of another. Viewed in this way, role differentiation on the basis of generation was rather weakly developed among the Iñupiat. If one had an uncle who was younger than oneself, which was quite possible, one treated that person more as a cousin than as an uncle. Absolute and relative age thus took precedence over generation as a factor influencing a person's behavior.

The ideal system was of course based on the premise that there would not be major discrepancies in absolute age among the members of a given generation. The key distinction was naturally between parents (dual *aŋayuqaak*) and their children (*qituŋat*). The former begat the latter, nurtured them in their infancy and youth, accompanied and guided them in their adulthood, and depended on them in their old age.[36] Nepotics—i.e., aunts and uncles, on the one hand, and nephews and nieces, on the other—operated rather like parents and children, especially if they lived in the same or neighboring houses, except that the obligation was not so strong in their case. At the next generational level, grandparents helped look after and teach their grandchildren while the latter were young, while grandchildren often played an important part in taking care of aged grandparents later on. Roles at the next and most distant generation level recognized by the Iñupiat, that of great-grandparents and great-grandchildren, were probably rarely filled. They were very vaguely defined, but, to the extent that they were, were similar to those of grandparents and grandchildren.

Sex

Role differentiation on the basis of sex is that between male and female in the generally accepted sense of those terms (Levy 1952:328).[37] Among the Iñupiat, a male was *aŋun* and a female was *aġnaq*. The differences in the activities and duties expected of individuals in the two categories was pronounced, and went far beyond the obvious biological necessity for males to inseminate women and for females to bear children. The differences began in childhood and continued throughout life.

Role differentiation on the basis of sex was manifested in differences in clothing style, dancing style, and the division of labor. During the day, at least, men and women did not spend a great deal of time in one another's company. Men were either out hunting, or else in the *qargi* (community hall), making or repairing equipment and/or listening to or telling stories. Women, on the other hand, performed chores around the settlement, or sat together in one of the houses, chatting, sewing, braiding sinew into line, or tending to other necessary tasks. Men and older boys usually ate dinner in the *qargi*, while females and younger boys ate at home.

A man was a big-game hunter who ordinarily hunted on foot. When he killed a caribou or other type of large terrestrial mammal, he left the carcass where it fell. When he returned home, he told his wife where it was. Following her husband's directions and tracks, she fetched it home with the aid of dogs, while he went to the *qargi*. There were a number of regional and seasonal variations on this basic theme, however. For example, seals killed on shifting sea ice were brought to the solid shore ice by the man who killed them. Men who hunted sea mammals in crews in early summer also brought the harvest to shore. Men who went on long caribou-hunting expeditions without their wives, as they did every summer along the Kobuk River, for example, had to process the harvest themselves before bringing it home. (When they went on hunting expeditions on foot with their wives, the men went ahead looking for caribou, while the women followed behind carrying the outfit.) Whales were so large that everyone had to help haul them up, butcher them, and place the meat and blubber in storage. But, in general, as far as big game is concerned, males hunted, and females retrieved and processed the harvest.

Women were in charge of meat and skins from the time they were first placed in their care until they were ultimately consumed as food or clothing. They cut up the meat, dried it or otherwise arranged for its preservation, stored it, cooked it as appropriate and necessary, and served it. They removed the hides, scraped them, stored them, and eventually shaped them and made them into clothing or other goods. It was their responsibility to make sure that all of the clothes worn by members of their family stayed in good order throughout the year.

Women also produced a substantial array of raw materials. They made, set, and tended snares for ptarmigan and hares around the settlement, and they gathered almost all of the vegetable products used for food, fuel, medicine, dye, or seasoning. Dogs were generally under the care of women. When traveling in winter, women helped the dogs pull the sled, while men either pushed from behind or went ahead to break a trail.

In general, males had greater authority than females. Although women now underwrite whaling crews, serve as mayor, and fill a variety of leadership roles in Iñupiaq communities, I have never heard of anything like that happening in early-contact times. The "chiefs" encountered by early Western explorers were always male, and I have never heard an oral account where that was not the case. Women were extremely important, indeed crucial, in helping their husbands achieve and retain leadership positions, but they rarely stood at the top of the political pyramid themselves.

Males were warriors. The responsibility for defense lay in their hands, and they were the ones who made up the war parties that attacked other nations. In most accounts of raiding and warfare, women are depicted as passive witnesses of the violence, and, if their men were defeated, as victims after it was over. Defeated males were usually killed outright. Females were often raped and tortured, and sometimes temporarily enslaved, before being put to death themselves.

In all Iñupiaq societies both men and women were actively involved in fishing, although the extent and nature of their respective involvement varied with the season and the district. Along the Kobuk River, for example, the summer salmon fishery was conducted entirely by women. The fall fishery, on the other hand, which was conducted with weirs, involved both men and women.

Both men and women could be shamans. My impression from the stories is that more men than women filled the shaman role, but many of the most powerful shamans were female. There seems to have been an age factor here. A woman's shamanistic power seems to have increased with age, whereas a man's seems to have remained about the same or declined over the course his career.

Girls were occasionally taught how to hunt by men who lacked sons, but whenever this happened, they still married and had children at the appropriate stages in their lives, and generally filled female roles as adults (M. Sage 1965). However, women sometimes served as members of whaling crews if there weren't enough men, and a few were recognized as being expert hunters (Aġviqsiiña 1940.1:53–54; Brower ms:182; J. Killigivuk 1940.2). I have never heard of Iñupiaq boys being raised as girls.

I also have not heard of a custom such as the two-spirit (formerly called "berdache") in plains Indian societies or the "third sex" of the eastern Canadian Inuit (Saladin d'Anglure 1986), whereby biological males filled female roles as adults. In 1826, however, Beechey saw a youth who had not had his lips perforated for labrets, and who "wore his hair in bunches on each side of the head, after the fashion of the women" (F. Beechey 1831, I:393–94). He also remarked that in his extensive travels along the coast of northwestern Alaska, this was the only case of the kind he saw.

Economic and Political Allocation

Role differentiation on the basis of economic allocation concerns who does what, and when, with regard to the production and consumption of goods and services (Levy 1966:210). The political counterpart concerns who has what power and responsibility at what times and over which activities (Levy 1952:333). Within both categories, although particularly the former, it is useful to distinguish between generalized and specialized roles. Generalized roles are those filled by everyone of the same absolute age and sex. Thus, among the Iñupiat, all adult males were hunters, and all adult females were seamstresses. Similarly, all individuals were either older or younger than someone else, and thus wielded power or bore responsibility depending on where they fit into the relative-age hierarchy.

Specialized roles, in contrast, are those that are not universally held by individuals of the same absolute age and sex. The role of shaman is one example. All shamans were also hunters or seamstresses, but relatively few hunters and seamstresses were also shamans. Since the generalized economic roles of the Iñupiat have been discussed in previous sections, albeit from a different point of view, this section is devoted to specialized roles. Since specialized economic and political roles were so closely entwined, it is useful to discuss them together.

Qaukłiich

A *qaukłiq* (sing.) was a family head. As is explained at some length in Chapter 3, there were three different levels of family organization in Iñupiaq societies. Moving from less to more inclusive, these were conjugal, domestic, and compound families. Briefly defined, a conjugal family consisted of a husband and co-resident wife (or wives), and their nonadult children. A domestic family consisted of two or more closely related conjugal families who shared a dwelling. A compound family consisted of two or more closely related domestic families whose members lived in two or more houses but operated as a single unit.

At the conjugal-family level, the *qaukłiq* was usually the husband, although widows could also fill the role. The notion of family head was more meaningful in the domestic-family context, in which the senior male member of the household usually had more authority than anyone else. And it was more meaningful still in the compound-family context, where the senior male member of the entire unit was usually the family head.

Family heads and their spouses at the various levels were the primary day-to-day managers in an Iñupiaq society. They determined what needed to be done, decided where it should be done, and specified who needed to do it. Then they, in combination with the other family members, carried out the plan. The most successful of family heads became an *umialik*.

Umialgich

Early Western visitors to northwestern Alaska encountered men who were better dressed than their companions, who bore themselves with a dignified air, and who were deferred to by others.[38] Following the Western custom of the time, they referred to these individuals in English as "chiefs,"[39] correctly surmising that they wielded more authority than anyone else. The Iñupiaq term for the role filled by these people is *umialik* (sing.).

Unfortunately, the term *umialik* has a number of meanings, including boat owner, leader, boss, and rich man. The Iñupiat could identify the specific sense in which the word was used by the context in which it appeared. That would be confusing in the present study, so I restrict my usage of the term to mean "rich man."

Umialgich (pl.) were family heads who acquired positions of unusual influence in the community "by being more thrifty and intelligent, better traders, and usually better hunters, as well as physically stronger and more daring" than almost everyone else (Simpson 1875:272). In addition to these personal abilities, they had to have the authority that accompanied seniority over groups of competent siblings, and they had to have one or more particularly competent spouses (Burch 1975a:209–19).

In comparative terms, an *umialik* was what Sahlins (1963) has called a "big-man," as opposed to a chief. In contrast to chiefs,

> Big-men do not come to office; they do not succeed to, nor are they installed in, existing positions of leadership over political groups. The attainment of big-man status is rather the outcome of a series of acts which elevate a person above the common herd and attract about him a coterie of loyal, lesser men (Sahlins 1963:289).

Following a suggestion of Elsa Redmond (1998:3–4),[40] I use the term "chieftain" in preference to "big-man" to refer to this role, although in this volume I usually employ the Iñupiaq term instead.

The power of an *umialik* was based primarily on wealth, which took the form of a large capital stock of equipment (e.g., boats, sleds, weapons, tools), a substantial surplus of food, a sizable quantity of trade goods (primarily in the form of furs), and a supply of beads—beads being the primary status symbol among the Iñupiat. This wealth, in turn, depended on the coordinated efforts of a sizable group of subordinate kinsmen as well as the *umialik*'s own personal production.

The *umialik* was important not only as a leading producer and consumer of goods, but also as a producer and consumer of services. The primary service he provided was effective management. He managed his compound family on a daily basis, using persuasion, negotiation, and example to keep the peace among the many adult siblings and cousins involved, as well as their spouses and children. By guiding the hunting activities of others, he made sure that the collective larder stayed filled. The *umialik* organized, underwrote, and usually directed the collective hunting activities, feasts, and ceremonies participated in by the members of his family over the course of a yearly cycle. The *umialik* was a consumer, on the other hand, of the allegiance, production, and support of the other family members; without them, he could not become or remain wealthy.

The abilities a man was required to demonstrate in order to become an *umialik* did not necessarily have to be perpetuated throughout his life. As long as his family continued to operate as a unit and support him, he retained his elevated status. For example, in January 1850, a party from the HMS *Plover*, which was spending the winter of 1849–50 locked in the ice near Chamisso Island, visited a chieftain named Selektutok at a village on Hotham Inlet:[41]

> We were carefully attended to by the chiefs [sic] eldest son a man of nearly 40 and we were at a loss at first to discover where the old chief was. We soon found the poor old man in one corner. He had long been bedridden, an unfortunate victim of Rheumatism, the disease had distorted some of the joints of his hands and had reduced him incapable of putting his food in the mouth. He spoke only when addressed, and then very little (Simpson 1850b: entry for Jan. 17).[42]

But he was still an *umialik*.

Ataṅġich

An *ataniq* (sing.) was someone who set limits on the behavior of someone else.[43] The term is often translated as "boss." It referred to the role filled by the person who was actually in charge of a specific collective undertaking, such as a caribou drive, whale hunt, beluga hunt, war party, or messenger festival. For present purposes, the term may be considered equivalent to "task group leader." An *ataniq* was often also an *umialik*, but that was by no means always the case. Charlie Smith (1970) explained the difference to me as follows: an *umialik* paid people to do his bidding, an *ataniq* did not.

From an economic perspective, an *ataniq* produced the services of direction and guidance without which large-scale enterprises could not have been undertaken successfully. From a political perspective, an *ataniq* had more authority than any of the other participants.

An *ataniq* was not necessarily a male, but, in practice, apparently was one most of the time. He could be, and probably usually was, also an *umialik*. But a successful *umialik* was smart enough to recognize and take advantage of the expertise of others. If someone within his sphere of influence was clearly more qualified than he to direct a particular enterprise, he (or she) was usually asked to do so. And during the time the enterprise was in progress, the *umialik* deferred to the *ataniq*.

Just how a person became the *ataniq* of an undertaking that transcended the compound-family level is not clear to me. There were relatively few occasions when this occurred, but they were important. One was the early-summer beluga hunts conducted annually by the Nuataaġmiut on the northern shore of Kotzebue Sound, and by the Kaŋiġmiut in Eschscholtz Bay. Both involved virtually all of the adult males in their respective nations, but the Nuataaġmiut hunt, in particular, was directed by a single individual. Another instance was a major invasion (as opposed to a small-scale raid) of a foreign territory, a project that involved the male members of many families. A third possibility was a caribou drive in which the members of two or more families were involved. A fourth was the construction of the road through the ice ridges that whalers built each spring to get their boats to the lead, or stretch of open water, where the whales were. This enterprise, too, must have involved a substantial segment of the entire population.

In the case of collective undertakings such as these, my impression is that there were two ways for a person to be recruited to the *ataniq* role. One was simple consensus. From lifelong familiarity, people knew each other's strengths and weaknesses even at the national level, and it may have been so obvious to everyone as to who should lead on a given occasion that there was not even any discussion of the matter. The difficulty my informants had in explaining how the process worked suggests that this may have been the usual procedure. Another possibility was for the *umialgich* to get together and negotiate the outcome. They did this from time to time in connection with disputes within the village, so it seems reasonable to suppose that they might have done so on other occasions as well.

Aŋatkut

An *aŋatkuq* (sing.) was a shaman, that is, "a specialist in healing, divination and allied social functions, allegedly by techniques of spirit possession and spirit control" (Gould and Kolb 1964:638).[44] There were several ways a man or a woman could become an *aŋatkuq*, all of which involved acquiring a "familiar" spirit (*qiḷa*). This spirit possessed the shaman, usually when asked to do so, and through it he or she could communicate with other spirits.[45] One could purchase a *qiḷa* from someone who already had it, receive it as a gift, or acquire it through inheritance. Occasionally, the familiar took the initiative and attached itself to a particular human without any effort on the person's part.

People could also seek an association with a spirit through ritual performances of various kinds, particularly if they were performed in localities known to be home to large numbers of spirits. In the Kivalina district, for example, a cave on the north side of Umagatsaiak Mountain (*uummagaatchiaq*) was such a place.[46] In the Shishmaref district, the upper Serpentine River area was similarly rich in spirit beings. The prospective shaman often tried to attract a spirit to come to him or her by various means, such as fasting, drumming and singing, or twirling a bull-roarer. In the cave near Kivalina, one entered the cave, uttered the phrase "*taaqtuq timaa*" ("its body is black") in a loud voice, and waited (A. Hawley 1976.2; B. Hawley 1989). After two or three days spent fasting in the cave, the supplicant might be accepted by a spirit. Such efforts were sometimes successful, sometimes not. Success could also turn into disaster, as when a spirit was so powerful that the human to whom it decided to become associated was not strong enough physically or psychologically to deal with it, and died as a consequence.

The *aŋatkuq* role was filled only by people who were associated with familiar spirits. Just how many such people there were at any given time is unknown. The only figure I have ever seen was Thornton's (1931:104) observation that in Wales in 1890 there were eight *aŋatkut* (pl.) in an adult population of 307, for a ratio of slightly more than one in forty. In nations whose populations were more widely dispersed, the ratio was probably somewhat higher.

An *aŋatkuq* performed a number of important services for the Iñupiat. The most common of these were identifying the causes of, and prescribing the cures for, a wide variety of calamities, including sickness, accidents, poor harvests, and bad weather. The causes were identified with the help of the *qiḷa*. The most common diagnosis was that someone had broken a taboo or failed to perform an important ritual. Equally often, the cure consisted of the imposition of one or more new taboos or rituals on one or more members of the community, either temporarily or permanently, although relatively simple problems could be fixed more directly through magic. The familiar spirit communicated the relevant information on both the cause and the cure to the *aŋatkuq*, who then transmitted it to the people involved. An *aŋatkuq* could also divine the future, perform spirit flights, and perform a variety of magical feats. The *aŋatkuq* usually collected a fee for his or her services. Since the Iñupiat paid in kind rather than with money, an *aŋatkuq* tended to be an unusually active consumer of a variety of goods, although he or she could also be compensated with services instead of things.

The special ability of an *aŋatkuq* to communicate with the spirit world and to impose taboos on the other members of the community were an important source of power. The others had to be willing to follow the shaman's instructions, of course, but they ran the risk of incurring the wrath of a malevolent spirit and possibly precipitating a disaster if they did not. On the other hand, an *aŋatkuq* was responsible to the other members of the community to use his or her power for the general good. One who did not was regarded as being extremely dangerous and ran the risk of being assassinated.

Iñuunniaqtit

Aŋatkuq is often translated by contemporary Iñupiat as "doctor" with reference to the healing function, or "witch doctor" with reference to the spirit medium through which he or she worked (Juul 1979; Keats 1976; Kirchner 1983). But the Iñupiat also had another kind of healer, one who did not use magic or work through spirit intermediaries during the course of his or her work. Traditionally, such a person was known as an *iñuunniaqti* (sing.); nowadays, he or she is referred to as a "tribal doctor."

An *iñuunniaqti* dealt with physical ailments through deep massage and manipulation (*saptaq–*) or bloodletting (*kapi–*), and sometimes with medicine.[47] Deep massage was used to treat stomach ailments, pain in the liver or other internal organs, sprains, and dislocations. It was also employed during pregnancy to ascertain and perhaps improve the position of the fetus and umbilical cord inside the womb. Bloodletting was performed with a small lancet. It was done to reduce swellings, cure headaches, remove pus from infected areas, and to remove "bad blood" from a patient's body. The *iñuunniaqti* ordinarily was paid either in kind or in service for his or her efforts. An *iñuunniaqti*, especially a good one, wielded some influence in the community, but was not nearly as powerful as an *aŋatkuq*.

Suġruich and Aŋuyaitch

A warrior who fought in open battle was an *aŋuyakti*, while a raider was a *suġruk* (see Burch 2005:98, 99). Both were generalized roles, as that concept was defined above, in that every adult male and teenage boy was expected to participate in both offensive and defensive combat. There was no specialized group of warriors set apart from the rest of the population. Fighting was a specialized activity, however, in that men did not engage in it very often; while they were engaged in it, their attention was focused almost exclusively on it.

Raids seem to have occurred often enough during the study period for virtually every Iñupiaq male to have to participate in one or more armed confrontations over the course of his lifetime. Toward this end, all boys were taught the techniques of shooting and dodging arrows, and they were trained to be tough enough to stand the stress of battle. They learned strategy and tactics during the course of many hours spent in the *qargi* listening to stories and discussions of previous encounters.

All adult males were involved in settlement defense, but I do not know what percentage was involved in aggressive actions toward an enemy nation. No one could force a man to participate in an attack on an enemy estate, so conceivably some men could have avoided participation in a raiding party. On the other hand, in the macho world of Iñupiaq males, it would have been quite remarkable for a healthy young man to stay home when all of his contemporaries were setting out on a raid; the pressure to go along would have been enormous. Iñupiaq men were at least as influenced by charges of cowardice as young American men are today (Simpson 1852–54: entry for Aug. 2, 1853).

Another role that is usefully discussed under the general heading of "warrior" is that of the *iññuqun*, or "prowler" (Burch 2005:91–99). An *iññuqun* was a man—I have never heard of a woman filling this role—who set off, either on his own or with a very small group of companions, to spy on, often to terrorize, and occasionally to kill people in another country. *Iññuqutit* (pl.) usually operated in mid- to late summer, setting out on foot to wander around an enemy estate, and to sneak up on people and observe what they were doing. If they could engage in some kind of mischief, such as slicing up a boat or stealing some food without getting caught, they often did so. If they found someone in a particularly vulnerable position, they might kill him or her. The terrorist element in these activities was in making the local people aware of the fact that an unknown number of enemy were in the neighborhood; unless they could be found and destroyed, they posed a threat of potentially serious dimensions.

People in every part of northwestern Alaska can tell dozens of stories about being victimized by *iññuqutit*, but I have yet to hear an account of the motivations and actions of an *iññuqun* from the aggressor's point of view. The percentage of people in any given nation who engaged in this type of activity is unknowable, therefore, but presumably it was rather small.

Menials

Eskimo societies are frequently characterized as being egalitarian, but in northwestern Alaska they were hierarchical. This hierarchy was based primarily on relative age, but family connections, or the lack thereof, were also a factor. The *umialgich* were at the top of the system of wealth and power, and what I call "menials" were at the bottom. Menials were not common, but they did exist.[48]

At the absolute bottom of the system was the *tigutaaluk*. This word was translated by my informants as "slave." Technically, a *tigutaaluk* was not a slave because he or she could not be bought and sold, but in most other respects the label is appropriate. Slaves were uncommon, but were found in some of the larger villages. The ones I have heard about were all males, who ranged in age from young boys to full adults. They were forced to live in a *qargi* and do all the dirty work required to support it: tend lamps, take out refuse, run errands, dump the chamber pot, and so on. They were entirely dependent on others for food, which, for them, consisted of scraps and leftovers, and for clothing, which was usually cast off. They were treated with contempt by everyone else. I have no certain information on how or with whom they lived during seasons when the *qargi* was closed, but presumably it was in the house or storm shed of the richest member of that particular *qargi*.

Only slightly above the *tigutaaluq* was the *savaktaaġruk*, or "servant." A servant could be either male or female and of any age from childhood on. He or she lived with a family in a house, or perhaps in the storm shed, rather than in a *qargi*. A *savaktaaġruk* was better clothed and fed than a slave, but was nevertheless required to do all the most menial tasks of the household. In times of hunger, the servant was the first to be placed on reduced rations.

The key factor in becoming a menial seems to have been a lack of supportive kin (Jensen 1970.6; Vestal 1970). Every one of the servants I have heard of was an orphan (*iḷiappak*). Just how one became an orphan in the Iñupiaq system is not mentioned in the stories, but famine, accident, and warfare, alone or in combination, could readily eliminate so many close relatives as to leave a person without support within the community. The few slaves I have heard about were from other nations, but I have no information on how they came to be in their unfortunate situation.

Religion

Role differentiation on the basis of religion concerns who does what, and when, with regard to belief in and the pursuit of ultimate goals (Levy 1952:337). This raises the question of what the ultimate goals of the early-19th-century Iñupiat might have been. I do not know the answer to that question with any certainty, but will offer three possibilities as hypotheses: (1) physical survival; (2) loyalty to one's blood kin; and (3) both of the foregoing (Simpson 1852–54: entries for Sept. 21, 1853, Feb. 12, 1854). In my judgment, the last alternative is the correct one. Compared to many other religions, these two goals may seem rather prosaic, but after pondering the matter for several decades, they are the best I have come up with.

The hypothesized ultimate goal of physical survival is at least partly consistent with the Iñupiaq belief that, after one dies, one is reincarnated in the form of another person. The afterworld, to the extent that it was conceived of at all, was thought to be a place where souls went to live temporarily while awaiting a new human form. Reincarnation in human form was automatic; it was not contingent on one's behavior either in life or in death. There was no heaven or hell to worry about, and there was no concern about being reborn as a mosquito, for example, or a lemming. To the extent one was concerned about the future, it was in this world, not another one. Thus, it is not surprising, as George Stoney (1900:834) reported, that "there is absolutely no knowledge or idea of a god or of a providence; nor is there worship of any kind, of animal, idol, or things." According to Simpson (1875:275), "they do not entertain any clear idea of a future state of existence, nor can they apparently imagine that a person altogether dies." He added that "they all agree in looking upon death as the greatest of human evils."

The hypothesized ultimate goal of loyalty to one's consanguineal, or blood, kin is consistent with early observations about the priority that such kin took over everyone else. For example, on the basis of his experience between 1848 and 1854, John Simpson (1875:247) reported that "beyond the sphere of their own family or hut they appear to have no regard." Similarly, George Stoney (1900:831–32) said that "relationship is binding; the most distant cousinship is recognized. The family never forgets its own no matter how far they may be separated."

Given the nature of Iñupiaq religion as I have described it, it should not be surprising that role differentiation on the basis of religion was minimal. Even the basic distinction between believers and the uninitiated was at a minimum; the former were simply adults who had grown up in the system, while the latter were infants and children who were still in the process of acquiring the beliefs of their elders. In a sense, the two kinds of "doctor," the *aŋatkuq* and *iñuunniaqti*, might be said to be religious specialists to the extent and in the respects that their expert knowledge enabled people to live longer than they otherwise might have. But beyond these rather basic considerations, I have not been able to discern any role differentiation on the basis of religion in a traditional Iñupiaq society.

Cognition

Role differentiation on the basis of cognition relates to differences in knowledge or understanding of a situation or phenomenon (Levy 1952:338–39). Here again, it is useful to distinguish between generalized and specialized roles. The former, it may be recalled, are those filled by everyone of the same age and sex; the latter are a residual category.

The generalized roles based on cognition in an Iñupiaq nation were those involving learners and teachers. The former generally were children and teenagers, while the latter were their parents, grandparents, aunts, and uncles. An important part of the ideology underlying the authority of seniors over juniors was based on the assumption that the former knew more than the latter.

Girls were taught how to sew, set snares, cook, butcher game, and perform myriad other tasks by their mothers, grandmothers, and aunts. Similarly, boys were taught how to track animals, hunt, and manufacture tools and weapons by their fathers, grandfathers, and uncles. This general education process went on all day, every day, from childhood to adulthood. As one achieved the level of knowledge required of an adult, one's role shifted from student to teacher, and one's students became the members of the following generation.

Knowledge was not evenly distributed among the adult members of an Iñupiaq society. Some people could do certain things—for example, sew, make sealskin rope, or carve—much better than others could. Expertise was recognized and admired, and everyone knew who knew most about doing what in the settlement, and often in the entire society. A widespread myth about Eskimos is that they were not competitive. In fact, the Iñupiat, at least, seem to have been quite competitive, not only in overt competitions in which there was a clear-cut winner, such as wrestling or football, but in just about everything. A new set of clothing, for example, was scrutinized and judged by every woman who saw it for evidence of the maker's skill (or lack thereof) in preparing skins and sewing clothing. Similarly, men did not submit the tools and implements they made to a jury for assessment, but everyone in the village made a critical appraisal of each man's work. One did not receive a formal grade, but one's abilities were duly noted and remarked on by everyone, usually behind one's back. Since every adult of the same age and sex had to perform the same set of tasks as everyone else in the same age and sex category, everyone was qualified to make informed judgments in such matters.

There were a few roles in an Iñupiaq nation that may be considered specialized with regard to cognition. Most notable, perhaps, were those of the two types of "doctor" discussed above, the *aŋatkuq*, or shaman, and the *iñuunniaqti*, or tribal doctor. The special knowledge of the *aŋatkuq* related to communicating with and influencing various entities in the spirit world. The special knowledge of the *iñuunniaqti* concerned the location and proper condition of the internal organs and blood supply, and the means of correcting problems in those areas.

A role that is sometimes confused nowadays with that of *aŋatkuq* is that of *iḷisiḷa* (sing.), which can be translated as "clairvoyant."[49] An *iḷisiḷa* was someone who had the ability to see and hear in real time things that were happening far away, that is, dozens or even hundreds of miles away. A special feature of this ability was an awareness of black magic being performed at some remote location, knowledge that enabled the *iḷisiḷa* to take counteractive measures before the magic was able to exert its harmful effects. *Iḷisiḷat* (pl.) did not work through familiar spirits, but through the power of their minds. They could do some of the things that shamans could, such as cure disease, but more often they acted to prevent evil shamans from achieving their goals. The power of an *iḷisiḷa* could not be purchased, inherited, or taught; it simply came to a person for unknown reasons and through unknown mechanisms. It is my impression that, for the most part, *iḷisiḷat* rarely exhibited their special power unless they were forced by unfortunate circumstances to do so. Shamans, however, could always tell who was an *iḷisiḷa* and who was not.

A specialized cognitive role that has been reported only from Point Hope is that of *ibrukok*, about which I have no independent information (Rainey 1940.20). According to the descriptions provided by Froelich Rainey's informants, an *ibrukok* seems to have combined elements of both the *aŋatkuq* and *iḷisiḷa* roles (Aġviqsiiña 1940.1:62–63, 103; Q. Dives 1940; Quwana 1940.1). Unlike the *aŋatkuq*, who used a drum to communicate with his familiar spirit, the *ibrukok* employed a magic stick to do so. The *ibrukok*'s belt was formed into a loop, with one end around the stick, the other around an afflicted person's head or injured limb. By lifting up on the stick, the *ibrukok* attempted to raise the afflicted person's head or limb, and posed questions to his familiar spirit while doing so. The spirit never entered the *ibrukok*'s body, but answered his or her questions, sometimes in a voice that everyone present could hear. On other occasions the spirit would communicate with the *ibrukok* without the intervention of the stick, in a manner reminiscent of an *iḷisiḷa*.

Another role that was specialized with regard to cognition was that of the *sivuniksriqiri* (sing.), which can be translated as "prophet."[50] A *sivuniksriqiri* was a person who could somehow see into the future. This person was not an *aŋatkuq*, who had to make a deliberate effort to work through his or her own familiar spirit to communicate with the spirit world. Rather, information about future events came to a *sivuniksriqiri* spontaneously, without any particular effort on his or her part. The most famous prophet in the study region was a man named Maniiḷaq, who predicted the arrival of Whites, the founding of the village of Ambler, and many other developments, long before they eventually came to pass (Pulu and Ramoth-Sampson 1981; Roberts 1978:115–23).

The final specialized role that was differentiated on the basis of cognition was that of storyteller, or *quliaqtuaqti* (sing.) (D. Jenness 1924:1; Ostermann 1942:163; Rainey 1947:269). The storytellers of an Iñupiaq nation were its major historians and entertainers. They were the repositories of the legends (*unipkaat*) and historical chronicles (*uqaluktuat*) that recorded the mythology and history of their people. They were also among a nation's foremost providers of entertainment, especially during the long nights of early winter. Storytellers were self-selected, and they trained themselves by observing and listening to their elders. When the elders who had taught them passed on, the new generation filled the gap.

Stratification

Stratification is the "particular type of role differentiation that differentiates between higher and lower standings in terms of one or more criteria" (Levy 1952:343). Several criteria used for ranking among the Iñupiat have already been mentioned: absolute age, relative age, generation, wealth, and knowledge. These are all characteristics of individuals rather than groups, and each individual in an Iñupiaq nation knew pretty well where he or she stood relative to everyone else with respect to each of them. Power entered into the calculation of rank through sheer physical strength, at the individual level, and through solidarity with a large number of kinsmen, at the group level.

An *umialik* and the members of his immediate family usually combined high ranking with respect to most or all of the above criteria to place them at the top of the system. An *umialik* was a mature adult who was a highly successful hunter and trader who gathered about him one or more spouses and several (usually) younger relatives, many of whom, individually, also ranked high on a number of scales. The power of an *umialik* in the community at large lay in numbers: the larger his family, the more wealth and power he and the other members of his family had.

Notes to Chapter Two

1. I am grateful to Ann Fienup-Riordan for comments on a draft of this chapter.
2. E. Curtis (1930:168), Q. Dives (1940), Elwood Hunnicutt (1970), D. Jenness (1924:183), J. Ningeulook (1981.2), Stoney (1900:845), Sun (1985:29). According to John MacDonald (1998:43–51), these stars were Altair and Tarazed, which belong to the constellation Aquila. At other times of year they can be seen in the evening in the western sky.
3. Aġviqsiiña (1940.1:37–38), Anderson et al. (1998:35), J. Savok (1986), Simpson (ms.e, 1851), C. Smith (1970), Stoney (1900:845).
4. Anderson et al. (1998:35), H. Anungazuk (1999.1), Gideon Barr (1982.1), Ramoth-Sampson (1987), Savok (1986), C. Smith (1970), Stoney (1900:846), Wells (1974).
5. Aġviqsiiña (1940.1), E. Attungana (1980), E. and P. Attungana (1980), Q. Dives (1940), S. Dives (1970), B. Foote (1992:11–18), David Frankson (1980), Hank (1959), Iviqsiq (1940), Jensen (1970.1, 1970.2, 1980.1), J. Killiguvuk (1960.2, 1960.4, 1960.7, 1961.1), Kingik (1980), Kowunna (1970, 1980), Kunuyaq (1940), Larsen and Rainey (1948:26–30), Larson (1995:208–11), Lisburne (1959), Lowenstein (1992:xxviii–xxxii; 1993:53–172), Nasugluk and Nasugruk (1940), Niġuwana (1940.1), Ostermann and Holtved (1952:120–23), Quwana (1940.1), Rainey (1940.16, 1940.17, 1947:244–68), S. Rock (1940), Tuckfield and Tingook (1960.1). See also Burch (1981).
6. A. Hawley (1970.1, 1976.4), J. Hawley (1976), M. Hawley (1965.1), Iviqsiq (1940), Jensen (1970.1, 1970.2), Kennedy (1984), E. Mills (1960.1), John Stalker (1965.1, 1970.1), Clinton Swan (1965.1, 1965.2), M. and M. Swan (1970), Milton Swan (1964.2), R. Walton (1965.1, 1965.2). See also Burch (1998a:23–57).
7. D. Adams (1986), Ashby (1970), Booth (1960.1:39), K. Burns (1960.2), M. Curtis (1970), L. Gallahorn (1969.1, 1970.3), Edna Hunnicutt (1960.1, 1960.2), Keats (1970.2), Robert Lee (1960.2), Luther (1960.1), McClellan (1970.2, 1986, 1987), T. Mitchell (1969), M. and D. Naylor (1960), Onalik (1986), John Stalker (1986), Wesley (1986). See also Burch (1998a:59–78).
8. D. Adams (1986), Booth (1960.1, 1960.2, 1960.4, 1961), E. Curtis (1930:195), T. Douglas (1986), Edna Hunnicutt (1960.2), Keats (1969.2, 1970.1, 1970.2, 1970.5), Luther (1960.1), J. Mitchell (1952.18), T. Mitchell (1969, 1970, 1986), Sampson (1970), Ella Smith (1970), John Stalker (1986), Martha Swan (1970), Wesley (1986). See also Burch (1998a:79–109).
9. H. Brown (1965), Cantwell (1887:28–32, 41–42), G. Cleveland (1965), M. Cleveland (1989), R. Cleveland (1965.5, 1965.7, 1970.1), Coffin (1970), A. Douglas (1976.3), Eliyak (1931), D. Foster (1970.2), Giddings (1956:5; 1961:31–46), Glover (1970.1, 1970.2, 1970.3, 1970.5), C. Lee (1970), NANA Cultural Heritage Project (1975a), Sheidt (1969.1), Sun (1970, 1985, 1989), Tingook (1960.4, 1965), Townsend (1887:86), J. Wells (1974), C. Wood (1931). See also Burch (1998a:123–70); Burch, Jones, Loon, and Kaplan (1999).
10. Anderson and Anderson (1982), W. Ballot (1970.1, 1970.2), E. Curtis (1930:225–28), J. Foster (1970, 1986.1), J. and F. Foster (1986), Kiana (1969, 1970), Ramoth (1970), C. Smith (1970), Wright (1969.2). See also Burch (1998a:221–43).
11. Anderson and Anderson (1982), Coffin (1970), J. Foster (1970), J. and F. Foster (1986), Kiana (1970), Ramoth (1970, 1986). See also Burch (1998a:245–58).
12. R. Cleveland (1970.1), D. Foster (1970.1, 1970.2), Glover (1970.2), NANA Cultural Heritage Project (1975f), Pungalik (1970), S. Thomas (1970). See also Burch (1998a:171–88).
13. Armstrong (1970), Carter (1986), P. Hadley (1986), Kialook (1964, 1970), Lee, Sampson, Tennant, and Mendenhall (1990:67–87), Lucier (1954:215), J. Savok (1986), Sunno (1951.63, 1951:101), E. Thomas (1986, 1987). See also Burch (1998a:259–84).
14. Beaver (1970.2), E. Curtis (1930:167–68), M. Curtis (1970), L. Gallahorn (1970.2), Glover (1970.5), Elwood Hunnicutt (1970), McClellan (1987), K. Mills (1989), L. Mills (1986, 1987, 1989), NANA Cultural Heritage Project (1975e), D. Naylor (1960.2), Northwest Iñupiat Elders Conference (1983b, 1983f, 1983g, 1983h), Jacob Stalker (1970), John Stalker (1986), Wright (1969.1, 1969.2). See also Burch (1998a:189–218).
15. E. Barr (1970), Gideon Barr (1991.1), Gilford Barr (1987), A. Karmun (1970), M. Karmun (1970), L. Mills (1986, 1987), T. Morris (1970), NANA Cultural Heritage Project (1975c), S. Thomas (1970), Vestal (1970). See also Burch (1998a:285–304).
16. Avessuk (1983.1, 1983.5, 1983.6), E. Barr (1970), Gideon Barr (1991), Eisler (1978:9–25), Eutuk (1983), Fair (1998), Heinrich (1963a:435–36), Hrdlička (1930:202), Kiyutelluk (1976), Koutsky (ms.a, ms.b, 1975a, 1975b, 1975c, 1981a), Nayokpuk (1991, 1999), H. Ningeulook (1983.2, 1983.3, 1983.4), Okpowruk (1983.4), Olanna (1983), D. J. Ray (1964:81–82), E. Tocktoo (1983), G. Tocktoo (1984), M. Tocktoo (1983.4), M. and V. Tocktoo (1999.1, 1999.2), V. Tocktoo (1983), Alex Weyiouanna (1983, 1999), A. and E. Weyiouanna (1999), Essau Weyiouanna (1983.3, 1983.4, 1987).
17. H. Anungazuk (1999.1), E. Curtis (1930:137–46), Koutsky (ms.a, 1976, 1981b), Nagozruk (1970), Nelson (1899:257), Oxereok (1999.1, 1999.2, 1999.3, 1999.4), D. J. Ray (1964:78–81), Thornton (1931:120–21, 130–38, 165–210), Weyapuk (1991.1, 1991.2).
18. Brower (ms:258), Dall (1866–67), Wells and Kelly (1890:24–25), Woolfe (1893:141).
19. The Sisualik fair has been described at length in Burch (2005:180–92). See that book for more information and detailed references.

20. In this volume I use the word "district" to refer to the several national estates relevant to this study.
21. Brower (ms:143, 157, 158, 160, 161), Grinnell (1901:49–51), B. Hawley (1982), Keats (1970.2, 1970.3, 1970.4, 1970.5), NANA Cultural Heritage Project (1975d), J. Ningeulook (1981.1, 1981.2), S. Obruk (1981), Stefansson (1914b:343), Stoney (1900:570–71, 813, 836–37), Thornton (1931:11, 220), Trollope (1855:874), Woolfe (1893:135, 137, 144).
22. As April progresses, even where the sun drops below the horizon, refraction keeps some light in the sky, and its effect is magnified by the snow covering the ground.
23. *Uvluq* can refer to both the period of daylight and the entire twenty-four-hour period.
24. According to John Hadley (1951), men used to sing a song just before daybreak each morning.
25. During the study period, before industrial haze reached the region, cloudless nights in northwestern Alaska were crystal-clear.
26. Overflow, or icing, occurs when a shallow river freezes to the bottom and the spring-fed stream is forced up through a crack to the top of the ice.
27. C. and R. Adams (1965), R. Adams (1965), H. Anungazuk (1999.1), Green (1969), A. Hawley (1965.16, 1965.17, 1973.2, 1973.3), Kennedy (1973), Ongtowasruk (1999), Sprott (1998:50–53), Clinton Swan (1965.5).
28. Anderson et al. (1998:95, 248), Brower (ms:380), K. Burns (1960.2:22), Call (1899:120–21), E. Curtis (1930:165–66), M. Curtis (1969), Geary (1976), Grinnell (1901:57), Jacobsen (1977:152), Kennedy (1965.3), N. Knox (1965), Niġuwana (1940.1:9–10), Ostermann and Holtved (1952:124–25), Rainey (1940.2), Simpson (ms.f, 1875:254), Stefansson (1914b:161–62, 178, 183–84, 208, 354–55, 386), Stoney (ms:92, 127–28; 1900:814–15), Charlotte Swan (1965.4), Martha Swan (1965.7), M. Tocktoo (1983.2), Wells and Kelly (1890:18), Weyer (1928: entry for Cape Prince of Wales, p. 16), Woolfe (1893:136).
29. John Simpson (ms.f) says that the people of Point Barrow did not tie the cord.
30. Aġviqsiiña (1940.1), Brower (ms:380), Call (1899:120–21), E. Curtis (1930:137–48), M. Curtis (1969.1), Q. Dives (1940:25–26), Hooper (1881:109), Niġuwana (1940.1), Ostermann and Holtved (1952:125), Rainey (1947:243), Simpson (1875:245, 249, 250), Sprott (1998:49, 51; 1999), Charlotte Swan (1965.2), Thornton (1931:85–88), Wells and Kelly (1890:18), Woolfe (1893:136).
31. H. Anungazuk (1999.1), Aġviqsiiña (1940.1:105), Avessuk (1983.3), L. Gallahorn (1969.1), A. Hawley (1970.2), Hooper (1881:109), Kuzuguk (1983), Lowenstein (1993:22), Nagozruk (1928), H. Ningeulook (1983.1), Northwest Iñupiaq Elders Conference (1983g:5, 105), S. and E. Obruk (1983.1), Ostermann and Holtved (1952:125), Rainey (1940.7, 1940.9), Stefansson (1914b:202, 346–47), Martha Swan (1984.1), M. Tocktoo (1983.5), Wells and Kelly (1890:18), Woolfe (1893:152).
32. Ostermann and Holtved (1952:125), Stoney (1900:831–32), Thornton (1931:59–60), Woolfe (1893:134, 137), Wells and Kelly (1890:18). Sprott (1998:50–51) has compiled a much more detailed list of the physical and emotional stages recognized in early childhood.
33. Aġviqsiiña (1940.1:74, 110), E. Curtis (1930:166), J. Mitchell (1952.1), J. Ningeulook (1983.3), Quwana (1940.1:7), Stefansson (1914b:340), Sunno (1951.1, 1951.52), Thornton (1931:79), Vestal (1970), Weyer (1928: entry for Cape Prince of Wales, p. 8).
34. Aġviqsiiña (1941.1:74), R. Cleveland (1965.8), E. Curtis (1930:166), Eliyak (1931), Gray, Cleveland, and Lee (1987), Grinnell (1901:76), Keats (1969.1, 1970.5), M. Konalook (1951), J. Mitchell (1952.14, 1952.15), Nagozruk (1928), Ostermann and Holtved (1952:126), Stoney (ms:127), Sunno (1951.77), Wells and Kelly (1890:127), Woolfe (1893:136).
35. H. Anungazuk (1999.1), Aġviqsiiña (1940.1:102–3), W. Ballot (1970.1), Brower (ms:136, 154–55, 186, 311–12), Call (1899:116, 126–27), Cantwell (1889a:66; 1889b:83), E. Curtis (1930:148–50, 66–167), M. Curtis (1970), Dall (1866–67: entry for October 12), Downey, Stalker, and Ashby (1987), L. Gallahorn (1970.3), Grinnell (1901:33, 39–40, 42, 70), A. Hawley (1966), Hooper (1881:113), Edna Hunnicutt (1970.2), Iviqsiq (1940), Jarvis (1899:67), Jensen (1970.2, 1970.3), Lee et al. (1990:17, 19), Luther (1976), Mitchell and Keats (1952), Nagozruk (1928), Nasugluk and Nasugruk (1940:8), H. Ningeulook (1983.4), Quwana (1940:38), Ostermann and Holtved (1952:126–27), S. Rock (1940), A. Skin (1970), A. Smith (1989), Stefansson (1914b:187, 316–17), Stoney (1900:830–31), Sunno (1951.15, 1951.41, 1951.42, 1951.43, 1951.81, 1951.109, 1951.115), Thornton (1931:105–7), Tingook (1961), Vestal (1970), Walton (1965.1, 1965.3), Wells and Kelly (1890:22), C. Wood (1931), Woolfe (1893:138).
36. C. Adams and R. Adams (1965), Green (1969), A. Hawley (1965.16, 1965.17), J. Killigivuk (1967), Clinton Swan (1965:5).
37. Brower (ms:129, 157), Keats (1970.4, 1970.5), Simpson (1875:252), Stoney (1900:813, 832), Thornton (1931:36, 86, 100), Seemann (1853, II:62, 66), Trollope (1855:874), Wells and Kelly (1890:17), Woolfe (1893:135, 144).
38. Aġviqsiiña (1940.1, 1940.2, 1940.3), E. Barr (1970), Cantwell (1889b:82), R. Cleveland (1970.3), J. Foster (1970), L. Gallahorn (1970.1), Glover (1970.5), A. Hawley (1965.9), Jensen (1970.6), Kiana (1970), R. Knox (1965), T. Morris (1970), C. Smith (1970), Clinton Swan (1965.3), M. and M. Swan (1970), Vestal (1970).
39. F. Beechey (1831, I:401, 458; II:280), Bertholf (1899a:24), Collinson (1889:332–33), Dall (1870a:556), *The Esquimaux* (1866–67:15, 16), Kotzebue (1821, I:208, 235–36), Maguire (1857:438, 454–55), McLenegan (1887:75), T. Moore (1851:29), Rasmussen (1933:312), Seemann (1853, II:135), Simpson (1875:272), Elijah Smith (1873), Stoney (1900:832).
40. Unfortunately, Redmond's discussion is a bit ambiguous on the difference between chief and chieftain.

41. If, as I believe, this is the person referred to in Simpson's 1875 paper (p. 245), he could not have been "less than eighty years of age. He had long been confined to his bed, and appeared quite in his dotage."

42. Punctuation (or lack thereof) follows the original without use of *sic*.

43. R. Cleveland (1970.3), J. Foster (1970), L. Gallahorn (1970.1), Glover (1970.5), A. Hawley (1973.2, 1973.4), Jensen (1970.1, 1970.6), T. Morris (1970), C. Smith (1970), M. and M. Swan (1970), Vestal (1970).

44. Aġviqsiiña (1940.1:63–65, 79–80), Beaver (1984), K. Burns (1960.2), Q. Dives (1940:37), Eliyak (1931), J. Foster (1970), L. Gallahorn (1969.2), Glover (1970.5, 1970.6), A. Hawley (1965.4, 1965.8., 1976.2), B. Hawley (1965, 1989), Jensen (1970.3), Keats (1970.7), Kennedy (1965.2), Lee et al. (1990:9), H. Ningeulook (1983.4), Northwest Iñupiat Elders Conference (1976.d:10–11), Stefansson (1914b:368), Stoney (1900:834–35), Sunno (1951.14, 1951.22, 1951.114), Martha Swan (1965.2), Vestal (1969, 1970), Wells and Kelly (1890:22–23).

45. Aġviqsiiña (1940.1:63–66, 79), Anungazuk (1999.4), K. Burns (1960.2), Q. Dives (1940:37), Glover (1970.6), A. Hawley (1965.1, 1976.2), B. Hawley (1989), Jensen (1970.3), Northwest Iñupiat Elders Conference (1976.d), Stefansson (1914b:367–68, 369–70), Sunno (1951.14, 1951.55, 1951.90, 1951.114).

46. The roof of this cave has now largely collapsed.

47. Beaver (1984), Dixon and Kirchner (1982), Keats (1976), Kennedy (1965.2), Lucier, VanStone, and Keats (1971:253–54), Martha Swan (1984.4, 1984.5), Wells and Kelly (1890:23).

48. Brower (ms:191), J. Foster (1970), B. Hawley (1982), Jensen (1970.6), Keats (1970.8).

49. Ballot (in Lee et al. 1990:5, 7), Glover (1970.6), Jensen (1970.3), Keats (1970.7), T. Morris (1970), Northwest Iñupiat Elders Conference (1976.a:4; 1976d:8; 1983a), C. Sheldon (1973–74.3, 1973–74.5, 1973–74.6, 1973–74.7, 1973–74.17).

50. R. Cleveland (1970.1), A. Douglas (1976.2, 1989.1), J. Foster (1970), Glover (1970.5), Jensen (1970.3), Keats (1970.9), T. Morris (1970).

Chapter Three

Solidarity

Individuals cannot live in isolation, but must be involved in relationships with other people in order to survive.[1] The pattern in terms of which these relationships are allocated among the members of a society according to their content, strength, and intensity is the structure of solidarity (Levy 1966:220). The study of solidarity involves the analysis of who does what with whom, and under what circumstances.

It is fruitful in a general analysis of any nation to distinguish between family relationships and all others. In highly industrialized nations, family relationships are important, but they are often overwhelmed, and they certainly are outnumbered, by obligations and relationships in the wider social sphere. In an Iñupiaq nation, the situation was exactly the opposite: family relationships were both the most numerous and the strongest from virtually every point of view (Simpson 1875:247; Stoney 1900:831–32). Consequently, most of this chapter concerns families and the relationships between and among family members. It is only toward the end that I broaden the scope of analysis to describe how members of different families related to one another.

Conjugal Families

A conjugal family (*aniqatigiich* or *qitungagiich*) is one involving a co-resident husband-wife pair and their unmarried children, if any. It is the type more commonly referred to as the "nuclear" family in the social science literature. The term "conjugal" focuses attention on the fact that the husband-wife bond is at the center of the system, and that it is the relationship that endures after the children grow up and have children of their own. Accordingly, it is with that relationship that I begin.

The Husband-Wife Relationship

The husband-wife (*ui-nuliaq*) relationship was established when a man and woman had sexual relations and started living together.[2] There was no wedding ceremony, although sometimes the man made gifts to the woman or to her parents when or before the couple got together. Among the Tapqaġmiut, it has also been reported that a newly married couple lived with the wife's parents for a year, during which the son-in-law did much of the hunting (J. Ningeulook 1983.3).

Most settlements were so small and isolated, and they were made up of such close relatives, that finding a suitable person to marry must have been a challenging task for most people. However, there seems to have been a general belief that marrying a close relative, even a first cousin, was desirable.[3] The rationale was that spouses who were unrelated would be torn by conflicting loyalties in case of an interfamily dispute or feud, since the tie of blood was stronger than the tie of marriage. Spouses who were blood relatives in the first place presumably would not have this problem.

Parents often tried to arrange their children's first marriage in order to create linkages with families they liked and respected. Most accounts indicate that women generally resisted getting "married" to their first suitor, whether chosen by the parents or not. I interpret such statements to mean that most girls were reluctant to lose their virginity, which male suitors probably tried to persuade them to do when they were in their early teens. In my time (i.e., the 1960s), the male perspective was that if a girl was physically big enough to have sex, she was old enough to have it. That view was not necessarily shared by girls, who often put up fierce resistance. It was not uncommon for a man to abduct a girl by force and essentially rape her to get the relationship started. If a woman's parents approved of the suitor, she had little choice. If they or her brothers opposed it, on the other hand, her wishes might prevail.

A few young women put up determined resistance to getting married because they were afraid of having sex. Such a woman was an *uiḷuaqtaq*, a term that seems to have been almost an epithet. There are many stories of such women being turned into some kind of supernatural creature as a penalty for their behavior. In other cases, they were beaten and gang-raped; ironically, the latter treatment was sometimes visited upon women who were promiscuous. I have never heard of a male counterpart to *uiḷuaqtaq*.

Most first marriages seem to have been temporary affairs, and both men and women typically lived with two or more partners before settling down with a spouse on a more permanent basis. Just as there was no marriage ceremony, so also there was no formal divorce procedure. People who wanted to separate (*avit–*) simply did so. If one spouse wanted to separate and the other did not, the situation was more complex. The ultimate outcome depended on which spouse desired the divorce, and the support or lack thereof from other family members. Once a child arrived, especially if it was a boy, the situation usually stabilized.

The sexual intercourse that was one of the foci of the husband-wife relationship was relatively straightforward. Ordinarily there seems to have been little foreplay if the interest was mutual or the man took the lead. If the woman took the initiative, she talked to her husband encouragingly and massaged his penis to arouse him. There seems to have been rather little variation in positions: intercourse was conducted prone and face-to-face. Most of the time the man was on top, but sometimes the woman was.

The husband-wife relationship was the social context in which the division of labor between the sexes was most sharply drawn. Just how it worked was summarized by Henry D. Woolfe (1839):

> Then the usual routine of Eskimo life begins; the husband goes out hunting, the wife sews garments and boots, sometimes accompanying her spouse on his trips and at other times remaining at home attending to her duties. In the evening or at dusk the husband returns and the wife repairs his clothing, dries his boots, and generally looks after his material comfort. During the winter and spring months the women go out on the ice to bring home any seals that may be captured, and in like manner they go inland with their husbands to convey to camp any deer that may be slain. For a male to drag a deer or seal into the village is a very

rare thing, unless he knows that the family is in need of food or that there are no provisions in the hut to enable him to get a meal on his return from the chase. Ordinary conditions prevailing, the women are always sent for the game. During the summer fishing and trading expeditions the women accompany the men on their trips, working with paddles and small oars in the canoe and otherwise assisting in the prosecution of the journey (Woolfe 1893:135).

The husband-wife relationship was also the context in which the sexual division of labor was most thoroughly counterbalanced through mutual dependence. Husbands hunted and made tools and other equipment, but they did so primarily for themselves and their wives. Wives sewed, looked after any game that had been harvested, and performed all the other duties appropriate to their sex—primarily for themselves and their husbands. Since men spent most of their time out hunting or in the *qargi*, husbands and wives spent relatively little time in one another's company except at night or when traveling.

Theoretically, the husband had authority over his wife. However, the political aspects of the relationship were not necessarily that simple. Woolfe (1893) had this to say on the subject:

> Eskimo home life in common with our own has many instances of "hen-pecked husbands," but the Eskimo's remedy when he tires of the continuous tirades and talk of his wife is to administer, if he is able, a sound thrashing with either his hands or a stick. Where a woman is believed to have the powers of a shaman, or medicine woman, she generally possesses control over a household (Woolfe 1893:134).

George Stoney (1900) commented as follows:

> The women have entire control of the food, regulating when it shall be eaten, the kind, and the amount. They are always consulted in all matters relating to trade, traveling and domestic affairs. Though apparently treated with indifference their influence is distinctly felt. Instances are numerous where a man's stout denial has been changed to ready assent after an interview with his wife (Stoney 1900:832).

These comments indicate that the allocation of power and responsibility between husband and wife was complex, but that, in general, wives held their own.

The mutual dependence of men and women, which was realized primarily in the husband-wife relationship, assured that few adults remained single for any length of time until they reached a fairly advanced age. The loss of a spouse through disease, accident, or divorce imposed a hardship on the survivor that was difficult to resolve except through another marriage. There is no way to know just how many times the average person married and remarried after the youthful experiments were over, but most people who survived into their sixties must have had two or more spouses along the way.

Spouses were expected to be fond of one another, but not necessarily in love as Westerners understand that concept. Emotions often ran high, however, and when one spouse failed to meet his or her obligations to the other, or was involved in an adulterous affair, the reaction by the aggrieved party was often intense indeed. Expression in such contexts ranged from crying and shouting to physical combat, this last usually, but not always, being won by the husband. Problems not resolved in a reasonable period of time resulted in divorce. However, couples who made it successfully through the early years of marriage and child rearing seem eventually to have reached a high level of mutual affection more often than not.

The husband-wife relationship was institutionalized as being weaker than relationships between consanguineal kin. That is to say, when one's obligations to siblings, parents,

children, aunts and uncles, or cousins conflicted with those to a spouse, the marital relationship was supposed to yield. On the other hand, the husband-wife relationship was relatively
strong when measured against relationships in the wider social sphere.

Children

The *ui-nuliaq* relationship was augmented as an element in a conjugal family by the relationships between parents and children, and by those between or among the children. The
subject is introduced by Figure 5, which consists of a simple kinship diagram using one form
of standard anthropological notation. In the figure, as in all subsequent diagrams of this
nature, a triangle represents a male, a circle represents a female, and a square indicates that it
does not matter whether the person in the indicated position is male or female. Vertical lines
represent biological descent, that is, passage from one generation to the next, while horizontal
lines with offshoots connect siblings. An equals sign indicates a relationship in which sexual
intercourse ideally plays a part. Ego is an imaginary person, in this case either a male or a
female, who serves as the point of reference. The "y" and the "o" within the symbols denote
younger and older, respectively, than the person who serves as the point of reference.

Figure 5 shows the eight types of relationship that could be found in a conjugal family in
addition to that of *ui-nuliaq*:[4] *aapa-igñiq* (father-son), *aapa-panik* (father-daughter), *aaka-igñiq*
(mother-son), *aaka-panik* (mother-daughter), *aapiyaq-nukatchiaq* (older brother–younger
brother), *aapiyaq-nayak* (older brother–younger sister), *aakiyaaq-nukatchiaq* (older sister–
younger brother), and *aakiyaaq-nayak* (older sister–younger sister).[5] Along with the marital
relationship, this yields a total of nine different types of relationship that could occur within
a conjugal family. However, the number of actual relationships in a real family varied according to the number of children involved.

Estimating the number of children born to the typical husband and wife in early-contact
northwestern Alaska is a problem because there are few hard data on the subject.[6] Since
the beginning of the 20th century, many Iñupiaq women are known to have borne large
numbers of children. For example, Chester Seveck (1973:9, 40) and his first wife, Tillie, had
eleven children, and Chester's second wife, Helen, produced nine children with her first
husband. These numbers were not unusual for women who were in their fifties when I first
went to Alaska in 1960, although the number of children who survived to have children of

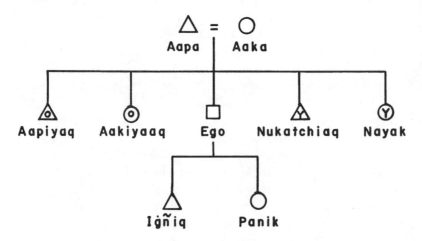

FIGURE 5. Parent-child and sibling relationships.

their own was often rather low at that time. The question is, were women having this many children during the period of interest here?

According to the few early observers who commented on the matter, 19th-century Iñupiaq women had very few living offspring. John Simpson (1875:254), who paid attention to such matters, said that "a couple is seldom met with more than three of a family, though inquiry may elicit the information that one or several 'sleep in the earth.'" Similarly, on the basis of observations made in the 1880s, Woolfe (1893:137) said that it was "rare to find a woman who has borne more than 4 children"; and Hooper, in 1880, reported that "[t]he women are not prolific; it is seldom that more than two or three children are seen in one family" (Hooper 1881:57; see also Hooper 1884:109). These anecdotes do not provide much in the way of hard information, but Simpson and Woolfe spent a lot of time with Natives, and they probably had good reason to write what they did. The obvious conclusion is that women with three or four children were exceptions rather than the rule; most must have had only one or two. The question then becomes the following: did Iñupiaq women have large numbers of children only to watch most of them die, or was the level of fertility low in the first place?

The standard opinion among the Iñupiat with whom I have discussed the matter is that their ancestors had had lots of children, but that many died while they were still infants. Certainly a high infant death rate seems plausible given the harsh conditions in which babies usually entered the world. Simpson (1875:254) reported that the greatest mortality occurred before a child's fifth year. He also noted that infant survival was strongly influenced by the condition of the mother, "according as the season is one of abundance or scarcity" at the time of birth (Simpson 1875:254). Seasons of scarcity occurred in most districts almost every year.

It was stated by some of my Iñupiaq informants that their ancestors used to commit infanticide when people were starving, when the baby was ill, and when the mother died in childbirth or shortly thereafter.[7] Girls were more likely to be "thrown away" than boys on the rationale that girls did not hunt.[8] These claims are corroborated by early Western observers. I wonder, however, just how often babies really were "thrown away" to die. My suspicions on this issue were raised during an interview with Emma Norton (1969), which went something like this:

Burch: Did they ever used to throw away their babies when they were starving?
Norton: Yes, they used to do that. It happened to me.
Burch: Excuse me?
Norton: When I was a baby we were starving. And my parents threw me away.
Burch: Then how did you get to be eighty-two years old?
Norton: My parents put me in the snow along the trail because they had very little food and they wanted it all to go to my older sister. Then some people came along and found me. They took me home and scolded my parents for what they had done. So my parents took me back and raised me.

Ernest Kignak (1976) said that much the same thing happened to him, except that he was adopted by the people who found him despite the fact that they already had a nursing baby of their own. These examples suggest that, although infanticide was sometimes attempted in extreme circumstances, the procedure was often carried out in such a way that the baby had a chance of being rescued and adopted by someone else.

Abortion may sometimes have been performed to prevent pregnancy from going to term. I never heard about this myself, nor did John Simpson (1852–54: entry for Jan. 11, 1853). However, the practice has been reported by others, primarily from the North Slope (Call 1899:121; Spencer 1959:229; Stefansson 1914b:201). It was carried out by kneading the abdomen, hitting the stomach with a flat stick, or jumping down from a high place. Otherwise, contraception was carried out by means of magic, as when certain songs were sung over a belt borrowed from a barren woman and then worn by the woman trying to prevent pregnancy. The success rate of these procedures is unknown, but was probably very low.

Most Iñupiat wanted to have lots of children, especially boys. The fact that so few did has convinced me that the birth rate itself was very low in early-contact times.[9] This conclusion is supported by Simpson's (1852–54: entry for Jan. 11, 1853) statement that "pregnancy is very infrequently observed among a large number" of women. This was probably because of certain practices and conditions. For example, women retrieved most or all of the big game killed by their husbands, and they helped pull the sled or boat while traveling. These tasks involved heavy lifting and pulling, and must have led to a high rate of spontaneous abortion among newly pregnant women within a day or two of conception; they would not even have known that they were pregnant. Prolonged breast-feeding, normally four to six years, must have resulted in a high frequency of what is known as lactational amenorrhea, a disruption of the menstrual cycle. This does not prevent pregnancy, but it greatly reduces the frequency of ovulation, hence the chances of becoming pregnant (Stefansson 1956). Nutritional stress must have been common in many districts each spring, partly from outright hunger, and partly because of a diet that was very high in protein; this, too, would have disrupted a woman's menstrual cycle, decreasing her chances of becoming pregnant (Speth and Spielmann 1983).

The fact that Iñupiaq couples had few living children thus seems to have been the result of a combination of several factors, the most notable of which were low fertility and a high infant death rate. These same factors no doubt combined with chance to produce a range of variation, with some couples having no living children at all, and others having perhaps four or five. This discrepancy was offset by the very widespread practice of adoption, whereby a couple with few or no children could obtain one from a couple with several, leaving most couples with two.[10]

The above considerations suggest that individual Iñupiat must have been involved in very few sibling relationships. However, certain other features of the system tended to increase that number. One was the very strong tendency for couples to live in houses with very close relatives, in which context most of the children acted as siblings even when technically they were cousins. Another possibility was in polygynous families in which the husband had two or more wives, each of whom might have two children. Similarly, although an adopted child was technically referred to as a *tiguaq*, in practice adopted children were treated and spoken of and to as though they were the biological offspring of the couple concerned. These matters are discussed more fully in later sections.

Parent-Child Relationships

The four types of parent-child relationships were listed above: *aapa-igñiq* (father-son), *aapa-panik* (father-daughter), *aaka-igñiq* (mother-son), and *aaka-panik* (mother-daughter).[11]

Infants and young children were given almost constant attention by both parents (dual, *aŋayuqaak*) as well as by other adults and older children. They were held, talked to, played with, and hugged a great deal. Since the father spent much of the day hunting or visiting in the *qargi*, the mother, assisted by other adults and older siblings, performed the bulk of child care, but fathers were attentive and expressive to their young children when they were home. Young children slept in the same bed as their parents, usually between them.

The amount of physical contact between mothers and infants was considerable. Children were nursed for four or five years or more. When a baby fussed, it was offered the breast; if that did not work, the mother placed it inside her parka, went outside, and either rocked back and forth in place, or strolled about the settlement until the baby calmed down. When outdoors, a baby was carried on the mother's back, naked (except for a diaper) against her skin. The baby could also be shifted around to the front so as to nurse while still inside the mother's parka.

At a somewhat later age, a youngster began to be dressed in light clothing, but it was still carried inside the mother's parka. When it wished to look around, its head was exposed to allow that, but at other times was completely enclosed in its mother's parka.

Weaning and toilet training seem to have been non-issues. As they developed, youngsters received gentle encouragement in the appropriate behavior. When they eventually crossed a particular developmental threshold, no ceremonial or other formal recognition was given to the event.

By the time children reached the age of perhaps three or four, there began to be some differentiation in treatment according to sex. Children in general were allowed considerable freedom of action as long as no danger was involved, but boys were particularly indulged. If not given what they wanted when they demanded it, or not permitted to do what they wanted when they intended to do it, boys could scream at their parents and hit them with fists or even sticks without being punished or even scolded. Stoney (1900) summarized the situation as follows:

> Parents are noticeably kind to their children. They work for them, help them, and do everything to please them. The male children are preferred; a father will exhibit his boy with the greatest pride but the daughter will be kept in the background and merely mentioned, yet each is treated with equal consideration in their bringing up (Stoney 1900:832).

Although his observations were made in Barrow, to the north of the study region, it is also worth quoting John Murdoch (1892) on this subject.

> The affection of the parents for their children is extreme, and the children seem to be thoroughly worthy of it. They show hardly a trace of the fretfulness and petulance so common among civilized children, and though indulged to an extreme extent are remarkably obedient. Corporal punishment appears to be absolutely unknown and the children are rarely chidden or punished in any way. Indeed, they seldom deserve it, for, in spite of the freedom which they are allowed, they do not often get into any mischief, especially of a malicious sort, but attend quietly to their own affairs and their own amusements (Murdoch 1892:417).

That pretty well says it all.

As youngsters approached their teenage years, boys began to spend progressively more time with their fathers and girls with their mothers. Thus they began their education in how to carry out the duties appropriate to adult members of their sex, and also in how they were supposed to act toward others as responsible adults. By the time puberty arrived, children were full-time apprentices to their parents. The emotional attachment between parents and children was no less intense at this stage than it had been earlier, but the intimacy that had characterized parent-child relationships when the children were young was replaced by greater formality. Teenage children were expected to listen to and obey their parents, and to treat them with respect. Respect—indeed, a measure of avoidance—ideally characterized mother-son and father-daughter relationships at this stage.

Just what happened when the children got married depended on the circumstances, and was probably the subject of considerable negotiation. As is made clear below in the section on domestic families, the members of conjugal families rarely lived in houses occupied only by themselves. Usually they started out living with one spouse's parents and/or siblings; later on, they typically lived with one or more of their own married siblings.

By the time they were teenagers, children had shouldered all of the responsibilities of adults in their society, sharing the work with any co-resident parents, parents-in-law, aunts and uncles, cousins, and adult siblings. Parents retained authority over co-resident married children, but, if they abused it, the children could exercise their right to set off on their own, or, more often, move in with other relatives.

As the parents began to reach an advanced age, the primary responsibility for keeping the family solvent was gradually assumed by the co-resident children. Simpson (1875), after noting that elders who had no children to look after them would have had a difficult time, described how elders were treated:

> For the tender solicitude with which their own infancy and childhood have been tended, in the treatment of their aged and infirm parents they make a return which redounds to their credit, for they not only give them food and clothing, sharing with them every comfort they possess, but on their longest and most fatiguing journeys make provision for their easy conveyance (Simpson 1875:249; see also Stoney 1900:829, 831, 832).

Many other early observers also commented on the solicitous care given to both the aged and to the physically impaired.[12]

Gerontocide, or the deliberate termination of an elder's life, was probably even less common in northwestern Alaska than infanticide was.[13] I have heard stories of elders who were too weak to travel being left behind when a family had to move in order to survive themselves, but they were always left with food—if any was available—and someone returned at the earliest opportunity to try to fetch them. That the return was not always made soon enough does not make this action a true case of gerontocide. Most elders who were abandoned seem to have been left behind while the family was on the move. They were too weak to continue, but the other members of the family ran the risk of starving if they stayed behind to look after them. I have never heard an account of an elder being deliberately put out in the cold to freeze or starve to death except when the entire family was in difficult straits.

One exception to the above statements was when people (of any age) who seemed to be on death's door were taken out of the house and placed in a separate shelter. The reason for this was not to kill them, but to have what seemed to be their imminent death occur outside the house. In most nations, it was believed that if a person died inside the house, the building had to be immediately and permanently abandoned by all of its inhabitants, along with most of its contents. This was a prospect no one welcomed, particularly in winter. Although this custom usually had the same effect as gerontocide—the accelerated death of the parent—the motivation was very different.

Parent-child relationships were arguably the strongest ties in Iñupiaq society, particularly from the child's perspective. In other words, when the obligations to one's parents conflicted with other considerations, those to the parents were supposed to take priority. A parent, however, if forced to choose between the obligations to his or her own parents and those to his or her children, might be in a quandary, but probably would choose in favor of the parents. I doubt if such conflicts arose very often, however.

Sibling Relationships

The four sibling relationships were those of *aapiyaq-nukatchiaq* (older brother–younger brother), *aapiyaq-nayak* (older brother–younger sister), *aakiyaaq-nukatchiaq* (older sister–younger brother), and *aakiyaaq-nayak* (older sister–younger sister).[14] Given the alleged low fertility rate, and particularly the element of prolonged nursing in contributing to it, one may assume that there often was a gap of several years, perhaps as many as five or six, between births. Thus, most people had few biological siblings, and those they did have probably were not particularly close to them in age.

There were many ways in which the number of people operating in sibling relationships could be increased. For example, when couples got divorced and remarried—which frequently happened—all of their children with either spouse were considered siblings. Or, a man or woman might die and the surviving spouse remarry, in which case any children of the second spouse were considered siblings of those born to the first. Likewise, all of the children born in polygamous marriages were considered siblings. Finally, since co-resident cousins and adopted children usually behaved as though they were siblings, sibling relationships were fairly abundant in most households, even if not always in conjugal families.

Sibling relationships were ideally dedicated to mutual aid and protection. Older siblings were taught to nurture and protect their juniors, and the latter were taught to cooperate with and obey their seniors. These patterns, established at an early age, were supposed to last a lifetime. If an adult Iñupiaq was in difficulty, whether it be predominantly political or economic in nature, it was to a sibling that he/she was most likely to turn for help.

Sibling relationships were emotionally intense, but affection was not supposed to be openly expressed. By the time they were in their teens, siblings were expected to communicate with one another in respectful tones. This behavior was most strongly institutionalized between brothers and sisters, who often did not even look directly at one another when speaking, especially during their teenage and early adult years. The pattern was weakest between sisters, who could laugh and joke together, at least if they were not too far apart in age.

In terms of strength, sibling relationships were second only to parent-child ties. In other words, the obligation to support one's siblings was greater than any other in the entire society except for one's parents.

Complex Conjugal Families

In addition to the "simple" type of conjugal family just described, the Iñupiat had two types of "complex" conjugal families in which there were two or more spouses of a given sex.[15] The more common type, by far, was a polygynous family with one man and two or more wives; much less common was a polyandrous family, with two or more men and only one woman. Both types resulted in the creation of new types of relationship.

The marital relationships that were created in complex marriage are noted in Figure 6. The upper diagram shows a polygynous marriage, with *ui* being the husband, *nuliaqpak* being his first wife, and *nukaġaq* being the second wife (and any additional wives). The relationship between the two wives was *aippaq-aippaq*, or *aippaġiik* (dual). A polyandrous marriage yielded an analogous set of relationships, with the one between the two men being that of *nuliaqan-nuliaqan,* or *nuliaqatigiik* (dual).

Polyandrous families existed in theory in the Iñupiaq system, but I have heard of only one that existed in practice. It involved a woman named Aġratquq (also known as Qayiayaq) and men named Nayukuuraq and Ukulii, all of whom were from Point Hope (Stefansson 1914b:206). No one could tell me how that particular marriage operated, or how polyandrous families in general were supposed to operate; my sources speculated, however, that there must have been considerable tension between the husbands in such a union. Apparently, this type of arrangement usually involved brothers who were too poor for each to support a separate wife (Rainey 1947:243).

The frequency of polygynous families in the study region in the early 19th century is unknown. Eliyak (1931) told Ira Purkeypile that when he was a little boy (presumably in the late 1850s), there were only four polygynous families in "Selawik country," which presumably included the estates of both the Kiitaaġmiut and the Siiḷviim Kaṇianiġmiut. Of the four, three men had two wives each, and one man had four, in a combined population of perhaps 1,000–1,200. John Simpson (1875:254) reported that, in the early 1850s, there were four polygynous marriages at Point Barrow in a total population of around 290; four at Cape Smythe (Utqiaġvik), with a slightly smaller population; and "several" at Point Hope, including one man with five wives, in a considerably larger population. Finally, Thornton (1931:63) reported that in Wales, with a population of 539 in 1891, one *umialik* had four wives, another had three, and "several others" had two. Since some of the wealthiest men in all of northwestern Alaska lived in the whaling villages of Point Barrow, Cape Smythe, Point Hope, and Wales, and since wealth was required to support more than one wife, we may assume that polygynous marriages in the study region were more common there than elsewhere.

Theoretically, a man took a second wife only when he was such a successful hunter and trader that one woman could not satisfactorily process his production. I have heard of overburdened women asking their husbands to take a second wife to help with the workload. While second wives were not invariably younger than the first, sometimes a man was attracted to a younger woman because of her sex appeal, and took her as a second wife. The first wife did not have to acquiesce, and apparently was not often consulted.

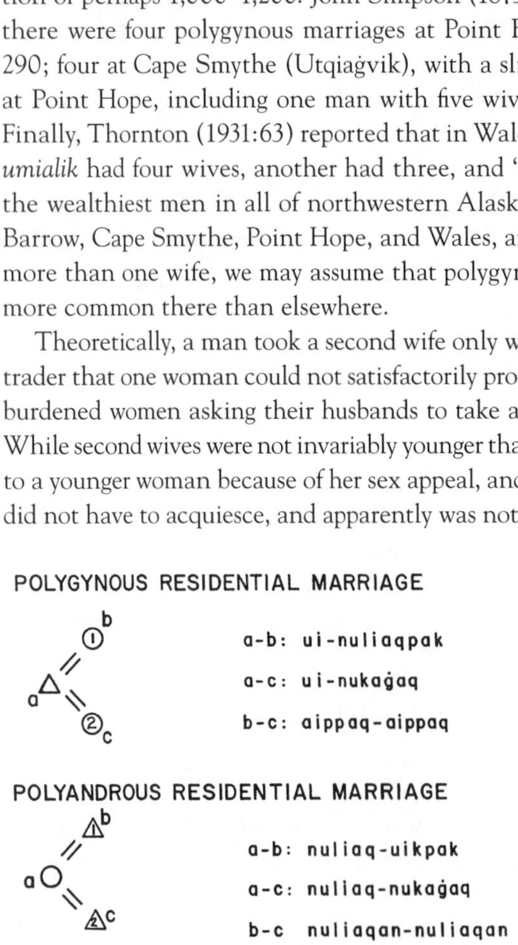

Ideally, co-wives were expected to work together and generally cooperate in performing chores around the house, in subsistence activities, in child rearing, and in helping transport the family's baggage from one place to another; they were supposed to act like sisters. However, the first wife was in charge whether or not she was older than the second. In practice, the ideal seems to have been largely realized in fact except when the husband exhibited a marked preference for the

POLYGYNOUS RESIDENTIAL MARRIAGE

a-b: ui-nuliaqpak
a-c: ui-nukaġaq
b-c: aippaq-aippaq

POLYANDROUS RESIDENTIAL MARRIAGE

a-b: nuliaq-uikpak
a-c: nuliaq-nukaġaq
b-c nuliaqan-nuliaqan

FIGURE 6. Complex marriage relationships.

second wife and discriminated in favor of her or her children. That certainly resulted in tension within the family, and, if it continued for any length of time, led to the departure of one of the women. Strains also could develop if the husband's parents or siblings demonstrably favored one wife over the other.

Children in complex marriages were expected to treat one another as full siblings. They addressed and referred to one another by sibling terms, and generally were supposed to act as though they were all born to the same woman. The two (or more) women were also supposed to treat one another's children as though they were their own. This ideal also seems to have been largely realized in fact except in time of crisis, especially famine. When there was barely enough food to go around, some mothers tried to hoard food for their own offspring and withhold it from the children of their co-wife (or co-wives). If discovered, this invariably led to conflict.

Domestic Families[16]

The members of a conjugal family almost never lived in a dwelling by themselves except during times of famine. The reason they sometimes did so during a famine is that people had to spread out as widely as possible, partly to spread the risk, and partly to increase the chances that at least someone would be able to find food. Ordinarily, however, conjugal families shared a dwelling with other very close relatives, and this larger unit is what I have called a "domestic family" (*igluqatigiich/tupiqatigiich*) (Burch 1975a:237).

Precisely how large domestic families were during the study period is unknown. Oral sources invariably said that "two or three families" used to live together in a house, but they could never tell me just how many people that involved. My interpretation of such comments is what they were really trying to say is that houses were rarely occupied by a simple conjugal family. Given the calculations discussed above, two statistically average conjugal families would have involved eight people, and three would have involved twelve.

For the purpose of calculating overall population size, in both this and other studies, I have assumed an average of eight people per household in fall/winter settlements (Burch 1981:14; 1998a:20–21). Although I believe this is a conservative number, I know of no hard evidence that would support a higher figure. The only reasonably hard data from anywhere near the study period are from Wales and Barrow. In Wales, Trollope (1855:873) estimated that each house was inhabited in 1854 by "at least 6 or 8 people, and in many 8 or 10." In 1891, the Wales population of 539 was distributed among 69 dwellings, for an average of 7.81 people per house (Thornton 1931:21, 219). In the Barrow district, Simpson (1875:237–38) determined that the average number of occupants per house in the two large villages there, Point Barrow and Barrow, was slightly less than six at the end of 1853. However, the populations of both settlements were under severe stress due to famine and disease at the time, and just how representative these numbers are of the early-19th-century situation cannot be determined. Later in the century, many households that were actually visited by outside observers in the study region held more than eight people. However, Westerners tended to stay with the wealthiest people wherever they went, so I presume that their observations were biased on the high side. Until some new evidence is found, therefore, I proceed on the assumption that average household size, and thus average domestic family size, was eight.

There were, however, a few extremely large domestic families, the generic term for which is *amilġaqtuayaat*.[17] The largest domestic family I ever heard of was in Point Hope, and was known as Iñugialiŋmiut. The couple who started this family had five sons, all of whom grew to adulthood, married, and had children; and all of them lived together in a single very large house that had two living rooms but a common entry. Given the usual numbers regarding conjugal family size and composition, this family may be understood to have developed considerable wealth and influence in the village.

Domestic families varied in composition, but some of the more frequent combinations are shown in Figure 7. Here, in Diagram A, we see a widow, two married sons and their wives and children, and an unmarried daughter. Diagram B shows a married couple, a married son and a married daughter, with their respective spouses and children. In Diagram C, the unit consists of two married brothers and a sister, with their spouses, and with the brothers' children. In the final example, Diagram D, we see two brothers, their wives and children, and the wife of one of the children. The different combinations, including several not illustrated here, add a number of new relationship types to the system. These include nepotic, cousin, multigeneration, and affinal relationships.

Nepotic Relationships

Nepotic relationships are those that involve aunts and uncles, in one generation, and nieces and nephews, in the next (Burch 1975a:150–54). In the Iñupiaq system, the relationships were *aŋak-uyuġu* (uncle-nephew/niece) and *atchak-uyuġu* (aunt-nephew/niece). The English terms are broadly interpreted here, since the Iñupiat regarded as "aunts" and "uncles" all their

A.

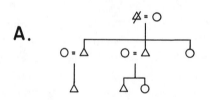

blood kin in their parents' generation, and as "nieces" and nephews" all their blood kin in the children's generation. If you encounter an Iñupiaq and, pointing to another man, ask, "Who's that?" you might be informed, "He's my uncle," and learn later that he is his father's cousin rather than brother. Your informant is not confused, he is just using English words to describe part of the Iñupiaq system which does not conform to the general American pattern.

B.

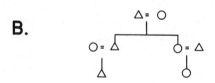

Nepotic relationships were almost identical to parent-child relationships, but in lesser degree.[18] While the nieces and nephews were youngsters, their co-resident aunts and uncles held and talked to and played with them just

C.

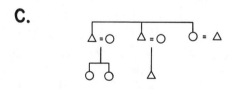

as their parents did. When the children got a little older, uncles were supposed to help protect, nurture, teach, and assist their nephews, who were expected to obey, enjoy, learn from, and help their uncles. The pattern for aunts and nieces was parallel in all respects. The only

D.

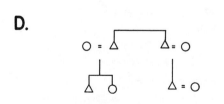

difference between parent-child relationships and nepotic relationships is that the obligation to live up to the ideals of the relationship was somewhat weaker in the latter than it was in

FIGURE 7. Examples of domestic families.   the former.

Cousin Relationships

The Iñupiat recognized three different types of cousin relationship, which are shown in Figure 8.[19] One involved the children of brothers, who were *aŋutiqatigiik* (dual), or what anthropologists call patrilateral parallel cousins. The second involved the children of sisters, who were *aġnaqatigiik* (dual), or matrilateral parallel cousins. The third cousin relationship involved the offspring of a brother and a sister, who were *iḷḷuġiik* (dual), or cross cousins. The same-generation descendants of people who belonged to one of these relationships were considered to be related to one another in the same way. In other words, the children of people who were *iḷḷuġiik*, for example, were also *iḷḷuġiik*. Thus, *iḷḷuġiik* could be second or third cousins, as well as first.

Just as the nepotic relationships were like parent-child relationships but to a lesser degree, so cousin relationships were like sibling relationships but to a lesser degree. In fact, as noted before, children who were raised in the same household typically acted as though they were siblings, and often referred to each other by sibling terms. In my time, this pattern was represented in English by statements such as, "He's my cousin, all right, but I call him 'older brother.'" Older cousins wielded authority over younger ones, but were expected to do so in a responsible way. Younger cousins were expected to obey their seniors, and all cousins were supposed to share things, and to support and assist each other whenever possible.

I have been unable to discover any differences in the way *aŋutiqatigiik* and *aġnaqatigiik* were expected to behave toward one another. If there was a difference, the information has been lost. *Iḷḷuġiik*, however, were definitely different. They were what anthropologists call "joking cousins," because teasing and practical jokes were a central feature of the relationship. Unfortunately, I do not know how this feature developed during childhood; all my information relates to adults.

Adult *iḷḷuġiik* could work together and be very fond of one another, yet still make one another the butt of ribald jokes and sarcastic commentary regardless of the sex of the individuals involved. This was done in both private and public contexts. The focus was often on weaknesses in the other person's character or personality, and criticism was sometimes leveled in the form of a derisory song. Particularly when carried out in front of an audience, such ridicule was often an effective means of correcting disruptive behavior. Within the confines of the typical small Iñupiaq household, one might think that perpetual joking of this kind would wear a bit thin after awhile. My sources admitted that sometimes it did, but ideally, one was never supposed to get mad at an *iḷḷuq* regardless of what he or she said.

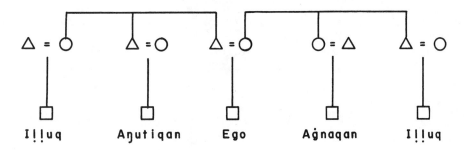

FIGURE 8. Cousin relationships.

Multigenerational Relationships

"Multigenerational relationships" is a phrase I coined to describe relationships involving relatives who are more than two generations apart (Burch 1975a:154). In the Iñupiaq system, the relationships were *aana-tutitchiaq* (grandmother-grandchild), *ataata-tutitchiaq* (grandfather-grandchild), and *amaułuk-iḷuliaġun* (great-grandparent–great-grandchild).[20] Actually, these relationships were more inclusive than the English terms suggest. An *aana* was really any female blood relative who was two generations older; thus, the category included great-aunts, in addition to grandmothers. Similarly, in practice, *amaułuk* seems to have been used to refer to practically any very old person, but there must have been very few of them during the study period.

Multigenerational relationships were similar, but not identical, to parent-child relationships. For example, parents tended to teach as much through demonstration as through admonition, while for grandparents the emphasis was more on instruction. Two particularly important components of the knowledge transmitted primarily from grandparents to grandchildren were genealogical information and historical data.

As children matured, relations between them and their parents became somewhat formal, whereas it stayed rather relaxed between elders and their grandchildren, at least on the part of the senior members. Grandparents often used pet names for their grandchildren even after the latter reached adulthood, which is something parents rarely did. Grandchildren, however, were taught to treat old people generally, and their grandparents specifically, with the utmost respect. Thus, it was not unusual to observe an elder gently teasing a young-adult grandchild, while the latter sat or stood still, eyes downcast, saying nothing.

A grandchild was often assigned, even as a youngster, to care for a particular grandparent (or great-grandparent) whose spouse had died. The two often lived together in a small house built a short distance away from the one the rest of the family occupied; the child brought food, fuel, and water to the grandparent, as necessary, and attempted to look after his or her every need. In every case of this I observed in my own time, the practice involved grandsons and grandmothers. Several stories I have heard from past times also fit this pattern, so it must be of ancient vintage.

Affinal Relationships

Affinal relationships are those established through marriage, as opposed to consanguineal relationships, which are established through birth or adoption.[21] The Iñupiat referred to affines as *iḷagiiksit* (pl.), and to consanguines as *iḷapiat* (pl.). The various relationships are introduced in Figure 9. This diagram is focused on an Ego who can be of either sex, hence is represented by a square rather than by a triangle or a circle. Since the diagram is rather complicated, I have listed the various relationships it indicates in Table 4.

The generic term for "spouse," as shown in Figure 9, is *tuvaaqan*. Since the relationship between spouses was discussed above, it is omitted from the present discussion.

Young married couples almost always lived with one set of parents or the other, so at least two in-law relationships occurred in almost every household. Just which two varied from one family to another.

The parent-in-law–child-in-law relationships were supposed to be rather similar to true parent-child relationships, particularly when the individuals involved lived in the same house. The father-in-law and son-in-law usually hunted together, or spent time together (and with other men) in the *qargi*, while the women cooperated in performing chores and other

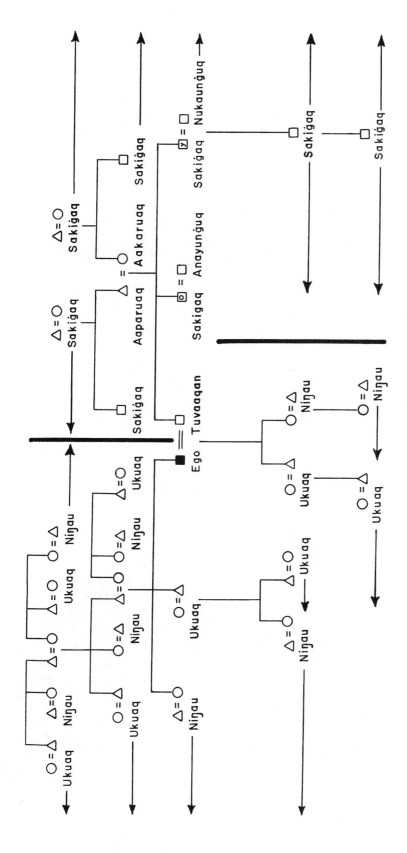

FIGURE 9. Affinal relationships. Modified from Burch (1975a:65).

Table 4. Affinal Relationships

aaparuaq-niŋau	father-in-law/son-in-law
aakaruaq-niŋau	mother-in-law/son-in-law
aaparuaq-ukuaq	father-in-law/daughter-in-law
aakaruaq-ukuaq	mother-in-law/daughter-in-law
sakiġaq-niŋau	consanguine/male in-law
sakiġaq-ukuaq	consanguine/female in-law
aŋyunġuq-nukaunġuq	co-affines
nulliq-nulliq	co-parents-in-law

daily activities. The members of the senior generation had authority over those in the junior generation, but were supposed to mentor and generally support them instead of bossing them around. The junior members were expected to obey their seniors, and to share with them the fruit of their labors. The people involved were supposed to be fond of one another, but to be rather restrained in expressing their affection. The mother-in-law–son-in-law and the father-in-law–daughter-in-law relationships were what anthropologists call "avoidant" relationships. Even when they lived in the same house, a man was not supposed to look directly at his mother-in-law; he spoke to her only when necessary, and then in quiet, respectful tones. The father-in-law–daughter-in-law relationship operated the same way.

The *sakiġaq-ukuaq* and *sakiġaq-niŋau* relationships were the most common affinal relationships because of the broad inclusiveness of the three categories. Technically, the category of *sakiġaq* encompassed all of the blood kin of one's spouse except for the parents-in-law; *ukuaq* and *niŋau* included any female and male, respectively, who were married to one's blood kin. As Figure 9 shows, these relationships could and usually did involve people of different generations and various degrees of collateral separation. The behavior appropriate to all of these relationships was supposed to mimic that expected of consanguineal kinfolk of the same age, sex, and generation. This was particularly so when the individuals involved lived together in the same house. One difference is that relations between in-laws of the opposite sex were even more restrained than those between siblings of the opposite sex. Another, perhaps more important, difference is that where obligations to one's blood relatives conflicted with those to one's in-laws, the former were always expected to take precedence.

An affinal relationship that has not been mentioned is the co-in-law, or *aŋayunġuq-nukaunġuq* relationship, which involved people who married siblings (A. Hawley 1965.11). Just who qualified for membership in this relationship is shown in Figure 10. Here we see two brothers, marked older and younger, and their respective wives. The wife of the older brother is the *aŋayunġuq*, and the wife of the younger one is the *nukaunġuq*. The same

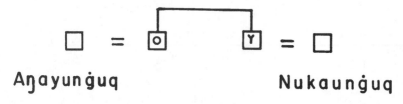

Aŋayunġuq   **Nukaunġuq**

FIGURE 10. The co-affine relationship.

relationship exists when the siblings are both females, or a male and a female. Since a large number of domestic families included married siblings, this relationship must have been rather common in traditional households. It was particularly active when the people involved were of the same sex, in which case the two men, or two women, spent a great deal of time in one another's company. They were supposed to act just like brothers or sisters. Apparently they often did except that, in time of stress, the tie of blood always took precedence over relationships created through marriage.

The *aŋayunġuq*—the person who married the older sibling—had authority over the *nukaunġuq* regardless of the relative ages of the affines involved. Thus, a thirty-year-old man married to a twenty-two-year-old woman was subordinate to a twenty-five-year-old man if the latter was married to her twenty-five-year-old sister. This is one of only two relationships in the entire Iñupiaq kinship system—the other being that of co-wives—where the intrinsic relative age hierarchy of the specific individuals involved was overridden by some other factor.

The final relationship in the affinal category is that of *nulliq-nulliq*.[22] This relationship involved co-parents-in-law, that is, people whose children were married to one another. I was unable to learn much about this relationship, beyond the usual platitudes to the effect that the people involved were supposed to act like blood kin. The relationship rarely occurred in the context of a single dwelling, and I suspect that it was not very well defined in any context.

Discussion

It is useful in trying to understand the mechanics of domestic family life to see how all of the relationships described above might combine in the case of a specific family. To illustrate the point, I reproduce in Figure 11 Family A from Figure 7, the only difference being that here the various positions are identified with letters, and the birth order of the adult siblings is indicated with numbers.

Figure 11 shows a domestic family involving nine people: a widow, her two married sons, their wives and children, and her unmarried daughter. This small organization contains thirty-six relationships of fourteen different types. These are listed, along with an indication of which specific individuals are related to each of the others in which way, in Table 5. I will not repeat the exercise with the three other families illustrated in Figure 7, but I believe it is easy to understand that each would be similar to this example but with a slightly different distribution of relationships.

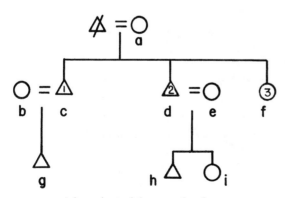

Domestic family life in early-19th-century northwestern Alaska was intense. The women and children were together for nearly twenty-four hours a day, every day, as were the men and teenage boys. If everyone lived up to the ideals of the relationships in which they were involved, life was good; a harmonious domestic family provided a wonderful, supportive social context in which to live. If,

FIGURE 11. A hypothetical domestic family.

Table 5. Relationships in a Hypothetical Domestic Family*

Marital relationships
1. *ui-nuliaq* (Hu-Wi): b-c, d-e

Parent-child relationships
2. *aaka-igñiq* (Mo-So): a-c, a-d, e-h, b-g
3. *aaka-panik* (Mo-Da): a-f, e-i
4. *aapa-igñiq* (Fa-So): c-g, d-h
5. *aapa-panik* (Fa-Da): d-i

Sibling relationships
6. *aapiyaq-nukatchiaq* (oBr-yBr): c-d
7. *aapiyaq-nayaq* (oBr-ySi): c-f, d-f, h-i

Nepotic relationships
8. *aŋak-uyuġu* (Un-Ni/Ne): c-h, c-i, d-g
9. *atchak-uyuġu* (Au-Ni/Ne): f-g, f-h, f-i

Multigenerational relationships
10. *aana-tutik* (GrMo-GrCh): a-g, a-h, a-i

Cousin relationships
11. *aŋutiqan-aŋutiqan* (Patrilat/Co): g-h, g-i

Affinal relationships
12. *aakaruaq-ukuaq* (Mo-in-La/Da-in-La): a-b, a-e
13. *sakiġaq-ukuaq* (spouse's blood kin—female married to same): d-b, b-f, h-b, i-b, f-e, e-g, c-e
14. *aŋayunġuq-nukaunġuq* (co-in-laws): b-e

* Keyed to Figure 11

on the other hand, any of the members failed to act the way they were supposed to, or to the extent that they failed to act properly, a domestic family could be the locus of considerable tension. The only solution in such cases was for the constituent conjugal families to separate and try to join other families; or, in the case of a particularly troublesome individual, to shun that person, to drive that person out, or, in the worst case, to kill him or her. Most families probably fell somewhere between the extremes.

Dwellings

The physical focus of domestic family life was the dwelling occupied by its members. Accordingly, this is an appropriate place to introduce the subject of housing. The house construction process is discussed in Chapter 4 under the more general heading of manufactured goods.

The Iñupiat built several different types of dwelling, varying with the season, the availability of construction materials, the degree of mobility required, the traditions of the nation concerned, and the specific needs of the particular individuals involved. The most substantial dwellings were large, semisubterranean sod houses built by people who spent the fall and winter months living on or very near the coast. Dwellings of this type usually were named, even in settlements consisting of a single house (Kunuyaq 1940:1; Simpson 1850b: entry for Jan. 16, 1850; Stefansson 1914b:309). In complex settlements, they were built in compound-family neighborhoods, which were also named. In both cases, the name of the dwelling or neighborhood served as a family name for those who resided in it.

At the opposite extreme were dwellings that were little more than tarpaulins made from several strips of seal intestine sewn together and stretched over a wooden frame; they were used in summer by people traveling overland on foot. In between were a variety of different types of dwelling covered with sod, logs, moss, mud, snow, and skins, or some combination of these.

From the viewpoint of solidarity, the main interest with respect to houses is the number of occupants, their social relationships to one another, and their physical relationships to one another within the building. In regard to the first two issues, my informants were unanimously of the opinion that fall/winter houses were almost always occupied by two or more married couples and their offspring, and that the married couples were virtually always linked by sibling, cousin, or parent-child ties. As noted above, just how many people this involved obviously varied. However, after considerable trial and error, I concluded that the figure of eight occupants per fall/winter house, on average, seems to account best for the evidence. Of the eight, at least four would have been adults.

Wealthy households included a larger number of people than the average. As noted above, the family known as Iñugialiŋmiut at Point Hope, for example, housed, at its peak, an elderly woman, her five sons, and their spouses and children, all within a single dwelling. The man at Point Hope who had five wives in 1854, presumably each with children, probably had them distributed among two or more houses (Simpson 1852–54: entry for Feb. 20, 1853). In the spring of 1885, when Charles Brower (ms:153) visited Point Hope, the rogue *umialik* Ataŋauraq also had five wives; the *nuliaqpak* lived in one house and the four *nukaġat* lived in another. Unusually large households sometimes included a nonfamily member, usually a male, who acted pretty much as a servant for the others in return for being housed and fed.

It wasn't always clear just where one house ended and another began.[23] For example, it was not unusual for two separate dwelling units to share a common entrance passage. It was also fairly common for two separate dwelling units to have one wall in common, either at the back or on one of the sides; people who lived in such a house were referred to as *tapittaġliġüch*. Houses were sometimes linked by covered hallways, which permitted people to go back and forth without venturing outside. At Point Hope, the houses of closely related people were often built so close together that several of them eventually coalesced into a single mound.

The spatial arrangement of individuals within a dwelling varied according to its floor plan. There were three basic patterns. In one, the main living area of the house was divided into two sections, a wide bench where everyone sat, slept, and ate, and a low area leading to a long entrance passage that usually contained alcoves for storage and cooking. When a family was very large, wide shelves were sometimes erected along the walls above the bench to serve as additional resting and sleeping platforms. A cutaway profile of such a dwelling is shown in Figure 12, with the living area on the right, and the storage/entryway on the left. A scale was not provided with the sketch, but, judging from the human figures in the living area, the interior of the building (including the entrance tunnel) must have been about 40 feet (12.2 m) long; about 30 percent of that was living area. This type of building was used primarily by the coastal-dwelling Tikiġaġmiut, Tapqaġmiut, and Kiṇikmiut.

Both the profile and the floor plan of a similar dwelling, which was excavated by Henry Collins (1937a:262–64) at the former Kiṇikmiut settlement of Miłłitaġvik,[24] is shown in Figure 13.

This house has a large foyer (A) with two entrances. The foyer held both storage and cooking areas, and was nearly as large as the dwelling portion of the house, which one reached by going through a narrow passage (B). In this case, the inner or dwelling room (C) was 17 feet 5 inches (5.8 m) long and 11 feet 3 inches (4.1 m) wide. As in Figure 12, a single wide sleeping platform extended 5 feet 7 inches (1.7 m) out from the rear wall.

The second pattern consisted of a square or rectangular open central area with a hearth around which one to three alcoves were situated. An elaborate example of such a "four-post-center" house, sketched by John Simpson (1875:255) in the winter of 1850, is shown in Figure 14, along with his explanation of its various components. The horizontal dimensions of the interior of this house were 16 by 20 feet (4.9 x 6 m). Ordinarily in such houses each of the alcoves would have been occupied by the members of a single conjugal family, but six such families were living in the house at the time of Simpson's visit.

Four-post-center dwellings were commonly erected in the Kotzebue district, and along the Kobuk, Selawik, upper Noatak, and Buckland rivers. They were rarely as elaborate or well constructed as the one pictured in Figure 14, but they were based on the same general floor plan.

The third main dwelling plan, which is not illustrated, consisted of a central hearth and undifferentiated space around it inside a building that was oval or circular in plan and domed in profile. People arranged themselves around the hearth in conjugal family units, sitting or lying on mats and sleeping bags placed on the floor. Dwellings of this type served as the basic dwelling only among the Kivalliñiġmiut, where they were sometimes 15 feet (4.6 m) across and 6 feet (1.83 m) high at the center (Brower ms:157). However, houses of this general style were used by people from many districts when traveling. Tipi-shaped dwellings, which were used by people from some interior districts in summer, also had a circular floor plan.

Heating considerations usually dictated that houses be no larger than absolutely necessary, hence most Iñupiaq houses were crowded no matter which floor plan was used. During the day and early evening, men and older boys were usually either out hunting, or else gathered in the *qargi*, which alleviated the space problem to some extent. When they ate at home, the men and older boys were served first, the women and younger children later; that also helped reduce crowding. At night, however, when everyone was at home, there was no escaping the press of people in the sleeping area.

Compound Families

A compound family was a family unit whose members occupied two or more dwellings, but still operated in terms of a single overriding family organization (Burch 1975a:237). The members of a compound family pooled resources, cooperated in all kinds of activities, and entered one another's houses without seeking permission. In most contexts, loyalty to one's compound family outweighed all other obligations and considerations in an Iñupiaq person's social life.[25]

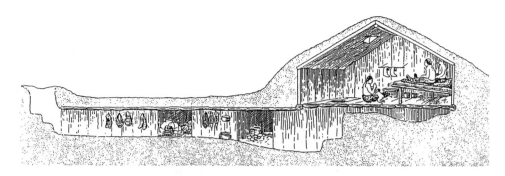

FIGURE 12. Profile of a semisubterranean sod house. Reproduced, with permission of the Smithsonian Institution, from Crowell (1988:197).

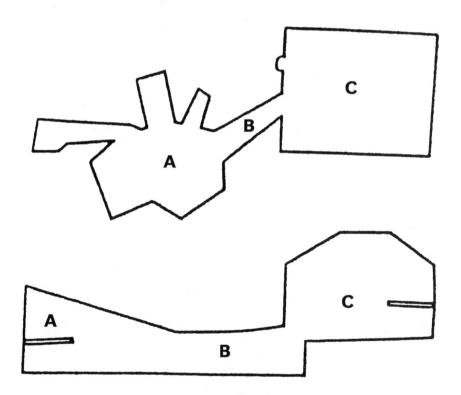

FIGURE 13. Floor plan and side profile of a house at the Kiŋikmiut settlement of Miłłitaġvik.

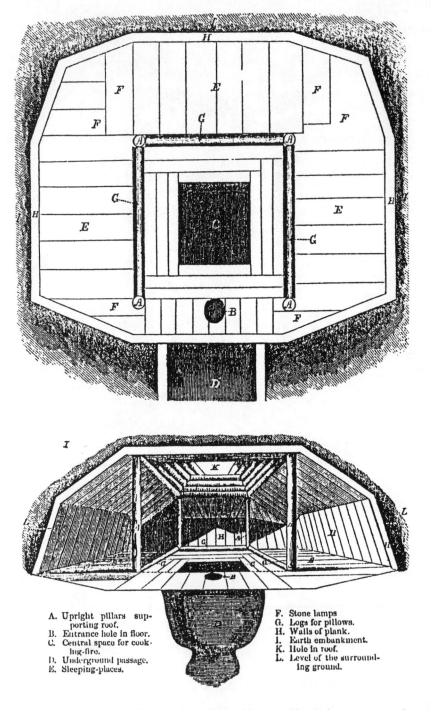

A. Upright pillars sup-
porting roof.
B. Entrance hole in floor.
C. Central space for cook-
ing-fire.
D. Underground passage.
E. Sleeping-places.

F. Stone lamps
G. Logs for pillows.
H. Walls of plank.
I. Earth embankment.
K. Hole in roof.
L. Level of the surround-
ing ground.

FIGURE 14. John Simpson's sketch of the floor plan and front profile of a four-post-center house at an unidentified Qikiqtaġruŋmiut settlement near the entrance to Hotham Inlet, 1849–50.

The Iñupiat identified a compound family by the suffix *-kut* appended to the name of the family head. Thus, the compound family headed by Samaruna was Samarunakut; it would be referred to in North Alaskan village English today as "Samaruna and them." A compound family was inherently larger than a domestic family, but otherwise was essentially the same in structure. In other words, the members of a compound family were linked by the same types of relationship that occurred in a domestic family; there simply were many more of them.

Just what a compound family was is best illustrated by example. This is provided in Figure 15, which shows an entire Nuataaġmiut settlement from about the mid-1880s.[26] I use this example frequently because it is the earliest one for which I have solid information. The thirty people in this settlement were organized in terms of nine conjugal families, which were nested within four domestic families, with the whole constituting a single compound family.

Figure 15 shows four households of closely related people. The members of the separate domestic families are enclosed within the broken lines. Average household size is 7.5 people, which is pretty close to the overall average of eight that I have used when estimating early-19th-century population size. However, the sibling groups represented here are quite a bit larger than what I have understood to be normal for the study period.

The thirty members of this family were involved in 435 relationships. I will not repeat the exercise carried out in Table 5, in which I showed exactly how each of the members of a family was related to each of the others. The set of relationships would be basically the same except for the addition of a polygynous marriage, but there would be many more examples of them. There are some general features worth pointing out, however. First, the foundation of this compound family was a set of relationships between siblings and cousins. Most of the people represented in the diagram are descendants of three brothers, which made them *aŋutiqatigiich* (patrilateral parallel cousins) to one another. Presumably the members of this senior generation were alive when the family was founded, but, as time passed, they and their spouses died. This is indicated by the slashes and the placement of the relevant symbols outside the boxes denoting the boundaries of the domestic units.

The founders had seven children, six of whom still belonged to the family during the period shown here. The seventh, a woman, evidently had gone to live elsewhere with her husband, but her daughter married the brother of the man who married her sister (House 4), and they lived here. The man represented by the blackened triangle, probably the oldest person in the group, was the family head, but his cousin, in House 2, was the only one with two wives. One of those wives brought along four of her siblings who, with their own wives and children, constituted the occupants of House 1.

Another important feature of this family was that its members made up an entire fall/winter settlement. (In most years, it was located near the mouth of Makpik Creek.) In this respect it was typical of the great majority of families and settlements. Indeed, the names of simple settlements were often considered to be nearly equivalent to Western family names (A. Douglas 1989.1). During hard times the unit divided along domestic family lines and spread out across the country looking for food. In desperate times even the domestic families split up. However, most of the time, except when visiting relatives elsewhere, these people stayed together all year round, following the rather arduous Nuataaġmiut annual cycle of movement (Burch 1998a:91–106). In all of these respects they were typical of compound families in northwestern Alaska.[27]

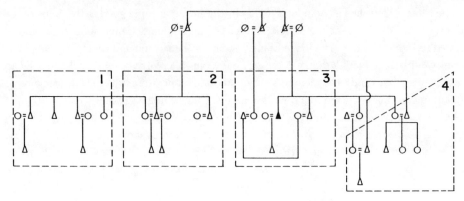

FIGURE 15. A Nuataaġmiut local family, ca. 1885. From Burch (1975a:256).

Discussion

Compound families were the major structural components of most (all?) hunter-gatherer societies. Indeed, Iñupiaq societies had what Elman Service (1975:70; see also Sahlins 1963:287) has called a "segmental" structure, meaning that they were "composed of equal and similar component groups (normally kin groups)," and lacked governments or other organizations of nationwide scope. The component groups were compound families. In the hunter-gatherer literature, they have been labeled "local bands" by June Helm (1965, 1968), "local groups" by Morris Opler (1955:180), "hunting groups" by Edward Rogers (1965:266; 1969:46), "hordes" by A. R. Brown (1918:222), and "camps" by Richard Lee (1972:350–56). Despite the variation in terminology, the unit being referred to by each author is a spatial grouping of kinfolk structured around a core of adult brothers and/or sisters, their spouses, and children (Helm 1968:121). In my view, if they are all the same kind of unit, they should be referred to by the same term.

These units also meet the criteria of most cross-cultural definitions of "family" (see Fallers 1965). In India, for example, this type of organization has been referred to as a "joint family" (e.g., by Kolenda 1968:346; Owens 1971:225), and in Mexico as a "great family" (Redfield 1941:194). I prefer "family" over most of the labels used in the literature on hunter-gatherers because it is more conducive to comparative analysis. In a previous publication I employed the label "local family" (Burch 1975a:237–38), but I now think that "local" is a bit confusing to people unfamiliar with hunter-gatherer ways of life. "Compound" implies that it is a large family unit created by the union of two or more smaller ones, which is exactly what it was.

Settlements

The Iñupiat made a distinction between villages and camps.[28] A village, or *nunaaqqiq*, was a place where at least some people ordinarily resided all year round. At certain times of year, villages were home to a mere handful of residents, often just a few elders and some children looking after them. They were, nevertheless, ordinarily occupied all year round by someone. A camp, or *piñiaġvik*, on the other hand, was a settlement so small that the seasonal movements of its inhabitants left it entirely devoid of residents from time to time every year.

Camps were usually characterized either by the season during which they were occupied or by the primary subsistence activity that occurred there. According to the first criterion, camps were designated as *upiṅġaksrivik* (spring camp), *upiṅġivik* (summer camp), *ukiaksrivik* (fall camp), or *ukiivik* (winter camp). According to the second, there were many possibilities, the most common of which were *natchiġñiaġvik* (seal-hunting camp), *tuttunniaġvik* (caribou-hunting camp), and *aqaluŋniaġvik* (fish camp). These basic distinctions were found throughout the study region, although the precise terms used varied to some extent from one dialect or subdialect area to another.

For purposes of the present study, it is useful to distinguish between "simple" and "complex" settlements. The former were settlements occupied by the members of a single domestic or compound family. They typically varied in population between about eight, in the case of an isolated household, to perhaps forty or fifty. Complex settlements, on the other hand, contained two or more compound families whose houses were built in separate clusters, or neighborhoods. These neighborhoods had names, which often served as family names for the people who resided in them (Kunuyaq 1940:1). To a significant extent, they may be viewed as two or more simple settlements that happened to be located very close together.

All villages (pl. *nunaaqqich*) were complex settlements, but only a few camps were. Unfortunately, it is impossible to know how many settlements fell into which category during the study period. The number could not have been constant anyway, changing seasonally and yearly. However, one can form a rough idea of what the possibilities were by looking at the statistics on settlement size.

The greatest regularity in settlement size from one year to the next was at the time of freshwater freezeup, so I begin with a consideration of the size of what I call "fall/winter settlements." Except when some extraordinary condition—such as a flood, an extremely early freezeup, or a battle—disrupted people's movements, such settlements were ordinarily occupied by essentially the same families every fall. If food remained plentiful in these locations, they might remain occupied well into the winter and possibly even into spring, hence the "fall/winter" designation. Even when they were abandoned for some reason during the winter, they were still considered to be a family's base of operations. Since people usually left their boats at these sites, it was to them that they returned in spring.

The basic data on fall/winter settlements over the study region as a whole are summarized in Figure 16. This is a graph showing the variation in size among settlements of this type as measured by the number of houses per settlement. I believe this measure is more reliable than any direct estimate of the population because evidence of the number of houses, in the form of ruins, lasts a lot longer than does evidence of how many people once occupied them. In every district covered by this study, a large number of 19th-century house remains survived into the late 19th and early 20th century. Many of my informants had seen these abandoned houses during their younger years and had asked more knowledgeable elders about them. Significantly, there was a high degree of agreement among different sources with regard to just how many houses were in any given location. The problems lie with the few large villages, which none of my sources saw at anywhere near their peak, and which were too large anyway for one to make accurate judgments about house numbers without actually doing a count. The figures for these villages are educated guesses.

Also difficult is the task of determining how many of the houses at a given site were occupied simultaneously. This is complicated by the fact that, in several nations, a house had to be abandoned if a person died in it; in some others, it was taboo to live in the same house for two years in succession. One is forced to rely on informants' judgments on this matter. Here again, I found the level of agreement to be very high.

Figure 16 summarizes the number of houses in the 284 fall/winter settlements that reportedly existed during the study period in the study region as a whole.[29] The range of variation was between one house, in 96 cases, and 75 houses, in a single instance (shown in the graph below as >10). As the graph shows, most of the settlements were tiny. Specifically, 246 of them, constituting 86.7 percent of the total, consisted of fewer than five households. It is reasonable to assume that the great majority, if not all of them, were simple in structure. Only ten settlements, or 3.5 percent of the total, contained ten or more households. Those ten were home to 27.5 percent of the total population of the study region, so it is reasonable to assume that all of them were complex in structure. That leaves us with twenty-eight fall/winter settlements, or just under 10 percent of the total, with five to nine houses; there is no way to know or even assume whether they were simple or complex without additional information.

The inhabitants of the study region were mobile hunter-gatherers whose annual movements followed a fairly regular pattern. In theory, people could settle anywhere they wanted within the borders of their nation's estate; fishing and hunting areas were open to all. However, there appears to have been a strong tendency for families to at least try to return to the same localities, if not the exact same sites, every year. The focus of this pattern in each of the several nations involved was the fall/winter settlement. Fall/winter settlements were the most regularly occupied locations in each district from one year to the next, and they were where the most permanent dwellings were built. To the extent that people identified themselves and were identified by others as being from a particular place, it was with the fall/winter

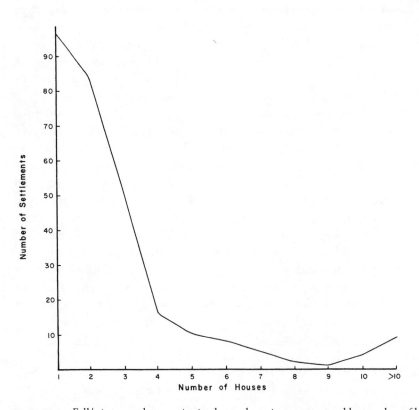

FIGURE 16. Fall/winter settlement size in the study region as measured by number of houses.

settlement. This was true even of the Nuataaġmiut, whose members actually might spend less than two months living in one of these locations in any given year.

During the course of their annual cycle of movement, the Iñupiat formed settlements of various sizes and degrees of complexity. In periods of famine, the inhabitants of even the largest and most complex fall/winter villages split up and spread out over the countryside. During this period, they lived in settlements of the utmost simplicity, often as isolated conjugal families. In some districts, tiny settlements were also the norm for at least part of every summer. Most Kivalliñiġmiut and Pittaġmiut, for example, dispersed over their respective estates in small family groups, hunting caribou and small game from late July to early September. The Akuniġmiut were divided into two types of summer settlement: fish camps of women, children, and elders along the Kobuk River, and wandering parties of men hunting caribou in the Noatak drainage. And finally, the members of both nations having estates along the Selawik River spent the summers spread out in fish camps, most of which were very small.

On the other hand, during the holiday season, the inhabitants of several simple settlements often merged into a single complex one, but only temporarily. And, during the summer fair and certain other events discussed later, practically the entire membership of several nations came together in one place. The point of all this is that, in order to survive at all, not to mention live as comfortably as they did, the Iñupiat had to be organized in such a way that they could aggregate on some occasions and disperse in others without undue disruption. The high level of economic and political self-sufficiency of domestic families was the mechanism making this possible.

The *Qargi*

The main focus of social interaction in an Iñupiaq village, other than the dwelling, was the *qargi*.[30] Some authors have referred to this type of structure as a "men's house," which, in some parts of Alaska, it was. However, in the study region, it is more accurately conceived of as a community hall. It is true that, during most days, it was a place where men and older boys spent their time if they were not out hunting or fishing. They worked on various projects, told stories, and took their meals there. It was the place where men discussed and debated the major issues of the day, and where troublemakers were interviewed and, if necessary, chastised. Women ordinarily entered only when serving food. But the *qargi* was also the place where dances, festivals, and feasts were held, and where major storytelling sessions took place. Most of these larger events involved both males and females, and children as well as adults.

Much of the attention given to *qargich* (pl.) in the literature focuses on those in the complex settlements of Wales and Point Hope, where they were permanent, named structures with distinct memberships. *Qargich* in these settlements were apparently founded by an *umialik* as a place where he and his male relatives could visit, work, and pass the time. Over the years, other people would be invited (or would request) to join, and most *qargich* that had been in operation for more than a few years included at least three or four *umialgich* among their members. As long as the founder was alive and active, he directed *qargi* affairs.

A group of men who were dissatisfied, for whatever reason, with the situation in the *qargi* to which they belonged could establish a new one. Once the founding member or members passed on, the surviving elders were in charge, although wealthy members of any age had considerable influence over a *qargi*'s members. In complex settlements, old men, bachelors, and older boys often lived and slept in the *qargi* during the seasons when it was open. Females were unwelcome except when serving food or on ceremonial occasions. Orphaned boys sometimes also lived in the *qargi*, where they worked as servants for the others.

Discussions of *qargi* in the literature almost always focus on complex settlements. However, my sources insisted that every settlement having more than one house had a gathering place, that is, a *qargi*, even if it was just an ordinary house. Most of the *qargich* in the study region must have been of this type. In this context, one did not think of membership in a *qargi*, since every male in the settlement was automatically entitled to use the facilities and participate in *qargi* affairs. In summer, a *qargi* was often nothing more than the downwind side of a boat placed on its side to serve as a windbreak. Wherever men gathered to chat and work on equipment was a *qargi*, as was any place where larger gatherings took place, regardless of whether it was enclosed or in the open air. When out-of-town guests were invited to participate in a festival of some kind, large but temporary (and often rather flimsy) buildings were erected so that the assembled multitude could fit inside more or less protected from the elements.

Simple Settlements

Socially, simple settlements were occupied by the members of a single compound family. Thus, they had the same basic structure as the Nuataaġmiut family shown earlier in Figure 15. Physically, they consisted of one or more occupied dwellings, perhaps a few temporary buildings (e.g., a menstrual hut, a birthing hut), and perhaps an abandoned house or two. Wherever material to build them could be obtained, racks were erected near the houses for various purposes: to dry fish or meat, and to store food, boats, and sleds to keep them away from dogs and other nuisance animals. Food storage pits were often dug nearby in the permafrost. Houses were usually constructed close together to permit easy visiting back and forth, and sometimes they were linked by tunnels or corridors. In most small settlements, one of the regular houses—usually the largest—served as the *qargi*. The beach or a gravel bar, or the frozen river, lagoon, or ocean surface, served as a playing field. Graves were placed anywhere that was convenient. Sometimes they were numerous enough and close enough together to justify the designation of graveyard; usually they were not. In summer, fresh water was obtained from nearby streams or, in some coastal settlements, from shallow wells. In winter, it was acquired either as liquid through holes chopped in the ice, or in the form of ice. The former was preferred since no fuel had to be consumed in its production. Garbage and human feces were dumped at a convenient nearby location, often to be consumed by dogs. Urine was kept in containers in the houses and used for washing and various other purposes.

In interior districts, houses were usually erected along and facing a stream or river, less often a small lake, on ground that was above spring flood level. They were also often built in the midst of or very near heavy willow growth, which served as a windbreak, source of fuel, a home to ptarmigan and hares that could be snared for food, and camouflage from enemy raiders. The plan of such a settlement that was inhabited during the study period is shown in Map 17. It is located at what used to be a good fishing place near the mouth of a small stream flowing from a lake into the Selawik River.[31]

As Map 17 shows, the site contains the remains of seven houses located on a grassy bank surrounded by willows and alders. The houses were of four-post-center type, with sleeping alcoves on either side of the central living area. This suggests that each was occupied by two conjugal families and perhaps an aged relative or two. According to my own sources, no more than three of the houses in this settlement were ordinarily occupied at any given

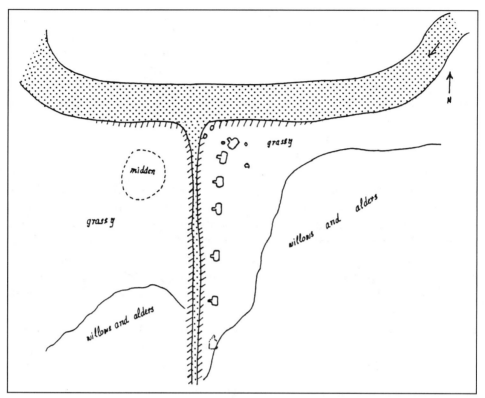

MAP 17. Field sketch (not to scale) of a small interior settlement. From Anderson and Anderson (1982:app. 2). Reproduced with permission.

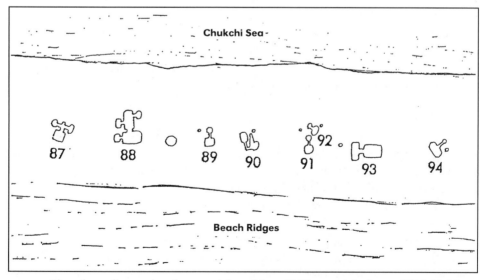

MAP 18. Plan of a small coastal settlement. Adapted from Giddings and Anderson (1986:41). House numbers from the original.

time. No building identifiable as a specialized *qargi* is apparent on the diagram, which is consistent with the village's small size.

On the coast, local terrain permitting, houses were usually built either facing the water or else oriented in a direction in which the prevailing winter winds would not cause drifting snow to cover the entrance. In most cases they were also situated on ground unlikely to be affected by storm surges, ice ride-up, or ice push.[32] Sometimes houses were located on the back side of the beach both to protect them from violent acts of nature and to render them less visible to seaborne enemy raiders.

Map 18 shows a sketch map of a coastal settlement that was probably occupied early in or just prior to the study period. The houses were not excavated by the archeologists who mapped them, so just how many were occupied at the same time cannot be determined; examination of their surface features suggests that they were roughly contemporaneous (Giddings and Anderson 1986:41). The dwellings show an interesting variety of sizes and shapes, as well as diverse orientations toward the shoreline. The large, more-or-less rectangular portions of the structures were probably sleeping and living areas, while the other portions were likely storage and cooking areas. House number 88 was a double house, probably with a wall between the two living areas. If three or four or more of these buildings were occupied simultaneously, one of the other structures probably served as a *qargi*. Given the settlement's location on the north side of Cape Krusenstern, where caribou, sea mammals, and fish were all available during different seasons, it is conceivable that this site was occupied for the greater part of the year.

Complex Settlements

Complex settlements were inhabited by the members of two or more compound families. As noted above, at least ten settlements almost certainly fell into this category. They are listed in Table 6. Note that at least three of the settlements in the list—Kuugruaq, Kuutchiaq, and Makkaksraq—were not ordinarily occupied on a year-round basis. Another twenty-eight settlements might have been complex in structure, or they might have been complex in some years and simple in others.

Complex settlements included people who were related to one another in terms of a number of relationships in addition to close kinship ties. This was sometimes true in simple settlements, but it was inevitable in complex settlements. Accordingly, this is the most appropriate section in which to discuss them.

Compound Families

Solidarity was stronger within each of the compound-family segments in a complex settlement than it was between them. The several families constituted factions between and among which a certain amount of tension often existed. The most extreme development of this pattern was in the large settlement of Point Hope, where some compound families may have involved more than eighty people. The children belonging to each unit formed play groups of youngsters of roughly the same age. As the individuals involved approached puberty, these groups sometimes formed gangs who fought youngsters from other families. A boy who was caught alone near the houses owned by the members of another family sometimes received a severe thrashing. Adults were at less risk, but were nevertheless ordinarily on guard when walking near or among the dwellings owned by the members of another family unless they were invited for a visit.

Offsetting the divisory effect within a complex settlement of the very strong solidarity existing within its resident compound families was the fact that the members of each family were linked to members of others through a variety of kinship ties. This was so because a person usually had to look beyond the limits of his or her own family to find a spouse; when married, one of the spouses had to go live with the other's relatives. When a young woman went to live with her new husband, for example, she was forced to focus her attention on the affairs of his family—her new family—during the ordinary course of daily life. However, she did not have to forsake altogether the ties she had with her own parents and siblings. Through a broad array of such connections, the members of every family in a complex settlement were linked to people belonging to each of the others. Although they were not as active as relationships existing within the separate compound-family units, these relationships helped hold the settlement together.

Leadership

Complex settlements lacked any settlement-wide council or other organization that might serve to coordinate the activities of its residents. In principle, the constituent compound families were completely independent of one another. However, all of the settlement's residents had to get along somehow if they were to live so close together successfully. The responsibility of keeping the peace fell on the different family heads, or *qauḱḷiich* (pl.), most of whom were relatively wealthy. I have no hard evidence on the point, but I suspect that compound-family heads living within the same complex settlement were not closely related to one another; if they were, they would have belonged to the same family.

Technically, a family head's span of control was limited to the members of the compound family he headed. His influence in the wider social sphere depended partly on the size of the family he headed, and partly on the personal esteem (or lack thereof) with which he was regarded by the community at large. Within his own family, a *qauḱḷiq*, with the help of his older relatives, tried to resolve conflicts and keep troublemakers under control. Externally, he

Table 6. Complex Settlements in Northwest Alaska

Settlement	Nation	No. Houses
Agianamiut*	Kiŋikmiut	25
Kiataanamiut*	Kiŋikmiut	35
Kuugruaq	Akuniġmiut	11
Kuupaamiit*	Kuuŋmiut	18
Kuutchiaq	Siilviim Kaŋianiġmiut	13
Makkaksraq	Kaŋiġmiut	20
Qayaina*	Akuniġmiut	14
Qigiqtaq*	Tapqaġmiut	20
Taksruq Saaŋa*	Qikiqtaġruŋmiut	20
Tikiġaq*	Tikiġaġmiut	75

* ordinarily had some residents year round

negotiated with other family heads on an ad hoc basis to sort out major problems, organize settlement-wide recreational activities (e.g., football games and other athletic competitions), and arrange for the common defense.

Qargich

Qargi involvement often served as a unifying force in a complex settlement.[33] In such settlements, the *qargi* was almost always a separate building because the dwellings were not large enough to hold very many men. In some complex settlements there may have been only one *qargi*, but in most there were two or more, each of which was named. As a rule, a *qargi* was built by the members of a single compound family under the direction of its head, and was considered the property of that family.[34] Its use was not necessarily restricted to members of that family, however, which is how it acquired its integrating function. For example, if a young man went to live with his wife's family when he married her, he might remain a member of his father's *qargi*; or, he might acquire membership in the *qargi* to which his father-in-law belonged. He could not belong to both, although he might be welcome in both on particular occasions. Over time, as people grew up, married, and became members of other families, *qargi* membership became more diffuse. Conversely, from time to time, dissension might arise within a *qargi*, in which case some individuals might leave and join another, or else try to establish a new one.

Changes were also introduced when a *qargi* washed out of a riverbank (inland) or beach ridge (coast), leading to its abandonment, and often to the redistribution of at least some of its members. For example, the large Tikiġaġmiut family mentioned above, known as Iñugialiŋmiut, built a *qargi* called Suaġvik. After a time, it was washed out. Its members then took over an abandoned *qargi* known as Uŋasiksikuaq. Its members had left town, but the newcomers kept the old name (Aġviqsiiña 1940.3; David Frankson 1980). Others, many of them from other families, gradually joined it as their own buildings also washed out.

Over the years and generations, the types of fluctuations described above increased the chances that, no matter how restricted a *qargi*'s membership might be at first, eventually several compound families would come to be represented in it. As this occurred, it increasingly became a forum of communication between and among different compound families and their heads. It also increased the chances that disciplinary actions imposed on troublemakers by *qargi* elders would have broad support within the community, and therefore would promote unity rather than divisiveness among the families concerned.

Doctors

For present purposes, I am using the English term "doctor" to include both *aŋatkut* (shamans) and *iñuunniaqtit* (tribal doctors) within the same general category. My interest here is the relationships existing between the doctors and their patients, as well as those between and among the doctors. These relationships could occur in simple settlements, but when they did, the individuals involved were usually very closely related, and they usually operated on a kinship basis. Many simple settlements lacked doctors altogether, however, and had to send for them in time of need. The population of every complex settlement included doctors of both types.

The doctor-patient relationship operated on a fee-for-service basis except when it involved close kin. A doctor was hired to solve a problem, and was compensated with food, equipment, or services. The fee was usually negotiated before a diagnosis was made and a cure suggested.

The services of *iñuunniaqtit* were always provided on an individual basis. In other words, a specific individual had a particular malady, such as a stomach ailment, and its treatment affected only that person. The services of an *aŋatkuq*, however, although frequently required because of one person's problem, often led to the imposition of one or more new taboos on that person's entire family, and sometimes on everyone in the settlement. Alternatively, a general calamity, such as flood or famine, might turn out to have been caused by one person's breaking of a taboo. The work of *aŋatkut* thus often involved fairly complex social dynamics, various aspects of which are discussed in subsequent chapters.

There seems to have been a certain amount of competition between doctors living in the same settlement. Obviously, a successful practitioner acquired a certain amount of prestige and influence, and also accumulated significant wealth. There was probably rather little competition between *aŋatkut* and *iñuunniaqtit*, because of their entirely different methods of diagnosis and treatment. Competition was more likely within, rather than between, specialties.

If someone had a severe stomach ailment, for example, who was to say at the outset whether it was caused by the breaking of a taboo or by something the person ate? Depending on the diagnosis, the treatment could vary dramatically. I do not know how this was sorted out during the study period, but I suspect it was rather like an incident that occurred more than a century later. In the spring of 1970, Charlie Lee, who lived in Shungnak, developed some kind of internal problem. He was flown to Kotzebue at government expense for treatment in the Bureau of Indian Affairs hospital. The doctors gave him some medication and sent him home. However, his condition continued to deteriorate. So, at his own expense, he flew back to Kotzebue to be treated by Della Keats, a well-known *iñuunniaqti*. She fixed the problem over the course of two or three days of treatment. In olden times, as in recent ones, afflicted people probably tried one kind of doctor first, and, if the treatment was unsuccessful, moved to the other.

Competition between *iñuunniaqti* living in the same settlement may or may not have been intense, but it probably was a divisive factor in community affairs only on rare occasions. Indeed, I never heard of it. Competition between and among *aŋatkut*, however, held at least the potential for causing major problems. On the one hand, it could be fairly straightforward and benign, as when two of them tried to outdo one another in performing dramatic feats of magic. On the other hand, it could be serious indeed, as when they tried to bring down supernatural forces on one another, potentially bringing harm to everyone in the settlement. This possibility is discussed in more detail in Chapter 5.

Whaling Crews

When hunting large animals, several people, usually but by no means always men, often worked together.[35] In a few cases, such as the beluga hunts of the Kaŋiġmiut and the Nuataaġmiut, practically every adult male in the nation was involved at the same time. In caribou drives, walrus hunts, and bearded seal (oogruk) hunts, "crews" were involved, but they virtually always consisted of family members. The same was true of duck and ptarmigan drives, although sometimes members of two or more families cooperated in these ventures (all of which are discussed in Chapter 4). The one organization in Iñupiaq societies that was not necessarily or automatically peopled exclusively by family members was the whaling crew, which was found primarily in the complex settlements of Wales and Point Hope.[36]

A whaling crew was recruited and underwritten by an *umialik*. The preference was to hire family members, both out of loyalty and for the increased returns that would accrue to the family if each crew member came from that family. However, a whaling crew was the one organization in an Iñupiaq society where skill was more important than kinship.[37] This was particularly true with regard to the harpooner. For that position, an *umialik* tried to recruit the very best person he could find, whether he was a relative or not. Good harpooners were expensive; they received not only a disproportionate share of the harvest, but were kept on retainer all year long.

Interestingly, and in contrast to what I was told, Rainey's Tikiġaġmiut informant Aġviqsiiña (1940.1:91) claimed that an *umialik* never asked a man to be on his crew. According to him, people requested to join a crew, and were either accepted or rejected by the captain. He claimed that crew members were less likely to quit if they did it that way.

Whaling crews were made up of a minimum of eight people, in the sense that eight people pretty much had to be in the boat at one time. There was one *aquti*, or helmsman, in the stern; one *kapukti* (*tavaqti*, in Wales), or harpooner, in the bow; and six *aŋuaqtit*, or crew-men (paddlers), in the middle, three on each side. The helmsman was usually the *umialik* himself. However, he could also be the harpooner, in which case the prime outside recruit would be the helmsman. The helmsman and harpooner were invariably men. The paddlers were usually men, although women served in that capacity from time to time.

The overall organization of a crew involved more than eight people, however. First, the *umialik*'s wife (or another woman, in Wales) had to perform or participate in a number of important rituals connected with the hunt, and she had to organize the transfer of food and other supplies from the village to the place where the hunters were operating. Each *umialik* usually also hired a shaman to look after the supernatural aspects of the enterprise. And one woman usually served as cook. In addition, for one reason or another, a crew member or two might be physically incapacitated or prevented by a taboo from working at a particular time, and would have to be replaced; or, especially toward the end of the season, crew members sometimes left to do something else. The *umialik* himself might have to return to the village occasionally, in which case someone else had to take his place at the helm and serve as *ataniq* (boss). Finally, several men were needed to help haul the boat and equipment two or three miles (3–5 km) or more over the rough ice to the lead (large crack in the ice) where the whaling was to take place, and even more to help bring the tons of meat, skin, and blubber back to the settlement after a successful hunt. Altogether, one crew could involve as many as ten to fifteen people or even more over the course of a six-to-eight-week whaling season. All of these people had to be fed and otherwise looked after by the *umialik* during the season itself, all got portions of the whale, and all were kept on retainer for much of the rest of the year.

Friendships

One relationship that often existed in complex settlements but almost never in simple ones was that of friendship.[38] Friendships were designated by different terms in different parts of the study area. For example, in the Kobuk River valley, *suunaaġiik* and *aññaġiik* (both dual forms) referred to friends who were both male or both female, respectively. In some other districts the term was *avilaitqatigiik* (dual), while in still others it was *avilaisuqatigiik* (dual), sex not being specified in either case. In order to be friends, two individuals had to be non-kin, or else very remote kin; usually (but not necessarily) of the same sex; and always of approximately the same age, usually meaning born in the same year.[39] These criteria permitted the individuals involved to relate to one another as equals, which was crucial to the successful operation of the relationship.

Friendships probably were usually initiated while the individuals involved were youngsters, and then developed over a lifetime. At their best, friendships consisted of people spending time together at work or at play, helping one another, sharing stories and jokes, and generally enjoying one another's company. The relationship was imbued with considerable intensity, meaning that friends typically were extremely fond of one another. However, it was also institutionalized as being very weak, which means that almost all of one's other relationships and obligations took precedence over this one. Friendship was more of a luxury than a relationship enjoyed by everyone on a daily basis.

Namesakes

Another relationship that often existed in a complex settlement was that of *atiqatigiik* or *atigiik* (dual), or namesakes.[40] All that was required for people to be namesakes was to have the same name. They did not have to be named after the same person, and they did not have to be name giver and name recipient; many babies were named after people who had recently died. However, given the magical qualities ascribed to names, it is not surprising that individuals who had the same one would regard one another as being linked together in some special way. Such individuals were expected to have similar personalities and character.

The content of this relationship was rather vaguely defined, as far as I could learn. Namesakes were supposed to be friendly to one another, and to give one another presents from time to time, but that is about all. Mostly, the *atiqatigiik* relationship seems to have been an option available to certain individuals. It gave them a basis on which to be in a special relationship, but it did not require them to be in one. Others could also use the relationship as a basis for interaction. Thus, someone who had the same name as one's spouse was designated *uumman* (heart). A man whose wife's name was Anausuk, for example, might give presents from time to time to someone else who was also named Anausuk, especially if that person was a woman. People in this relationship also sometimes danced together on formal occasions.

Marriage in Lesser Degree

Virtually every complex settlement included relationships created through what Albert Heinrich (1963a:80) called "marriage in lesser degree." There were various possibilities here, but the context in which these relationships were usually created involved either (a) co-marriage, or spouse exchange, or (b) marriage, divorce, and remarriage. The primary results of these arrangements are shown in Figure 17.

The relationships created by co-marriage are shown in the upper diagram in Figure 17.[41] Here we see two residential husband-wife pairs (a-b, d-c) who, on at least one occasion, changed sexual partners with one another. The change created the relationship of *aippaġiik* (dual) between the two women, and that of *nuliaqatigiik* (dual) between the two men. The same two relationships, it may be recalled, were also created by polygynous and polyandrous marriages. A fourth relationship, that of *uiŋuraq-nuliiraq*, or co-spouses, was created between each man and the other's wife. Finally, once even a single exchange had taken place, the children of any of the adults involved were related to one another as *qataŋutigiitch* (sing. *qataŋun*).

Theoretically, co-marriages could exist in simple settlements. However, the tight kinship network that existed in such settlements usually prevented them from becoming recognized.

No such restraint existed in complex settlements. There is no way to determine the extent to which co-marriages took place, but they must have been fairly common.[42] They usually involved people who were good friends, and who wanted to replace the institutionally weak tie of friendship with the stronger bond of kinship. They also enjoyed the diversion provided by having more than one approved sexual partner. The exchanges usually were overnight affairs, although they could be repeated as frequently as the individuals involved wished.

Qataŋutigiitch were supposed to interact pretty much as siblings did, and they typically addressed one another by sibling terms. However, they usually lived in separate dwellings or different settlements when they were members of the same society, and the relationship was often rather weak. When they belonged to different societies, on the other hand, the relationship was institutionalized as being rather strong. When social (e.g., a feud) or environmental (e.g., a famine) problems arose in one's homeland, one could go visit a *qataŋun* in another nation and expect to receive shelter and support.

The second major form of marriage in lesser degree is shown in the lower diagram in Figure 17. Here we see a case where a husband and wife (a-b) were divorced, as indicated by the diagonal line across the equals sign, and both remarried. Remarriage also resulted in the creation of relationships between the two women and the two men involved, these being exactly the same ones that existed in both forms of complex residential marriage and in co-marriages. In this case the children of the various individuals involved usually considered each other to be siblings rather than *qataŋutigiitch*, the former being the stronger of the two possibilities. Divorce and remarriage did not result in the replacement of one set of

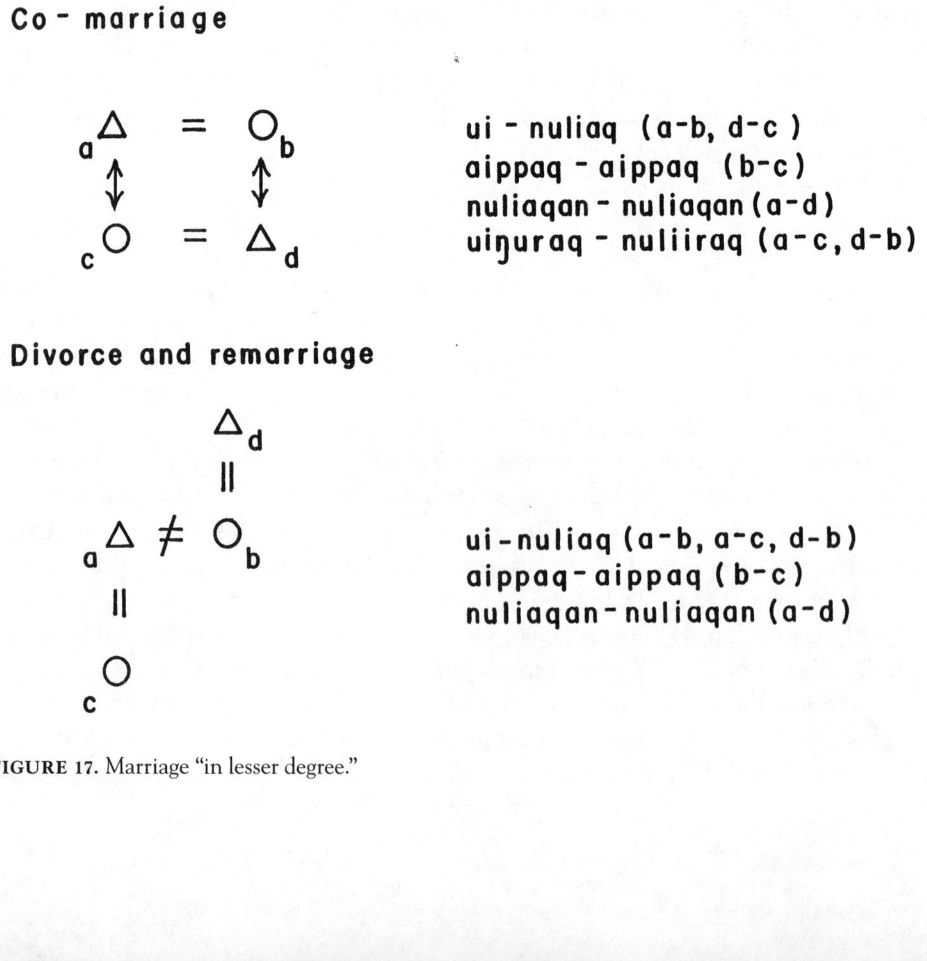

Co - marriage

$$
\begin{array}{ccc}
{}_a\triangle & = & \bigcirc_b \\
\updownarrow & & \updownarrow \\
{}_c\bigcirc & = & \triangle_d
\end{array}
$$

ui - nuliaq (a-b, d-c)
aippaq - aippaq (b-c)
nuliaqan - nuliaqan (a-d)
uiŋuraq - nuliiraq (a-c, d-b)

Divorce and remarriage

$$
\begin{array}{c}
\triangle_d \\
\| \\
{}_a\triangle \neq \bigcirc_b \\
\| \\
\bigcirc \\
{}_c
\end{array}
$$

ui-nuliaq (a-b, a-c, d-b)
aippaq- aippaq (b-c)
nuliaqan- nuliaqan (a-d)

FIGURE 17. Marriage "in lesser degree."

relationships by another, but with the addition of a new set of relationships to the first. This was the point of Heinrich's (1972) article on "divorce as an alliance mechanism."

Once a man and a woman had sexual relations, they and any children either of them ever had were considered to be related in one or another of the ways listed above—forever. The relationships might become inactive or even hostile—the latter particularly in the case of divorce and remarriage—much of the time, but they were there nevertheless. A *nuliaqan*, an *aippaq*, and especially a *qataŋun* was someone who could be called upon in time of trouble and be expected to provide support.

There was also a third form of marriage in lesser degree. This involved sexual intercourse conducted without the knowledge of the principals' co-residential spouses. On the face of it, this was cheating. However, in the Iñupiaq scheme of things, clandestine sex theoretically created the very same relationships that were associated with institutionalized co-marriage. The key issue was the extent to which these relationships were publicly acknowledged. Apparently there was considerable variation in this regard. Short-lived affairs usually had no lasting implications. Those that continued for some time, on the other hand, usually became common knowledge, particularly if they produced children. The relationships that had been theoretically created were then either accepted by the jilted spouses or they were not. In the latter case, trouble usually ensued in the form of shouting, wife beatings, fights, divorces, or some combination of the four. If the jilted spouses accepted their situation, however, an acknowledged co-marriage could be the result. No matter what the outcome was in other respects, any children any of the participants ever had were *qataŋutigiich*, whether they chose to act as such or not.

Nicholas Gubser (1965:117) once wrote that the Iñupiat sought "sexual variations in partners rather than in practices," and all the evidence I have been able to gather on the subject supports that view. Variation in partners was achieved both institutionally, through co-marriage, and illegitimately, through extramarital affairs, if one can use that phrase in the Iñupiaq context. There is of course no way to know the prevalence of either type of activity during the study period, but extramarital affairs seem to have been fairly common. One might be tempted to believe that the best hunters, or handsomest, or strongest, most active men and the physically most attractive women were the ones who most frequently indulged themselves in this way. Evidence from my own time (1960s) does not support such a conclusion, however. Some of the most sexually active men I knew were indeed outstanding hunters, but others were among the least productive human beings I have ever heard of. The most sexually active women were neither particularly young nor especially good-looking. When I inquired among the men what the attraction was, I received responses like "Good rhythm," or "She sure knows how to do it!" I did not feel that I knew any women well enough to pose the same question, but I presume that I would have received analogous responses.

Partners

Partners, or *niuviġiik* (dual), were individuals of either sex who agreed to exchange specified goods with one another on a regular basis (Burch 1970a; 1988a:104; 2005:155–59). Usually the exchanges took place regularly at specific times of year, but they could occur whenever one partner was in need and the other had the wherewithal to help. The goods that served as the focus of the exchanges between partners were those that were not equally available to the individuals involved. Thus, if one person lived in an area where caribou were often abundant and the other did not, caribou skins typically made up one side of the equation.

The other side might consist of sea mammal products. Since the conditions necessary for a productive partnership rarely existed within a given district, most partnerships linked individuals who were members of entirely different nations.

Variations in skill could also serve as the basis of partnership. For example, if one man was an excellent carver but a poor hunter, and another man's skills were just the reverse, they might form a partnership to take advantage of their respective strengths and offset their respective weaknesses. This type of partnership could occur within a nation, and also within a complex settlement. However, it must have been uncommon, since other family members were usually able to provide the necessary skills, and kinfolk always took precedence over partners.

Kiŋigin

The largest and most complex fall/winter settlements in the study region were the major centers of Kiŋigin (Wales), just north of Cape Prince of Wales on Bering Strait, and Tikiġaq (Point Hope), near the tip of Point Hope. Both were occupied all year round, although the number of people in residence fluctuated dramatically over the course of a yearly cycle. During the study period, they usually were occupied between about mid-July and late August by only a few people, whereas during the whaling season in April and May, they were home to virtually every member of their respective nations. Their exceptional nature justifies special treatment here. This section focuses on Kiŋigin, the following one on Tikiġaq.

Kiŋigin was the main village of the Kiŋikmiut, located just north of Cape Prince of Wales on the shore of Bering Strait.[43] Actually, it was composed of two different settlements, Kiataanamiut and Agianamiut, that were located very close to each other.

A diagram of how Kiŋigin might have appeared in the early 19th century is shown in Map 19, which is keyed to Table 7.

Table 7. Key to Map of Kiŋigin*

TERM	REFERENT	TRANSLATION
Agianamiut	"hillside village"	"village/people to south"
Ałłagazamiut	abandoned site	"separate place"
Anaġiaqtuġik	locality C	"place to defecate"
Azrviisi	locality D	[just a name]
Ilulinaaq	cove	"indentation"
Iŋiġuq	long, low rise in ground	?
Kiataanamiut	"lower village"	"place to north"
Kuuŋmiut	stream, and locality F	"river people"
Maġaġvik	island	"mud place"
Nigraamiut	locality E	"people with decorated clothes"?
Niiqłavaat	locality A	"northern, northerly"
Qargitaġvik	abandoned village	"place with old qargi"
Singaġrugmiut	locality B	"channel people"
Singaugaaġruk	Mission Creek	"channel that goes inland from the sea"

* Keyed to Map 19.

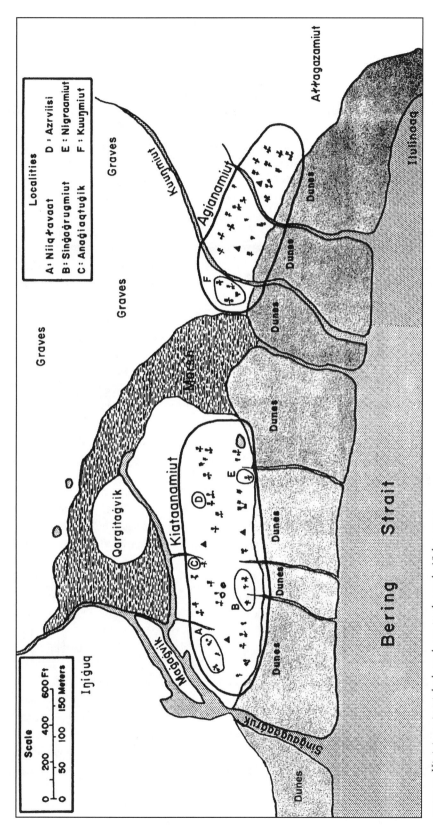

MAP 19. Kiŋigin as it might have been in the early 19th century.

Map 19 was developed from an aerial photograph of the modern village and its surround-ings. The landscape was then modified according to information reported to me by Herbert Anungazuk and Ernest Oxereok, along with other considerations discussed below, to show how this same area might have looked in the early 19th century.[44]

Kiataanamiut and Agianamiut were separated from one another by a marshy area that formerly was quite unsuitable for house sites, but which has now largely dried up. A third settlement, Qargitaġvik (or Qargitaġviŋmiut), was located inland from Kiataanamiut, on what was formerly an island. At the time it was occupied, it could be reached in summer only by boat, via Sinġaugaaġruk creek. It has been abandoned throughout the contact period, but just when it became so is uncertain.[45] H. Greist (n.d.: ch. II, pp. 2–3) estimated that it was inhabited until about 1845, but he does not indicate the basis on which he came to this conclusion. Recent archeological research suggests that the site was abandoned around AD 1500 (Harritt 2003a; 2004:173); legend says that its inhabitants fled to avoid annihilation at the hands of the Kiataanamiut, with whom they were feuding (E. Curtis 1930:136).

Kiŋigin is located on the shore of Bering Strait near the westernmost point of North America. Immediately to the south rises the upland forming Cape Prince of Wales. Toward the west, in clear weather, one sees the rugged escarpments of the two Diomede Islands and Fairway Rock, and, in the distance, the cliffs of easternmost Asia. To the east and north, the upland recedes, and the country opens up into a broad, swampy plain extending the whole way to Cape Espenberg, nearly 150 miles (240 km) away. The country is carpeted with a mosaic of tundra vegetation that, although seemingly sterile, provides a wide array of plant foods within a few minutes' walk of the settlement. What is now a broad beach in front of Kiŋigin formerly was broader still, and included a wide band of sand dunes between the bluff and the more level beach near the waterline. Weyer (1928) described the dunes as being parallel to the shore, about four feet (1.2 m) high, and covered with sparse, stabilizing grass; marshy tundra filled the depressions between the ridges. The dunes were reportedly more substantial still a century earlier. Fresh water was provided by creeks flowing through the village, and by a spring located some distance up the hill to the south.

Situated on the border between the Arctic high-pressure climate regime to the north and the Bering Sea low to the south, Kiŋigin is notorious for its stormy weather (H. Anungazuk 1999.1; Thornton 1931:6–7, 12–14; Weyer 1928). A strong southerly alongshore current (*quŋiq*) in summer, and a northerly one (*uŋavriq*) in winter, combine with brisk winds to make travel on Bering Strait a hazardous enterprise all year round.[46] According to Arthur Nagozruk, Sr., winter ice conditions here were so dangerous that most men were in their late twenties before they had acquired sufficient knowledge to be able to venture very far out on it on their own (Lucier 1969). With regard to boat travel, the people of Kiŋigin have the most fully articulated set of emergency procedures of any Eskimos I have ever met; I presume that they were developed a long time ago. Despite the harsh climate and the other hazards of living there, Kiŋigin was one of the largest concentrations of people in northwestern Alaska because of its access to large numbers of migratory sea mammals: bowhead whales, walrus, beluga, and seals.

The southern village, Agianamiut, was located on the lower slopes of the upland, and its houses were distributed in an irregular pattern according to the lay of the land. Kiataanamiut was on fairly level ground. Houses there were erected on well-drained locations in irregular lines roughly parallel to the shore. The buildings depicted were sketched as representing the Kiŋikmiut pattern of a large freestanding dwelling unit and a long entrance tunnel usually having one or two alcoves. Some houses are shown as sharing the entrance tunnel with a neighbor. An example of such an arrangement was the house in which Trollope stayed in 1854, where the separate dwelling units were occupied by the conjugal families of two brothers.

Trollope (1855:873) estimated that there were twenty to thirty houses each in Agianamiut and Kiataanamiut. Since it is universally believed now that Kiataanamiut was larger than Agianamiut in the early 19th century, as it was toward its end (Thornton 1931:20), I have represented it as having thirty-five dwelling units, as opposed to twenty-five in Agianamiut. At the presumed average of eight residents per house, Kiataanamiut would have had a population of 280, and Agianamiut a population of 200, for an overall total of 480. Several localities had names, as shown in Map 19 and explained in Table 7. In addition, each house reportedly had a name.

According to Trollope (1855:872), the two villages combined had four *qargich* in 1854. However, Weyer (1928) was told that previously there had been three *qargich* in Kiataanamiut and two in Agianamiut. That is more consistent with my understanding of the relative numbers of people in each settlement. *Qargich* are shown as triangles in Map 19, although their location is pure guesswork.

Each *qargi* had a name, although none of the early-19th-century names is remembered today.[47] Toward the end of the century, when both the population of Kiŋigin and the number of *qargich* it could support had declined, Kiataanamiut had one *qargi* named Kaiyuwatuuq, while Agianamiut had one named Ugiyuataġik and another named Tutuŋaliq (H. Anungazuk 2002; Nagozruk 1971; Oxereok 1999.1, 1999.2).

Other features included cold storages dug into the permafrost, one and sometimes two or three per house. More visible were the many racks for storing food, sleds, and other paraphernalia near the houses. In 1890 there were fifty-one large, open boats (pl. *umiat*) in the village (Thornton 1931:125), and there would have been at least that many racks on the beach on which they could be stored out of the reach of dogs. In the early 19th century the number of boats, hence racks, might have been even greater. Graves were placed on the hillside behind the village in areas where there is an abundance of frost-shattered rock. Bodies were wrapped in walrus skin and covered with rocks.

Agianamiut and Kiataanamiut seem to have been two separate villages that happened to be situated very close together. According to some reports, there was considerable animosity between the two. Trollope (1855:873), for example, said that people in Agianamiut spoke disparagingly of their neighbors in the winter of 1854. E. W. Nelson (1899:257; see also Nelson 1877–81: entry for July 12, 1881), who visited Wales very briefly in the summer of 1881, reported that "the people of these two villages had a standing feud that occasionally broke into open quarrels. Those of the 'spit village' [Kiataanamiut] were the most aggressive, and were hated and feared by the others." Subsequent visitors made similar observations (E. Curtis 1930:136; H. Greist ms: ch. II, pp. 2, 3; Thornton 1931:20).

Despite the reported antagonism, people from the two settlements encountered one another daily without apparent difficulty, and there seems to have been a fair amount of intermarriage between them (H. Anungazuk 1999.1). The inhabitants of both villages also participated in communal games and athletic contests in which the inhabitants were divided into two teams, each of which included people from both settlements.

I interpret these apparently contradictory observations as follows: Kiŋigin was composed of several compound family factions that combined at a still higher level to form "super-factions," which constituted the settlements of Agianamiut and Kiataanamiut. Despite occasional disagreements, the members of the two super-factions were united with one another and with the inhabitants of several smaller settlements in the nation of Kiŋikmiut.

Tikiġaq

Tikiġaq (Point Hope) was the main settlement of the Tikiġaġmiut, and was the largest settlement in northern Alaska.[48] In contrast to Kiŋigin, which was located next to the high land of a cape, Tikiġaq was situated at the tip of a triangular peninsula of low, tundra-covered land extending more than fifteen miles (24 km) out from the mainland. The nearest visible uplands are Cape Thompson, about twenty-seven miles (43 km) to the southeast, and the highlands of the western Lisburne Peninsula, nearly as far away toward the northeast. The climate was colder than that of Kiŋigin, but it was generally not quite as stormy. Here, as at Kiŋigin, the main attraction for people was access to large numbers of sea mammals. Bowhead whales passed close offshore in April and May; walrus regularly hauled out on the north side of the spit in June, July, and sometimes September; seals were common from November to July; and bearded seals were common from March to July. Caribou also wandered out onto the spit from time to time.

A reconstructed version of early-19th-century Tikiġaq is shown in Map 20. Since changes in the terrain here have been much more dramatic than at Kiŋigin, it is necessary to digress briefly on how I did the reconstruction.

My starting point was a map made in 1939–40 by Helge Larsen and Froelich Rainey (1948: between pp. 20 and 21).[49] I compared that with the situation I observed at Point Hope in the spring of 1970 and a map of the same area made by Raymond Newell (1985: fig. 1) in 1984. The differences among the three indicate that the northern shore of the point was wearing down at an average rate of roughly 4.7 yards (4.3 m) per year, and that the southern shore was building up at less than half that rate between 1940 and 1984. Assuming constant rates between the early 19th century and 1940, the northern shore would have been 580 yards (535 m) farther out in 1815 than it was in 1940, and the southern shore would have been about 275 yards (250 m) farther in. The point would have been much thicker then than it is now. This last conclusion is consistent with Beechey's chart made in 1826–27 (1831, I: end map), a hand-drawn map prepared for me by David Frankson (1980), and Donald Oktalik's (1970) remark that, during his sixty-two years of life, the spit had gotten a lot smaller on the north, but had changed rather little on the south.[50] The only discrepancy was in Frankson's map, which shows a slight northward hook to the point.

It is known that the houses were embedded in large mounds constructed on top of parallel beach ridges. Therefore, I began with the four rows of ridges and mounds actually shown on Larsen and Rainey's map, extended them toward the west, and added more house mounds to them. I then added three more ridges and rows of house mounds on the north. I think that the result is a realistic depiction of what Tikiġaq might have been like around the beginning of the 19th century. However, it is possible that the houses on the eastern end of the southernmost row, as shown in Larsen and Rainey's map, may have been built a bit later.

Many, probably most, of the houses were incorporated into large mounds of earth containing one or more dwelling units.[51] The mounds were built along the tops of the ridges that constitute the Point Hope chenier, hence were strung out in rows separated by depressions, most of which were swampy in early summer. Each house had a name, although I do not know if the name applied to the entire mound or to the separate dwelling units within it (Stefansson 1914b:309). Storage racks were built next to or right on top of the mounds, and

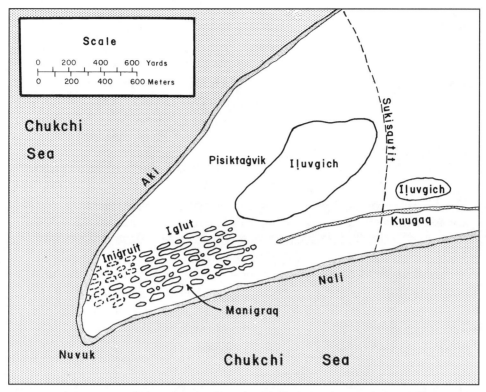

MAP 20. Tikiġaq as it might have been in the early 19th century. *Aki* = north shore; *iglut* = houses; *iḷuvgich* = graves; *iniġruit* = ruins; *kuugaq* = slough; *manigraq* = playing field; *nali* = south shore; *nuvuk* = point; *pisiktaġvik* = archery range; *sukisautit* = sharpened spikes placed in the ground.

cold storages were excavated in the permafrost nearby. Drinking water was obtained from snow, in winter, and from shallow wells, in summer (Jensen 1970.1, 1970.2).

Seven *qargich* were distributed at various locations in the settlement during the early 19th century, but their names have been forgotten.[52] At a later time, although I don't know just when, there were four in the southernmost row of houses, these being Qargiġruaq, Agraktaġvik, Suaġvik, and Uŋasiksikaaq (David Frankson 1980). Qaġmaqtuuq and Kaṇiḷiqpak were located in the row just to the north. It is more than likely that at some point there were one or two more in the rows farther north as well, but they were destroyed so long ago that their former existence has been forgotten. In any case, the number of *qargich* was not constant, because they, like the houses, kept washing out on the western end of town. Sometimes new ones were rebuilt to replace those that had been destroyed; sometimes they were not. The outcome apparently depended on fluctuations in the overall population as much as or even more than on the political dynamics of the village. (Due to the declining population of the settlement during the second half of the 19th century, the number of *qargich* dropped from six to two.[53])

Exactly how large Tikiġaq was at any given time is impossible to determine. In 1940, Larsen and Rainey (1948:20) counted the ruins of seventy houses in the ancient village, whereas Knud Rasmussen (Ostermann and Holtved 1952:47) had counted 122 in 1924 (see also Lowenstein 1993:32–35). This means a loss of fifty-two houses in only fifteen years. If one extrapolates back in time from 1924, adding fifty houses every fifteen years, the total for 1800 would have been an extraordinary 480 dwellings. At an average of eight people per house, the total population would have been 3,840, an unlikely figure indeed. Beechey, whose expedition visited Tikiġaq in 1826 and 1827, and who was an excellent observer, did not describe a village of anywhere near that size. In fact, Beechey's nephew Richard (quoted in Bockstoce 1977:107) said that only thirty or forty houses seemed to be in good repair at the time. That suggests a population only in the range of 240 to 320 people, which seems much too small. However, none of the records of Beechey's expedition even mention the enormous graveyard situated east of the houses (see below), which suggests that neither he nor any of his subordinates reached the eastern end of the settlement.

In 1939–40, Larsen and Rainey (1948) noted that the refuse on the ancient site reached a depth of eight to ten feet (2.5–3 m), and was composed of innumerable whale bones, stones, sod blocks, driftwood logs, thousands of artifacts, decayed meat and skins, a conglomeration of the refuse accumulated through centuries of occupation (Larsen and Rainey 1948:20).

They also stated that, "for the most part, it is impossible to recognize individual house mounds" (Larsen and Rainey 1948:20). This was exactly my reaction when I examined what was left of the site in 1970. This probably results from the fact that mounds containing only one dwelling unit were uncommon. Most held two or more dwellings, plus storage spaces and possibly a *qargi* as well. One of the mounds that I saw in 1970 seemed to contain seven subunits, each with a separate entrance; some were connected to one another inside the mound, some were not. The near impossibility of recognizing individual dwelling units from outside before their roofs caved in casts doubt on all of the eyewitness estimates. However, if what Richard Beechey counted was thirty to forty *mounds*, many of which contained two or more dwelling units, his observation might be accurate. Fifty mounds are shown in my reconstruction, and these would have contained both dwelling units and *qargich*; some of the mounds on the northwestern part of the village would have been uninhabitable because of erosion, and are shown in the diagram as ruins.

The variable relationship between house mounds and their constituent parts is illustrated in Figure 18. Here we see a sample of seven mounds from the Thule culture archeological site of Qariaraqyuk, in northern Canada, which was investigated by Peter Whitridge. These particular mounds were selected by me from a much larger number to illustrate the range of variation exhibited at the site. As the figure indicates, all of the mounds except the one on the extreme left contain two or more subunits. Most of these subunits were dwellings, but those that are blackened on the diagram were apparently *qargich*, as indicated by the fact that they lacked sleeping platforms (Whitridge 1999:211). On the basis of my own observations in Point Hope in the spring of 1970, it would be reasonable to project this general pattern onto the mounds shown in the Tikiġaq map in Map 20. However, some of the Tikiġaq mounds were even larger, and presumably contained correspondingly more numerous and more complex subunits. Neighboring dwellings at Tikiġaq were characterized by the Iñupiat as *upsiksut*, meaning that they were densely packed together.

FIGURE 18. House mounds vs. dwelling units. Adapted, with permission, from Whitridge (1999:148).

A complication in calculating Tikiġaq's size is the fact that the north side of the spit was eroding away, and periodic storm surges carried seawater some distance into the settlement. Every few years, people who lived in the northwestern part of the settlement had to abandon their homes and move to the opposite end of the village. On Beechey's (1831, I:365) first visit there, in 1826, he was led by the few people in residence at the time "between heaps of filthy and ruined habitations, filled with stinking water, to a part of the village which was in better repair." His remark suggests that, at any given time, a whole section of the village, not just a few houses, was in the process of being destroyed, hence was uninhabitable. Sixty years later, Woolfe (1893:132) observed that "within the past 25 years the extreme end of Point Hope spit has been carried away by the movement of the spring ice, and there were several storehouses and huts swept off on one occasion."

Still another complicating factor is the strongly held Tikiġaġmiut belief that a house in which a person died had to be abandoned. People attempted to deal with this by removing the old and sick from their home before they died. However, they must have waited too long on a number of occasions. This would have resulted in there being at least some uninhabited but otherwise habitable dwelling units scattered about the village at any given time.

Both of the above factors would have led to the presence of a large number of uninhabited dwellings in the village, most, but not all, of which would have been in the northwestern part of town. Thus, even a systematic count of the mounds existing in, say, 1826, would not have yielded an accurate number of the functioning dwelling units existing in the village.

With all of the above caveats in mind, and since no one has produced evidence showing it was wrong, I am sticking with an estimate I made several years ago, that Tikiġaq contained an average of approximately seventy-five occupied dwelling units and a population of about 600 people during the study period.[54] A more impressionistic but probably more accurate way to characterize the size of the population is that it was so large that not everyone who lived there knew everyone else (David Frankson 1980). Samuel Dives (1970) told me that at one point, so many people used to live there that they cleaned the game animals out of the nearby countryside, forcing many families to move elsewhere to be assured of the necessities of life.

An interesting feature of Tikiġaq was an enormous graveyard (*iḷuvġich*) or, somewhat more accurately, set of graveyards, to the north and east of the dwellings.[55] The largest one contained thousands of burials in most of which the body was wrapped in a cover of walrus or bearded seal skin, or placed in a wooden box. Charles Brower (ms) described what he saw there in the spring of 1885:

> We had seen the uprights as we came along the beach on our way down. I thought at the time they were wood. When I did get close enough to get a good look at them, they were all jaw bones of whales, standing upright in the ground. Mostly they were of the smaller ones, not over ten feet [3 m] long. To these were lashed the lower jaw of a walrus. In the walrus jaw there was laid pieces of wood and on these were laid other pieces, making a platform, where most of the bodies had been placed. Some few bodies were on the ground, where they had been dragged on some old sled belonging to the person, or their family. The bodies were all wrapped in some old sleeping skins. When ever any one died all their personal things that were in daily use were left at the grave, as for instance, if it were a woman, her sewing gear, her *oo-lu-ra* or womans [sic] knife, and some times her cooking pots or her personal ornaments, beads, earrings were all buried.

> If a man, his hunting implements, sometimes his Kyack, his pipe, or his Keloun [drum]. If a child, all his toys were left. Always whatever was left at the grave was broken so to be of no more use to any one alive, even the sled was broken at the grave.
>
> What interested me as much as anything, was the size of the graveyard. It extended for miles up toward the base of the point, and looked like a forest of small trees with the tops cut off. There were thousands of these whale jaw bones, and it seemed to me as if it must have taken a great many years to accumulate such a large number. Many had no bodies on them, and these were so old that the bodies had decayed and fallen down or been eaten by the ground squirrels that infested the grave yard, in the summer (Brower ms.:154).

In winter, when the ground was frozen, many bodies were just placed on the surface; some were buried later, others were not. During warmer seasons, the coffin or body bag was placed on a platform with the deceased in a supine position, knees and arms flexed, facing east. The graves were not tended, and at any given time, the great majority were in a state of disrepair.

Three other features of early-19th-century Tikiġaq worthy of mention include a playing field, an archery range, and a defense perimeter.[56] The playing field (manigraq) was a relatively level, dry area between the first and second beach ridges on the south side of the village. This is where football, baseball, and other outdoor games and contests were held. The archery range (pisiktaġvik) was located north of the houses and west of the graves; this is the only settlement I have heard of in northern Alaska where a specific area was set aside for target practice. The final feature of note was the defense perimeter. This consisted of several rows of pointed and sharpened bone or baleen stakes (sukisautit) set upright in the ground, with only the tips showing. This was the Iñupiaq equivalent of a minefield whose borders and pathways were known to the residents of the village, but not to outsiders. Night raiders approaching the village across the flat terrain who stepped on them pierced their feet, which rendered them unable to walk. Most raiders knew that they had to approach the village via the relatively narrow avenue of the beach, where stakes could not be kept from washing out. This restriction on invader maneuverability made village defense much easier than it would have been had the entire surface of the spit been open to enemy passage.

The Tikiġaġmiut presented a unified and very powerful front to the general social world of northwestern Alaska, but they were sharply divided internally along compound family lines. These divisions were particularly pronounced within the settlement of Tikiġaq. There is no way to know precisely how many compound families occupied the site in the early 19th century, but one can make an educated guess. In 1908, the population consisted of 179 people, who were organized in five compound families and three isolated domestic families (Burch 1975a:260–69). The compound families had 66, 49, 24, 16, and 8 members, respectively. It is likely that the average compound family size was smaller in 1908 than it had been a century earlier because at the earlier time, "individual survival depended upon the support of a powerful family" (Rainey 1947:242), whereas in 1908 that was much less the case. Therefore, in 1808, when the population was more than three times its 1908 size, it is reasonable to suppose that there were at least ten to fifteen large compound families at Tikiġaq, with no unaffiliated households even at the margin.

The compound families whose members occupied Tikiġaq during the study period constituted factions between and among whom there was a fair amount of conflict.[57] The site had been occupied continuously for hundreds of years, and individuals and families had had ample time to acquire a lengthy set of grievances against one another. Disputes between members of different domestic units within a compound family could be mediated by elders in the *qargi*, but Iñupiaq societies lacked a formal mechanism for the peaceful resolution of conflicts between the members of different compound families. Disputes at this level occasionally resulted in armed confrontations and bloodshed within the village, which of course provided the basis for further disputes later on.

Flexibility

Eskimo social organization has sometimes been characterized as being "flexible," which I take to mean responsive to change, or adaptable (Burch 1975a:61–62, 195–97). This was certainly true in northwestern Alaska, and it is worth devoting a few paragraphs to describing both the sources and the consequences of this feature of the system.

The first source of flexibility was the presence of large numbers of people to whom one could theoretically relate on some sort of kinship basis. For example, although it was argued earlier that the average number of biological offspring born to each married couple was probably very small, the number of people who could appropriately act as siblings could be compounded many times over through adoption, and through parental divorce and remarriage, polygamous marriage, and co-marriage. Through the same mechanisms, the number of one's cousins could be multiplied to an even greater degree. Thus, a person with only a single full biological sibling and four full biological first cousins could arrive at maturity with a dozen de facto siblings and several dozen de facto cousins. This provided the ordinary adult with a large supply of individuals to whom he or she could justifiably relate on some sort of important kinship basis (Heinrich 1963:100–11; 1972).

The second source of flexibility was the functional diffuseness of Eskimo kin relationships. A functionally diffuse relationship is one in which the activities or considerations or rights and obligations that are covered by the relationship "are more or less vaguely defined and delimited" (Levy 1952:255–58). The reader may recall the all-encompassing nature of the various family obligations described earlier in this chapter. I stated that relatives were supposed to support and protect one another, but I was not very precise about just what that meant. Such vague descriptions are unavoidable where functionally diffuse relationships are concerned.

The third and final source of flexibility was the high level of autonomy accorded to individual Iñupiat, even as children.[58] To a degree scarcely fathomable in the contemporary United States, Iñupiat were free to decide what they would do, how they would do it, and with whom they would do it. Of course, one's counterparts had equal freedom of choice, which meant that a person could deviate only so far from generally accepted norms of behavior without being made an outcast. The actual result in each case was achieved through a combination of trial and error, more or less self-conscious negotiation, and simple common consent, all worked out over the course of a lifetime.

The three features discussed above gave Iñupiat unusual latitude for deciding whom they would relate to even as offspring and siblings, as well as how they would operate in terms of the relationships concerned. People were also free to strike out completely on their own, abandoning virtually all their relatives. Such a course of action was suicidal, however, and everyone knew it; one simply could not survive without the help of close kinsmen. This consideration put an outer limit on one's freedom of choice with regard to the selection of significant others.

Furthermore, relationships that are functionally diffuse to the degree manifested in the Iñupiaq kinship system are extremely time-consuming because there is practically no limit on what is required of the members. There is a fairly narrow limit on just how many people a given individual can "support and protect" twenty-four hours a day, seven days a week, all year long, in meaningful terms. Thus, of all of one's many potential siblings, cousins, aunts, uncles, and even parents in some cases, one could actually afford the time to connect significantly with only a few. Thus, one had to make choices.

The way the above factors seem to have worked out in most cases was that, initially, priority was given to one's biological parents, offspring, siblings, cousins, and nepotics. (People who were adopted gave the priority to the adopting family members.) It was during crises that the system's flexibility came to the fore. For example, if one's biological parents or siblings died in an accident or raid, or from starvation, institutionally approved alternatives were usually available.[59] Flexibility was thus a crucial source of stability during times of catastrophic change, and was probably a major factor in the Eskimos' long-term survival in the harsh environment of the far north.

National Solidarity

The highest level of solidarity in early-19th-century northwestern Alaska was the nation, or society. In considering this matter, it is useful to recall that the number of people who had to relate to one another on the national level was very small. National populations are estimated to have ranged between only about 300 (Napaaqtuġmiut) and 1,300 (Tikiġaġmiut) people, with an average of just over 560. Since nearly half of the members of each nation consisted of subadults (as defined by the Iñupiat), the number of individuals effectively involved in maintaining solidarity at the national level was between only about 150 and 650.[60]

One major problem Iñupiaq nations had in maintaining national solidarity was the absence of governments and other unifying organizations. A nation consisted of a number of highly self-sufficient families operating more or less independently of one another much of the time. The families were linked by a variety of kinship and other ties, but there were no nationwide mechanisms for resolving interfamily disputes or for dealing with troublemakers. The potential for fragmentation was thus considerable, and, indeed, there are stories from ancient times of whole sections of a population packing up and leaving during periods of interfamily strife.[61] However, there were also powerful constraints against fragmentation, since flight to another nation's estate was a dangerous proposition even for a large group of people. Most of the time, therefore, family heads negotiated solutions to interfamily disputes, and the potential for fragmentation seems rarely to have been realized in fact.

A second problem in maintaining national solidarity was the necessary physical dispersal of the members among tiny isolated settlements for most of the year. However, settlement isolation was by no means absolute. In most cases, settlements were close enough to one another to permit visiting back and forth without much difficulty. In addition, men from neighboring villages often encountered one another when hunting.

Some years ago I identified three concepts that are useful in considering the apparent isolation of Iñupiaq settlements (Burch 1981:62). The first is the settlement, which is the area occupied by the dwellings and associated features. The second is the catchment zone, which is the area around a settlement within which the hunting activities of its inhabitants normally take place. The third is the scanning zone, which is the area monitored for its subsistence potential by the inhabitants of a settlement.

Among the Tikiġaġmiut sea mammal hunters of the Point Hope district, for example, the catchment zone typically encompassed an area of about 80 square miles (ca. 210 km²), while the scanning zone was approximately 315 square miles(ca. 815 km²). In general, neighboring settlements among the Tikiġaġmiut had overlapping catchment zones, and they definitely had overlapping scanning zones. Among caribou hunters, such as the Nuataaġmiut, the catchment and particularly the scanning zones were quite a bit larger, while among fishermen, such as the Kiitaaġmiut, they were probably considerably smaller. In most but not all cases, the catchment and scanning zones of neighboring villages overlapped. When hunters from neighboring villages met, they of course stopped to talk, and through that mechanism alone there was a fairly steady flow of information throughout each nation. Families visited back and forth from time to time, and they encountered one another when conducting regular seasonal movements. During the holiday season of late November to early January, intervillage contacts increased by an order of magnitude. Through these mechanisms, people had a fairly good idea of what was happening over quite large areas much of the time.

Large gatherings known as *katirut* or *katittut* were also built into the yearly cycles of several of the nations included in this study.[62] These were gatherings of the general membership of an entire nation, usually for a few days of feasts, games, and general socializing. Such events were held annually by the Kiitaaġmiut, Kivalliñiġmiut, and Tapqaġmiut in early July, and by the Kivalliñiġmiut, Kiŋikmiut, Qikiqtaġruŋmiut, and Tikiġaġmiut in September.[63] Such events were also held on an ad hoc basis in every nation, although they usually occurred during the early-winter holiday season (late November to early January).

The festivals held at the end of the whaling season by the Tikiġaġmiut can also be included in the *katirut* category, as can the concentrations of people in Kiŋigin and Tikiġaq for the whaling season itself. Another pattern is provided by the Nuataaġmiut. Probably the most widely dispersed of any people during the winter, most of them spent practically the whole time from May until the end of August living and traveling together in one large group.

Seasonal movements brought together virtually the entire membership of many nations for a certain period each year. Although not ordinarily designated as *katirut*, these occasions served many of the same functions. For example, almost all of the Nuataaġmiut traveled to the coast together each spring, and remained camped together while they were there. Similarly, the entire Napaaqtuġmiut and Qikiqtaġruŋmiut populations traveled as units from their spring seal-hunting stations to the trade fair at Sisualik, and they also lived in separate nationality-bounded camps while they were there.

Through the various processes described above, the Iñupiat developed and maintained a high degree of national identity and a sense of national distinctiveness. The members of each nation thought their own estate was the most bountiful and beautiful district in the world, and they thought of themselves as being more intelligent, stronger, faster, and better-looking than anyone else, and as superior providers, dancers, storytellers, and lovers (Elwood Hunnicutt 1970; T. Mitchell 1970; Vestal 1969). Although the tie to family was stronger than the tie to country (Simpson 1875:247), nationalism was sufficiently well developed in northwestern Alaska for people confronted by an outside threat to be willing to lay down their lives in defense of their homeland and fellow countrymen. This solidarity was evidently fairly stable over time, since the nations covered by this study seem to have endured for many generations, and possibly even for centuries (Burch 1998a:318).

There were, however, some variations, since there were at least three types of membership in every nation. The first was hereditary membership, which was acquired by people who were born to members of the nation concerned and who spent their entire lives as members. It is my understanding that at least 80 percent, and probably more like 90 percent, of the members of each nation were in this category. Hereditary members were not only the largest segment of the population, but also the primary repository of knowledge about the national estate and its history.

The second type of membership consisted of immigrants, people who married in or otherwise joined a nation (usually as adults) from an origin somewhere else. To the extent that they still thought of themselves and acted as members of their nation of birth, these people remained members of that nation, although they had also become members to at least some extent of the nation to which they had moved. Perhaps 5 percent of the members of each nation were in this category.

The third type of membership was expatriate, meaning people who were born into one nation but who later married into or otherwise became members of another. About 5 percent of the members of each nation were probably in this category.

An interesting question is the loyalty of the immigrant and the expatriate members if and when they had to choose between their nation of birth and the nation they subsequently joined. People did not have to make this choice very often, if at all, during the course of their daily lives, but during a raid or a battle they sometimes did. Accounts of hostile encounters indicate that such people usually tried to intercede to prevent confrontations from resulting in bloodshed, and apparently they were often successful in this regard.

Immigrants were under considerable pressure to conform to their adopted country's patterns of speech, dress, and general demeanor. I have no information on how long it took for the ordinary immigrant to begin to identify himself or herself as a member of an adopted country, but hereditary members apparently tended to regard immigrants as outsiders for a long time. Della Keats, who was born in 1907, told me that when she was a girl, elderly Nuataaġmiut used to ridicule her as being a Kuulugruaġmiu despite the fact that her ancestors had immigrated to the upper Noatak district from the Meade River (Kuulugruaq) district a whole century before (Burch 1998a:372).

Notes to Chapter Three

1. I thank Ann Fienup-Riordan for comments on an earlier version of this chapter.
2. R. Adams (1965), M. Brown (1976), E. Curtis (1930:148, 166), Eliyak (1931), R. Gallahorn (1952.8), Green (1969), A. Hawley (1964.2, 1964.6, 1965.13, 1965.18), Heinrich (ms:box 1, folder 10, p. 10), Keats (1970.2), Killigivuk (1940.2, 1959.2), Niġuwana (1940.1), Northwest Iñupiat Elders Conference (1976a:3, 8–9; 1976b:2, 4–6; 1976c:2–6, 13, 15–17), Rainey (1940.4, 1940.5, 1940.6, 1940.11, 1940.18, 1940.19, 1947:243), Jessie Ralph (in Lee, Sampson, Tennant, and Mendenhall 1990:85), Simpson (1875:254), John Stalker (1965.1, 1965.2), Stoney (ms:126; 1900:830), Sunno (1951.116), Clinton Swan (1965.4; 1965.5), M. and M. Swan (1970), M. Thomas (1964), Thornton (1931:63–64, 99), Vestal (1969), Walton (1965.3), Wells and Kelly (1890:10, 19, 21), Weyer (1928), Woolfe (1893:135).
3. Aġviqsiiña (1940.1:96), Killigivuk (1940.2), Kunuyaq (1940:1); cf. Gubser (1965:64–65).
4. Agnabooguk (1999), A. Douglas (1989.3), Foster (1970), L. Gallahorn (1970.2), Green (1969), A. Hawley (1965.9, 1965.11, 1965.13, 1965.15, 1966, 1967), M. Hawley (1965.2), Heinrich (ms, 1955a, 1955b, 1960, 1963a), Jensen (1970.6), Keats (1970.5), Kennedy (1965.2), J. Killigivuk (1940.2, 1967), C. Lee (1970), Rainey (1940.5, 1940.6, 1947:242), Rock (1940), T. Sage (1965.2), Sprott (1998), John Stalker (1965.1, 1965.2, 1965.3), Clinton Swan (1965.3, 1965.4), L. Swan (1965), Martha Swan (1965.3, 1965.5, 1965.6, 1970), M. and M. Swan (1970), Milton Swan (1965.1), O. Swan (1965), A. Thomas (1965), Walton (1965.2). The reader should be warned that kinship terms vary to some extent between and among dialects and subdialects, and that usage has changed quite a bit in many districts since the 19th century. Describing these variations is beyond the scope of this book.
5. The term *nukatchiaq* can refer to both younger sisters and younger brothers, but I have never heard of *nayak* referring to anyone except a younger sister. To simplify the discussion here, I have artificially restricted the use of the former to refer to younger brothers only.
6. I thank Lawrence Hamilton for comments on an early version of this discussion.
7. Brower (ms:362), A. Douglas (1989.2, 1989.3), A. Hawley (1966), Edna Hunnicutt (1970.2), Keats (1970.3), Seemann (1853, II:65–66), Simpson (1875:250), Stoney (ms:127–28). See also Hamilton, Seyfrit, and Bellinger (1997).
8. Killigivuk (1940:2). According to Lawrence Kaplan, the Iñupiaq term for this is *iktaq*, meaning "something thrown away," "cast out," "discarded."
9. Cf. Murdoch (1892:39), Stefansson (1956). Aldrich (1889:158) claimed that Iñupiat women had a baby every summer, but he was in the north only one summer, during which he spent most of his time on a whaling ship.
10. R. Adams (1965), Aġviqsiiña (1940.1), A. Hawley (1965.13), Keats (1970.3, 1970.4), Nasugluk and Nasugruk (1940), Sheidt (1969.2), Simpson (1852–54: entry for Jan. 11, 1853), Martha Swan (1965.5), Thornton (1931:91), Elsie Weyiouanna (1983.2).
11. R. Adams (1965), Cantwell (1889b:82), A. Hawley (1964.3, 1965.12, 1965.16, 1965.17), Hooper (1881:109), Simpson (1875:249–50), Sprott (1999), Stoney (1900:831–32), Clinton Swan (1965.5), Thornton (1931:89, 91), Woolfe (1893:134–35, 137).
12. F. Beechey (1831, I:360, 384, 390, 394, 402; II:302), Cantwell (1889b:82), Simpson (1850b: entry for Jan. 17, 1850), Stoney (1900:832), Thornton (1931:21, 75), VanStone ed. (1977:91), Woolfe (1893:152).
13. Aġviqsiiña (1940:1), A. Hawley (1966), Seemann (1853, II:66), Simpson (1875:250), Thornton (1931:75).
14. C. and R. Adams (1965), R. Adams (1965), A. Hawley (1965.5, 1965.11, 1965.14, 1965.17, 1965.18), Killigivuk (1940.2), Clinton Swan (1965:5). As noted above, in most districts the term *nukatchiaq* refers to both younger brothers and sisters, but *nayak* always indicates a younger sister.
15. Eliyak (1931), A. Frankson (1940), Green (1970), A. Hawley (1965.6, 1965.9, 1965.11, 1965.13, 1965.15, 1965.18), M. Hawley (1965.1), Rainey (1940.19), Stoney (1900:830), Martha Swan (1965.4, 1965.5, 1965.6), Walton (1965.3), Wells and Kelly (1890:21), Woolfe (1893:134, 135).
16. Eliyak (1931), J. Foster (1970), M. Hawley (1965.2), Keats (1969.2, 1970.5), C. Smith (1970), E. Smith (1976), R. Walton (1965.3).
17. W. Ballot (1970.2), J. Foster (1970), L. Gallahorn (1970.2), Glover (1970.2), Green (1969), Jensen (1970.7), Keats (1970.4), Kowunna (1970), C. Lee (1970), D. Oktalik (1970), John Stalker (1965.1), Martha Swan (1965.6), M. and M. Swan (1970).
18. R. Adams (1965), A. Hawley (1965.11, 1965.14, 1965.15, 1965.16, 1965.18), Clinton Swan (1965.5).
19. R. Adams (1965), A. Douglas (1989.1), A. Hawley (1965.5, 1965.7, 1965.11, 1965.14, 1965.15, 1965.16, 1965.18, 1976.6), M. Hawley (1965.2), C. Lee (1970), John Stalker (1965.1, 1965.2, 1970.3), C. Sheldon (in Northwest Iñupiat Elders Conference 1976c:10–12), Clinton Swan (1965.5), Martha Swan (1965.3, 1965.6).
20. C. and R. Adams (1965), A. Hawley (1965.16), T. Mitchell (1969), Martha Swan (1965.4), M. Tocktoo (1983.6).
21. C. and R. Adams (1965), J. Foster (1970), Green (1969), A. Hawley (1965.11, 1965.16, 1965.17, 1965.18), C. Lee (1970), Clinton Swan (1965.5), M. and M. Swan (1970). See also Burch (1975a:160–64).
22. Beaver (1967), M. Curtis (1969), A. Hawley (1967), Keats (1970.3), Clinton Swan (1967).
23. A. Hawley (1965.9, 1965.11, 1965.13, 1965.15), M. Hawley (1965.2), Martha Swan (1965.5, 1965.6), Trollope (1855:874).
24. Collins describes the structure in exquisite detail; only a small portion of his account is presented here.

25. Aġviqsiiña (1940.3), Kunuyak (1940), Quwana (1940), Rainey (1947:240–41), Rock (1940).

26. The information on which this chart was based was provided by Della Keats (1970.1). The founders of this family were descendants of refugees from a famine in the Meade River district of the North Slope that probably occurred sometime in the first decade of the 19th century (Burch 1998a:372). The descendants of the people shown here belonged to what became the Booth, Bundy, Howarth, Mitchell, and Sage families of Kivalina, Noatak, and Kotzebue in the early 20th century.

27. For other examples of compound families, see Burch (1975a:262–76).

28. Anderson and Anderson (1982:35–36), H. Anungazuk (1999.1), R. Cleveland (1970.3), J. Foster (1970), L. Gallahorn (1970.1), A. Hawley (1965.11, 1965.13), Keats (1970.3), C. Lee (1970), Clinton Swan (1965.3), Martha Swan (1965.4, 1965.6), M. and M. Swan (1970).

29. For settlement size in the NANA Region, see Burch (1998a); for comparable data on the Point Hope district, see Burch (1981). Comparable data on the Shishmaref and Wales districts were obtained separately for the present study.

30. Aġviqsiiña (1940.1, 1940.2), R. Cleveland (1965.8, 1970.2), E. Curtis (1930:146), Q. Dives (1940:30–33), S. Dives (1970), *The Esquimaux* (1866–67:15), D. Foster (1970.1, 1970.2), J. Foster (1970), L. Gallahorn (1969.2, 1970.1), Glover (1970.4, 1970.5), A. Hawley (1965.9, 1965.17), M. Hawley (1965.2), Edna Hunnicutt (1970.1), Jensen (1970.2, 1970.6, 1970.7), C. and L. Jensen (1980), Keats (1969.2, 1970.2, 1970.4), Killigivuk (1959.2, 1960.9), Kingik (1980), Kunuyaq (1940), Larsen and Rainey (1948:26), C. Lee (1970), Nagozruk (1971), Quwana (1940), Rock (1940:9), Seemann (1853:59), Simpson (1875:259–60), C. Smith (1970), John Stalker (1965.1), Thornton (1931:109–10, 113), Trollope (1855:868–69, 872, 873), R. Walton (1965.2, 1965.3).

31. The identity of this site is not given in order to help protect it from looters.

32. Ice ride-up and ice push are different ways in which sea ice is forced up over land.

33. Aġviqsiiña (1940.1), S. Dives (1970), David Frankson (1980), Heinrich (1955:17–24), Jensen (1970.1, 1970.6, 1970.7, 1980.1, 1980.2), Kingik (1978:18; 1980), Larson (1995), S. Rock (1940), Simpson (1875:259).

34. The best early evidence on this point comes from Barrow, which is outside the study region (Brower ms:146; Simpson 1852–54: entries for June 25 and 26, 1853; 1875:259; cf. Murdoch 1892:79).

35. H. Anungazuk (1999.1, 1999.2, 1999.3), Brower (ms:168–76), E. Curtis (1930:137–40), Foote and Williamson (1961:50), L. Gallahorn (1970.1), A. Hawley (1973.1), Jensen (1970.6), J. Killigivuk (1961.1), Larsen and Rainey (1948:27–28), Rainey (1947:257–62), Sereadlook (1999), Thornton (1931:165–67, 170), Woolfe (1893:147).

36. The crews that hunted whales at the Kivalliñiġmiut settlement of Nuvua and the Tikiġaġmiut settlement of Uivvaq were probably made up of family members, although I have no solid information about the membership of crews operating in these locations.

37. It now appears that in an earlier publication (Burch 1975a:22–24) I overstated the extent to which crews were composed of kinsmen.

38. R. Cleveland (1970.3), A. Douglas (1989.1), J. Foster (1970), A. Hawley (1965.13, 1965.15), Keats (1970.8), Sours (1984), John Stalker (1970.2), Clinton Swan (1965.3), Martha Swan (1965.6).

39. As people aged, the notion of being the "same" age gradually expanded, eventually coming to mean having been born within a few years of one another.

40. J. Foster (1970), L. Gallahorn (1969.1), A. Hawley (1965.11, 1965.15, 1970.2, 1976.1), B. Hawley (1964.2), Niġuwana (1940.1), Martha Swan (1965.6).

41. C. and R. Adams (1965), R. Adams (1965), Burch (1970b), Green (1969, 1970), A. Hawley (1965.5, 1965.7, 1965.9, 1965.14, 1965.16, 1965.18, 1966), M. Hawley (1965.1), Jensen (1970.6), Kennedy (1976), Nagozruk (1928), Northwest Iñupiat Elders Conference (1976c:8–10), Rainey (1947:242), T. Sage (1965.1), Clinton Swan (1965.5), Martha Swan (1965.4; 1965.6), R. Walton (1965.3), Vestal (1970).

42. I now believe that co-marriage was more widespread than I did when I wrote my book on Eskimo kin relationships (Burch 1975a:106–11).

43. H. Anungazuk (1999.1, 1999.4, 1999.5, 1999.6, 1999.7, 2000.1, 2000.2, 2000.3, 2000.4, 2000.5), T. Anungazuk (1991), E. Curtis (1930:136), Dumond (2000), H. Greist (ms:ch. II, pp. 2–3), Heinrich (1963a:12, 430–34), Lucier (2000b), Nagozruk (1971), Nelson (1887–81: entry for July 12, 1881; 1899:257), Oxereok (1991, 1999.1, 1999.2, 1999.3, 1999.4), Thornton (1931:20), Trollope (1855), Weyer (1928:67–69, 77–78). Harritt (2003b) has recently published an historical and geographic summary of Wales that is usefully compared with the account presented here.

44. An unpublished sketch map of Wales made by Diamond Jenness in 1926 was also useful in preparing Map 19. This map was provided by David Morrison to Roger Harritt, who kindly shared it with me.

45. The explanation for the abandonment of Qargitaġvik is that someone from this village killed one of the Agianamiut. Fearing retribution from that much larger group, Qargitaġviŋmiut shamans produced a thick fog bank under the cover of which the entire population of the settlement fled by boat. Reportedly, the refugees ended up at Point Barrow.

46. Current names from Oxereok (1999.4).

47. Nagozruk (1971), Thornton (1931:109–13), Trollope (1855:873), Weyer (1928).

48. Aġviqsiiña (1940.1, 1940.2, 1940.3), F. Beechey (1831, I:365–67), Brower (ms:154), S. Dives (1970), Edson (1895:471), David Frankson (1980), Gough (1973:152–53), Jensen (1970.1, 1970.2, 1970.6, 1970.7, 1980.1, 1980.2), Kingik (1978:18), Kisautaq and Kean (1981:69–70), Knapp (1904:727), Larsen and Rainey (1948:14,

19, 20, 26, 175), Larson (1995), D. Oktalik (1970, 1980), Ostermann and Holtved (1952:47–48), Rainey (ms, 1947), S. Rock (1940), Rowe (1904:48), Shinkwin and the North Slope Borough Planning Department (1978), Tuckfield and Tingook (1960.1), VanStone ed. (1977:58), White (1889).

49. I am also grateful for information provided by David Frankson (1980).

50. See also Lowenstein (1993:28–32).

51. The houses examined in the Point Hope Ethnology Project 1984 were built later than the period of relevance here (Newell 1985).

52. Aġviqsiiña (1940.1), S. Dives (1970), David Frankson (1980), Hopson (1978:18), Jensen (1970.1, 1970.6, 1980.1), Kingik (1980), Larsen and Rainey (1948:26), Larson (1995), Rainey (1947:244), Quwana (1940.1), E. Rock (1980), S. Rock (1940), Spencer (1959:49), Wells and Kelly (1890:10).

53. S. Dives (1970), Hopson (1978:18), Jensen (1970.1), Rainey (1947:244), Spencer (1959:186), Stefansson (1914b:342).

54. The actual estimate was 77 houses and 616 people (Burch 1981:14).

55. Bertholf (1899a:25), Brower (ms:154–55, 186), Call (1899:127), S. Dives (1970), Jensen (1970.2), Klengenberg (1932:121), Knapp (1904:727), Larsen and Rainey (1948:20, 175), Nelson (1899:322), Woolfe (1893:138). The human and other remains in the enormous 19th-century graveyard were subsequently concentrated in a much smaller area under missionary guidance.

56. S. Dives (1970), David Frankson (1980), Jensen (1970.6), Niġuwana (1940.1).

57. Aġviqsiiña (1940.1, 1940.3), S. Dives (1970), A. Hawley (1964.4, 1964.5), Jensen (1970.6), Kunuyaq (1940), Rainey (1947:240–42), S. Rock (1940).

58. Bodenhorn (e.g., 1997, 2000) has written extensively on individual autonomy.

59. Although isolated orphans figure prominently in Iñupiaq folklore, they actually must have been fairly rare because of people's willingness to adopt.

60. For a discussion of societal membership, see Levy (1952:122–27).

61. The flight of the Qargitaġviŋmiut from Wales is one example.

62. Here I am using Iñupiaq verbs as English nouns.

63. W. Ballot (1970.2), M. Hawley (1965.1), Elwood Hunnicutt (1970), Jensen (1970.1), C. Smith (1970), Thornton (1931:124).

Chapter Four

The Economic Process

The economic process consists of the production and consumption of the goods and services making up the income and the output of a social system (Levy 1952:330, 389).[1] As that definition suggests, the two major divisions of the economic process are production, which consists of the accrual of goods and services to a social system, and consumption, which consists of the ways in which goods and services are used or dissipated by the members of that system.

Economic analysis can be complicated because production and consumption occur at the same time. For example, when an Iñupiaq hunter killed a caribou, he produced a variety of raw materials, but he also consumed clothing and weapons (among other things) as he did so.[2] When his wife went out to butcher the carcass and bring it home, she produced a service while simultaneously consuming her clothing and utensils, and usually a sled and the services of dogs as well.

In an effort to simplify the presentation, I have divided this chapter into sections in which production is the primary focus. However, in the course of discussing the production of particular goods and services, I provide information on the consumption of others without making a special point of it. I also try to go somewhat beyond the specific focus of a given section to indicate what the next steps in the process are. Later, when I return to the same process further down the line, the reader will be able to pick up the discussion without much difficulty.

More information is available about the economic process than about any other aspect of traditional Iñupiaq life; indeed, more than on all the other aspects combined. This fact is reflected in the length of this chapter. The presentation is by no means exhaustive, however, and interested readers will benefit from an examination of the sources cited here.

Raw Materials

Raw materials are objects that exist in the nonhuman environment, and are either directly dissipated upon their acquisition or are dissipated in the production of other goods or services (Levy 1952:393). The familiar guessing-game litany of "animal, vegetable, or mineral?" pretty well sums up what is involved here and, indeed, those are three of the four main categories in which the material is presented. The fourth is liquids.

Animals

The Iñupiat were hunter-gatherers with only one domesticated animal, the dog. All of their clothing, most of their food, and the components of many of their utensils, weapons, tools, and other accoutrements were derived from animate sources.

The complexity and variety of the means whereby animals were harvested differed considerably from one species or group of species to another, and the presentation that follows reflects this diversity. Some sections are devoted to a single species, while others deal with groups of species that were harvested by similar techniques.

Each section begins with a very brief description of the animals involved. It then proceeds to a more detailed description of how they were hunted and at least the initial processing procedures. In the case of collaborative efforts, there is a discussion of the various roles, relationships, and leadership associated with the relevant activities. That is followed by a discussion of how the harvest was allocated among the people involved, and a brief indication of the uses to which the harvest was put. In the section on manufactured goods, I pick up the sequence at that point and follow the various products to their ultimate destination.

Caribou

Barren ground caribou (*Rangifer tarandus granti*), or *tuttu* (sing.), are medium-sized deer that undertake long seasonal migrations (Hemming 1994). Within the study region, adult bulls in good condition average 350 pounds (ca. 150 kg) or more, while adult females weigh somewhat more than half that. They undergo significant changes in weight over the course of a yearly cycle, generally being fattest (and heaviest) in late summer and early fall, and leanest (and lightest) in late winter. During the study period, caribou were hunted by people in all of the nations of northwestern Alaska, although they were present in most estates for only part of the year.

The Drive Fence

Several techniques were employed to harvest caribou, the most productive of which were based on the animals' tendency for strong directional movement, particularly during seasonal migrations.[3] The challenge was to influence this movement so that the animals would enter a trap; the primary mechanism whereby this was achieved was the drive fence.

A drive fence consisted of an array of "scarecrows," or *iñuksuit*,[4] erected in two rows making up a huge V.[5] If rocks were abundant, *iñuksuit* consisted of cairns; where rocks were rare or difficult to obtain, *iñuksuit* were made of bunches of shrubs tied together, often wrapped with old caribou skins. The "arms" of this V were sometimes several miles long, and perhaps as much as a mile apart at the open end. This open end faced the general direction from which caribou ordinarily came at a particular time of year, or at a place where local topography regularly influenced caribou movements. As the lines of *iñuksuit* converged toward the closed end of the V, the caribou were channeled toward a very specific place where there was either a corral or a body of water deep enough to force the animals to swim; and, sometimes, both.

After the fence was erected, caribou had to be located, so hunters spread out to survey the countryside. When a suitable band of caribou was found, it was monitored by the hunters, whose intent was to slowly herd it toward the open end of the V. As the band approached, hunters who were particularly fast runners attempted to guide the animals toward the open end of the V. If the runners managed to get the animals moving into the trap, people who had been hiding jumped up and assisted. Still others, hiding behind the *iñuksuit*, stood up and shouted, frightening the animals into moving at a still faster pace.

In winter, the sides of the *iñuksuit* facing the open end of the V were plastered with snow so as to be almost invisible to caribou from that direction; the other sides of the *iñuksuit* were left exposed. The object was to make the caribou, whose eyesight is not particularly good, think that the *iñuksuit* were people when they looked back in the direction from which they had come. This caused them to panic, running farther into the trap. When sufficient snow was on the ground, small snow houses where hunters hid were erected beyond the outermost *iñuksuit*, observing developments through peepholes.

The drive fence for a corral often led across a stream—which caused the animals to bunch together—and then up and over a hill, the corral beginning at the top or just over the brow.[6] A corral consisted of a series of tall stakes driven into the ground in a circle, a semicircle, or open square, the design varying according to the terrain. Often there were two or more rows of stakes. Where stakes were not available, piles of rocks or bunches of shrubs tied together served the same purpose. In all cases, the uprights were separated by enough space for a caribou to pass between them.

Each opening through which an animal could pass was guarded by a snare (*nigaq*) made of heavy skin rope, the butt end of which was firmly anchored to an object placed in the ground. When the animals tried to escape through the openings, the stanchions holding the snares bent or fell over, releasing the snares to capture the caribou. Alternatively, the snares were held open by weak twine, which broke when the animal tried to pass, releasing the snare. Snared animals were dispatched by lance-wielding hunters. Animals that tried to get past their snared companions were either caught in a second row of snares, or shot with bow and arrow. Snares used when snow was on the ground were bleached white; those used in summer or early fall were not.

A somewhat idealized illustration of a drive fence and corral, apparently drawn by Knud Rasmussen, is shown in Figure 19. Here the drive fence consists of poles rather than cairns or bundles of willows. It guided the animals across a stream, then up a hill and into more than

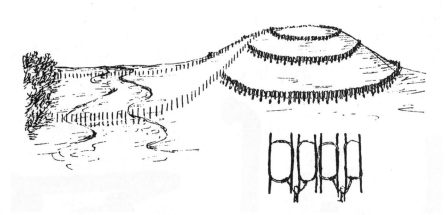

FIGURE 19. Caribou drive fence and corral. The method of anchoring snares and holding them open is shown in the lower right side of the sketch. From Ostermann and Holtved (1952:33), reproduced with the permission of the Department of Ethnography, National Museum of Denmark. Another elegant drive fence is depicted in Stefansson (1914b:385).

200 snares arrayed in three semicircles around its slopes. This sketch depicts an unusually elaborate arrangement, but it illustrates clearly the principles involved.

An alternative to corraling was to drive the animals into a lake or deep river. Caribou are good swimmers and take readily to water. Except for the Kobuk, most of the rivers in the study region are shallow enough for caribou to ford without swimming, so often they were driven into lakes or, near the coast, into lagoons.[7] In locations where there was a small lake and many people, individuals were placed around the lake in an effort to prevent escaping caribou from emerging from the water (E. Curtis 1930:144–45). In all cases, lance-wielding kayakers lay in wait. After the first few animals had entered the water, the hunters emerged from their hiding places, chased the swimming caribou, and speared them. Just one or two well-directed strikes at the kidneys with a lance either killed an animal or rendered it helpless. Since caribou carcasses float high in the water, the men could keep on hunting until they either had enough or until the rest of the animals had escaped. Then they retrieved their harvest and brought it to shore.

A special form of water drive was employed at Imuruk Lake, a sizable body of water in Pittaġmiut country located in an extensive lava field (T. Morris 1970; Vestal 1970). There is a large peninsula on the northwest side of the lake, with a lava ridge along one side of it. Caribou would not cross the lava; it is believed they feared injury to their feet. So, the hunters simply waited for the animals to arrive and then chased them toward the lava flow. The lava deflected their movement, and led the animals to the lake just where hunters were waiting in kayaks.

Caribou drives into water obviously took place during the summer and early fall. Drives into corrals could occur at any time of year, depending on the whereabouts of the animals.[8] In the northern part of the study region, drives into corrals were usually performed in the fall. Farther south, they were more likely to occur during the winter.

A caribou drive, whether into water or a corral, was a cooperative enterprise involving as few as five or six people or as many as two dozen or more. The greater the number of participants, the greater the chances of success. A drive fence was considered the property of the head of the compound family whose members conducted the hunt. The actual hunt, however, was usually directed by the oldest man present, who acted as the *ataniq* (boss), whether or not he was the family head.[9] It should be noted that drives were by no means always successful, frequently being aborted in the early stages when the caribou decided to head in a direction other than the one desired by the hunters. On the other hand, when they were successful, they could yield dozens or even hundreds of animals in a short period of time (Tuckfield and Tingook 1960.1).

Other Techniques

A less productive caribou-hunting technique, but one requiring only one person and relatively little effort after the initial investment, was the snaring of individual caribou.[10] In areas where there was thick brush along a creek bed or through a stretch of forest, the hunter created a clearing through which caribou could find easy passage. (A naturally occurring passage through thick undergrowth could also be used.) One or more snares were set across the opening and anchored. Sometimes the rope was stiff enough for the noose to stay open without external support; alternatively, it was held open by a few twigs or light twine. The hunter then went about his business, perhaps setting snares in other locations, hunting caribou with bow and arrow, fishing, or working around the house. Every day he checked his snares, dispatching any captured caribou with a lance.

As indicated earlier, bow and arrow was another method for killing caribou.[11] According to Tuckfield and Tingook (1960.1), the traditional Iñupiaq bow could kill a caribou at 150 yards (135 m). If properly struck, a wounded animal might run for a short distance, but soon died.

Winter hunting with bow and arrow was difficult, since the sound of a hunter's footprints on the snow carries a long distance in very cold weather. This made the animals difficult to approach close enough for a shot.

Summer hunting was easier. In warm weather, caribou congregate in cool areas, such as snowbanks, and in windy or shady areas, in an effort to keep from overheating and to escape biting insects; animals who find a spot where they are comfortable are loathe to leave it. This made perfect conditions for bow-and-arrow hunting by experienced stalkers. Lingering snowbanks occur at the same locations almost every year, and hunters sometimes erected blinds nearby to help them approach the animals without being seen. Hunters also took advantage of the almost trancelike state that caribou go into in summer when overheated and tormented by insects; the animals are easily approached and shot when in this condition.

Caribou were also obtained with pitfalls (pl. *qargisat*).[12] A prerequisite for this type of hunting was the presence of deep, hard-packed snow. The hunter excavated a deep pit in the snow and placed sharpened caribou antlers, or wooden or bone spikes, upright on the bottom. The pit was covered with a thin layer of hard-packed snow, making it almost invisible. The "bait" was human urine, the smell of which attracted the curiosity of passing caribou. An animal who approached and fell into the pit was fatally pierced by the spikes. A variation was to dig a rather small pit such that the front legs fell into the hole without touching bottom (Killigivuk 1960.1). The animal remained suspended, held up by its head, neck, and hindquarters, until dispatched by the hunter. Sometimes a line of pits was dug into a long snowdrift, and caribou were driven toward it. To my knowledge, the only district within the study region where this technique was widely employed was that of Point Hope, home of the Tikiġaġmiut.

Another technique for obtaining caribou was employed in the Kobuk River valley, where extensive areas of deep, soft snow form in mid-winter in wooded areas or at the bottom of ravines. Hunters on snowshoes drove the animals into an especially deep snowbank, where they became bogged down. Because of the snowshoes, hunters could approach the struggling animals and dispatch them with a lance or with bow and arrow (Anderson et al. 1998:203; R. Cleveland 1965.7).

The easiest technique of all was used by the Nuataaġmiut, of the upper Noatak River district (T. Mitchell 1970). The upriver portion of their estate was bounded on the north by Howard Pass, a low, wide gap in the mountains linking the Noatak valley with the North Slope of the Brooks Range. Frequent strong winter winds flow through the pass, bringing cold, heavy air from the high-pressure atmospheric regime of the North Slope to the relatively lower-pressure regime of the Noatak River valley. After a particularly violent winter storm, Nuataaġmiut living in the vicinity went into the pass to look for dead caribou. Frequently they found some, because the windchill had been so severe that even caribou froze to death. All the people had to do was pick up the frozen carcasses and haul them back to camp.

Division of the Harvest

In general, caribou carcasses were divided equally among the hunters involved in a collective enterprise, but kept by individual hunters otherwise (B. Hawley 1984; Keats 1970.9; T. Mitchell 1969). In a corral, snares sometimes were individually owned and marked, in which case each hunter kept the animals caught in his snares, plus any he shot with bow and arrow.[13] The corral's owner, however, sometimes took a few animals over and above the ordinary portion to keep for himself.

Usually, most of the people involved in a collective hunt belonged to the same compound family, so most of the resources produced were usually pooled among the constituent domestic units—exactly who killed what was not so important (Iviqsiq 1940; T. Mitchell 1970; Stefansson 1914b:385). Since dozens or even hundreds of animals could be killed in a single drive, a successful hunt meant plenty of caribou for everyone.

Processing

When a caribou was killed the throat was cut, it was skinned, and the much-desired back fat and back sinew were removed (Brower ms:255; Stoney 1900:842). Just how caribou were processed beyond that depended on the season, the purpose for which they were taken, and the means available to transport the harvest back to the settlement. There may also have been differences between nations, but my information is not sufficiently detailed to make distinctions at that level.

Caribou taken between early fall and late spring were processed in essentially the same way regardless of how they were killed unless destined from the outset to become dog food.[14] In the latter case, they were simply cut up into chunks. Otherwise, the hide was removed by making a cut up the belly from the anus to the throat, with slits down the front of the front legs and the back of the rear legs. If the skin was to be used to make a parka, a cut was made under the jaw and around the muscle below the eyes, and the head skin was left attached to the body skin. Otherwise, the cut was from behind the ears and across the back of the head and around under the neck. The fat, back sinew, tongue, eyes, and internal organs were removed and saved. The stomach contents, a major source of vitamin C, were saved if it was cold enough to preserve them, or discarded if not. Intestines were cleaned and dried. The head was cut off low around the shoulders and hung on a pole, if possible, and the legs were removed. Rib cages were left for the dogs. Carcasses that could not be eviscerated fairly quickly were used for dog food.

What happened next depended on the temperature. In early fall or late spring, the meat was cut into strips and dried in the sun or in the house. The dried strips were then stored in seal oil if there was enough on hand. In the fall, if it was cool but above freezing, the meat was wrapped in skins, placed in holes in the ground, and covered with rocks. It fermented there to some extent, and was eaten later as *quaq*, or frozen raw meat. If the animals were killed some distance from the settlement, the carcasses were cached, more often than not, to be retrieved later. If it was cold enough for meat to freeze quickly, it was deboned, cut into large pieces, and placed in a cache. By mid-fall, it was often necessary to bring the carcass into the house to thaw it before it could be completely butchered. The leg bones were saved. Toward the end of the season, the bones were smashed and boiled. Sometimes the resulting stock was consumed warm as soup, while at other times it was left to cool. In the latter case, the fat congealed at the water's surface, then was removed and stored for later consumption.

Most processing of caribou meat between late fall and early summer involved some combination of the elements just described, regardless of the way in which the animals were killed. The warmer the weather, the greater the necessity to cut the meat into strips and dry it. The colder the weather, the greater the extent to which it could be cached underground or frozen aboveground. Surplus meat acquired during the winter had to be sliced thin and dried in the spring or it would rot. Skins destined for later use were dried or frozen, as discussed in a subsequent section.

The processing of caribou killed in the summer was usually quite different from the pattern just described.[15] In the first place, the primary goal of most summer hunts was the acquisition of hides for clothing, particularly those of fawns of the year. Furthermore, most hunters living in the study region had to walk dozens, and sometimes hundreds, of miles to find caribou at this time of year. Then, having made a successful hunt, they had to pack the harvest the whole way back home again. In some districts, they traveled by boat part of the way, the balance on foot.

The overwhelming emphasis on skins and the difficulties of transport imposed stringent limitations on just what could be accomplished. Skins, virtually all of which were destined to become clothing, were carefully removed and dried (Brower ms:242). Fat, too, was removed and dried, as were some of the sinews. Some meat was dried and carried along as food, but most of the meat and all of the bones usually were abandoned.

There were variations, however. For example, sometimes the marrow was removed from the bones and placed in the stomachs, which served as containers. Sometimes hunters also saved the tongues, hearts, eyes, and intestines, all of which were cleaned and dried.

Drying took two or three days in good weather (Foote and Williamson 1961:24). Since both the degree of preservation and the weight of whatever materials were to be carried home were dependent on how dry they were, it can be understood that a wet summer could have a devastating impact. However, once dried, the hides could be kept in fairly good condition if rolled up properly, and any meat or other parts around which they were wrapped were protected from the elements.

The preservation and storage of caribou meat and other body parts varied with the season. From mid-fall to mid-spring, people in most districts kept them in bundles on elevated storage racks, where they simply froze. In some districts, especially along the coast, they were also kept in ice cellars, where they could be kept frozen more or less indefinitely. Otherwise, meat had to be dried to at least some extent if it was to last more than a few days. If it was even partially dried, it could be preserved more or less indefinitely if stored in seal oil (although considerable attention had to be devoted to the proper care of the pokes containing oil and dried meat). Thoroughly dried meat could last for months if kept dry. Another procedure was to keep meat in a storage pit (as opposed to an ice cellar) dug into the ground. If the pit was lined with willows or strips of wood, covered with soil, and not exposed to direct sun, meat stored within it lasted for several weeks, possibly even months. From the Iñupiaq point of view, a modest amount of putrefaction actually made raw and frozen meat taste better.

Just how many caribou were required to sustain one family for a year is uncertain. There was, of course, considerable variation from one nation to another in the extent to which people depended on caribou for food, inlanders generally having a greater need than coast dwellers. For clothing, however, the requirements were pretty much the same everywhere. Della Keats, who had discussed the matter with her mother, estimated that forty caribou per hunter for both food and clothing, or eighty for an average domestic family of eight (or ten per person), was the Nuataaġmiut's minimum annual requirement (Keats 1970.5; cf. R. Cleveland 1965.10; D. Foote 1965a, II:296–97). Additional hides would have been required for clothing to wear on special occasions and for international trade. Furthermore, most of these hides had to consist specifically of fawn or mid-summer to early-fall adult cow skins for parkas and pants. Hides of bulls were required for footgear. If these calculations and my population estimates are correct, the ideal annual harvest must have been on the order of twenty caribou per person, or a total of 146,400 animals for the population of the study region as a whole. I doubt that this figure was reached very often.

Uses

Stoney (1900) succinctly summarized the many uses to which caribou were put:

> Every part of the deer has its uses. The skin furnishes material for huts, tents, boats, clothing, bedding and rope; the sinew, thread; the antlers, sinkers, tool handles, etc.; the hoofs, as small boxes; the hair, mixed with tobacco, is smoked; the bones, crushed and boiled, yield oil; the marrow gives grease and hair oil; from the contents of the stomach a soup is made and the flesh is eaten raw or roasted or boiled (Stoney 1900:842).

The procedures whereby the raw material was transformed into these products are discussed in later sections of this chapter.

Fish

Fish were an important source of food for both people and dogs in all parts of the study region.[16] Indeed, after traveling up and down the coast of the study region during two summers in the mid-1820s, Beechey (1831, II:300) felt justified in characterizing the Iñupiat as being "a nation of fishermen." The species that were harvested are listed in Table 8. Their distribution varied geographically and, with a few exceptions, seasonally in each district. To describe the details of this variation is beyond the scope of the present volume. What is important here is the means by which fish were harvested, processed, and stored. The same basic procedures were known by the inhabitants of every district, but they were applied in ways that were most suitable to local conditions.

Weirs

A weir (sapun) is a fence built across a stream or river to prevent or guide the passage of fish past a particular point.[17] The Iñupiat built weirs of upright poles inserted into the streambed placed close enough together to prevent fish from passing through; brush was placed upstream of the poles to aid in blocking fish passage. Alternatively, they erected a barrier of young spruce trees or willow shrubs (with the branches left on) butt ends up. In either arrangement, a narrow opening was left for the fish to pass through, where they were speared, captured with a dip net, or caught in a trap.

The most efficient approach was to leave an opening in the fence just large enough to hold the end of an elongated basket, or fish trap (taluyaq), about four to six feet (1.2–1.8 m) long, made of slender willows. The mesh of the basket, like that of the weir itself, was sufficiently open to let water, but not fish of the size being sought, pass through. The end of the trap facing the direction from which the fish were coming was filled with a funnel-shaped framework (iggiaq) made of stakes or baleen lashed together. Fish passed through the funnel into the trap, then either could not figure out how to get out again or injured themselves

Table 8. Fish Harvested by the Inhabitants of the Study Region

English Name		Scientific Name	Iñupiaq Name*
Alaska blackfish		*Dallia pectoralis*	*iłuqiñiq*
arctic grayling		*Thymallus arcticus*	*sulukpaugaq*
burbot (ling cod)		*Lota lota*	*tittaaliq*
char & trout	arctic char	*Salvelinus alpinus*	*aqalukpik*
	Dolly Varden char	*Salvelinus malma*	*aqalupiaq*
	lake trout	*Salvelinus namaycush*	*aqalukpak*
	"old man" char	*Salvelinus alpinus*	*aŋayukaksraq*
cod	arctic cod	*Boreogadus saida*	*aqaluaq*
	saffron cod	*Eleginus gracilis*	*uugak*
flounder	(several)		*nataaġnaq*
longnose sucker		*Catostomus catostomus*	*kaviqsuaq*
northern pike		*Esox lucius*	*siulik*
Pacific herring		*Clupea pallasi*	*uqsruqtuuq*
salmon	chum salmon	*Oncorhynchus keta*	*aqalugruaq*
	king salmon	*Oncorhynchus tshawytscha*	*taġyaqpak*
	pink salmon	*Oncorhynchus gorbuscha*	*amaqtuq*
	red/sockeye salmon	*Oncorhynchus nerka*	*sayak*
	silver/coho salmon	*Oncorhynchus kisutch*	*sikayuġraq*
sculpin	(several)	*Cottus* spp.	*kanayuq*
smelt	capelin	*Mallotus villosus*	*paŋmagraq*
	pond smelt	*Hypomesus olidus*	*iłhuaġniq*
	rainbow smelt	*Osmerus mordax*	*iqauniq*
whitefish	arctic cisco	*Coregonus autumnalis*	*tipuk*
	broad whitefish	*Coregonus nasus*	*qausriluk*
	humpback whitefish	*Coregonus pidschian*	*qaalġiq*
	least cisco	*Coregonus sardinella*	*qalusraaq*
	round whitefish	*Prosopium cylindraceum*	*quptik*
	sheefish/*inconnu*	*Stenodus leucichthys*	*sii*

* There are many local and regional variants of these terms.

on the sharp endpoints of the funnel when they tried. They were speared, pulled out by dip net, or hauled out in the basket into which the funnel had been set. The advantage of this type of arrangement was that it did not have to be continuously monitored, just checked from time to time, the frequency being dictated by the intensity of the fish run. Sometimes several traps were placed in a single weir.

An alternative to the trapping method was to leave an open gap in the weir. A series of split stakes, with the light-colored (split) side up, was placed on the bottom of this opening to make the fish more visible as they passed through. The fish were caught with a long-handled dip net (*qalu*). Still another variation was to spear fish passing through the opening, a procedure employed most commonly when large fish were involved. These techniques were employed primarily in winter, when people could stand on the ice observing developments below.

In most districts, the best time of year to use weirs was just after freezeup. Water levels often rise and fall dramatically over the course of an ordinary summer, which complicated the construction, maintenance, and use of weirs; in winter, the ice is usually too thick. However, as soon as creeks and feeder streams begin to freeze in the fall, water levels drop considerably, and remain fairly stable for some time after, while the ice is still thin. Thus, weirs could be built with some confidence that they would not be ruined or overwhelmed by flooding, and without too much work. The ice helped anchor the tops of the stakes or trees with which the fence was made. Freezeup also initiated the downriver movement of many fish species, providing yet another reason to emphasize the use of weirs at this time. These generalizations applied least in the Selawik valley, where much of the use of weirs was on sloughs, and where major fish movements were from small lakes out through sloughs in late summer (J. Foster 1986.2; Ramoth 1986; C. Smith 1970).

Seines

Another important fishing technique involved use of a seine (*qaaktuun*).[18] This was a net ranging from 20 feet (6 m) to as much as 75 feet (23 m) in length, with a height of about 3 feet (1 m), with approximately a one-inch (2.5 cm) square mesh. Wooden floats were attached to the top line, and sinkers made of ivory, caribou antler, or bone were affixed to the bottom. Wooden spreaders spanning the desired distance between the top and bottom lines were placed at the ends and at appropriate intervals along the length of the net.

Seines were used in rivers where a gravel or sand bar sloped gradually down into a deep pool (*qaglu*), or along the ocean or lagoon shore where the bottom sloped gradually downward from the beach. When a school of migrating fish was observed coming up the river or along the beach, people in a boat poled out at a right angle to the shore just ahead of the fish. As the boat progressed, the seine was played out behind, the shore end being attached to a long line held by people assisting from shore. When the seine had been suitably stretched out ahead of the fish, the boat was turned in the direction from which the fish were coming and the net was played out parallel to the shore. When the fish hit the net, the boat continued on a bit farther, then headed in to shore. When the bottom of the seine reached the sloping bottom of the gravel bar or beach, the fish were trapped. At that point people standing on shore rushed into the water, grasped the spreaders, and pulled the seine toward shore, eventually scooping the fish out onto the gravel.

Seines could also be used without boats. Figure 20 shows a technique observed by E. W. Nelson on Kotzebue Sound in September 1881 (see also Hooper 1881:59). The shore end of the seine was held by two men standing at the water's edge. The other end was kept away from shore by a man wielding several floating poles lashed together to form a single long

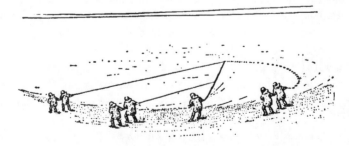

FIGURE 20. Seining without a boat on Kotzebue Sound. From Nelson (1899:186).

one. The net was drawn forward—toward the left in the illustration—by men pulling two long lines, one attached to the seine itself, the other to the mid-point of the pole. They drew the net along the beach for one or two hundred yards (90–180 m), then hauled it in to the beach, thus trapping the fish.

Still another method was employed by elders at Point Hope who were left behind in summer while everyone else was away hunting or trading (B. Foote 1992:44–45). One end of a gill net or short seine was attached by a line connecting the spreader at one end of the net to a deadhead on shore. A long line at the other end was run through a loop in a rope tied around a heavy rock placed as an anchor some distance from shore, then back to shore. Another line connected people on the shore to the spreader at the far end of the net. When fish hit the net, all the people had to do was pull on the end of this second line. That brought the net and the fish to shore. When they wanted to reset the net, they simply pulled on the line running through the loop on the anchor.

The size of the harvest provided by one haul of a seine varied according to the number of fish that were in the school, the length of the seine, and the number of fishermen. On more than one occasion, I have seen nearly a ton of Dolly Varden char caught with a single haul of a sixty-foot (18 m) seine in the Wulik River, in the Kivalina district.[19] Obviously, seining could be extremely productive. However, during the study period, seines were rarely as long or as strong as the ones I saw in the 1960s. Sometimes only a few people were available to help with the work, which often meant that many fish escaped. High water in the rivers or a surf on the coast made it difficult to locate fish, and nearly impossible to use a seine. Thus, even a light rain or a moderate breeze could bring seining operations to a halt.

Gill Nets

Seining could be very productive, but it required the active involvement of several people to do even at a minimal level. A device that could be employed by just one or two individuals, and that did not require constant attention, was a gill net (*kuvraq*).[20] This was a long net similar in structure to a seine, with floats attached to the top line, sinkers on the bottom, and spreaders at appropriate intervals to keep the mesh open. However, instead of being actively maneuvered, it was simply anchored in the water at a right angle to the shoreline, like a floating wall. Fish swimming along the shore tried to pass through it; if they failed and tried to back out, their gills caught on the line and they were trapped. The size of the mesh was critical here: fish can swim right through openings that are too large; they cannot get their heads far enough in for the gills to catch if the openings are too small. Therefore, gill nets were made and used with a specific size of fish in mind. While the net was doing its work, the people could set about doing other tasks. The net had to be checked two or three times a day to remove any fish that had been caught; debris that had been caught in the mesh had to be removed as well, since its presence served to warn approaching fish of danger.

Gill nets were used in both freshwater and saltwater, and they could be used after freezeup as well as during the time of open water. Setting and maintaining a gill net under the ice was a tricky business, however. In the winter of 1884, Charles Brower (ms) learned how it was done by the Kivalliñiġmiut:

> Fishing through the ice in winter is quite a job, especially when the ice is four feet [1.22 m] thick. The holes through the ice are cut in the fall when the ice is just thick enough to bear the weight of a man, are not more than eight feet [2.5 m] apart, so as the ice gets thicker the nets can be set with greater ease. After

cutting holes in a row long enough to set the net, a long line with a weight on the end is dropped through the end hole, then a stick with a hook at the end is poked through the hole next to it and the line is caught and brought through, hauling enough slack on the line so that the same operation can be done over till the line is stretched through all the holes, the full length of the net under the ice. Then the net is hauled through the first hole which is always the largest land [sic] set. Great care is always taken to see that the net is so weighted that it will not float up and freeze to the ice. If this happens, the net has to be cut out or abandoned (Brower ms:158; see also p. 248; A. Douglas 1976.5; and Anderson et al. 1998:186–89 for illustrations).

Checking the net was nearly as difficult as setting it in the first place, particularly in very cold weather. However, like snares set for caribou, gill nets worked all the time without requiring constant attention.

Other Fishing Techniques

Several other techniques were used for catching fish. Although rarely as productive as the procedures already described, under certain conditions they were often the most effective.

One technique was the hook and line.[21] Hooks consisted of a lure resembling what we would call a plug (used in conjunction with a bait casting or spinning rod), with a hook (niksik) of metal, bone, ivory, or tooth or toenail of certain animals (e.g., beaver) inserted into it. The lure, in turn, was attached to a line the other end of which was connected to a short stick one to three feet (30–90 cm) in length. Sometimes a leader made from baleen connected the line to the lure. Using the stick, the lure was jerked up and down, or "jigged," in the water. Fish striking the bait were hauled in as fast as possible. Another technique used for catching large fish, at least along the Kobuk River, was to tie a small fish to a stick attached to the end of a line. When the fish swallowed the bait, the fisherman jerked the line, turning the stick crosswise inside the prey, and thus capturing it (Grinnell 1901:23).

Hooking was done from kayaks, in summer, and through holes chopped in the ice, in winter. When the prey consisted of arctic or saffron cod ("tomcod"), which were pursued enthusiastically along the coast during the winter months, hooking was fairly productive, sometimes yielding several dozen fish in less than an hour. This was an activity in which both children and elders could participate effectively. Often a small snow house was built over the fishing hole, partly for the comfort of the angler, and partly to reduce the extent to which the water in the hole would freeze when unattended overnight. When the prey was pike, the returns were less frequent, but the fish were much larger.

Another variation was to use a set line (qaǵruqsaq) with a baited hook attached (Keats 1970.9). The line was anchored to the shore or to stakes in the ice and left overnight. Alternatively, people employed a trot line, which consisted of a main line with a series of shorter lines attached to baited hooks running off it.[22] This was usually done in pursuit of ling cod, in which case each hook was embedded inside a piece of meat or fish, which served as bait. One end of this line was anchored to the bottom. During the peak of the ling cod run, each hook set the night before was likely to have a fish on it by morning.

Lures were used without a hook in conjunction with a leister, or three-pronged fish spear (kakiat), or with a long pole tipped with a detachable barbed point connected to a shaft by a short line (kapuqqaun).[23] The fisherman jigged the lure, which attracted fish to within spearing range. Spears were also used—generally without the use of lures—to catch fish in shallow streams or shallow water in large streams. In still another variation, a man traveling in a kayak took a fish spear along and threw it more or less at random ahead of him as he proceeded. Usually it floated up empty, but occasionally a fish was skewered. This technique was particularly common on the Kobuk River, which had a substantial run of large sheefish.

Various other techniques were used to catch fish as the situation demanded or opportunities arose.[24] Small fish, such as smelt, that mass in large schools at certain times of year were often caught with dip nets. Dip nets were also used to catch almost any kind of medium- or small-sized fish in shallow streams. Bows and arrows were sometimes used to kill large fish spawning in shallow streams; apparently this was a favorite occupation of young boys.

But the possibilities continue. In both the Selawik and Kotzebue districts, for example, whitefish move into ponds and small lakes during the spring flood. When the water level drops they are trapped, making them easy prey for anglers (Elwood Hunnicutt 1970). The Kivalliñiġmiut, whose coastline was bordered by lagoons separated from the ocean by a barrier beach, took this a step further (Martha Swan 1984.2). They dug a hole on the barrier beach side of a lagoon about three to four feet (1.22 m) deep and eight or more feet (2.4 m) across. Then they made a trench between the hole and the lagoon, lining it with wood to prevent the sides from caving in. Fishermen kept watch, and when they saw that the hole was full of fish, they removed the liners, causing the walls of the trench to collapse, trapping the fish. Then they just waited as the water level in the hole dropped. As many as 1,500 to 2,000 pounds (680–910 kg) of fish could be caught at one time in this way, just before, during, or just after freezeup.

Division of the Harvest

Just how fish were divided during the study period is not known with certainty, but the few indications I have suggest that similar patterns prevailed then as in more recent times (B. Hawley 1984; Walton 1965.1, 1965.3). The basic rule seems to have been that fish were divided equally among the people who contributed to the fishing effort. Thus, fish caught by hook and line, or by spear, were kept by the person who caught them. Those caught in a gill net were kept by its owner. Fish caught by seine were divided equally among those who shared in the work, plus an extra portion for the boat owner. If the seine was owned by a single individual, that person was entitled to a share for the seine, as well as a share for his/her effort in catching the fish. Often, however, several people contributed segments of netting, which were combined to make a seine, in which case the owner of each section received an extra portion. Finally, in the case of a weir, all those who contributed to its construction and use received a share. I suspect, but do not know for certain, that in the case of weirs built through the collective efforts of members of several different families in a complex settlement, that each household, rather than each person, received a share.

A discussion of the division of the fish harvest is almost meaningless because it was invariably pooled, certainly at the domestic-family level, and usually at the compound-family level. Thus, if six members of a family each caught fish by hooking, the individuals did not segregate their catch, but placed it in the common larder. Fish caught in a gill net were likewise added to the common store, regardless of who actually made the net or who tended it. Seining was usually done by members of a single compound family; the catch might be divided equally among the households for processing and storage, but the harvest was regarded as being common property. Much the same procedure was followed when weirs were involved. The only exception might have been in the complex settlements along the Kobuk River, where substantial weirs were required because of the river's size, and where their construction involved members of several different compound families.

Processing

Fish invariably ended up as food for humans or dogs, but there was some variation in just how they progressed from initial acquisition to ultimate consumption. The simplest situation occurred in winter, when fish froze whole within a few seconds of being removed from the water. Much of the time these fish were stored in a cache, where they remained frozen, and they were eventually consumed raw and frozen by both people and dogs. Alternatively, they were thawed and boiled.

A variation on the frozen fish scenario was when fish were caught just around freezeup. At that time, whole fish were often simply placed on a gravel bar to freeze overnight, and then thaw again the following day (Anderson et al. 1998:183; M. Karmun 1970; McClellan 1970.2). They fermented a bit, but that was all right, because they were intended to be consumed as *quaq*.

In summer, the most common procedure was to air-dry fish.[25] Scales were removed by scraping the fish with a sharp-edged wood chip. The next step was to remove the head, after which lengthwise slits were cut through the body on both sides of the backbone, beginning at the tail and working toward where the head had been. These three cuts removed the head, viscera, and backbone, while leaving the meat intact and still attached to the skin in two strips connected at the tail. Transverse cuts were then made in the meat (but not the skin) to provide greater air access, and the whole was hung on a rack to dry.[26] Roe was dried separately, often by being suspended in an old net. Along the Kobuk, dried fish and roe were usually placed on racks in a shed and lightly smoked for several days to keep the meat from becoming flyblown. Under good conditions, fish were dry enough after three days to be stored in oil for later use. If oil was not available, another day or two of drying was required. Thoroughly air-dried fish were tied in bundles and placed in a cache. Smaller fish, such as smelt, were placed whole on sandbars to dry. In all cases, offal was fed to the dogs.

Freezing and drying, the most common procedures, were not the only ones. Most others involved some sort of putrefaction. For example, the Kiŋikmiut sometimes buried salmon in the sand until they got so ripe that the backbone could simply be pulled out, at which point they were considered ready to eat (Van Valin 1944:183). Along the Kobuk and Selawik rivers, and the northern shore of the Seward Peninsula, it was common in the summertime to dig a hole several feet into the earth, line it with grass, sticks, and/or moss; place dozens or hundreds of freshly caught whole fish inside; and cover them with moss, then dirt or sand.[27] The fish were removed the following winter and consumed as *quaq*. Apparently, this procedure was used primarily with smaller fish, or with the heads and/or roe of larger ones. A fish was considered "done" when its eyes became red (H. Anungazuk 2002).

One interesting way to process fish was employed in summer by people in at least the Selawik and Kobuk river drainages.[28] They cut the head off the fish, let the carcass sit for two or three days, then removed the skin, peeling it back toward the tail without tearing it. The skin thus formed a bag, open at one end. It was blown up like a balloon, and tied shut at the open end to keep the air inside, and hung to dry. Meanwhile, dozens or hundreds of fish stomachs were placed in a large wooden pot, where they were boiled by placing heated rocks in water. After boiling for awhile, the water was left to cool; fat rose to the top and was spooned off into another bowl. Roe, which had been sun-dried, was mixed with the oil. This mixture was placed in the dried fish-skin bags, which were again tied shut. (Dried fish eggs and oil were also stored in dried caribou stomachs.) The bags were placed in a deep hole in the ground, and covered with bark and sod or dirt. They were removed and their contents eaten the following winter. Unfortunately, I did not learn how the meat was disposed of, but presumably it was sun-dried.

Storage

The Iñupiat were "delayed-return" hunter-gatherers (Woodburn 1982) who acquired most of their raw materials at one point in time, and consumed them at a later one. Food was sometimes consumed a year or more after it was placed in storage. During the intervening period, three basic problems had to be solved: preservation, access, and protection.

Preservation was a problem especially for fish acquired in summer. As indicated above, this was effected primarily by drying the meat and storing it in oil. Properly dried fish stored in seal or fish oil can easily last a year if the sealskin or fish-skin poke holding the product is kept in a cool, shady place. Where oil was not available, it was essential to keep the fish thoroughly dry. That usually required the construction of some sort of storehouse (*sigluaq*), either elevated or partly underground.[29] The dried fish were tied in bundles and hung from the roof or a frame. The preservation of frozen fish was not a problem until the spring thaw arrived, by which time very little usually was left.

A critical factor in the preservation of fish was the Iñupiaq tolerance of, indeed preference for, partially decomposed food. The key was to keep the decomposition rate low enough to get the product reasonably intact to freezeup, at which point deterioration essentially stopped. Storage pits and semisubterranean storehouses evidently were satisfactory for this purpose.

Access to the stored supplies was another problem. After a good summer and fall, the supplies owned at the end of October by the members of even a single household could weigh in the tons. In some districts, particularly along the Selawik and Kobuk rivers, these supplies consisted mostly of fish. This was far too much for people to transport given the means at their disposal. One obvious solution was to stay home, meaning at the fall/winter settlement. Another was to go back and forth between the location where supplies were stored and where people wanted to be. These, indeed, were the strategies most often adopted. If and when supplies ran out, people were no longer constrained by this factor.

Protection, for the most part, meant protection from various fur-bearing animals, domesticated dogs, and bears when they were not in hibernation. In most cases, elevated caches, subterranean storehouses, and pits were adequate for the purpose, although bears could get into anything if they wanted to; a watch had to be kept. Dogs were a perpetual problem, however. Storehouses and elevated caches were as much to keep dogs away as they were to deter wild animals. In interior districts north of the tree line, people made "nests" in the fall by weaving willow branches into circular frameworks several feet across, and held in place on the ground by stakes (Walton 1965.3). Frozen or nearly frozen fish were placed inside and covered with a latticework mat of willows. These nests were often located at some distance from the settlement so that dogs wouldn't bother them, and, by the time they were built, bears were about to go into hibernation. Still another procedure just after freezeup was to place a layer of fish on the ice, sprinkle it with water (which promptly froze), cover that with more fish and more water, and so on (Giddings 1956:32). The ice preserved the fish and protected it from scavengers and predators. Finally, a hole was sometimes chopped in the ice, frozen fish were placed inside, and ice and snow were placed atop the fish (Sunno 1951.51).

Seals

Six species of seal were found in the waters off northwestern Alaska, of which two—the ribbon seal (*Phoca fasciata*) and the harbor seal (*Phoca vitulina*)—were only occasional visitors. The Steller sea lion (*Eumetopias jubatus*) was also a rare visitor. These three are not discussed further. The other three—the bearded seal, ringed seal, and spotted seal—were common, and were of major importance in the early-contact economy of the region.

Bearded seals (*Erignathus barbatus*) are the largest seals found in northwestern Alaska. The Iñupiaq term for bearded seal is *ugruk*. In northwestern Alaska, this seal is universally referred to in English as "oogruk." I follow that practice henceforth in this volume.

Oogruks average about ninety-three inches (2.4 m) in length, and attain weights of more than 750 pounds (340 kg) at their heaviest, which is during the winter (J. Burns 1994a). They appeared off the coast of northwestern Alaska in late winter. Adults remained there until the ice left in July, when they followed it north. However, many young animals remained in the region throughout the summer and into the fall. During the study period, large numbers of young oogruks were found around the head of Kotzebue Sound and in Hotham Inlet in early fall. Many entered the Kobuk delta and lower Kobuk River, Selawik Lake, and the lower Selawik River.[30]

The ringed seal (*Phoca hispida*) was the most widespread and most abundant seal found in the study region, but it was also the smallest. (In Iñupiaq, the ringed seal is known as *natchiq*; it is usually referred to in English simply as "seal," as opposed to oogruk and spotted seal.) Ringed seals rarely exceed five feet (1.5 m) in length, and 150 pounds (68 kg) in weight (Eley 1994). Like the bearded seal, the ringed seal is at its heaviest in winter. Ringed seals appeared along the coast of the study region when ice began to form in the fall, and they remained there until it left the following summer. A few remained during the summer, but most followed the sea ice to the north.

The spotted seal (*Phoca largha*) is known in Iñupiaq as *qasigiaq*. Adult spotted seals generally weigh between 180 and 240 pounds (80–110 kg), although the largest may approach 270 pounds (125 kg) (J. Burns 1994b). They were present in the study region primarily during the season of open water, that is, from mid-July to late September. They were often seen near the mouths of rivers or inlets, but some ascended the larger rivers for a considerable distance (Cantwell 1887:50).

Seals were hunted in all of the coastal districts of the study region.[31] Just where and when can be quickly surmised through a brief review of the yearly cycle maps in Chapter 2. At least some of the people living at every settlement located on the coast were there to hunt seals. The issue before us here is how they went about it, for they had a variety of techniques at their disposal (F. Beechey 1831, I:344, 454; II:308).

Ice-Edge Hunting

There were two times of year when hunters standing on the sea ice pursued seals swimming in open water.[32] The first was in fall, when ice started to form along the shore. The second was in spring, when the ice began to melt, creating pools and cracks, but hadn't really begun to break up.

The techniques employed were essentially the same. In both situations, the hunter was on the ice and the seal, or oogruk (only in the spring), was in the water. The basic procedure was to build a hunting blind of snow blocks right next to the water's edge, with a peephole or two through which the hunter could watch for prey. When a seal or oogruk swam by, the hunter attempted to strike it with a harpoon dart. If successful, he hung on for dear life until the animal was exhausted. At that point, the seal or oogruk was dispatched with a thrusting spear or club. Tuckfield and Tingook (1960.2) reported that seals used to come very close to hunters, and estimated that experts could plant a dart in a seal at a range of about twenty-five feet (7.5 m).

A man could hold on to a seal, but it was much easier to do so if there was an adjacent ice pile or other solid object around which he could wrap the line. However, an oogruk was very difficult for one man to hold on to. Partly for that reason, men often hunted oogruks in pairs, not only to hold the line attached to the wounded animal, but also because it was difficult for one person to get such a large creature out of the water. If a lone hunter managed to kill an oogruk and needed help getting it out of the water, he climbed onto an ice pile and started to holler; hunters who heard the call converged on the scene, and those who actually helped the successful hunter received a portion of the harvest.

Breathing-Hole Hunting

From about freezeup until early to mid-March, ringed seals were the only pinniped species present in the waters of northwestern Alaska. They swam about in leads and pools; until rifles arrived in the region, they were very difficult to hunt there because they were usually out of harpoon range. The alternative was the breathing-hole technique, which was the one most widely employed during the winter.[33]

Being mammals, seals need to breathe directly from the air. This is often impossible in an ice-covered ocean unless they tunnel through the ice to the surface. This is exactly what they do; in fact, most seals create a series of breathing holes.

The first problem for the hunter was to find a breathing hole, which was not easy because the holes quickly become covered with a thin layer of ice. Accordingly, dogs were sometimes used to locate them. Once a hole had been discovered, the hunter had to stand by it on a three-legged stool (*nikivġautaq*), motionless, with a poised harpoon, until the seal returned. Several hours, or even a whole day or more, could pass before this happened; it was a very tedious process. If a seal came up to breathe, the hunter thrust the harpoon blindly into the hole and hoped for the best. If the hunter flinched when the animal suddenly appeared without warning, it recoiled and went to another hole. If the strike was successful, the hunter hung on until the animal became exhausted, then dispatched it with a lance. Several men often hunted in the same general area so that several holes were attended simultaneously. Seals have to breathe in the open air, so the hunters knew that eventually one of them would be successful.

Nets

A more sophisticated, and often more productive, technique was to use a net (*natchiqsiun*) designed primarily for ringed seals.[34] In early fall, before freezeup, long nets were set out at right angles to the shore, rather like the gill nets used for fish, but made of much stronger sealskin twine with a larger mesh. During the winter, on the other hand, nets about 15 feet (5.5 m) long, made of sealskin line with 10-inch (25 cm) mesh, were set in parallel pairs ("gill-net approach") or in rectangles beneath ("corral approach") the ice around breathing holes (Brower ms:283–85). If holes made by a seal could not be located, the hunter sometimes dug one himself.

The gill-net approach was apparently effective throughout the twenty-four-hour day during the fall, whereas the corral approach was productive only in darkness, meaning the absence even of moonlight. In the latter context, seals were sometimes lured by men making scratching noises on the ice surface. The seals became entangled in the nets, and either drowned or were clubbed to death by men actively tending the nets.

It was often worth the effort to make and deploy such expensive equipment. Charlie Jensen (1970.1; cf. Ostermann and Holtved 1952:122) told me that he once got forty-five seals in one night using a net, and that he knew of others who had taken nearly a hundred over the same span of time (see Brower ms:395). Thus, under the right circumstances, a productive one-night session could yield from 6,000 to nearly 15,000 pounds (2,700–6,800 kg) of meat and blubber to a single hunter. On the other hand, all of the work involved in making and setting the net could yield a return of zero if there were few seals in the area.

Stalking

Beginning in mid- to late March, both seals and oogruks begin to sun themselves on the ice surface, either right next to a hole or alongside a lead or open patch of water, all serving as potential escape routes from predators. As the season advances, they spend progressively more time on top of the ice. Although they sleep much of the time, they awaken every few seconds, lift their heads, and look around for danger. Thus, they are difficult to approach and kill. Fortunately for the hunter, seals and oogruks have poor eyesight, which makes them vulnerable. Oogruks, which are much larger than seals, were the primary target under these circumstances.

Hunters approached oogruks sunning themselves on top of the ice by mimicking their actions.[35] Wearing a parka of bleached sealskin (*qatigniñ*), the hunter approached as closely as he dared on foot. Then he lay down on his side on a piece of polar bear skin, with the fur side down, and started to act like an oogruk, pretending to sleep for a few seconds, then lifting his head to look around. From time to time he lifted his feet, mimicking the oogruk raising its hind flippers. Every time the oogruk took one of its brief naps, the hunter slid slowly forward on the bear skin. When the oogruk raised its head again, he stopped and pretended to be sleeping. The hunter carried a harpoon and either a lance or a club, holding them against (and parallel to) his body with one hand. In the other hand he held a "scratcher" (*argaun*) made from seal or oogruk claws. Periodically, the hunter gently raked the ice with the scratcher, which got the oogruk's attention.

If all went well, the oogruk became so used to seeing the hunter that it directed its search for predators elsewhere. The hunter continued to move forward when the prey was sleeping until he was within striking distance. However, when the hunter got this close, the seal often kept one eye open even when its head was down. The hunter watched the eyes, and the second the oogruk looked away, he hurled his harpoon, hoping to embed its head in the oogruk. The animal immediately dove into the water, and the hunter jumped up and ran to the nearest ice pile or little rise and wrapped the line around it. When the line was about to become taut, the hunter sat down and braced himself. If no mounds were available, he placed the scratcher on the snow, wrapped the harpoon line around it, and sat on it. Alternatively, the hunter carried a special grip around which he wound the line so that he could hold it without injuring his hand. Eventually the oogruk had to come up for air, at which point the hunter drew in the slack in the line. After a quick breath, the oogruk dove again, and the hunter braced himself once more. This process continued until the oogruk was out of breath and exhausted, at which point the hunter speared or clubbed it to death.

Danger

Hunting on the sea ice was one of the most dangerous activities in which Iñupiaq hunters engaged (A. Hawley 1965.10; Killigivuk 1960.8; Rainey 1947:253), and it is appropriate to say something about what the danger was. When the ocean first freezes in late fall or early winter, it is usually very calm, and its surface, hence the newly formed ice, is very smooth. The ice often remains so in protected bays and inlets, but on the outer coast, and particularly at exposed locations such as Point Hope and Cape Prince of Wales, the initial situation does not last. Soon the tide, current, and wind break up the ice and move it about.

The process and its results were eloquently summarized by Harrison R. Thornton (1931), who observed them at Wales:

> One who has never been in the Arctic would very naturally imagine an ice-field to be almost perfectly level; but such is very far from being the case—at least in Bering Strait. The different floes are continually being hurled against one another by the wind and tide and current; for, in these narrows, there is not room enough for any two of them to slip past each other. Accordingly, when two ice-fields come into collision, the edges of one, or of both, are broken into huge blocks, which are forced up on to the unbroken ice and lie there in rows or piles of non-descript arrangement (Thornton 1931:133).

When these powerful forces were actively at work, hunters were not even tempted to venture onto the ice. However, a day could begin calmly, then deteriorate suddenly after a number of men were already some distance from shore. Thus, ice movement, and the conditions that presaged changes in ice conditions, were the subjects of intense and prolonged study by all those who made their living by hunting on it. At Wales, sea-ice conditions were so complex that boys, who were taught about the ice from infancy on, typically reached their late twenties before they were considered qualified to venture out on it without the guidance of a more experienced hunter (Lucier 1969).[36]

The greatest danger, other than being crushed by piling ice, was drifting out to sea. Piling and grinding ice makes noise that warns even the most foolhardy to stay on land. But ice can break off from the land-fast ice and drift out without a sound, and with no apparent warning. Even if the ice field on which he was marooned remained intact, a drifted hunter ran the risks of starvation, hypothermia, and, particularly, severe dehydration if he was out there for any length of time (D. Norton 1965). Another danger was coming ashore in a foreign country, where strangers were usually treated badly. Iñupiaq history is full of stories of drifted hunters being tortured and killed after coming ashore in the estate of an enemy nation. As an indication of just how dangerous ice hunting was, Thornton (1931:21) reported that in the decade 1881–91, sixteen men from Wales were carried away by the ice and lost, although their precise fate remained unknown. A final danger was the risk of being killed by polar bears, which are known to have stalked humans who themselves were stalking seals.

By Boat

Coastal Iñupiat had two basic kinds of boat: a large, open boat known as an *umiaq*, and a one-man, decked canoe, or kayak (*qayaq*). Both were used to hunt seals and oogruks, but the techniques differed to some extent depending on which type of boat was involved.

Kayaks were used to hunt seals in the fall, when ice first began to form along the shore; to hunt both seals and oogruks when cracks formed in the ice in late spring; and to hunt spotted seals in the rivers and lagoons in summer.[37] The procedure was to paddle or drift quietly along and harpoon any animal that came within range. The harpoon line remained attached to the harpoon handle, which served as a drag on the fleeing animal, and as a locator beacon when it floated to the surface. The animal had to come up to breathe from time to time, and every time it did so, the hunter rushed toward it to keep it from catching its breath. Eventually, the exhausted animal remained on the surface in order to catch its breath, and was dispatched with a lance or club. The carcass was then either inflated, with the help of an instrument described later in this chapter, or attached to floats to keep it from sinking, and towed to shore-fast ice or land.[38]

Umiat (pl.) were used for seal hunting primarily in the spring and early summer, when there was still lots of ice around, but when there was also a considerable amount of open water.[39] They were used by crews hunting oogruks, although seals were also taken as targets of opportunity. A crew consisted of four to eight or more men, depending on the size of the boat and the availability of people. A harpooner (*kapuqti*) was in the bow, a helmsman (*aquti*) was in the stern, and the others (pl. *aŋuaqtit*) paddled. If an oogruk was spotted in the water, they tried to get close enough for a strike from the boat. If the strike was success-ful, a float attached to the harpoon line was thrown overboard, and the procedure was the same as it was with kayaks; or, the line was attached directly to the boat, which the stricken animal pulled until exhausted. Alternatively, and more commonly, oogruks hauled out on the ice and, while sunning themselves, were stalked by a harpooner acting alone. However, as soon as the harpooner made a strike, others rushed forward to help hold it. Then, while the harpooner rested, the others towed the carcass to the boat.

Hunting by boat in leads and openings in the ice was much safer than hunting on the ice on foot, but it was not without danger. The pans of ice could close, for example, crushing a boat between them. Or, if a breeze rose up, the whole field of ice could be blown out to sea. For this reason, if for no other, hunting by *umiaq* was safer than hunting by kayak, because two men could keep watch while the others napped. Since spring hunts often lasted forty-eight to seventy-two hours or more at a stretch, napping was an integral part of the exercise.

The Hunt at Imahaaq

Where the modern town of Kotzebue is located, a hunt took place several times a year that, to my knowledge, was unique (Elwood Hunnicutt 1970, 1984; K. Mills 1989; L. Mills 1989, 1991). In the early 19th century a lagoon called Imahaaq was located in a place where streets and houses now stand. It had three outlets. A current of clear water, evidently spring-fed, flowed through the lagoon and the outlets. The place was a favorite resort of spotted seals and young oogruks in the late summer and early fall. Animals of both species cruised in the lagoon and outlets, and spotted seals often hauled out on the beach.

People kept watch, and when a large number of animals had congregated in the lagoon on a calm sunny day, young men ventured out into the adjacent ocean wearing sealskin wet suits, with headdresses of gull or loon heads (L. Gallahorn 1970.3; Elwood Hunnicutt 1970, 1984). Beginning at the settlement, which was then some distance south of the lagoon, the men partly walked and partly swam parallel to the shore. When they got to the channels, the animals viewing them underwater took them for seals; those watching them from above water could see only the gull or loon heads. Neither perspective warned of danger. If carried out properly, the advance ultimately placed a line of hunters across the mouths of each channel. The men then moved into the lagoon and speared or clubbed as many animals as they could. Several were taken almost every time they tried this.

Division of the Harvest

Just who claimed what in connection with a seal harvest depended on the circumstances of the hunt and the species of seal.[40] In general, in the case of either ringed or spotted seals, the person who made the kill kept it. Seals caught in a net owned or operated by several people were divided equally among the men involved, although if only one of them owned the net, he might get an extra portion. If seals were killed as targets of opportunity by members of an oogruk-hunting crew, they were often shared for immediate use, although any leftovers were kept by the man who made the kill.

Oogruks, which were normally hunted by two or (usually) more men working together, were shared equally between or among the hunters. If they had hunted by *umiaq*, its owner would get an extra share for the boat. If two men working together harvested a single oogruk, each kept half; the senior person kept the rear half of the animal, the junior the front. If several men working together secured only a single oogruk, they divided equally both the meat and the skin. The skin was first stretched and dried, then cut into pieces of a size suitable for making boot bottoms; these were divided equally among the members of the crew. Since oogruk-hunting crews almost always consisted of men from a single compound family, the division had less to do with the ultimate disposition of the harvest, which was pooled, than it did with sharing the work of processing it, which was divided more or less equally among the family's female members.

Processing

Seals killed on the ice during the winter were dragged home or transported via small sleds (B. Foote 1992:54; Tuckfield and Tingook 1960.2). In the former case, one end of a line was attached to the animal's snout, while the other was connected to a strap placed around the hunter's chest. Only one adult seal could readily be retrieved in this manner. Sleds employed for this purpose were about two to three feet (60–100 cm) long and eight inches (20 cm) high, and pulled by the hunter using a harness similar to the one employed in dragging. On flat ice, one man could pull a load of eight frozen seals or one frozen oogruk on such a sled (Tuckfield and Tingook 1960.2). Over broken or piled ice, or when the animals had not yet frozen, the load had to be much smaller. In fact, getting the harvest over the ice piles that often abutted the shore-fast ice was often a major problem. In severe cases, the men from the village probably cooperated in building a trail through the ice piles, although the only certain knowledge I have of such an enterprise was the road built in spring by the whaling crews.

During the period of open water, seals and oogruks killed by a kayak hunter were secured to floats and dragged home. Seals, and especially oogruks obtained by a crew, were loaded into the *umiaq* and brought to shore. If several were taken, they were often eviscerated before being placed in the boat because doing so lightened the load. If the women were ready to work on them, the carcasses were taken immediately to wherever they directed. If there was a processing backlog, carcasses were anchored to lines and kept in the cold water until there was room for them at the butchering site. Seals and oogruks killed by people living out on the sea ice in spring were stored whole in ice pits until the women were ready to process them.

The processing of seals and oogruks proceeded along somewhat different lines, relating to both the size of the animal and the purpose for which it was being processed. Consequently, it is useful to discuss the two species separately. Since spotted seals were processed in pretty much the same way as ringed seals, they do not receive separate treatment. Processing in general was fairly complicated, and only a brief summary is presented here. For more detailed treatment, the reader is advised to consult Berit Foote's excellent illustrated book.[41]

For readers unfamiliar with sea mammals, it is appropriate to make a few introductory remarks about their anatomy. Sea mammals are very different from terrestrial mammals. For example, the meat of domesticated cattle is often "marbled" with fat; with sea mammals, the meat and the fat are completely separate. Caribou, even in their prime, have lean meat, but they also have a layer of fat on their hindquarters, and other fat deposits in their viscera. In contrast, virtually all of the fat, or blubber, of sea mammals is concentrated in a distinct layer located between the skin and the meat. From the outside in, then, a sea mammal can be conceived of as being made of skin, blubber, meat, and bones, in that order, each layer being clearly differentiated from the one next to it. Viscera constitute a fifth category. It should also be mentioned that the blubber of seals and oogruks is self-rendering. That is, if you cut raw blubber into cubes and place them in a container, cover it, and keep it in a cool place for a month or so, it turns into oil without any additional processing being required.

Oogruk skins were used for four purposes, and they were removed in a specific way for each one. For skins intended for boot soles, a cut was made around the head above the eyes, another around the hind flippers, and a longitudinal cut was made along the belly between the two circular cuts. The skin was removed without the blubber, beginning at the belly cut and working down both sides toward the spine. When the fore flippers were reached, the joints were severed, and the flippers were removed with the skin. The inner side of the skin was scraped clean of residual blubber, and stretched to dry.

For skins intended to be used as boat covers, a single cut was made extending from the lower jaw down the belly and forking out toward the hind flippers. The skin was removed without the blubber. Oil was rubbed into the hair side of the skin, which was then folded and stored in a relatively warm place. Two or three weeks later the skin was retrieved, and the epidermis, hair, and excess oil adhering to it were scraped off. The skin was then hung to dry without being stretched. Later, it was soaked in water shortly before being made into a boat cover.

Skins intended to be made into rope were those of males. Three circular cuts were made: one around the head, one around the hind flippers, and one around the animal's midsection. The two main sections were removed by peeling them toward the tail and the head, respectively. Then the blubber was removed from each section, and the hide was treated similarly to the skins being used for boat covers.

The final use of oogruk skins was to protect meat and blubber intended for storage. In this case, the skin, meat, and blubber were cut away together, and then divided into four to six units. These were rolled into bundles, skin side out and meat side in, with the edges sewn together. The bundles were then placed in cold storages dug into the ground for later consumption.

Oogruk meat that was not placed in cold storage was usually sliced into thin strips, air-dried, and stored in oil. At times it was left with some blubber attached, cut into small chunks, and placed in oil. A third possibility was to dry the meat partially, then cook it lightly before placing it in oil. The hind flippers were sometimes kept intact, placed in the sand for a few days to ferment, and then eaten raw. As far as I know, none of the viscera were eaten by humans, although some may have been fed to dogs. The intestines, however, were emptied, cleaned, and blown up like balloons to dry.[42] They were subsequently used to make waterproof garments.

Turning now to ringed seals, there were again three ways of skinning them depending on their final use. Skins that were to be made into floats, storage bags, or pants were processed by a procedure observed in 1884 by Charles Brower (ms):

> The skins used in making these floats were skinned from the animal, by cutting around the head, then skinning the rest of the body through this incision, care being taken not to puncture the hide, as the skin was cut from the body it was hauled back and finally turned inside out. The last thing done was to cut the hind flippers from the body (Brower ms:171; see also 280).[43]

Net-caught seals were preferred for this purpose because their skins had not been damaged by a weapon (H. Anungazuk 2002).

Skins intended to become rope were removed as follows: a cut was made across the ventral surface of the seal between the two front flippers. The skin was removed with the blubber attached by cutting between the meat and blubber at the head end and drawing the front portion of the skin over the head. The remainder was pulled toward the tail flippers, and cut free from the carcass at the flippers. The blubber was then separated from the skin, and from there the skin was treated in the same way as oogruk skins destined to become rope.

Skins that were to be used for most other purposes (e.g., boots, trade) had cuts made around the head and the tail flippers, with a longitudinal cut down the belly between the two, and the skin and blubber were peeled back from there. The blubber was then removed from the skin; the latter was cleaned with human urine and stretched to dry. Flippers that were not reserved for food were cleaned and made into ditty bags or canteens.

Seal meat was cooked and eaten fresh; cut into strips, dried, and stored in oil; or frozen. In general, seal meat seems to have been consumed relatively promptly, whereas oogruk meat was usually dried and placed in storage. Ringed seal liver and kidneys were considered delicacies, the latter often being eaten warm and steaming right out of a newly killed animal. Sometimes the liver and intestines were placed on flat boards to freeze, then eaten raw and frozen (H. Anungazuk 2002). The cleaned and dried intestines were also cooked and consumed as food. Beyond that, as far as I know, viscera were fed to the dogs.

Seal and oogruk meat acquired in late spring and early summer was typically dried and placed, along with cubes of blubber, into sealskin bags, or "pokes" (sing. *puuq*). Kenneth and Ethel Mills (1960) estimated that, on average, one oogruk or six seals gave enough oil for one poke. Inside the poke, the blubber soon turned to oil. The pokes were kept as cool as possible by being covered with skins while being transported by boat, or by being placed in holes in the ground and covered with sand or dirt otherwise. If properly cared for, meat and oil stored in a poke were just as edible a year later as the day they were put in the poke.

Stefansson (1951:265) estimated that in the spring the average family would lay away three to seven pokes of dried meat and oil for the following winter. He also guessed that the average poke weighed about 300 pounds (136 kg). However, the size of a poke varied with the size of the seal from which it was made. Bob Hawley (1970), who actually weighed pokes for the Kivalina Native Store, found that only the very largest pokes weighed 300 pounds; the average was about 200 pounds (90 kg). Three to seven of those, of course, totaled 600 to 1,400 pounds (270–639 kg) of meat and oil.

Uses

Ringed seal and oogruk skins and flippers were made into rope, footgear, parkas, pants, containers, floats, boat covers, tent covers, tarpaulins, and various other goods.[44] The meat and some of the internal organs served as food for both humans and dogs. Oil provided fuel for lamps, food for people and dogs, and served as a preservative, as medicine, and as an insect repellant. Pokes of meat and oil were a major item of trade between coastal and inland peoples. Spotted seal meat was dried or frozen and used primarily for dog food, since people did not like its taste (Brower ms:137, 295–96). The blubber made perfectly good fuel, however, and the skins were sometimes used for clothing and storage bags.

Baleen Whales

Baleen whales are whales that lack teeth (Carroll 1994). Instead, they have two rows of plates of a hornlike substance, known as baleen, which hang down in racks from each side of the upper jaw. The inner margins of the plates are fringed with fine bristles. The whale feeds by filling its mouth with water, which it then forces out through the baleen. The bristles filter out zooplankton contained in the water, these microorganisms constituting the huge mammals' sole food.

Several species of baleen whale were found off the coast of the study region, but only two, the bowhead (*Balaena mysticetus*) and the gray whale (*Eschrichtius robustus*), were found in significant numbers (Carroll 1994; Frost 1994). The Iñupiat hunted gray whales only as targets of opportunity during the summer. Dead animals of either species that washed ashore were used for dog food and—very rarely—as emergency human food. However, the bowhead, or *aġviq*, was systematically sought, and was a major element in the economy of the study region. Accordingly, the treatment that follows deals exclusively with that species.

Bowhead whales reach a maximum length of about 60 feet (18.3 m) and a weight of over 60 tons (54,430 kg) (Carroll 1994; see also Lowenstein 1993:xv–xx). They have thick (1.5 ft/.5 m) blubber and thick skulls, the latter being used to break the sea ice so that they can breathe.

Bowheads spend the winter in polynyas (areas of consistently open water within pack ice) in the Bering Sea, and migrate north through Bering Strait in late March and April, following leads in the ice. They spend the summer in or near the ice pack in the Arctic Ocean. In the early 21st century this is usually a considerable distance north of the study region, but during the early 19th century, it was not nearly so far away. The whales return south in the fall, mainly on the Asiatic side of Bering Strait. The prime hunting season for bowheads in the study region is and was during the northward spring movement, although the Tikiġaġmiut sometimes hunted them in the fall as well (Jensen 1970.1; Larsen and Rainey 1948:28–29; Rainey 1947:263).[45]

Ice conditions, which were controlled by the wind and by ocean currents, ordinarily permitted bowheads to be regularly hunted in the spring at only four locations within the study region (see Map 21). Two of them, Uivvaq and Nuvua, rarely fielded more than two or three crews. In general, the people at these two sites were there primarily to hunt oogruks, but whales appeared often enough to justify the extra time and effort required to prepare a whaling outfit. Whaling was of secondary importance in the overall scheme of things at Uivvaq and Nuvua, although, as may be readily understood, any whales taken had an enormous impact on the local economy. The other two whaling villages, however, Point Hope

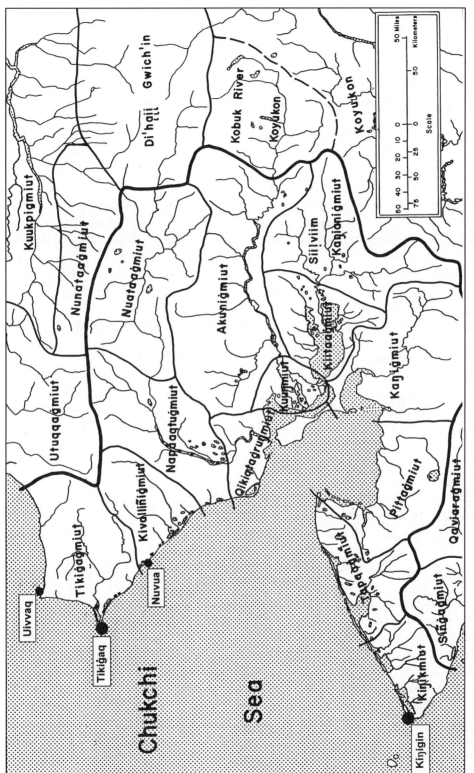

MAP 21. Political map of the study region, ca. 1800, showing the locations of the whaling stations of Uivvaq, Tikiġaq, Nuvua, and Kiŋjgin.

and Wales, were major centers where anywhere from ten to twenty crews were out on the ice each spring. The balance of this section is devoted to whaling at those two places.

The Spring Hunt

Spring was heralded along the coast of Northwest Alaska by the arrival of the first snow buntings and perhaps some eider ducks. This occurred at Wales in late March, and at Point Hope in early April. The birds were followed by beluga swimming north in the offshore leads, which signaled that bowheads were about to arrive (Foote and Williamson 1966:1065; Rainey 1947:257; VanStone 1962b:44–45). From then on a twenty-four-hour watch was kept until they appeared.

Spring whaling was done at leads, or passages of open water in the sea ice.[46] The location and extent of the closest lead varied according to wind and ocean currents, but it was usually located two or three miles (2–5 km) from shore. To reach it, the whalers had to haul their boats and all of their gear across a series of ice ridges and hummocks marking the boundary between land-fast ice and the moving ice beyond. This was usually a difficult proposition, so members of the several crews cooperated in building a road through the worst of the ridges.[47] Once through, the crews spread out along the lead, and worked more or less independently of one another until a whale was struck.

Camps were established on the ice very close to the lead, and a watch for whales was kept twenty-four hours a day as long as the weather was favorable. The hunters did not use tents, but sheltered themselves from the wind with walls made from snow blocks (Jensen 1970.4). They slept in their clothes, since if they were in sleeping bags, the whales might pass before they could crawl out and launch the boat.

When whales appeared, boats were launched as quietly as possible. The hunters attempted to approach a whale from behind and slightly to one side, hoping to reach it just as it rose to breathe. A whale allegedly can neither see nor hear a boat approaching from that direction. If everything went just right, the harpooner thrust the point of a large, heavy harpoon into the whale. If it stuck, a designated paddler sitting behind him threw overboard three drag floats attached to the harpoon head by a long line. Then, if not before, the whale dove, taking the line and floats with it.

After the strike, the hunters did not know for certain where the whale was until the floats reappeared on the surface. By this time, or soon thereafter, any unengaged boats whose crews could see what was happening converged in the same part of the lead. The primary objective at this point was to get additional harpoons and drag floats attached to the whale, which increased the chances of actually taking it, and which guaranteed the other crews a share of the harvest. They also wanted to harass the animal, which was barely wounded at this point, so that it wouldn't spend enough time on the surface to catch its breath. If everything went well, the whale became exhausted from dragging the floats through the water and from lack of oxygen. Eventually it came to rest on the water's surface. At that point the boat that made the first strike moved in, the harpooner now wielding a heavy lance. With the first few cuts he attempted to hamstring the whale so that it could not move its tail, thus rendering it immobile. Subsequently, he tried to cut the animal's backbone, or strike a vital organ, such as the aorta, which led to the animal's demise. The fore flippers were then tied across its belly for ease in towing. Several crews attached lines to the tail and towed the carcass to a suitable spot at the lead's edge.[48]

Processing the Harvest

If the hunt was successful, the next problem was to get the whale out of the water, at least to the extent that butchering could begin. One step the Iñupiat took to minimize this problem was systematically to pursue juveniles in the 23-to-26-foot (7–9 m) range rather than adults two or three times that size.[49] Smaller whales apparently also cannot go as far between breaths as larger ones can, thus rendering them easier to kill (Aġviqsiiña 1940.1:50). A juvenile still weighs some 23 to 24 tons (11,000 kg), however, which makes it difficult enough to haul out of the water.

When the whale had been towed to a suitable place, a ramp was cut in the edge of the ice to ease the hauling-out process. Walrus-hide ropes were attached to the tail, and people—who by this time included most of the village—started to pull it out. Whenever they could go no farther, they stopped, fastened the lines to ice piles to keep the carcass from sliding back into the water, and began to remove skin, blubber, and meat from the top side of the tail; the underpart was left intact so as to make the carcass easier to slide. Then they turned the whale around and removed the baleen. The next step is described in the words of Charles Brower (ms):

> As soon as the lips were off, two slits were out [sic] through the blackskin [sic] on the back of the head, then two toggles were made in the ice back ten feet [3 m] or so from the edge [of the ice]. Two pieces of ice four feet [1.2 m] high were then placed near the edge. Walrus line was rove through the slits in the head, over the blocks of ice, and through the toggles in the ice, back and forth several times. A piece of drift wood was used as a heaver, and both lines were twisted at once. Anyone who knows what a spanish windlass is, will understand what a purchase this rig will give (Brower ms:177).

The process continued, pulling the carcass up a bit, cutting off some meat and blubber, then pulling it up some more. The skin and outer layer of blubber were removed as quickly as possible, partly to release the body heat (which causes the meat to rot) and partly to lighten the load. If weather conditions permitted the work to continue to its conclusion, the end result was several tons of meat and blubber in cold storage, a major addition to the baleen supply, and jaw and rib bones that could be used in house construction and for other purposes.

Of course, things did not always go well. The harpooner could miss, or a properly struck whale could escape somewhere under the ice and be lost. Or, wind conditions could change, closing the lead and forcing the crews to haul their boats out to keep them from being crushed, or open the lead so wide that the whale had plenty of room to make its escape. Other possibilities were for the whale to thrash its tail, capsizing the boat, or to come up underneath a boat and lift it right out of the water, spilling its contents into the sea, or to smash the boat when it went into its death throes. (Fortunately for the Iñupiat, bowheads are unusually peaceful creatures who, despite their enormous size, rarely, if ever, attack their pursuers.) Even a successful hunt did not guarantee a successful harvest, because the butchering process took several hours to complete. During that time the weather could change for the worse, bringing work to a halt, forcing people to abandon a partially processed carcass.

Most of the meat, blubber, and *maktak* (bowhead skin with blubber attached) were cut into manageable chunks and hauled to the village, where they were placed in cold storage until needed. Some meat intended to be used as dog food over the summer was sun-dried, although much of it was usually flyblown by the time it was consumed by the dogs. Most of what was needed for the whaling festival in late June or early July was simply kept covered and in a cool, shady place until the festivities began. And finally, some meat was cut into thin slices and intentionally fermented to form the delicacy known as *mikigaq*, which was consumed at the festival.

Division of the Harvest

The division of a whale was conducted according to a customary set of rules as interpreted either by the *umialik* of the first crew to strike it or by an elder requested by that *umialik* to direct the process. I have been unable to find out the rules governing the apportionment of a bowhead in Wales, but I am aware of seven accounts of how it was done at Point Hope. The most detailed were obtained by Berit Foote (1992:31–32), James VanStone (1962b:48–53), and Rosita Worl (1980:317–20); two were contained in the field notes of the late Don Foote (ms.a, ms.b); and the sixth and seventh were provided to me by Amos Hawley (1973.1) and Clinton Swan (1984.2).[50] The several accounts do not agree precisely with one another, but they are very similar. One may assume that the people of Wales followed rules that incorporated the same basic principles, although the details may not have been identical to those followed in Point Hope.

The division of a bowhead whale is summarized in Table 9 and Figure 21, which is keyed to Table 10.[51] Figure 21 and both tables are informed primarily by Berit Foote's account, which is the only one I have seen in which late-20th-century and more traditional patterns are clearly differentiated.

There is no need to review in the text the information that is presented in the figure and tables. However, it is appropriate to point out that the *umialik* and crew of the first boat to strike the whale ended up with the most and the best. The crews of the next seven boats to strike the whale were entitled to something, however, but in descending order of precedence.[52] This worked out satisfactorily, because it often required the cooperative efforts of several crews to bring a whale to the point at which it could be killed, and to tow the huge creature to the ice edge. The *umialik* of the first boat, who received much more than any other individual, was under a heavy obligation—indeed, an outright imperative—to share much of his portion with the general public, partly right away, and partly at subsequent feasts and festivals. Thanks to the use of ice cellars dug into the permafrost, the meat and blubber could be kept in good condition for a year or more after a whale was taken (see Brower ms:179). An astute *umialik* attempted to keep as much meat and *maktak* under his direct control as possible during the butchering and transporting stages—without appearing to be stingy—so that he would have more to give away to the general public later at festivals, or to families in need, thus enhancing his influence in the community.

Size of the Harvest

The success of a whaling season was determined only partly by the number of passing whales. At least as important were ice conditions, which, governed by wind and ocean currents, could vary radically from one year to the next.[53] Under really poor conditions, a year could pass when few if any whales were taken. It was the fluctuations, and particularly the lean years, that really mattered over the long run.

There are, of course, no statistics on the bowhead whale harvest for any location or any time during the study period. Don Foote (1965a:290) estimated that Point Hope whalers averaged 10.5 whales per year. That strikes me as very low for the early 19th century, before American whalers decimated the stock. Rainey's (1947:261) informants suggested the more likely figure of fifteen to eighteen, apparently as a maximum number. According to Herbert Anungazuk (2002), the oral history of the Kiŋikmiut records that it was a marginal year if only eighteen were taken at Wales. They got only five at Point Hope in the spring of 1880, which I believe is the earliest hard figure we have (Hooper 1881:27). However, in 1885, they harvested twelve (Brower ms:188). At that point, the whale population had been reduced by more than two-thirds from its estimated early-19th-century size (Bockstoce and Botkin 1983). Already in 1852, in fact, some Tikiġaġmiut informed Maguire (1854:165) that whales had "become very scarce on the coast" in the four years that American whalers had been pursuing them.

With regard to whaling at Wales, the only useful information was provided by Thornton (1931). He reported that

> Three whales were captured by the Wales natives in 1889, 0 in 1890, and 1 in 1891. Furthermore, those that were struck and not secured, or that were just missed and would probably have been got with better appliances, were: 12 in 1889, 2 in 1890, and 29 in 1891 (Thornton 1931:170–71).

The 1891 figure for near misses seems to me to be phenomenally high, although Thornton was actually in Wales that year, and he must have had some basis for this number. The only other early figure I have from Wales is eight whale calves (juveniles?) in the spring of 1902 (*Eskimo Bulletin* vol. 5: May 1902). All of these figures date from decades after the American onslaught on the bowhead population began.

Toothed Whales

Toothed whales, as the name implies, are those having teeth instead of baleen. Several species of toothed whale occur in the waters off the study region, but only one, the beluga or white whale (*Delphinapterus leucas*), or *sisuaq*, is present in significant numbers.[54] Accordingly, it is the only one discussed here.

Adult male beluga range from 11 to 15 feet (3.4–4.6 m) in length, and weigh from 1,000 to 2,000 pounds (450–900 kg) (Lowry 1994). Females are much smaller, seldom exceeding 12 feet (6.1 m) in length. The animals are gray when born, and lighten as they age, becoming white around the age of five or six years.

Belugas arrive in the waters of the study region just ahead of the bowheads, following leads north in the spring, and usually spend much of the summer there. Typically they traveled in small pods of five or six animals, but herds of several hundred were observed from time to time. During the study period belugas were apparently much more abundant in Northwest Alaska than they are now, regularly entering Hotham Inlet and Selawik Lake, and the lower portions of the Kobuk and Noatak rivers (Ramoth 1970). Particularly large concentrations were found in early July off Sheshalik Spit, on the northern shore of Kotzebue Sound, and in Eschscholtz Bay, in the southeastern corner of Kotzebue Sound.

The Hunt

Two basic techniques were used to obtain belugas.[55] One was pursuit by harpoon-wielding hunters in kayaks, while the other was by net (*sisuaqsiun*). Both techniques were used in all coastal districts of the study region.

Kayak hunters took advantage of the belugas' tendency to swim in pods relatively close to shore or near offshore shoals. People kept a watch, and when a pod was seen heading in their direction, the men launched their kayaks, paddled some distance out, and waited. When the whales arrived, the hunters tried to herd them into shallow water—practically

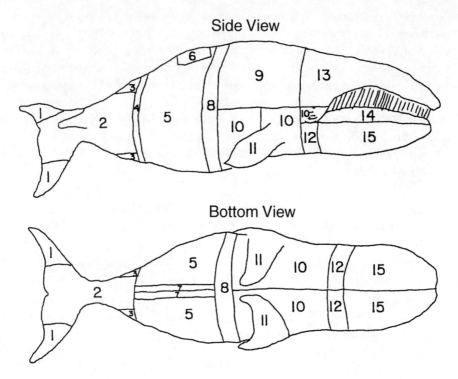

FIGURE 21. Division of a bowhead whale. Keyed to Table 10.

Table 9. Division of a Bowhead Whale: I

baleen	The *umialik* whose boat made the first strike kept one side, while the other side was divided up among all the other boats.
blowhole	Given to anyone who wanted it.
eyes	Given to the second and third boats to strike the whale.
heart	The *umialik* of the first boat to strike the whale kept it, for distribution to the general public at the whaling feast in June.
intestines	Divided among the crews of the first, second, and third crews to strike the whale.
kidneys	A small part of each kidney went to the *umialik* whose boat made the first strike, while the balance was divided among the crews of boats two and three.
liver	Given to anyone who wanted some for use as dog food.
lungs	One lung was given to the crew of the *umialik* whose boat made the first strike, while the other was shared between boats two and three.
stomach	Given to anyone who wanted some.
tongue	Shared between the second and third boats to strike the whale.

Table 10. Division of a Bowhead Whale: II*

1. *avarraq*: The tail flukes were cut up and handed out by the *umialik* at the festival marking the end of the whaling season.

2. *aŋiruk*: The tails of whales killed by *umialgich* with fewer than five whales to their credit were divided and passed out to anyone who wanted some when the slush ice began to form the next fall. *Umialgich* who had taken five or more kept them in storage, then shared them with anyone who wanted some at a festival the following March.

3. *suluġaq*: One side of the tail section was kept by the *umialik* of boat number one, the other side was given to the captains of boats two and three to strike the whale.

4. *ahluna*: This was a circular cut three fingers wide which the *umialik* of the lead boat could give to whomever he wanted.

5. *uati*: This was kept by the *umialik* whose boat struck the whale first.

6. *iġikigraq*: This piece was taken from the share of the *umialik* whose boat made the first strike while the whale was being butchered, cooked on the ice, and eaten by the people helping haul it out.

7. *iŋi*: This cut belonged to the *umialik* whose boat struck the whale first. Half of it was given to the shaman who performed the rituals associated with the hunt.

8. *tavsiñaaq*: The eighth boat to strike the whale got a circular cut above the *uati*. Its width was measured either by the length of a mukluk (boot), or by the distance between the outer sides of the palms when the tips of the outstretched thumbs touch.

9. *qimiġluk*: This portion was divided equally among the members of the crew (everyone but the *umialik*) of the first boat to strike the whale.

10. *siḷvik*: This part, which includes the eye, was divided equally among the *umialgich* and crews of the second through the fifth boats to strike the whale.

11. *taliġuk*: The largest part of the fore flippers went to the crew of the boat that struck the whale first, the smaller section to the crews of boats number two and three.

12. *tirraġiagrak*: This section was cut out for later distribution as gifts by the *umialik* of the first boat to strike the whale.

13. *niksiutaq*: The head has highly valued skin with blubber attached (*maktaq*), but little meat. Much of this portion was cooked on the ice and eaten by anyone who wanted some.

14. *qaġlu*: The sixth and seventh crews to strike the whale received a lip each.

15. *qaa*: The bottom section of the head was divided between the fourth and fifth crews to strike the whale.

* Keyed to Figure 21

right up onto the beach—where they could not escape by diving. If a large number of men was involved, a few crews in *umiat* attempted to keep the pod in shallow water, while their companions in kayaks chased individual animals.

Beluga hunters employed the harpoon in the same way that bowhead hunters did: by attaching a line and a float to the animal, then dispatching it with a lance after it became exhausted. The difference is that a beluga hunter used lighter equipment, and usually operated from a kayak rather than from the stronger platform of an *umiaq*. In beluga hunting, *umiat* were ordinarily used to help herd the animals to a desired location, and to help haul the harvest to the butchering site. In very shallow water, the harpoon stage was often eliminated, and hunters tried to kill the animals directly with a lance. This was a bit risky, however, since dead beluga rarely float. On the other hand, if beluga were numerous, hunters could often kill more animals faster with lances than with harpoons.

After the hunt concluded, the men had to perform the laborious task of towing the dead animals back to camp, although this was sometimes done by crews in *umiat*. In some districts women helped haul in the harvest; in others they did not. The largest drives took place at Sheshalik, where the entire male population of the Nuataaġmiut participated annually in a coordinated hunt, and in the inner sector of Eschscholtz Bay, where the entire male population of the Kaŋiġmiut did likewise.[56]

Nets were set along the coast for beluga during the period of open water, primarily from June to early November.[57] Nets made of strong twine were set out at right angles to the coastline. Beluga swimming along the beach became entangled in the mesh. People waiting on land saw the nets' floats bobbing, whereupon hunters in kayaks or *umiat* promptly set out and dispatched the animal(s) with lances. Sometimes people threw stones from or chased the animals with kayaks to try to frighten them into the net. Most netting was done either by the Tikiġaġmiut on the shores of Lisburne Peninsula, or by people living in districts along the northern shore of the Seward Peninsula; most kayak hunting was done in the inner reaches of Kotzebue Sound.

Division of the Harvest

There were two alternative procedures for dividing the harvest.[58] In one, each hunter kept for himself the animal(s) he killed. In the other, the animals were divided equally among all the households in the camp. The former procedure was the one followed by the Kaŋiġmiut in their large-scale hunt in Eschscholtz Bay, despite the fact that it was a coordinated effort involving many hunters. The latter procedure was followed by the Nuataaġmiut in their large-scale hunt at Sisualik.

When only a few hunters were involved, the harvest was divided equally among the households in the camp, whose residents usually belonged to a single compound family. Or, if a beluga was taken by a whaling crew during the bowhead season, it often served to supply the men with food while they were out on the ice. On the other hand, among the Nuataaġmiut, who conducted a large-scale organized hunt, the harvest was divided equally among every domestic family represented at the site whether or not any of its members had participated in the hunt.

Processing the Harvest

The carcass was hauled ashore on its side, tail first.[59] The initial cut was made around the base of the head. Then two cuts were made up the back from the tail to remove the skin and blubber along the backbone. The tail flipper was then removed: part of it often was cut into small pieces and eaten immediately, raw. Forward of that cut, pieces of skin with blubber attached, and meat, were cut off in sizes that were easy to carry. After most of the meat and blubber had been removed, the animal was turned over and eviscerated. Then the head was skinned. The tongue, stomach, heart, liver, and intestines were saved for human consumption. The lungs were dried for dog food.

Beluga meat was cut into strips, rinsed, and dried on racks or on grass. It was more difficult to dry than either seal or oogruk meat, and quickly became flyblown. Iñupiat generally were not particularly fond of the meat anyway, however, and used it primarily for dog food (Elwood Hunnicutt 1970). Consequently, they often did not take the special care with it that they did with, say, oogruk meat. Sometimes, however, if the kill was made close to a family's fall/winter settlement, some of the meat was put in cold storage. The back sinew was kept separate from the meat and blubber, and was used to make thread or twine.

In contrast to the meat, the *maktaaq* (beluga skin with the blubber attached) was a favorite food, and was processed much more carefully. It was cut into strips, washed, partially dried, cut into squares, boiled, dried again, and stored in pokes of seal or beluga oil. Unlike seal or oogruk blubber, that of the beluga is not self-rendering. The women had to cook it in order to transform it into oil. This was a time-consuming and laborious process, so they often just placed cubes of blubber in the poke. However, *maktaaq* stored in beluga oil is particularly tasty, so an effort was usually made to prepare at least some in this way.

Uses

Beluga provided meat for human and (particularly) dog food, *maktaaq* and blubber for human consumption, sinew for twine, and membranes for containers (R. Adams 1984; B. Hawley 1984). Although beluga were generally of importance to people whose estates lay along the coast, the Nuataaġmiut, whose estate was a considerable distance inland, were probably the dominant consumers of beluga in the entire region. (As noted earlier, the Nuataaġmiut had an easement to conduct an annual hunt at Sheshalik, in the estate of the Qikiqtaġruŋmiut, during a season when the latter were on the Chukchi Sea coast hunting oogruks.)

Walrus

The Pacific walrus (*Odobenus rosmarus divergens*), or *aiviq*, is a large sea mammal with ivory tusks. Adult males often approach two tons (1,800 kg) in weight, while females may exceed one ton (900 kg) (J. Burns 1994c). They spend the winter in the Bering Sea, move north following breakup in May and June, and return south in the fall. They generally avoid the relatively protected waters of Kotzebue Sound, preferring the main current flowing north out of Bering Strait. Within the study region, they were commonly available only to the Kiŋikmiut of Wales and the Tikiġaġmiut of Point Hope, but were pursued as targets of opportunity by the Tapqaġmiut and the Kivalliñiġmiut.

The Hunt

There were three basic contexts in which walrus were hunted: when they were swimming in the water, hauled out on an ice floe, and hauled out on the beach. The first two were more common near Bering Strait and Cape Prince of Wales; the third was more common near Point Hope.

In contrast to oogruks, walrus typically haul out on the ice or beach in large groups rather than as individuals. When they do, they often go to sleep; alternatively, they are involved in fairly intense social interaction among themselves. In either case, they are fairly easy to approach.

An unidentified member of the Western Union Telegraph Expedition who observed walrus hunting at Wales in the spring of 1867 described how they were pursued when hauled out on the ice:

> Taking the direction of the sound [of walrus barking], they paddle until the object of their search can be seen (basking in the sun), in large numbers on the ice floes, barking and playing with their young. Arrangements are now made for an attack; a strong walrus skin rope (with a seal skin buoy attached to each end) is extended from stem to stern, alongside the gunwales; harpoons, spears, guns, etc., are placed where they can be seized instantly; kapituks or shirts made from the intestines of the walrus or seal, with hood attached, are put on and closely drawn about their face, and every dark object hidden as much as possible from the animals' view. Paddling swiftly and noiselessly, the boat shoots its bow upon the floe among the walrus, who commence their boisterous barking and tumble into the water. Each Indian [sic] hurls his [harpoon] into [an] animal, and fastens the line attached to it to the rope connected with the buoys, which is then thrown overboard, the hunter [?] of it only retained and held in the bow. The animals, infuriated at this treatment, splash, bellow, and swim along beneath the surface of the water, turning the boat around at a furious rate. As they reappear on the top they are run through with lances or shot in the head; the young ones being shot or harpooned as they swim around the mother for protection. When they are all killed they are towed to a large flow, hauled out, skinned and quartered in a trice (*The Esquimaux* 1866–67:47–48).

This must be the method of hunting used during the period of concern here, except for the fact that firearms were not yet available then.

Hunting a swimming walrus in the absence of ice pans was essentially like hunting a bow-head whale; the animals were pursued by boat and harpooned by the bowman.[60] According to the unidentified reporter for *The Esquimaux* (1866–67:48), during periods when there were no ice pans around, all of the boats from Wales formed up in a line a few yards apart, then paddled in unison, first in one direction and then in another, until a herd was spotted. The animals were harpooned when they came to the surface to breathe.

Isolated animals were also spotted from time to time by hunters in pursuit of other prey. There were three ways to deal with them, according to the circumstances. One method was to attach a drag float to the walrus with a harpoon, and the animal would eventually become exhausted. Another was to attach to it a very long and exceptionally strong line, quickly carry the line onto a nearby ice floe, and wrap it around a large block of ice. A third procedure was to attach the walrus to the boat; the wounded animal pulled it along as it tried to escape, often enabling the hunters to get within striking distance of other animals. In each case, as long as the harpoon head and line held, the animal could not escape unless it went under the ice. Ultimately, the walrus was dispatched with either a club or a lance, the former apparently being preferred because less blood was lost (E. Curtis 1930:142).

Getting a walrus out of the water, although easier than handling a bowhead whale, was not an easy proposition. It required heavy walrus or oogruk lines and a pair of Native blocks and tackles. The latter consisted of two sharpened ivory or heavy bone stakes driven into the ice. A line was attached to the base of each stake, run down through slits cut in the hide of the walrus's back, then back up through a hole in the top of the stake. If three or four men pulled on the end of the line, the carcass emerged from the water.[61]

There were two elements of danger in hunting walrus by boat. First, although their natural tendency is to try to escape, walrus are quite willing to stand and fight if necessary, using their tusks as weapons (F. Beechey 1831, I:402; II:308; T. Sage 1965.1). A whole herd of walrus thrashing about in the water attempting to flee, or trying to protect the young or the wounded among them, was a serious threat to the crew of even a large *umiaq*. Second, the floating ice in Bering Strait was itself a hazard, for the wind and current could jam it together, crushing the boat; or, it could trap the boat in a small pool and carry it an unknown distance downwind along with the rest of the ice pack. For these reasons, Kiŋikmiut walrus hunters butchered the animals as fast as they could and loaded the carcasses into the boat.

The main context in which walrus were hunted farther north was when they were hauled out on the beach. Major hauling grounds were located on the northern shore of Point Hope spit in the spring, and on the western side of Cape Lisburne and near Cape Thompson in early fall.[62] In these locations, hundreds of animals often rested on the beach at the same time. But walrus also haul out in smaller numbers, or even individually, almost anywhere. Smaller groups are often more difficult to approach than are larger ones because the animals' alertness declines with increasing numbers.

When the prey was on the beach, hunters approached as stealthily as they could, often on foot, then rushed among the sleeping animals trying to kill them with clubs and lances. This could be a dangerous activity, with dozens of the huge beasts thrashing around trying to escape. It could also result in just a few hunters acquiring tons of meat and several tusks within the space of a few minutes.

Few historic records on walrus harvest exist for any portion of the study region. However, Thornton (1931:179) reported that the Kiŋikmiut killed 322 in 1890, and 109 the following year. These kills were made at a time when the walrus population had been severely reduced by American whalers (Thornton 1931:179; Wells and Kelly 1890:26; Woolfe 1893:146), so the numbers presumably could have been much greater fifty years earlier. Thornton's figures also suggest that there could be a wide range of variation in harvest between one year and the next, that of 1890 being nearly three times as great as that of 1891.

Processing the Harvest

There was some variation in how a walrus carcass was butchered depending on the circumstances under which the animal was killed and the specific uses for which the hide was intended. If an animal was harvested by a boat crew in dangerous ice conditions, the viscera were often quickly removed and thrown away to lighten the load, and the rest of the animal was butchered as quickly as possible. If, on the other hand, the animal was killed on the beach, processing could occur at a leisurely pace.

The initial cuts ordinarily made on a walrus carcass whose hide was to be used in a boat cover (usually that of a female) are shown in Figure 22, a sketch drawn by Herbert Anungazuk, from Wales. The flippers were left intact and removed whole from the carcass (H. Anungazuk 1999.3, 2000.1; Avessuk 1983.1; Thornton 1931:138, 170). After any residual blubber had been removed, the hide was placed in a warm place for a week or more to season. It was then stretched on a large frame and split in half, resulting in an inner and an outer skin. This was a task demanding considerable skill and effort on the part of the women who did the work, and requiring extremely sharp knives.

Hides (usually those of young males) to be made into rope were removed by a different procedure. The front and rear flippers were removed roughly as shown in Figure 22, but there was no linear cut down the front. Instead, the hide was divided into three sections by four circular cuts going the whole way around the body: one just above the tail, one about the navel, one across the chest, and one at the base of the front flippers. Each of these sections was removed intact and made into rope by a procedure discussed in a later section of this chapter.

A hide that was not destined to become a boat cover or rope was cut approximately as shown in Figure 22, except that it was

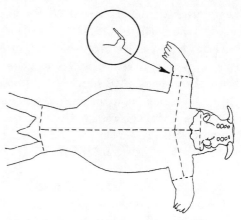

FIGURE 22. Initial cuts on a walrus. Sketch by Herbert Anungazuk.

divided into a number of smaller pieces. These had slits cut in them for ease of handling. The pieces were later sliced into still smaller pieces, boiled, and stored with oil in pokes for later consumption.

Walrus meat was cut into strips, partially dried, boiled, and stored, with blubber, in sealskin pokes (H. Anungazuk 2002; Ongtowasruk 1999). The heart, liver, intestines, kidneys, and lungs were dried, cooked, and stored in pokes. Walrus blubber was aged for a few days, then cut into small pieces and also stored in pokes. The pokes were either placed in cold storage or in a shallow pit dug into the soil. In the latter context, the meat fermented to some extent before freezeup. The cheeks and flippers were also frequently placed in the ground for a few days to ferment before being eaten. Any stomach contents (which would have consisted of clams) were normally consumed by the crew shortly after the kill.

Division of the Harvest

The raw materials obtained from a walrus hunt were divided among the participants in the hunt. Unfortunately, I have no information on how the division was carried out when walrus were killed on the beach. Presumably each animal belonged to the person who killed it, with portions being given at the hunter's discretion to those who helped butcher the carcass and haul the products back to the village. In the great majority of cases, the helpers would have been close relatives of the hunter.

I have more certain information on what happened in the case of walrus that were hunted by boat. In contrast to the situation in whaling, where several crews had to work together to bring in a single whale, walrus hunters typically were members of a single crew who often secured more than one animal during a single hunt. Walrus were hunted in larger boats than were used for whaling, and the boats were usually manned by larger crews.

According to Knud Rasmussen (Ostermann and Holtved 1952:121), at Point Hope, the person who owned the boat got the head and tusks, strips of hide, and pieces of blubber. Rasmussen did not mention meat, but surely the boat owner received a portion of that as well.

At Wales, the division of a walrus was much more at the discretion of the *umialik* of a successful crew than was the case in whaling, and there was probably a fair amount of variation among crews in how it was done (H. Anungazuk 1999.3, 2000.1, 2000.2, 2000.3, 2000.4; Thornton 1931:170). Walrus crews were usually made up of men from a single compound family, in which case the harvest was pooled. It was less a question of dividing the meat and other products than it was a matter of apportioning the work associated with processing and storing the meat and other products. This was done under the direction of the *umialik's* wife. To the extent that the meat and other products were divided among the crew, higher-ranking members received larger and/or more choice portions than lower-ranking members, always at the discretion of the *umialik* or his wife. Rank was based primarily on skill, but also in part on the basis of one's actual contribution in a particular hunt. The *umialik* ranked first, followed by the harpooner, followed by the several crew members in an order determined by the *umialik*. There was a fair amount to be apportioned, as practically every part of a walrus except the gall bladder was consumed in one way or another. The choice parts were the hide, tusks, flippers, and a large triangular piece of meat cut off the chest and upper abdomen.

Uses

Walrus meat and blubber were consumed as food by both humans and dogs.[63] The heart, liver, flippers, and lungs were also eaten. Whole tusks were made into pickaxes, while tusks, penis bones (bacula), and mandibles were used as clubs. Mandibles were also made into sinkers for gill nets. Tusks and penis bones were cut into smaller pieces, then carved into the components of a variety of tools, weapons, and other items. Boat covers, tent covers, tarpaulins, body bags (coffins), "blankets" for the blanket toss (*nalukataq*), and heavy-duty line were made from the hides. Hides were also cut into small pieces, fermented, and eaten. Skylights and drum covers were made from the membrane of the intestine or stomach, and containers were made from the stomach and the flippers. Intestinal membrane was also used to make waterproof clothing.

Bears

Three species of bear are found in Northwest Alaska: black bear, brown bear, and polar bear. The black bear is restricted to forested regions today, and may not have been present in the study region at all in the early 19th century (Johnson 1994; C. Smith 1970). If it was present, it was likely restricted to the extreme upper Kobuk River, a district inhabited at the time by Athapaskans rather than by Iñupiat. Black bears therefore do not figure further in this account.

Brown Bears

The brown bear (*Ursus arctos*), often called the "grizzly," is *akłaq* to the Iñupiat. It is a large, fierce, and enormously strong mammal that is, and apparently was, found in all sectors of northwestern Alaska (C. Smith 1970). In the study region, adult males weigh up to 900 pounds (410 kg) in early fall, when they are extremely fat, and may stand nearly 9 feet (2.7 m) tall; females are three-quarters the size of the males (Eide, Miller, and Reynolds 1994). Most brown bears enter dens in the fall and hibernate until early spring.

Brown bears were routinely hunted as opportunity presented, but were specifically pursued at two times of year.[64] One was in the late summer and early fall, when they were at their fattest. The best place to find them then was in or near shallow rivers where salmon or char were spawning. All the hunters had to do was wait, and a bear was likely to appear eventually. The other time to hunt them was in the spring, just before they emerged from their dens, when they are said still to be quite fat. The locations of dens were often known to the people living in the district. Several men would surround one, open it up, and kill the often-drowsy bear as it emerged.

Killing a brown bear was rarely a simple matter, and often involved two or more hunters working together. Usually, the bear was first shot with bow and arrow, more than once, if possible. This was partly to try to kill it, but also partly to try to provoke it into standing up. If and when it did, the hunter quickly moved forward with a heavy spear, knelt, planted the butt end on the ground, and tilted the point at the animal's heart. When the bear dropped down to attack or flee, it impaled itself on the spear. Unless this maneuver was instantly fatal—which it often was—the hunter tried to stay out of the enraged animal's way. Eventually, weakened from loss of blood and damage to its internal organs, the bear expired. Should the bear decide to charge the hunter instead of standing up, the spear was used in essentially the same way, although aimed at the collarbone; it was much more difficult to brace properly against an onrushing animal than against one standing on its hind legs.

The only other technique I have heard of for killing brown bears is with snares. A snare used for this purpose would have to be remarkably strong and well anchored; only walrus or thick oogruk line would do. Snares were deployed in two contexts. One was to set the snare along a riverbank, where bears looking for fish in summer often traveled. The most effective method was to attach the snare to a nearby tree in such a way that when the bear struggled, it would fall over the bank and hang itself. Snares were also placed near caches of human food that bears might be tempted to raid prior to going into hibernation. Still another technique was to build an enclosure of logs, put a dead animal inside as bait, and set snares in the opening (Ostermann and Holtved 1952:116).

Brown bears were too large to carry home, so they had to be butchered on the spot. The hide was removed by rolling the bear onto its back, slitting it up the belly from the crotch to the throat, with side cuts down the legs, and peeled back from there (Anderson et al. 1998:216–17). The carcass was then dismembered, with practically all parts except the brain, lungs, and liver being saved (E. and P. Attungana 1980). The meat and organs were divided equally among the men who participated in the hunt, but the hide went to the person who made the most decisive move in killing the animal. The head was never brought into the village; it was either buried or impaled on a small tree or shrub (Anderson et al. 1998:291).

Most brown bears were killed by people who lived some distance from the sea, and who therefore had to trade with coast dwellers in order to acquire oil (Keats 1969.2; Paneak 1970; Martha Swan 1970).[65] Accordingly, one of the most sought-after products of a bear hunt was fat (R. Cleveland 1965.10). This was removed from the mesenteries, body, and viscera, and rendered into grease by cooking. It was stored in bags made from the stomachs of caribou or other animals, and then placed in the ground to keep reasonably fresh. The back and tail fat were eaten raw with dried fish or meat. The meat and organs were not dried, but were boiled prior to consumption. In the fall, bear meat and organs could be frozen and thus kept for awhile, but had to be consumed reasonably promptly in the summer. Teeth and claws were made into fishhooks. Hides were cleaned and softened, and used intact as mattresses and door covers. They were also cut into rope and made into dog harnesses.

Polar Bears

The polar bear (*Ursus maritimus*), white bear, or *nanuq* of the Iñupiat, is another formidable creature that is so closely associated with the sea ice that it is often characterized as a sea mammal. Polar bears do venture out on land periodically, however, and the odd one appears fifty miles (80 km) or more inland from time to time. Polar bears are generally slightly heavier and taller than brown bears (Lentfer and Lowry 1994). They do not hibernate, although pregnant females create a den in the snow prior to giving birth, usually in December, and they remain there with their cubs for three or four months.

The close association between polar bears and sea ice means that they were ordinarily present in the study region only between October and late June, and then only on the ice or near the coast. Most polar bear hunters had to contend not only with a dangerous prey, but also with the various hazards attendant on sea-ice hunting. The main centers for polar bear hunting were Wales, Point Hope, and Cape Lisburne, which project the farthest out into the sea, but all the people living in estates bordering the sea encountered polar bears from time to time.

Polar bears were usually encountered, or located by their tracks, by seal hunters. This is logical, because both bears and humans were pursuing the same prey. Such was the prestige associated with killing a polar bear that, unless one's family was starving or out of fuel, a properly equipped seal hunter who came across fresh polar bear tracks immediately altered his priorities. Alternatively, hungry bears sometimes walked right into a settlement looking for food, in which case the entire male populace would muster to defend the place.

Polar bears were taken with a combination of spears and bows and arrows, but almost never with snares.[66] The objective was to use bow and arrows to bring the animal to bay and stand up, then coax it into impaling itself by falling on a spear. The best time to approach a bear was when it had just finished gorging on a seal, but hunters on the sea ice rarely had the luxury of choosing the time and place when an encounter would occur.

Occasionally, polar bears were taken by crews hunting in *umiat* among the floes as the ice pack was breaking up in late spring.[67] According to Edward Curtis (1930:144), a harpoon was thrown at the hindquarters of the swimming bear, after which the crew often had to paddle backwards to keep away from the enraged animal, and also to keep the line taut. He claimed that heavy stones on loops were slid down the line until the bear sank with the weight and drowned. I have a bit of trouble with his account, however, because I cannot imagine what crews hunting oogruks and walrus would be doing carrying such heavy stones in their boat.

There is little in the way of solid information on which to estimate polar bear harvests. At Wales, Thornton (1931:158) said that in 1892, "only" nineteen were killed out of thirty-two that were seen, and that eleven had been taken the year before. It should be noted that these numbers reflect the harvest of a populace armed with firearms, which are a much more effective weapon against bears than arrows or spears. On the basis of his observations in the 1880s, when firearms would have been used most of the time, Woolfe (1893:150) estimated that "an average 60 to 100 polar bear skins" were obtained every year along the entire coast from Bering Strait to Barrow.

Polar bears had to be butchered at the kill site because of their size, and, as far as I know, they were processed in essentially the same way as brown bears (B. Foote 1992:35). Any fat attached to the skin was left, to be removed later in the village. The meat was shared equally among the hunters present, but the hide and skull belonged to the man who saw the bear first (H. Anungazuk 2002). The meat and internal organs (except for the liver) were consumed as food; hides were used as rugs, mats, and door covers (E. and P. Attungana 1980).

Polar bear meat had to be thoroughly cooked before being eaten; the liver was never eaten. We know now that polar bear meat is dangerous because the animals have a high incidence of trichinosis; that is why it has to be well cooked. Consumption of polar bear liver causes hypervitaminosis A, which causes illness and even death if very much is consumed. The Iñupiat knew the consequences of failing to follow these procedures, but attributed the problem to supernatural forces rather than to empirical ones. I do not know what use, if any, was made of the other organs, but the teeth and claws were often made into fishhooks. The skins were used for clothing, mattresses, door covers, and blankets.

Fur-Bearing and Miscellaneous Mammals

The Iñupiat of the study region harvested a number of mammals that fit into the broad categories of fur-bearing and small game animals. They are listed in Table 11, and discussed individually or in convenient groups below.

Table 11. Fur-Bearing and Miscellaneous Mammals

English Name	Scientific Name	Iñupiaq Name
beaver	*Castor canadensis*	*paluqtaq*
fox, arctic	*Alopex lagopus*	*tigiganniaq*
fox, red	*Vulpes vulpes*	*kayuqtuq*
hare, Alaskan	*Lepus othus*	*ukallisugruk*
hare, snowshoe	*Lepus americanus*	*ukalliq*
lynx	*Lynx canadensis*	*nuutuuyiq*
marmot, Alaska	*Marmota broweri*	*siksrikpak*
marten	*Martes americana*	*qaviatchiaq*
mink	*Mustela vison*	*tigiaqpak*
muskrat	*Ondatra zibethicus*	*kigvaluk*
otter, river	*Lutra canadensis*	*pamiuqtuuq*
porcupine	*Erethizon dorsatum*	*iuqutaq*
squirrel, arctic ground	*Spermophilus parryii*	*siksrik*
weasel, least	*Mustela nivalis*	*naulayuq*
weasel, short-tailed	*Mustela erminea*	*itigiaq*
wolf	*Canis lupus*	*amaġuq*
wolverine	*Gulo gulo*	*qapvik*

Marmots

The Alaska marmot (*Marmota broweri*) weighs about 10 pounds (4.5 kg) or more and may exceed 24 inches (61 cm) in total length (Curby 1994). These animals live in colonies, with their dens located on talus slopes in upland districts. They are and were particularly common in the mountains and foothills of the Brooks Range, and, at least formerly, they or their close cousin the hoary marmot (*Marmota caligata*) were widespread in the uplands in the interior of the Seward Peninsula.[68] Marmots hibernate from late September to late April, and thus were accessible to hunters for only about five months a year.

Marmots were hunted primarily at two times of year.[69] The first was in late April, when they had just emerged from hibernation. The adults are allegedly fat and good to eat at this time of year, and the young animals have excellent skins for parkas. The second major marmot-hunting season was between mid-August and late September, when they were fat and their skins were in prime condition for the coming winter. They might be shot with bow and arrow, but they were usually taken with snares or deadfall traps set near den openings. Men who were looking for caribou or sheep in the mountains frequently came across marmot colonies, and hunted marmots with snares or deadfalls while still actively pursuing the larger prey. Marmots were kept by the person who caught them.

A marmot was skinned and gutted, and the carcass hung for partial drying (Anderson et al. 1998:29; Paneak 1970). The skin was scraped clean and hung separately to dry. The stomach and intestines were discarded, but the meat, heart, lungs, liver, kidneys, eyes, and brain were eaten after being boiled or roasted. The fat was rendered into grease and stored in caribou stomachs. The skins were used to make fancy parkas (R. Cleveland 1970.1; D. Foster 1970.1).

Ground Squirrels

The arctic ground squirrel (*Spermophilus parryii*) is about 14 to 18 inches (35–45 cm) long, and weighs up to about 2 pounds (.9 kg) (Alaska Geographic Society 1996:110–11). Ground squirrels live in colonies in well-drained areas all across the study region. They hibernate from September or October to April or May.

Ground squirrels were caught primarily with snares (*maksruksaq*) placed near den openings.[70] Sometimes several dozen squirrels could be taken from one colony in just a few days by a single hunter. Often the hunters were women and children, who could set and monitor the snares while the men hunted larger game.

I have no certain information on how ground squirrels were skinned, but it was probably with the casing method used for muskrats (see below). The viscera were removed, and the rest of the animal was cooked whole and eaten. The hides were pieced together to make clothing, particularly for young children. They were also made into beautiful fancy dress parkas for women.

Muskrats

Muskrats weigh from 2 to 4 pounds (0.9–1.8 kg) and measure 10 to 14 inches (26–36 cm) in length (excluding the tail) (Willner et al. 1980). They live in marshy areas containing shallow lakes and sloughs throughout the study region, but are and were particularly common in the Selawik and Kobuk river valleys, and in the lower Noatak basin.

Muskrats were hunted primarily in the spring, shortly after freshwater breakup, by men or older boys in kayaks.[71] They were taken chiefly with bow and arrow, but also with three-pronged spears identical to those used to hunt waterfowl. When the local muskrat population was high, a hunter could take several dozen animals in just a few days. Another approach was for the hunter to open a muskrat house or hole in the bank, and hide behind a blind made from caribou hides. When a returning muskrat was about to surface, he shot it with an arrow tied to a long piece of twine. The hunter pulled the muskrat in without changing his own location (Stone 1976). Muskrats were kept by the person who killed them.

Muskrats were skinned by the casing method (Anderson et al. 1998:220; Nelson 1899:125; Towkshjea 1960.2). This involved making a slit down the back of one hind leg, and across and up the other. The skin was then peeled away, inside out, forward over the body and the head. It was then placed on a frame and dried.

Muskrats were taken more for food than for the pelt during the study period.[72] The carcasses were skinned, gutted, and hung to dry for three or four days, then either roasted or boiled; the viscera was fed to the dogs. The skins were used to make clothing, or as trim for clothing, especially by people living in the Selawik drainage (C. Smith 1970). The sinews in the tail were separated and used for thread, or braided into twine.

Hares

Two types of hare are found in the study region, the snowshoe hare and the arctic hare (Best and Henry 1994). Snowshoe hares average around 18 to 20 inches (45–50 cm) in length and weigh 3 to 4 pounds (1.3–1.8 kg). Arctic hares are 22 to 28 inches (55–70 cm) in length and weigh 6 to 12 pounds (2.7–5.4 kg). Both turn white in winter. Since the two species were pursued and used in the same way, they are not differentiated in the following account.

Hares were unevenly distributed over the study region. Geographically, they were rare or even absent in the upper Noatak River valley, in mountainous districts, and in areas very near the coast. On the other hand, they were ordinarily found in some numbers in floodplains having substantial shrub growth. Over time, hare numbers fluctuate enormously, from almost zero one year to several thousand in the same district a few years later.

Hares were rarely pursued in summer, but they were routinely hunted all winter long with snares.[73] Whenever a new camp was made the women or youngsters set out snares in nearby willow thickets. Less frequently, hares were pursued with bow and arrow, often by young boys learning to hunt. Hares were also taken with an organized drive and a net. A net resembling a gill net was set up across one end of a long but narrow willow patch. Then several people, starting at the far end of the patch, moved slowly toward the net, shouting and striking the willows. This frightened the hares, who, in panic, ran into the net, became entangled there, and were killed, either by being clubbed or by having their neck wrung. When the local hare population was high, several dozen animals could be taken in a single drive. Hares were kept by the people who caught them; in a drive, they were divided equally among the participants.

Hares were skinned using the casing method described above, then cleaned and dried. The hide was used to make soft clothing for infants, socks, mittens, clothing trim, and as trim around the open end of sleeping bags. Hides were sometimes cut into strips and woven into blankets. The eviscerated carcass was boiled, roasted, or dried. Everything except the intestines and stomach were eaten. Hares are usually too lean to provide a fully balanced diet, but in late winter they were sometimes the only available food.

Beavers

Beavers generally attain a weight of 40 to 70 pounds (17–32 kg) and a length of 3 to 4 feet (0.9–1.2 m), of which 10 inches (254 cm) or so consists of tail (Alaska Geographic Society 1996:19–20; Shepherd 1994). Beavers live in lakes, ponds, sloughs, and streams, occupying dens in the bank, or houses made out of sticks and mud away from shore. They are active all year-round, but during the winter they live mostly in their dens or houses, venturing forth under the ice to retrieve food stored the previous summer. During the study period they were fairly common in the Selawik and Kobuk valleys, but rare or absent elsewhere (Tickett 1970.1; C. Smith 1970). They were subsequently exterminated in the region, but recently have returned and repopulated it.

Beavers were occasionally hunted in winter by chopping open their houses and shooting them with bow and arrow (Anderson et al. 1998:228; R. Cleveland 1970.3; Keats 1970.9). They were primarily hunted in spring, however, during the freshwater breakup process. They were pursued by men in kayaks who either speared them or shot them with bow and arrow. Beavers were kept by the person who killed them.

During the first half of the 19th century, beavers were hunted primarily for food; it was only later, as the fur trade grew, that their pelts became important. Indeed, I am not aware of any use to which the pelt was put during the study period. After being skinned, the carcass was eviscerated and the stomach was thrown away. The rest of the organs, and the entire head, were boiled. The meat was prepared for eating by boiling, roasting, or half-drying followed by boiling (Anderson et al. 1998:293; Keats 1970.9). The teeth and claws were carved into fishhooks or used as components of tools.

Foxes

Two types of fox live in the study region, the arctic or white fox, and the red fox. The arctic fox is small, weighing from 6 to 10 pounds (2.7–4.5 kg) and averaging 28 inches (71 cm) in length, not including the tail (Stephenson 1994a). Red foxes range from 22 to 32 inches (55–80 cm) in length, not counting the tail, and weigh from 6 to 15 pounds (2.7–6.8 kg) (Jennings 1994). Arctic foxes are found on the mainland north of the tree line, and on the sea ice. Red foxes are found throughout the terrestrial portions of the study region. Since both species were hunted and used in approximately the same ways, they are combined in this discussion.

Foxes were hunted with snares and deadfall traps, although I understand neither species was particularly actively hunted during the study period.[74] They were also taken with nets. Bait was set, surrounded on three sides by a net (puuġu). The hunter hid nearby, and when the animal approached the bait, he ran forward, shouting. The animal became entangled in the net while trying to escape and was killed with a club. The main interest was in the pelts, which were used to make fancy-dress clothing and for trim. Certain magical qualities were attributed to foxes, and bits of fox fur were sometimes affixed to a person's clothing in order to bring good luck. In general, fox meat was used as human food only in time of famine.

Mustelids

Mustelids found in the study region include the wolverine (Taylor 1994), river otter (Solf and Golden 1994), marten (Shepherd and Melchior 1994), mink (J. Burns 1994d), least weasel, and short-tailed weasel (ermine) (Lieb 1994). Wolverines were widely distributed across the study area, but the others were more numerous in forested districts than on the tundra. All were taken primarily with deadfall traps (naniġiapiat), although bow and arrow and snares were also employed. The animal was kept by the person who caught it.

Otter, mink, and marten were sought both as food and for their pelts, whereas the other species in the list were hunted only for their fur.[75] The pelts were used to make parka trim, and sometimes to create entire outfits for youngsters. Otters, which have elongated bodies, also provided sinew that was used to make ptarmigan snares (John Stalker 1965:1). All mustelids were believed to have certain magical powers, weasels in particular. Shamans, as well as ordinary people, often carried one or two weasel pelts with them for protection against evil forces (E. and P. Attungana 1980; C. Sheldon 1973–74.4). Wolverines were also considered to embody mystical properties, and several taboos related to their capture and processing (Ostermann and Holtved 1952:36, 114).

Wolves

Wolves were found throughout the study region, although they were probably more common in forested districts than on the tundra (Stephenson 1994b). Wolves were often taken with a special device known as an *isivruġaq* or *qaġruqsaq*, a thin sliver of baleen, sharpened at both ends, coiled in a tight loop, and held in place by sinew.[76] Meat and fat were packed around it, and the whole was frozen in the shape of a small ball. It was then left in an isolated place, where a wolf coming along would discover and eat it. As the meat, fat, and sinew digested in its stomach, the baleen uncoiled, piercing the wolf's stomach. Although it might take the stricken wolf a day or two to die, the carcass could be located by following its tracks. Wolves were also taken with deadfalls (Ostermann and Holtved 1952:113–14) and spring traps (discussed below).

Wolves ordinarily were not eaten, but were sought for their fur, which was used as parka trim, particularly for the ruff around the front of the hood (Ostermann and Holtved 1951:26). The hide was kept by the person who killed the animal. Numerous taboos and rituals were associated with the killing and processing of wolves (Ostermann and Holtved 1952:36, 114).

Lynx

The lynx is a large cat weighing up to 40 pounds (18.2 kg) (Berrie, Earnest, and Stephenson 1994). Lynx were found throughout the study region, but were more abundant in forested districts than on the tundra. Generally, they were found in the greatest numbers wherever and whenever the hare population was high. They were caught primarily with deadfalls, and kept by the person who trapped them.

During the study period, the lynx seems to have been pursued primarily as a source of food (Anderson et al. 1998:226–27, 293; Woolfe 1893:150). The meat was cooked by boiling or roasting. All parts were consumed except for the stomach and the intestines. The fur was used to make parkas and as trim.

Porcupines

Porcupines are large rodents weighing up to 25 pounds (11.5 kg). They were distributed in low numbers all across the study region, but were probably more numerous in forested districts than on the tundra (Bromley and Osborne 1994).

Porcupines have a slow, meandering gait, and are easily taken with a club, which need be no more elaborate than an unmodified rock or piece of wood. They were so easily taken that they could be pursued by young boys learning to hunt, and by people weakened from famine (Anderson et al. 1998:218; Gray 1976; C. Sheldon 1973–74.15).

Porcupines were cooked by boiling or roasting. Virtually everything was consumed except the stomach and intestines and, of course, the spines. Porcupines were also used for a variety of purposes other than food. The unexcreted feces were removed from the intestines and saved to be eaten as a cure for diarrhea; the bladder was used to "wax" sled runners; and the bones were cleaned and saved to help cure aching joints (Anderson et al. 1998:294; Gray 1976).

Discussion

The economic status of many of the animals discussed in this section changed significantly over the course of the study period because of the expansion of the fur trade. Sought at least as importantly for their food value as for their fur at the beginning of the 19th century, they became increasingly valuable as a medium of exchange for trade goods as the century progressed. The most significant changes came after the study period was over, however.

Dall Sheep

Dall sheep (*Ovis dalli*), or the *ipniaq* of the Iñupiat, were distributed throughout the Brooks Range. During the study period, they also made seasonal visits to the foothills west and south of the mountains, particularly around Capes Lisburne and Thompson, and to the Cosmos Hills and Angayucham Mountains, in the upper Kobuk valley.[77] During the second half of the 19th century, sheep were exterminated in the Baird Mountains, and their numbers were drastically reduced everywhere else. Recently they have made a significant recovery in many districts.

Before the advent of firearms, sheep were hunted with bow and arrow and with snares, primarily in summer.[78] Because they frequented rugged, open terrain, they were difficult to approach close enough to shoot. However, they were drawn to mineral licks in the valleys, many of which were known to the Iñupiat. Hunters patient enough to await their arrival could ambush a flock, sometimes killing several individuals before the others escaped.

Another technique was based on the understanding that sheep are extremely alert for danger coming from below, but almost oblivious to it coming from above. After spotting sheep on a mountain, one or two hunters of a group would separate and go to the other side of the mountain, climb to the top, and wait. After awhile, the remaining hunters would reveal themselves, and the sheep would run uphill to escape. There, of course, they encountered a hail of arrows fired by the men who awaited them.

Still a third situation in which sheep were hunted was on the trails they used to cross lowlands when passing from one ridge to another. This is where snares could be used most productively, but sometimes it was also possible to ambush the animals with bow and arrow as they passed by. The harvest was ordinarily retained by the person who owned the snare or did the shooting, except in a cooperative hunt, in which case it was divided equally among the people involved.

Sheep were hunted primarily for their meat, which the Iñupiat found particularly tasty.[79] Rams in prime condition weigh up to about 300 pounds (136 kg), while the ewes are about half that size (Heimer and Whitten 1994). Thus, they provided a fair return for the hunter's effort, particularly if taken by snares. In summer, the meat was dried. As far as I know, the Iñupiat ate everything but the stomach, which was used as a container for storing tallow. A particularly prized item was a big knot of fat behind a ram's neck called the *tugliq*. It was dried and taken along by hunters to nibble as they walked about the country. The hides were used to make parkas, footgear, socks, and mittens, and as trim on fancy-dress clothing.

Birds

More than 150 species of birds occur in the study region, roughly 80 of which were of some economic significance to the Iñupiat.[80] The particular species involved probably have not changed significantly since the early 19th century, although the population size of a given species, and the relative proportions of the different species in the Iñupiaq economy, certainly have. There is, and surely always has been, considerable variation in species distribution within the study region from one district to another.

Waterfowl

The largest class of birds having significance in the Iñupiaq economy was migratory waterfowl, which includes ducks, geese, swans, loons, and grebes. The specific species in this group that were of the greatest economic significance are listed in Table 12.[81]

Northwestern Alaska holds the nesting grounds of substantial populations of waterfowl. The flats in the Selawik and lower Kobuk river drainages have a very high density of nesting birds, with the lower Noatak and lower Buckland valleys and the Espenberg Peninsula

Table 12. Waterfowl of Economic Significance

English Name	Scientific Name	Iñupiaq Name
brant, black	*Branta bernicla*	*niġliġnaq*
bufflehead	*Bucephala albeola*	*nunuqsiġiiaq*
eider, common	*Somateria mollissima*	*miituk*
eider, king	*Somateria spectabilis*	*kiŋalik*
eider, Steller's	*Polysticta stelleri*	*igniqauqtuq*
goldeneye, common	*Bucephala clangula*	
grebe, horned	*Podiceps auritus*	*suġliq*
grebe, red-necked	*Podiceps grisegena*	*suġlitchauraq*
goose, Canada	*Branta canadensis*	*iqsraġutilik*
goose, snow	*Chen caerulescens*	*kaŋuq*
goose, white-fronted	*Anser albifrons*	*kigiyuk*
harlequin duck	*Histrionicus histrionicus*	*saġvaq tiŋmiaq*
loon, arctic	*Gavia arctica*	*malġi*
loon, common	*Gavia immer*	*taatchiŋiq*
loon, red-throated	*Gavia stellata*	*qaqsrauq*
loon, yellow-billed	*Gavia adamsii*	*tuutlik*
mallard	*Anas platyrhynchos*	*ivugasrugruk*
merganser, red-breasted	*Mergas serrator*	*paisugruk*
oldsquaw	*Clangula hyemalis*	*aahaaliq*
pintail	*Anas acuta*	*ivugaq*
scaup, greater	*Aythya marila*	*qaqłukpalik*
scoter, common or black	*Melanitta nigra*	*uviññauyuk*
scoter, surf	*Melanitta perspicillata*	*tuunġaaġruk*
scoter, white-winged	*Melanitta deglandi*	*killalik*
shoveler	*Anas clypeata*	*ivugaq*
swan, whistling or tundra	*Cygnus columbianus*	*qugruk*
teal, green-winged	*Anas crecca*	*qaiŋiq*
widgeon, American	*Anas americana*	*uggiihiq*

being not too far behind. Tens of thousands of other birds pass through the area or along the coast every spring on their way to nesting grounds farther north.

Waterfowl were hunted with a variety of techniques, depending on the species, the time of year, and the physical context within which they were pursued. Along the coast, a major waterfowl hunt was undertaken during the spring migration, which targeted both birds destined to nest within the study region and those headed farther north.

Along the coast, by which I mean the shoreline exactly, not a few yards inland, a major hunt was undertaken in the spring when birds were flying north.[82] The ocean is still ice-covered at this time, although the ice is beginning to melt down and break up. Many of the flocks following this route fly only two or three feet (.5–1 m) above the water or beach, varying their altitude to some extent according to the direction of the wind and the presence of obstructions in their path. Hunters lay in wait for them, often behind a pile of ice shoved up on shore, or on the north side of a point over which the birds often took a shortcut. The birds had to alter their altitude slightly upward to fly over the obstruction, and were caught either with bolas or with long-handled nets by the lurking hunters.

Inland, before the waterfowl began to nest, they were hunted by kayakers wielding either bow and arrow or special bird spears, both of which were usually directed at swimming birds.[83] The spears usually had three prongs at the point, and another three about halfway back on the shaft, although sometimes there was just one set or the other. With this weapon, even a near miss often produced some results.

A major hunt was conducted in many districts in July, when the adult birds were molting and unable to fly, and the young had not yet mastered flight.[84] Several techniques were brought to bear during this season. In some districts, particularly the Shishmaref district (Tapqaġmiut), several kayakers cooperated in rounding up the birds and in driving them slowly across and eventually out of the water toward others on shore who were hiding, but manning a long net. As the birds approached the net, the pursuing hunters made a rush, the panicked birds tried to flee, and ran right into the net. Another technique used during this season was to set a series of baleen snares across a grassy area on the margin of a lake or pond, often with the use of decoys.[85] One arrangement was to set the snares upright, which caught the birds by the neck. The other was to lay the snares on the ground, slightly elevated by blades of grass; this caught them by the feet. The final technique was to pursue the birds in kayaks with a spear or bow and arrow.

Ducks were kept by the person who caught them, except in the case of an organized drive, in which case the participants shared equally in the returns. The birds were usually plucked and eaten fairly promptly.[86] The meat was prepared by boiling as a soup or thin stew, roasting, or partial drying followed by cooking. The skin, head, feet, and most of the viscera of ducks and geese were also cooked and eaten, except for intestines that were full when the bird was killed. Loons and grebes were skinned, with the fat left on the skin. The skin was then cut into small pieces and cooked with the bird's meat. Loon and grebe skins were sometimes made into socks, waterproof pouches, or waterproof parkas (Beaver 1976.2). Duck or goose fat was often aged and used as a medication. Eggs were boiled and stored in seal oil (E. Mills 1960.4). The feathers and heads of loons were often used in the costumes made for special dances (E. and P. Attungana 1980).

Sea-Cliff Nesting Birds

Sea-cliff nesting birds live in colonies, sometimes of several thousand, on the faces of cliffs rising directly above, or very near, the ocean. During the 20th century there were nearly forty of these colonies within the study region, the greatest concentrations of which were located around Capes Thompson and Lisburne (Paul and Lehnhausen 1994; Sowls, Hatch, and Lensink 1978). The same colonies probably existed during the early 19th century, although the number of birds involved apparently was much greater then than it is now. The main species nesting in these colonies are listed in Table 13.

Table 13. Sea-Cliff Nesting Birds of Economic Significance

ENGLISH NAME	SCIENTIFIC NAME	IÑUPIAQ NAME
cormorant, pelagic	*Phalacrocorax pelagicus*	*iŋitqaq*
guillemot, pigeon	*Cepphus columba*	
murre, common	*Uria aalge*	*akpaliq*
murre, thick-billed	*Uria lomvia*	*akpaluuraq*
puffin, horned	*Fratercula corniculata*	*qilayaq*
puffin, tufted	*Fratercula cirrhata*	

Sea-cliff nesting birds were hunted primarily in the spring, during their northward migration, by the same techniques used to hunt migrating ducks, that is, with nets and bolas; they were also taken with slingshots.[87] Sometimes they were caught with nets suspended over the cliffs or wielded by men lowered down the cliff face on ropes (Nelson 1899:133; Wells and Kelly 1890:25). However, the birds' main significance was as a source of eggs. Collecting them was a risky business, because people had to scale the cliffs from below, or descend them holding onto ropes suspended from above (Nelson 1899:133; see Phebus 1972:58 for a sketch of this operation). Nevertheless, egging was carried out by a significant number of people, including elders, every year. Although the number of nesting pairs of birds probably varied from year to year, people could visit the cliffs with the certain knowledge that they would find food there.

The harvest of both birds and eggs was divided equally among those hunting together.[88] Eggs were hard-boiled and stored in a poke in seal oil (Hooper 1884:41; Jensen 1970.1; Clinton Swan 1984.1). Adult birds of most species were skinned and gutted, and promptly cooked and eaten, or else stored raw in seal oil. Baby birds were gutted, and stored in seal oil, skin and all. Cormorants were eaten, but their skin has a bad odor, and it was thrown away.

Grouse

This category contains two subgroups: true grouse and ptarmigan. Each is represented in the study region by two species. True grouse include the ruffed grouse (*Bonasa umbellus*), or *ituqtuuq*, and the spruce grouse (*Canachites canadensis*), or *napaaqtum aqargiq* (Ellison 1994). Within the study region, these birds occur primarily in the forested portions of the Kobuk River valley, and are often found roosting in trees. Ptarmigan include the rock ptarmigan (*Lagopus mutus*), or *niksaaqtuŋiq*, and the willow ptarmigan (*Lagopus lagopus*), or *aqargiq* (Weeden 1994). The willow ptarmigan is found in tundra districts throughout the study region, whereas the rock ptarmigan is found in treeless areas in the interior only. Ptarmigan are almost always found on the ground, usually in willow patches, except during nesting season, when they spread out all over the tundra.

Ptarmigan were an important source of food everywhere except on exposed sections of coast where there are no shrubs.[89] In late winter, ptarmigan were often the only creature available to sustain human life. One of the primary ways they were caught between September and May was with snares (pl. *nigatchiat*) set by women and children near virtually every camp made near a patch of shrubs. Another technique consisted of an array of snares set along the ground, which caught the birds by the foot. Ptarmigan were also shot with bows and blunt-tipped arrows, pursued with enthusiasm by young boys learning to hunt (L. Greist 1970; T. Mitchell 1969).

The most productive way to take ptarmigan, however, was with nets.[90] A long net (*puuġuaq*), perhaps 30 to 100 feet (9–10 m) long and about 18 to 36 inches (45–90 cm) high, was placed around the end of a willow patch, held upright with sticks thrust into the snow. Usually this long net consisted of two or more shorter ones strung together, the sections having been made by, and belonging to, different women. Women and children started at the opposite end of the willow patch and slowly drove the birds forward. Since ptarmigan prefer to flee by running rather than by flying, the birds could be gradually herded toward the net. Sometimes the stuffed bodies of hawks were carried on poles to frighten the ptarmigan and prevent them from flying. As the ptarmigan approached the net, the drivers began to shout and run forward, scaring the birds into it. Many of the birds became entangled, and were caught and killed by their pursuers. This technique was particularly productive when the hunters were able to drive the birds into the wind, sometimes hundreds being taken in one drive.

Another variation was used just at the beginning of mating season, when male ptarmigan become quite combative (Stoney 1900:839). Several birds were shot, skinned, stuffed, and tied to a net placed out on the tundra. When male birds attacked the decoys, they became enmeshed in the net. Still a third variation was to cut a number of willows and thrust them into the snow in an area, such as a frozen and snow-covered lake surface, where they did not grow naturally. Ptarmigan migrating northwards in the spring were often attracted to these artificial willow patches, and were netted there (C. Smith 1970; Sunno 1951.76).

Ruffed and spruce grouse were nowhere near as important in the traditional Iñupiaq economy as ptarmigan, but they were hunted, usually as targets of opportunity, in the Kobuk valley. The only technique I have heard of for taking them is with bow and arrow.

Ptarmigan and grouse were kept by the person who snared or shot them. In the case of a drive, they were divided among the people who cooperated in the project and who supplied the nets. I do not have certain evidence on the point, but I strongly suspect that the owner of the net, or of each section of net, got a special share for its use as well.

Grouse and ptarmigan were plucked, then often boiled or roasted without being eviscerated (Anderson et al. 1998:296; Woolfe 1893:149–50). Sometimes a ptarmigan was dried whole, but this was not true of grouse. Ptarmigan and ruffed grouse eggs were boiled and eaten, but spruce grouse eggs were not eaten. Ptarmigan leg feathers were often used to temper pottery (Keats 1969.2), and ptarmigan sinew was sometimes used to make line for snares (J. Evok 1970; Clinton Swan 1984.2).

Shorebirds

The category of shorebirds consists of the long-legged little birds typically seen in summer running back and forth up and down the ocean beach as waves ebb and flow. The species that were of economic significance to the Iñupiat in the study region are listed in Table 14.

Shorebirds were taken by snare and by bow and arrow.[91] However, most of the time they were probably obtained by young boys with slingshots who were learning how to hunt. Since they had to stalk the birds, taking cover, noise, range, and wind direction into account as they did so, the boys learned lessons that would stand them in good stead when hunting larger game later on. Otherwise, shorebirds seem to have been taken more as targets of opportunity by men going about other business, by people who for some reason were out of food, or by people seeking a little change in diet. Eggs were probably taken more often than the birds themselves.

Shorebirds and their eggs were kept by the person who initially acquired them. The birds were plucked, boiled whole, and consumed in their entirety except for the bones, bill, and feet. The eggs were boiled.

Table 14. Shorebirds of Economic Significance

ENGLISH NAME	SCIENTIFIC NAME	IÑUPIAQ NAME
curlew, Eskimo	*Numenius borealis*	
dowitcher, long-billed	*Limnodromus scolopaceus*	*siyukpalik*
dunlin	*Calidris alpina*	*siyukpaligauraq*
godwit, bar-tailed	*Limosa lapponica*	*turraaturaq*
killdeer	*Charadrius vociferus*	*talikvak*
phalarope, red	*Phalaropus fulicaria*	*auksruaq*
plover, American golden	*Pluvialis dominica*	*tullik*
plover, blackbellied	*Pluvialis squatarola*	*tullikpak*
plover, semipalmated	*Charadrius semipalmatus*	*qurraquraq*
sandpiper, Baird's	*Calidris bairdii*	*nuvuksruk*
sandpiper, pectoral	*Calidris melanotos*	
sandpiper, rock	*Calidris ptilocnemis*	
sandpiper, semipalmated	*Calidris pusilla*	*liaviliaviluurak*
sandpiper, spotted	*Actitis macularia*	*iksriktaayuuq*
sandpiper, western	*Calidris mauri*	*kipiluguksiuyuk*
snipe, common	*Gallinago gallinago*	*kukukiaq*
turnstone, black	*Arenaria melanocephala*	
turnstone, ruddy	*Arenaria interpres*	*tullignak*
whimbrel	*Numenius phaeopus*	*siituvak*
yellowlegs, lesser	*Tringa flavipes*	*tiŋmiam qipmia*

Gulls and Terns

Gulls and terns of economic significance in northwestern Alaska are listed in Table 15.[92] They were taken by bow and arrow or gorget (see below). They were plucked, boiled whole, and eaten in their entirety except for the bones, bill, and feet. However, their primary value was as a source of eggs. Gulls and terns, whether nesting on sea cliffs or on the ground, take flight rather quickly when approached by humans.[93] This makes it fairly simple to locate their nests, hence their eggs. The eggs were hard-boiled and stored in seal oil.

Table 15. Gulls and Terns of Economic Significance

ENGLISH NAME	SCIENTIFIC NAME	IÑUPIAQ NAME
gull, Bonaparte's	*Larus philadelphia*	*aqargigiaq*
gull, glaucous*	*Larus hyperboreus*	*nauyasugruk*
gull, herring	*Larus argentatus*	*qiġitiġiaq*
gull, mew	*Larus canus*	*nauyatchiaq*
gull, Sabine's	*Xema sabini*	*aqargiyiaq*
kittiwake, black-legged*	*Rissa tridactyla*	
tern, arctic	*Sterna paradisaea*	*mitqutaiaq*

* often found nesting on sea cliffs

Raptors

Raptors are birds of prey, and several species of hawks and owls were of some significance to the Iñupiat. The species involved are listed in Table 16.

Table 16. Raptors of Economic Significance

ENGLISH NAME	SCIENTIFIC NAME	IÑUPIAQ NAME
eagle, bald	*Haliaeetus leucocephalus*	*tiŋmiaqpak*
eagle, golden	*Aquila chrysaetos*	*tiŋmiaqpak*
falcon, peregrine	*Falco peregrinus*	*kirgavich kiriat*
goshawk, northern	*Accipiter gentilis*	*kirgavik*
gyrfalcon	*Falco rusticolus*	*kiliagvik*
hawk, rough-legged	*Buteo lagopus*	*qilġik*
osprey	*Pandion haliaetus*	*qaluksiuġayuk*
owl, great gray	*Strix nebulosa*	*naataq*
owl, great horned	*Bubo virginianus*	*nukisaġaq*
owl, short-eared	*Asio flammeus*	*nipaiŋuktaq*
owl, snowy	*Nyctea scandiaca*	*ukpik*

Most raptors were taken by bow and arrow, often lured by a stuffed ptarmigan hung from a pole.[94] Owls, however, were usually caught with snares placed on tussocks or small mounds on the ground. A third technique was to employ a gorget (Nelson 1899:133; Quwana 1940:10; VanStone 1976:15, 30; 1980:30; 1990:11). The gorget was a small spike of antler, bone, or ivory sharpened at both ends, with a groove for lashing in the center. It was embedded in a piece of fish or meat, and connected via a piece of twine tied around the groove to a shrub or anchor of some kind. The bird ate the piece of meat or fish and tried to fly away, turning the spike in its throat. This prevented the bird's escape, and often killed it.

The meat was boiled and eaten as soup, although owl heads were not cooked. Certain species, particularly eagles, and to a lesser extent gyrfalcons, were acquired more for their magical properties than for their value as food. Eagle feathers and dried eagle skins were used in ceremonies and worn on ritual regalia; the feathers were also inserted in headbands worn by raiders who were about to launch an attack.

Miscellaneous Bird Species

A few additional bird species were significant for the Iñupiat but which, as a group, do not fit easily into any of the other categories relevant to this volume. Accordingly, they are discussed individually.

One species in the miscellaneous category is the lesser sandhill crane (*Grus canadensis*), or *tatirgaq*, which is a long-legged wading bird standing about three feet (0.9 m) tall (Paul, Rosenberg, and Rothe 1994). I have no certain information on how cranes were hunted during the study period, although bow and arrow is one obvious possibility. They definitely were hunted, however. Douglas Anderson et al. (1998:296) report that the meat was roasted or boiled for soup and eaten, as were the heart, lungs, eyes, brain, and liver. Beaks were used for making points, especially for fish spears. The hollow leg bones were used to make a child's toy blowgun, and the wings were dried and used as a whisk broom or fan. Crane eggs were boiled and eaten.

A second major bird species was the common raven (*Corvus corax*), or *tulugaq* (Schwan 1994). Ravens are highly intelligent, inquisitive birds who played a prominent role in Iñupiaq folklore.[95] I do not know how they were taken, but they are easily attracted by small pieces of meat or shiny objects, and it would have been a simple matter to lure them to within easy range of a bow and arrow, snare, or gorget. Only a shaman could kill them without causing a calamity, but even shamans apparently took them only when they were needed for specific magical purposes (E. and P. Attungana 1980). In 1826, Beechey (F. Beechey 1831, I:458) noted that raven beaks and claws were frequently attached to ornamental headbands and belts. Dried raven skins were important in the rituals associated with whaling and in the black magic involved in placing a curse on enemies (Brower ms:176, 188; Wells and Kelly 1890:24; Woolfe 1893:148).

I have very little information on the use of other bird species. Anderson et al. (1998:297) report that, in the Kobuk valley, some small birds, such as pine grosbeaks and rusty blackbirds, were roasted or boiled for soup, and that tree swallow meat and nest material were used for medicinal purposes. No doubt similar uses were made of other small birds, but the information has either been lost or simply not recorded.

Invertebrates

The Iñupiat of the study region harvested sea slugs, squid, three varieties of mollusk, five kinds of crab, and six species of shrimp.[96] Although I have Iñupiaq names for most of these creatures, I have been unable to identify corresponding English or scientific names for any of them. Therefore, the following discussion will be very general.

The various types of invertebrate listed above were obtained primarily by the Kiŋikmiut and Tikiġaġmiut.[97] Only crabs were systematically harvested, usually by children and elders, in February and March. The main crab-catching technique was to use a small, circular, wooden-rimmed net or baleen grid baited with seal fat or a seal nose. It was lowered to the bottom through a hole chopped in the sea ice. After a time, crabs attracted to the bait were slowly hauled to the surface while they were eating. Another technique was to lower a dead tomcod attached to a weighted line to the bottom. After a crab seized the fish with its claws, it was slowly raised to the surface and landed on the ice. Crabs were kept by the person who caught them. They were eaten either boiled or frozen and raw.

The other types of invertebrate, mostly mollusks and shrimp, were not actively sought. Instead, they were gathered in late summer and fall by beachcombers, who found them washed up on the beach after severe onshore storms. Clams were also found in certain lakes far in the interior, where they were gathered by people wading in the water (Anderson et al. 1998:301). As far as I know, all of these creatures were boiled before being eaten. However, mollusks removed from the stomachs of slaughtered walrus were usually eaten raw by walrus hunters.

Vegetables

For a region located so far north, northwestern Alaska hosts an unusually large number of plant species.[98] The greatest number and variety grow in the central and upper Kobuk valley, which is home to at least 368 species of flowering plants, a number of tree and shrub species, and an undetermined but extensive array of mosses, lichens, and liverworts. The number and variety of vegetable resources decline toward the west, reaching their lowest levels in the Point Hope district, in the northwestern corner of the study region.

The Iñupiat made significant use of the vegetable resources available to them, more so than generally has been recognized by outsiders.[99] This bias is unfortunately perpetuated in the present study, partly through my own ignorance of botanical matters, partly because of the limitations of the literature, and partly because Iñupiaq knowledge of many relevant matters had been lost by the time of this research. Two volumes that helped offset my own limitations in this area are Anore Jones's (1983) book on edible plants in northwestern Alaska, and Douglas Anderson et al.'s (1998:285–86) volume on subsistence in the Kobuk valley (see also J. Anderson 1939).

The information on the production of vegetable raw materials is presented below under six headings: large trees, small trees, shrubs, berries, miscellaneous flowering plants, and a residual category of grasses, mosses, lichens, and fungi.

Large Trees

Stands of northern boreal forest are found in the Kobuk, lower Noatak, Selawik, Buckland, and Kiwalik river valleys. These forested areas are home to an array of plant species, among which the most important large trees to the Iñupiat were white spruce (*Picea glauca*), or *napaaqtuq*; black spruce (*Picea mariana*), also *napaaqtuq*; and paper birch (*Betula papyrifera*), or *urgiiliq*.

Despite the existence of this resource, standing timber (*uummaq*) was almost never harvested. Instead, driftwood (*qiruk*) was the primary source of wood used by humans throughout the study region.[100] In forested regions, it was supplied by the annual spring flood, which washed out trees living along riverbanks, depositing them on sandbars and islands farther downstream, or carrying them out to sea. Along the coast, driftwood was supplied by the region's own rivers, and by the mighty Yukon. The latter reaches the sea a considerable distance south of the study region, but it transported an enormous amount of wood to the Bering Sea. Ocean currents then carried much of it northward through Bering Strait, and eventually deposited it on the beaches of northwestern Alaska. Before the Iñupiat started using wood-burning stoves to heat their houses (around the turn of the 20th century), driftwood was abundant on the shores of the Chukchi Sea.[101] Only the Nuataaġmiut, who lived in the upper Noatak valley, lacked direct access to driftwood in their homeland. However, they visited the lower Noatak valley and the Kotzebue Sound coast every summer, and, through these travels and through trade, were able to acquire the wood they needed.

Use of driftwood eliminated much of the labor involved in chopping and hauling, and driftwood was lighter in weight and easier to shape than green timber (Giddings

1952:64). It also made it easier to select precisely the type of wood that was needed for particular purposes.

> Bowed logs such as had grown over a river bank could thus be chosen for the tough compression wood required for bows, resilient [boat] frames, and the like, straight-grained wood for flat work, and roots for implement handles, bowls, and other utensils and tools of special form (Giddings 1952:64).

The Iñupiat lacked axes (Giddings 1967:238), so logs had to be cut to the desired length by alternate techniques. One of them, as described by Charlie Smith (1970), was as follows:

> They cut logs with fire. They build a little fire; they want to cut the log, they cut some kind of green willow; and they put [the willow] fire underneath the log and keep it going all the time, clean up, and don't let that fire spread to the side. That willow moving all the time to where the fire is. And take them off ashes on top of the log, so that the fire was cutting through in a small place (C. Smith 1970).

Another technique was to saw the wood with a stone saw apparently made out of a thin slab of schist (R. Cleveland 1965.7).

Logs were split with wedges and mauls, and dressed with adzes, chisels, gouges, and, for finer work, whittling knives (Giddings 1967:238). They provided firewood, and the raw material out of which house frames, walls, bows, arrows, tent poles, cutting boards, boat storage scaffolds, drum frames, masks, handles, harpoons, spears, pegs, spear throwers, burial scaffolds, meat scaffolds, sleds, amulets, drying racks, boat frames, snow goggles, paddles, oars, net and seine floats, buckets, pots, spoons, dishes, ladles, snowshoe frames, platters, and shovels were made.[102] White spruce was preferred for most of these items because of its size and hardness, although suitable pieces of black spruce and birch were also used (Anderson et al. 1998:236–37).

Wood was not the only part of a tree that was useful to the Iñupiat. Green spruce boughs provided insulative covering for tent and house floors, and were used in weir construction. Spruce needles, sap, and pitch were used for medicinal purposes. Pitch was also used as glue and as the equivalent of our chewing gum. Bark taken from standing trees provided roofing material for summer shelters, caches, and drying racks. Thick spruce roots were made into sun goggles, while thin roots were used for sewing birch-bark baskets.[103] Where available, birch bark was cut and peeled from standing trees; it was made into baskets, cups, and buckets, and was used to cover canoes.[104]

In general, large logs and bark taken from standing trees were acquired and worked by men and older boys. Boughs gathered for insulation, needles, pitch, and roots were typically gathered by women. Firewood could be collected by anyone, but apparently was acquired mostly by women and children. All of these materials normally were kept by the family whose members initially acquired them.

Small Trees

Two species of small to medium-sized (commonly 30–50 ft/9–15 m) tree were economically important to the Iñupiat. These are the balsam poplar/cottonwood (*Populus balsamifera*), or *ninŋuq*, and the quaking aspen (*Populus tremuloides*). Stands of the former grew in suitable habitat in the valleys of rivers and their larger tributaries throughout the study region, while the latter was restricted to the middle and upper Kobuk. Small trees, like young trees of larger species, were sometimes cut down to provide poles for fish camps or the construction of weirs. This was done by girdling with an adze or by uprooting (Giddings 1952:64).

Cottonwood, often cut as standing timber, was used for a variety of purposes, particularly in districts such as the upper Noatak, where large trees are absent. It was used to make boat frames, boat storage racks, meat and fish drying racks, sled runners, and house frames. Cottonwood was not a good fuel because it leaves a heavy ash, although it was useful in making smudge fires to keep mosquitos away.[105] The wood was carved into net floats and sun goggles, the inner layer of the bark was eaten as a laxative, and the leaf buds were gathered in winter as medicine for a sore throat.

Aspen was used as firewood, but the wood is too soft for much wider application. The inner bark was chewed as a laxative (Anderson et al. 1998:302).

Shrubs

Shrubs grow in profusion along the rivers, streams, and sloughs of Northwest Alaska, and on protected (usually south-facing) banks away from the waterways. At least five varieties were of economic significance to the Iñupiat.

The most important and most ubiquitous shrubs everywhere in the study region were the feltleaf willow (*Salix alaxensis*), or *uqpik*, and the diamondleaf willow (*Salix planifolia*), or *kanuŋniq*. Several other *Salix* species, most of them known as *uqpik* in Iñupiaq, were less widely distributed, but generally used for the same purposes.

Standing willows, both green and dead, were harvested by being cut down or broken off; willows were also acquired as driftwood. Like trees, willows could be split with wedges and mauls, and dressed with adzes, chisels, gouges, and whittling knives. Dead willows were used primarily for firewood. Green willows were used for a variety of purposes: frames for dome-shaped houses and tents, dip net handles and frames, skewers, insulative floor covering, weirs, basket rims, fish traps, snowshoe frames, withes for stringing fish, and "scarecrows" in caribou drives.[106] The inner bark was cut off in long thin strips, twisted into line, and made into seines and gill nets.[107] The bark was eaten from young shoots.[108] The young leaves (*sura*), which are rich in vitamins C and A, were eaten fresh in large quantities, or stored in oil and eaten later with meat. During famines, the white inner bark was scratched off in shreds, mixed with oil or grease, and eaten as an emergency food (L. Gallahorn 1970.2; Jensen 1970.2). Willow buds also provided a cottonlike material that was used as tinder to start fires (Beaver 1976.1; Stoney 1900:845). Willow ashes were placed in socks to help prevent sweaty feet, which are prone to freezing in cold weather (Charlotte Swan 1964).

Another type of useful shrub was the American green alder (*Alnus crispa*), or *nunaŋiaq*, which was harvested by the same techniques used for willows. Alders were generally too crooked to use for many of the purposes to which willows were put.[109] However, the wood made better fuel than willow wood because it burned hotter and longer. Probably the main use of alders, though, was to make a red dye to color the leather side of animal hides; for this, the bark was shaved off and boiled. The leaves were also chewed and applied as a compress to alleviate the discomfort of wasp stings and mosquito bites.

The final types of shrub are the common juniper (*Juniperus communis*), or *tulukkam asriaq*, and Labrador tea (*Ledum decumbens*), or *tilaaqqiuq* (Anderson et al. 1998:304; Gray 1976). The leaves of both plants were plucked and used for medicinal purposes. The same was true of juniper berries, which were most efficacious if picked during the winter.

Berries

Berry bushes are technically shrubs, but they are usefully separated from other shrubs because the majority of them were dwarf plants from which the most desired product was their fruit, which was consumed as food. There is one exception to this rule, the cranberry, which was equally if not more important for its medicinal qualities. The specific species of shrub that I have included in the berry category are listed in Table 17.

The different berry species are distributed unevenly over the study region, but each one occurs to some extent in every district. Different kinds of berry ripen according to different schedules, but, in general, they were picked in August and September pretty much everywhere; in some cases, particularly with cranberries, the previous year's crop could also be picked just after the snow melted in spring. Regardless of when and where they ripened, they were usually picked by women and children.

Salmonberries and blackberries were carefully picked by hand, but the others were picked quickly and in a seemingly chaotic manner.[110] Women placed small baskets or buckets beneath the shrubs. The shrubs were then stroked with a special instrument resembling a short-handled pitchfork (illustrated by Anore Jones 1983:87), or whacked with a spoon or a dipperlike implement known as a *qalutaq*. This knocked the berries off the stems and into the container without damaging them. A considerable quantity of leaves and twigs inevitably fell into the container as well. The berries were periodically separated from the leaves and twigs by pouring them slowly from the small container, held two or three feet (60–100 cm) high, into a larger container resting on the ground.[111] If there was even a light breeze, the detritus was blown away, leaving the container full of nothing but berries.

All kinds of berries were eaten raw, often as they were being picked; they were also processed in various ways and stored for later consumption. Some were made into soup, while several were mixed with whipped tallow to make *akutuq*, or "Eskimo ice cream." Almost all were put into containers of various kinds, often with seal oil, fish oil, or caribou grease, and placed in cold storage. If kept cool enough until cold weather arrived, the berries remained edible until at least the following spring.

Table 17. Berries of Economic Significance*

ENGLISH NAME	SCIENTIFIC NAME	IÑUPIAQ NAME
bearberry	*Arctostaphylos uva-ursi*	*tinnik*
bearberry, alpine	*Arctostaphylos alpina*	*kavlaq*
bearberry, red-fruited	*Arctostaphylos rubra*	*aŋutvak*
blackberry, crowberry	*Empetrum nigrum*	*pauŋaq*
blueberry, bog	*Vaccinium uliginosum*	*asriavik*
cloudberry, salmonberry	*Rubus chamaemorus*	*aqpik*
cranberry, bog	*Vaccinium oxycoccus*	*qunmun asriaq*
cranberry, highbush	*Viburnum edule*	*uqpiŋñaq*
cranberry, lowbush	*Vaccinium vitis-idaea*	*kikmiññaq*
currant, american red	*Ribes triste*	*niviŋŋaqutaq*
nagoonberry	*Rubus arcticus*	*tuuŋaum asriaq, ivgum asriaq*
rose, prickly	*Rosa acicularis*	*katitaǥnaq*

* Technically, all of these are shrubs.

Cranberries also served a variety of medical functions.[112] They were used, along with seal or fish oil, to cure loss of appetite; they were mashed into a paste and placed around the neck to cure a sore throat; and they were similarly wrapped around a person's abdomen to cure a potentially fatal affliction known as *siksisaq*.

Miscellaneous Flowering Plants

This is not a natural category, but one I invented to help organize the material. The specific species involved are listed in Table 18. This is a rather diverse set of plants, and they are discussed below either separately or in groups, as descriptive convenience warrants. Most of the plants discussed in this section were normally harvested by women.

The Eskimo potato, or *masru* (*masu*), was a favorite food.[113] The roots of this plant are about an inch (2.5 cm) in diameter and several feet (ca. 65–90 cm) long. They were obtained in one of two ways. The first was to dig them up with a mattock or pick. The best times to do this were just after the first heavy frost in the fall, and just before new growth started in the spring. (Roots dug up by people were known as *argaat*.) The second method was to raid a cache of roots independently excavated by voles and stored by them for the winter.[114] (Roots dug up by voles were known as *nivit*.) When this was done, some kind of alternative food was left for the voles in gratitude for their effort. In either case, the roots were cut into suitable lengths and stored either dry in an elevated cache, or in a container with seal oil (near the coast) or bear grease (inland) placed in the ground.

Another root crop was cottongrass (*Eriophorum* spp.), which was gathered almost exclusively by voles and then stolen from them by humans.[115] Unlike *masru*, the roots of this plant contain numerous hairs, which have to be scraped off prior to storage and consumption. The roots were cleaned, dried, and stored in oil or grease. Cottongrass tufts were also mixed with ashes to serve as the tinder used to start fires with bow drill or flints. This came in the

Table 18. Miscellaneous Flowering Plants of Economic Significance

English Name	Scientific Name	Iñupiaq Name
celery, wild	*Angelica lucida*	*ikuusuk*
chive, wild	*Allium schoenoprasum*	*paatitaaq*
cottongrass	*Eriophorum* spp.	*pikniq, pitniq*
Eskimo potato	*Hedysarum alpinum*	*masru, masu*
fireweed	*Epilobium angustifolium*	*quppiqutaq*
fireweed, dwarf	*Epilobium latifolium*	*pamiuqtaq, pautnaq*
greens, beach	*Honckenya peploides*	*atchaaqłuk*
lousewort, woolly	*Pedicularis lanata*	*qutliutaq, qutliiraq*
lovage, sea	*Lingusticum scoticum*	*tukkaayuk*
pink plume	*Polygonum bistorta*	*ippiq*
rhubarb, wild	*Polygonum alaskanum*	*qusrimmaq*
roseroot	*Sedum rosea*	*liviaqłuk*
saxifrage, Brooks	*Saxifraga punctata*	*asriatchiaq*
sour dock	*Rumex arcticus*	*quaġaq*
sourgrass	*Oxyria digyna*	*quŋuluk*
wormwood, common	*Artemisia tilesii*	*sargich*

form of the "cotton" that gives the plant its English name. The tufts were collected during the summer and stored in a dry place for future use.

The leaves of several plants were consumed raw with seal oil. This group includes sea lovage, wild celery, pink plume, Brooks saxifrage, fireweed, dwarf fireweed, and wild chive.[116] Raw leaves were also stored in seal oil, and eaten with dry meat. The precise techniques used to pick the leaves and the best time of year to gather them varied to some extent from one species to another; the details need not concern us here, since Anore Jones (1983:13–30) has done an admirable job of presenting that information. The main points to make here are that women spent a great deal of time gathering these leaves every summer, and that the leaves are very rich in vitamins C and A (or pro-vitamin A).

Another convenient grouping of plants is sour dock, beach greens, sourgrass, and wild rhubarb. In each case, the leaves were picked, chopped into small pieces, boiled into a paste, and left to ferment before being eaten.[117] Berries, especially blueberries and blackberries, were often mixed into the paste as well. If stored in a cold place, the mix remained edible and nutritious all winter.

Roseroot and woolly lousewort also form a convenient group. In the former case, both the stem and leaves were used, whereas in the latter it was the young flower tops. In both cases, the raw plants were placed in a water-filled container and allowed to ferment for two or three weeks. The resulting concoction lasted for some time if kept in a location cool enough to keep the fermentation process from going too far (Anore Jones 1983:53–57; Ongtowasruk 1999).

The final category of miscellaneous flowering plant consists of a single plant, the common wormwood (*Artemisia tilesii*), or *sargiq* (or *sargiġruaq*), also known locally in English as "stinkweed."[118] This plant was picked in September, when the leaves were nearly dead. They could be used immediately, but normally were dried and stored for later use. The uses were entirely medicinal, but the plant had a wide range of applications within that sphere. The leaves were wrapped or directly applied as a poultice on open sores, boils, swollen joints, or sprains; they were wrapped and used with a heated rock as a hot pad for an earache; and they were boiled to make a curative tea for colds, sore throats, lung problems, bladder problems, and as a general tonic.

Miscellaneous Plants

This is a residual category that includes mosses, grasses, lichens, and fungi of various kinds, most of which I have been unable to identify with respect to species name. As far as I was able to determine, the inhabitants of even the most marine-oriented nations within the study region did not eat seaweed, although they sometimes used it to flavor soup (H. Anungazuk 2002; E. and P. Attungana 1980; Weyer 1928).

Several kinds of moss were used by the Iñupiat. Moss was picked by hand or with a special type of shovel made of spruce during the driest period of summer (R. Cleveland 1966). Its most widespread use was as house insulation. Many of the winter houses of the Kivalliñiġmiut and Nuataaġmiut, and the summer houses of the Kiitaaġmiut and Siiḷviim Kaŋianiġmiut, were entirely covered with a layer of moss or a combination of moss and grass.[119] Moss was also used to cover meat placed in storage pits to keep it from coming into contact with the soil (Brower ms:129). The most common moss used in house construction was sphagnum moss (*ivruq*). A different kind, reindeer moss (*ivrauraq*), was eaten after soaking, drying, and storing for a time in seal oil (Beaver 1976.1). Tussock moss, known as *maniq*, and another kind of moss known as *ipiġaksraq* were used to make lamp wicks (Anderson et al. 1998:234;

J. Ralph in Lee et al. 1990:87). Finally, sponge moss (*tininniq*) was used as diaper material, held against the skin by a leather panty. When soiled, the moss was thrown out and replaced (Anderson et al. 1998:235; J. Ralph in Lee et al. 1990:87).

Grass also had a variety of uses. It was used to line meat storage pits, and (often in combination with moss) as a house insulating material (Anderson et al. 1998:305; C. Smith 1970). Grass was braided in long rows linked together to form a sleeping mat placed on top of the willow-covered floors. In some districts, grass was braided into baskets (Dinah Frankson 1980; Keats 1969.2). The Kiitaaġmiut and Siiḷviim Kaŋianiġmiut piled grass against a wooden frame in the spring to serve as a windbreak when sleeping out of doors (C. Smith 1970). Finally, dried grass was used as an insulating material in boots (Dall 1866–67; Dinah Frankson 1980; Seemann 1853, II:52).

This section concludes with lichens and fungi, which, although not exactly plants, are close enough for inclusion here. Birch fungus (*Polyporus aplanatum*), or *avaatchiqiq*, was used as a fire starter in emergencies and burned inside a house or tent as a mosquito repellent (Anderson et al. 1998:305). Reindeer lichen (*Cladonia rangiferina*), or *niqaaq*, was eaten as an emergency food (Anderson et al. 1998:306; E. and P. Attungana 1980). More generally, lichens were harvested, usually mixed with other vegetable products, in the form of the stomach contents of caribou; these were often eaten by people, who obtained a rich supply of vitamins in the process (Anore Jones 1983:130).

Minerals

Mineral resources may be broadly defined for present purposes as anything used by humans that comes from the earth. Materials that might be included under this heading range from igneous rock, which is formed deep within the planet, to soil, which is formed on or near the surface through the interaction of rocky material, vegetation, water, and air. Other possibilities include fossil plants and animals, and organic substances whose composition or appearance have been altered by geologic processes.

The Iñupiat did not use many minerals. However, they did employ as many as their technology allowed, and the uses to which they put them showed a sophisticated understanding of their physical properties. The Iñupiat evidently studied the landscape to see what it had to offer, and they experimented with everything they found to see how it might be usefully employed.

The Iñupiat did not create mines for the extraction of mineral resources. However, they were always on the lookout for suitable materials in the beds of streams or on rocky outcrops, and picked up potentially useful items as they were encountered. Deposits of high-quality materials of various kinds came to be well known over the generations, and at least some of them were used to such an extent that they developed into quarries. Larger pieces of rock found at the quarries were reduced to more manageable sizes by being smashed against one another or against some other kind of hard object. Further reduction was handled by processes discussed below in the section on manufactured goods.

Unfortunately, most of the traditional knowledge of geologic resources and their uses has been lost. With the advent of Western manufactured goods and materials in the mid-19th century, the need for many local mineral resources gradually declined, and so did the knowledge relating to their extraction and use. I failed to investigate the subject myself until the 1980s. I was fortunate to learn what I did, but the present treatment must be viewed as a very cursory coverage of a much larger subject. Hopefully, Iñupiat, archeologists, and geologists, working together, will be able to add to the material presented here.

The minerals I have learned about are listed below, along with what I have learned about what they are, where they can be found, the methods whereby they were extracted and modified, and the uses to which they were put. The various resources are listed in alphabetical order using English terms, where known, and Iñupiaq terms otherwise.[120]

Alugvik: *Alugvik* is a white rock that is not too hard. Mountain sheep apparently love to eat it. It is said that if a person puts some on his finger and tastes it, and repeats the act one or two times, that person's hunger is satisfied (A. Douglas 1989.1; L. Mills 1989).

Amber: Amber is a relatively hard, brittle fossil resin, usually yellowish to brownish in color, and translucent or transparent, that originated as sap in coniferous trees.[121] In Northwest Alaska it is found in widely scattered small pieces on the ocean beach or in streambeds, and it was also obtained in trade from people on the North Slope. Usually, pieces of amber are rounded due to wave or current action, which rolls them along the beach or stream bottom. The Iñupiat of Northwest Alaska drilled them and used them as beads. On the North Slope, pieces of amber were also used as charms: they were hung over the chest to prevent coughs, or sewn on to clothing to provide magical assistance in hunting. Amber might have had similar uses within the study region.

Chert: Chert (*aŋmaaq*) is a type of hard, extremely dense sedimentary rock that occurs primarily as a small lump, or nodule, in limestones and dolomites. In Northwest Alaska it is widely distributed as cobbles in streambeds and gravel bars, as well as in outcrops of bedrock.[122] In many districts suitable pieces were simply picked up from streambeds examined for the purpose during periods of low water. In other districts, specific deposits were quarried for this material. For example, Hall and Mull (1976) have described one chert quarry along a small tributary of the Kelly River, and Edwin S. Hall, Jr. (pers. comm. April 15, 1988) has found another, much larger and more heavily mined quarry near Wrench Creek, another tributary of the Kelly. Nodules in these localities are already loose or separated from the surrounding matrix. Native miners apparently simply picked out the best pieces, perhaps reduced them to blanks for ease of transport, and carried them home. The blanks were chipped or flaked later, as needed, to make arrow and spear points, scrapers, knives, gravers, and other tools. Pieces of chert were also struck against pyrite to start fires.

Clay: Clay is a very fine rock or mineral fragment or detrital particle of any composition. It forms a plastic, moldable mass when finely ground and mixed with water. Clay is discussed below under the headings *mamaqtaq*, *nuġġiġvik*, pottery clay, and *siaquya*.

Graphite: Graphite is a naturally occurring crystalline form of carbon; it is opaque, lustrous, greasy to the touch, and iron black to steel gray in color.[123] It occurs in veins or bedded masses in metamorphic rocks. Its distribution in Northwest Alaska has not been reported. Graphite was used by the Iñupiat as a lubricant for such things as bowstrings. Pieces of graphite were placed on the eyes of the deceased (Woolfe 1893:22). F. W. Beechey (1831, I:360) also reported that it was ground up, mixed on a piece of slate with a little saliva, and used to blacken the edges of women's eyelids.

Hematite: Hematite (*ivisaaq*), or red ocher, is a common iron mineral that occurs in a variety of forms, and is found in igneous, sedimentary, and metamorphic rocks. It has a distinctive cherry-red to reddish-brown color, and a characteristic brick-red color when ground into powder. It is the principal ore of iron. Deposits of hematite are scattered widely over Northwest Alaska. Pieces were broken (to keep them from exploding in the fire), heated in a fire, ground to powder, mixed with water, and used as paint.[124]

Iitaaq: *Iitaaq* is a rock that was ground into powder and used as a pigment to make black or blue-black paint (Lucier 1989). Just what type of mineral is involved is not known. It has been reported only from the Buckland district.

Kannuyaq: *Kannuyaq* is a kind of rock that resembles jade but which is softer (A. Douglas 1989.1; Hall 1988a; Jackson 1989; Clinton Swan 1984.1). Its composition and origin are unknown, although it might be copper. Its distribution in Northwest Alaska is also unknown, but it has been reported from the Kivalina, central Kobuk, and Selawik districts. It was used to make pipe bowls.

Kayułuk: *Kayułuk* is a cream-colored rock that is "hard," and that has a physical structure similar to a sponge ("lots of bubbles"); presumably it is pumice (S. Evok 1987). Its distribution in Northwest Alaska is not known, but apparently it is fairly widespread. It was used like sandpaper to soften skins after the scraping had been completed, and like a wood file in the early stages of smoothing wood to make arrow and spear shafts.

Kitik: *Kitik* occurs in deposits found in various localities throughout the study region.[125] Several deposits are located along the Kobuk River near Kiana, another is near Deering, and there are two near Wales, but there are apparently many others as well. Some rocks covered by this term consist of gypsum, while others are metalimestone fragments. A sample I sent to Susan Karl (1990), of the U.S. Geological Survey, proved to be calcareous sand (from limestone). No doubt any type of rock that is relatively soft and that can be smashed and ground to powder after first being heated in a fire was called by this term, regardless of its precise chemical nature.

Kitik was retrieved as pebbles, burned in a fire, then smashed and ground. It was used primarily in dressing skins, but it was also used to temper pottery.

Limestone: Limestone is a sedimentary rock wholly or primarily composed of calcium carbonate (D. Anderson 1988a). Many beds of limestone are ancient shell banks or coral reefs. Outcrops occur in many sectors of Northwest Alaska, and pieces can be found in streambeds and riverbeds. Limestone rocks were used to line hearths, and apparently also in dressing skins (see *kitik,* above).

Mamaqtaq: *Mamaqtaq* is a muddy substance that reportedly smells like caribou fat. It melts in the mouth, and is pleasant to taste. It was eaten from time to time. Sometimes it was consumed out of curiosity; at other times, it served the very serious purpose of keeping one's stomach juices working during a time of famine. *Mamaqtaq* has been reported only from the Selawik region.

Mammoth teeth: The remains of the Pleistocene cousins of modern elephants are relatively widespread in alluvial and beach deposits in Northwest Alaska, and they are occasionally washed out by wave or river action (D. Anderson 1988a; L. Mills 1989). They are not old enough to have become fossilized, but are often stained by chemicals in the soil. They were carved to make fishhooks and objects of personal adornment.

Marble: Marble is a metamorphic rock consisting predominantly of fine- to coarse-grained recrystallized calcite and/or dolomite, and is found in various places in Northwest Alaska. The Iñupiat used it to make labrets (Lucier 1989).

Nephrite: Nephrite (*isiŋnaq*) is an exceptionally tough, compact, fine-grained greenish or bluish rock that occurs in igneous and metamorphic rocks. It is the less rare, hence less valuable, kind of jade (the more valuable kind being jadeite). In Northwest Alaska, nephrite occurs only in the north-central Kobuk valley: as pebbles, cobbles, and boulders along several northern tributaries (e.g., Jade Creek, Shungnak River, and Dahl Creek) of the Kobuk

River, and as lode deposits in Jade Mountain.[126] There is also a locality just above Ambler where jade reportedly occurs in thin sheets. The central Kobuk is one of just three areas in the United States where nephrite is found (Loney and Himmelberg 1985).

The Iñupiat picked up pieces from streambeds, and ground and polished them to make adze blades, arrow- and spearheads, lance blades, maul heads, knife blades, whetstones, and labrets. Sheet nephrite was made into ulus (women's knives). Nephrite and objects made from it were an important item of international trade.

Nuġġiġvik: *Nuġġiġvik* is a soft white substance, either a very soft clay or a thick liquid, that oozes from the ground (P. and E. Atoruk 1989). It reportedly tastes good; people sometimes ate it just for fun. Taken in larger quantities, it served as a laxative. A deposit is located near "Coal Mine," along the Kobuk River a short distance above Kiana.

Obsidian: Obsidian (*salliñ*) is a black or dark-colored volcanic glass. It does not occur naturally within the study region, but was obtained in trade from Koyukon Indians living in the Koyukuk valley.[127] However, there is another rock with characteristics similar to those of obsidian and known by the same Iñupiaq name that is found in an outcrop on a little hill called Suqliirat, which is located between the southern end of the Kallarichak Hills and the Kobuk River. It is easy to find there after a rain because the wet rock glistens in the sun.

At various times in the prehistory of Northwest Alaska, obsidian was chipped or flaked to make arrow and spear points, although it was rarely used for these purposes in the 19th century. However, it was sometimes used to make lancet blades for therapeutic bloodletting.

Pottery clay: Deposits of clay suitable for making pottery (*qiku*) are found in banks of streams and rivers in many parts of Northwest Alaska, but the best material is said to come from the Buckland and lower Selawik districts.[128] Several deposits also occur in the central Kobuk valley; some are white, others are red, and a few are yellow.

The material was dug out of the bank with shovels, and used to make pots, bowls, and lamps. Clay was also packed around whole fish prior to its being baked in campfire coals.

Pyrite: Pyrite (*ikniñ*) is a common brassy yellow mineral; it is the most widespread and abundant of the sulfide minerals, and occurs in many kinds of rock. In Northwest Alaska, it is found in many outcrops in the mountains. The Iñupiat used to strike it against chert to produce a spark to start a fire (P. and E. Atoruk 1989; F. Beechey 1831, I:345, 360; D. Oktalik 1980).

Qauqtaq: *Qauqtaq/qaḷiñiq*, or "old ivory," is ancient walrus or mammoth ivory that is buried in the ground.[129] It is often stained by chemicals in the surrounding soil, but is not old enough to have become fossilized. Old walrus ivory is rare but present along the shores of Kotzebue Sound, and occasionally washes out on the beach. Mammoth ivory is much more widely distributed, and is frequently found in stream bottoms or projecting from riverbanks. Both types of ivory were carved to make labrets, fishhooks, handles, dippers, needles, and components of tools, utensils, weapons, and jewelry. Because of its distinctive color, old ivory was considered more valuable than new (walrus) ivory.

Qayuŋnilik: *Qayuŋnilik* is a hard crystalline rock similar to quartzite that is found on the surface in the Baird Mountains, where it is reported to be fairly common. It was used to make sharpening stones and labrets (P. and E. Atoruk 1989; A. Douglas 1989.1).

Quartzite: Quartzite (*qaummaḷuk?*) is very hard sandstone that occurs in both metamorphosed and unmetamorphosed forms. In the former case, it has been recrystallized by regional or thermal metamorphism; in the latter, the quartz grains have been so completely cemented with secondary silica that the rock breaks across or through the grains rather than around them. Pieces are common in the streambeds of Northwest Alaska, and deposits are exposed in outcrops in many districts.

During the study period pieces of quartzite were used in many districts as cooking rocks.[130] They were heated in a fire and then placed in a water-filled wooden or birch-bark container, where they heated the water without damaging the container. The first set of rocks got the water boiling; after the addition of a second or third set, the meat was cooked. Quartzite was especially useful for this purpose because it does not explode or fracture when placed in a hot fire. People sometimes also heated rocks before putting out the fire, since they retained their heat for some time afterward. Quartzite was also used occasionally to scrape skins.

Sand: Sand (*qaviaq*), which is usually composed of finely ground quartz, is widely distributed along the streams and rivers of Northwest Alaska, along the beaches in the western sector of Kotzebue Sound, and along the northern shore of the Seward Peninsula. It was used as a grinding material in the manufacture of slate and jade tools, to temper pottery, and to remove hair from skins (P. and E. Atoruk 1989; D. Oktalik 1980).

Sandstone: Sandstone (*siuġaq?*) is a medium-grained clastic sedimentary rock composed of abundant rounded or angular fragments of sand set in a matrix and more or less firmly united by a cementing material. It is found along many streambeds, and in rock outcrops in many parts of Northwest Alaska. It served as a whetstone for grinding and sharpening knives and spear points (D. Anderson 1988a; Giddings 1961:143–44; 1967:305, 312; Lucier 1989). In some districts sandstone was the primary material out of which lamps were made.

Schist: Schist is any strongly foliated crystalline metamorphic rock that can be readily split into thin flakes or slabs. The Iñupiat used thin, evenly shaped slabs of schist to cut (by sawing) other types of mineral, such as slate and jade, and presumably such other hard substances as ivory (Giddings 1967:312; Lucier 1989).

Serpentine: Serpentines form a group of minerals that are derived by the alteration of magnesium-rich silicate minerals, and are found in both metamorphic and igneous rocks. There are outcrops of serpentine along the Kobuk River, and along the appropriately named Serpentine River, in the Shishmaref district. The rock was occasionally used to make lamps (Lucier 1989).

Siaquya: Siaquya (*sikuyuk?*) is evidently a type of clay. Its precise composition is unknown, as is its distribution within Northwest Alaska. It has been reported from the Selawik and central Kobuk districts, and from a locality just below the mouth of upper Noatak Canyon. The raw material was dried, ground to powder, mixed with seal oil, and rubbed on boat seams as waterproofing (Anderson et al. 1998:306; NANA Cultural Heritage Project, Selawik 1975g: sites G3 and H4). It was also used as paint.

Slate: Slate (*ulugraq*) is a compact, fine-grained metamorphic rock that can be split into slabs and thin plates. Most slate was formed from shale. In some sectors of the study region, such as the Point Hope district, outcrops are common; in others, such as the central Kobuk district, they are absent. People living in the latter district acquired slate through trade. The Iñupiat pried slabs of slate out of the matrix, and cut, ground, and polished them to make knives, spearheads and arrowheads, fine-grained whetstones, and scrapers.[131]

Sod: Sod, or turf, consists of the upper layer of soil bound by grass or other plant roots into a thick mat. During the study period it was cut into blocks and stacked over the outside of wooden winter house frames in many districts to serve as insulation (Lucier 1989). Sod was also used to bank ground-level or subterranean food caches, and as a foundation for campfires made on the ice at spring seal-hunting camps.

Stones: Unmodified or slightly modified stones were used in a variety of ways (Anderson et al. 1998:306; S. Dives 1970; Lucier 1989; T. Mitchell 1969). The following list is a sample:

- Small round stones were used as sinkers for gill nets, seines, and fishing lines; makeshift whetstones; sling projectiles; bolas stones; hammers; and in juggling games.
- A weight-graded series of oblong stones was used in weight-lifting contests and in general physical conditioning.
- Medium-sized round or tabular stones were used to hold down the bases of tents.
- Relatively small but variably sized rounded stones usually found in streams were drilled and made into spinning tops.
- Medium-sized tabular stones were used in the construction of deadfall traps for fur-bearing animals.
- Medium-sized to large tabular stones were used to construct meat caches and underfloor vaults for the safekeeping of valuable items. In some areas they were used to construct house floors, and, in localities where wood was hard to come by, the walls of houses.
- Medium-sized to large stones, both tabular and round, were used to construct cairns. Cairns were occasionally used as guideposts, but were more frequently used as "scarecrows" along the wings of caribou drive fences and in the corral at the ends of those fences. Similar stones were also used in some districts to construct above-ground graves.
- In districts where people used an open fire in the main living area for heating rocks and cooking, the fire pit, or hearth, was lined with flat rocks.
- Hafted to a wooden handle, stones served as clubs to kill wounded animals.

Sukisaġnaq: *Sukisaġnaq* is some kind of rock that was ground and polished to make arrowheads. Its distribution in the study region is unknown; it has been reported only from the Kotzebue district.

Talc: Talc is an extremely soft, light green or gray mineral with a characteristic soapy or greasy feel; it is easily cut with a knife. In English it is often referred to as soapstone. Deposits occur in the Jade Mountains and Cosmos Hills, just north of the Kobuk River, and on the eastern Seward Peninsula (Grybeck 1977; Till 1990; Till et al. 1986). At least one deposit is also reported in the lower Noatak valley. Most of the soapstone used in northern Alaska was imported from Canada, however (Kingik 1980; D. Oktalik 1980).

Talc is so soft that it is easily weathered, and will not form knobs or peaks; consequently, it is often difficult to locate. This fact, along with its restricted distribution in the study region, kept it from being extensively used. However, in both the Kobuk and Buckland districts it was carved into seal-oil lamps (Foote 1965b; L. Gallahorn 1969.2; Sunno 1951.112). Along the Kobuk River lamps were always hidden when winter houses were vacated for the summer (R. Cleveland 1965.4), with the result that many of the lamps that were made and used there have not been found in archeological excavations.

Tinaakatiisruuk: *Tinaakatiisruuk* is a slate-like rock that outcrops on the lower Pah River. It was used as a sharpening stone for knives (Anderson et al. 1998).

Liquids

The Iñupiat made use of a limited number of liquid resources. These may be usefully grouped under the following headings: water, urine, blood, saliva, hot springs, and mineral springs. Sea mammal oil, which is also a liquid, and which was of major importance in the economy, is discussed in several other sections of this chapter.

Water

The Iñupiat identified three basic types of water: *taġiuq*, or saltwater; *imaq*, or unpotable water (usually brackish); and *imiq*, or freshwater. The only use of saltwater that I have heard of was to bathe wounds (Gregg, in Northwest Iñupiat Elders Conference 1983g), and its use was of course restricted to people living on the seashore. Freshwater had a much wider variety of uses.

Freshwater is abundant in much of northwestern Alaska, but not always in a form that readily lends itself to human consumption, and not necessarily at all times of year. For more than half of the year, much of the freshwater is locked up in the form of ice or snow. Even during the period of open water, rivers and streams are often fouled with dirt and debris, such as during breakup in spring and rainy periods in summer. Some ponds apparently contained microscopic organisms that cause stomach or intestinal problems ("beaver fever") and had to be avoided.

Twentieth-century Iñupiat always impressed me with their desire for high-quality drinking water, and I presume that their 19th-century ancestors were similarly particular. Because of their year-round high-protein diet, the dryness of the air during cold weather, and the general lack of alternatives, they drank a great deal of it.[132]

In summer, especially when the water level was low, good drinking water was easily obtained by people living along rivers and streams; all they had to do was go out and scoop it up. For people hunting in or traveling through hills and mountains, however, water was often a problem, particularly late in the season, after the previous winter's snow had melted. Their solution was to make canteens out of caribou or seal stomachs, bladders, or seal flippers, and take water with them. This enabled them to travel in areas where they otherwise would have had some difficulty.

In winter, people living inland cut holes in river ice, keeping them open as long as they could. They often erected small snow houses over the holes, or else placed a block of snow over the hole, which kept the water from freezing over as quickly or as thickly as it otherwise might (Iviqsiq 1940).

If water was unavailable, ice was preferred over snow as a source, since snow contains countless tiny pockets of air and shrinks dramatically when heated. Snow can also be scorched if heated too fast, which imparts an unpleasant taste to the water. For a given quantity of water, a much greater volume of snow than ice must be collected, and snow is usually more difficult to transport than ice. Both snow and ice were normally melted simply by being kept for awhile in a watertight container inside the house. However, people in more of a hurry placed heated rocks in pots containing snow or ice. In camps located away from sources of water or ice, water was acquired by placing a hard mass of snow on a stick leaning over a watertight container near the flames of an open fire (Giddings 1961:137).

In many coastal areas freshwater was a precious commodity in both summer and winter. In some places, such as Wales, springs and streams on the nearby hillside and behind the village provided what was needed.[133] At Point Hope and Shishmaref, on the other hand, it was often necessary either to melt snow or to travel some distance to get suitable ice (Jensen 1970.1, 1970.2; Kowunna 1970). Men hunting out on the sea ice in all coastal districts had a major problem, since cold air is very dry and freshwater ice was rarely available; it was snow, saltwater ice, or nothing. Consequently, hunters on the ice frequently suffered from dehydration. The observations made by U.S. Navy personnel stationed at Barrow in 1881–82 are pertinent in this regard:

> as the season advanced and water became scarce we were daily besieged by the
> seal hunters coming in from the sea and begging for a drink of water, of which
> there is great scarcity after the frost has sealed up all sources of supply. The scarcity
> of fuel, together with their inadequate means for melting ice and snow, causes
> them to suffer under a constant water famine from October to July (P. Ray 1988:
> lxxv–lxxvi; see also Bockstoce ed. 1988, I:222; Seemann 1853, II:60).

The situation for seal hunters in the Point Hope, Shishmaref, and Wales districts must have
been much the same as Ray described for Barrow.

Over the course of the winter, the salt in sea ice percolates downward, with the result
that the upper layers of ice gradually become fresh and can be melted for drinking water. In
late spring, when the ice begins to melt, pools of freshwater form on the ice surface; as long
as the ice remains, drinking water is abundant along the coast.

Many coastal areas also had a shortage of freshwater in summer, particularly on barrier
beaches such as those on the northern shore of the Seward Peninsula, and along much of
the coast between Kotzebue Sound and Point Hope. Many of the smaller coastal lagoons
contained freshwater during the spring thaw and breakup, but became brackish later in the
season. In some areas, one could get freshwater by digging a well in the sand (F. Beechey 1831,
I:383; A. Hawley 1965.3); Jensen 1970.1). In other areas, freshwater ponds provided what was
needed, although they frequently dried up if not replenished periodically by rain.

Cold water was the primary liquid consumed by the Iñupiat. Water was also the primary
medium in which food was cooked. Meat and fish were often eaten raw and/or frozen, but
when cooked, they were usually prepared in water made hot by heated stones.[134] The leftover
water was usually consumed also, but the cooking was so light that it rarely constituted a broth
(Glover 1970.3, 1970.4). Bones and other body parts were frequently boiled to render the fat
they contained; as the water cooled, the fat rose to the surface and congealed; it could then be
skimmed off and eaten, stored, or used as lamp fuel (Iviqsiq 1940; T. Mitchell 1969). Finally,
water was used in cleaning and otherwise preparing skins for various uses, and for softening
sealskins or caribou hides to be made into boat covers (Wells and Kelly 1890:26).

Water was also required for dogs. In winter, dogs usually looked after themselves by
eating snow, although in bitterly cold, dry weather they sometimes needed to have some of
the liquid form provided to them. In summer, dogs did not need to be fed too often unless
they were working (which they often were), but they were often in desperate need of water.
They tolerated a wider range of water quality than people did, but nevertheless had to be
provided for much of the time by people living or traveling along the coast or crossing a
range of hills or mountains.

Urine

Human urine had a number of important uses. It was the primary liquid used for bathing,
although bathing was not frequently indulged in.[135] Urine was collected in a special container,
which was simply a wooden pot kept inside the main house or an alcove off the entrance
tunnel. It was used by both men and women "without the slightest approach to reserve"
(Woolfe 1893:144; see also F. Beechey 1831, I:407; Murdoch 1892:420–21). The urine pot
differed from the chamber pot, in which feces were also deposited, and whose contents were
thrown out on a regular basis.

One particularly crucial time urine was used was in washing newborn babies (Stoney
ms:127–28; Woolfe 1893:136). As Woolfe (1893:136) noted, "this ablution was about the only

one that the natives of some villages ever received throughout their lives." In the absence of soap, urine was the only liquid the Iñupiat had that could cut seal oil.

Urine was also used in treating skins to be made into clothing (Murdoch 1892:300; Nelson 1899:116, 117; Spencer 1959:57). Sealskins, for example, were soaked in urine to remove the fat adhering to them, although scraping was required to complete the job. Similarly, the flesh sides of caribou hides and the skins of other animals were wetted with urine prior to being scraped clean of meat and fat.

Urine was an important element in the manufacture of goods out of bone, antler, and ivory. The material was soaked thoroughly in urine to soften it, and was frequently wetted with urine during the manufacturing process (Nelson 1899:196).

Finally, urine was placed around cuts, where it was intended to act as an astringent and as an antiseptic (Hild 1983). It may have worked in the latter capacity, but was probably counterproductive in the former.

Saliva

To most readers, human saliva might seem like even less of a raw material than human urine. However, certain important uses should be mentioned: these were primarily in magical procedures performed by shamans. Some examples from my field notes will show how it was both produced and consumed.

The first example was supplied by Edith Kennedy, a person of Nuataaġmiut ancestry whose family used to go to Point Hope to work for the American whalers there in the 1890s, when she was a little girl. One year they were attending the whaling festival. Edith's father, Aqsiataq, was sitting next to a little old man, who was evidently a shaman, and they were having a conversation.

> Her father told him that Edith was a rather sickly little girl. So, the little old man told her to stick her feet straight up. He took some of his saliva and rubbed it around on the bottom of her foot. That's all he did. Shortly thereafter she started to get better, and stayed that way (Kennedy 1965.2).

Kennedy died in 1992, just a few months short of her 100th birthday.

The second example was provided by Tommy Sage (1965.1), who was technically Edith's nephew, but who in fact was a few months older than she was. He was also of Nuataaġmiut ancestry, but was living in Kivalina at the time of this event. It was late June when people noticed a large piece of ice drifting past with hundreds of walrus on it. Tommy's boat was the first to get there. Suddenly the water around the boat was full of very angry walrus, and the men began to fear for their lives. But a noted Kivalliñiġmiut shaman, Kukik, was at the helm. He spit on his hand and rubbed it along the side of the boat, and that kept the walrus from harming them.

These examples show the usual way that saliva was used for magical purposes: the shaman spit on his hand or a finger and rubbed it on the object or person needing protection or a cure. Sometimes, however, one spit a greater distance. For example, when a crew struck a whale, the captain spit into the water to make his magic song (intended to kill the whale) go down into the water to where the fleeing whale was located (Aġviqsiiña 1940.1:52; Rainey 1947:260). And when a hunter on the frozen ocean heard the ice cracking around him, he spat to both the left and right to protect himself (J. Killiguvuk 1959.2).

Blood

As hunters of caribou and sea mammals, the Iñupiat had access to large quantities of blood (F. Beechey 1831, I:343–44; Glover 1970.3, 1970.4; Woolfe 1893:140). If their ancestors were anything like the women I saw butchering caribou or seals in the late 20th century, they rarely wasted a drop of it. Blood was kept in wooden or pottery containers, or bags made out of caribou stomachs. It was made into a nutritious soup (*qayuq*), often mixed with oil.

Hot Springs

Hot springs (*uunaqtuat*) are found within northwestern Alaska on the Reed River (a tributary of the Kobuk), near the head of the Selawik River, and near the head of the Serpentine River in the Shishmaref district. They were used for therapeutic, hygienic, and recreational purposes.[136] Hot water has a beneficial effect on sore muscles and aching joints. This fact was well known to the Iñupiat who, when suffering from aches and pains, immersed themselves in hot springs where the temperature was not too severe. The springs, which never freeze, also provided a welcome source of winter water to big game as well as to human travelers.

Travelers sometimes cooked food in a hot spring simply by immersing meat in it for awhile. My sources contended that, from time to time, hunters cooked ptarmigan in the Upper Division Hot Springs, which is located near the head of the Selawik River. They placed whole birds in the water, weighed down with rocks, and hauled them out—cooked—about fifteen minutes later.

Mineral Springs

"Mineral spring" is my translation of the Iñupiaq word *mamaiḷaq*.[137] It has been described to me as a yellowish-orange, malodorous liquid that oozes out of the ground, discoloring the adjacent soil or snow, and any water into which it flows. Springs producing this liquid have been reported to me from the western part of the Igichuk Hills (on Mamelak Mountain), and the upper Wulik River, in the Kivalina district. The liquid was consumed, often mixed with seal oil, as a laxative. Only a small quantity was required to purge the system.

Manufactured Goods

Manufactured goods are all goods modified by human activities for human purposes from a raw material state (Levy 1966:233). For example, berries that are eaten directly upon being picked are not manufactured goods. "Eskimo ice cream" made from mixing uncooked berries with whipped tallow *is* a manufactured good. Willow branches cut from shrubs are raw materials, but tent frames or weirs made from such branches are manufactured goods.

A given raw material often passes through a series of stages in the manufacturing process, such as when the hide is removed from a caribou carcass, and successively dried, scraped, cut, and sewed into a garment; at each step of the way, it is a bit more manufactured than it was before. The first steps in the manufacturing process of many goods were described in the previous section. In this section, I pick up the various processes and take them to their conclusion. It should be noted that there was some variation in manufacturing techniques from one nation to another, depending partly on differences in local tradition, and partly on the differential availability of particular materials. A detailed discussion of this variation is beyond the scope of the present study.

My research in northwestern Alaska rarely focused on traditional manufacturing processes, with the result that I cite rather few elders as sources of my information here. Fortunately, others filled in the gap, and their reports are my primary sources on many items.[138]

Tools

A tool is a good that is employed in the deliberate modification of one or more other goods (cf. Levy 1966:12). A large number and variety of objects can be classified as tools.[139] John Driggs (1905), the first missionary at Point Hope, listed some of the possibilities:

> The first knives were of flint, jade and slate; the boring tools of flint; the adze of jade; hammers were made mostly from jade and wedges from bone; white flint was used to saw the jade, and the brown variety was employed for tools. The women's knives were largely of slate, but sometimes of jade, and their needles of ivory or bone (Driggs 1905:95–96).

Some tools, such as arrow shaft straighteners, were highly specialized, while others, such as drills, had a variety of applications. In order to simplify the presentation, this section focuses on tools having a wide range of uses. More specialized tools are discussed in later sections where their significance is more apparent.

For Work in Stone

The tools used in making implements of stone varied according to the type of rock involved and the implement's purpose. In all cases, however, the raw material either had to be discovered in a size in which it could be easily handled, or it had to be reduced to a manageable size by being smashed against other rocks; or it could be fragmented with a hammerstone (which was usually unhafted when used in this context). In being reduced by a hammerstone, the rock to be broken was usually held in the left hand, which was protected by a leather guard, and the hammerstone was struck against it (Murdoch 1892:287; Sunno 1951.95). The resulting blank was then modified by one or a combination of three basic processes: pecking, flaking, and grinding.

Pecking involved the repeated striking of one rock against another, or the more precise technique of striking it with a hammer and chisel (Booth 1960.2; Giddings 1952:78; Nelson 1899:91). It was usually used to shape coarse rocks, such as sandstone, or smoother material, such as talc, that does not lend itself to flaking. A small, sometimes tiny, piece of the subject rock was removed with each blow. Through lengthy repetition, the object eventually acquired its desired shape. The process was relatively crude, and was employed primarily either to rough-shape items that were later finished by grinding, or in the production of such large items as hammerstones, adzes, and lamps, which were difficult to produce by grinding and flaking. It was also employed to make lashing grooves in adze heads, mattock blades, and other large tools, and in stone sinkers for nets.

Flaking was employed in work with very hard, brittle rock, such as the various materials commonly known as flint—or, more accurately, chert—which can be reduced systematically only by concoidal fracture. The tool used to do this was the flaker, or flaking tool.[140] This consisted of a short, straight rod, or bit, of a hard material, such as bone, iron, or antler, fitted into a deep groove drilled in the end of a (usually) curved wooden or ivory handle, and held there by a simple lashing. An example of a flaker is shown in Figure 23. This particular one consisted of an antler grip to which a bone blade was lashed with sealskin twine.

The material to be shaped was held in the left hand and pressed against the palm, which was covered by a thick mitten or piece of leather for protection. The flaker was grasped well forward in the right hand with the thumb on top of the blade, and pressed firmly and steadily against the edge of the blank. This made flakes of the desired size break off from the under surface. Alternatively, the blank was held in a groove cut in a log, which served more or less as a vise. This procedure was repeated, moving back and forth from one side of the blank to another, until the implement reached the desired shape. Products of this technique included arrow points, lance heads, drill bits, and a variety of scrapers.

FIGURE 23. A flaking tool. The original was about seven inches (18 cm) long. From Murdoch (1892:289).

Grinding involved the patient rubbing of the subject rock back and forth, or in a rotary motion, against a coarse rock, a sandy surface, or a relatively smooth rock covered with fine sand that progressively wore away its outer layers (Giddings 1967:305, 312). As the object approached its desired form, progressively less coarse grinding material was employed so as to produce a smoother finish. The process was particularly useful in the shaping of slate and jade, neither of which can be worked by flaking. Both materials were often split with a wedge prior to being ground (Giddings 1952:64).

The grinding process was also used to hone the edges of slate and jade tools, except that the grinding surface employed was much smoother than the one used in basic shaping. The primary tool here was the whetstone (*ipiksaun*), which could be made of any hard, fine-grained material.[141] Indeed, it could consist of merely a river or beach pebble of the appropriate texture, but most people preferred high-quality jade or slate implements specifically shaped for the purpose. A whetstone was often drilled so that a line could be run through it for attachment to the owner's belt.

An interesting way to polish jade was sometimes used by the Akuniġmiut (A. Douglas 1989.1; Giddings 1967:312–13). They tied the partly shaped stone to the end of a stick that had a flattened area at the opposite end. They tied the stick to a long line, with the flattened end facing upstream, and anchored it above a sandbar in a swift, shallow section of the river. The current made the stick, hence the jade, move back and forth, and the weight of the tool kept it against the sand's surface.

A special form of grinding was performed with a stone "saw."[142] A saw was usually a narrow slab of schist that was drawn back and forth across jade, slate, ivory, bone, antler, or wood, wearing a progressively deeper groove into the material, eventually cutting through it. In essence, it was a grinding tool that did its work along a very narrow plane. According to Driggs (1905:95–96), flaked chert blades also were used to saw jade. Stefansson (1914b:393) confirmed this, and added that the chert blade was periodically dipped in water and then in dry sand when used for this purpose. By the early 19th century, some toothed metal saws of foreign manufacture had arrived in Northwest Alaska; as they became more numerous, they replaced the cruder saws of traditional design.

For Work in Ivory, Antler, and Bone

Ivory (both walrus and mammoth), antler, and bone were softened prior to being shaped by being soaked in urine or hot water, a procedure that was repeated several times during the modification process (Driggs 1905:94; Nelson 1899:80, 196). Then, depending on the size and shape of the object being made, the material was cut laterally with a stone saw, scored with an engraving tool or chisel, and/or split longitudinally with wedges. The end result of these processes was usually a blank. This was then shaped more precisely by being carved with a stone or metal knife, etched, rubbed against a grindstone, and/or drilled. An enormous number and variety of objects were made of these materials. Antler and ivory were also important as components of larger implements, whose other components were wood and/or stone. Just to show how effective these tools were for working in such a hard substance as ivory, I cite an example reported from Point Barrow by John Simpson, in the winter of 1854. An Iñupiaq friend of his named Iqsiñġa was in desperate need of a piece of walrus tusk for one of his crew members. Simpson gave him a tusk one day and got it back the next. In the meantime, Iqsiñġa had

> taken off as much as he wanted, which was about one third divided lengthwise and effected very regularly with only a knife in a way a saw could not be applied in consequence of the natural curve of the [tusk] (Simpson 1852–54: entries for Feb. 13 and 14, 1854).

The virtuosity of Iñupiaq carvers was illustrated by their ability to make a chain out of a solid piece of ivory (F. Beechey 1831, II:310; Bockstoce 1977:90; Simpson 1850b: entry for Jan. 18, 1850).

For Work in Wood

Most of the wood used by the Iñupiat was driftwood collected from either the beach or a riverbank, as noted earlier. Thick logs were cut by being burned through with a carefully focused fire.[143] From there, the wood was split with chisels or wedges driven with mauls, and shaped with adzes.[144]

An adze (*ulimaun*) is a wood-cutting tool in which the blade is set at a right angle to the handle.[145] It was used for cutting along the grain rather than across it. There were two basic types: those in which the blade was lashed directly to the handle, and those in which the blade was inserted into a head that was lashed to the handle. A small example of the former, with a handle only four inches (10 cm) long, is shown in Figure 24.

Adze blades were made of a hard material, such as jade, fine-grained schist, serpentine, metal, or antler. They were flattened on the bottom for hafting, and scored above for lashing. Handles, usually made of wood, but sometimes of antler or bone, were drilled with one or more holes at the upper end to receive the lashing.

A maul (*kautaq*) is a heavy hammer. In northwestern Alaska, mauls were used for driving wedges, pounding stakes, crushing bones, and various other purposes.[146] Some mauls had heads made of ground and polished hard stone, while others had heads made from beach or river pebbles modified just enough to be lashed onto the end of a wooden handle. Some had heads of heavy bone, while a few were carved out of a solid piece of ivory or wood. Two examples are shown in Figure 25.

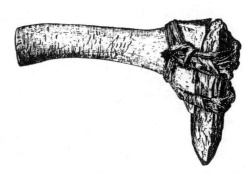

FIGURE 24. An adze with an antler handle and a jade blade. From Murdoch (1892:168).

The upper one had a 7.2-inch (18.3 cm) handle of hardwood, the lower one an antler handle about 4.7 inches (11.9 cm) long. The heads of both tools were lashed to the haft with sealskin twine.

Wedges were made of wood, bone, antler, and ivory, and were used for major splitting operations (Giddings 1952:64, 78; Nelson 1899:88). Chisels were usually made out of bone or stone, shaped with spatulate working ends, and a bone handle made to fit into the palm of the hand.[147] They often had a hole drilled in them to receive a thong so that they could be hung from the owner's belt. They were used to incise grooves in wood in preparation for splitting with a wedge, and for finer shaping of wood after coarse reduction by an adze.

For still finer work in wood a whittling knife was employed. This tool was the so-called "curved" or "crooked" knife (*mitlik*). Its form and use were succinctly described by Murdoch (1892).

> The knife consisted of a small blade, set on the under side of the end of a long curved haft, so that the edge, which is beveled only on the upper face, projects about as much as that of a spokeshave. The curve of blade and haft is such that when the under surface of the blade rests against the surface to be cut the end of the haft points up at an angle of about 45%.... The knife is held close to the blade between the index and second fingers of the right hand with the thumb over the edge, which is toward the workman. The workman draws the knife toward him, using his thumb as a check to gauge the depth of the cut. The natives use these knives with very great skill, taking off long and very even shavings and producing very neat workmanship (Murdoch 1892:157; see also Thornton 1931:139; VanStone 1976:20; 1980:41).

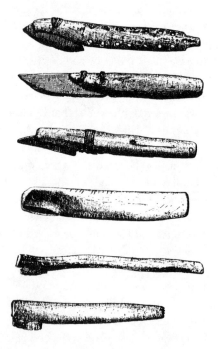

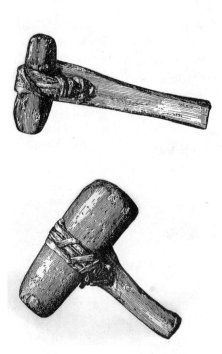

FIGURE 25. Two examples of stone mauls. From Murdoch (1892:95).

FIGURE 26. Some examples of "crooked" knives. The top two had slate blades, the middle two had metal blades, and the bottom two had flint blades. All of the handles were about six inches (15 cm) long. From Murdoch (1892:159, 160, 161).

Some examples of crooked knives are shown in Figure 26.

During the early 19th century, the blades of most crooked knives were made from imported metal. Handles were variously made from bone, antler, or wood. This knife was "the principal tool used in fashioning and finishing a great variety of boxes, dishes, trays, tubs, spear-shafts, bows, arrows, and frames for umiaks, kaiaks, sledges, and other woodwork" (Nelson 1899:85). Another tool used to finish long pieces of wood was a two-handed scraper made from caribou leg bone, which was used in the manner of a spokeshave (Giddings 1952:77).

Grooves and hollows were made in wood with a gouging tool made from a beaver's incisor set into a wooden handle, the so-called "beaver tooth" tool (Giddings 1952:78; Nelson 1899:89; VanStone 1976:21). Holes were made with bow drills (Giddings 1952:78; Nelson 1899:89; VanStone 1976:21). F. Beechey (1831, II:310) noted that there were a variety of other tools for work in wood, including "instruments for breaking wood short off," but he did not describe them.

For Work in Skins

Work in skins was initiated with knives, which were used to remove the hide from the carcass and in subsequent shaping. If the cutting was done by a male, it was usually with a knife (*savik*) having an oblong blade of slate or iron, sometimes of chert or jade, fastened onto the end of a wood or antler handle, or placed between two pieces of wood wrapped around with cords of baleen or rawhide.[148] These knives resembled modern sheath knives, and were, indeed, often carried in leather sheaths. Two examples of knives with slate blades hafted with caribou sinew to wooden handles are shown in Figure 27.

If the cutting was done by a woman, it was usually, perhaps invariably, done with an ulu.[149] This was a knife made from slate, shale, or iron that was flat on one edge, and curved, crescent, or semi-lunar in shape on the other. A wooden, bone, or ivory handle was affixed to the flat edge. The blade, on the curved edge, was beveled. Examples of ulus are shown in Figure 28.

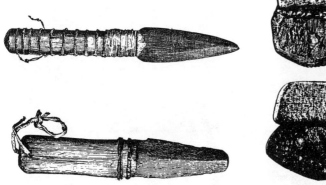

FIGURE 27. Examples of slate-bladed knives. The lower one had a haft four inches (10 cm) long and a blade three inches (7.6 cm) long. The upper one had a haft five inches (12.7 cm) long and a blade 3.5 inches (8.9 cm) long. From Murdoch (1892:151).

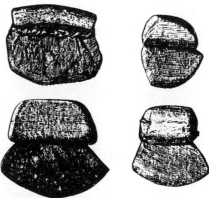

FIGURE 28. Women's knives, or ulus. The one on the upper right had a wooden handle, while the others had antler handles. All of the blades were made from slate. The blades ranged from 2.25 inches (5.7 cm) to 3.75 inches (9.5) in width. From Murdoch (1892:162).

Residues of flesh and fat were removed from hides with ulus; the hides were then softened with a series of scrapers.[150] For preliminary work, a bone or ivory scraper with a sharpened edge was used. Sometimes a small oblong ivory cup with a sharpened edge on one end was used for this purpose; in addition to scraping particles off the skin, the cup retained any accompanying oil for other uses. The second phase was performed with a two-bladed scraper made from caribou leg bone from which a lateral piece was removed and the resulting edges sharpened. The third step was performed with a scraper made from a circular, pipe-shaped piece of metal fitted onto a short wooden handle. The final phase of scraping and particularly softening was done with a blunt-end scraper made from chipped flint hafted onto a handle of wood or ivory. With the third and fourth types of scraper, the skin was placed across the worker's left thigh, and the tool was grasped firmly with the right hand and pushed away from the worker. Scraper handles were precisely shaped to fit comfortably into the hand of a specific individual (Brower ms:243). An example is shown in Figure 29.

Other primary tools used in skin work consisted of bodkins and needles. A bodkin (*kapun*) was an implement with a wood, bone, or ivory handle at the end of which a very sharp point of metal, ivory, jade, or flint was inserted. Bodkins were used to punch holes in the hide through which thread was then drawn with triangular-shaped needle (*quagrulik*) made of bone or ivory.[151] Accessories included thimbles (usually made of hide), thimble holders, cases for needle storage, and combs used to pull the hair from caribou skins (Keats 1960.3; Nelson 1899:109; VanStone 1980:47–48).

For Work in Soil

The Iñupiat had to work in soil to build semisubterranean houses, excavate cache pits and cold storages, and to dig roots. Their primary digging tools were the pick (*sikḷyaq*) and the mattock (*ulimaun*). These consisted of a wooden handle to one end of which was lashed a pointed (pick) or broad-bladed (mattock) piece of bone, ivory, or jade.[152] A root pick was simply a smaller version of a pick. A mattock is illustrated in Figure 30.

Picks and mattocks were used to loosen the soil, if thawed, or cut it into blocks, if frozen. In the former case, loose soil was removed with a shovel (*piksrun*), which was usually made from wood tipped with bone or ivory, or a broad bone taken from a whale.[153] In the latter case, blocks were pried out with poles or cut out with picks and removed intact.

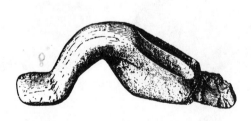

FIGURE 29. A skin scraper with a flint blade and a handle of old ivory. The original tool was slightly more than five inches (12.7 cm) long. From Murdoch (1892:297).

FIGURE 30. A mattock with a whale-rib blade hafted with oogruk rope to a 24.5-inch (62.2 cm) pine handle. From Murdoch (1892:303).

Drills

Drills were used to make holes in bone, ivory, antler, jade, slate, and wood.[154] Drills have been mentioned several times in earlier sections, but it is appropriate to describe them here. The drill (*pattaq*) consisted of a wooden shank (*siku*) into the end of which a sharpened bit of metal or very hard stone was inserted. The opposite end of the shank fit into a bone or ivory socket set in a wooden mouthpiece (*kiŋmiaq*), which the operator held between his teeth (see Figure 31).

A drill was powered by a bow (*pattaqtuun*) made from a curved piece of wood, bone, or ivory, and a leather thong, the latter being wrapped two or three times around the shank. The operator held the bit against the object to be drilled with the mouthpiece, and rotated the shank by drawing the bow back and forth. A workman could operate the drill with one hand and his teeth, the other hand being free to hold the object being drilled. Some drills were larger and were worked by two men, one holding the bit in place, the other drawing the bow; these were used in making large holes in boat and sled frames. According to Thornton (1931:151), one could hardly drill wood faster with a modern brace and bit. Jade, however, was not so easily dealt with. That material was drilled very slowly, with sand being used to augment the cutting power of the drill, the shank being sprayed with water to keep it from overheating (Weyer 1928: Wales).

Some drills were designed to make fires. For this purpose, the shank was made of hardwood sharpened to some extent at the working end and not fitted with a bit. It was held against a drill bearing, which was a piece of softer wood on the margin of which small holes had been cut to receive the sharpened end of the shank. By rotating the shank, the worker created intense heat. This eventually produced a glowing ember in the moss or other flammable material held against the drill bearing. By blowing gently on this ember, the operator induced the flame to spread.

Another type of drill was powered by pumping rather than by drawing a bow. It had two crosspieces through which the shank was inserted. The lower crosspiece was fixed in position, although the shank was free to rotate within it, and was used to hold the shank in place. The upper crosspiece could be moved up and down. A cord was attached to each end of the upper crosspiece, and coiled around the shank. Moving the upper crosspiece in a rapid up-and-down motion caused the shank to rotate. This type of drill was apparently used primarily to start fires (VanStone 1976:22, 87).

FIGURE 31. A bow drill and mouthpiece made from spruce, and a spruce shank with a bone ferrule held on with two bone pegs. The bit was made from steel. From Murdoch (1892:176).

Clothing

Iñupiaq clothing was made from skins. The most commonly used material was caribou hide, but ringed seal, oogruk, dog, fox, wolf, mountain sheep, marmot, ground squirrel, beaver, otter, muskrat, marten, otter, lynx, hare, mink, duck, and fish skins, as well as seal and oogruk intestines (for rain gear), were also employed, either as the basic material out of which the garment was made, or as trim.[155] Thread was made of sinew, usually, but by no means exclusively, from caribou. The sinew was dried, shredded into very thin strips with a special instrument resembling a comb, and spliced together for this purpose (Driggs 1905:98; D. Naylor 1960.5; VanStone 1980:45; 1990:15).

To be made into clothing, skins went through a complex process of being scraped as clean of fat and oil as possible; then successively soaked in urine, water, or fish broth; scraped again; and dried.[156] The process was repeated a number of times, but with a series of progressively smoother scrapers and eventually the application of the pulverized white rock known as *kitik*, until the material was soft and pliable enough to serve its intended purpose. Then the skins were measured, cut with an *ulu* to the appropriate size and shape, and sewn with bodkins and needles. Sometimes the flesh side of land-mammal hides was colored with a reddish dye made from alder bark (E. and P. Attungana 1980; O. Knox 1984; Northwest Iñupiat Elders Conference 1976d:12). Alternatively, skins—especially sealskins—could be bleached almost white through a process of alternately wetting and freezing.[157] The oogruk- or walrus-skin soles of boots were shaped with the aid of a special tool known in English as a "boot-sole creaser" (Bockstoce 1977:74–75; Nelson 1899:108; VanStone 1980:45). Berit Foote (1992:79–114) has compiled an illustrated account of how skins were measured, cut, and sewn to make clothing.[158] Interested readers are advised to consult her book for details.[159]

The basic outfit consisted of a hooded frock (parka), pants, mittens, socks, and boots.[160] Beyond that, clothing varied according to gender, season, national custom, occasion, and availability of materials. This variation was created through the choice of material used, the precise cut of the clothing, the season, the pattern of skin arrangement, and the trim.

A man's parka hung well over the pants, was cut evenly around the bottom, and had a rounded hood. Figure 32 pictures a rather elaborate example, with tassels just below special trim around the bottom and on the arms. The two white strips (*manusiñak*, dual) on either side of the neck were a nearly ubiquitous feature of 19th-century male parkas. A woman's parka (see Figure 33) similarly hung down over the pants, but instead of a straight cut, had a small rounded flap on the bottom in front, a much larger one on the bottom in back, and sides cut almost to the hips. The hood was pointed. The example shown in Figure 33 is fairly elegant, with tassels, trim, and different-colored skins placed to create a pleasing pattern.

FIGURE 32. A man's parka with the hood pushed back. From Murdoch (1892:113).

The sleeves of both men's and women's parkas fit so loosely that the wearers' hands could be pulled inside and their arms crossed over their chest for extra warmth without having to remove the garment. The woman's parka also had extra fullness in the back just below the hood so that an infant or young child could be carried there, protected from the elements. The baby was held in place by a large belt around the mother's waist outside the parka. There was also enough fullness in a woman's parka for infants to be swung around from the back to the breast without being exposed to the cold air.

Men's breeches came to a short distance below the knee, and had drawstrings at the waist and at the knee. Their boots (see Figure 34) normally had long uppers that extended to the bottom of the pant legs, although sometimes much shorter and fancier ones were worn on special occasions. In contrast, women's pants and boots were a single garment. Moss or grass was placed in both men's and women's boots, sometimes with skin insoles, to provide cushioning and insulation.

Both men's and women's parkas were usually trimmed with wolf or wolverine fur. Belts, made of claws or teeth sewn onto a backing of sealskin, were worn around the parka.[161] One or more amulets, and often the tail of some animal, were usually attached to the belt, the former in front or on the sides, the latter behind.

In winter, people wore two layers: an outer layer with the fur side out, and an inner one with the fur side in.[162] In summer, only one layer of clothing was worn, and it was often made of lighter material (such as seal, ground squirrel, or muskrat skin) instead of caribou hide. Summer was also the time when old, worn-out clothing was used. Waterproof sealskin boots were in widespread use in summer, although footgear was often dispensed with altogether in warm weather, as were mittens.

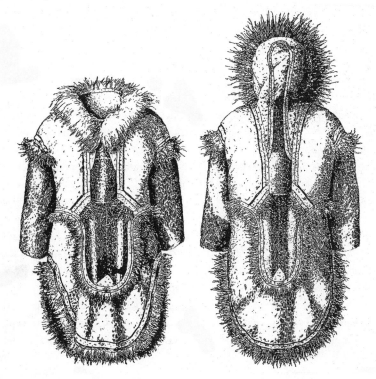

FIGURE 33. A woman's parka, front view on the left, rear view on the right. From Murdoch (1892:118).

FIGURE 34. A sample of men's boots. From McLenegan (1887).

Nationality was usually expressed in some detail of the cut, the precise arrangement of the skins, or in decoration (Simpson 1875:242; Wells and Kelly 1890:17). Although Westerners could not always detect these differences, the Iñupiat could identify a stranger's nationality from afar simply on the basis of his/her clothing. Unfortunately, no information on just what patterns characterized the dress worn by people from specific nations has survived.

The occasion affected what one wore in a variety of ways. For example, during festivals and celebrations, clothing made from only the best skins was worn; it was often made of skins of contrasting colors pieced together in an elegant pattern.[163] During major dances, men sported headbands supporting one to three eagle feathers, and special mittens equipped with rattles. In battle, or when fearing an assassination attempt, men wore ivory or bone plate armor or vests made from eider duck skins under the parkas, or caribou skin or fur vests over the parkas, in order to deflect or impede the penetration of enemy arrows. When conducting raids or in battle, men wore headbands and two feathers, one inserted above each ear.[164] In rainy weather, long waterproof parkas made from seal or oogruk intestines, or from loon skins, were worn over regular clothing.[165] In late winter and spring, when the intense glare of the sun on the snow can cause severe eye pain and even blindness, one wore goggles (dual *irigaak*) carved out of soft wood, shaped to fit the wearer's face, and scored with narrow slits for viewing. People who frequently had to launch or land boats in ocean surf wore waterproof sealskin waders (dual *pauŋŋaak*) (Thornton 1931:34–35).

A detailed discussion of variation in Iñupiaq clothing is beyond the scope of this work. However, a general idea of the possibilities can be conveyed with reference to types of footgear. This is done in Table 19, which is based on information obtained from a single source, Della Keats (1970.4).[166] More extensive investigation would no doubt have yielded a much longer list. As the table shows, footgear varied in the length of the upper, in the material from which both the upper and the bottom were made, and in whether the hair side of the

Table 19. Varieties of Iñupiaq Footgear

Name	Description
atulaaq	Insole or short caribou hide sock
atulapiaq	Long caribou hide sock.
atuŋalik/ugrulik	Unbleached oogruk bottom.
attutik	Waterproof sock of oogruk intestines.
isik	Just like *isiktuq*, but to just above ankles.
isiktuuq	Boot with four strips of skin extending to knee, any kind of bottom.
kamaapak	Has *isiktuuq* tops, unshaped oogruk bottom, with hair on. Used with snowshoes.
kiplautchiaq	Fancy boots with alternating white and black skins, with hanging strips of wolverine skin; fancy top, oogruk bottom. Short. Worn by men.
mamiligauraq	Just like *mamilik*, but comes to just above ankle.
mamilik	Caribou with hair inside, soft bottom. Worn by men.
natchiviaq	Low-quality water boot with upper made from fresh sealskin, hair outside. Rush job for spring use.
puugruaq	Boot made of an old poke, hair outside.
pauŋaak	Waders (come to waist).
piñiġaq	Just like *qaqlik* but short.
qaqlik	Water boots, with bleached top, black sealskin uppers (no hair), oogruk bottoms.
tuttulik	Term refers to bottom only; soft caribou skin with hair inside.
ugrulik/atuŋalik	Unbleached oogruk bottom.
ulitchuiaq	Caribou skin uppers extending to knee, hair inside, oogruk bottoms. Oiled outside for waterproofing.
ulitchuiauraq	Same as *ulitchuiaq*, but goes only to just above ankle.

skin faced in or out. For walking across smooth ice or hard-packed snow, Iñupiat sometimes "tied a loop of rawhide around their boot near the ball of the foot, then passed the free end around the ankle and tied it over the arch of the foot" (Sunno 1951.60).

Iñupiaq clothing was admirably suited for protection against the cold. Direct insulation was provided by the material out of which it was made. The insulating effects were significantly enhanced through application of the air-capture principle. Thus, warmth created by the wearer's body was prevented from escaping by the series of overlapping elements (parka over pants over boots) and ultimately by the tight fit of the hood around the face. The fur ruff around the hood significantly reduced the effects of wind on the wearer's face. Stefansson (1955) estimated that an Eskimo could remain comfortable in bitter cold wearing an outfit that, in its entirety, weighed only about ten pounds (4.5 kg) (see also Jarvis 1899:53). When food supplies ran out and men had to venture some distance from home in an effort to locate game, they simply took some food, an extra pair of boots, and two pieces of caribou hide with the hair left on. At night, if no shelter was available, they sat on the hair side of one piece of skin, placed their feet on the hair side of the other, pulled their arms inside their parka, leaned forward, and slept reasonably comfortably right out in the open air (Paneak 1970).

Iñupiaq clothing was less satisfactory for summer wear (Woolfe 1893:150). Even a single layer of lightweight clothing was often uncomfortably warm, particularly in the interior, but its removal exposed the person to the swarms of mosquitoes that infest northwestern Alaska in summer. For this reason, Western-style clothing was adopted for summer use well before its eventual adoption for winter wear.

As a final note it is appropriate to mention that the manufacture of clothing was significantly affected by adherence to taboos. One could not simply make or mend clothes when convenient or necessary. The details varied from one nation to another, but the following list will provide a general idea of the possibilities: women could not make or mend clothing while men were hunting beluga or bowhead whales (Jensen 1970.1); when a woman was sewing, one could not pick grass (M. Naylor 1960.1); one could not do any sewing if a person in the settlement was sick.[167] Transgression of the first taboo in the list resulted in the death of the seamstress. In the second case, it resulted in someone's death, although not necessarily that of the seamstress. And in the third, it resulted in the death of the sick person. Obviously, rules with these implications could not be broken lightly.

Food

Iñupiaq food benefited very little from human manufacture beyond the effort involved in acquiring the raw material, initial processing, and storage. As Hooper (1884) put it:

> Food is eaten without the slightest regard to its condition. Rancid oil, rotten eggs, putrid meat, and decayed fish are staple articles of food, and are eaten from the same wooden bowl, or kantag [*qattaq*?], which is used for all purposes, from the chamber to the kitchen (Hooper 1884:104).

Most meat and fish were eaten raw in a dried, frozen, and/or fermented state with seal oil, caribou tallow, fish oil, or bear grease as a condiment.[168] Cooking was usually confined to boiling, most of the time by means of heated rocks placed in containers holding water and pieces of meat, fish, and/or animals' internal organs (K. Burns 1960.2; Giddings 1961:136–37). One method used to acquire fat to go with the lean meat available was to boil smashed bones or internal organs, allow the broth to cool, and skim off the congealed fat that floated to the surface. Roasting over an open fire was an occasional alternative, particularly for families whose members lived in houses with open interior hearths, or who were traveling. However, roasting had the disadvantage of losing into the flames some of the fat that might otherwise have gone into the broth.

The Iñupiat also consumed more plant foods than did their Inuit relatives to the east.

> Another popular error exists in the belief that the Innuits [*sic*] eat no vegetable food. The fact is they eat large quantities of berries, willow and alder leaves, sorrel, scurvy-grass, and a small bulbous root which in appearance, smell, and taste, resembles wild parsnip. These articles are generally eaten raw, although they are sometimes cut up and allowed to ferment before being eaten (Hooper 1884:104).

Much of the time people had to eat what was available, such as fish when the salmon or char were running, caribou when a successful drive had been completed, and berries when they were in season. Although they truly liked their food, they tired of eating the same thing all day every day for weeks at a time. Variation was created by storing different kinds of raw materials in the same container, such as dried oogruk meat and different kinds of leaves in seal oil, and allowing them to age together. Some examples of "special" foods intended to provide variety are listed in Table 20.

Table 20. A Sample of "Special" Foods

akutuq: Caribou back and especially visceral fat were cut into small pieces and mashed to a paste with the hands, sometimes with a bit of seal oil, then whipped, by hand. From that point, one or some combination of several other items could be worked into it: berries; *masru* that had been chopped and cooked; dried and shredded caribou meat; or fish—boiled, drained, the bones and skin removed, and the meat thoroughly mashed (Anderson et al. 1998:233; B. Foote 1992:153; Anore Jones 1983:127–129; A. McClellan 1970.2; E. Mills 1960.4; D. Naylor 1960.7; Towkshjea 1960.2; Woolfe 1893:145).

auruq: Summer fish that had been stored whole in the ground and left to rot and eventually freeze. Eaten raw and frozen (John Stalker 1986).

ittukpalak: Mashed fish eggs and cranberries mixed with seal oil and whipped by hand (Anderson et al. 1998:297, 298; Nellie Russell in Lee et al. 1990:207).

kaktuaq: Raw fish livers, fish eggs, and blueberries mixed together in a wooden container and eaten without further processing (R. Cleveland 1966).

miġnaq: Fish that had slightly decomposed, then frozen solid for quite awhile, then completely thawed out for a day or two (Lowell Sage 1984).

mikigaq: Bowhead whale meat was cut into small pieces and placed into a pot with pieces of skin, tongue, and blubber. The mix was then allowed to ferment for several days, with periodic stirring and taste-testing. When the taste was about right, it was placed in cold storage to prevent it from fermenting further. Eaten without cooking (B. Foote 1992:151, 152; Koenig 1984; O. Swan 1984.2).

niġukkaq: The back meat and the liver of a freshly killed caribou were cut into strips. The viscera were removed, and the rib cage cleaned out. Then the sliced meat, liver, and stomach were put into the rib cage. Everything was left there for two days to "cook," then was ready to eat (Anore Jones 1983:130; Clinton Swan 1984.1).

puiñiq: This was made by boiling marrow and smashed caribou bones, and letting the broth cool so that the fat congealed on the water's surface. The fat was then skimmed off and stored in a caribou stomach to await consumption (Iviqsiq 1940; Keats 1970.1, 1970.2, 1970.5; E. Mills 1960.4; T. Mitchell 1969; D. Naylor 1960.7).

qalluaq: Loon or grebe skins, with the fat left on, were cut into small pieces and cooked with the bird's meat. The liquid fat was skimmed from the broth, left to cool, and eaten with the meat (Anderson et al. 1998:296).

tinniugaq: A mixture of burbot liver, eggs, and stomach, mashed together (sometimes with berries) and boiled (Anderson et al. 1998:300).

utniq: Fermented oogruk flipper: First they cut off the flipper. Then they laid the skin out with the blubber and some meat attached to dry in the sun. After a day or so, a layer of dry blubber and meat was removed from the rest, and wrapped around the flipper. Then the whole thing was stored beneath the sand for a couple of days until it got ripe (B. Foote 1992:152; A. Swan 1983:123).

yuuqqaq: Some caribou meat was boiled, and then fresh blood, fat, and some pieces from the dark part of the stomach were stirred into the pot containing the meat and water (B. Foote 1992:153).

If supplies were good, the Iñupiat could serve several types of food at a meal. However, there were many taboos restricting foods that could be cooked or eaten together, which limited freedom of action in food selection.

The traditional Iñupiaq diet of game, fish, and sea mammal meat was rich in protein and omega-3 polyunsaturated fatty acids, and low in saturated fat.[169] Internal organs, and often stomach contents, were good sources of vitamins and minerals. The various plant products yielded vitamins, minerals, and fiber. The minimal cooking and other processing left the nutritional value of the food largely intact; much of what was removed through boiling was retained in the broth, which was likewise consumed.

Fermented food carried some risk of botulism (Dolman 1960), although, over time, the Iñupiat learned how to store their food supplies safely. People I talked to about this claimed that it was only after contact, when they tried to store fermenting food in metal containers, that botulism seems to have become a serious problem (Martha Swan 1964). Some foods, such as polar bear meat, carry a high risk of trichinosis (Rausch 1970), but people learned through painful experience that these substances had to be cooked with unusual thoroughness in order to be safe. Similarly, polar bear liver contains such a high concentration of vitamin A as to make it toxic, but by the time period of interest here, its consumption had long since been tabooed. Despite these problems and its highly restricted composition, the Iñupiaq diet was "capable of furnishing all the nutrients essential for nutritional health" (Draper 1977:309; see also Draper 1978), provided that it was prepared according to traditional methods and that it was available in sufficient quantity.

Food, of course, was not always available in sufficient quantity. Lean periods occurred in some districts almost every year, and in every district in some years. Along the coast, unfavorable winds could keep the sea ice in perpetual turmoil or solidly packed against the shore, making sea mammal hunting difficult or impossible. In the interior, caribou, which are notoriously fickle in their movements, could depart for other lands, leaving the people behind with little or nothing in the way of food. If saltwater breakup on the ocean came early in the spring and the ice moved out, the crucial spring sea mammal hunt ended prematurely. If freshwater freezeup came early, it prevented people from boating to their intended fall hunting stations. In summer, the fish runs in the rivers might be rendered inaccessible by heavy rain and high water. In every district, powerful winter storms could keep people from hunting or fishing for weeks at a time. Whenever and wherever any of these developments occurred, if food supplies were low when they began, famine was the inevitable result. Cantwell stated (1889a) that

> my personal observation of these natives leads me to believe that while it is true
> that they can consume large quantities of food when it is plentiful, they are also
> capable of going without food for much longer periods than the *average* white man
> (Cantwell 1889a:65; italics in the original).

When famine struck, there were three basic options. One was to move to another part of one's own district in the hope of finding better hunting or fishing grounds there. As the Kivalliñiġmiu elder Regina Walton (1965.2) told me, "We never stayed the whole winter along the river when there were no caribou and no fish either. Then we had nothing to eat. The people spread around looking for ptarmigan, staying wherever they found some." The second option was to flee to another, presumably better-endowed, district, and hope to connect there with a trading partner (*niuvik*) or relative. The third was to hunker down and hope for the best. The first two alternatives were predicated on the assumption that the people involved had the strength to make the trip; the third was not.

When ordinary food supplies were exhausted, people turned to emergency foods in order to survive.[170] One option was to kill and eat their dogs, who also would have been starving. This was the route taken on many occasions, but of course people who did this ended up without any dogs. A second option was to eat the white, inner bark of willows, scratched off in shreds and mixed with seal oil, if they had any. A third was to eat reindeer moss dipped in seal oil, if they had any. And a fourth was to eat ptarmigan or hare droppings. If they were able to kill any small animal or bird, people did so. And in the most extreme situation, they ate the remains of their deceased relatives (Edna Hunnicutt 1960.1). Extreme hunger was familiar enough to the Iñupiat that, when food somehow arrived after a severely lean period, they knew enough not to gorge themselves, but to begin with broth, gradually working up to solid food.[171]

Buildings

The Iñupiat had four basic types of walled and usually roofed structures: dwellings, *qargich*, workshops, and caches. Before proceeding to the details, two general observations are in order. They apply specifically to dwellings, but the same basic points can be made with regard to all Iñupiaq buildings.

The first is that the labels the Iñupiat used for different types of house can be confusing to the uninitiated. For example, any kind of dwelling with a dome-shaped frame was a *qaluuġvik*. However, if the frame was covered with a tarpaulin made of caribou hides, it could also be called an *itchalik*; if it was covered with moss or sod, it could be called an *ivrulik*. And if it was the type of house normally occupied in winter, it could be called an *ukiivik*; or in summer, an *upinġivik*.[172] The terminology is further complicated by dialectal and subdialectal differences. My own failure to understand these matters once led me to claim greater national distinctiveness in house types than likely existed in fact (Burch 1983:118).

The second general point was expressed by archeologist J. L. Giddings (1961) after excavating several prehistoric houses in the Kobuk River valley. He said that a fall/winter house was never

> duplicated exactly in its details. The style of a house, given a basic idea of construction, seems to have been left entirely to the discretion and taste of its builder. Size may have been determined by the number of individuals to be housed, by the inequality of effort of the several builders, by the depth of frost in the ground, and by any number of other factors at which we can only guess. The builders had no "blueprint" to follow other than their knowledge of what a house generally should look like, and they probably used only the roughest of measures in planning an excavation, lengths of timbers, and the like (Giddings 1961:127).

Similarly, Andrew Sunno (1951.56) told Charles Lucier that houses differed from one another not only in size, but in such matters as depth of excavation, the location of the peak of the roof, and in overall plan.

For present purposes, Iñupiaq dwellings are usefully divided into four general types: semisubterranean houses, surface frame houses and tents, snow houses, and makeshift shelters.[173] Some of these were illustrated in Chapter 3.

Semisubterranean Dwellings

Semisubterranean houses (pl. *igluǵruat*) were built by excavating a large hole in the ground, erecting a framework of timber or whale ribs around the hole's perimeter and over its top, covering the frame with wooden walls and roofing, and covering the whole with moss and the soil produced during the excavation. Woolfe (1893) summarized how it was done:

> In order to build one of these huts a vast amount of digging with picks made of whale rib or walrus tusk is required, as after the surface of the ground is removed hard frozen earth is encountered within a few inches [cm] of the top. A space is excavated of an oblong form, generally to a depth of 3 or 4 feet [90–122 cm], while a tunnel for an entrance is dug at one side or at the end of the oblong, according to the locality from which the heaviest snowdrift comes, so as to make the entry on a lee side. Timber is used for framing, and in form these huts resemble an inverted bowl, with a square hole left on top to provide light. Sods and moss are utilized for covering the frames, and any interstices are chinked with moss or brush (Woolfe 1893:144).

Some of these houses were substantial. In January of 1850, John Simpson (1850b: entry for Jan. 17, 1850) visited a Qikiqtaġruŋmiut house in which, at one point, he counted forty-six people in addition to his own party and the building's regular occupants.

Basic procedures were similar in each district where semisubterranean houses were built, although the earthmoving tools were sometimes made of different materials.[174] In places such as Point Hope, where good timber was not always available, whale ribs were often substituted for wood in house construction. Among the Akuniġmiut, Kiitaaġmiut, Kuuŋmiut, Napaaqtuġmiut, Qikiqtaġruŋmiut, and Siiḷviim Kaŋianiġmiut, semisubterranean houses were built on the four-post-center plan, with a central cooking and working area and alcoves on the sides, and sometimes also at the rear, for sitting and sleeping.[175] Among the Kaŋiġmiut, Kiŋikmiut, Tapqaġmiut, and Tikiġaġmiut, houses were built on a rectangular plan with benches at the back of the main living area for sitting and sleeping. Entrance passages often had one or two alcoves for storage or cooking.

The permafrost had to be thawed before much excavating could be done. To do this, a fire was built on the ground and sustained until the frost was gone. Loose soil was removed with shovels, but blocks of frozen ground were broken off around the initial hole with picks, or pried off with long poles with sharpened ends used somewhat like a digging iron.

The timbers used to make the walls were split and placed vertically, smooth side in, the tops notched to hold the cross beams. The timbers forming the roof were similarly placed smooth side in. Moss, which served as insulation and kept soil from falling through the cracks, was placed outside the wooden framework with the root side out before being covered with the soil or blocks of sod removed during the excavation process.

Varying with the size of the building and the number of available workers, construction of a basic semisubterranean house took four or five days to complete if pursued aggressively (Giddings 1961:126; Glover 1970.1; C. Smith 1970). In the major coastal settlements, where houses were typically occupied for several winters in succession, they were usually more elaborate than those built in the interior, and they took much longer to build.

Surface Frame Houses and Tents

Surface frame houses and tents consisted of a framework of logs or poles over which one or a combination of several different types of cover were laid or stretched. There was considerable variation in the structures included in this category.

Log Cabins

The most substantial house in the surface category seems to have been the log cabin, built only in the forested sector of the lower Noatak River valley (Brower ms:160; L. Gallahorn 1970.2). Apparently this house was similar in structure to a European log cabin, except that there was no chimney or window. Instead, there was a hearth in the center of the living area and a removable skylight directly above it. People slept on the floor around the back and sides of the room.

Four-Post-Center Houses

A more common pattern was a dwelling that was a four-post-center house similar to the one described above, but built on the ground surface rather than in an excavated pit. It was ordinarily much smaller than most semisubterranean houses, had little in the way of an entrance passage, and generally was a less substantial structure.[176] Such houses were usually built in winter, when it was too cold to thaw and dig into the ground.

The construction of these houses was usefully summarized by John Simpson (1875):

> [O]n the rivers, where trees grow, structures of a less permanent kind are erected.
> Then the smaller trees are felled, cut to the length required, and split; then laid
> inclining inwards in a pyramidal form, towards a rude square frame in the centre,
> supported by two or more upright posts. Upon these the smaller branches of the
> felled trees are placed, and the whole, except the aperture at the top and a small
> opening on one side, is covered with earth or only snow. The entrance is formed
> of a low porch, having a black bear-skin hanging in front, leading to a hole close
> to the ground, through which an unpracticed person can hardly creep, farther
> protected from the breeze by a flap of deer-skin on the inside. In the hilly districts,
> near the source of the Spafareif [sic] [Kiwalik] River, this sort of snow-covered
> hut was in use, and the inland tribes on the Nu-na-tak [Noatak], are described
> as living in dwellings of a similar kind, constructed of small wood, probably built
> afresh every year, and not always in the same locality (Simpson 1875:258–59).

In fact, in most districts, such houses were erected at each place people stopped with the intention of staying more than one or two nights. Since a family normally built several of these houses every winter, their construction consumed an enormous amount of time and energy over the course of the season.

Houses that were intended for only brief use often did not have an entrance passage, but just a heavy (usually bear) skin over the door. All houses in this category had a fireplace in the middle over which was a skylight made from the intestines of some animal. The skylight was removed while the fire was burning, and subsequently replaced to retain as much heat as possible. Rocks forming the hearth, the ground around it, and perhaps heated cooking rocks continued to radiate heat for some time after the fire was extinguished.

The cover of this type of house seems to be a matter of some confusion. In the passage quoted above, Simpson says earth or snow. Some of my own sources (e.g., Walton 1965.2) said that the framework was covered with a layer of grass, over which was placed a layer of moss, upon which some gravel was sprinkled to keep the moss from blowing away. Others maintained that it was covered with sod. Theoretically, it could have been grass and moss in some cases, and sod in others. However, there is a question in my mind about the meaning of the Iñupiaq word *ivruq*. It is often translated as "sod," but sometimes as "moss." Once when Clinton Swan and I visited a place on the Wulik River called Ivruqtusuq, he pointed to a bed of sphagnum moss and said decisively that that was *ivruq*. When Alfred

Stone (1976) stated that when people walked on *ivruq* "they'd sink down about a foot and a half," he was clearly talking about a thick bed of moss, not sod (see also Anderson et al. 1998:235). Moss makes more sense, because these houses were made repeatedly all winter long, when moss was difficult, but sod was next to impossible, to obtain. When I asked Thomas Mitchell (1969) if the moss wouldn't blow away, he responded that these houses were usually built in the midst of thick willows, where wind had little impact.

A variation on this type of house was built in the Kobuk River valley at the summer fish camps occupied by women, old men, and children.[177] The first step was to collect spruce (occasionally birch) bark to serve as the house cover. It was acquired by cutting with an adze two rings around a standing tree about six feet apart, making a vertical slit with a knife between the rings, and peeling off the bark. After a sufficient supply had been obtained, the bark was brought to the village, placed on damp moss, and held flat there with rocks. While the bark was seasoning, a rectangular framework was built of two end posts and four corner posts with joining rafters over which a layer of willow branches was laid. The flattened spruce bark was then placed upon the framework, a hole being left in the center of the roof as a vent. Wet moss was then spread over the bark to keep it from drying and curling. Gravel, laid over the moss, held everything in place. The door was covered with a bear skin to keep out mosquitoes, and the smoke hole was closed except when a smudge fire was built inside. Cooking was ordinarily done outside.

Dome-Shaped Houses

Dome-shaped houses, or *qaluuġviich* (pl.), had a framework made from slender poles whose ends were inserted in the ground in a pattern ranging from circular to elliptical.[178] The poles were bent over and tied together to form arches, and reinforced along the sides with horizontal wooden strips. The framework was then covered with either a tarpaulin made of caribou hides or sealskins; a layer of grass, moss, or sod, or some combination of the three, which was often covered with a layer of snow; or a layer of spruce bark.

Depending on the type of cover, a dome-shaped house could be used during any, or every, season of the year. In most districts it was used by families who were traveling, in both summer and in winter. The building was erected whenever travelers stopped for the night, then disassembled and brought along on the sled or in the boat when they moved on. In areas where neither saplings nor suitable timber were available locally, people often used poles they had acquired elsewhere, and lived in a dome-shaped house all winter long.

The third possibility was a dome-shaped house covered with birch or spruce bark. This last was found only along the Kobuk River, and only in summer (R. Cleveland 1966; C. Lee 1970; Sun 1970). This was basically a variant of the type of Kobuk summer house discussed above, but with a dome-shaped framework; it was built according to the same basic principles.

Conical Tents

Conical tents (sing. *tupiq*) were used in summer by people belonging to several different nations.[179] In July of 1881, E. W. Nelson (1877–81) observed a large number of these tents at Sisualik, on Kotzebue Sound, and described them as follows:

> These [tents] are invariably covered with deerskins sewed together, the hair on
> [the] outside and laid over a framework of converging sticks which are supported
> midway up their length by a hoop to which the sticks or poles are lashed as fol-
> lows: the apex being about 10 feet [3 m] from ground and the diameter at base

some 12 to 15 feet [3.7–4.6 m], and they are usually occupied by from one to two families each and not more, but generally by one family (Nelson 1877–81: entry for July 16, 1881).

Nelson's illustration of a conical tent frame is shown here in Figure 35.

Nelson (1899:261) also reported that the tents he saw at Hotham Inlet were covered by untanned winter caribou hides sewn together in squares of six, with several squares comprising the cover of a single tent.

Snow Houses

The snow house (*aniyutyaq*) was not the primary winter dwelling anywhere in northwestern Alaska during the study period. However, it was commonly used in certain circumstances, as listed below:

FIGURE 35. Sketch of a tent frame seen at Hotham Inlet. From Nelson (1899:261).

- When the Kivalliñiġmiut, Napaaqtuġmiut, and Qikiqtaġruŋmiut moved onto the sea ice to hunt seals in the spring (Elwood Hunnicutt 1970; Jensen 1970.2; C. Luther 1960.1);
- When the Kuuŋmiut and Kiitaaġmiut moved onto the ice of Hotham Inlet and Selawik Lake, respectively, to hook for sheefish in the spring (D. Foster 1970.1; C. Smith 1970);
- When people without tents traveled through or lived in an area lacking suitable poles for frames (M. and D. Naylor 1960; Stoney 1900:812; Walton 1965.2; Woolfe 1893:144);
- As emergency shelter when caught by bad weather or when drifted out on the sea ice (D. Norton 1965);
- To hide in when driving caribou (A. Hawley 1965.9; Luther 1960.1);
- When traveling light to attack people in another country (Jensen 1970.6);
- To cover good fishing holes to help keep them from freezing over and to help keep the fishermen warm (S. Thomas 1970);
- To house pregnant women about to give birth (K. Burns 1960.2);
- To house seriously ill people so that they would not die in the regular living quarters.

A precondition to snow-house construction is snow of suitable homogeneity and compactness. In general, the best snow was found in drifts in windy, treeless areas. The basic pattern was to cut blocks about two feet square and eight inches thick with a special shovel. The blocks were placed upright on the snow in a circle around the area from which they had been removed.[180] They were placed leaning slightly inward. Successive layers of progressively smaller blocks were added, gradually closing at the top. A door was then cut in the wall, with a small outside passageway of snow blocks added to protect the entry.

Less elegant snow shelters were also built. These were more or less ad hoc in shape, built on the spur of the moment. These were often square or rectangular in plan, built of upright walls of snow blocks over which a roof of flat slabs of snow was laid. On other occasions, the ends were made a bit higher than the side walls, a ridge pole was placed across them, and slabs of snow were laid from the side walls to the ridge.

Miscellaneous Shelters

The Iñupiat used a variety of shelters in addition to those described above.[181] Most of them do not properly fit under the rubric of "building," but this is an appropriate place to discuss them.

The most substantial dwelling in the miscellaneous category was a true building made primarily of rock (T. Mitchell 1976). This type of dwelling was built by people living in the barren areas around the large lakes in the upper Noatak district. The rock was covered with moss, then with mud to hold the moss in place. Sod, apparently, was not used.

The remaining dwelling types were all temporary shelters, most of which were used only in special circumstances. The Kivalliñiġmiut, for example, when they walked inland to hunt caribou during the summer, carried a lightweight tarpaulin made from oogruk intestines (Walton 1965.2). It was easily made into a tent by placing it over a framework of willows. Alternatively, they constructed temporary shelters by piling up pieces of shale for corner posts, then placing a large slab of shale on top of them (J. Stalker 1970.1). When the days began to get warm in the spring, the Kiitaaġmiut of the lower Selawik district often made what was really nothing more than a windbreak by placing a number of poles into the snow in a circular pattern and weaving grass between them (C. Smith 1970). People slept and ate there in the open air. Finally, people living in forested areas often made temporary shelters by cutting down several small spruce trees and either leaning them up against the limbs of a larger tree to form a lean-to, or stacking them together tipi style (Giddings 1961:46, 127). Temporary shelters of this nature were used only in special circumstances. The general Iñupiaq policy was to erect dwellings that would last for prolonged periods; one could never be sure when a storm would arrive in either summer or winter, and it was best to be prepared for it.

Qargich

The *qargi*, or community hall, was a feature of almost every Iñupiaq settlement. Complex settlements usually had more than one, the number being loosely correlated with the settlement's population. As Trollope (1855:872) discovered in 1854, the number of *qargich* was a "very expressive manner of estimating the extent and the population of a place."

In general, *qargich* were constructed along the same lines and by means of the same techniques as the dwellings in a community.[182] In other words, if the houses in a settlement were semisubterranean, so was the *qargi*. If, on the other hand, the dwellings were dome-shaped tents, so was the *qargi*.

The only fundamental difference between a dwelling and a *qargi* was the presence of a sleeping area in the former, and its absence in the latter. However, permanent *qargich* in large settlements, and temporary *qargich* erected for special events, such as a messenger festival, usually had at least one bench, and sometimes two, around at least three of the walls. In the latter case, there would be a lower one perhaps three feet (1 m) above the floor, and another one several feet above that. But these benches were seats for spectators, not beds for people to sleep on. In summer, the *qargi* was usually not a building at all, but simply an outdoor space protected by a windbreak—often consisting of a few large boats turned on their sides—or a large tent quickly thrown up and speedily dismantled.

John Simpson (ms.a) provided an early description of a *qargi* that he visited around the middle of the 19th century. Apparently either in the fall of 1849 or early summer of 1850, Simpson visited a small settlement on Hotham Inlet, which he called Sinerak, or Beach Town. He counted eight summer tents and five winter huts, indicating that the residents were either preparing to return to their houses for the winter or had just moved out of them for the summer. The reason that this small settlement is worthy of note is that its residents had erected a separate building to serve as a *qargi*. Simpson (ms.a) reported that the building was in a "tolerable state of repair," but that the materials "were very rotten":

> The karigi is fifteen feet by eighteen [4.6 x 5.5 m] and the walls start at 7 [feet; 2.1 m] from which the roof slopes upwards on all sides to a flat top of eight feet [2.4 m] square and nearly ten [3 m] high. There is a window on the south side of the sloping roof and near the same side of the door is the round aperture in the floor for entering by the subterranean passage now full of water [since it was summertime]. There is also a bench eighteen inches [46 cm] wide running round the four walls at the height of three feet [90 cm] from the ground and the floor is made of planks reaching from side to side (Simpson ms.a).

Such a building was too large to serve this small community as its regular meeting place. Therefore, we may suppose that it had been erected for the specific purpose of hosting a messenger festival some years previously. That would explain both its size and its apparent deterioration; it was no longer needed. *Qargich* erected for specific events were often torn down afterwards, their constituent parts being used for other purposes.

In 1854, Henry Trollope (1855) described a somewhat larger *qargi* he visited in Wales:

> We were followed by at least 150 people, and very civilly invited into the dancing houses, poa-llalley tupucs, as we came to call them: these were very far superior to the one at Sin-na-ra-mute, where we were detained so long, the entrance or passage higher or broader, so that it was sufficient to stoop low instead of going down upon hands and knees; the interior was really clean and cheerful, a spacious room 20 feet [6 m] square, with brilliant lights in troughs of seal oil, the wicks formed of moss placed in a row at the edge, and fed by a piece of blubber hanging within reach of the flame; the light was excellent; I was reminded of the jets of gas often seen in shop windows, and the heat was far more than I could have believed, outside the temperature was –25°, and within it was +36°.... There were eight or ten people in the place making snow-shoes, fitting spears, bows and etc; we went into two others which were not quite so large, and equally comfortable (Trollope 1855:873).

The only other description of the interior of a *qargi* in the study region from any time near the period of interest here is also from Wales. At the beginning of November 1866, the settlement was visited by a party from the Western Union Telegraph Expedition, which was based at Port Clarence. The men arrived cold and wet, but after having their clothing tended to and a hot meal, were invited to the *qargi*.

> After a rest we were invited to the Paloly, or dance house, by the Chief at whose residence we were stopping.[183] To give a correct description of this exhibition, is beyond our power. The house was about twenty feet [6 m] square, built with an underground entrance; around the walls were placed seats or shelves for the spectators, one side of which was occupied by the musicians; two raised platforms at the side served as galleries for the youth, who laid on all fours, and thus looked at the performance (*The Esquimaux* 1866–67:15).

Workshops

The main workshop was the *qargi*. Almost all small goods—weapons, tools, household implements—were manufactured there. Any item that could be brought into or removed from the building through the door or via the skylight was usually made in the *qargi*. The one item that could not be made there was an *umiaq*. For that, at least in winter, a special structure had to be built.

Two settlements within the study region where special workshops had to be constructed were Wales and Point Hope, the two major whaling centers. At both places, whaling boats had to be made ready during the winter for use in the spring. Minor repairs could be made outside, but new boats were built in a shop. Unfortunately, the only early description I have of a special workshop comes from Barrow, well to the north of the study region. Rochefort Maguire described a workshop he and John Simpson visited in the spring of 1854 where a man was building a new *umiaq* frame. He said it was a

> very ingeniously contrived workshop hollowed out in the snow with an entrance by a square trap door and passage similar to the usual snow houses, it was a little longer than the boat, which was 32 feet [9.75 m] in extreme length, and nearly six feet [2 m] high, with a flat roof covered with seal skins and snow over all—the side towards the sun at the time of their working hours was effectually lighted by six ice windows which admitted a beautiful soft light (Bockstoce ed. 1988:358).

When the boat frame was finished, all they had to do was knock down a snow wall and pull it out. Presumably, men at Wales and Point Hope erected a similar building for this purpose. People from other regions usually did not need their boats until after breakup, and worked on them in the open air, under a tent cover, or behind a windbreak.

Caches

Several kinds of cache were built in northwestern Alaska, varying to some extent with the season, the district, and the nature of what was being stored. Perhaps the most impressive were the cold storages (sing. *siģluaq*) that were built at the major whaling centers at Wales and Point Hope. I have never seen or heard a description of those at Wales, but Brower (ms) gave a firsthand account of how they were built at Point Hope:

> Each family had one of these, some as deep as fifteen feet [4.6 m], dug in the frozen ground. Some that I saw were two stories, a floor having been built half [way] down, fastened to corner posts. The [whale] blubber with the blackskin attached was lowered to the bottom, the pieces always laid in pairs with the blubber or blackskin together to keep them from freezing so hard that they could not be separated when wanted later for food. The meat was all put in each piece separate and allowed to freeze hard, then it was all put in one pile. It took only a short time to freeze so hard that it had to be cut up with their stone adzes and pried apart with a bone instrument made for that purpose, generally from a short piece of a whale's rib (Brower ms:179).

As might be imagined, it took a considerable amount of work with picks and shovels to build these storages, and they were maintained with great care.

Another type of cache was the food storage pit, also known as *siģluaq*. This was made by digging a rectangular hole in the ground, and lining it with grass, willow branches, rocks, or skins.[184] Sealskin or fish-skin pokes containing oil, dried meat or fish, berries, or other foods were placed inside, and the whole was covered with additional lining material over which was placed a layer of dirt. More elaborate cache pits were lined with split logs. Meat and fish that were not stored in oil fermented to some extent in these caches, but they were relished later when eaten raw and frozen.

One variation on the storage pit in soil was the storage pit in river ice (Sunno 1951.51). Its construction simply involved chopping a hole in thick river ice with an ice pick, placing fish or meat inside, and covering it with slabs of ice and snow.

Another variation on the storage pit was a small, semisubterranean log cabin (*saiyut*) (Anore Jones 1983:124; Kialook 1964; C. Smith 1970). After a hole of suitable dimensions was excavated with picks and shovels into the upper layer of permafrost, a building with log walls rising some distance above ground level was built in it. A small door was made in one wall above ground level, and the building was capped with a peaked wooden roof. Finally, dirt was piled around the bottom to help keep the cold from the permafrost from escaping. As long as such a building was built into frozen ground, food stored within it would not deteriorate to an unacceptable level.

The final type of cache was an elevated platform, of which there were two basic types. One was simply an open platform (*ikiġġaq*), as described from Wales by Thornton (1931):

> Four poles—each of which is 20 or 25 feet [6–7.7 m] high and 8 or 10 inches [20–25 cm] in diameter at the butt-end—are firmly sunk in the ground; then stout cross-pieces are attached, which in turn support the two floors—one being about 7 feet [2.1 m] from the ground and the other some 5 or 6 feet [1.5–1.8 m] above that. All the fastenings, as well as those about the houses, are made with thong. One of the four uprights serves as a ladder, the projecting knobs and stumps of limbs taking the place of rungs; or, if these protuberances are insufficient, notches are cut.
>
> On the lower level sleds, kayaks, spears, nets, ice-scoops, etc. are kept, in order to prevent the dogs from eating the thong or hide that is used in their construction; on the upper furs and skins, the two latter being wrapped in walrus, or oogarook, hide to protect them from the weather (Thornton 1931:227; see also J. Grinnell 1901:49).

Old boat covers served as tarpaulins to cover goods stored on the top platform (E. Curtis 1930:162).

A more elaborate version of elevated cache differed from the one just described in that it had a little log cabin instead of a platform on top (*uŋaluuraq*).[185] Along the Kobuk River, these were constructed as follows:

> The pilings are approximately six-foot [3 m] spruce logs, notched on the upper ends to receive two horizontal spruce poles. Smaller spruce poles span the pilings to form a floor. The irregular logs are ideal for a cache, because air easily circulates through the unchinked cracks. Split logs . . . may also be used for the walls (Anderson et al. 1998:236).

Split logs were also used to make the gabled roof. A notched log or ladder up to the small door provided access to the storage area.

Household Goods

The category of household goods includes items normally used within the house, plus a few others that do not fit well into any other category. No doubt many of these items were included in what Beechey (1831, I:405) referred to as the "variety of nameless articles always to be found among the Esquimaux."[186] It is appropriate to note here that the few early Western observers who commented on the internal condition of fall/winter houses found them clean and neat, even if characterized by what to them was a very unpleasant smell created by fermented food and chamber pot contents.[187]

Racks

Prominent objects in most households were racks made from willow switches or thin pieces of wood lashed together in a rectangular framework and suspended from the ceiling.[188] Racks had two contrasting purposes: as a place to dry wet clothing, and as a place to put blocks of snow or ice to melt (the drops falling into a bucket placed underneath). Alternatively, frozen meat or fish could be thawed on a rack (or on a stand at the back of the house). The rack's effectiveness was contingent on the ambient heat in the upper level of the dwelling chamber.

Bedding

Bedding consisted of two basic elements. One was a "mattress," which, in most districts, was a mat made of long blades of grass collected during the summer and braided into strands six to eight feet (1.8–2.4 m) long.[189] To make the mat, the strands were hung in parallel rows from the ceiling or a frame, and attached to one another at intervals with thin thread woven in a double over-and-under pattern. The finished mat was placed directly on the sleeping bench in a sod house, or on a layer of brush insulation in other types of dwelling. Where suitable grass was not available in sufficient quantity, caribou hides were used.

The other bedding element was the bedding proper.[190] In coastal villages, this usually took the form of caribou-skin blankets. In the interior, the same material was more often made into sleeping bags, hair side in, with twisted hare skin sometimes sewn around the opening. Occasionally, blankets were made entirely from hare skins, which were warmer and softer than caribou-hide blankets, but which required a large number of skins. All were made using the sewing techniques and equipment described above in the context of clothing.

Lamps

The oil lamp (*naniq*) was the primary source of light, and often of heat, in Iñupiaq buildings.[191] In some districts cooking was done in pots suspended over oil lamps, while in others it was done over a wood fire. Another variable was the location of the cooking area: in four-post-center houses it was usually in the center of the main room; in semisubterranean sod houses, it was often in an alcove off the entry tunnel.

Most lamps were made by pecking a depression into a stone having roughly the desired shape; the margins were often modified as well. Sandstone, serpentine, and talc were the primary raw materials. Sometimes lamps were made of pottery, which is discussed in a separate section below. Rarely, they were carved out of wood.

Lamps were usually semi-lunar, sometimes oval, in shape (see Figure 36). They ranged from about six inches (15 cm) to more than three feet (1 m) in length and perhaps three inches to a foot (7–30 cm) in width. The smallest ones were carried by travelers, while the largest were usually owned by coast dwellers who lived in houses to which they returned every year. Some of the larger lamps had bowls that were divided into two or more sections, each of which was basically

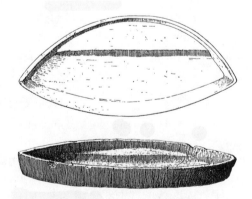

FIGURE 36. A soapstone lamp. The original was 17 inches (43 cm) long and 1.5 inches (3.8 cm) deep in the center. From Murdoch (1892:106).

a separate lamp. In some districts the lamp was placed on a stand, and a pan was placed beneath it to catch any oil that might drip out.

The most desired fuel was seal oil, in lieu of which fish oil, caribou tallow, marmot fat, bear grease, or mountain sheep tallow were used (R. Cleveland 1970.1). A major problem was the fact that all of these substances were also important forms of food.

When fuel was abundant, there sometimes were as many lamps in use in a house at any given time as there were married women living there, each of whom owned and tended one. In the interior, particularly among the Nuataaġmiut, the supply of oil was sufficiently low that only one lamp burned unless it was exceptionally cold. But everywhere, when supplies fell short, the number of lamps was reduced, often to just one. When famine struck, light and heat sometimes became secondary considerations, even during the dark days of early winter.

In a *qargi*, the lamps were managed by men; the number varied with the size of the building and the kind of activity going on. During special events, the *qargi* was brightly lit. Under ordinary circumstances, just enough lamps were lit for the men to do their work. If food, particularly fat, was in short supply, the *qargi* was closed.

Wicks were made from dry tussock moss (*maniq*), which was collected during the summer, dried, and stored in lumps (B. Foote 1992:156). When a wick was needed, a suitable amount of moss was removed and crushed between the fingers to the consistency of coarse tobacco. A piece was soaked in oil, ignited, and pushed with a special stick close to the edge of the oil (roughly the center of the straight side) in the lamp. Additional wick material was added in thin lines on both sides of the burning piece until the wick was nearly as long as the bowl. By dripping oil on this additional material, the flame could be gradually extended nearly the whole way along that side of the bowl. Once the fire was burning, oil was drawn out of the reservoir and into the wick by capillary action. Care was taken to keep burned wick out of the oil reservoir, which would have spoiled the oil for any other purpose, such as food.

Lamps fueled with fish oil, or with caribou or bear grease, presumably would have been more difficult to ignite because those substances congeal at higher temperatures than sea mammal oil does. However, I have never heard or read how this problem was solved. Once started, lamps were easily kept going by skewering a piece of fat or blubber on a stick and placing it over the flame where it dripped into the lamp as it melted. The wick was trimmed by adjusting its location relative to that of the oil.

According to Berit Foote (1992:156), there was "no smoke or smell from the lamp, just a pleasant scent of tundra from the wick." Similarly, Diamond Jenness (S. Jenness 1991:49) reported that an oil lamp "hardly smoked at all, and gave a light equivalent to two ordinary candles." Trollope (1855:873) compared the light to "the jets of gas often seen in shop windows" in mid-19th-century England. John Murdoch (1892:107), at Barrow, reported that "two such lamps burning at the ordinary rate give light enough to enable one to read and write with ease when sitting on the banquette, and easily keep the temperature [of a sod house] between 50° and 60° F. in the coldest weather." Despite this positive testimony, oil lamps had to have been the source of the black lung disease from which Iñupiat in general and women in particular seem to have suffered.[192] In contrast to the sources cited earlier, Grinnell (1901:50) complained that "the penetrating smell of burning seal oil is very stifling."

Fire

An open fire was employed for cooking in many districts and provided heat and at least some light while the cooking was in progress.[193] In houses with long entrance tunnels, cooking was usually done on a stone hearth (*igniqaġvik*) located in an alcove adjoining the entrance tunnel; the living quarters were lit and heated with lamps. In four-post-center houses, the hearth was located on the floor at or near the center of the living quarters. In all cases, hearths were located under a skylight or smoke hole, opened to vent the smoke while the fire was burning.

Fires were started with an ember generated on softwood by bow drills (see Figure 37) or by striking together two pieces of iron pyrite. The ember or spark was then placed on a small bed of tinder and gently fanned or blown into a flame. Over the course of the study period, these methods were gradually replaced by flint and steel. Tinder consisted of fine plant material (cottongrass, willow catkins, or various other plants) obtained during the summer and stored for later use.

There was usually only one cooked meal per day. A fire was usually built only to prepare that meal. Meat was occasionally roasted over an open fire, but most cooking was done by boiling. Where stone or metal pots were available, they were suspended over the fire (or lamp) and heated directly. More commonly, several rocks were heated in the fire and then placed in a wooden or pottery container holding meat or fish and water.[194] Hot rocks were handled with wooden tongs (*kigilġutaq*) made of two pieces of wood lashed together near one end. They were turned from time to time until they were extremely hot, then placed in the pot. When the rocks cooled and the water ceased boiling, they were removed from the water and put back in the fire. Three—and sometimes only two—cycles of heating and boiling were required for most cooking.

Sometimes a fire was kept burning for awhile after dinner had been cooked if it did not produce too much smoke. Alternatively, the rocks were heated an extra time since they radiated heat long after they were removed from the fire. However, since the air circulation in most Iñupiaq houses was ineffective, by the time the cooking was over the interior was often uncomfortably smoky. The fire was allowed to die down, the embers were thrown out through the skylight (with the same tongs used to handle the rocks), and the skylight re-covered.

Buckets

Buckets were made in a variety of sizes, round or oval in shape, and were used to carry or store water, human waste, food, oil, and berries.[195] Most households had several, each designated for a different purpose. Buckets were also used for cooking with water and hot rocks, as described above. They usually had handles, typically made of antler or ivory, which were often carved with designs or the shapes of animals (Bockstoce 1977:79).

A bucket (*igavaun*) was made from a thin piece of straight-grained spruce that had been split from a log with wedges, dressed with an adze and chisel, and finished with a crooked knife. It was then soaked in water to soften, after which grooved sticks were placed over each end to prevent their splitting. The

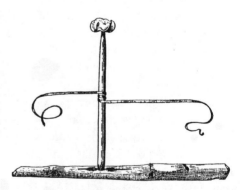

FIGURE 37. A fire drill. The 12-inch (30 cm) shaft was made of pine; the mouthpiece was a caribou astragalus bone. The drill was powered by hand using a 40-inch (1 m.) strip of oogruk skin. From Murdoch (1892:289).

board was then bent over the maker's thigh until the ends slightly overlapped. Rawhide ropes were tied around the cylinder so that it would retain its shape, and the grooved sticks were removed. Two parallel rows of holes were punched in the overlap, and spruce root was drawn through the holes to hold the cylinder together.

The bottom was made of a similar but slightly thicker piece of wood that was carefully shaped with a crooked knife, and beveled on the edges. It was inserted from the top, and pushed down until the edges fit neatly into a groove previously cut near the bottom of the cylinder. Finally, the bucket was soaked in water and allowed to dry slowly. It was then usually watertight. Any small leaks were repaired with spruce pitch.

Dishes and Platters

The flat containers the Iñupiat used to hold, carry, and serve food are variously described in English as dishes, platters, or trays, depending on their size.[196] The longer they are, the more likely they are to be characterized as platters. There were two basic types: those made from two pieces of birch bark, and those made from a single piece of wood.

A two-piece dish or platter was created from birch bark in the same way as a bucket, as described in the previous section. In other words, a piece of birch bark was shaped, steamed, or soaked, and bent into an oval or circular shape, the ends were sewn together, and a bottom inserted. A bucket differed in that it had a much higher side than did a dish or platter, often had a handle as well, and was more carefully made as it was intended to hold liquids.

A one-piece dish (*puggutauraq*) or platter (*alluiyaq*) was carved out of a single piece of soft wood or root. A blank was prepared with the various woodworking tools in the Iñupiaq kit, then shaped with precision with a crooked knife. These objects were made in a wide variety of sizes and shapes.

Pots

A cooking pot (*piktaliq*) was sometimes carved out of wood, but most were made of pottery.[197] The main ingredients for the latter were clay, sand, and tiny feathers from a ptarmigan or duck breast or leg. In some districts moss, blood, and seal oil scraped from the outside of a poke were also included. All of these were thoroughly combined. When the mixing was complete, the mass was formed into a ball. The maker thrust one hand into the ball, and shaped it by beating the outside with a stick held in the other hand. Finishing touches were executed with a smoother made of skin. When completed, the pot was either placed beside a small fire and slowly dried, being turned periodically so that the heat would be evenly distributed, or else it was placed directly in a fire to harden.

Pots ranged from about four to eighteen inches (10–46 cm) in height, and three to nine inches (7.6–23 cm) in width at the mouth (see Figure 38), and were roughly one-quarter-inch (6 mm) thick. In many districts pots had flaring rims, which made them easier to lift. Sometimes they were made with holes through which lines could be run so that they could be suspended from a ceiling or a tripod. Decoration tended to be nonexistent or minimal, although in some districts exterior markings were made with special batons or paddles prior to firing. In general, the pottery made in northwestern Alaska was flimsy and easily broken. The strongest and handsomest pots were produced by the Kaŋiġmiut and Kiitaaġmiut, who often made them for export.

Baskets

Baskets were made to carry or store a variety of items, such as leaves, berries, sinew and other sewing materials, and personal possessions. There were two basic types varying with the raw material, which was either birch bark or grass.

A birch-bark basket (*qallivik*) was made from a single piece of bark that was steamed or soaked to soften (A. Jones 1983:125; VanStone 1976:25–26; 1980:51). It was then bent upwards around the edges, folded at the ends, and stitched with spruce or willow root to a split-root rim fastened to both the inner and outer edges of the bark. Larger baskets were sometimes made with encircling strips of bark or willow (see Figure 39).

Baskets (sing. *aguupmak*) were also made of grass, at least in the southern half of the study region (J. and M. Konalook 1951.1; Nelson 1899:204). Regarding their construction, it is difficult to improve on the description provided by E. W. Nelson (1899):

> A strand of grass is laid in a coil forming the warp, the woof is then woven in by interlacing grass stems, and the coil is continued until the flat bottom is completed. The coils are then superimposed one upon the other until the basket is built up to the top, where it is narrowed in to form a circular, oval, or square opening. Frequently the coil is commenced on the bottom around a vacant space, from an inch to three inches in diameter, into which is sewn a piece of rawhide. The rim at the top has the grass brought over and neatly turned in on the under side, forming a smoothly finished edge (Nelson 1899:204; for illustrations, see plate LXXIV opposite p. 202).

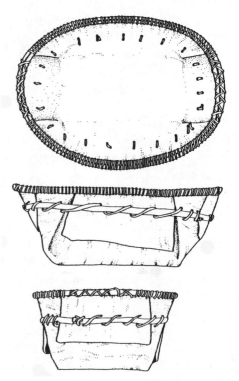

FIGURE 38. A clay pot from Kotzebue Sound with a capacity of approximately three gallons (11 liters). From Nelson (1899:201).

FIGURE 39. A birch-bark basket 13.6 inches (34.6 cm) long and 4.7 inches (12 cm) high. From VanStone (1980:51). Reproduced with permission of the Field Museum of Natural History.

The grass was collected in the fall, and kept wet during manufacture so that it would not break (VanStone 1980:50–51). Baskets were made in a variety of sizes and shapes, and some were fitted with lids.

Bags

Bags were made in a wide variety of shapes and sizes for storing or transporting all manner of goods, ranging from small items—such as spruce pitch, fire-making equipment (flint and steel or pyrites, dry willow catkins), fishing gear, sewing equipment (including needles, thimbles, thread), and lance points—to large items, such as bedding and clothing (see Figure 40).[198] The raw materials of which they were made were equally variable, including grass and virtually every kind of skin available, including fish skin. Many bags were plain, but others displayed ornamental patterns resulting from the variety of skins having different colors and textures, and some were made from skin from the entire head of an animal (such as a wolf). Many had elaborately carved ivory or bone handles. The manufacturing processes included the regular ones involved in sewing and carving, as described above.

Boxes

Wooden boxes of various sizes and shapes were made for the safekeeping of tools, needles, thread, jewelry, arrowheads, and other small items (Nelson 1899:93, 98; Sunno 1951.97; VanStone 1976:11; 1980:28). Rectangular boxes were sometimes carved from single blocks of wood, but others were made from five pieces of carefully shaped wood. In the latter, the ends were dovetailed into the sides, and the bottom was held in place with wooden pins. Boxes of this type were often decorated with inlaid ivory figures. Circular or oval wooden boxes were typically made by bending a thin piece of wood into the desired shape, presumably after steaming or soaking, with the overlapping ends sewn or pinned together. The bottom was inserted as with the birch-bark buckets described above. Lids were attached either with rawhide hinges, by strings run through holes in the bottom, or slid into slots carved in the sides. Wooden boxes were often shaped like animals, or decorated with carved figures and inlaid beads or pieces of ivory on the top or sides.

The Iñupiat also made containers to hold particularly small items inside the larger boxes (Sunno 1951.49, 1951.72; VanStone 1980:47). Items such as beads and fishhooks might be kept this way. Some of these so-called "trinket boxes" were simply smaller versions of the larger boxes. Others were made from a piece of caribou antler hollowed out with a beaver-tooth tool. Bottoms were flush with the sides, and held in place with wooden pins. The close-fitting tops were carved from wood.

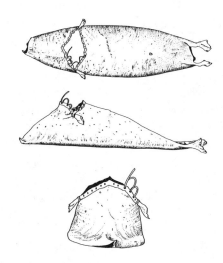

FIGURE 40. A clothing bag made from an entire spotted seal skin. From VanStone (1980:49). Reproduced with permission of the Field Museum of Natural History.

Sewing Equipment

Every Iñupiaq woman was a professional seamstress. Accordingly, she owned an array of equipment necessary to pursue her craft, as well as containers in which to store it. Three items in this array—scrapers, needles, and bodkins—were discussed above in the section on clothing.

Needles were kept in special tubular cases (sing. *uyamik*) made from antler or ivory.[199] In some instances needles were loose in the case, held there by wooden, bone, or ivory stoppers. Alternatively, they were inserted in a leather strap, the ends of which projected from the case (see Figure 41). To remove the needles, one pulled the strap at one end; to return them, one reversed the process. Women often carried the cases attached to their belt. Needle cases typically were carved with figures or designs.

Thimbles were usually made of skin, preferably that of a seal. As described by Nelson (1899:109; see also p. 110, and plate XLIV), they had "a slit extending across one edge, forming a loop-like strap, through which the forefinger is thrust, so that the strap rests across the nail and the pad of skin in the inner side of the finger." Thimbles were kept on a hook-shaped holder made of bone or ivory, usually attached by a cord to the needle case or a work bag.

Thread was made from sinew, preferably from a caribou, but alternatively from almost any species of mammal or even bird (Brower ms:158, 243; Murdoch 1892:311–12; Nelson 1899:110–11). The sinew was dried, then beaten with a maul to loosen the fibers. The fibers were divided with a small comb carved from ivory or bone, and cleaned. Two or three, or occasionally four, strands were then twisted or braided together to make the thread. The finished product was stored on a wooden, bone, or ivory shuttle-like object until needed.

Utensils

The Iñupiat had a variety of utensils for handling liquids, variously referred to in English as spoons, dippers, ladles, and scoops, usually according to the size of the bowl portion of the object.[200] Spoons, generally, were carved from a single piece of wood (wooden spoon, *qayuttaq*), although ivory, bone, and even jadeite were also carved for the purpose. Dippers, ladles, and scoops were typically carved from a single piece of wood, although many were made out of the horn of a mountain sheep that was boiled for some time, then hollowed out or molded into the desired shape (see Figure 42); some were even made out of ivory.

Another procedure used for making ladles, and also cups, was to thin a piece of wood at one end, boil that end, and bend it around, following the same procedure described above to make buckets. A wooden bottom was inserted later, while the part that was not bent was whittled into a handle. Cups were also made in a similar manner from baleen (see Figure 43), which is more flexible

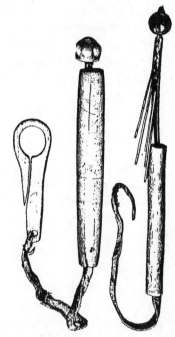

FIGURE 41. Two needle cases. The one on the left has a belt hook and is nearly closed. The one on the right is open, showing the needles inserted in the leather strap. From Murdoch (1892:321).

than wood, hence did not require boiling. Cups were also carved from tree roots or burls, and made out of birch bark.

The snowbeater was an another important utensil in an Iñupiaq household (Bockstoce 1977:74; Nelson 1899:77–78; VanStone 1976:28; 1980:53–54). When one entered a house with snow on one's clothes, the snow melted, weakening the material of which the clothing was made, and creating the need to dry it thoroughly before it could be worn again. To prevent this, snow was beaten from clothes before the wearer entered the heated part of the dwelling. The utensil employed for this task was usually a long, thin piece of wood flattened over much of its length, but with a narrow, rounded grip. There were many variations, however. Beaters could be made from ivory, antler, and bone, and they could be curved as well as straight. Some had special grips lashed onto the handle, and some had rawhide loops attached to the handles so that they could be worn on a belt. Many were carved with designs or figures.

The final item in the list of utensils is the back scratcher. The Iñupiat were infested with lice, which, I am told, itched annoyingly, as did various other skin irritations. The back scratcher was used to deal with this problem. As a rule, it consisted of a straight rod with a small, circular antler or ivory disk attached across one end (Nelson 1899:310; VanStone 1976:28–29; 1980:54).

Toys

A final category of goods found in most households consisted of toys.[201] The most common were models of items that youngsters would use in earnest later in life. Boys had model sleds, kayaks, *umiat*, slingshots, and small bows and arrows. Girls played with dolls (sing. *iñuuraq*) that were carved into human shapes from ivory, wood, antler, or bone, and often dressed with clothes mimicking adult garments. They also had model dishes and household utensils for their amusement. Realistically rendered animal figurines were also common. There were also various types of buzz toys. The most prominent of these was the so-called "bull roarer" (*imigluktaaq*), which consisted of an elongated, thin wooden board notched along the edges, and attached by a line to a stick. One held the stick and whirled the board around, which

FIGURE 42. A dipper made from the horn of a mountain sheep. An antler peg is driven into the handle to serve as a hook by which to hang the dipper from the edge of a bucket. From Murdoch (1892:101).

FIGURE 43. A cup made from a strip of baleen bound around a spruce bottom. The ends were sewn together with strips of baleen. The original was 4.6 inches (11.7 cm) in diameter. From Murdoch (1892:101).

produced a buzzing sound. Tops, other types of buzz toys, and darts round out the basic list. The Iñupiat were creative, and improvised diverse other gadgets, including mechanical ones, for the amusement of their children.

Hunting Equipment

This section deals with the weapons used primarily to kill mammals and birds, and with various related items of equipment. Fishing equipment is discussed in a separate section. Nets, which were used to capture fish, some birds, and some mammals, are dealt with in still another section that appears after the discussion of the manufacture of thread, twine, and line.

Bows and Arrows

The bow-and-arrow complex consisted of bows, arrows, quivers, waterproof bags in which to carry the bows, and wristguards, plus a set of tools needed for the manufacture and maintenance of the weapons. These were important items in a man's kit for, as Kashevarov (VanStone ed. 1977:89) observed in 1838, "The Eskimo devotes every spare moment to making or repairing his weapons. Wherever he goes he takes his bow and quiver of arrows with him."

Bows were made from wood that was progressively reduced from its original form to the desired size by means of the woodworking tools and procedures described earlier. They ranged from about forty-three to fifty-four inches (110–138 cm) in length, and were of two basic types (see Figure 44).[202] The simple bow (*aiyakpak*) was "made from one piece of wood, and depend[ed] entirely upon the elasticity of the wooden arm for the cast of the arrow" (T. Hamilton 1970:43, 45). The complex bow (*pisiksi/qalluiññaq*) was made from one or more pieces of wood, but instead of being a simple curve, it had a staff that resembled a simple bow in the center, but also had a siyah (straight rigid extension) on each end, and "knees" (or bends) at the junctures. To produce this distinctive shape, the wood was wrapped in shavings soaked in water and positioned over a fire. When the wood had softened, it was pegged down on the ground in the desired form, and left to cool (F. Beechey 1831, II:309; see also Bockstoce 1977:21).

Bowstrings were made from caribou sinew. The string of a simple bow was in contact with the wood only at the tips, whereas the string of a complex bow was "in contact with about a foot [30 cm] of the wood at each end" (F. Beechey 1831, II:309). The siyahs made the complex bow a more powerful and efficient weapon than its simple counterpart,

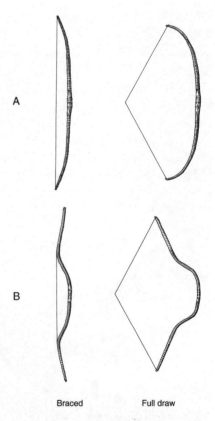

A

B

Braced   Full draw

FIGURE 44. Sketches of simple (A) and complex (B) bows, braced and at full draw. Sketches by Jack Scott.

but when the released string hit the staff, it "made a report that would be fatal to secrecy" (F. Beechey 1831, II:309).

While some simple bows had sinew backing, all complex bows did. Backing consisted of a complex network of braided caribou sinew (or sometimes baleen) stretched along the length of the bow to add strength and resilience. The addition of the sinew backing was very intricate, as described by Murdoch (1892):

> Having the bow sprung back one end of a long piece of sinew twine was made fast temporarily to the upper nock, leaving an end long enough to finish off the bowstring. The other end was carried round the lower nock and the returning strand half-hitched round the first snugly up to the nock, and then carried round the upper nock and back again. This was repeated, each strand being half-hitched round all the preceding at the lower nock until there were eight parallel strands, and an eye fitted snugly to the lower nock. The bight was then slipped off the upper nock, the end untied and the whole twisted tight. This twisted string is now about 2 inches too long, so the upper eye is made by doubling over 2 inches of the end and stopping it down with the free end mentioned above, thus making a long eye of seven strands. With the end, six similar strands are added to the eye, each being stopped to the twist with a half hitch. The end is neatly tucked in and the strands of the eye twisted tightly together (Murdoch 1892:198; Bockstoce 1977:21–22 has close-up photographs of backing).

The result was a cable stretching the length of the bow, held in place on the front of the frame by half hitches. Additional reinforcement was sometimes provided by placing pieces of antler, bone, or hide beneath the cable. Seemann (1853, II:53) reported that the Iñupiaq bow was "most ingeniously strengthened by thongs of deer-sinew," and Murdoch (1885a:169) characterized the sinew-backed bow as a "marvel of complication and perfection."

Proper tension on the cable was a crucial factor in the amount of spring in the bow, hence the power imparted to an arrow. Moisture caused the cable to expand, thus reducing the spring, so men were very careful to keep their weapons dry. But atmospheric conditions and ordinary use also affected the tension, therefore requiring frequent adjustments. These were effected by means of a marlinespike and two sinew twisters. A marlinespike was a small (3–7 in/7.6–17.8 cm), sharp-pointed rod made of ivory or hard bone (Bockstoce 1977:24–25; Murdoch 1892:292). A twisting rod was a small (ca. 4–5 in/10–13 cm) blunt rod of the same material having four flat sides and a small ridge at each end, the ridges facing in opposite directions from one another (Bockstoce 1977:26–27; Murdoch 1892:292–94; VanStone 1980:27–28). The marlinespike was forced among the strands of backing to allow for entry of the twister. Murdoch (1892) described how the twister was used:

> The end is inserted between the strands at the middle of the bow, so that the ridge or hook catches the lower strands, and the end is carried over through an arc of 180%, which gives the cable a half turn of twist. This brings the twister against the bow, so that the twisting can be carried no further in this direction, and if the tool were to be removed for a fresh start, the strands would have to be held or fastened in some way, making the process a slow one. Instead, the tool is slid back between the strands till the other end comes where the first was, so that the hook at this end catches the strand, and the workman can give to the cable another half turn of twist. This is continued until the cable is sufficiently twisted, the tool sliding back and forth like the handle of a vise. The tools are used in pairs, one being inserted in each cable and manipulated with each hand, so as to give the same amount of twist to each cable (Murdoch 1892:293).

Arrows were usually made from spruce, almost always acquired in the form of driftwood (Bockstoce 1977:27–29; Cantwell 1889b:86; Murdoch 1892:201). The wood was reduced to the shape of a cylindrical rod some twenty-five to thirty inches (64–75 cm) long with the woodworking tools and techniques already described. Then it usually had to be straightened. This was done with a special tool carved out of ivory or antler (Bockstoce 1977:31–31; Nelson 1899:88; VanStone 1980:41). An arrow-shaft straightener was a (roughly) rectangular antler or ivory rod widened sufficiently near one end so that a hole could be cut that was large enough to fit an arrow through; the opposite end served as a handle. Straighteners were often carved in the shapes of real or fanciful animals, and decorated with designs of various kinds.

Before a straightener could be used, the shaft of the prospective arrow was bound in a spiral direction with fine wood shavings, immersed in water, and held over a fire (Belcher ms, quoted by Bockstoce 1977:31). When the wood was judged to be ready, the shavings were stripped off and the straightener applied. When the shaft had acquired the desired form and cooled, a nock was cut in the end, and feathers were attached. To do this, the shaft of a feather six or seven inches (15–18 cm) long was split and the web trimmed to an aerodynamic taper. Then, with yet another special tool (Bockstoce 1977:32–33; Murdoch 1892:294), the two, sometimes three, feathers were wedged into slits cut near the end of the shaft and bound in place with fine sinew or baleen.

Arrowheads took a wide variety of forms depending on the purpose for which the weapon was to be used.[203] Arrows for caribou were tipped with ivory, bone, or chert. Arrows used for bears had heavier shafts, were a bit longer than caribou arrows, and were tipped with iron or chert. Arrows intended for large birds were usually tipped with antler or ivory, while for small birds, arrows had blunt tips that would kill the bird without damaging it. Finally, fish arrows had two or three antler or ivory prongs on the tip in the general form of the head of a leister. The arrowhead was placed in a slit in the end of the shaft and held there by sinew lashing.

Four more items completed the bow-and-arrow complex. One was a quiver, which was a long, straight sealskin or caribou-skin bag stiffened with a wooden or ivory rod held in place by ties, and equipped with a shoulder strap for carrying (Murdoch 1892:207–9; VanStone 1976:13). The second was a waterproof case for the bow, an important item because the backing and bowstring stretched if wet. The quiver and case were often attached to one another. The third item was a wristguard, which was a small shield of bone, antler, or baleen strapped onto the forearm of the hand holding the bow to protect it from the snap of the bowstring (Murdoch 1892:209–10; VanStone ed. 1977:89). The final item was a three-fingered glove worn on the hand pulling the drawstring (Campbell 1998: figure 37).

Harpoons

A harpoon is a spear to which the head is not permanently attached.[204] When prey is struck, the head detaches from the shaft. This eliminates the torque that a thrashing animal would place on the rest of the weapon, which might dislodge the head or break the main part of the spear. After a successful strike, the shaft either floats to the surface or, if attached to the retaining line, serves as a drag. The harpoon head remains embedded in the prey, while the hunter, or the shaft, or a float, remains attached to the harpoon head via a retaining line.

Iñupiaq harpoons were sophisticated weapons having several components. These, and the raw materials of which they were usually made, are listed in Table 21. The materials and the ways in which they were acquired and modified were all discussed previously. As far as I am aware, no special tools were required to make a harpoon.

Table 21. Harpoon Components

COMPONENT	MATERIAL(S)
blade	chert, slate, ivory
finger rest	ivory
foreshaft	ivory, walrus baculum, antler
head	ivory, bone, antler
ice pick	walrus baculum, ivory
lashings	sealskin line, baleen, caribou sinew
retrieval line	seal, oogruk, or walrus skin line
shaft	wood (spruce)
socket piece	walrus baculum, ivory

The arrangement of the various components on the weapon itself is illustrated in Figure 45, which shows two different models. Figure 45A shows a sealing harpoon dart about 60 inches (150 cm) long. This type of harpoon was ordinarily used by men hunting in kayaks or stalking sleeping seals on the ice, and has a comparatively short and light shaft. The head is a single piece of ivory in which tangs have been cut; the absence of a toggle shows that it was intended for use against small seals, which lacked the strength to dislodge a barbed point. There is no blade. Once the head had penetrated the prey, it disengaged from the end of the shaft, while remaining attached to it by the retrieval line, which is twisted around and ultimately tied to the shaft in the diagram. As the seal tried to escape, the line unwound, and the animal ended up pulling the shaft behind. This acted as a drag and helped exhaust it. More commonly, the retrieval line was attached to the middle of a separate line that was connected to the shaft at two different points. This caused it to be pulled at right angles to the seal's course, which increased the drag. Sometimes the retrieval line was attached to a small float made from a walrus intestine or stomach. That increased the drag even more, and made it easier for the hunter to locate his prey.

Figure 45B is a sketch of a heavy ice-hunting harpoon about 80 inches (200 cm) long. This type of harpoon was longer and heavier than the one illustrated in Figure 45A. It was used

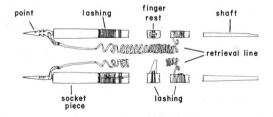

A. Sealing harpoon dart

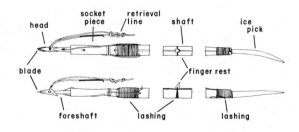

B. Ice hunting harpoon

FIGURE 45. Two types of harpoon and their components. Adapted from VanStone (1980:21, 24). Reproduced with the permission of the Field Museum of Natural History. Keyed to Table 21.

by men hunting on foot on the sea ice, and could be either thrust or thrown. The proximal end is an ice pick used to test the thickness of the ice as the hunter moved about on it. At the distal end, an iron blade is set in a toggling head that is designed to turn sideways to the direction of the drag on the line when implanted in the prey. This weapon has a foreshaft, which gave way when the animal was struck, thus helping release the point from the shaft without damage to the latter, and allowing it to float to the surface; the head remained embedded in the seal.

Variations in harpoon structure included differences in the thickness and length of the shaft, the presence or absence of a foreshaft, the flexibility of the foreshaft when present, the presence or absence of a large basal spur and/or blade on the head, the presence or absence of an ice pick on the proximal end of the shaft, and the presence or absence of drag floats. The largest prey, the bowhead whale, was pursued with harpoons having heavy shafts, fixed foreshafts, toggle heads, slate or chert blades, and retrieval lines made of heavy oogruk- or walrus-skin rope attached to three inflated sealskin pokes. The smallest prey pursued with harpoons were ringed seals, which were taken with weapons such as the one represented in Figure 45A.

Other Spears and Lances

In addition to harpoons, the Iñupiaq collection of hunting equipment included a variety of thrusting and throwing weapons with long shafts. Like harpoons, they varied in the number of component parts, the form of the head, the material used to make the head, and the size. In contrast to harpoons, all of these weapons had fixed heads. The materials of which they were constructed were generally the same, however: wood for the shafts, and slate, chert, ivory, antler, or bone for the other components. To my knowledge, no special tools were required for their manufacture.

Thrusting spears, 5 or 6 feet (1.5–1.8 m) long, were used to dispatch caribou caught in snares, or to spear them while swimming.[205] A longer and heaver version of this weapon was used to kill bears, particularly brown bears. Essentially, a thrusting spear was little more than a very long-handled knife, with a large chert, slate, ivory, or occasionally jade blade (see Figure 46) inserted in a socket at the distal end and lashed with sealskin or rawhide line.

Killing lances were similar in structure to thrusting spears, but were a bit heavier, and apparently had particularly wide and elegantly made chert blades (Booth 1960.1; B. Foote 1992:48, 49). Both Brower (ms:171) and Woolfe (1893:147) referred to the blades as being as "large as a man's hand," and "beautifully flaked." They were used to dispatch large wounded sea mammals, such as walrus and bowhead whales, which had become exhausted from pulling drag floats and being too harassed by the hunters to catch their breath. The lances used to kill bowheads had shafts 12 feet (3.65 m) long.

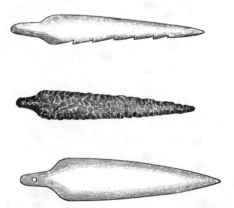

FIGURE 46. A series of spear blades. The one on top was carved from antler; the one in the middle was made from flint; and the one on the bottom was made from jade. From Cantwell (1889b: plate 1).

Bird spears were employed to kill molting birds unable to fly (Cantwell 1889b:86; Thornton 1931:142; VanStone 1976:13; 1980:28, 30, 31; 1990:10–11). Designed to be thrown, they had relatively light shafts 60 to 66 inches (155–170 cm) long. The head consisted of a single antler, bone, or ivory point barbed on one side (see Figure 47). In addition, there were three barbed prongs extending outward in a triangle around the shaft, located toward the middle or even the proximal end.

FIGURE 47. Segment of a bird spear. From VanStone (1980:31). Reproduced with permission of the Field Museum of Natural History.

FIGURE 48. Segment of a fish spear. From VanStone (1980:31). Reproduced with permission of the Field Museum of Natural History.

The final weapon to be discussed here is the fish spear, or leister (Booth 1960.2; Giddings 1952:41; VanStone 1976:17; 1980:35; 1990:12). This spear had three antler or ivory prongs at the distal end, one in the form of a point projecting beyond the end of the shaft, and the other two as barbed side prongs on opposite sides (see Figure 48). It was usually employed to spear fish attracted to a lure dangled through a hole in the ice, or from a kayak.

One more item that is usefully discussed in this section is the throwing board, or atlatl (F. Beechey 1831, I:445; Belcher ms:65; Bockstoce 1977:44–46). This was not a weapon, but an instrument designed to improve the power of certain spears. The throwing board was a narrow wooden platform carved in the shape of a long (ca. 18 in/45 cm) triangle (see Figure 49). A grip extended beyond the wide end, a hole was cut for the forefinger, and there was a notch for the thumb. A groove extended down the middle to an ivory catch at the narrow end.

FIGURE 49. Two throwing boards. From Murdoch (1892:217).

The weapon was placed in the groove, and the catch fit into a groove carved in the butt end of the spear. Throwing boards were typically used with bird spears and the lighter types of harpoon as an extension of the hunter's arm. By providing greater leverage, they greatly increased the weapon's thrust.

Miscellaneous Sealing Gear

Several items of equipment, in addition to harpoons, were employed by seal hunters. By placing them in a miscellaneous category I do not mean to imply that they were optional or trivial, because they were not; it is just an organizational convenience. Seal nets, which might have been included here, are discussed along with other types of net in a separate section below.

Men hunting seals at their breathing holes in the sea ice sat or stood on a triangular-shaped, three-legged wooden stool (*nikivġautaq*) (B. Foote 1992:51; VanStone 1990:7). A triangular hole was cut out of the center, and all the edges were beveled to reduce its weight. A small strip of ivory was inserted in one side of the top to use as a scraper in removing ice from the hunter's boots; an amulet was often attached to the bottom for luck in hunting; and a shoulder strap of sealskin was pinned to the seat for ease in carrying. Sealskin rope was wound tightly around the legs; when a hunter had drifted out and could find a small piece of ice he could kneel on, he thrust the ice pick end of his harpoon (or an ice staff) between this rope and the seat and used the stool as paddle.

Men hunting on the sea ice usually employed a harpoon that had an ice pick on the proximal end, but sometimes they did not (B. Foote 1992:53; VanStone 1976:15). In this case, they carried a long-handled ice pick (*unaaq*) to test the strength of the ice, which frequently was not as great as it appeared to be even to the experienced eye. The pick consisted of a long wooden staff tipped with a rod of ivory, antler, or bone.

Hunters on the ice seeking seals in the water often made use of a special scratcher (*argaun*) (VanStone 1976:11; 1980:26). This was usually a curved piece of wood, wider at one end than the other, with two or (usually) three "fingers" cut out of the wider end. A seal claw was lashed onto the end of each finger. The narrower end of the implement was a grip. The hunter lay on the ice, harpoon at the ready, and scratched the surface of the ice with this device. Curious seals that approached to investigate the source of the sound were harpooned.

Seals, as noted above, were virtually always taken with a harpoon or dart rather than a lance. The harpoon attached the prey to a line, which was either held by the hunter or attached to a harpoon shaft or a drag float. Pulling it eventually exhausted the seal, at which point it became possible to kill it with a club. Sealing clubs were of two different types. The simplest one consisted of a round stone with a hole drilled through it, and a short sealskin line passing through the hole (B. Foote 1992:49). The hunter inserted his hand through a loop at the other end of the line, grasped the straight part with his hand, and hit the seal on the head with the stone. More elaborate clubs had a wooden or bone handle to which a knob of bone or ivory was attached (VanStone 1976:11; 1980:26).

Having killed a seal on the ice, the next problem was to get the carcass home, or at least onto solid shore ice where the hunter's wife could retrieve it. This was done by dragging, which was feasible due to the animal's streamlined shape and tough skin. It was done with a drag line, of which there were two basic types. The simpler version consisted of a line, usually made from oogruk skin, with a loop at one end, and a small ivory toggle at the other. A slit was cut from the seal's eye through the roof of its mouth, through which the loop was placed and coiled over the muzzle (H. Anungazuk 2002). The hunter then grasped the toggle at the other end of the line, dragging the seal behind him (Bockstoce 1977:66–67; VanStone 1976:11–12; 1980:26–27; 1990:9–10). Toggles, more commonly known as "drag handles," were almost always carved into the shapes of animals or decorated with designs.

The more elaborate type of drag line consisted of an oogruk-skin strap having three parts: "a shoulder strap, a pulling rope, and a short piece of hide made into two permanent loops, one slightly smaller than the other" (B. Foote 1992:53, 54). The larger loop went through a cut in the seal's lower jaw and over its snout, while the smaller loop was attached to the pulling rope. The other end of the pulling rope was attached to loops at each end of the shoulder strap, which went across the hunter's chest and around his shoulders. Once everything was set, the hunter placed the strap across his chest and dragged the seal to shore-fast ice, where it was retrieved by his wife.

The final item to be discussed in this section is the so-called "probe." Dead seals float in winter, but, no longer buoyed by a thick layer of blubber, sink in spring and summer. Therefore, men hunting seals by kayak would have considerable difficulty getting their harvest home if they did not have some means of floating the carcass to tow behind their boat. To deal with this problem, slits were made at various points in the seal's skin, and a long curved rod of antler, pointed at one end, was inserted to loosen the blubber from the skin over a space perhaps 12 inches (30 cm) square (Nelson 1898:131; Sunno 1951.73; VanStone 1976:12; 1990:10). A hollow tube made from the wing bone of a bird was used as a straw to blow air into, and thus inflate, the space so created. A wooden plug was quickly inserted to prevent the air from escaping. The creation of several such spots kept it from sinking and made it easier to tow to shore.

Miscellaneous Whaling Gear

Other types of equipment in addition to harpoons were required to harvest whales. These are conveniently grouped into a miscellaneous category, which, as in the previous section, does not imply that they were optional or insignificant.

One important item was an ice pick (Brower ms:176; B. Foote 1992:50; Woolfe 1893:147). This consisted of a wooden shaft about 8 to 10 feet (2.5–3 m) long with an ivory point hafted onto the distal end. The working end of the point was carved from the part of the tusk that had been in the walrus jaw, since it was harder than the pointed end. This tool was used to make a path through the piles of ice to an open lead where whales were to be found, and also to make a ramp in the ice up which a dead whale could be hauled.

Flensing tools were used to butcher whales. There were two types (B. Foote 1992:55–57). One was a long-bladed (16 in/42 cm) ivory butchering knife sharpened on both edges that was attached to a long (90 in/226 cm) wooden pole. This was used to mark off shares on the whale's skin, and to slice through the blubber and meat. The other was a spade-shaped ivory or bone knife in which the cutting edge consisted of chert chips set into a piece of bone. The handle was 8 to 10 feet (2.5–3 m) long (Brower ms:171–72). It was used to separate the meat from the bones.

Whale meat, skin, and blubber were cut into large chunks that were too heavy and slippery to handle easily. The tool devised to help deal with this problem was the blubber hook (Bockstoce 1977:73–74; Brower ms:172; B. Foote 1992:56, 58). It consisted of a wooden pole at the distal end of which an ivory, bone, or antler rear-facing spike was lashed at an angle away from the pole. To provide a better grip, the proximal end of the shaft was either bent at a right angle, or else equipped with a bone or antler handle lashed onto the shaft.

The final item in the miscellaneous whaling equipment list is the float, which was the same as a poke except that it was filled with air rather than food. Three such floats, made of inflated whole sealskins, were attached to a harpoon head's retrieval line to serve as a drag on the struck animal and as an indicator of its location. They were essential to the success of the whaling enterprise.

Charles Brower's description of how the skin was removed from a seal to make a poke was quoted earlier in this chapter. I now continue with his account of how the float was made:

> The skin was then carefully cleaned of all blubber, the hind and front flippers
> removed, an ivory plug with a round hole in it then lashed in the skin, usually
> under one of the front flippers, and all the other holes in the skin were then care-
> fully sewn up. The last thing done was to fit a small piece of wood in the opening
> at the head around which the skin was lashed tightly. All this done the float was
> then blown full of air and the plug tightly jambed [sic] in the ivory plug (Brower
> ms:171; see also B. Foote 1992:55–56; VanStone 1976:10, 12; 1990:8).

The ivory plugs, known as inflation nozzles, were often carved in the shapes of humans or
animals (Bockstoce 1977:67–68).

The largest of the three floats was attached to the very end of the retrieval line, and the
two smaller ones were tied, side by side, a bit farther down the line. The large float often had
a wooden disc with the face of a person or animal carved on it attached to the neck opening.
When a whale fled, the spirit in the disc was supposed to call out and lead its owner to the
wounded animal (Bockstoce 1977:69; Rainey 1947:257).

Snares

Snares were employed to catch ptarmigan, ducks, ground squirrels, hares, marmots, foxes,
caribou, mountain sheep, and brown bears.[206] Their value lay in the fact that, once set, they
did their work while the hunter who owned them could attend to other business. When
triggered, they captured the prey, often killing it via strangulation.

The basic component of a snare was a line whose length and thickness varied according to
the size and strength of the intended prey. A snare for small game (*magluqsaq*), for example,
was short, and usually made of braided sinew or baleen fibers. A snare for caribou or mountain
sheep (*nigaq*), on the other hand, was sometimes 20 feet (6 m) or more in length and made
from braided oogruk line. Snares used for bears were made from extra-thick oogruk line.

In most cases the noose was formed by running one end of the line through a knotted
loop at the other. For small game, however, it was sometimes formed by fastening one end
of the line to a wood or bone cylinder, forming a loop, and running the free end back
through the cylinder. The trick was to keep the noose open in such a way that the prey
would place its head through it, then draw tight around its neck. With small snares this
was often done with blades of grass or twigs; sometimes snares were placed in hollow
logs into which the prey was lured with bait. Another technique was to put bait inside a
snowbank, set the snare in front of it, and cover the whole with a thin layer of snow; an
animal trying to dig out the bait would spring the snare. Large snares were held open by
poles that were strong enough to bear the weight of an empty noose, but weak enough to
yield when the prey's head went through it.

The free end of a snare had to be attached to an anchor. For caribou, sheep, and bears,
this was often a deadman—that is, a rock or log placed in a hole, covered with soil and
water, and frozen in. Alternatives included large rocks, or the base of strong willows or
cottonwoods. For small game the base of a nearby shrub sufficed. However, most snares for
small game were attached to the end of a flexible pole, one end of which was placed in the
ground, and the other end bent over and held in place by a hook or weight that was tripped
when the animal got caught, lifting it up and strangling it.

In most cases, the line and the cylinder (for small game) were the only items prepared
in advance; sometimes decoys, particularly for ptarmigan, were prepared as well. All of the
remaining components of an effective snare set usually were made on the spot. These items
could include, in addition to anchors and springs, appropriately sized fences of wood or rock

to guide the prey toward the snares. Molting ducks swimming along the grassy margin of a pond were often caught by a string of snares attached to a log.

Traps

The most commonly used type of trap for catching foxes, otters, lynx, minks, martens, and wolverines, and occasionally brown bears, was the deadfall.[207] This was a trap so constructed that a heavy weight fell on the prey, holding it so it couldn't escape, and often killing it outright. The larger the intended prey, the larger and heavier the deadfall had to be.

The basic deadfall was made of two logs, one placed flat on the ground, the other held directly above it by a vertical "support stick," which, in turn, was placed on the flattened end of a "trigger stick." The opposite end of the trigger was sharpened to a point. The weight of the raised log was often increased by rocks lashed to it. Bait was placed on the pointed end of the trigger. When an animal took the bait, it moved the trigger, which released the support, causing the weighted log to fall, pinning the animal, and sometimes killing it.

There were many variations on the basic theme. One was to use rocks instead of logs. Another was to bevel the interior edges of both logs to a sharp edge, so that the animal would be held more firmly. For large animals the ground was sometimes cut away below the lower log and covered with twigs and snow. When an animal was pinned but not killed, its frantic movements to escape knocked away the twigs and snow, leaving it suspended by the neck. Fences were often built to guide the intended prey so that the trap could be approached from the direction in which it would be most effective.

A more elegant device was the spring trap, which, unlike the deadfall, required a fair amount of advance preparation. Spring traps were used primarily to kill wolves. This item is sufficiently complex that, instead of describing it myself, I present E. W. Nelson's illustration of one in Figure 50, and his description of how it worked.

> 1–1 is a cylinder of wood, that material or bone ordinarily being used for these traps; 2–2 are crosspieces of wood or bone, bound together by strong sinew cords;

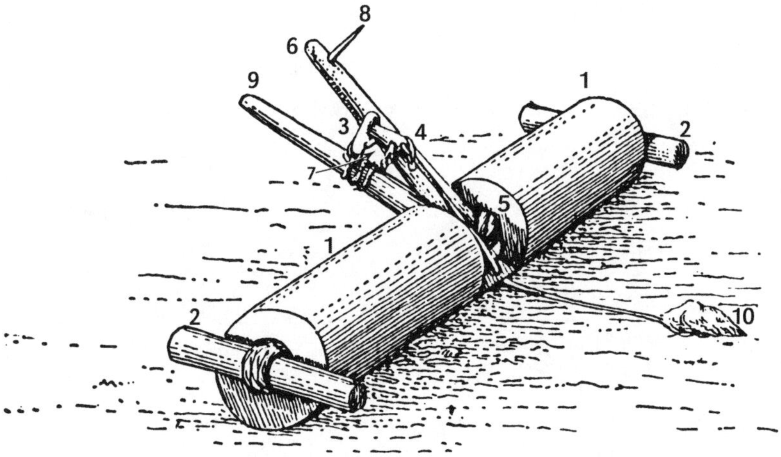

FIGURE 50. A spring trap. From Nelson (1899:123). See also Thornton (1931:218) and VanStone (1976:15).

3 is an ivory or bone block; 4 is an ivory or bone pin, fitting into 3, and is attached to a cord passing through a hole in the cylinder to the bait at 10; 5 is a slot cut through the side of the cylinder; 6 is a stout lever of bone with a knob at its inner end, which is inserted through the cords connecting 2–2; 8 is a pointed spike of bone or ivory . . . ; 7 is a peg projecting from the side of the lever. 2–2 are twisted in opposite directions until the twisting of the connecting cords, which pass around them and through the cylinder, causes a strong tension, thus holding the crosspieces so firmly against the ends of the cylinders that they cannot slip back. This also draws the cord so taut in the cylinder that when the lever, 6, is drawn back to lie parallel with 9, a great resistance is encountered, acting like a spring to throw it back to its first position. The lever, 6, is held in position next to 9 by passing 4 over 7 and into 3. The bait is tied to the end of a cord attached to 4 at 10, so that it lies just within 8. The trap is then fastened firmly to the ground and concealed with earth, but care is taken to insure the free working of the lever. The bait is then exposed in line with the lever and when a slight pull is given, the pin, 4, is freed and the lever springs sharply over, burying the spike set in its end in the skull of the animal (Nelson 1899:123).

Bolas

A bolas (*qiḻamitaun*) consisted of several lines of braided sinew or sealskin about 3 feet (1 m) or more long tied together, sometimes with feathers, at one end (see Figure 51).[208] At the other end, the lines were tied individually to small stones, or pieces of bone, antler, or ivory. Where stones were involved, grooves had to be pecked around the sides for the attachment of the lines. Bone, antler, or ivory pieces had to be cut into equivalent sizes and shapes, and then drilled, to serve as weights.

Holding onto the knotted end, the hunter twirled the bolas around once or twice, then hurled it up into the flock of waterfowl as it passed overhead. As the device lost speed the weights spread out. As Nelson (1899:134–35) described it, when one of the weights or its cord touched a bird, "the other [weights] appeared as if endowed with intelligence; their course was rapidly changed, and the bird enwrapped as completely as it if had been struck squarely by the sling." The bolas was a very effective weapon for capturing low-flying waterfowl near the end of points of land along the coast.

Thread, Twine, and Line

Thread, twine, and line were crucial to survival in the rugged conditions of northwestern Alaska. The diverse uses to which these goods were put have been mentioned in earlier sections of this chapter, but little has been said about how they were made.

The manufacture and maintenance of thread, twine, and line required considerable skill and a major investment of time, particularly on the part of women. These products were made from a variety of raw materials and produced in different thicknesses and strengths according to the uses for which they were intended. For purposes of convenience, the following discus-

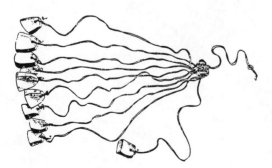

FIGURE 51. A bolas. From Cantwell (1889b:plate II).

sion proceeds generally from thinner to thicker through the somewhat arbitrary headings of thread, twine, and line. Items in each category could be enlarged and strengthened by braiding several of them together.

Thread

Sinew taken from the back or legs of a caribou, and from beluga, seals, and ptarmigan, were made into thread, but suitable sinew from almost every type of animal could be used for the purpose.[209] Regardless of its source, the sinew was dried and beaten with a maul to loosen the fibers. The fibers were then divided with a small comb and pulled off with the fingers. Irregularities and loose fibers were removed by hand.

The thread resulting from the above process was too thin and weak for most purposes. In order to strengthen it, two or more fibers were twisted or braided together through one of a variety of procedures, and two or more pieces were spliced together to attain the desired length.[210] The heaviest thread was used to make fishing lines and thread for sewing oogruk- or walrus-skin boat covers. Three or four pieces of thread could be braided together to form twine, which could be used to make gill nets.

Twine

Twine, or relatively thin rope, was made from a variety of substances, including sealskin, caribou skin, baleen, bark, and roots.[211]

Sealskin Twine

The strongest and most versatile twine was made from sealskin. It was used for lashing together the components of sleds, boats, and other objects; constructing seal and beluga nets; in making medium-strength snares and harpoon lines; and for a variety of other purposes. Sealskin twine was invaluable to the Iñupiat because of its strength and flexibility, and was a major item of trade between coastal districts and the interior.

The initial preparation of sealskin to be made into rope, as discussed in an earlier section of this chapter, yielded what amounted to a tube of hide. The tube was placed in some kind of a container or wrapped in an old boat cover, and placed in a warm place for several days to season, along with enough blubber to keep it moist. When it was ready, the by-now quite odiferous hide was removed, and the epidermis, hair, and any remaining oil were scraped off. It was then ready for cutting.

Cutting required the close cooperation of two people—often, but not necessarily, husband and wife. One person, usually the husband, was the cutter, and the other, usually the wife, was the puller. To begin with, the tube of skin was turned inside-out, which gave the participants a somewhat better grip. Using a crooked knife, the cutter made a slit in the edge of the skin the width of the desired twine, made a hole in it, and placed a small stick or similar object through the hole to serve as an initial grip for the puller.

The two then sat facing each other, each holding with one hand the narrower (rear) end of the skin tube. The cutter, with his free hand, placed the knife into the already prepared slit. The puller, with her free hand, grasped the stick and began to pull, slowly and very steadily, on what was to become the twine. As this was done, the skin tube rotated around the two people's hands so that the twine was removed from its upper edge in a continuous piece. When it could be pulled no farther, the puller stopped, moved the hand up to a point near the tube, gave the line a few turns around another stick to serve as a grip, and pulled some more. The process was repeated until the tube had been completely transformed into twine. If done properly, the procedure resulted in twine of uniform thickness, hence strength, throughout. If the puller varied the speed with which the line was drawn, or the cutter failed to hold the knife at exactly the same angle throughout the exercise, the result was an unsatisfactory twine in which some portions were too strong, and others were too weak.

The twine was then coiled, and soaked in water to remove any dirt particles and/or residual oil. After a brief time, it was removed, and the water squeezed out. The final step was to hang the line between two poles that were erected parallel to the ground. It was not stretched taut, but allowed to droop just a bit in the middle. The necessary stretching was performed by gravity. When dry, the line was somewhat thinner than it had been when it was first hung. It was then either placed into immediate service, or coiled and placed in a safe place until needed.

Caribou-Skin Twine

Caribou skin was also made into twine (Murdoch 1892:302; Northwest Iñupiat Elders Conference 1976d:2–9; Tingook 1960.4). Ideally, the process began with a fawn or yearling hide that had not dried out. The hair side was wet with warm water, and the hide was rolled up, hair side in, and stored in a warm place for three days. (If it was stored for longer than that, the rope would be too weak.) Then it was unrolled, and the by-now easily removed hair was scraped off. The preliminary phase concluded with the hide being thoroughly washed.

One way to produce the rope was to begin by making a hole in the center of the skin. From there, the cutter worked around the hole, moving progressively outwards, cutting the skin into the desired thickness. Another way was to trim the edge of the hide to even it out, then remove the twine from the outside. As in making sealskin rope, the cutter had to focus intently on the angle of the knife and the thickness of the line, guiding the work with a thumbnail. Another person rotated the skin, pulling off the line as it was cut, making certain to pull at a very steady rate of speed. I was unable to learn if the new line was suspended between poles for a few days after being cut.

Bark Twine

Twine was also made out of the inner bark of willows, primarily in interior districts, for use in gill nets and seines.[212] The bark was peeled from willows during the winter or spring, when it was easily removed in long, narrow strips from the trunk. A special barking tool made from the radius of a lynx or the lower leg bone of a loon was used for this purpose. The outer bark was removed, and the strands of stringy inner bark were rolled into a ball for storage.

When it was time to make the nets, the strands were removed from the ball and soaked in water. From this point on, they could not be allowed to get too dry or they would turn to dust. On the other hand, if they stayed soaking wet for too long, they would stretch and break.

Strings were spliced together by overlapping the ends of two pieces, twisting them around each other, and rolling them between the palms of the hands. Whenever work was interrupted, the twine was rolled back into a ball. Women living along the Kobuk and Selawik rivers, particularly, used to spend a considerable portion of their time collecting bark, making twine, and using the twine to make and repair nets and seines.

Other Forms of Twine

Spruce roots were excavated, removed from the tree trunk, and split into strips (Giddings 1961:35; Northwest Iñupiat Elders Conference 1983d:9). The strips were then soaked until soft. They were used to lash together the components of temporary boat frames, and to sew pieces of birch bark into containers of various kinds. Strips were also braided together with willow-bark lines to make the top and bottom lines of seines and gill nets.

Twine was also made from baleen (Brower ms:419; B. Foote 1992:58–59, 61). Long thin fibers were cut from the plates and spliced together. Baleen twine was used to make fishing lines, snares, and lashings of various kinds.

The final form of twine was made from the quills of bird feathers, particularly those of loons or seagulls (Driggs 1905:92–93; B. Foote 1992:61). The quills were sliced into very thin strips, and tied together to form a line. This type of twine was used almost exclusively with fishing lures.

Line

Line, or heavy rope, was made from oogruk and walrus hide (B. Foote 1992:118; M. and M. Swan 1964.1). With these two large species, instead of removing the entire skin as a single tube, the skin was cut into three tubes, each of which was removed separately. Beyond that, the process was essentially the same as making sealskin twine, except that the material was heavier and more difficult to cut.

Splices

It was often necessary to splice segments of twine or line together when greater length was needed. This was done in one of two ways. The first was to connect the two cords directly together by a slit splice, as shown in Figure 52. This was effected by cutting a slice in each of the two cords and running the lines through them in such a way that their tips were essentially woven together.[213]

The second method was to use small ivory blocks to link two lines together. An example is presented in Figure 53 (Nelson 1899:144; VanStone 1980:25; 1990:10). Here one can see that the line on the right is permanently attached to the block, which is carved in the shape of a seal. The line on the left has a loop, the end which is run through a hole in the block and around a knob, which holds it in place. This type of arrangement had the advantage of permitting both a solid connection and the possibility of an easy disconnect.

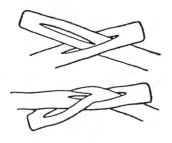

FIGURE 52. A slit splice. From Murdoch (1892:302).

FIGURE 53. A cord splicer. From Nelson (1899:144).

Nets

The Iñupiat employed nets to catch a variety of creatures: seals, beluga, fish, ptarmigan, migratory waterfowl, sea-cliff-nesting birds, hares, and foxes.[214] The material (baleen, sealskin, sinew, bark) of which the twine was made, the size of the mesh, and the size and shape of the finished net varied according to the size and strength of the prey being sought. Accordingly, most families owned several different sizes and types of net, particularly in the Kobuk and Selawik drainages. However, the same basic manufacturing techniques and equipment were involved regardless of the purpose for which a net was to be used, and it is these that concern us here.

Net-making equipment consisted of two basic items: a shuttle and a net gauge. A shuttle (*nuviḷḷaun*) was a long, flat reel of antler or wood, the ends of which were double horned, the horns bending in toward each other but not quite touching (see Figure 54). It was used for carrying the twine during net construction, and varied in size according to the thickness of the twine being used. The gauge (*kuvriñ*) was a device used to measure the size of the mesh, and consisted of both a handle and a measuring segment (see Figure 55).

Gauges were made from antler, ivory, wood, baleen, bone, or some combination of the five, either in one piece, or in two pieces lashed together.

Berit Foote (1992) described the procedure for making a fish net as follows:

> First, the net-maker winds the line twice around the gauge, then he makes a knot and pushes the line off the gauge, so that a loop twice the size of the gauge is produced. Holding the loop in an oval shape with the knot at one side, he ties on a strong piece of line at the top of the oval. This line is fastened to [a stationary object]. Now the line is stretched over the gauge, with the first loop hanging loose, and the shuttle is passed through it from below. The net-maker pulls the line up against the gauge and makes the knot for the second mesh while holding the line in place on top of the gauge with the thumb. The line is laid over the left hand, and the shuttle is passed through the second loop from below. It must pass in front of the line, for otherwise no knot will be formed.

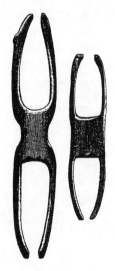

FIGURE 54. Two net shuttles, both made of caribou antler. From Murdoch (1892:313).

FIGURE 55. Three mesh gauges. The upper two were made of antler. The one on the bottom had a wooden handle and a bone blade. From Murdoch (1892:314).

> When about 35 meshes have been made in this way, one has obtained a standard depth for the net. It is now taken off the line around the [stationary object] and, picking up all the meshes between the knots, the net maker secures them collectively to this line.
>
> Now work on the length of the net begins. The meshes are left on the gauge until all 35 have been made, then they are pushed off and a new row is added. This process is repeated until the net reaches the desired length (B. Foote 1992:58).

Heavy lines were then threaded through the top and bottom rows of mesh for attaching the floats and sinkers.

Floats and sinkers were used on seines, gill nets, seal nets, and beluga nets. Sinkers were stones, or pieces of caribou antler or ivory lashed to the bottom line. Floats were pieces of wood or bark tied to the top line to keep it at or near the water's surface. Wooden spreaders were placed at each end, and sometimes in intermediate locations as well, to aid in keeping the top and bottom lines separated by the desired distance (see Figure 56). Nets that were not used in the water, such as those employed to catch ptarmigan, hares, and ducks, had spreaders, but of course did not need sinkers or floats. Dip nets, by contrast, had mesh that was curved around in a cone shape, closed at one end, and open at the other, with the open end attached to a frame that, in turn, was connected to a handle. But the basic technique for constructing the mesh was pretty much the same for all types of net.

Fishing Equipment

Equipment employed for catching fish included seines, gill nets, leisters, weirs and traps, and hook and line. The manufacture and use of most of these items have been described already, and need not be discussed again. Instead, attention is focused on goods not covered so far: dip nets, ice chisels, ice scoops, lures, and scalers.

The manufacture of the mesh for dip nets has already been described, but the overall implement has not. The following account is of the Kiitaaġmiut version.

> The dip net [*qalu*] had a rim diameter of four feet [122 cm]. The handle was about fifteen feet [4.6 m] long, and was attached to the rim by lashing with the aid of a crosspiece that crossed rim to rim by lashing off-center in a T-arrangement with the handle. The cone shaped small mesh dip net was one-and-a-half fathom[s] or nine feet [2.7 m] long. The rigid elements of the dip net were made of wood (J. Konaluk 1951.1).

An essential item for seal netting and fishing (with either a gill net or hook and line)

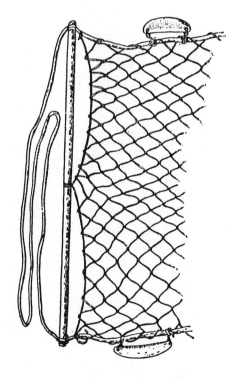

FIGURE 56. The end of a seine from Wales, with a 30-inch (76 cm) spreader, wooden floats (top), and ivory sinkers (bottom). From Nelson (1899:189).

anytime between freezeup and breakup was an ice chisel, or pick (*tuuq*) (Giddings 1952:40; Murdoch 1892:307–8). This consisted of a point of sharpened antler or ivory inserted into a hole drilled in the end of a spruce pole, reinforced at the distal end by lashings. The pole itself had to be long enough for the fisherman to chop through perhaps as much as three or four feet of ice just to get to the water's surface.

A related item was the ice scoop. Most winter fishing was done when the air temperature was below freezing, sometimes far below. This meant that ice kept forming on the water in the hole, and had to be scooped out in order that fishing could continue for more than just a few minutes. The device used to deal with the problem was the ice scoop, a typical example of which is shown in Figure 57 (Murdoch 1892:308–9; VanStone 1976:18–19; 1980:37, 38). The basket was made from a piece of antler that was thinned, shaped, soaked in water, and bent around to form a rim. The overlapping ends were sewn together with thin strips of baleen to form a loop, which was lashed to the pole with baleen. Pairs of holes were drilled around the lower edge of the loop. Through them, baleen strips were strung to form a mesh that was tight enough to catch pieces of ice, but loose enough to let water pass through.

Lures were another important item of fishing equipment. They were made of ivory, animal teeth, antler, stone, and bone, and often some combination of the five.[215] Typically, they were carved into interesting shapes and fitted with inset pieces of some other material to represent eyes, and connected to beads or rings to provide an additional attraction to fish (see Figure 58). Leaders were made from baleen or the split quill of a large feather. Lures were used in

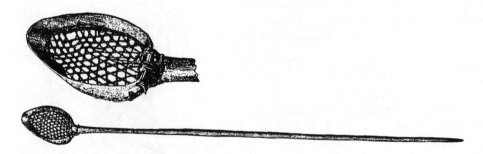

FIGURE 57. An ice scoop. From Murdoch (1892:308).

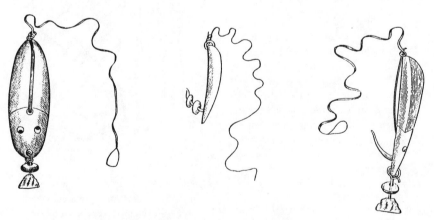

FIGURE 58. A sample of fish lures from the Kobuk River. The one in the center was made from ivory, the other two primarily from stone. From Cantwell (1889b:plate II).

two ways. One was to attract fish to within striking distance of a leister. Alternatively, lures were provided with barbless hooks and used to catch fish directly. In the latter case, the size of the lure varied according to the size of the fish being sought. Both techniques involved suspending the lure in the water and jigging it up and down, for which purpose a rod 1 to 2 feet (30–60 cm) in length was attached to the other end of the line (B. Foote 1992:61, 62; VanStone 1976:18; 1990:12–13). Lures not heavy enough to sink on their own were weighted with sinkers (VanStone 1976:18; 1980:39; 1990:13–14).

The final item to be discussed under the heading of fishing equipment is the scaler (Giddings 1952:40; Stefansson 1914b:320–21). This consisted of either a caribou scapula modified to some extent to increase its effectiveness, or a caribou rib sharpened on one edge.

Means of Transport

The Iñupiat traveled frequently and widely over the course of a normal yearly cycle, often with all or most of their goods and chattels. As one might presume after reading the descriptions of their manufactured goods up to this point, a family's possessions could be quite substantial; to move them required rather sophisticated means of transport, which varied from one season to another. In this section I briefly summarize how the various items used for transport were constructed. In a later section on travel, which appears under the more general heading of "services," I describe how they were used.

Boats

The Iñupiat had three basic types of boat: a large open boat, or *umiaq*; a decked canoe, or *qayaq* ("kayak"); and an open canoe, or *umiaġriatchiaq*. They also made rafts and other watercraft under certain circumstances.

The *umiaq* was the main means of water transport throughout most of the study region.[216] It consisted of a wooden frame over which an oogruk- or walrus-hide cover was stretched. *Umiat* varied from about 20 to some 50 feet (6–15 m) in length, although the majority were about 30 to 35 feet (9–10.5 m) long. They ranged from about 4 to 8 feet (1.2–2.4 m) in beam, and 30 to 36 inches (75–90 cm) in depth. In general, *umiat* made for travel primarily along rivers were longer and narrower than those built primarily for travel along the coast; *umiat* built as whaling boats were smaller than those constructed for travel. The most robust craft were built by the Kiŋikmiut, who were the only people in the study region who regularly ventured significant distances from shore.

Umiaq frames (see Figure 59) were made from driftwood by men, "each part being cut and fitted with the utmost nicety" to the others (Thornton 1931:125–26). The stem and stern pieces specifically were often made from a tree trunk and a large attached root, which had a natural curve even prior to shaping, as well as considerable strength. The components were lashed together with sealskin twine. This produced a strong frame, while slip joints made it flexible enough to withstand considerable stress without breaking.

The *umiaq* cover consisted of several oogruk or walrus hides from which the hair had been removed. They were soaked in water to soften, then measured against the boat frame and trimmed as necessary. The prepared skins were united with double waterproof seams by several women working together.[217] Men briefly soaked the completed cover in water again, then fitted it over the outside of the frame. By means of oogruk or baleen twine run through slits cut along the cover's edge and around the gunwale, it was stretched tight and lashed to the frame. When the cover dried, it shrank and fit the frame as tightly as a drumhead. The seams were rubbed with seal oil for additional waterproofing. *Umiaq* covers that were too

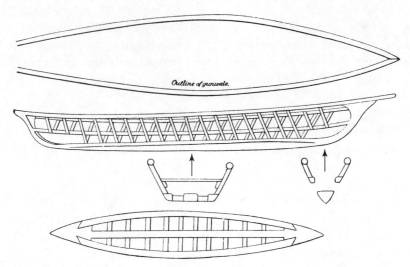

Outline of gunwale.

FIGURE 59. Frame of a model *umiaq*. From Murdoch (1892:336).

worn to serve their original purpose made excellent tarpaulins, and had a variety of other uses (T. Mitchell 1986).

The Iñupiat reckoned the size of an *umiaq* by the number of skins required to cover it. Six oogruk skins were used to cover the average 30-to-32-foot (9–9.75 m) traveling boat, while the smaller craft used for whaling usually had five-skin covers. At the other extreme, I once heard of an *umiaq* made by a wealthy Nuataaġmiu trader that required fifteen skins (M. and M. Swan 1970).

Among the Kiŋikmiut, the material of choice was split walrus hide rather than oogruk, the inner layer for the bow and stern, the outer for the rest. Splitting the hide was a difficult task requiring a great deal of time and skill. Otherwise, the construction procedure was the same as with an oogruk-skin-covered boat. Three walrus hides were required to cover a 25-to-30-foot (7.5–9 m) frame, and five for a 45-foot (14 m) frame (H. Anungazuk 2002.1).[218]

An empty 30-foot (9 m) *umiaq* drew about three or four inches (7–10 cm) of water, and was light enough for four people to lift without too much difficulty. Such a craft could carry 3,000 pounds (1,360 kg) of freight and six people (Wells and Kelly 1890:27). When fully loaded, it drew only six to eight inches (15–30 cm) of water. In both oogruk- and walrus-hide boats, additional strips of skin about a foot (30 cm) high were often sewn to the gunwales and held upward by sticks to prevent water from splashing into the craft in rough seas (Wells and Kelly 1890:27; Woolfe 1893:149). Inflated sealskin pokes or kayaks were sometimes lashed to the outside of the gunwales for greater stability.

An *umiaq* was propelled by river current, by dogs attached to the gunwale by a long line, by people tracking the boat with a similarly long line, by men using paddles, by women using oars, by sails, or by some combination of these.[219] For tracking along a beach or riverbank, whether pulled by dogs or people, a long line was attached to the gunwale on the shore side about a third of the way back from the bow. The other end of the tracking line had loops to serve as chest straps if people were pulling the boat, or the line was tied to dog harnesses.

Oars and paddles were made from driftwood. Narrow-bladed oars were attached to the gunwale by two long loops of twine, and prevented from chafing the skin cover on the gunwale by a long plate of bone or a thick layer of hide. Often there was only one oar. Its purpose was to keep away from shore a craft that was being tracked by dogs or people who were on the shore. The paddles used during the study period had blades with something of an elongated teardrop shape, although the one used to steer the boat was sometimes rounder. Paddles were often decorated with stripes of black and/or red paint to identify their owner.

Square-rigged sails, usually made from dehaired caribou hide, were rectangular in shape (Thornton 1931:125–26; Woolfe 1893:149). The single mast was held in place at its foot on the centerboard by the lower jawbone of a walrus (or similar object), and at the top by four thongs of oogruk rope attached to the gunwales and/or the stem and stern posts. The back stays were adjustable (Bockstoce 2002). A long pole, or yard, was lashed to the top of the mast. The sail was suspended from it, with the lower edge being held in place by an oogruk line at each end tied to the gunwales. Sails were used only in following winds; *umiat* could not tack upwind or hold a course on a downwind reach.

The second type of boat used in Northwest Alaska was the kayak. In general, kayaks were used for hunting rather than for travel, although sometimes two or three were rafted together for stability and used for river travel. Rafted kayaks could carry a heavier load than a group of single craft. Kayaks were ordinarily taken along as part of the freight of an *umiaq* in case they were needed for hunting.

Kayaks were made from driftwood frames over which covers of ringed seal skin, and occasionally caribou skin, were stretched.[220] The construction process was analogous to that employed in making *umiat*, with obvious adjustments for the kayak's smaller size and much more streamlined shape, and the use of lighter materials. In the study region, kayaks usually had a single hatch; otherwise they were entirely decked over (see Figure 60). They generally were about 18 inches (45 cm) wide, and ranged between about 17 and 19 feet (5.2–5.8 m) in length. Six ringed seal skins, or three large bull caribou hides, were required to cover a full-sized kayak. A waterproof parka or apron of seal intestines worn by the paddler was attached to the coaming around the cockpit, preventing water from getting inside. Kayak paddles ordinarily were double-bladed, and the blades were often ornamented with colored stripes. Kayaks frequently had various accoutrements to assist the hunter, such as sealskin deck straps to hold paddles or harpoons when not in use, ivory harpoon rests, and circular wooden racks to keep harpoon lines in good order (VanStone 1976:33; 1980:63; 1990:18–20).

The third type of boat used in Northwest Alaska was the open canoe, or *umiaġriatchiaq* (or *qayaġiaq* or *umiaġiiraq*) (see Figure 61). Such boats were built and used solely along the Kobuk and Selawik rivers. In both districts they were the primary means of water transport; for many families, they were the only means.

Open canoes had a frame of young spruce or birch whose components were acquired and shaped by men, and lashed together with split spruce roots.[221] The cover was made from overlapping pieces of birch or spruce bark placed on the frame in transverse sections. The pieces were held together and lashed to the frame by spruce roots or willow twine run through holes punched through the bark. The seams were waterproofed with spruce pitch. These canoes, which were partially decked near the bow, were between 8 and 12 feet (2.5–3.5 m) long, and about 2 feet (60 cm) wide at their broadest point. They were propelled by one or two people using single-bladed paddles, or, in very shallow water, by two rods pushed against the river bottom. These boats were not large enough to carry much of a load, and families making a major shift in location had to make several trips back and forth to complete the journey. Like kayaks, two or three open canoes could be lashed together for stability.

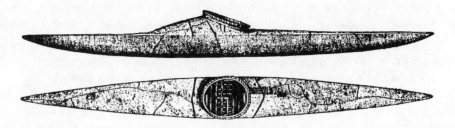

FIGURE 60. A kayak. The original was 19 feet (5.8 m) long and 18 inches (46 cm) wide amidships. From Murdoch (1892:329).

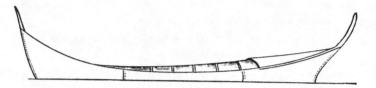

FIGURE 61. An open canoe. Sketch from Cantwell (1889b:plate III).

Rafts were built and used primarily by men living along the Kobuk River who made long hunting expeditions on foot to the Noatak River valley, returning over the mountains to a point upstream from their homes. When they reached a tributary of the main river, they built a raft and floated downstream with their summer harvest of hides and meat. Similar craft were sometimes made by people living on the lower Noatak River and the Selawik River when they needed to move a large quantity of goods some distance downstream.

The standard raft (*umiaġluk*) consisted of perhaps a dozen poles 16 to 18 feet (4.8–5.6 m) long, with the smaller ends lashed together and to a crosspiece to form a bow perhaps 4 or 5 feet (122–152 cm) wide.[222] A platform was built across the wider middle and rear part of the raft to hold people and their loads. Rafts were propelled primarily by the current, and steered (and sometimes propelled) with poles.

The only other type of watercraft I have heard about in Northwest Alaska was a make-shift boat with a cottonwood or willow frame whose components were lashed together with willow roots (Keats 1970.1; Robert Lee 1961.1). The cover was made from several caribou hides sewn together with caribou sinew. The cover was lashed to the frame with twine made of sealskin, oogruk skin, or even caribou skin. The seams were waterproofed with caribou fat or a mixture of charcoal and oil. This type of craft was usually built for one-time use by people who found themselves with large loads far upriver of their intended destination during the period of open water. The Nuataaġmiut, who lived above the forested part of the Noatak River valley and hence could not make rafts, seem to have been the primary people to use this type of craft.

Sleds

The Iñupiat had two basic types of sled. One was a flat sled, or *qamun*, and the other was a railed sled, or *uniapiaq*.

FIGURE 62. A *qamun*, or flat sled. From Murdoch (1892:355).

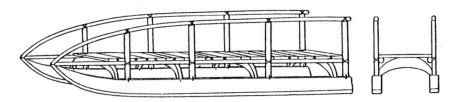

FIGURE 63. An *uniapiaq*, or basket sled. From Murdoch (1892:354).

The *qamun* (see Figure 62) was a heavy-duty sled with solid driftwood runners about 8 inches (20 cm) high, 2 inches (5 cm) wide, and 6 to 16 feet (2–5 m) long, the length depending on the particular use for which the sled was built.[223] The runners were joined by cross slats about 25 inches (64 cm) long, which extended two inches (5 cm) beyond the runner on each side. They were lashed to the runners with sealskin, oogruk, or baleen twine passing through holes drilled in the wood. Sometimes a longitudinal strip was lashed across the top of the crosspieces on each side. The number of cross slats varied with the length of the sled. Sled runners were shod with strips of ivory, whale jawbone, or wood, all fastened with pins. In very cold weather, these were sometimes coated with a layer of ice to help reduce friction.

The *qamun* was used primarily to haul *umiat*. One occasion was at whaling time, when the boats had to be hauled across the ice to and from the water's edge. It was also employed to carry large loads of whale meat and blubber back to the village. The other main context for *qamun* use was on journeys that were intended or expected to straddle breakup; the people went out by sled hauling the boat, and returned by boat carrying the sled. Shorter and lighter versions were sometimes built to help individual hunters haul a heavy load, such as an oogruk or several seals.

The second type of sled in widespread use was the basket sled, or *uniapiaq* (see Figure 63).[224] The runners were made from planks 2 to 3 inches (5–7.5 cm) wide and 6 to 7 inches (15–18 cm) high that were bent upward in front after being soaked in water to soften. Along the sides, four or five stanchions were mortised into the upper edge of the runners and projected upward 30 to 36 inches (75–90 cm). Bow-shaped pieces of wood made from tree roots were mortised into the tops of the two runners, linking them together; like the stanchions, they were held in place by wooden pins. Rails were lashed to the tops of the stanchions, and bent downward to meet the front of the runners. Two lengths of planking were lashed to the inside of the stanchions, and to the rail across the front. The slats were then placed on top of and lashed to these planks. Basket sleds were between 2 and 3 feet (60–90 cm) wide, and 10 to 14 feet (3–4.2 m) long. People in most districts used spruce to make their sleds; those living in forested districts tended to use birch. Runners were shod with ivory, whale jawbone, or hardwood slats, held to the wood with pins. The finished sled was waterproofed with red paint made from crushed ocher (NANA Cultural Heritage Project 1975b).

Pedestrian Transport

Sleds and boats were used throughout Northwest Alaska, but, as noted above, they often were powered by people and/or dogs on foot. This was true universally of sled travel, and was generally true for people traveling upriver by boat. In addition, at certain seasons in most districts, at least some people had to travel on foot over fairly long distances without the help of either sleds or boats. In all of these cases, special equipment was used.

Snowshoes (dual *tagluk*) were important items in districts where deep, soft snow—as opposed to windblown, hard-packed snow—predominated.[225] Deep, soft snow was particularly common in the Kobuk, lower Noatak, and Selawik valleys, but was found in willow patches and isolated pockets in most other districts as well. Without the aid of snowshoes, winter travel in such areas would have been almost impossible.

John Simpson (1875) described the most common type of snowshoe found in the study region as follows:

> [T]wo pieces of alder, about two feet and a half [75 cm] long, curved towards each other at the ends, where they are bound together, and kept apart in the middle by two cross-pieces, each end of which is held in a mortice. Between the cross-pieces is stretched a stout thong, lengthwise and across, for the foot to rest upon, with another which first forms a loop to allow the toes to pass beneath; this is carried round the back of the ankle to the opposite side of the foot, so as to sling the snow-shoe under the joint of the great toe. . . . Some are five feet [150 cm] long by fourteen inches [35 cm] wide, rounded and turned up at the toe, and pointed at the heel, neatly filled in before and behind the cross-bars with a network of sinew, or of a very small thong made from the skin of the small seal, nat'-sik (Simpson 1875:243–44).

Alternative materials included birch and spruce, for the frame, and caribou-hide rope, for the webbing. Grinnell (1901) characterized Iñupiaq snowshoes as "models of symmetry and neatness" (J. Grinnell 1901:44).

The long type of snowshoe described by Simpson was known as *taglupiaq*, an example of which is illustrated in Figure 64. Another type, known as *putyugiaq*, had a short, sharp-nosed frame. In interior districts, it was used to break the trail for dog teams and to walk behind sleds (Anderson et al. 1998:126). A coastal variation of this form was used for walking across thin saltwater ice (VanStone 1980:58, 59). According to Stefansson (1914b:345), snowshoes without any toe or heel webbing were used during the spring when daytime thaw alternating with nighttime freezing created a crust on the snow.

Other equipment used for pedestrian travel included backpacks made from hides or old boat covers for people and dogs, and tumplines and harness made from rope for people and dogs respectively. These items are discussed below in the section on travel.

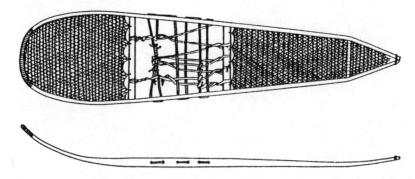

FIGURE 64. A *taglupiaq* type of snowshoe. From VanStone (1980:59). Reproduced with the permission of the Field Museum of Natural History.

Personal Adornment

The Iñupiat of Northwest Alaska manufactured a variety of items of personal adornment. The diversity of these objects and the frequency with which they were worn seem to have been significantly greater in the early years of the 19th century than toward the end; they also seem to have been greater along the coast than they were in the interior. If the information were available, I would not be surprised to learn that details of personal ornamentation differed slightly from one nation to another. However, the same basic pattern seems to have prevailed everywhere, and that pattern is what I describe here.[226]

Labrets

To European visitors to Northwest Alaska, the most noticeable item of personal adornment was the labret (*tuutaq*).[227] This was a piece of jewelry worn by men on the lower lip. Most men who had labrets wore two, one on each side, although there seems to have been no requirement, aesthetic or otherwise, that they do so. There was also no requirement or expectation that the two labrets worn by one man match in material, size, or style.

Labrets were made from a variety of materials, including ivory, bone, and several types of soft stone, sometimes decorated with a bead or a stone of a different color. Each had a flat or slightly concave end that rested against the wearer's lower gum, which held the labret in place. The other end, which was the decorative one outside the lip, was oval or round, and of varying length. Three examples are shown in Figure 65, with the outer, or decorative, end on top in each case. Example 1 is a simple stone plug in which the end worn next to the gum was larger than the decorative end. Example 2 is a jade plug whose decorative end was substantially larger than the gum end. Example 3 was made from ivory and glass. Labrets were made from the various materials with the tools and techniques for working ivory and stone described earlier.

The holes in the lower lip through which labrets were worn were usually opened when a male was in his early teens. The operation was performed with a lancet and a piece of wood. One man held the boy's head from behind, while another held the piece of wood inside the lip and cut a hole from the outside by pressing the lancet through the lip into the wood. The result was a small hole, which was temporarily filled with a wooden or ivory plug, the flat end of which was placed against the gum. The recipient had to stay outside the house after the operation, living in a tent or snow house for several days while the wound healed. Until the wound had healed completely, it was necessary to rotate the plug daily to keep it from sticking. If the plug was removed during this period, the boy would die (T. Mitchell 1987). After the wound had healed, the plug was replaced by a small but otherwise regular labret. The hole was enlarged over a period of years through the use of progressively larger labrets, and sometimes through additional cuts in the lip. Labret holes in the lips of an older man could be as much as a half inch (1.27 cm) in diameter.

The size of a labret signified a man's wealth and status in the community; the more important he was, the larger the labret. The largest were about 2 inches (5 cm) in diameter. Older men of considerable status sometimes wore at least one labret that was so large it made the lip hang down, exposing the teeth.

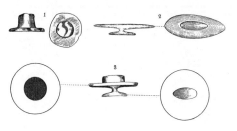

FIGURE 65. Examples of labrets. From Cantwell (1889b:plate V).

Labrets were not necessarily worn all the time. For example, they were ordinarily removed at night. If they were not replaced in the morning, the men walked around with saliva oozing from the holes. Labrets were very uncomfortable to wear outside in cold weather, and men planning to spend a long time out of doors in winter temporarily replaced them with wooden plugs.

Hair Care

Women's hair, which was usually parted down the middle and tied in a bunch or braid on each side of the head, was dressed with combs (Murdoch 1892:149–50; Nelson 1899:57–58). These were variously made from flat pieces of walrus ivory, caribou antler, or bone, into which fine teeth were cut or incised. Examples of combs are shown in Figure 66.

Men's hair was shaved off on the crown of the head with very sharp knives. It was allowed to grow around the sides, where its length was adjusted by someone using a knife and a piece of wood for an anvil (Brower ms:493).

Tattoos

Tattoos are not ordinarily considered manufactured goods or items of personal adornment, but they surely are elements in personal adornment, and this is a convenient place to discuss them. They need to be mentioned because tattoos were at least as common among women as labrets were among men. A Napaaqtuġmuit woman reported to Stefansson (1914b:202) that she had been taught that if girls "did not tattoo the chin, the chin would grow long to disfigurement."[228]

A tattoo (*tavluġun*) was created by drawing a piece of thread blackened with soot underneath the skin with a needle, usually between a woman's chin and her lower lip. The result was a line that appeared blue. The most common pattern was three narrow, roughly parallel, vertical lines down the chin.

Girls often began around the age of puberty with just one line, then added more later. Sometimes they ended up with only two lines, and in other cases the middle line consisted of several thin ones made so close together as to present the appearance of a single broad stripe. Yet another pattern was a single broad stripe down the chin, with no narrow counterparts. Although the total number of lines eventually reached three or four in most cases, it apparently could reach as many as thirty. The pattern differed to some extent from one region to another, and perhaps even from one nation to another, but there is not enough information from the study period to know what the variations were at the national level.

Other variations included patterns tattooed on the arms or the back of the hands, often made by the woman herself. A few men had tattoos on the face, usually in the form of X's, triangles, or "raven tracks" near the corners of the mouth. Another male pattern was a "rectangular bar an inch and a half long, extending from the corners of the mouth toward the ears" (Wells and Kelly 1890:16). Among men, tattoos were apparently most common among elders who had had successful careers as whalers.

FIGURE 66. Examples of hair combs made from walrus ivory. From Murdoch (1892:150).

Other Ornaments

Many other ornaments were worn by both men and women.[229] Most involved beads of glass, amber, jet, turquoise, and/or ivory. Glass and turquoise beads had to be obtained through trade with the Chukchi, but material for the others could be acquired either locally or in regional trade. Turquoise beads were considered particularly valuable, and a person who had just one or two was regarded as being wealthy.

Beaded ornaments included ear (sing. *taquupik*) and nose (sing. *qiŋaġun*) ornaments, both of which consisted of beads strung on a thread suspended either directly from a hole drilled through the earlobe or septum, or from a small hook inserted into the hole. Some examples of ear ornaments, all made of colored glass beads, are shown in Figure 67. A nose ornament is shown in Figure 68. Wealthy men sometimes had beads attached to a headband.

Bracelets (sing. *tayaq*) worn around the wrist, finger rings (sing. *qitiqłiaġun*), and necklaces (sing. *uyamitquaq*) were similar in construction to ear and nose ornaments, and were worn primarily by women. A particularly elegant piece also worn primarily by women was a long string of beads suspended from both ears that hung down below the chin. Men sometimes wore a pendant around the neck. Women sometimes wore large bracelets (sing. *taliġaq*) around the forearm, these usually being made from an imported material such as copper or iron.

Both men and women wore strings of beads around the head, and women who braided their hair often bound the braids with strings of beads. Only men wore headbands (sing. *niaquun*), which were made from seal or caribou hide from which the hair had been removed. Headbands of this type were regarded as a general sign of wealth and importance, and accordingly were worn by relatively few on a daily basis (F. Beechey 1831, I:396, 458; Eliyak 1931; Glover 1970.5). Shamans sometimes wore headbands made from ermine skins while performing feats of magic. Special headbands were often worn by participants in dances and ceremonies, and warriors about to launch an attack wore headbands into which one eagle feather was inserted behind each ear.

FIGURE 67. Examples of ear ornaments. From Cantwell (1889b:plate V).

FIGURE 68. An example of a nose ornament. From Cantwell (1889b:plate V).

Ceremonial Objects

The Iñupiat made and used a variety of ceremonial objects, the most ubiquitous of which was the tambourine drum (qiḷaun).[230] The frame for this drum was made from a thin, flat strip of wood 60 to 80 inches (150–200 cm) long and about an inch (2.5 cm) wide, cut and shaped with the various woodworking tools described earlier. The wood was soaked in water, steamed, then bent around until the two ends met or overlapped. The ends were held together in various ways. With overlapping ends, the simplest arrangement was to drill holes through the overlap and run twine through them. Another way was to fasten the overlapping ends to a strip of ivory on the inside of the hoop and secure it to the wood with stitches of baleen or sinew. When the two ends met instead of overlapping, they were beveled to wedge-shaped points that were inserted into slots cut into a short piece of ivory of the same width and thickness as the frame; they were held in place by lashings. The handle consisted of a round 4-to-6-inch (10–15 cm) rod of ivory, antler, or bone that was usually carved into the shape of a person or animal. A square notch was cut in its upper surface to receive the lower edge of the frame. It was held in place by lashings run through holes in both the frame and the handle.

The drum head consisted of the membrane from a bowhead whale liver, or the lining of a caribou or seal intestine. It was dampened and stretched over the top of the frame, where it was held in place by braided sinew cord set in a groove running around the rim. The drumstick was a slender elastic wooden wand about 2.5 feet (75 cm) long.

The tambourine drum, almost always accompanied by singing or chanting, was used in practically every ceremony, dance, shaman's séance, or other special event in Iñupiaq life. A more special instrument was the box drum (kaḷukaq).[231] This was a rectangular box having zigzag ornaments on the top. It was made of thin, knotless spruce boards about 3 feet (90 cm) long held together by wooden pins. One side had a circular hole cut in it. On the side opposite the hole was a striking platform consisting of either a pad of fur or a pole fastened to the box. The drumstick was a small club. This drum was played only in special ceremonies, usually during a messenger festival, and then by only one man at a time. It did not rest on the floor, but was suspended from the qargi ceiling so that it could be moved back and forth while being struck. This instrument reportedly made an impressive deep booming noise.

The wooden mask (kiiñaġuq), carved from driftwood, was another important type of ceremonial object.[232] Like the box drum, a mask was ordinarily used solely for ceremonial purposes. Most masks were carved either in the size and shape of a human or animal face, or, more often, in the oversized image of a spirit that had been encountered by a shaman during a visit to the nonempirical world. Masks carved to represent an animal were often thought to imbue the wearer with the particular attributes of the species or entity concerned. Some masks cleverly combined realistic and surrealistic elements, such as one simultaneously representing both a human face and the shape of a bowhead whale. Many of the images, particularly those representing spirits, were grotesque.

Most masks were carved by shamans or by expert craftsmen hired by shamans for the purpose. However, masks were sometimes created by ordinary people for the purpose of amusing an audience. Such masks typically depicted some peculiarity of an individual or group in a ridiculous way and were used in satirical performances. Masks were often colored with hematite, soot, or a dye made from alder bark. Teeth, made from carved ivory, antler, or bone, were sometimes added, as were fringes or tufts of animal hair or feathers. Masks were either suspended from the ceiling of the qargi, or, more commonly, worn by dancers or shamans, held on the head by a leather headstrap attached to holes drilled in the wood.

Ceremonial gorgets were made from thin strips of wood 16 to 20 inches (40–50 cm) long and perhaps 5 inches (13 cm) high (Murdoch 1892:370–72). The lower rim was usually carved in a convex curve with a serrated edge. The upper rim had a straight edge, but rose upward from the ends to the middle. Gorgets were held in place by one cord around the neck and another around the chest. They were typically painted with scenes of the people and/or the animals that were the focus of the ceremony in which they were used.

Rattle mittens were long stiff mittens made from dehaired sealskin that reached to the elbow (Murdoch 1892:366; Ray and Blaker 1967:28; Sunno 1951.104). In the study region, rattle mittens were worn primarily by men. A number of puffin beaks or thin ivory or bone strips were attached to the mitten in such a way that they dangled. When a dancer moved his arms vigorously in time to the music, the suspended objects struck the outside of the mittens and made a rattling sound.

The list of ceremonial objects also includes a variety of headpieces.[233] Some headpieces were special hats made solely for use in dancing. Tanned animal hides, with the skin from the head completely intact, were sometimes worn on the heads of dancers. Hides of wolves, wolverines, bears, foxes, and lynx were commonly used in this capacity. Another type consisted of the stuffed heads of birds, with the skin attached but sometimes with the feathers removed, which were worn on the head and over the shoulders. Loons and ravens, in particular, seem to have been preferred for this use. Finally, there were ornamental fillets of skin or feathers attached to the front of a headband. Dancers so attired frequently performed with rattle mittens.

The Iñupiat also made a number of mechanical devices for use in ceremonies (Murdoch 1892:372; Nelson 1899:341, 342, 344; Ray and Blaker 1967:28–29). Many of them were carved wooden or ivory animals or birds that nodded their heads, pecked at a board, flapped their wings, or performed other acts when manipulated by hidden strings. Others were made in the image of humans and had movable appendages.

Knud Rasmussen (1933) witnessed a ceremony in a *qargi* in Point Hope that illustrated some of the possibilities:

> A carved wooden image of a bird hangs from the roof, its wings being made to move and beat four drums placed around it. On the floor is a spinning top stuck about with feathers; close by is a doll, or rather the upper half of one, and on a frame some distance from the floor is a model skin boat, complete with crew and requisites for whaling.
>
> The proceedings open with the singing of a hymn; then a man springs forward and commences to dance; this, however, is merely the signal for mechanical marvels to begin. The bird flaps its wings and beats its drums with a steady rhythmic beat. The top is set spinning, throwing out the feathers in all directions as it goes; the crew of the boat get to work with their paddles; the doll without legs nods and bows in all directions; and most wonderful of all, a little ermine sticks out its head from its hole in the wall, pops back in again and then looks out, and finally runs across to the other side to vanish into another hole, snapping up a rattle with a bladder attached as it goes (Rasmussen 1933:332–33).

Although this was in 1924, it is my understanding that what Rasmussen saw is representative of the *kind* of event that took place a century earlier.

Similarly, at Wales the following took place in 1902:

Under the shadow of the central lamp on the floor were mechanical figures of diminutive men, sea parrots and a twelve-inch wooden whale. The whale was made to imitate spouting by five blades of grass being blown from the hole in its head. The wooden sea parrots marked time to the music by turning their heads from side to side, and the little men moved heads and arms in the same manner as the real ones (Ray and Blaker 1967:29, quoting Suzanne Bernardi).

A final item that is appropriately included in this section is the so-called "shaman's helper" (*kikituk*).[234] This was a wooden object carved in a shape resembling that of a thick-tailed weasel, often with inset bone or ivory teeth or eyes. Such objects were typically painted red and black. They apparently contained considerable magical power, and were used by shamans to try to assassinate particularly powerful competitors in their profession. Presumably any ceremony associated with this process would have been private.

Amulets

An amulet (*aanġuaq*) was an object imbued with magical power.[235] This property arrived in the object spontaneously, or was placed there intentionally by a shaman. In general, amulets were used to ward off potential danger or to bring good luck. Many amulets, such as dead bumblebees, feathers, or small stones, were naturally occurring objects whose magical power was discovered through shamanic ritual or by accident. Others, such as a dried animal or bird skin, were deliberately modified, but their magical qualities developed either spontaneously or through shamanic action. Skins of ravens, ermines, wolves, and eagles apparently were inherently associated with sufficient magical power to qualify as amulets without human intervention. However, some objects were deliberately created to serve as amulets.

Manufactured amulets were made from wood, ivory, bone, or stone. Many were created in the shape of an animal. An amulet intended to bring good luck in whaling, for example, might be carved in the shape of a whale. In general, the older an amulet was, the more powerful it was considered to be, having stood the test of time.

Amulets were worn as pendants, sewn into clothing, hung on the back, attached to a strap worn obliquely across the torso, suspended from the ceiling of a house or *qargi*, placed on a stake out of doors, lashed to the bow of a boat, or attached to a net. Their size varied according to the context in which they were intended to be used. Almost all manufactured amulets (except those chipped from stone) had one or more holes drilled in them so that they could be suspended from, lashed to, or sewn onto some other object. Since the magical power of each amulet was very restricted in its application, most individuals and households owned a considerable number.

The Tobacco Complex

When Otto von Kotzebue (1821, I:239; see also p. 209) arrived in Northwest Alaska in the summer of 1816, he found the Iñupiat to be "exceedingly fond of tobacco: they chew, snuff, smoke, and even swallow the smoke." He was surprised to find tobacco there despite the apparent fact that no Westerners were known to have visited the region prior to his expedition. However, as Dorothy Jean Ray (1975b:97–102) has so interestingly described, the tobacco found in Northwest Alaska in the early 19th century was leaf tobacco (*taugaaqqipiaq*), at least some of which came the whole way around the world from the southeastern United States, arriving in Alaska by way of Siberia. However, in order for Iñupiat to consume this imported commodity, they had to manufacture a certain amount of paraphernalia themselves.

Tobacco was smoked in a pipe (*paipak*), the components of which were manufactured locally or imported.[236] Cantwell (1889b) succinctly described how pipes were made:

> The bowl is made of iron, brass, ivory, or stone, cylindrical, with its top flanged and two lugs on the lower end, over which the lashing passes which secures it to the stem. The bore of the bowl is from one-fourth to one-half inch in diameter and holds, when full, about a thimbleful of very finely pulverized tobacco. The stem is from twelve to eighteen inches [30–45 cm] in length, and is made by splitting a branch of alder or soft piece of wood in two and making a groove in each part. The two parts are then put together so that the grooves lie opposite each other and are securely lashed in this position with sinew (Cantwell 1889b:89; see also Giddings 1961:141; VanStone 1976:43–44).

Cantwell also noted that a woman's pipe (*kuiŋiq*) was longer than the one used by men.[237] Each pipe, whether men's or women's, was furnished with a short steel or ivory pricker for clearing the bowl when fouled.

Some examples of pipes seen by Cantwell in the 1880s are shown in Figure 69. Number 1 in the sketch is just a simple tube without a bowl. Number 2 has a stone bowl, numbers 3 and 5 have brass bowls, number 4 has a jadeite bowl, and number 6 has an inlaid stone and ivory bowl; otherwise, they are all of the basic construction described above. Numbers 5 and 6 were women's pipes, while all the others belonged to men. The mouthpieces in the illustration were all short tubes carved from ivory or bone.

Alternate materials for mouthpieces included wood, stone, brass, and iron. One may assume that metal bowls were less common in the region earlier in the century than they were when Cantwell was there in the 1880s. On the coast, pipe stems were frequently carved out of ivory, and were decorated with designs and figures, both etched and in relief.[238]

Other items in the tobacco complex included a container, either a pouch (*iraqsraun*) or a box, to hold tobacco, snuff, and a mortar and pestle to grind tobacco leaf and fungus to make quids (for chewing) (VanStone 1976:43–44; 1980:65–67). The boxes were usually attractively carved with images of various kinds, and the bags were often made of different skins arranged in an attractive pattern. Snuff tubes were made from the hollow wing bones of large water-fowl. The last item in the tobacco complex was a wooden mortar in which tobacco was crushed to powder with a wooden pestle and mixed with other ingredients to create the precise blends desired for smoking, snuffing, or chewing.

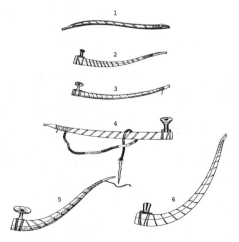

Military Equipment

The weapons used in battle were essentially the same as those employed in hunting, which have already been described.[239] However, there were some differences. Particularly along the coast, special arrowheads were sometimes made for use in warfare. One type was a tanged chert arrowhead that would have been difficult to remove from a wound. Another was a bone

FIGURE 69. Examples of smoking pipes. From Cantwell (1889b:plate IV).

or ivory arrowhead that was deliberately weakened near the base so that it would break off inside the victim's flesh, requiring surgery for its removal.

A more conspicuous item of military equipment was plate armor (*mannisaq*).[240] This consisted of a vest made from several dozen thin, rectangular plates of ivory (usually), wood, antler, or bone linked to one another in series around the torso by twine run through holes drilled around the plate edges. The vest was held in place by leather shoulder straps. If properly made, it was proof against arrows. At Point Barrow in the fall of 1853, the English were shown such a vest that was made from steel plates rather than locally available raw materials, but this instance may have been unique (Bockstoce ed. 1988, I:295; Simpson 1852–54: entry for Oct. 16, 1853).

Plate armor was worn primarily by men living along the coast. However, inlanders, and even some coast dwellers, made vests of furs or duck skins (with the feathers left on), or caribou hide (F. Beechey 1831, I:340; II:284, 285). These greatly impeded the progress of an arrow into the wearer's body, and sometimes prevented it altogether. Another alternative was a vest made from oogruk hide (T. Morris 1970).

Two final items of specialized military equipment were the stockade (*avalġusiq*), and the movable wall. The former was an enclosed wall of poles or stakes placed in the ground behind which warriors were protected from enemy assault as long as their own projectiles were able to keep the enemy at a sufficient distance to prevent high arcing shots from raining down on them.[241] The movable wall was constructed of willows lashed together and lined with thin slabs of slate (Giddings 1961:124–25). Archers were protected as they moved it forward toward the enemy. Curiously, the wall seems to have been denoted by the term *mannisaq*, the same one used for plate armor.

Services

A service is defined as an effort.[242] Given this broad definition, the production of raw materials and manufactured goods also involves the production of services. However, the focus of attention in such activities is on the goods that result, not on the effort required to produce them. There are other activities, however, such as health care and travel, in which the focus is on the services as such. In the former case, production of goods is the goal; in the latter case, goods may provide some of the means, but their production is not the focus of attention. This distinction makes it possible to avoid needless repetition of material that has already been covered. The presentation below concentrates on those activities in which the attention of the people involved was primarily on the service.

The goal of avoiding needless repetition also influences the internal organization of this section. Many of the activities that are considered here from an economic perspective are also viewed in other chapters from other perspectives, such as the political one. Several are more usefully treated in detail in those chapters than they are here. In a few cases where prior discussion is absent, a short presentation covers the relevant material sufficiently for present purposes. I therefore begin this chapter with a section of "brief treatments." Presented in alphabetical order, the topics included under this heading are clothing and equipment maintenance, education, entertainment and recreation, food services, management, rituals and ceremonies, warfare, and waste removal. Singled out for more detailed presentation subsequently are distribution, health care, and travel.

Brief Treatments

Clothing and Equipment Maintenance

The production of clothing was described in an earlier section of this chapter. What was not mentioned there was the fact that most people had only one or two outfits to wear for ordinary use for an entire year, with some seasonal adjustments, and perhaps one set of fancy-dress clothing for special occasions.[243] Consequently, particularly given the harsh climate of northwestern Alaska, proper clothing maintenance was a matter of crucial importance.

Clothing maintenance was the responsibility of women, who spent a considerable amount of time engaged in it.[244] Indeed, clothing was inspected almost every day to see if it had been damaged; if it was, it was ordinarily tended to immediately. However, clothing repair, like clothing manufacture, was often complicated by taboos. For example, in some districts when someone died, no sewing was permitted for several days (Hobson 1855:886).

Maintenance involved two basic types of activity. One was dealing with wet clothing. First it needed to be dried, then it had to be softened or it was likely to be both uncomfortable and brittle. If brittle, it was prone to tearing. Softening was usually accomplished by holding the dried piece with both hands and moving the hands back and forth in opposite directions. In extreme cases, a scraper might have to be brought into play. The second type of maintenance activity was sewing tears, and sometimes patching them for added strength.

Certain other goods, in addition to clothing, were ordinarily repaired by women. These included nets, torn skin bags, torn boat covers, and any other damaged items made from animal hide. Otherwise, most equipment was manufactured and maintained by men. Just what was required varied according to the item involved (Collinson 1889:74; Murdoch 1892:89, 90–91, 386; VanStone 1980:53). In many cases a component part or lashing had to be replaced. In others, holes or gaps were patched with an appropriate material placed over the rift and sewn on with baleen or some other kind of thread. This was often necessary with wood or bark containers, which sometimes broke, and frequently cracked. Sometimes a crack was repaired by drilling a hole on each side and lashing the two sides together. In the case of broken stone pots or lamps, which were difficult to acquire in the study region, a piece precisely shaped to fill the gap was cut and put in place, held there by lashings run through holes drilled in the material.

Data on the subject are difficult to come by, but it is my impression that repairs were made as the occasion demanded, and that proactive inspection of equipment by men (such as women did with clothing) was uncommon. Major exceptions to this generalization were bows and arrows, *umiaq* frames and covers, and harnesses and sleds, all of which received daily or even more frequent inspections when in active use.

Education

The education process in Northwest Alaska was informal and diffuse. There were no formally designated instructors, and no specialized locations where teaching took place. Education was pervasive in that it went on continuously almost everywhere. Children spent most of their time in the company, or at least the proximity, of adults—parents, aunts and uncles, grandparents—from birth on, and they learned a great deal simply by watching and listening. As they grew older, they tried to emulate their elders. They also received instruction from older relatives in how to do things, in how to read the weather and other environmental signs, in animal behavior, and in how to behave toward other people. Detailed knowledge of the countryside was acquired during the course of the annual cycle of movement. Many place-names related to historical people or events; learning them and the stories behind them conveyed extensive historical knowledge. The daily exchange of information among adults helped them educate each other, as well as any youngsters who happened to be within hearing distance, about current events. Finally, the stories told in the *qargi* by the best-informed individuals in the community gave everyone access to the received wisdom and knowledge of their people.

The education process is discussed in greater detail, and with references, in Chapter 6.

Entertainment and Recreation

The Iñupiat liked to have a good time, and over the generations they invented a large number of ways to do so. Singing and dancing were perhaps the most common of these, followed by feasting and athletic competition. Listening to stories in the *qargi* at night was another very popular activity. Less common, but at least as enjoyable, was the blanket toss, which was somewhat similar to bouncing on a trampoline except that the participants were thrown into the air from a fairly rigid walrus hide rather than from the recoil of a flexible surface. Even the ceremonies and rituals that occurred over the course of the year, however serious their purpose and conduct, provided a diversion from daily life, and hence some recreation to the participants and onlookers. Entertainment and recreation are discussed at some length, and with references, in Chapter 6.

Food Services

George Stoney (1900:832) expressed the basic principle of food services among 19th-century Iñupiat in a single sentence: "The women have entire control of the food, regulating when it shall be eaten, the kind, and the amount." He might have added that this control was exercised from the moment the raw material entered the village or, in many cases, from when a woman went out to where her husband had made a kill and fetched it home. Women processed and stored the harvest, prepared the food for consumption, and served it.[245]

Ordinarily, there was only one cooked meal a day, in late afternoon or early evening. The men and older boys ate together. Women, older girls, and youngsters usually ate separately, after the men were finished. Infants were fed meat that had been partially chewed by adults, usually their mothers. If the food supply permitted, everyone ate until satiated. At other times of day people helped themselves to dried or raw frozen fish or meat, or to leftovers from the night before. When people were traveling, everyone usually ate at the same time.

Trollope (1855) described a typical evening meal at a house in Wales where he was a guest in January of 1854:

> The women soon brought the dinner in, hot and hot [sic] at intervals of 20 minutes: it consisted of large pieces of seal stewing in rich gravy, and looked very good: seven or eight sat down on the floor, and began to eat away with great gusto, fingers in the dish, knife at the mouth, with which they sliced away in a manner that had we tried it, our lips, noses, and fingers would have been in great danger: the last dish was hot gravy soup, which they helped themselves to with wooden ladles holding about a saucer-full, apparently as hot as they could well bear it (Trollope 1855:874; see also Thornton 1931:213).

If the men were in the *qargi*, their wives took the food there, and the men helped themselves from one another's pot.

There were also impromptu meals, such as when hungry hunters made a kill. Kotzebue (1821) observed an instance of this in the summer of 1816:

> A seal which had just been killed was put in the middle [of a group of men]; they cut open its belly, and one after the other put in his head and sucked out the blood. After they had sufficiently drunk in this manner, each cut himself off a piece of flesh, which they devoured with the greatest appetite... (Kotzebue 1821, I:236).

During feasts or other formal occasions, instead of encircling a common pot and helping themselves, people sat in rows. Each person had a separate plate or bowl, and was served by women circulating among the crowd. If the people attending the feast were from different communities, and certainly if they were from different nations, the interesting problem of conflicting food taboos arose between or among the various groups assembled. It never occurred to me to inquire about this, but Stefansson (1951) did comment on the general situation:

> When people of different districts met at a meal, some one, perhaps the hostess, would recite all the taboos which she knew which were appropriate to that meal, and then would ask one of her guests whether he knew any in addition. He would then contribute such as his hostess had omitted; then a second guest would be appealed to, and when all the taboos which all those present knew of had been clearly called to mind, the meal would go on. Then the next day, if one of them had a headache, or if the cousin of another broke a leg, they would say to one another, "What taboo could it have been that we broke?" (Stefansson 1951:411)

This problem was not unique to international gatherings, however, since taboos applied differently even among the members of the same family.

On the other hand, there is some evidence that the Iñupiat believed that many taboos were geographically restricted (Keats 1969.1). To the extent that was true, a person from one nation who was visiting people in another was subject to the local taboos, not to those of his/her own country. In this instance, the host and hostess would be presumed already to have attended to the taboos relating to their feast, and their guests would be taken care of accordingly. Unfortunately, there is no way we can know just how people dealt with situations like this.

Management

For present purposes, the term "management" refers to the planning and supervision of the production process. This subject is discussed from the political perspective in some detail, with references, in Chapter 5. In that chapter the key concepts are power and responsibility, of which management in the present sense is only one element.

The key management roles in Iñupiaq societies were filled by family heads and their wives. There were three levels of family unit—conjugal, domestic, and compound—and, accordingly, three levels of management focus. Compound-family heads and their wives had more management authority and responsibility than any others. They were the ones who made the strategic decisions about where to live, when to move, what raw materials and equipment had to be produced, and what rituals needed to be performed. They also provided the guidance and direction necessary for their strategy to be carried out, and moderated stresses and strains that developed among family members.

A family head (*qauḷiq*) at any level could not force anyone to do anything. Domestic and conjugal families, and even individuals, could pack up and leave larger units at any time. The alternatives were to strike out on their own, or, with permission, join another domestic or compound family. Since life in isolation was extremely risky, joining another unit was the usual choice.

There was, however, something of a snowball effect here. The more effective the management of a compound family was, the more other conjugal families and individuals were tempted to invoke kinship ties to join it. This increased the authority and broadened the span of control of the family head and his wife, since the new members had to contribute to the common good or be expelled. On the other hand, if the management was poor, people moved elsewhere. In these family-oriented societies, most individuals and conjugal families had alternative kin with whom they could affiliate, although the alternatives were rarely all uniformly appealing. At any given time, family size was a good indicator of the relative management effectiveness of the various family heads, always with the caveat that the number of people involved could not long exceed the (seasonal) carrying capacity of the local environment.

Task groups involving people from more than one family operated under the supervision of an *ataniq*, or boss. This was a man who had consistently demonstrated superior knowledge, judgment, and skill in the relevant activity over a long period. He held his position by consensus in recognition of his ability. An *ataniq* could and did give directions to his companions, usually after consulting with the most knowledgeable among them, but he could not force anyone to do anything. However, since failure to comply might lead to the collapse of the enterprise, there was considerable pressure on individuals to conform. The primary contexts in which this type of management occurred include large-scale beluga drives, large-scale caribou drives, and raids and battles. Whaling crews, which were largely family based, operated under the direction of the boat owner, or *umialik*.

Rituals and Ceremonies

The Iñupiat performed a bewildering array of rituals and ceremonies. Some were intended to bring game or good weather, while others were employed to avoid or prevent suffering or harm. Some rituals took just a few moments to perform, while others required months for their preparation and several days for their execution. Some could be performed by a single individual in private, some were performed by a single individual in public, some required the participation of both husbands and wives, and still others required the participation of dozens of people. Rituals and ceremonies varied to some extent from one nation to another, but the overall pattern was consistent throughout the study region.

Some rituals could be performed by anyone: a hunter might sing a special song to bring him luck in hunting or utter a special saying to keep an evil spirit at bay. Respectful treatment of dead animals was important in ensuring future success in the chase. Such rituals were usually performed by individuals in private. Most shamanistic rituals, however, although performed by a single individual, were conducted before an audience. The objective of these events typically included the diagnosis of an illness (or some other calamity) and the prescription of a remedy.

Ceremonies and rituals involving two or more people typically were intended to bring hunting success. The most complex were those involved in preparation for whaling, of which there were several scattered over the fall, winter, and spring months. The whaling captains and their wives had featured roles in most of these affairs, but other crew members participated in some.

The largest ceremonies were embedded in major events usually referred to in English by the term "feast," but which in reality were often several interrelated feasts, dances, and other ceremonial activities. Chief among these were the messenger festival, the whaling feast, and the feast for the dead. It is also appropriate to include here the annual gathering of all or most of the members of a nation, known as *qatirut*, which involved dancing, athletic competition, and feasting. Rituals and ceremonies are discussed at greater length, with source references, in Chapter 6.

Warfare

International hostilities took three basic forms: terrorism, raiding, and open battle. These are summarized to some extent in Chapter 5, but at much greater length in another volume (Burch 2005:207–19).

Terrorism was carried out by single individuals or, less often, groups of two or three men (pl. *iññuqutit*), who stealthily invaded foreign territory with the intent of causing mischief, if not outright harm, to people living there. Sometimes murder was committed, but more frequently such activities as stealing food, damaging caches or boats, and other acts of vandalism were intended to intimidate and disconcert the local folks. This made people feel vulnerable, which seems to have been the terrorists' primary objective. *Iññuqutit* operated primarily during the period from about mid-July to mid-September. When terrorists were caught they were usually killed.

Raids were the primary form of international violence in the early 19th century. They were carried out, usually in mid- to late fall, by a party of perhaps a dozen men from one nation who stealthily invaded the territory of another. The objective was to approach a small settlement under cover of darkness, trap the inhabitants inside their houses or, preferably, gathered together in the *qargi*, and kill them all. The threat of such raids was one reason why Iñupiat men carried their weapons with them all the time.

Open battle involved a much larger number of combatants than a raid, but the goal was just the same: wipe out the enemy, including any women and children who had the misfortune to be in the area. The two forces drew up in lines opposite one another and attempted to wear each other down through maneuvers and long-distance archery. If one side began to get the upper hand, it closed on the opposing force and attempted to dispatch its members with spears, clubs, and knives in a series of individual actions. Like raids, open battles usually took place in early fall, that is, after freezeup but before the days grew too short or the snow became too deep. Unlike raids, they almost always occurred during daylight hours. However, they could occur at any time of year and at any time of day.

Fighting was only part of the effort required in international hostility. Before any fighting could occur, the aggressors had to travel to the enemy homeland. This required pedestrian expeditions of several tens of miles, as a minimum, and sometimes as much as 200 or 300 miles (320–480 km) (Burch 2005:87–88). What happened afterward depended on the outcome. If the aggressors were victorious, they had to retreat to their home estate, transporting their wounded and living off the land as they went, all while keeping an eye out for enemy attacks. If, on the other hand, the defenders prevailed, only one or two deliberately released aggressors had to worry about returning home. If the fighting had taken place right in a settlement, victorious defenders had to tend to their own dead and wounded and remove the bodies of their deceased enemies. If the battle had occurred outside a settlement, the victors tended to their own casualties, dispatched any surviving members of the enemy force, and either threw the enemy bodies onto a pile, or left them where they lay.

Waste Removal

Waste removal is a subject that is absent from ethnographic accounts of early-contact northwestern Alaska.[246] I did not deliberately collect any information on the subject myself, perhaps because it seemed so obvious. But, when I began to write this chapter, it occurred to me that, for a people as beset with taboos as the early-19th-century Iñupiat were, nothing should be considered obvious. I tried to fill the gap by perusing archaeological reports, but most of them are not much more informative on this topic than the ethnographic accounts. My treatment of this subject is brief primarily because of lack of relevant information.

The potential for waste accumulation varied considerably from one nation to another. For example, along the middle Kobuk River, people built a new house every fall some distance from the one they occupied the year before. All or most of the Kaŋiġmiut, Kiitaaġmiut, Kivalliñiġmiut, Kuuŋmiut, Napaaqtuġmiut, Pittaġmiut, Qikiqtaġruŋmiut, and Tapqaġmiut spent a month or two living on the ice of the Chukchi Sea, Hotham Inlet, or Selawik Lake each spring, and any waste they produced while there disappeared when the ice went out. In the coastal settlements of the Kiŋikmiut, Tapqaġmiut, and Tikiġaġmiut, on the other hand, houses were typically occupied at least seasonally for several years in succession. Obviously the potential for waste accumulation, hence the need for waste disposal, was much greater in these last three nations than in any of those listed previously. In general, one may assume that the more frequently people moved over the course of the yearly cycle, the less of a problem they had with waste accumulation.

The material that had to be disposed of included human waste; dog waste; old, worn-out animal hides from boat covers and tents; large quantities of animal bones; pieces of broken or worn-out equipment of every kind; chips and flakes from the manufacture of stone tools; slivers of ivory, bone, and antler; shavings and other debris from the manufacture of various wood products; worn-out clothing; and, in some districts, ashes and charcoal.

Waste was regularly removed from *qargich* and house floors using the wing of a large bird as a whisk broom. The question is, where did people put it? With the exception of animal bones, the quantity of material involved probably was not very great, at least on an annual basis. Over longer periods of time, however, the volume would have been considerable. This was especially true of the ancient coastal villages of Wales, Shishmaref, and Point Hope.

When I first went to Northwest Alaska in 1960, human waste was fed to the dogs, at least in the smaller villages, and was eagerly consumed by them. I suspect the same procedure was followed in the 19th century, except that urine was kept for tanning hides and other purposes. Dog feces were not normally consumed by dogs, at least in my time, and people cleaned up the winter's accumulation after the snow melted and the ground dried. Presumably a similar cleanup occurred 200 years ago, although the number of dogs, hence the quantity of feces, would have been very modest compared to what I observed in the early 1960s. Another major form of dog waste was hair, which was shed annually in huge quantities. However, in June and July, when shedding was at its height, most people were traveling with their dogs, so that the hair would have been spread around the countryside rather than accumulating in one place.

Bowhead whale skulls were dumped in the ocean following the performance of a brief ritual. Other whale bones were variously dumped in the ocean after the meat had been removed; used as structural members of buildings, caches, and graves; or retained to be made into sled runners. Beluga bones were either burned, taken offshore and dumped in the sea, or placed some distance away behind the beach, the custom differing from one nation to another. Bones from caribou, fish, seals, and other animals consumed as food by both humans and dogs would have produced a substantial amount of waste. No doubt most were fed to the dogs, but even they could not consume everything. Dogs, and particularly free-ranging puppies, probably spread the bones around a bit, but the remaining litter in the village would still have been considerable. It must have been systematically removed.

My 1970 notes on the remains of 19th-century Point Hope, the largest settlement in the study region, suggest that a great deal of waste other than human feces was simply thrown outside the house, usually at the sides or in the back, and sometimes even on the house itself. Larsen and Rainey's (1948:20; Rainey 1947:261) observations in the early 1940s, and the recent excavation of a midden at the former Tikiġaġmiut settlement of Uivvaq, near Cape Lisburne (Hoffecker et al. 2000; Reynolds 2001), seem to support this conclusion. On the other hand, it is possible that the remains of the abandoned 19th-century village of Point Hope became a garbage dump for the early-20th-century village, located some distance to the east; when occupied, it may have been kept much tidier.[247] This hypothesis is supported by F. Beechey's (1831, I:365) observation made in 1826 that the abandoned western portion of the settlement was filled with "heaps of filth," whereas he did not make a similar comment on the eastern portion, where the houses were in good repair.

At the large permanent settlement of Wales, winter waste from houses on the ocean side of the shore was placed on the sand dunes in front of the houses, while waste from houses on the back side of the lower village was placed just below the riverbank (H. Anungazuk 2001; Collins 1937b:63). In both cases, it was washed out to sea during the spring thaw. During the summer most of the residents were traveling, and rain, waves, and wind would have kept the beaches swept reasonably clean of any garbage placed there by those who remained behind. One had to be careful, though. In Point Hope, for example, it was taboo to throw hair shaved from caribou hides on the sea ice, the hair being said to block the breathing holes of seals and be offensive to whales (Aġviqsiiña 1940:45, 95; Rainey 1947:274).

I have no specific information on waste disposal in the large coastal settlement of Shishmaref. Kotzebue (1821, I:200–2) examined the settlement rather thoroughly in the summer of 1816, but made no mention of refuse littering the site. Since he was not inclined to be charitable toward the local people, I think he would have commented if he had seen much in the way of garbage.

In the interior, people moved around more, and settlements occupied one year or season were often unoccupied the next. Giddings (1956:47) reports that, in the Kobuk valley, when a fall/winter house was about to be abandoned every bit of its contents was either stored in an elevated cache, loaded on the sled to accompany its occupants on their travels, or thrown onto the river ice to be carried away by the spring flood. Since it was taboo to reoccupy the same house, the long-term accumulation of waste would have been minimal. In a few interior settlements enough waste built up to form a midden; where this occurred, most garbage seems to have been dumped at a designated site a short distance from the houses (Anderson and Anderson 1982; Giddings 1952:14). Charcoal left from extinguished fires was simply thrown through the skylight to fall on top of the house (Giddings 1961:33; Hickey 1968:48–50).

Distribution

The distribution process concerns the transfer or conveyance of the goods and services produced by the members of a society to the person or persons who will consume them.[248] The subject is examined at three levels: intrafamily, interfamily, and international.[249]

Intrafamily Distribution

It will be recalled (from Chapter 3) that there were three levels of family unit: conjugal, domestic, and compound. A conjugal family consisted of a husband and wife and their nonadult children. But conjugal families rarely lived separately. The vast majority of Iñupiaq households consisted of two or more closely related conjugal families, creating what I call a domestic family. More generally, most settlements consisted of two or more interrelated domestic families who also functioned as a single unit, creating what I call a compound family. This was the unit within which most distribution occurred.

From an economic point of view, the core of the system consisted of husband-wife pairs. As is noted repeatedly in earlier sections of this chapter, the production of raw materials, manufactured goods, and services was generally sharply divided along gender lines. However, there was almost no specialization beyond this; each man or woman had to produce essentially the same goods, and most of the same services, as every other. Different goods and services that husbands and wives produced were distributed to each other and to their subadult children for consumption. However, when two or more closely related conjugal families were united in a domestic unit, most raw materials and many manufactured goods were pooled, that is, contributed to a common stock. And when two or more domestic families were joined together in a compound family, many goods and services were pooled at that level as well. But the pooling that occurred was restricted to the family unit. It just so happened that the great majority of settlements were inhabited by the members of just one (compound) family. Thus, intrafamily distribution and settlement-wide distribution usually coincided.

A couple of hypothetical examples will show how the system worked. When a man hunting alone killed several caribou, he owned the carcasses. When his wife went out to retrieve them, they came under her control. Once she brought the carcasses home, however, the meat and hides ceased being regarded as uniquely hers or theirs. Rather, they were viewed as belonging to all members of the family: conjugal, domestic, or compound. Partially processed materials were placed in storage under the direction of the family head's wife, and they could be withdrawn and consumed by any family member who needed them—with at least the tacit approval of the family head's wife. Similarly, if a man made an adze or other utilitarian object, it was considered to be his unless he gave it to someone; but every member of the family felt free to use it without asking permission.

Pooling did not guarantee an equal distribution of goods or services among family members, particularly at the compound-family level. Family heads and their wives received the most and best of everything. Or, to put it more accurately, since distribution was largely conducted under their supervision, they took the most and the best for themselves (as they were expected to). The larger the family, the greater the quantity of goods that were produced, hence the more from which they had to choose. In well-managed families, this accumulation of wealth at the top was actively supported by other family members; those who did not approve either departed or refrained from comment. In poorly managed families, on the other hand, such an asymmetric distribution was resented, and eventually led to the dissolution of the unit.

Not all property was pooled. Clothing, amulets, and magic formulas or songs, for example—which were usually either created by the owner, received from a close relative, or purchased—were considered the property of individuals. Beyond that, the lines between private and pooled goods were more obscure. Kayaks, utensils, tools, weapons, nets, and implements of all kinds made by family members either for their own use or for the use of specific other family members might be considered "marginally private" property. In the first instance, they belonged to the person who made them or the person for whom they were made, that person being the primary user. But it was expected that such items would be used for the common good. When not actually in use by the "owner," they could be used by any family member without requesting permission. Some items, such as seines and *umiat*, were manufactured and theoretically owned and maintained by individuals, but they required several family members to use effectively, and all family members received a portion of the income produced with them. Houses and *qargich* were both built and used by family members functioning as a team.

Use of individual property marks to identify the owner of a particular item would seem to contradict the pooling concept. However, as Franz Boas (1899:601) noted, marks were placed almost exclusively on "weapons used in hunting, which, after being dispatched, remain in the bodies of large game" (see also Giddings 1952:46; Stefansson 1914b:390). Thus, marks were found on harpoons, lance heads, arrows, floats attached to harpoons, and sometimes fishhooks, but rarely on tools or utensils. Boas (1899:601) correctly concluded that the "object of the property mark [was] to secure property-right in the animal in which the weapon bearing the mark [was] found." A mark established the right of the hunter to the game or to a portion thereof vis-à-vis other hunters;[250] but, once taken home, the harvest was placed in the common stock belonging to his family.

Property marks were also used by beachcombers. A man walking along the beach who found a high-quality piece of driftwood simply hauled it away from the water and carved his property mark in it (Brower ms:360). It was then considered his property, and he could return and fetch it when circumstances permitted. If anyone else took it, the act was considered a theft.[251]

The basic concept underlying distribution within a family is usually represented in English by the word "sharing" (see Kishigami 2004). But it is important to understand that the altruism implied by that word was seldom a factor. As Stoney (1900:832) observed, lending within families was *obligatory*. It was not necessarily an expression of generosity or goodwill; it was something that people were expected—indeed required—to do. Nicolas Peterson (1993) has referred to this practice as "demand sharing." Among the Iñupiat, I doubt that many were conscious of the obligatory element in pooling; like breathing and sleeping, it was just something one did.

Notions of obligation and demand sharing raise the question of what happened if someone consumed a disproportionate amount of the common stock of food or failed markedly to contribute to it. Stefansson (in Pálsson 2001:124) seemed to think that no one cared. I don't believe it. In the early 1960s, more than a century after the study period, the Iñupiat held to the same principle of sharing that their ancestors allegedly held. Indeed, sharing was often cited to me as one of the primary ideals of Iñupiaq life. But that did not prevent people from doing some "ledger keeping," meaning that they were aware of variations in contributions to and withdrawals from the common stock. Although they often did not do anything about them, they noted and resented both stinginess and greed. I doubt that their ancestors behaved any differently.

My most elderly informants repeatedly pointed out to me, when my questions or comments apparently suggested otherwise, that some of their ancestors were much less intelligent, energetic, capable, and productive than others. Everyone knew who both they and the more productive people were. When times were good and food was plentiful, the disparity was recognized but generally ignored. When the food supply deteriorated, however, this changed.

Widespread and prolonged hunger, or famine (niqailaq), led to the breakdown of the institutionalized distribution system in even the largest settlements.[252] Instead of contributing food to the common stock, people began to hoard it. The breakdown began at the compound-family level when members of the constituent domestic units withheld food from the general supply. Sometimes they tried to steal food from other households, and in extreme cases committed murder in order to obtain food.

The members of the least productive households were the first to run out of food and the first to die. The members of the most productive families kept what little they had for themselves, and were the most likely to survive.

The breakdown continued within the domestic family. As the famine worsened, women started to hoard food for themselves, their husbands, and their offspring, and to keep it from their housemates (M. Hawley 1965.1). What little there was was secreted in various hiding places rather than placed in a common storage area, and was distributed and consumed surreptitiously. In extremis there was a breakdown even within the conjugal family, although at that level there was a fairly well-institutionalized set of priorities. Active adults were supposed to receive the most of whatever food there was; older children came second, youngsters third, and infants, invalids, and elders last. In each category, males ranked ahead of females. The chances of dying were the reverse of this sequence. In the most extreme situation, people ate the bodies of dead relatives in order to survive themselves (Edna Hunnicutt 1960.1).

The subject of death brings us to the last topic under the heading of intrafamily distribution: inheritance (kiŋuvaannaq–, "to inherit").[253] Items the deceased used in daily life were usually placed beside or atop the body: weapons and tools with men, household implements with women, and personal clothing with everyone. So, the question of inheritance relates to other types of good, of which there was often a considerable quantity and variety.

As far as I can determine, there was no fixed pattern of inheritance beyond the fact that almost everything stayed within the family—certainly the domestic unit. Houses continued to be owned and lived in by the domestic family who did so during the life of the deceased unless the death occurred there; in such a case, the house had to be abandoned altogether. Individuals could declare who should get what before they died, but often failed to do so. However, sometimes individuals, anticipating imminent death, did give away prized personal possessions, such as amulets and magic songs. Much depended on the composition of the membership of the deceased's household. Umiat, kayaks, dogs, nets, and sleds tended to pass to the widow or widower (if there was one), but otherwise passed down through the male line. In practice, that meant to the oldest son living with the deceased at the time of his/her death. If there was no adult son or grandson living with the deceased at the time of his/her death, such items were ordinarily inherited by daughters. Although I have no specific information on the subject, I suspect that when an entire family died without survivors, whatever possessions were left, with the possible exception of dogs, remained where they lay.

Interfamily Distribution

Interfamily distribution consisted of exchanges between compound families, whether they lived in the same or different settlements.[254] It is important in understanding interfamily exchanges at this level to realize that Iñupiaq families were highly self-sufficient economically. This was particularly true of large compound families; their members produced most of the goods and services that they needed to get along. This explains how they could live in near or complete isolation for weeks and months at a time. Economic self-sufficiency was not complete at the family level, however, so people periodically sought goods or services from members of other families. Interfamily exchanges that were satisfactory to both sides also strengthened the ties between unrelated families, in which case they were often prompted as much by political considerations as economic ones. Finally, interfamily trade was a means whereby ambitious individuals could increase their wealth if they were able to outsmart the people with whom they were dealing.

Distribution at the interfamily level was carried out on an individual rather than a collective basis. However, because of the pooling that occurred within families, and due to the authority wielded by the *umialik* and his wife, external distribution of family resources had to be carried out by them, or with their approval. This is why *umialgich* were the primary traders. As Cantwell (1889b:82) put it, the *umialik* was the "chief trader and general business agent" of the Iñupiat. If a trade was arranged by any other person, it had to be done in consultation with the other family members or else be limited to personal property. Except when conducted between very close relatives or between "trading partners," most interfamily exchanges were commercial in nature. At the interfamily level, goods and services were bought and sold, not given away.

When a family had a surplus of anything for which there might be a market, its members tried to sell (*tuni–*) it. Conversely, when a need for a particular item could not be satisfied within a family, its members sought to buy (*tauqsiq–*) it. Gross supply of a particular commodity was not the only factor influencing demand, however; quality was also considered. People who were particularly skilled at making, say, sealskin rope, were often approached by others hoping to buy some.

Most transactions were carried out in public. Thornton (1931) described the process:

> As soon as a trade is agreed upon, everybody feels at liberty to inquire into the transaction. Even while the negotiation is going on, bystanders do not hesitate to proffer suggestions and advice nor to express their opinion concerning the price offered for the article. This takes the place of published quotations; thus every man, woman and child in the village keeps posted as to the market price of sundry articles (Thornton 1931:69; see also Brower ms:227, 244).

However, since the Iñupiat lacked a generalized medium of exchange, or money, calculating the correct price of a particular item was often difficult. Again, I quote Thornton (1931):

> The great trouble lies in the lack of a common standard in which all values may be expressed. For instance, a native offers us a dozen ptarmigan and wants caps in return. We are out of caps at the time and suggest that he take needles instead. He thinks that he knows the market price of grouse in terms of caps, and so he has to work out a problem something like this: If *a* caps equal 12 ptarmigan and

b caps equal *c* primers and *d* primers equal *e* beads and *f* beads equal *g* needles,
how many needles are equal to 12 ptarmigan? This example would probably puzzle
most freshmen and likewise many sophomores; hence it is little wonder that poor
Lo takes a long time to solve it. If one lets him, he will take half the day; for,
especially when the wind is unfavorable for hunting, time is no object with him
(Thornton 1931:71–72).

This example is taken from the early 1890s, but if one substitutes wolverine skins for caps,
and sealskins for primers in the above passage, it applies equally well to the study period.
Thornton could have added that prices of many goods changed dramatically over the course
of a year according to seasonal variations in supply.

There was a considerable amount of gamesmanship involved in interfamily exchanges.
Coming out ahead in a trade was often more important to the participants than acquiring a
badly needed item. But the lack of a generalized medium of exchange often made it difficult
to know who came out ahead; it was clear only later on. The haggling over a transaction
could go on for hours or even days, and, as Thornton's remarks quoted above indicated, it
usually took place in a public forum in which onlookers provided suggestions and criticism.[255]
Among the talents required to become and remain an *umialik* were negotiating skill, and the
ability to judge more accurately than others the correct values of different commodities.

In some interfamily exchanges, the Iñupiat bought and sold things on credit (*akiqsruq–*).
The primary examples of this were on the Kobuk and Selawik rivers (R. Cleveland 1970.3;
Glover 1970.5). In both instances, the main international traders lived on upper sections
of the river. After breakup, they descended to Kotzebue Sound, acquiring but not paying
for goods to sell at the Sisualik trade fair (see below) from families met along the way. The
people from whom they acquired these goods typically placed an order (*qanniq–*) for goods
they desired in return. The traders conducted their business at the fair, then paid off their
debts on their way home, presumably extracting a commission for their services. It would
be fascinating to learn the details of these sequential transactions, but I have been unable
to locate any information on the subject.

Services as well as goods were for sale at the interfamily level. If one needed the services
of a shaman or *iñuunniaqti* who was not a family member, for example, one had to pay
(*akiliq–*) for them. Conversely, if a shaman who was not a particularly good carver needed
a mask, he/she hired someone to make it. Members of whaling crews—particularly expert
harpooners—were hired, and women sometimes were hired to help sew *umiaq* covers if a
family did not include a sufficient number to do it on their own.

There were other, less common, forms of interfamily distribution as well. One of them was
the giving of gifts as part of certain ceremonial dances (*maġlak–*), as discussed in Chapter 6.
Another was the exchange of goods between "trading partners" (*niuviġiik*), which was much
more common in international trade and hence is discussed under that heading below. The
third form was theft.

Theft (*tiglik–*, "to steal") consisted of taking goods without permission from a family of
which one was not a member (Aġviqsiiña 1940.1; Simpson 1875:247–48; Thornton 1931:49,
228). Almost by definition, it could take place only in complex settlements, since simple settlements were occupied by only a single family. There is no way to know just how widespread
stealing was, but Simpson (1875:247) said that it was common in the complex settlement
at Point Barrow, and that it was only the "certainty of detection" that prevented it from
being even more prevalent. Theft was usually limited to meat and oil, since ownership was

marked on weapons, and most utensils and other equipment were easily recognized by the owner and other people as well. Preventive measures included tying dogs around caches, and placing booby traps in entrance tunnels. When discovered, a thief was required to return the stolen goods, and suffered a decline in public opinion. Sometimes he or she was beaten. Those who repeatedly stole things sometimes had their fingers smashed with rocks. Theft of food in the midst of a famine sometimes resulted in the offender's being killed. Stoney (1900:833) claimed that he never even heard of theft, but almost all of his experience was either in simple settlements containing only a single compound family, or in complex settlements where a festival was in progress.

Distribution at the national level consisted of the sum of the exchanges conducted at the interfamily level. There were no national forums established specifically for the exchange of goods and services. However, the settlements at Wales, Point Hope, Buckland, and Shishmaref were large enough for interfamily exchanges to occur throughout the year, with the *qargi* being the primary venue for such activities. Many of the nations whose members were widely dispersed for much of the year held annual or semiannual gatherings when everyone came together, and these were always occasions when interfamily exchanges took place. And, in all cases, people from different settlements visited one another throughout the year, and exchanges of one kind or another virtually always occurred at such times. Even though there were no formal mechanisms for distributing goods and services throughout an entire society, the informal ones appear to have been rather effective.

International Distribution

The resource base of each nation in Northwest Alaska differed to some extent from that of all or most of its neighbors. These differences created regional disparities in the supply of and demand for many types of raw material, and also of some locally manufactured goods. By 1800 there was also differential access to goods manufactured by Europeans. These differences created the foundation of an extensive international trade network. This network encompassed not only the entire study region, but extended outward to the north, east, and south, in Alaska, and west into Chukotka.[256] I have described this system in some detail in another volume (Burch 2005:207–19), and accordingly limit the present discussion to a brief summary.

Distribution at the international level was conducted in the context of two contrasting social frameworks. The first was the same type of interfamily exchange arrangement described above. In other words, distribution was by means of interfamily commercial transactions, except that, in this case, the people involved were of different nationalities. The only difference I am aware of is that attempts to cheat seem to have been much more common in the international context.[257] For example, in August 1826, some Iñupiat on Kotzebue Sound tried to sell F. Beechey (1831, I:391) "fish-skins, ingeniously put together to represent a whole fish, though entirely deprived of their original contents" (see also F. Beechey 1831, II:306; Kotzebue 1821, I:211, 222, 226, 235; VanStone ed. 1973:84–85). Not surprisingly, attempts to detect cheating were also more common in the international arena. Attempts at outright theft seem to have been more frequent when people of different nationalities were in close proximity to one another (F. Beechey 1831, I:397; II:278, 279).

The other social framework for international distribution was the so-called "trading partnership" (dual *niuvigiik*).[258] This was a relationship between two individuals, male or female, usually although not necessarily from different nations, who exchanged goods annually or semiannually. As I have noted elsewhere (Burch 2005:155–59), this relationship would be more accurately characterized by the phrase "giving partnership," since the exchanges involved were usually well below market prices. Whenever they got together, partners made requests of one another for things they would like to receive the next time they met. For example, someone from a nation whose estate was along the coast might request beaver skins from a partner who lived in the upper Selawik district, while the latter might ask for a poke of seal oil. Each person was obliged to fulfill the other's request if it was at all possible to do so. The beauty of this arrangement was the minimization of risk. On the one hand, the supplier knew what the demand for a particular good was long before he was expected to satisfy it; on the other hand, the person seeking that good knew that the supplier would do everything he could to provide it.

International exchanges took place primarily in two contexts, trade fairs and messenger festivals (Burch 2005). Trade fairs took place every summer at various coastal locations in northern and western Alaska. The largest was at Sisualik, on Kotzebue Sound.[259] Here nearly 2,000 people from all parts of the study region and beyond gathered every year for a week or two of feasts, dances, athletic competitions, and, of course, exchanges of goods. Messenger festivals took place in winter, usually during the holiday season of late December and early January. They normally involved people from two nations, the people from one having invited specific families from another to participate. Messenger festivals, like fairs, involved feasting, dancing, athletic competition, and the exchange of goods.

Exchanges between partners took precedence over commercial transactions at both the fairs and messenger festivals. Once the obligations of partnership were met, people were free to buy and sell on the open market. Commercial transactions were more common at fairs than at messenger festivals because the fairs involved a much larger number of people who were not partners. Fairs also took place in summer, and people could transport greater quantities of goods by boat than they could by sled to a messenger festivals.

Discussion

The subject of distribution raises the issue of communism, which Richard Lee (1988), among others, has claimed was ubiquitous among hunter-gatherers. More specifically, it has been claimed for the Iñupiat. For example, after observing Iñupiaq life in fairly close quarters for over a year in the early and mid-1880s, George Stoney (1900:832) wrote that "a sort of communism exists among the natives in a village; all articles are used in common, and borrowing and lending are obligatory and customary." Stefansson, after greater (although later) experience, also used the word "communism" with reference to the Eskimo distribution system:[260]

> [M]y experience with Husky [i.e., Eskimo] communism is likely to make me a convert (at least, a mild sort of one) to the general doctrines of communism. The seemingly very strong objection to C[ommunists]—that some are lazy and will become parasites—seems to have little force in the actual life of the H[uskies]. Some . . . are more energetic than others, and accomplish more, but all try and all do something. The fact that one works harder than another worries neither of them, nor the community in general (in Pálsson 2001:124).

How does one reconcile these assertions with my reconstruction of how the system worked? The answer is quite straightforward. Both Stoney and Stefansson acquired most of their experience living in simple settlements, that is, settlements consisting of just a single compound family. They did not think of it as a family, however, because it was much larger and more complex than most Western families. Instead, they thought of it as a village. Given the pooling of resources that occurred in such settlements, it is not surprising that the notion of communism came to the observers' minds. Once one realizes that the whole settlement was occupied by just a single large family whose members pooled resources, the notion of communism loses most of its analytical value.

More pertinent is what went on in complex settlements, that is, settlements inhabited by the members of two or more compound families. In my earlier discussion of this subject, I asserted that the distribution of goods and services between families was carried out primarily on a commercial basis. John Simpson (1875:247) put it in stronger terms when he wrote that "perhaps it is not too much to say that a free and disinterested gift is totally unknown" among the Iñupiat. In other words, on an interfamily basis, one could not get *anything* unless one paid for it. That is not communism in any sense of the word.

The government teacher in Point Hope in 1911–12 reaffirmed this view:

> [The Natives of Point Hope] cannot be said to be just in their dealings, as they are, at all times, willing to take advantage of a stranger's ignorance concerning local prices. They show no gratitude to their benefactors should they perceive that the latter is in immediate need of a certain article or service, but raise the price as high as they can.[261]

In 1928, Weyer was told by an informant identified as "Mazen," evidently a White person who apparently had spent time in Selawik, on the Kobuk River, and in Wales, that the Iñupiat "may divide the meat freely, but after it is once in their hut it is *theirs*. You can eat all you want day after day in a hut and nothing will be said, but you must not take any away" (Weyer 1928; emphasis his).

In contrast, H. R. Thornton (1931:79), on the basis of his experience in the complex settlement of Wales, claimed that "during times of scarcity . . . no one goes hungry as long as anybody else has anything to eat." There was, indeed, a notion of charity, which, in the Iñupiaq case, meant giving food to hungry people who were not members of one's own compound family. However, it was possible only in a few large settlements where there were some very affluent people. Making charitable gifts of food during hard times was considered a good thing, and conveyed prestige on the *umialik* who made them, but they were made only in exceptional circumstances, not in ordinary daily life. Such a gift did not impose any specific debt on the recipient, but did, in a more general way, make him/her beholden to the donor. And gifts would be made only until the *umialik*'s family began to experience shortages, after which the *umialik* looked after his own. Referring to the practice as "communism" does not strike me as being particularly useful.

Health Care

The notion that Alaska Natives "enjoyed a pristine state of good health" prior to contact with Europeans has been effectively put to rest by Robert Fortuine (1990:1; see also Fortuine 1975:3; 1986/87; Woolfe 1893:143).[262] Although generally free of infectious diseases such as smallpox, measles, influenza, and tuberculosis, the Iñupiat still had to contend with a formidable array of health problems. These included arthritis, blindness, boils, botulism, broken bones, burns, cancer, chronic lung disease, colds, constipation, cuts, diarrhea, dislocated joints, earaches, frostbite, headaches, hearing problems, hypothermia, impetigo, internal parasites, periodontal disease, difficulties with pregnancy and childbirth, rabies, respiratory problems, rheumatism, snow blindness, sprains, stomachaches, strokes, trichinosis, and urethral stones, to mention only some of the possibilities. Dealing with these and other afflictions was an important element in Iñupiaq life.

This section discusses in a general way the arsenal of weapons at the Iñupiat's disposal for contending with health problems, and the ways in which they were delivered. The material is presented under three main headings: medicines, surgery, and magic.[263]

Medicines

Medicines are substances or preparations used in treating disease.[264] The most common medicines employed by the Iñupiat were infusions (or teas) made from boiling certain leaves, berries, or other substances in water. Far and away the most widely used of these throughout the study region was a tea made with the leaves of *Artemisia tilesii*, known in Iñupiaq as *sargiq* or *sargiġruaq*, and in colloquial English as common wormwood, stinkweed, or sage (J. P. Anderson 1939:716; Fortuine 1988b:215; Charlotte Swan 1965.1, 1965.2, 1965.3). The tea was drunk to treat bladder problems, bone aches, head colds, joint pain, lung problems, sore muscles, sore throats—in short, almost any imaginable ache or pain. As a compress, it was used to cure burns.

A distant second to wormwood leaves as a source of multipurpose medicinal infusion were leaves of Labrador tea (*Ledum decumbens*), known to the Iñupiat as *tilaaqqiuq* (J. P. Anderson 1939:715; Fortuine 1988b:210; Anore Jones 1983:60–61). Other plant materials used to make medicinal teas were the berries, leaves, and stems of the juniper bush (*Juniperus communis*, or *tulukkam asriaq*), spruce sap (*suġliaq*), and spruce needles (*qisiqsiutit*). Juniper berries were most effective if collected in winter, but wormwood and Labrador tea leaves had to be collected in summer or fall. I do not know if season mattered in the case of spruce sap or needles. More esoteric items used to make medicinal teas, sometimes in combination with one or more of the materials mentioned above, included unexcreted droppings removed from the intestine of a dead porcupine, and dog feces.

Plant materials were also used to make poultices applied to burns, open wounds or sores, insect bites, sprains, and sore throats, a poultice being "a soft, moist, usually warm mass applied to a lesion of the skin" (Fortuine 1988b:191). Again, wormwood leaves were the most commonly used substance. However, in the case of insect bites, alder (*Alnus crispa*, or *nunaŋiaq*) leaves, chewed into a paste, were thought to be more effective. A poultice of mashed lowbush cranberries (*Vaccinium vitis-idaea*, or *kikmiññaq*) placed around the neck was used to cure sore throats. Blackberry (*Empetrum nigrum*, or *pauŋaq*) juice was squeezed into the eye to relieve the symptoms of cataracts and snow blindness. In some districts a jelly made from algae was used to treat swellings and inflammations. Spruce sap was used to heal cuts. It was warmed, molded to the area of the cut, and held in place with a skin bandage.

Another important class of medicines, used both internally and externally, consisted of oils. Seal oil was the most common of these, although in many interior districts, fish oil was equally or more important. Taken internally as medicine (as opposed to food), these substances had to be consumed in excess, in which case they acted as laxatives. This cleaned out the gastrointestinal tract, and, theoretically, at least, any afflictions contained within it. Oil was also used externally as an ointment to heal cold sores, cuts, insect bites, frostbite, rashes—in short, skin problems of all kinds. Duck or goose body-cavity fat was apparently as useful as seal or fish oil in dealing with skin problems. Earaches were treated by placing a few drops of warmed oil into the ear, and the neck of someone with a sore throat was rubbed with oil.

Certain mineral substances were used as laxatives, although they were not widely available. One was the odiferous mineral water known as *mamaiḷaq*. The other was a very soft white clay known as *nuġġiġvik*. I have not been able to find scientific identifications of either substance.

A final medicine that needs to be mentioned is urine. Fresh, warm urine was used to clean wounds, and is said to have helped reduce bleeding after bloodletting or lancing. It is also said to have been useful in softening porcupine quills prior to their being pulled out of a person's flesh.

The identification and use of medicines were part of the general lore of the Iñupiat. Knowledge of how to locate materials, process them, and use them was passed down from one generation to the next within families, and was by no means restricted to specialists. I have no definite information on the point, but my impression is that women tended to have greater expertise than men in obtaining the raw material for, prescribing, and preparing medicines. Many medicines, particularly leaves that were to be used to make infusions or poultices, had to be collected during the summer or fall months, dried, and stored. Some plant medicines were more abundant in forested areas than in tundra zones, hence were an important item of international trade. Spruce pitch, in particular, has been identified in this context (F. Beechey 1831, I:345, 406), although it had a number of uses in addition to medical applications.

Surgery

Surgery is concerned with diseases and conditions requiring or amenable to manual procedures. In Northwest Alaska surgery took five main forms: manipulation of the internal organs, or deep massage; lancing; bloodletting; amputation; and what I call "repair work." These procedures were usually performed by a specialist, most commonly a "tribal doctor," or *iñuunniaqti*, but sometimes by a shaman (*aŋatkuq*). Each type of specialist was paid in kind for this service, the price being negotiated prior to treatment. An *aŋatkuq* could apparently demand higher wages than an *iñuunniaqti*, which may be part of the reason the latter were more often hired to perform this service. Both men and women could be tribal doctors or shamans.

Deep massage, or manipulation, was used to deal with major problems affecting the internal organs that could not be treated with, or did not respond to, a laxative or enema.[265] My sources specifically mentioned problems with the appendix, gall bladder, small intestine, stomach, and uterus as being amenable to such treatment. If one assumes that the technique used in Northwest Alaska in recent times was derived from the one employed in the 19th century, the basic procedure was as follows. Long enough after eating for the stomach to have emptied, the patient was made to lie on his or her back with the knees raised. The doctor, sitting or kneeling beside the patient, slowly but firmly pressed down with the fingers into the area of the apparently afflicted organ in order to ascertain its boundaries and to confirm the preliminary diagnosis. Then, after softening the general area by moving the hands in a circular motion, the organ was deliberately moved through downward

FIGURE 70. An example of a lancet. The original was about 4 inches (10 cm) long. From Nelson (1899:310).

or forward pressure "to give it more room." Sometimes the procedure was more effectively performed from the back, in which case the patient sat on the floor and the doctor worked from behind and below the rib cage.

Lancing is the "surgical incision of the skin with a point or blade in order to drain out an accumulation of pus or other pathologic fluid, such as that from an abscess" (Fortuine 1985:32). The instrument used to perform this procedure in Northwest Alaska was a lancet, or *uŋuyun*, an example of which is shown in Figure 70. It was made of a small, thin, double-edged blade that was inserted in the split end of a short wooden handle and wrapped tightly with twine.[266] Each lancet was made to fit the hand of the person who was to use it, so there was considerable variation in length from one to another. There was a high level of agreement among my sources that lancet blades were most commonly made from jade in the early 19th century; or, if jade was not available, from slate. However, as the century progressed, iron gradually became the material of choice.

A boil was believed to contain a living being in the form of a worm. It was important not to irritate the boil when it began to grow, for that might cause the worm to burrow deeper into the flesh. That made it more painful and more difficult to extract. When the boil was ready to erupt, it was softened with oil and saliva, lanced very carefully with a cruciform incision, and sometimes drained with a hollow goose quill. The "core" was delicately removed and disposed of through a complex series of procedures.[267]

Bloodletting was similar to lancing, and was performed with a lancet, but was used for different purposes and resulted in a different outcome. Many afflictions—such as backache, bone aches, headaches, joint pain, snow blindness, and swellings and inflammations of all types—were attributed to "blocked blood" or "bad blood." The indicated cure in such cases was to release the blockage or remove the bad blood. Prior to the procedure, the blade was warmed by holding it in the hand, which made the procedure less painful. The lancet was then held in the butt of the doctor's palm, with the thumb up alongside the blade to control the depth of the cut. The point was forced through the skin, the depth and angle of the insertion varying according to where on the body the procedure was being performed. The cut could be three inches (7.5 cm) deep straight into a hip, for example, or only an eighth of an inch (5 mm) deep and at a sharp angle on the side of a head. Great care had to be taken, especially around joints and the spine, not to cut tendons or major nerves. If properly made, the cut was followed by a substantial flow of blood from the wound, thus releasing the blockage or removing the bad blood.

The fourth type of surgery performed by the Iñupiat was amputation (Call 1899:121–22; Fortuine 1984:24; 1985:35–36). This was required primarily in cases of severe frostbite, when areas of flesh, digits, or limbs were frozen beyond recovery. Frozen flesh was allowed to become gangrenous. When it had dried, the damaged flesh was partly cut away with a knife, and partly allowed to slough off. The removal of a limb was more complex, as described by George Stoney (1900):

> An assistant holds the patient and the medicine man performs the operation, cut-
> ting off the frozen part. The limb must mortify before cutting so that all the tissues
> will be contracted; no live flesh is ever cut. The instruments used are a knife and
> a saw and nothing is placed over the cut except a little seal oil. The invalid must
> stand the pain without flinching or uttering a sound (Stoney 1900:833).

This brings us to what I call "repair work," a phrase that covers suturing, splinting, and bandaging.[268] Severe cuts were sutured with an ordinary sewing needle and very fine thread made from caribou sinew. When a limb or digit was amputated, flaps of skin were left beyond the bone and sewn together to cover the wound. Splints consisted of lengths of wood, baleen, or rolled caribou hide lashed to the affected member both above and below the break. Rainey's informant Sam Rock (1940:7) described a case in which a man's skull had been smashed by a brown bear, but his brother molded it back into roughly its normal shape with his hands, and the man apparently recovered. Bandages usually consisted of softened caribou hide, often soaked in oil, and tied with sinew.

Magic

Magic is the use of means that are at least partly nonempirical to achieve empirical ends (Levy 1966:357).[269] An example would be people living in a drought-stricken area performing a special dance to bring rain. People and dancing are empirical and so is rain, but there is no empirical basis on which a dance and any ensuing rain can be causally linked to one another. In Northwest Alaska, dealing with situations containing nonempirical elements was the special province of the shaman.

Magic was an important element in Iñupiaq health care. In very serious cases, magic was immediately invoked. However, it was expensive and risky, and usually adopted as a last resort. It was invoked primarily in situations in which other treatments had failed, and in cases in which the symptoms defied empirical diagnosis. There is no end to possible situations in which all other treatments failed. Examples of maladies that would have been difficult or impossible for the Iñupiat to diagnose or treat empirically include cancer, internal parasites, lung and heart diseases, and stroke; no doubt there were many others as well.

The shaman's first challenge was to make a diagnosis. It was invariably determined that the affliction had been caused by a spirit, usually because the patient had broken a taboo or failed to perform a ritual, and had thus offended that spirit. The problem was to ascertain which taboo had been broken or which ritual had not been performed. This was not easy, since the possibilities were almost endless. As Stefansson (1914b:127) once remarked, "there are probably no things, actions, or relations that are thinkable to the Eskimo mind that are not subject to becoming aglernaktok" (*agliġnaqtuaq*), meaning tabooed or subject to mandatory ritual treatment. At any given time, people could be aware of only a few of them.[270]

Diagnosis usually proceeded in one of two ways. In relatively simple cases, the patient was made to lie down. The shaman then took his own belt and looped it over the patient's afflicted part—head, arm, or leg. The ends of the belt were tied to a strong stick about 6 feet (2 m) long. The shaman sat beside the patient and lay the stick across his/her thighs. He/she then posed a question to an invisible spirit (presumably his/her own familiar spirit, or *qila*), about the problem. Using the stick across his/her thighs as a lever, the shaman then tried to lift the patient's afflicted part off the ground. If it rose, the answer was considered a "yes"; if not, a "no." Proceeding in this way for as long as it took, the shaman learned both the cause of the problem and its cure. An alternative and much more elaborate procedure was for the shaman to beat his/her drum, sometimes don a mask, sing magical songs, utter magical formulas, and go into a trance. In that state, he or she could hold a direct dialogue with the familiar spirit about the patient's problem.

Having made a diagnosis, the shaman had to determine and try to effect a cure. Sometimes this was fairly simple. For example, the shaman might be able to withdraw the affliction from the patient's body simply by putting his/her lips against the patient's skin and sucking.

In other cases, rubbing the shaman's saliva over the affected area did the job. More often, the cure was more complicated, and involved at least two steps. The first was to inform the patient about which taboo he or she had broken. The second was to get the patient to confess that he or she had, indeed, broken it. Without a confession, a cure was in doubt. Often there was a third step, which was to impose one or more additional taboos on the patient so as to placate the offended spirit. If any of these solutions worked, the patient was cured. If not, the whole process had to be repeated. Ultimately, the patient either recovered, continued through life with a chronic affliction, or died.

A still more complex, and expensive, way to cure a sick person was to perform a séance. An observant but skeptical D. Henry Woolfe (1893) described what occurred during such an exercise:

> The modus operandi of these shamans differs very slightly. For the least sickness or ailment one or more are called upon to drive away the evil spirits or devils that are supposed to have located themselves in that part of the body where the pain lies. In treating a patient only the members of the household and invited guests are in the home or tent. . . . The hut being darkened, the shaman enters with a slow step and a solemn face. Desultory conversation ensues for a while, and, assuming a grave and portentous air, he produces a drum made of walrus or hair-seal bladder stretched over a hoop. With a thin, flat stick he strikes the drum, producing a doleful sound, and amid the noise he commands and exhorts the evil spirit. The performance is usually inaugurated with mournful sounds, but as the shaman proceeds, he is encouraged by the approval of the audience, who make responses to the incantation, such as "go ahead", "yes, that's so", and queries as to the location of the devil. Gradually he warms up, his utterances become thick and quick, and the symptoms that are supposed to be essential to the driving out of the spirits now appear. The shaman rolls his eyes, his tongue protruding and body quivering, and his whole frame seems to be in a hysterical and highly nervous condition. Many of these impostors at this juncture cover their heads with a coat of seal gut, shaking it to and fro and under its cover emit ventriloquial sounds, such as the quacking of a duck, barking of a dog, blowing of a whale, and other nondescript noises. With foam exuding from his mouth and features distorted, he extends his arms toward the patient, who lies in the center of the hut or tent. He breathes upon or touches the parts where pain is supposed to be located, drawing his hands from the body upward and downward, as if to drag the pain away. Again ventriloquism is brought into play, and a conversation with replies ensues between the shaman and the evil spirits. With a whoop and a jump he finally declares that the devil has left the patient and then sinks to the ground exhausted. There is a great amount of exaltation and peculiar hysterical conditions visible during these performances, and the shaman, after an extended seance, exhibits all the symptoms of a faint or an epileptic fit. The entire nervous system seems to be unstrung and limp (Woolfe 1893:139).[271]

If one shaman proved unsuccessful, others were called until either health was restored, the family could no longer afford to pay the medical expenses, or death ended the proceedings.

Magic was also invoked as a disinfectant. People who were thought to be sick or liable to get sick for some reason were made to stand over a small smudge fire. After a few minutes, their clothing became permeated with smoke, and the threat was considered removed (Goodwin 1970; Grinnell 1901:41).

Travel

Most Iñupiat moved about a great deal over the course of a normal yearly cycle, and travel consumed a considerable amount of their time and energy (Burch 1975b). When they moved from place to place, they took a substantial percentage of their goods and chattels with them: shelter, food, sleeping bags, weapons, fishing equipment, cooking rocks, and all the tools, utensils, and containers they needed to live comfortably, not only at their destination, but at each stop along the way. This policy of "traveling heavy" required considerable effort, but it also enabled people to deal with a variety of unforeseen problems—such as storms and floods—that they might meet along the way. If they got stuck someplace, they had the wherewithal to cope with the situation (Stefansson 1951:56). Implementation of this policy required not only sophisticated equipment, but carefully worked-out procedures for moving it and using it. Regardless of whether they moved by sled, by boat, or on foot, people usually traveled in groups to provide mutual support in times of trouble.

In this section I summarize what I have been able to learn about early-19th-century travel under three main headings: sled travel, boat travel, and foot travel. Since dogs were important in all three, and since they have not been singled out for attention so far, I begin the discussion with them.

Dogs

Dogs were the only domesticated animal owned by the Iñupiat. They were used to track boats along the coast and up the rivers in summer, to pull sleds in winter, and to serve as pack animals in summer. In small settlements they served as sentinels to warn people of the hidden presence of strangers, and they were killed and eaten in time of famine. The pelts of dogs that died or were killed were skinned to supply ruffs for parkas or material for men's pants. Dogs were theoretically owned by men, but were raised, fed, and generally looked after by women (Brower ms:148).

Dogs were major consumers of food, the same kinds of nonvegetable food eaten by their owners. When working in winter, they needed a daily ration of at least three pounds (1.35 kg) of meat, fish, or blubber—whatever was available locally—to supply the energy needed to keep them sufficiently vigorous and warm (Anderson et al. 1998:127–28; Giddings 1961:145; Thornton 1931:156). The Napaaqtuġmiut reckoned one medium-sized dried salmon per dog per day in winter (K. and E. Mills 1960). If they were working hard, or if it was extremely cold, dogs required more. The food requirements made dogs expensive to keep, especially during hard times, which is what resulted in their low numbers. In interior districts, teams usually contained one to three working dogs; on the coast some teams included as many as five, but rarely more.[272] Females generally were not used as draft animals, and a significant percentage of females was probably put to death at or shortly after birth. The rest were used for breeding.

The dogs owned by the Iñupiat are usually referred to as "huskies." The early-19th-century huskies were what Natives in my time characterized disparagingly as "heavy-duty," that is, large and powerful, but slow. Certainly they were much larger than the racing dogs used in the late 20th century (Anderson et al. 1998:127; Rausch 1951:162; Thornton 1931:154). Most working males probably weighed in the range of 60 to 90 pounds (27–40 kg), while some weighed well over 100 (45 kg). Stoney (1900:565), who actually weighed his dogs, considered a 75-pound (34 kg) animal to be of "moderate" weight in the mid-1880s. Females generally were at or below the normal weight range for males.

Huskies had strong necks, broad, deep chests, and bodies that tapered somewhat toward the hindquarters.[273] The paws were broad, and there was webbing between the toes; they were good swimmers. Huskies had broad heads topped by pointed ears. These were upright and aimed forward most of the time, but they could be laid flat against the head when the animal was frightened, angry, or working hard, or they could be moved around more or less independently of one another when the animal was bored or indifferent to what was going on. The tail normally curved up over the back, but was held relatively straight when the animal was working or angry, and between the legs when it was frightened or submissive. The most desirable coat consisted of a layer of extremely thick short hair and a much thinner layer of long hair. As long hair tended to get full of snow during stormy winter weather, which could result in frostbite, there was some selective breeding against it. Fur colors included black, white, brown, rust, and tan, sometimes separately, sometimes in combination.

Huskies made a wide range of vocalizations that changed according to mood and circumstances. They apparently barked only when confronting a polar bear (Brower ms:417);[274] otherwise their repertoire of noises consisted of a variety of whines, howls, and growls. These sounds, and the various angles at which they could hold their tails and direct their ears, made them remarkably expressive.

Litters seem to have averaged between five and eight pups. Often pups were left to their mother to look after (Thornton 1931:157). However, if dogs were in short supply in a settlement, or if a family had a team of aging animals, puppies were carefully nurtured. In cold or stormy weather they were sometimes kept with their mother in the entrance tunnel of the house or in a shelter built especially for them. Women sometimes chewed meat or fish to soften it for pups approaching the weaning stage. Dogs were named soon after birth, usually after deceased humans or characters in legends. By the time a dog reached adulthood, it knew its name (Murdoch 1892:357; Stefansson 1914b:284).

Dogs were allowed to run free until they were about six months old, at which point they began to be introduced to their lifetime occupation of work. Huskies generally reached their peaks of strength and endurance between the ages of three and six years, and gradually declined thereafter. A major factor in their aging was the wearing down of their teeth from eating so much frozen fish and meat over the years; some dogs died of starvation simply because they could no longer chew their food.

Most dogs spent their entire lives out of doors, regardless of the weather. In general, they were kept tied when not working.[275] This kept them out of trouble, available when needed, and easy to feed. Unfortunately, huskies enthusiastically ate anything made of leather, and all the rope, twine, clothing, bags, tarpaulins, boat covers, and many other goods were made of that substance (J. Grinnell 1901:48). To deal with this problem, a collar, made of diamond-leaf willow bark or, more often, sealskin or caribou hide, was tied to a stick three or four feet (90–122 cm) long. The other end of the stick was attached to a shrub, stake, or log. Another way to connect the stick to the dog was with a forked stick, the crotch of which was tied around the dog's neck. In either case, the animal was held in place, but could not reach the edible substance either around its neck or around the anchor. It was also limited in its movements to pivoting around the anchor. The only places where dogs were observed to run free were at the settlement of Shishmaref, which is located on an island (Kotzebue 1821, I:200), and along the west side of Kotzebue Sound (Kotzebue 1821, I:232). These animals probably were left to fend for themselves during the summer. The same animals were probably tied in winter.

Just how the Iñupiat treated their dogs, as judged by Western standards, is the subject of some debate. Murdoch (1892:358) and Seemann (1853, II:31), for example, said that dogs were treated well. Thornton (1931:150, 155–56, 160), on the other hand, in an otherwise even-handed account, claimed that dogs were treated with brutality. If there were differences among settlements in this respect, perhaps both views were correct. Huskies were beaten with whips to stop them from fighting, but rarely otherwise. They were bred to work, and healthy, well-cared-for animals rarely needed any encouragement to do so.

Huskies were strong and they were tough. As noted above, working dogs were mostly male, and relatively young, usually less than seven years in age. This combination of traits ensured that they would be quarrelsome, and preventing and halting fights was a major preoccupation of canine husbandry.[276] Dogs were sometimes muzzled to keep them from fighting (Thornton 1931:160; VanStone 1976:34). Gelding, which might have alleviated the problem, was not practiced.

Sled Travel

Virtually all winter travel was done with the help of a sled. People who did not have a sled were reduced to packing their things on their backs, or to dragging a shrub or animal hide behind them with a few goods resting on it (Stone 1976). The only other alternative was not to travel at all. This raises the question, why *did* people travel in the harsh conditions of an arctic winter? The answer is, for one or a combination of several reasons. The most common was to relocate to an area where game was more abundant than it had become at the current location. A related reason was to move to the locality where a major harvest of seals, fish, or caribou had been made (some miles away from home); it was often easier to move the settlement to where a large kill had been made than it was to bring the harvest to the settlement. A third possibility was to visit friends or relatives, or to attend a messenger festival. A fourth reason people traveled in winter was to position themselves for anticipated spring and early-summer hunting; the best areas were usually at some distance from the best wintering places. Finally, people traveled in winter for a change of scene, to get some variety in the diet, or to escape an oppressive social environment.

As noted earlier in this chapter, two types of sled were used in Northwest Alaska, the railed (or basket) sled (*uniapiaq*) and the flat sled (*qamun*).[277] However, the former was by far the more common. Flat sleds were sometimes used by people who had to move *umiat* from their winter settlement to a spring camp prior to breakup, or from the settlement to a lead in the ice for whaling. However, most basket sleds were made wide enough to be used in this way as well. The traditional basket sleds also had straight rails, and they lacked crosspieces between the rails at the rear of the sled. These features made it much easier to nest an *umiaq* between the rails of a 19th-century sled than those of a 20th-century model.

Ideally, sleds were pulled exclusively by dogs. In reality, they were almost always pulled by one to three dogs and one or more people, with another person pushing and guiding the sled from behind.[278] Even when there were enough dogs to pull the sled unaided, someone—usually the woman who raised and fed them—had to walk in front to guide and encourage them. (The Iñupiat did not begin to train dogs as leaders until the late 1880s.) In interior districts where the snow was deep and soft, a person had to precede the entourage on snowshoes to break a trail. In very deep snow, it was necessary for trailbreakers to travel back and forth several times to prepare the way.

In most districts, dogs and humans pulled sleds using a single tandem hitch.[279] This consisted of a towline attached to the sled, to which dogs and/or people were alternately connected via shorter lines, or traces. In other districts they used a paired tandem hitch, in which people or dogs were connected to the towline in the same way, but in pairs. In a few districts, such as Wales, they used a fan hitch, in which the trace from each dog was connected directly to the sled. When favored with a good trail and a following wind, sails were sometimes raised to help propel the sled (Brower ms:149).

Dog harnesses were made from strips of sealskin, bear hide, or caribou hide to fit the specific dog that was to wear it. VanStone has described and illustrated a rather crude harness made of two strips of sealskin joined at the rear end and separated at the front by two short pieces of sealskin; the dog's head fit between the crosspieces (VanStone 1980:63). More common were harnesses with two broad straps running along the back, with thinner extensions down around the neck and across the chest, then back up behind the front legs toward the rear of the harness. There they were fastened together. Crosspieces linked the straps so that they fit closely around the head and across the chest (B. Foote 1992:145; Thornton 1931:131). In all cases, a trace, or line, ran from the rear of the harness to the towline or the sled, depending on the hitch in use. Antler or ivory swivels (see Figure 71) kept the traces from twisting. The harness used by humans to pull a sled consisted of a broad strap of sealskin or caribou hide that went across the chest, with the trace being attached at the back. Leather whips were sometimes used to keep dogs from straying from the chosen path, but mostly to stop them from fighting (Sunno 1951.4).

People traveling in winter were almost always up before daybreak, particularly during the short days of November, December, and January. After a meal that usually consisted of oil and frozen raw fish (*quaq*), they loaded the sleds with all of their goods and chattels, hitched up the dogs and themselves, and proceeded on their way. Infants were carried in the back of their mothers' parka. Young children and incapacitated elders rode on the sled, but everyone else who was not actively pulling or pushing the sled walked behind it or went ahead on snowshoes to break a trail.

Speed of movement varied radically depending on the size of the load, the number and condition of the people and dogs in harness, and the quality of the trail. Under perfect conditions, three healthy dogs and two healthy adult humans might be able to move a load of 500 pounds (225 kg) at an average rate of between two and three miles (3.2–4.8 km) an hour. With a heavier load, a less-than-perfect trail, and/or inclement weather, the rate of progress was much slower. When people and dogs were weakened by hunger, progress was slower still, and rest stops were more frequent.

Travelers took the easiest trail that was available in the direction they wanted to go. Coastal travel was usually on the ice of the lagoons behind the beach ridges until the ocean froze in December. Later, sea ice along the shore was often equally or more suitable; in many areas, ice piles were grounded a hundred yards (90 m) or more offshore, leaving a smooth

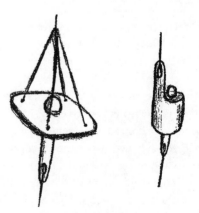

FIGURE 71. Examples of swivels. From Sunno, Hadley, and Konalook (1951). Reproduced with the permission of Charles Lucier.

stretch near the beach. Usually the ice was thick enough here to be quite safe; dangerous areas of thin or moving ice were found beyond the grounded ice piles. On the other hand, sea ice was sometimes driven right up onto the beach by onshore winds. Around the faces of headlands, the ice was often extremely rough and nearly or absolutely impassible. Traveling through such areas was not only difficult, it risked serious damage to the sled and injury to people and dogs. Therefore, travelers often had to circumvent such places, going inland, up and over the back of any headlands.

Travel inland was usually on frozen waterways: creeks, rivers, and lakes. The frozen tussock fields that covered much of the land surface made for a rough road until sufficient snow accumulated to fill in the spaces between tussocks (which often was not until February or March). Riverbanks were avoided if at all possible because of the usually heavy willow growth there. Meanders in most of the rivers posed a problem because the distance along the river's course was several times greater than it was if one took a straight line. The solution was to take shortcuts by cutting across the base of the many peninsulas created by the river's loops. Over several generations of use, fairly good shrub-free trails were created across the bases of meander loops, thereby reducing the distance that people had to travel when going up- or downstream.

Areas of thin ice or open water were a special problem for travelers in the interior (Stoney 1900:586). In the fall, the ice was thin everywhere, and had to be checked frequently. In some places, the current was too swift for the river to freeze at all. In bitterly cold weather it was dangerous to cross such areas because of the likelihood that frozen toes or feet on the part of both humans and dogs would result. Sometimes, however, travelers had no choice, so a crossing had to be followed by an immediate change of footgear and special attention to the dogs' feet.

A more common problem was what is variously known as "icing," "aufeis," or "overflow." This occurs in the many spring-fed rivers of Northwest Alaska that freeze to the bottom in shallow places. This dams the water flowing down from above, ultimately forcing it up through cracks and over the ice surface. If a thin layer of ice formed on top of the overflow, the procedure was to cover it with a "bridge" of saplings two or three feet (60–90 cm) apart augmented with a layer of brush on top. One or two people crossed the bridge with a long line attached to the towline and began to pull the dogs across. When the animals reached the bridge, they moved quickly of their own accord to get past the water.

The final problem encountered by travelers in the interior was steep terrain. Although people tried to avoid this, sometimes it was necessary to cross a range of hills or mountains to get to one's destination. When the trail became too steep, it was necessary to stop, unload the sled, and pack its contents over the pass (Stoney 1900:569; Sun 1970). This might require several trips back and forth. Descending steep slopes with a heavily loaded sled was easier but more dangerous, since the sled might accelerate downhill, overrunning the dogs and people pulling it, crashing into an obstruction, and/or dumping the load. Consequently, on very steep slopes, the dogs were unhitched, and people tried to slow the sled's downhill momentum by restraining it with ropes attached to the rear of the sled (Brower ms:307).

The day's journey usually ended either when game was sighted, or when a good camping place was reached after several hours of travel. The ideal camping place had freshwater or freshwater ice close by; willows to provide a windbreak and possibly game in the form of hares and ptarmigan; and convenient access to seals, caribou, or fish. Travelers often had to stop before they reached such a place.

Sled travel in clear weather was feasible twenty-four hours a day even during the short days of early winter. This was because, in the pollution-free skies of early-19th-century Alaska, the light from the moon and stars reflecting off the snow made the coarse-grained vision required for slow-speed sled travel easily attainable. The only problem was tripping over small drifts or in shallow dips in the snow, which were sometimes difficult to see in the absence of shadows. As the days grew progressively longer in March, darkness became even less of a constraint on human movement.

As the weather warmed and darkness vanished in late April, the snow often became so soft during the day as to constitute an impediment. People sank into it, and dogs suffered from the soft snow jamming the spaces between their toes. Consequently, most travel was carried out in what would have been nighttime hours in February because, although there was light all the time, the sun dipped low enough for the temperature to drop several degrees, refreezing the snow and firming the trail. The problem here was that when the snow surface freezes at night it contains lots of ice crystals, which, unless the dogs wore leather booties, cut the pads on the dogs' feet (Weyer 1928:71). Unfortunately, dogs preferred eating booties to wearing them. Travelers sometimes were in a quandary on how to deal with the situation.

Setting up camp was an enterprise that usually took several hours.[280] The first step was to tie the dogs so that they could not eat their harness (or anything else made of leather). The second step was to erect a house. Along the coast or in windswept areas, the temporary houses of travelers were often made of blocks of wind-packed snow. In the interior, they more frequently consisted of oval dome-shaped frames made from plaited willows covered by caribou skins or a layer of moss. (Any moss had to be dug up from beneath the snow, which took considerable time and effort.) In both cases, a layer of snow was usually thrown over the initial cover to provide added protection from the elements.[281] After work on the house or shelter was completed, the sled was unloaded and its contents placed inside. The dogs were then fed, and the people settled down inside for a hot meal and rest.

The first day's routine was repeated every day thereafter until either the intended destination was reached, or until fish or game were discovered. Travelers generally had to live off the land regardless of the purpose of their trip, so extended journeys were necessarily halted from time to time so that people could hunt or fish. Often, of course, the whole purpose of a trip was to move to a more productive area than the one left behind. In such cases, the discovery of a good fishing hole or a large band of caribou meant that at least one phase of the expedition was concluded. On the other hand, when the purpose of a trip was to attend a messenger festival, there was considerable compulsion to keep moving. Some of these journeys covered distances of nearly 300 miles (480 km) as the crow flies, and considerably more than that on the ground (Burch 2005:176).

Food was not the only problem that had to be attended to by sled travelers. Sleds were frequently damaged by rough terrain or through careless handling, and halts had to be called for their repair. Clothing—especially footgear—tore or wore out and had to be repaired or replaced. Other equipment was damaged and required repair. Underfed people and dogs became exhausted or suffered injuries. Babies were born and elders died. In short, life went on as people moved from place to place, all of which made sled travel a slow and difficult process, but one still better than the alternative.

Boat Travel

Long-distance boat travel in Northwest Alaska was conducted in *umiat*, the 30-to-40-foot (9–12 m) open boats made of wooden frames and oogruk- or walrus-hide covers.[282] *Umiat* were used both on the sea and in the rivers, but the procedures followed in the two contexts differed to some extent. With regard to ocean travel, as Woolfe (1893:149) observed many years ago, "with the exception of the tribes at Cape Prince of Wales and on Diomede, King, and Sledge islands [the last three being outside the study region], the Eskimo are not venturesome in proceeding seaward out of sight of land." But for most, there was little need to go out of sight of land. The groups just named, however (mostly from the Bering Strait area), had to travel between the islands and the mainland, and to cross Bering Strait to Asia. They propelled their boats with square-rigged sails made from caribou hide or sealskin, paddles, and oars when at sea, and tried to travel as fast as possible until reaching the proximity of land.

Most *umiaq* travel on the ocean was conducted along the shore, which, in most of the study region, consisted of a relatively gently sloping gravel beach.[283] With a following wind a sail was used. Otherwise, the boats were tracked by humans and/or dogs, paddled by men, and/or rowed by women. For tracking, dogs in regular harness were attached via traces to a long towline connected to the boat. A boat that was being tracked reportedly could make about four or five miles (6–8 km) per hour in good conditions (Hooper 1881:29), although one has to wonder how long the humans who were placed ashore to lead the dogs and keep them from eating their towline and traces could maintain that pace while trotting on a sand or gravel surface. Thornton estimated that a loaded *umiaq* under sail could make seven to ten miles (11–16 km) per hour traveling directly downwind (Thornton 1931:126).

The greatest hazards to *umiaq* travel both out at sea and near the shore were strong winds and the resulting rough water. The boats were not stable enough to withstand a heavy sea, and, when under sail, they could not tack or hold a crosswind course. Flaps of sealskin or walrus hide were sewn along the gunwales and raised on sticks to keep water from splashing in. Kayaks or inflated sealskin pokes were sometimes tied outside the gunwales for greater stability (Collinson 1889:74). But when the wind got too strong or the sea too rough, boats headed for shore.

When landing in breakers, *umiat* were run straight onto the beach. People immediately jumped out, and before the next wave came along, turned the boat broadside to the surf. As soon as it could be done, two long poles were placed under the boat at right angles to the waves to keep it from sinking in the sand. Each ensuing wave pushed the boat a bit farther up the beach (on top of the poles), and people standing along the landward gunwale prevented it from drifting back out with the retreating water. Eventually it was high enough to be unloaded safely. After being emptied, the boat was either carried away from the water's edge or rolled away on top of an inflated sealskin poke. Later, if it was deemed safe to travel but the surf was still up, the launching procedure was the reverse of the one used in landing, except that the long poles were used to push the craft away from the beach.

In many districts, if water conditions became too rough on the ocean, it was possible to portage the boat and its contents across the beach ridge to a relatively calm lagoon and continue on. When rounding a headland, however, it was necessary to put the dogs on board and either sail or paddle the craft until a smoother shoreline was reached on the other side. In rough weather, boat travel ceased at headlands.

In freshwater, the mode of travel depended on whether the boat was heading down- or upriver.[284] Most downriver travel was done on the spring flood, just after breakup. The current provided most of the energy, while the crew paddled just enough to maintain steerage way. The dangers here were from ice jams when the departure was made too early in the season, and from submerged logs and roots that could not be seen in the murky water.

The basic procedure for traveling upriver was to track the vessel along the bank using the same procedures and equipment as on the ocean shore. However, it was more complicated in this context. Stoney (1900) described how it worked:

> A boy goes ahead as a dog leader and a man follows as driver; the latter's position is not an easy one; sometimes a dog will go to one side of a bush and the next dog the other side, or the head dogs will go over a fallen tree and the others under it, causing trouble and a dog fight and necessitating a delay to straighten out again. About two miles [3.2 km] an hour is made in tracking; delay is caused by the dogs having to be shifted often from one bank to the other in order to get good footing. Occasionally in places dogs cannot be used and recourse is had to poles and paddles. Whenever the wind is fair sail is made (Stoney 1900:837).

Much depended on the river's depth. When the water level was down, the flow was reduced and long gravel bars were exposed on many of the region's rivers (with the notable exception of the Selawik River). These bars provided good footing for the trackers and little in the way of shrubs or other obstacles. When the water level was high, however, the gravel bars were inundated, the current was strong, and the trackers, whether human or canine, had to travel on the usually willow-covered bank. It often took two or three times as long to ascend a river a given distance with high water as with low.

In attempting to understand boat travel, whether on the sea or in a river, it is important to recall that about half the trips took place at a time of year when there was little or no darkness. Weather conditions, not the amount or timing of daylight, were the primary factors influencing movement. By late August, and certainly in September, however, darkness increasingly became an impediment restricting the hours during which people could travel, although even then weather was the more important factor. People traveling upriver in late summer and early fall made frequent halts to eat, rest, or seine for fish, and a regular camp was usually made every evening. However, travelers who were behind schedule or worried about an early freezeup, and thus in a hurry, usually slept under overturned boats, resuming their progress early the next day.

At any point in the season, whether traveling on saltwater or fresh, whenever it was decided to stop for awhile, the *umiaq* was unloaded, carried away from the water's edge, and turned on its side. Its sides were banged with a long pole to loosen any gravel that might have gotten inside and wedged between the cover and the frame; any residue was flushed with buckets of water. Gravel wore holes in the cover if it was not removed on a regular basis. The cover also needed to be dried out periodically or else it, and particularly the seams holding the skins together, would rot. This was apparently a greater problem in freshwater than in salt. The dried cover was rubbed with seal oil from time to time to help maintain its waterproof quality.

Umiat were usually heavily loaded for long-distance travel, which almost always included trade as a major objective. By placing poles along the sides, it was possible to raise the load as much as four feet (120 cm) above the gunwale. However, it was risky to have a load this high in a boat out on the ocean even when kayaks or inflated sealskin pokes were lashed to the gunwales as outriggers.

Estimates of the payload of an average *umiaq* range from five to seven tons, plus a crew of six people (Stefansson 1944:37; 1951:106; Stoney ms:162; Thornton 1931:125). Obviously, larger boats could carry more than smaller ones. Over the course of a summer, some *umiat* covered distances of 500 to 1,000 miles (800–1,600 km) with loads of this size.

Echoing F. Beechey's (1831, I:404–5) account, Hooper (1884) summarized his 1880 observations of *umiaq* travel as follows:

> The carrying capacity of the oomiac is enormous. When used in traveling it contains a tent of drilling or deer-skin, guns, traps, spears, bows and arrows, a kyack, a seal-skin poke filled with water, a quantity of dried meat or fish, and, in the warm season, a lot of birds and eggs; a sled, several pairs of snow-shoes, a fish-net and some smaller nets for catching birds, a shaman drum, and several bags of skin clothing. Perhaps, in addition, a stock of oil, whalebone [baleen], ivory, or furs is taken along for the purpose of trading.
>
> The *personnel* consists of three or four men, about as many women, and two or three children. Add to these two or three dogs, each with a litter of puppies, and some idea may be formed of what a traveling oomiac contains. The working dogs are generally left on shore to follow on foot, which they do, keeping up a continual and most dismal howl. If the wind comes ahead, and the natives desire for any reason to continue their journey, they catch and harness the dogs, and attach them to the oomiac after the manner of a canal-boat and horses, and continue on their way, making four or five miles [6–8 km] an hour. When they wish to stop for a night or day they land and pitch the tents; the oomiac is unloaded and turned up on the shore, and the Innuits are as much at home as if in their winter houses (Hooper 1884:102; italics original).

People who traveled by *umiaq* were prepared for just about anything.

When the season for boat travel came to an end, the *umiaq*'s skin cover was removed, dried, folded, and placed inside the boat's frame. The whole was then placed on a framework of poles high enough to keep it beyond the reach of dogs. The following spring, when the season for boat travel was about to begin, the cover was taken out, soaked in water to soften, patched if necessary, and lashed back onto the frame.

Foot Travel

Extensive travel on foot was conducted in the summer and fall in three major contexts.[285] One involved groups of men moving to and from summer caribou-hunting grounds, requiring journeys of anywhere from several tens to hundreds of miles, and lasting from one to two months or more. The primary practitioners of this activity were Akuniġmiut men, who annually traveled in small groups from the central Kobuk district to the upper Noatak and back. But men from almost every nation in Northwest Alaska traveled on foot from time to time, over shorter distances, and at less regular intervals. In either context, they were usually accompanied by one to four pack dogs, each of which could carry a load of up to about fifty pounds (22.7 kg).[286]

The second context for extensive foot travel involved entire families, or, more accurately, the able-bodied members of families, on caribou-hunting expeditions. Invalids and elders were left behind with a few children to help look after them. These family hunting expeditions involved trips of several tens of miles, and sometimes more, and they could last from four to six weeks. Family hunting trips occurred occasionally in almost every district, but the primary practitioners of this particular pattern were the Kivalliñiġmiut, the Pittaġmiut, and, to a lesser extent, the Tikiġaġmiut. The Kivalliñiġmiu Regina Walton (b. 1885) described her own experience as a young girl:

> When they got up to where there were lots of caribou, they made camp there, and made a house while drying the meat. When the meat was really dry, they wrapped it up. They took the meat off the ribs and the belly and packed it tightly with rope. The packs were almost too heavy to lift. When a man was going to pack the meat, he wrapped it in an old kayak skin [*qayyiñģaq*]. There were two ways to pack the meat: one was with a tump line across the forehead, and one was with a strap across the chest.
>
> When they got a lot of caribou, and the people dried the meat, they took it to where they were going to camp for the next night. When they couldn't take it all in one load, they would come back to get the rest. While they were drying the meat, they ate only what was left on the bones, saving the rest to take home.
>
> When they wanted to do that, the husband and wife, when they wanted to go home, they packed the meat on their backs, stopping after one day's travel. They left the meat there, then went to get some more, bringing it to the same place. When there was a young child or anyone staying with them [i.e., a baby-sitter], they could usually pack the meat in one day and return again.
>
> While they were doing like that every day, they ate just the bones. They never ate the real meat, just tried to finish the bones. When the last meat was eaten from the bones, they would start to eat the heaviest pieces from the good meat. They continued thus, carrying and eating the meat (R. Walton 1965.2).

The third and final context involved parties of men intent on raiding the people of another nation. Their forays covered anywhere from several tens to several hundred miles.

People traveling on foot took as little in the way of equipment and other paraphernalia as possible. The simple and obvious reason for this was that they and their dogs had to carry everything on their backs, often over difficult terrain. The basic equipment consisted of a full set of weapons, a bedroll, an extra set of waterproof boots, a tarpaulin made of several caribou or seal intestines sewn together, oil, and dried fish or meat. Oogruk flippers or caribou bladders were used as canteens. Fishhooks and lines, small dip nets, and light snares (for ptarmigan, ground squirrels, and hares) helped the travelers live off the land as they went. People on hunting expeditions also carried heavy-duty oogruk-line snares for caribou.

Women and girls carried infants, and all the equipment and supplies in caribou-hide or sealskin bags held on the back by a strap (*natmautaq*) across the chest. When heavily loaded, they used a tumpline (*kavraġmiutaq*) across the forehead as well. Dogs carried their loads in pouches suspended on both sides of their body, with a broad strap across the back connecting the two, and a thin strap across the chest to keep the pack from sliding backwards. Until a supply of meat had been obtained, the men and older boys walked some distance ahead of the rest of the party carrying only their weapons, looking for game. When all of the travelers were males, the younger ones went ahead to search for game, and the older men and dogs followed with the loads.

The people who traveled with the least equipment were raiders (*suġruich*) and soldiers (*aŋuyaktit*). They had to travel fast, both going to and coming from an attack, and they could not take along pack dogs to help carry the load. Some of these excursions were made over long distances, perhaps as much as 300 miles (480 km) one way as the crow flies, and the men dared not let impediments slow them down. While they were in enemy territory, warriors also had to travel surreptitiously. This meant that they had to avoid the easiest routes and best camping places, and that they could not build fires to warm themselves or cook.

Caribou hunters on the way out carried little more equipment than did warriors. However, they hoped on the return trip to have huge loads of caribou hides and as much dried meat and fat as they and their dogs could carry. The primary objective was to obtain hides; consequently, most meat and organs, and all bones, were either consumed immediately or left behind. People carried staffs to help them maintain their balance when fording rivers and streams, and for support when walking in rough terrain.

When people got tired or hungry they stopped, ate, rested and perhaps napped, then proceeded. They were not limited by darkness in either hunting or traveling until well into August, after which darkness rapidly increased its influence on human activities, especially on hunting. No matter what they were doing, people were plagued with mosquitoes (and black flies in some districts) until late August.

Foot travelers stopping for one night often slept in the open air unless it was raining, in which case they made shelters out of willow branches or rocks, and/or the lightweight tarpaulins they brought with them. If the harvest was big enough for them to stay in the same place for awhile, they erected a house with a willow frame and a moss or tarpaulin cover. Such an establishment provided some relief from insects through the use of a smudge fire inside the house. A caribou stomach sometimes served as a cooking vessel: meat and water were put in the stomach and a hot stone was dropped in to bring water to boiling temperature (Foote and Williamson 1961:24). Alternatively, meat was roasted. If it was raining too hard to make a fire, food was eaten raw.

Whenever a kill was made, people stopped and set up a base camp. There they butchered the carcasses, and dried the hides and meat on willow branches or frames made from willow branches. In good weather, this took two or three days, during which time those not actually involved in processing the harvest hunted outward from the base camp. In wet weather, the hides could not dry properly, which greatly increased the weight of the loads the men had to carry on their return trip.

If kills continued to be made in the vicinity of the base camp, people stayed there. Usually, however, hunting ceased to be productive after a few days, in which case they moved on. If the first base camp was located near the intended route home, the initial harvest was stored there under rocks, to be retrieved on the return trip. Otherwise, it had to be carried along as people moved from place to place. Dried hides were rolled into huge but relatively light bundles, with dried meat and fat stored in the middle.

As the load accumulated, it eventually became too great to carry. When this point was reached, the procedure was to move forward in relays (*natmaktuq–*). People and dogs headed out in the morning carrying the largest loads they could manage, and walked about half a day. Then they cached their loads and returned to pick up the remainder. In an unusually productive summer they might have to proceed in a triple relay rather than a double one. By repeating this process day after day, they eventually made it home.

Discussion

The evidence summarized in this chapter suggests that the early-contact Iñupiat were master hunter-gatherers and craftsmen. That, however, is a somewhat idealized view. As my senior informants repeatedly reminded me, only some individuals had the skill, talent, and energy to operate at the highest level, whether it be in hunting seals or sewing clothes. Others were lazier, less competent, and/or less motivated than their fellow countrymen, and they accordingly operated at lower levels. With regard to any particular ability, individuals ranked along a continuum from the highest level to the lowest. In my time (1960s), the people who were the most competent at one type of activity generally were the most competent at several others; they tended to have the most capable spouses as well. It is my impression that the same was true in earlier periods.

The variation among individuals might have been characterized by a bell-shaped curve, with a few people represented at the bottom, a few at the top, and the majority somewhere in between. Alternatively, the variation might have been characterized by a bimodal curve. In the latter case, there would have been a fair number of very capable people at one end of the continuum, a similar number at the opposite end, and relatively few in between. My impression is that the latter was actually the case, but this could result from a bias of my research methods. In any event, an impression cannot stand as evidence. The main point is that, in either scenario, there was considerable variation in energy and skill among the members of even these very small populations.

Despite the variation among the individuals involved, the fact that the Iñupiat and their ancestors successfully lived in the harsh north Alaskan environment for at least a thousand years (and probably much longer) stands as proof that a significant percentage of them not only knew what they needed to do, they did it. It is difficult to imagine how they could have been more effective in acquiring the raw materials and manufacturing the goods required to survive given the means at their disposal.

The material presented in this chapter might suggest that the Iñupiat were people who rationally analyzed their circumstances and problems and devised ways to deal with them (Burch 1994b). And so they were. From this perspective, the main obstacles to success were environmental. The rivers could be full of fish, for example, but the water so high that people could not seine for them. Caribou might exist in huge numbers, but choose in any given year to migrate along rarely frequented routes. The coastline might be very conducive to *umiaq* travel in good weather, but virtually impassable in bad. A solid ice pack in the eastern Chukchi Sea could drive most of the seals, hence most of the polar bears, over to Chukotka, leaving the people on the Alaskan coast with little or nothing.[287] Hundreds of bowhead whales could be migrating past a whaling station, but wind and ice conditions could prevent the hunters from reaching them. In short, unpredictable environmental factors could conspire to prevent all the rationality in the world from being effective.

The Iñupiat tried to reduce environmental uncertainty by placating the hostile invisible forces controlling the weather and the animals on which they depended. The primary technique for doing this was to adhere to the enormous number of taboos or perform the myriad rituals they believed were required of them by these invisible forces. However satisfactory this approach may have been in helping the Iñupiat sustain their motivation to carry on, adherence to these taboos also interfered "seriously with the prosperity of the people" (Thornton 1931:165). In the remainder of this section I indicate in a general way the nature of the economic impact of taboos and rituals on the Iñupiaq way of life. They are discussed from different points of view, and at greater length, in Chapters 5 and 6.

Relatively few taboos or rituals affected the production of raw materials, but huge numbers related to the consumption of those materials, particularly where animate resources were involved. (Whaling was an important exception to this generalization, as discussed in

Chapter 6.) However, if the requisite taboos were broken or the prescribed rituals were not performed, the spirits of the animals of one or more species became offended and refused to permit any more of their kind to be taken until they were placated. Placating spirits usually required the intercession of a shaman, and often the imposition of still more taboos or rituals. A few examples are presented below to illustrate.

Caribou hunting, in general, was relatively unconstrained by taboos or rituals. From the moment an animal was killed, however, numerous rules applied. Among the coastal Tikiġaġmiut, these included the following: People had to use different weapons to kill and different tools to process caribou than they used for sea mammals. Caribou hair and scraps of caribou hide were not allowed to be thrown away between about early October and mid-May or seals would be driven away from the coast and whales would be offended. Women could not scrape caribou hides the same day an oogruk had been killed. Eating a caribou windpipe whose rings had not been split would kill a dog. Women could eat any part of a caribou except when menstruating, during which time they could not eat any part of a caribou head. If a caribou was killed while people were hunting beluga, it had to be cooked at a special place some distance from the dwelling (Aġviqsiiña 1940.1:95; B. Foote 1992:50; Rainey 1947:274; Stefansson 1914b:196, 273).

In the interior, among the Nuataaġmiut and Akuniġmiut, the rules were somewhat different. Caribou caught in snares had to be skinned with stone knives only. The ear cartilage could not be separated from the head, while the skin of the ears had to stay attached to the rest of the hide. The head could not be severed from the trunk until the body had been cut in half through the lower part of the chest. The meat of snared deer had to be eaten raw, roasted, or boiled in a pottery kettle, not a metal one. Women were forbidden to eat certain parts of a caribou. Caribou meat could not be cut with an axe, nor could it be cooked inside the house; it had to be cooked outside, and passed in through the skylight (Ostermann and Holtved 1952:36, 117; Stefansson 1914b:320; Stoney 1900:569–70, 837–38).

The taboos and rituals relating to whales, brown bears, and wolves were considerably more onerous than those for caribou.

A final example illustrating the constraining effect of taboos and rituals on the economic process comes from Point Barrow. That is outside the study region, but similar customs seem to have prevailed there as in the area of present concern. The example is significant because, as far as I know, it is the earliest attested case, coming from 1853–54. In Point Barrow it was taboo to do any work for five days after any person in the settlement died (Brower ms:182; Simpson 1852–54: entries for Nov. 25, 1853, Mar. 29 and 31, 1854). "Work" included hammering. But hammering, it turns out, included such things as knocking the ashes out of a pipe, tapping the ground with a walking stick, chopping ice, and striking one's feet together when sitting on a bench. In other words, this one taboo meant that life had to practically grind to a halt in the entire village. Given the fact that Barrow was enduring a severe famine at the time, with people dying of starvation practically every week, this taboo alone had to have had a major dampening effect on an already severely depressed economy.

I believe that the sample suffices to show that following the rules must have held the productivity of Iñupiaq nations far below the level it would have reached if rationality and environmental variables had been the controlling factors.

Notes to Chapter Four

1. This is a shortened and simplified version of Levy's definition. I use the phrase "economic process" instead of Levy's "structure of economic allocation," but we are writing about the same thing.

2. There is a tendency in conventional speech to equate "consumption" with the ultimate dissipation of a good or service, and the "consumer" as being the person at the end of the line. Given the definitions used here, there is usually a whole series of steps involving both production and consumption between the initial production of a service or (especially) a good and its ultimate consumption.

3. W. Ballot (1970.1), Gideon Barr (1987), F. Beechey (1831, I:344; II:307), Koutsky (1981a:25–26), Stoney (ms:139–41; 1900:837–38), Sunno (1951.16), Tuckfield and Tingook (1960.1), Wells and Kelly (1890:25), Woolfe (1893:146).

4. Anderson et al. (1998:201–2), E. Barr (1970), Booth (1961), Booth, Lee, and Towkshjea (1960), J. Foster (1970), Giddings (1952:42), A. Hawley (1965.5, 1965.9, 1976.3), M. Hawley (1965.2), Edna Hunnicutt (1960.3), Iviqsiq (1940:4–5), Jensen (1970.1), Lucier (1954:215), Luther (1960.1), E. Mills (1960.1), Ostermann and Holtved (1952:33, 116–17), C. Smith (1970), Stone (1976), Stoney (1900:837–38), Sunno (1951.16, 1951.39), Tickett (1970.2), Tuckfield and Tingook (1960.1), Wells and Kelly (1890:25).

5. Rows of cairns can still be seen in hilly or mountainous parts of the region. Most of the willows were used as fuel by reindeer herders early in the 20th century.

6. Anderson et al. (1998:202), Booth (1960.2), B. Foote (1992:34), A. Hawley (1965.5), Iviqsiq (1940), Luther (1960.1), E. Mills (1960.1), Ostermann and Holtved (1952:33), John Stalker (1965.1), Stefansson (1914a:385–86), Walton (1965.2).

7. E. Barr (1970), Gideon Barr (1987), Booth (1960.2, 1960.3), Brower (ms:464–65), E. Curtis (1930:144), B. Foote (1992:35), Keats (1970.1, 1970.2), Killigivuk (1960.1), T. Mitchell (1970), T. Morris (1970), Sunno (1951.16), S. Thomas (1970), Tuckfield and Tingook (1960.1).

8. According to some sources (Jensen 1970.1; Rainey 1947:266), the Tikiġaġmiut, in the extreme northwestern corner of the study region, did not use the corral method at all. According to others (Tuckfield and Tingook 1960.1), however, they did. Stefansson's (1914b:385) plan of an elaborate caribou drive was apparently sketched from a model made by a Tikiġaġmiu.

9. A. Hawley (1965.5, 1965.9), J. Killigivuk (1960.7), Keats (1970.4), M. and M. Swan (1970), Walton (1965.2).

10. Anderson et al. (1998:202), Booth (1960.4), R. Cleveland (1965.7), B. Foote (1992:34), L. Gallahorn (1970.3), Edna Hunnicutt (1960.1, 1960.3), Elwood Hunnicutt (1970), Jensen (1976), Keats (1970.2, 1970.4), T. Mitchell (1969), T. Morris (1970), Sun (1985:70), Sunno (1951.16).

11. Anderson et al. (1998:201, 202, 211), W. Ballot (1970.1), Emily Barr (1970.1), B. Foote (1992:34–35), Monroe (1960), Sunno (1951.16), Martha Swan (1970), Tuckfield and Tingook (1960.1).

12. Brower (ms:353), Driggs (1905:97), B. Foote (1992:34), Foote and Williamson (1961:29), Killigivuk (1960.1), Ostermann and Holtved (1952:34, 113, 115), Tuckfield and Tingook (1960.1).

13. Arrows also had ownership marks.

14. Anderson et al. (1998:201, 203, 208–9, 211), P. and E. Attungana (1980), Brower (ms:252), B. Foote (1992:35), Iviqsiq (1940), Keats (1970.4), Killigivuk (1960.9), T. Mitchell (1969), D. Naylor (1960.5), Stefansson (1914b:345), Stoney (1900:842–43), Martha Swan (1970), J. Towkshjea (1960.1, 1960.3), Vestal (1970).

15. Anderson et al. (1998:201), Armstrong (1970), Avessuk (1983.4), Gideon Barr (1987), R. Cleveland (1965.7, 1970.1), B. Foote (1992:35), Glover (1970.1, 1970.2, 1970.4), Myra Hawley (1965.1), Jensen (1970.1, 1970.4), Kiana (1970), C. Lee (1970), E. Mills (1960.2), T. Mitchell (1969, 1970), Quwana (1940.1), Rainey (1947:244, 266), Tuckfield and Tingook (1960.1), Walton (1965.2).

16. See Anderson et al. (1998:180–98), Bockstoce (1977:57–62), and Phebus (1972:sketches 38–46) for both information and a number of excellent sketches of different ways of fishing. Another comprehensive account is NANA Elders Conference (1979.1).

17. D. Adams (1960.2), A. and P. Attungana (1970), Cantwell (1889b:81), A. Douglas (1976.5), Foote and Williamson (1961:25), D. Foster (1970.1), Giddings (1956:31–32), Glover (1970.1, 1970.3, 1970.4), Grinnell (1901:23), Edna Hunnicutt (1960.3), M. Karmun (1970), Keats (1970.9), Kiana (1970), A. McClellan (1970.1, 1970.2), T. Morris (1970), Pungalik (1970), C. Smith (1970), J. Stalker (1965.1), Stoney (1900:841), Sun (1985:23–24), Sunno (1951.9), Tingook (1960.3), Walton (1965.3).

18. Anderson et al. (1998:147, 160–62, 164–67, 180–82), Andrews (1939:177), Booth (1960.1, 1960.4), Cantwell (1889b:80–81), L. Gallahorn (1970.3), Giddings (1961:129), Keats (1970.9), Robert Lee (1960.2), K. and E. Mills (1960), T. Morris (1970), M. Naylor (1960.1), J. Ningeulook (1981.1), Sheidt (1969.1), Stoney (1900:841–42), Sunno (1951.9), Tingook (1960.4), Walton (1965.3).

19. In the 1960s, fish in Kivalina were divided into portions using a washtub as the unit of measurement. After actually weighing a few tubs full of fish, all I had to do was count the total number of tubs and multiply that number by the average weight per tub to estimate the total weight of the harvest.

20. Anderson et al. (1998:146–47, 158–60, 167–70, 180–82), A. Douglas (1976.5), Hooper (1884:105), Elwood Hunnicutt (1970), Keats (1970.9), Kialook (1964), C. Lee (1970), K. and E. Mills (1960), Ostermann and Holtved (1952:35), Rainey (1947:268), S. Thomas (1970), Thornton (1931:128, 129, 208), Tuckfield (1960), VanStone ed. (1977:62). For sketches see Phebus (1972:68–69); the captions identifying the net as a seine are incorrect.

21. Anderson et al. (1998:154–55, 184–86), Booth (1960.2), E. Curtis (1930:142–43, 163), S. Dives (1970), A. Douglas (1976.5), Edna Hunnicutt (1960.3), Elwood Hunnicutt (1970), M. Karmun (1970), Keats (1960.3), Kialook (1964), Larsen and Rainey (1948:27), Rainey (1947:25), Stoney (1900:841), S. Thomas (1970), Thornton (1931:95–97). For sketches see Phebus (1972:61, 65).

22. A. Douglas (1976.5), D. Foster (1970.1), J. Hawley (1984), Keats (1969.2), A. McClellan (1970.1), Stefansson (1914b:390).

23. Anderson et al. (1998:150), Booth (1960.2), A. Douglas (1976.5), Edna Hunnicutt (1960.2), Keats (1970.9), E. Mills (1960.3), J. Ningeulook (1981.1, 1981.2), Russell in Lee et al. (1990:209), Stoney (1900:841), Sun (1985:24), Sunno (1951.48), Thornton (1931:208).

24. Anderson et al. (1998:150), C. Armstrong in Lee et al. (1990:69), Coffin (1970), Keats (1970.9), E. Mills (1960.3), M. Morris (1951.1), Sunno (1951.9).

25. Anderson et al. (1998:148–49, 171–74, 182–83), F. Beechey (1831, I:441), Cantwell (1887:42; 1889b:81), R. Cleveland (1965.7), L. Gallahorn (1970.3), Giddings (1956:14–15), Glover (1970.1), Gough (1973:230), Kialook (1964), Kiana (1970), K. and E. Mills (1960), Stoney (1900:841), Tingook (1965). There was some variation in processing fish according to the season and the district.

26. A considerably more complex procedure involving at least seven cuts was sometimes used by residents of the Kobuk valley (S. Cleveland 1965).

27. Anderson and Anderson (1982:40), Anderson et al. (1998:173), Avessuk (1983.1), A. Douglas (1976.5), Glover (1970.3), C. Smith (1970).

28. E. Ballot in Lee et al. (1990:27, 29), Beaver (1976.2), Glover (1970.4), Kiana (1970), Tingook (1965).

29. Anderson et al. (1998:153), Cantwell (1889b:80), Giddings (1961:129–30), C. Smith (1970), Tingook (1960.3).

30. D. Foster (1970.1), L. Gallahorn (1970.3), Elwood Hunnicutt (1970, 1984), Ramoth (1970).

31. The most comprehensive account of seal hunting in the study region is Lucier and VanStone (1991b).

32. Brower (ms:187), E. Curtis (1930:162–63), Foote and Williamson (1961:30), Larsen and Rainey (1948:29), Rainey (1947:253, 264), Tuckfield and Tingook (1960.1, 1960.2).

33. Brower (ms:259, 345), B. Foote (1992:40), A. Hawley (1970.2), Jensen (1970.1), Larsen and Rainey (1948:26, 27), A. McClellan (1970.2), J. Ningeulook (1981.1), Quwana (1940.2), Rainey (1947:253), John Stalker (1965.1), Clinton Swan (1970), Tuckfield and Tingook (1960.1, 1960.2).

34. F. Beechey (1831, I:454), Brower (ms:283, 395, 567), E. Curtis (1930:145, 146), Q. Dives (1940:6–16), S. Dives (1970), M. Hawley (1965.2), Edna Hunnicutt (1960.3), Jensen (1970.1), J. Killigivuk (1960.2), A. McClellan (1970.2), T. Morris (1970), Nelson (1899:126), Ostermann and Holtved (1952:122), E. and B. Oxereok (1998), Rainey (1947:255), S. Thomas (1970), Thornton (1931:137), Tuckfield and Tingook (1960.1), Vestal (1970), Wright (1969.2).

35. Aġviqsiiña (1940.1:59), Brower (ms:500), K. Burns (1960.2), S. Dives (1970), L. Gallahorn (1970.3), Hooper (1881:59), Edna Hunnicutt (1960.3), Elwood Hunnicutt (1970), Kialook (1964), Larsen and Rainey (1948:29), Robert Lee (1960.2), Luther (1976), A. McClellan (1970.2), J. Ningeulook (1981.1), Rainey (1947:263–64).

36. Lucier got this information from Arthur Nagozruk, Sr., who was born and raised in Wales.

37. E. Curtis (1930:168), S. Dives (1970), Foote and Williamson (1961:32), L. Gallahorn (1970.3), Kialook (1964), A. McClellan (1970.2), J. Ningeulook (1981.1), Rainey (1947:253), Thornton (1931:128).

38. Dead seals float during the winter, but sink fairly quickly in spring and summer.

39. S. Dives (1970), Foote and Williamson (1961:32), L. Gallahorn (1970.3), Kialook (1970), A. McClellan (1970.2), Thornton (1931:128).

40. B. Hawley (1984), Keats (1970.8), Okpowruk (1983.4), Ostermann and Holtved (1952:121), Rainey (1947:262); Tuckfield and Tingook (1960.1); cf. E. Curtis (1930:142).

41. B. Foote (1992:63–77). Other sources for this section include a number of my own observations made in northwestern Alaska, and the following: H. Anungazuk (2002), Gideon Barr (1987), K. Burns (1960.2), Edna Hunnicutt (1960.3), A. McClellan (1970.2), E. Obruk (1981), Okpowruk (1983.4), Clinton Swan (1964), M. and M. Swan (1964.1, 1964.3), Milton Swan (1964.2), M. Thomas (1965).

42. For the full process, see B. Foote (1992:66, 68).

43. This is the same procedure described by Avessuk (1983.4), Keats (1970.5), E. and B. Oxereok (1998:6), and M. and M. Swan (1964.1).

44. E. and P. Attungana (1980), M. Curtis (1970), B. Hawley (1984), Clinton Swan (1965.1), Thornton (1931:213–14).

45. Unfortunately, I have no information on how fall whaling was conducted at Point Hope.

46. The only eyewitness account of spring whaling done with precontact types of equipment and procedures is that of Charles Brower (ms:169–87), made in Point Hope in the spring of 1885. Other sources for this section include Aġviqsiiña (1940.1), Aldrich (1889:176), H. Anungazuk (1995), E. Curtis (1930:137–42), Fair (2003), Foote (ms.a), Lowenstein (1993:xxi–xxvi), Ostermann and Holtved (1952:122–23), E. and B. Oxereok (1998:15–17), Quwana (1940.1, 1940.2), Rainey (1940.14, 1940.15, 1947:257–62), S. Rock (1940), Clinton Swan (1984.2), O. Swan (1984), Thornton (1931:165–71), Tingook (n.d.), Wells and Kelly (1890:25–26), and Woolfe (1893:146–49).

47. For photographs of such a "road" and the kind of ice piles through which it had to be cut, see Gibbs (1906:78) and Jarvis (1899:90).

48. For a sketch of towing a whale, see Phebus (1972:23).
49. Aġviqsiiña (1940.1:58), Rainey (1947:261), Savelle (2000), Savelle and McCartney (2003).
50. See also Kisautaq and Kean (1981:340–42). Hawley got his information from Roy Vincent, Leonard Lane, and Patrick Attungana, all of Point Hope.
51. I have been unable to discover who got the bones. Some were probably dumped in the ocean, but whale ribs were often structural members of houses north of the tree line and they were used in platform graves. Jawbones were cut to make sled runners, so there must have been some rule(s) about who got what.
52. I do not know how these basic rules were modified when fewer than eight crews were involved.
53. J. Simpson (1875:263–64) notes the impact of fluctuations in ice conditions at Barrow in the 1840s, before American whalers had had any impact on the bowhead population.
54. The famous beluga caviar comes from a sturgeon (genus *Huso*), which is a fish.
55. The most comprehensive published account of beluga hunting in the study region is Lucier and VanStone (1995). Additional sources include Armstrong (1970), Booth (1960.1:39–41; 1960.2:40; 1960.4:39–42), Brower (ms:126), E. Curtis (1930:163–64, 195), L. Gallahorn (1970.3), Geary (ms), Hooper (1881:24–25, 59, 105), Edna Hunnicutt (1960.3), Elwood Hunnicutt (1970), Keats (1970.2), Kialook (1964, 1970), Lee et al. (1990:71), Luther (1960.1:53–54), A. McClellan (1970.2), T. Mitchell (1969), Morseth (1997:245–47), Northwest Iñupiat Elders Conference (1983.d:12–13), Sunno (1951.32), Towkshjea (1960.3).
56. Regarding the Sheshalik beluga hunt, see Burch (1998a:91–94); regarding the Eschscholtz Bay beluga hunt, see Burch (1998a:273–77).
57. Aġviqsiiña (1940.1:60–61), S. Dives (1970), B. Foote (1992:43), Foote and Williamson (1961:23), Lucier (1954:215), Morseth (1997:247), Rainey (1947:244, 265), S. Thomas (1970), Thornton (1931:179).
58. B. Hawley (1984), Elwood Hunnicutt (1970), Keats (1970.9), Kialook (1970), McClellan (1970.2).
59. The most detailed account of beluga processing is Morseth (1997:248–50). Other sources include C. and R. Adams (1984), E. and L. Adams (1984), R. Adams (1984), H. Anungazuk (2002), B. Foote (1992:43), B. Hawley (1984), Elwood Hunnicutt (1970), Keats (1970.3), Kialook (1964), Lena Sage (1964.1, 1964.2), and Towkshjea (1960.3).
60. H. Anungazuk (1999.1, 1999.3), E. Curtis (1930:142–44), *The Esquimaux* (1866–67:47–48), Sereadlook (1999), Thornton (1931:172–78), and Wells and Kelly (1890:25). For sketches of walrus hunting, see Phebus (1972:28, 29, 30).
61. For sketches of how this worked, see Phebus (1972:32–33).
62. S. Dives (1970), Green (1959:12), Jensen (1970.1, 1970.4), Kowunna (1970), Larsen and Rainey (1948:25, 29), Rainey (1947:264, 266).
63. H. Anungazuk (2000.1, 2000.2, 2000.3, 2000.4), E. Curtis (1930:145), *The Esquimaux* (1866–67:48), Glover (1970.4), Jensen (1970.2), Keats (1970.6), F. Ongtowasruk (1999), Oxereok (1999.1), Sereadlook (1999), Thornton (1931:109–10, 149, 225).
64. Anderson et al. (1998:214), P. Ballot (1970), R. Cleveland (1965.7, 1970.1), Coffin (1970), Driggs (1905), D. Foster (1970.1), F. Glover (1970.4), Jensen (1970.2), Kialook (1964), C. Lee (1970), Lee et al. (1990:141), T. Mitchell (1969, 1970), Monroe (1960), Stone (1976), Stoney (1900:838–39), Sun (1985:73–74). For sketches of bear hunting, see Phebus (1972:39–42).
65. Anderson et al. (1998:291–92) published a detailed list of how different brown bear parts were used.
66. E. Curtis (1930:144), B. Foote (1992:35), Jensen (1970.1), Kowunna (1970), Larsen and Rainey (1948:27), Rainey (1947:256), Thornton (1931:132, 158), Tuckfield and Tingook (1960.3), Woolfe (1893:150).
67. E. Curtis (1930:144), Tuckfield and Tingook (1960.3).
68. Anderson et al. (1998:229), P. Attungana (1980), Curby (1994), Kingik (1980), Wells and Kelly (1890:9).
69. Anderson et al. (1998:229), R. Cleveland (1970.1, 1970.2), J. Evok (1970), D. Foster (1970.1), Keats (1970.2), C. Lee (1970), E. Mills (1960.4), T. Mitchell (1969), Ostermann and Holtved (1952:115), Sun (1985:72–73; 1989:35), Wells and Kelly (1890:35).
70. Avessuk (1983.4), G. Barr (1982.2), E. Curtis (1930:143, 168), D. Foster (1970.2), Jensen (1970.2), M. Karmun (1970), Keats (1970.2), Kowunna (1970), T. Mitchell (1969), Paneak (1970), S. Thomas (1970), Woolfe (1893:145, 150). See Phebus (1972:48) for a sketch of a ground squirrel snare.
71. W. Ballot (1970.2), R. Cleveland (1970.1), Eliyak (1931), D. Foster (1970.1), L. Gallahorn (1970.3), Kialook (1964), Kiana (1970), R. Skin (1970), C. Smith (1970), Towkshjea (1960.2), Woolfe (1893:145, 150).
72. D. Foster (1970.1), Kiana (1970), Towkshjea (1960.2), R. Skin (1970), C. Smith (1970).
73. Anderson et al. (1998:218–19, 295), Armstrong (1970), E. Barr (1970), E. Curtis (1930:227), Eliyak (1931), D. Foster (1970.1), J. Foster (1970), Glover (1970.1), Elwood Hunnicutt (1970), Keats (1969.2, 1970.1), Kialook (1964), C. Lee (1970), A. McClellan (1970.2), T. Morris (1970), Ostermann and Holtved (1952:114), C. Smith (1970), S. Thomas (1970), Tingook (1960.4, 1965), Vestal (1970), Wright (1969.2). See Phebus (1972:49) for a sketch of a hare ("rabbit") snare.
74. Anderson et al. (1998:227, 228, 229, 230), E. Curtis (1930:168), Driggs (1905:93), Eliyak (1931), D. Foster (1970.2), Keats (1970.2, 1970.4, 1970.6), Kiana (1970), Kowunna (1970), McClellan (1970.2), Martha Swan (1970), Ostermann and Holtved (1952:34–35, 114, 116), Stefansson (1914b:388), Stone (1976), Sunno (1951.47, 1951.108), Wells and Kelly (1890:25), Woolfe (1893:148).

75. Anderson et al. (1998:292–93), D. Foster (1970.2), McClellan (1970.2), Ostermann and Holtved (1952:36), Wells and Kelly (1890:16–17), Woolfe (1893:145, 150).

76. Keats (1970.2), Nelson (1899:121), Ostermann and Holtved (1952:34, 114), Sunno (1951.103).

77. Anderson et al. (1998:217), Brower (ms:194–95), Jensen (1980.2), N. Walker (1986).

78. Ahgook (1970), Brower (ms:195), R. Cleveland (1965.7), L. Greist (1970), T. Mitchell (1969), NANA Cultural Heritage Project (1975d), Paneak (1970), Sun (1985:70–71, 76).

79. Jensen (1970.4), T. Mitchell (1960), D. Naylor (1960.4), NANA Cultural Heritage Project (1975d), Paneak (1970), Stoney (1900:839), Wells and Kelly (1890:15).

80. United States Department of the Interior, Alaska Planning Group (1974a:377–78; 1974b:605–17; 1974c:581–601; 1974d:485–91; 1974e:569–78; 1974f:52–62, 509–17).

81. Patten and Rosenberg (1994), Paul and Tankersley (1994), Rosenberg and Rothe (1994), Rothe (1994a, 1994b), Rothe and Matthews (1994).

82. E. Curtis (1930:143), Driggs (1905:92), B. Foote (1992:53), Jensen (1970.2), Larsen and Rainey (1948:28, 29), McClellan (1970.2), T. Morris (1970), Quwana (1940:10), Rainey (1947:262, 265), Thornton (1931:194–95).

83. Glover (1970.1), T. Mitchell (1969), J. Ningeulook (1981.1), Ray (1964:81), Sunno (1951.3, 1951.31), Thornton (1931:128).

84. D. Foster (1970.1), Glover (1970.1), T. Mitchell (1969), J. Ningeulook (1981.1), Ostermann and Holtved (1952:35, 115), Ray (1964:81), C. Smith (1970), Stone (1976), Stoney (1900: 840), Sunno (1951.3), Thornton (1931:128), Tuckfield (1960).

85. For a sketch of this type of snare, see Phebus (1972:57).

86. This paragraph is based primarily on Anderson et al. (1998:295–96).

87. E. and P. Attungana (1980), Brower (ms:194), S. Dives (1970), Driggs (1905:93), B. Foote (1992:17), Foote and Williamson (1966:1058), Hooper (1881:48; 1884:41), Jensen (1970.1, 1970.2), Kellett (1850:12), Larsen and Rainey (1948:28, 29, 30), T. Morris (1970), Quwana (1940:27), Rainey (1947:266), Seemann (1853, II:101), VanStone (1980:28).

88. E. and P. Attungana (1980), Jensen (1984.2), E. Mills (1960.4), Tuckfield and Tingook (1960.1).

89. P. Ballot (1970), Booth (1960.1, 1960.2), K. Burns (1960.2), E. Curtis (1930:167), M. Curtis (1969), Driggs (1905:93), McClellan (1970.2), E. Mills (1960.2, 1960.3), Quwana (1940:10), Sampson (1970), C. Smith (1970), Stefansson (1914b:388), John Stalker (1965.1), Sunno (1951.76), Tingook (1965), Wells and Kelly (1890:25), Woolfe (1893:149).

90. Brower (ms:157), E. Ballot in Lee et al. (1990:30, 31), P. Ballot (1970), Ostermann and Holtved (1952:35, 114), John Stalker (1965.1), Sunno (1951.5), Clinton Swan (1984.2).

91. Anderson et al. (1998:297), E. and P. Attungana (1980), E. Curtis (1930:164), A. Hawley (1965.9).

92. Anderson et al. (1998:469), E. and P. Attungana (1980), E. Mills (1960.4), C. Smith (1970).

93. Glaucous gulls often nest on sea cliffs.

94. Anderson et al. (1998:297), E. and P. Attungana (1980), Kialook (1964), E. Mills (1960.3), Stefansson (1914b:392), Woolfe (1893:148).

95. R. Gallahorn (1952.4, 1952.5, 1952.15, 1952.16, 1952.17, 1952.18), A. Harris (1952.5, 1952.7), J. Mitchell (1952.13), Sunno (1951.79), Wells and Kelly (1890:7–8).

96. Some of these may actually have been different age classes of a single species rather than different species.

97. E. and P. Attungana (1980), E. Curtis (1930:143, 145), B. Foote (1992:44), Foote and Williamson (1961:21, 23), Larsen and Rainey (1948:27), Rainey (1940.3; 1947:255, 256), Stuck (1920:121), Thornton (1931:209–10), VanStone (1962b:35), Weyer (1928).

98. P. Anderson (1982), United States Department of the Interior, Alaska Planning Group (1974b:97, 625–30; 1974d:46, 497–507; 1974e:583–84; 1974f:523–29).

99. Giddings (1961:135), Kiana (1970), Stoney (1900:842–44), Woolfe (1893:130–31, 145).

100. Anderson et al. (1998:301), D. Foster (1970.1, 1970.2), Dinah Frankson (1980), Giddings (1952:64; 1967:43–44, 238), E. and B. Oxereok (1998:5), Seemann (1853, II:53), Simpson (1852b), C. Smith (1970).

101. E. and P. Attungana (1980), F. Beechey (1831, I:345, 370, 374, 380, 383, 387, 413, 418, 419, 420, 454, 463, 457; II:251, 266, 269, 309, 316, 317), Berkh (1983:18), Dinah Frankson (1980), Hooper (1884:104), Kotzebue (1821, I:205–6), T. Moore (1851:28), Stefansson (1914b:8).

102. Anderson et al. (1998:301–2), Beaver (1976.1), R. Cleveland (1970.1), S. Dives (1970), D. Foster (1970.1), Dinah Frankson (1980), L. Gallahorn (1969.2), Glover (1970.1, 1970.5), Keats (1969.2, 1970.1, 1970.4, 1970.5), C. Kiana (1970), C. Lee (1970), A. McClellan (1987), Ralph in Lee et al. (1990:87), Sheidt (1969.1), C. Smith (1970).

103. Anderson et al. (1998:301–2), Beaver (1976.2), F. Beechey (1831, I:406–7), Coffin (1970), A. Douglas (1976.6, 1976.7), Giddings (1961:35), Kiana (1970), C. Lee (1970), McClellan (1987).

104. Anderson et al. (1998:237), Coffin (1970), Giddings (1961:36–39), C. Lee (1970), C. Wood (1931).

105. Anderson et al. (1998:174–75, 302), A. Douglas (1976.6, 1976.7), Keats (1969.2, 1970.1, 1970.5), Kiana (1970), T. Mitchell (1970).

106. Anderson et al. (1998:233, 235, 302), Coffin (1970), Keats (1969.2, 1970.9), C. Lee (1970), T. Morris (1970), C. Smith (1970).

107. Beaver (1976.2), R. Cleveland (1965.2, 1966), Coffin (1970), D. Foster (1970.1), L. Gallahorn (1970.3), Giddings (1961:30, 35), Elwood Hunnicutt (1970, 1984), Kiana (1970), C. Lee (1970), Sheidt (1969.1), C. Smith (1970), Stoney (1900:840–42), Sun in Mendenhall et al. 1989:39), Tingook (1965), Townsend (1887:86).

108. Anderson et al. (1998:302–3), B. Hawley (1984), Anore Jones (1983:7–12), E. Mills (1960.3), Ongtowasruk (1999).

109. Anderson et al. (1998:302), E. and P. Attungana (1980), A. Douglas (1976.6, 1976.7), O. Knox (1984), Northwest Iñupiat Elders Conference (1976d).

110. Anderson et al. (1998:232–33, 303), E. and P. Attungana (1980), Avessuk (1983.1), Beaver (1976.1, 1976.2), R. Cleveland (1970.1), E. Curtis (1930:164), A. Douglas (1976.1), D. Foster (1970.1), Keats (1970.2), Kiana (1970), C. Lee (1970), E. Mills (1960.3), Ongtowasruk (1999), Russell in Lee et al. (1990:209), Seemann (1853:54), Stone in Lee et al. (1990:95, 169), Stoney (1900:844), Sunno (1951.45), VanStone ed. (1977:62), Woolfe (1893:130–31).

111. This entire process is illustrated in Anore Jones (1983:79).

112. Anderson et al. (1998:303–4), Beaver (1976.1), A. Douglas (1976.6, 1976.7), Geary (1976), Gray (1976), Keats (1970.2), Stone in Lee et al. (1990:95).

113. Anderson et al. (1998:234, 304), E. and P. Attungana (1980), R. Cleveland (1970.1), Anore Jones (1983:114–18), Keats (1970.4), Loon (1990), E. Mills (1960.3), Ongtowasruk (1999), Martha Swan (1984.3).

114. Probably voles, but usually called "mice" in Northwest Alaska.

115. E. and P. Attungana (1980), Beaver (1976), Dinah Frankson (1980), Anore Jones (1983:119–20), L. Oktalik (1980).

116. Anderson et al. (1998:234, 304–5), E. and P. Attungana (1980), Dinah Frankson (1980), Anore Jones (1983:13–30), Ongtowasruk (1999).

117. Anderson et al. (1998:304), R. Cleveland (1970.1), D. Foster (1970.1), Dinah Frankson (1980), Anore Jones (1983:33–51), Keats (1970.2), Kiana (1970), C. Lee (1970), E. Mills (1960.3), B. Mouse in Lee et al. (1990:219, 221), Ongtowasruk (1999), Martha Swan (1984.3).

118. Anderson et al. (1998:305), Beaver (1976.2), A. Douglas (1976.6, 1976.7), Geary (1976), Gray (1976), B. and S. Hawley (1984), Ongtowasruk (1999), Charlotte Swan (1965.3).

119. Anderson et al. (1998:305), E. and P. Attungana (1980), Keats (1969.2), C. Smith (1970), Walton (1965.2).

120. Unless otherwise noted, all of the technical descriptions of minerals in this section come from Bates and Jackson (1980). They present the information in alphabetical order, so page references are unnecessary here.

121. D. Anderson (1988a), F. Beechey (1831, I:360), Bockstoce ed. (1988, I:183, 210), Hall (1988b).

122. P. Attungana (1980), Hall (1988a), McClellan (1987), D. Oktalik (1980), Clinton Swan (1984.1).

123. D. Anderson (1988a), F. Beechey (1831, I:345, 408), Giddings (1952:79), Woolfe (1893:131).

124. P. and E. Atoruk (1989), F. Beechey (1831, I:345), Giddings (1952:78, 79), Jackson (1989), Lucier (1990), NANA Cultural Heritage Project (1975g: Selawik, site H5), D. Oktalik (1980), Sunno (1951.74), Clinton Swan (1984.1).

125. P. and E. Atoruk (1989), A. Douglas (1989.1), Guthrie and Matthews (1978:475), Karl (1990), Lucier (1989), McClellan (1987), L. Mills (1989), D. Oktalik (1980).

126. E. Anderson (1945), P. Attungana (1980), P. and E. Atoruk (1989), Jackson (1989), A. McClellan (1987).

127. P. and E. Atoruk (1989), D. Clark (1972), A. Douglas (1989.1), Hall (1988a), Jackson (1989), Patton and Miller (1970).

128. P. and E. Atoruk (1989), A. Douglas (1989.1), Jackson (1989), Lucier (1989), L. Mills (1989), D. Oktalik (1980), Clinton Swan (1984.1).

129. P. and E. Atoruk (1989), F. Beechey (1831, I:393), J. Hawley (1984), Stoney (1900:817), Clinton Swan (1984.1).

130. D. Anderson (1988a), Coffin (1970), A. Douglas (1989.1), Keats (1969.2), Lucier (1989), T. Mitchell (1969), Paneak (1970), C. Smith (1970).

131. P. and E. Atoruk (1989), P. Attungana (1980), David Frankson (1980), Jackson (1989), Lucier (1989), D. Oktalik (1980), Clinton Swan (1984.1).

132. Glover (1970.3, 1970.4), Hooper (1884:104), Thornton (1931:214–15), Trollope (1855:876).

133. H. Anungazuk (1999.1), Oxereok (1999.1). H. Anungazuk (2002) says that the hillside stream becomes foul by about midwinter, and is not used as a water source again until the following summer.

134. Coffin (1970), Keats (1969.2), Kiana (1970), Paneak (1970), Sheidt (1969.1), C. Smith (1970).

135. Brower (ms:383), Seemann (1853, II:62), Trollope (1855:876), Whymper (1869a:168; 1869b:161).

136. C. and S. Attla (1991), J. and F. Foster (1986), Stoney (1900:577–78), A. and E. Weyiouanna (1999).

137. B. Hawley (1989), McClellan (1970.2), L. Mills (1989), V. Swan (1989). More generally, the term mamaiḷaq refers to any foul-smelling substance.

138. Rainey's field notes contain an excellent set of sketches of (Rainey 1940.12) and a list of terms for (Rainey 1940.13) a wide array of manufactured goods.

139. Rainey's informant, Niġuwana (1940.1:17–31), provided him with a comprehensive list of descriptions and terms for tools of all kinds, as well as other equipment. This list is too long to reproduce here, but it is acces-

sible in the Alaska and Polar Regions Department at the University of Alaska Fairbanks. See also Rainey (1940.12, 1940.13).

140. Bockstoce (1977:48), Brower (ms:422), Cantwell (1889b:87), Driggs (1905:94–95), Giddings (1952:74–76), Iviqsiq (1940), D. Keats (1970.6), Murdoch (1892:287–88), Stefansson (1914b:203), Sunno (1951.95, 1951.111), VanStone (1990:45). For illustrations of flakers, see Nelson (1899:91), Murdoch (1892:288, 298).

141. Giddings (1952:64, 78), Nelson (1899:92), Stefansson (1914b:393), VanStone (1976:21).

142. Giddings (1952:66, 69, 78; 1967:312), D. Oktalik (1980), VanStone (1976:21; 1980:42). For a photograph of saws, see Giddings (1952: plate VI.)

143. Giddings (1952:64, 77, 78), Nelson (1899:86, 88), C. Smith (1970), VanStone (1976:21; 1980:42).

144. Giddings (1952:77, 78), Nelson (1899:88), Thornton (1931:149), VanStone (1976:19; 1980:39–40; 1990:14).

145. Giddings (1952:77, 79–80), Sunno (1951.27), VanStone (1976:19; 1980:29–40; 1990:14). For illustrations of adzes, see Bockstoce (1977:72), Murdoch (1892:175–72), and VanStone (1976:82).

146. Driggs (1905:95–96), Giddings (1952:75, 78), Murdoch (1892:93–99, 182), Nelson (1899:75, 88), VanStone (1976:19).

147. F. Beechey (1831, II:310), Giddings (1952:77), Murdoch (1892:173–74), Nelson (1899:86, plate XXXVIII, no. 14), VanStone (1976:21; 1980:42).

148. Bockstoce (1977:70–71), Cantwell (1889b:87), Giddings (1952:76–77), Hooper (1884:106), Iviqsiq (1940), T. Mitchell (1969), Murdoch (1892:150–53), Nelson (1899:152), Sunno (1951.61, 1951.95), Thornton (1931:39), VanStone (1976:20; 1980:40–41).

149. Cantwell (1889b:87), Driggs (1905:95–96), Giddings (1952:77), Thornton (1931:150), VanStone (1976:20; 1980:41–42)

150. Bockstoce (1977:77), Brower (ms:242–43), Giddings (1952:68, 76, plate XL), Murdoch (1892:294–95, 299), Nelson (1899:112), Sunno (1951.95), VanStone (1976:22–23; 1980:43, 112–13).

151. Driggs (1905:95–96), Giddings (1952:78–79, 82–83), Nelson (1899:106), VanStone (1976:21; 1980:42), Woolfe (1893:150).

152. Bockstoce (1977:72–73), Cantwell (1889b:88), Giddings (1952:77–79), E. Mills (1960.3), Thornton (1931:149), VanStone (1976:20, 83; 1980:40, 108), Woolfe (1893:138, 145).

153. Driggs (1905:97), Giddings (1952:78), Luther (1960.2), Nelson (1877–81: entry for July 18, 1881), C. Smith (1970), Thornton (1931:149).

154. Bockstoce (1977:79–86), Cantwell (1889b:87), B. Foote (1992:174), Giddings (1952:74, 75), Glover (1952.4), Murdoch (1892:289–90), Nelson (1899:81), Stefansson (1914b:393), Thornton (1931:150–51), VanStone (1976:21, 22; 1980:42–43; 1990:14–15).

155. Avessuk (1983.5), Beaver (1976.2), F. Beechey (1831, I:340–41), Cantwell (1889b:83–84), R. Cleveland (1970.1), Eliyak (1931), Giddings (1961:139), Hooper (1884:101–2), Keats (1970.4), McClellan (1987), NANA Elders Conference (1979.1), Niġuwana (1940.1), Jessie Ralph in Lee et al. (1990:83), Simpson (1875:242–43), Thornton (1931:32), Wells and Kelly (1890:17), Woolfe (1893:150).

156. C. Allen (1960:70–71), Driggs (1905:97–98), Nelson (1899:116–18), Ralph in Lee et al. 1990:83), Stefansson (1914b:148), Sunno (1951.65), Wells and Kelly (1890:26), Woolfe (1893:150).

157. E. and P. Attungana (1980), Elwood Hunnicutt in Northwest Iñupiat Elders Conference (1976d:12), O. Knox (1984), Sunno (1951:65).

158. Patterns have also been published by Chaussonnet (1988:215, sketches a and b) and Murdoch (1892:113, 118). Rainey's (1940.12) unpublished field notes also contain an excellent set of pattern sketches.

159. Issenman (1997) illustrates various types of stitching used in Eskimo sewing on page 90, and patterns used for clothing in Barrow, Alaska, on page 26. Oakes and Riewe (1995:60) illustrate an Alaskan-type boot and show the kind of stitching used to attach the upper to the bottom.

160. Avessuk (1983.4, 1983.5), F. Beechey (1831, I:340–41, 396), Belcher (ms:69), Brower (ms:573–74), Campbell (1998:43, 44), Cantwell (1889b:83–84), Dall (1866–67), Hooper (1884:101–2), Jarvis (1899:53–54), Moore and Johnson (1986:110–14), Ralph in Lee et al. (1990:85), Simpson (1875:242–45), Thornton (1931:17–18, 32–35), VanStone (1976:30–32; 1980:55–58; 1990:17), Wells and Kelly (1890:16–17), Woolfe (1893:150).

161. F. Beechey (1831, I:340–41), Belcher (ms), Bockstoce (1977:94–95), VanStone (1976:30–31; 1980:56).

162. Avessuk (1983.4), Hooper (1884:101), Simpson (1875:242), Wells and Kelly (1890:16–17).

163. F. Beechey (1831, II:396), Dall (1866–67), Simpson (1875:243), Thornton (1931:35), VanStone (1976:30, 31; 1980:55).

164. F. Beechey (1831, I:340; II:284–85), Nelson (1899:330), Sauer (1802:247), Simpson (1852–54: entry for April 5, 1854), VanStone ed (1977:89).

165. Beaver (1976.2), F. Beechey (1831, I:240), Bockstoce (1977:92–94), Hooper (1884:102), Thornton (1931:32–33), VanStone (1976:30; 1980:55–56; 1990:17).

166. Cantwell (1889b: plate III), Dall (1866–67), B. Foote (1992:85–101), Thornton (1931:17–18), VanStone (1976:32; 1980:57–58).

167. Grinnell (1901:29), Hooper (1881:24–25), T. Mitchell (1986), M. Naylor (1960.1), Woolfe (1893:147–48).

168. Beaver (1976.2), Cantwell (1889b:83), L. Gallahorn (1970.2, 1970.3), Giddings (1952:85), Keats (1969.2, 1970.1), E. Mills (1960.4), T. Mitchell (1969, 1986), E. Obruk (1981), Stefansson (1914b:344), Sunno (1951.25), Woolfe (1893:145).

169. Christensen (1989), Christy (1982), Draper (1977, 1978), Egeland, Feyk, and Middaugh (1998:10–14), Gadsby (2004), Geraci and Smith (1979), Anore Jones (1983:132–33), Mala (1984).

170. E. Atoruk in Lee et al. (1990:179), P. Atoruk in Lee et al. (1990:187, 189), Beaver (1976.2), K. Burns (1960.2), M. Curtis (1970), L. Gallahorn (1970.3), Gooden in Lee et al. (1990:229), Edna Hunnicutt (1960.1), Jensen (1970.2), D. Keats (1970.4), T. Mitchell (1986), M. Naylor (1960.2), Russell in Lee et al. (1990:199, 201), Stone in Lee et al. (1990:169), Clinton Swan (1984.1), Martha Swan (1976), Thornton (1931:192), N. Wood (1986).

171. K. Burns (1960.2), T. Mitchell (1969), Mouse in Lee et al. (1990:215, 217, 223), Stone in Lee et al. (1990:177).

172. Nowadays, these terms refer to winter and summer camps, respectively.

173. Lee and Reinhardt (2003:73–113) employ a somewhat different schema.

174. Anderson and Anderson (1982:47–49), P. Attungana (1980), F. Beechey (1831, I:366–67), Bockstoce (1977:24), Chamisso (1986:19), R. Cleveland (1965.2:9–10; 1966; 1970.1), Collins (1937a:262–64), E. Curtis (1930:162, 208–9, 225), S. Dives (1970), Edson (1895:471), Foote and Williamson (1961:27), David Frankson (1980), Giddings (1956:29–30; 1961:40–41, 125–26), Glover (1970.1), Jensen (1970.2), Kotzebue (1821, I:200–1), NANA Elders Conference (1976.2), Newell (1985), Rowe (1940:48), Seemann (1853, II:57–58), Simpson (1850b: entry for Jan. 17, 1850; 1875:258), C. Smith (1970), Sunno (1951.56), Thornton (1931:219–23), Townsend (1887:86), VanStone ed. (1977:56, 84), White (1889: entry for July 12). Sarah Kingik has compiled a detailed lexicon of house-component terminology for Point Hope (in Newell 1985:162–65).

175. See C. Young (2002) for an extensive discussion of the four-post-center dwelling.

176. Booth (1960.2), R. Cleveland (1965.2), A. Douglas (1976.3), L. Gallahorn (1970.1, 1970.3), Giddings (1961:126), Edna Hunnicutt (1960.1, 1960.2, 1960.3), Keats (1969.2, 1970.4, 1970.5), T. Mitchell (1969, 1976, 1986), Ella Smith (1976), Sunno (1951.2).

177. R. Cleveland (1965.2, 1966), E. Curtis (1930:209), A. Douglas (1976.3), Giddings (1956:5; 1961:35, 48, 127), Sun (1970).

178. Booth (1960.2), Brower (ms:157), R. Cleveland (1965.7), E. Curtis (1930:209, 225), Giddings (1961:127), Grinnell (1901:49–50), Edna Hunnicutt (1960.3), Jensen (1970.5), Keats (1969.2, 1970.2, 1970.10), J. Killigivuk (1960.7), M. Naylor (1960.1), M. and D. Naylor (1960), Nelson (1899:260), C. Smith (1970), Sunno (1951.98).

179. Booth (1960.2), E. Curtis (1930:162), Hillsen (1983:34), Edna Hunnicutt (1960.3), C. Lee (1970), T. Mitchell (1986), Nelson (1899:260, 261), Vestal (1970).

180. Brower (ms:132, 135, 349, 356), Glover (1970.4), Edna Hunnicutt (1960.3), Jensen (1970.2), Luther (1960.1), Stoney (1900:812); cf. Brower (ms:262, 349) and P. Ray (1988:lii, lxxix) for the North Slope.

181. See Sun (1985:32–59) for a discussion of various types of shelter.

182. Jensen (1970.1), Larsen and Rainey (1948:26), Sunno (1951.56).

183. I have been unable to discover a Native word that might correspond to "paloly."

184. Anderson and Anderson (1982:29), Anderson et al. (1998:231), E. Curtis (1930:162), C. Lee (1970), T. Mitchell (1969, 1970).

185. Anderson and Anderson (1982:49–50), Anderson et al. (1998:235), D. Foster (1970.1), Grinnell (1901:49), Kotzebue (1821, I:218), C. Lee (1970).

186. They were "nameless" in English, not in Iñupiaq.

187. F. Beechey (1831, I:367), Kotzebue (1821, I:200), Murdoch (1892:420), Thornton (1931:223), Trollope (1855:873), VanStone ed. (1977:56, 84).

188. Murdoch (1892:74), Thornton (1931:223), VanStone (1976:28), Woolfe (1893:144).

189. Keats (1969.2), J. and M. Konalook (1951.1), Nelson (1899:202–3), Thornton (1931:152), VanStone (1976:26–27; 1980:54).

190. Keats (1969.2), E. Mills (1960.3), M. Naylor (1960.2), Murdoch (1892:74–75), Sunno (1951.34).

191. Bockstoce (1977:91), Booth (1960.2), Brower (ms:246), Cantwell (1889b:88), B. Foote (1992:156), L. Gallahorn (1969.2), Giddings (1961:128, 143–44), Hooper (1884:103), Edna Hunnicutt (1960.1, 1960.2), Keats (1969.2), J. Konalook (1951.2), Lucier and VanStone (1991a), T. Mitchell (1969), Seemann (1853, II:58), C. Smith (1970), Sunno (1951.64, 1951.110, 1951.112), Thornton (1931:223), VanStone (1980:53), Walton (1965.2), Woolfe (1893:144). Lucier and VanStone's (1991a) article is a useful illustrated summary of what is known about lamps in the study region.

192. Zimmerman and Aufderheide (1984:61); Zimmerman, Jensen, and Sheehan (2000:59); cf. Ammitsbøll et al. (1991:95).

193. Beaver (1976.2), Brower (ms:247), Cantwell (1889b:88), R. Cleveland (1970.1), Giddings (1956:32–33; 1961:137–38), Glover (1970.1, 1970.2), Hooper (1884:104), Edna Hunnicutt (1960.2), Keats (1969.2, 1970.1), J. and M. Konalook (1951.2), Murdoch (1892:291), NANA Cultural Heritage Project (1975b), Sheidt (1969.1), Simpson (1875:243), C. Smith (1970), Stoney (1900:570–71), Sunno (1951.38), Tingook (1960.4, 1965), Walton (1965.2), Woolfe (1893:131, 144).

194. Coffin (1970), Keats (1969.2), Sheidt (1969.1), C. Smith (1970), Sunno (1951.38).

195. Cantwell (1889b:87), Coffin (1970), Giddings (1961:136, 142–43), Glover (1952.2), Simpson (1852:a), VanStone (1976:23; 1980:45–46, 46–47). For illustrations, see Murdoch (1892:86–87) and Nelson (1899: plate XXXII, opp. p. 82).

196. Cantwell (1889b:87), E. Curtis (1930:162), Dall (1866–67), Glover (1952.2), C. Lee (1970), NANA Cultural Heritage Project (1975b), Ralph in Lee et al. (1990:87), C. Smith (1970), VanStone (1976:26, 28; 1980:51–52). For illustrations, see Murdoch (1892:88, 89, 99–101), and Nelson (1899:plates XXXI and XXXII).

197. The major source on pottery in the study region is Lucier and VanStone (1992). Other sources on pots: Anderson et al. (1998:236), Booth (1960.2), E. Curtis (1930:197), Driggs (1905:96), L. Gallahorn (1969.2), Giddings (1952:92, 94, 102; 1961:143), Edna Hunnicutt (1960.1, 1960.2), Iviqsiq (1940), Keats (1960.1, 1969.2, 1970.5), Larsen and Rainey (1948:177), Lucier (original source not cited; 1951), NANA Cultural Heritage Project (1975b), M. and D. Naylor (1960), Nelson (1899:201–2), Ostermann and Holtved (1952:36), E. and B. Oxereok (1998:22), J. Ralph in Lee et al. (1990:87), Stefansson (1914b:312), Sunno (1951.75), Thornton (1931:152–53), and Walton (1965.2).

198. Beaver (1976.2), Bockstoce (1977:75–76), B. Foote (1992:114), Giddings (1961:37), Keats (1960.3), J. and M. Konalook (1951.2), Nelson (1899:93, 104), VanStone (1976:23–24; 1980:48–50; 1990:12, 16).

199. Burch (1984:314, fig. 20), Nelson (1899:103–4), Sunno (1951.72), VanStone (1976:28; 1980:47; 1990:16).

200. Bockstoce (1977:78–79), Cantwell (1889b:81, 87, 88), Coffin (1970), Giddings (1952:87), Murdoch (1892:101–5), D. Naylor (1960.4), Nelson (1877–81: entry for July 18, 1881; 1899:65–72), Stefansson (1914b:393), VanStone (1976:26; 1980:52–53; 1990:16).

201. Cantwell (1889b:89), Murdoch (1892:376–85), Nelson (1899:330–35, 341–47), D. Ray (1977:110–11, 113), Sunno (1951.33, 1951.40, 1951.70), VanStone (1976:44–45, 96; 1980:67–68; 1990:22).

202. F. Beechey (1831, I:340; II:309–10), Bockstoce (1977:20–24), Campbell (1998: plate 37), Driggs (1905:93–94), Murdoch (1885a, 1885b, 1892:195–207), Nelson (1899:155–57), VanStone (1976a:12–13, 77, 78; 1980:27, 28, 100), Varjola et al. 1990:294).

203. Bockstoce (1977:27–31), Cantwell (1889b:86), Giddings (1952:41), Glover (1952.1), E. Mills (1960.2), Murdoch (1892:201–7), VanStone (1976:13, 17–18, 78; 1980:28, 36; 1990:12).

204. Bockstoce (1977:33–43), Brower (ms:170–71), E. Curtis (1930:139–40), B. Foote (1992:48–49), Murdoch (1892:214–40), Nelson (1899:135–45), Thornton (1931:142–43), VanStone (1976:8–10; 1980:20–25).

205. Bockstoce (1977:46, 47), Cantwell (1889b:86), Eliyak (1931), VanStone (1976:11).

206. Bockstoce (1977:63–64), Brower (ms:158), E. Curtis (1930:168), Eliyak (1931), B. Foote (1992:55), Keats (1960.2, 1970.1), Luther (1976), E. Mills (1960.2, 1960.3, 1960.4), K. and E. Mills (1960), Nelson (1899:122, 124–25, 131–32), VanStone (1976:14; 1980:30, 32; 1990:11–12).

207. Anderson et al. (1998:227), Booth (1960.2), Cantwell (1889b:86–87), Keats (1970.2), McClellan (1970.2), E. Mills (1960.4), Towkshjea (1960.2).

208. Belcher (ms:65), Bockstoce (1977:48–50), Brower (ms:240), Cantwell (1889b:86), B. Foote (1992:53), T. Morris (1970), Murdoch (1892:244–46), VanStone (1976:15; 1980:28), Wells and Kelly (1890:25).

209. Brower (ms:158; 1899), B. Foote (1992:119), Driggs (1905:98), McClellan (1970.2), D. Naylor (1960.5), Nelson (1899:110–11), Tingook (1960.4), Utqiaġvigmiut Aġviqsiuqtit Aġnaŋich (2000).

210. For the best discussions and illustrations of sinew twisting and braiding, see B. Foote (1992:119–22) and Utqiaġvigmiut Aġviqsiuqtit Aġnaŋich (2000:36–39). Other sources include Murdoch (1892:311–12), Nelson (1899:110–12), Ostermann and Holtved (1952:35).

211. B. Foote (1992:64–65, 119), B. Hawley (1965), Kennedy (1964.2), Clinton Swan (1964), Martha Swan (1964), M. and M. Swan (1964.1, 1964.3), Milton Swan (1964.2), M. Thomas (1964).

212. Anderson et al. (1998:91, 235), Beaver (1976.2), R. Cleveland (1965.2:3–5; 1966), Coffin (1970), D. Foster (1970.1), L. Gallahorn (1970.3), Giddings (1956:14–15; 1961:35, 141–42), Elwood Hunnicutt (1970, 1984), Kiana (1970), C. Lee (1970), Sheidt (1969.1), C. Smith (1970), Sun in Mendenhall et al. (1989:39), Tingook (1960.4, 1965).

213. B. Foote (1992:121–22) has published very useful sketches of how this was done, including one of a more complicated form of slit splice than the one shown here.

214. F. Beechey (1831, I:295), Bockstoce (1977:50–57), Brower (ms:157–58), Cantwell (1887:42; 1889b:81), B. Foote (1992:50–51, 58–59), L. Gallahorn (1970.3), Giddings (1956:9–10, 35, 36), Jensen (1970.1), Kiana (1970), J. Konalook (1951.2), McClellan (1970.2), E. Mills (1960.3), Murdoch (1892:312–16), Nelson (1899:185–94), E. and B. Oxereok (1998:4), Quwana (1940.1), Sheidt (1969.1), Stoney (1900:841), Clinton Swan (1984.1), S. Thomas (1970), Thornton (1931:137), Tingook (1960.3, 1965), Townsend (1887:86), VanStone (1976:14–15, 17; 1980:25–26, 31–32, 34–36; 1990:12), C. Wood (1931).

215. B. Foote (1992:61–62), Giddings (1952:40), Keats (1960.3), VanStone (1980:36, 39; 1990:14).

216. H. Anungazuk (1999.3, 2002), Avessuk (1983.4), F. Beechey (1831, I:389–90), Belcher (ms:64), A. Hawley (1965.1, 1965.7), Hooper (1881:28; 1884:102), Jensen (1970.3), Keats (1970.2, 1970.4, 1970.5), McClellan (1970.1, 1970.2), Murdoch (1892:335–37), D. Naylor (1960.2), Nelson (1898:217–18), Seemann (1853, II:55–56), Sereadlook (1999), Sunno (1951.28), M. and M. Swan (1970), Thornton (1931:125–26), Trollope (1855:875), VanStone (1976:33; 1980:64), Wells and Kelly (1890:27), Woolfe (1893:149). Snaith (1997) presents a well-illustrated mix of information on traditional and recent *umiat*.

217. The best account I have seen of *umiaq* cover construction within the study region was published by Berit Foote (1992:132–16). See also Utqiaġvigmiut Aġviqsiuqtit Aġnaŋich (2000).

218. See Smith and Smith (2001:298–99) for an example of a Kiŋikmiut *umiaq*, probably dating from the early 1890s.

219. F. Beechey (1831, I:346), Hooper (1881:28; 1884:102), Murdoch (1892:339), Nelson (1892:224), Woolfe (1893:149).

220. V. Adams (1964), Booth (1960.1), Edna Hunnicutt (1960.2), Keats (1970.3, 1970.4), M. Naylor (1960.1), Sun (1970), Thornton (1931:127, 129), VanStone (1976:33; 1980:63; 1990:17–19), Woolfe (1893:148), Zimmerly (2000:63–65).

221. Anderson et al. (1998:118), W. Ballot (1970.1), Cantwell (1889b:60, 84–85), Giddings (1961:36–38, 145–47), C. Smith (1970), Sun (1970), C. Wood (1931). Photographs of relatively modern (canvas-covered) versions of such craft have been published by Giddings (1952:60; 1956:22).

222. Anderson and Anderson (1982:39), Anderson et al. (1998:117–18), Giddings (1956:18–19; 1961:147), C. Sheldon (1973–74:11), Sun (1985:65–66).

223. Brower (ms:170, 177), B. Foote (1992:139), Edna Hunnicutt (1960.2), D. Keats (1970.3, 1970.5), T. Morris (1970), Murdoch (1892:355).

224. Cantwell (1889b: plate III), B. Foote (1992:138), Hooper (1884:103), Keats (1960.2, 1960.3, 1970.3, 1970.5), J. Konalook (1951.3), Murdoch (1892:353–55), Nelson (1898:206–2), Seemann (1853, II:56), Sunno (1951.80), Thornton (1931:130).

225. Anderson et al. (1998:126), Cantwell (1889b:85), Giddings (1952:60), Glover (1952.5), C. Lee (ms), Northwest Iñupiat Elders Conference (1976d:7–9), Simpson (1875:244), Tingook (1965), VanStone (1976:34, 1980:58). VanStone (1980:60–62) has published detailed sketches of webbing.

226. F. Beechey (1831, I:341, 343, 360, 393, 394, 405–6, 456), Bockstoce (1977:87–90), Cantwell (1889b:88), Dall (1866–67), Giddings (1952:88–90; 1961:140), Hooper (1881:57; 1884:101), Jensen (1970.3), Kotzebue (1821, I:209–10, 227–28), McClellan (1987), L. Mills (1987), T. Mitchell (1987), Murdoch (1892:143–49), Nelson (1899:44–50), Northwest Iñupiat Elders Conference (1983a:2; 1983c:2), Simpson (1875:241), Stoney (1900:829–30), Thornton (1931:30–32), VanStone (1976:42; 1980:64–65; 1990:21), Wells and Kelly (1890:15–16), Woolfe (1893:151).

227. Aġviqsiiña (1940.1:73), F. Beechey (1831, I:339, 341, 343, 360, 384, 422, 455, 458; II:304–5), Brower (ms:489, 673), Cantwell (1889b:88), Hooper (1881:56–57), Jensen (1970.3), Kotzebue (1821, I:209–10), McClellan (1987), L. Mills (1987), Nagozruk (1928), Nasugluk (1940:18), Nelson (1899:49), Simpson (1875:239–40), Stoney (1900:830), Thornton (1931:32), Wells and Kelly (1890:15–16), Woolfe (1893:151).

228. Aġviqsiiña (1940.1:74), F. Beechey (1831, I:360, 384–85, 407), M. Morris (1951.2), Nelson (1887–81: entry for July 15, 1881), Niġuwana (1940.1:6), E. Norton (1969), Simpson (1875:241), Stefansson (1914b:154), Stoney (1900:829), Sunno (1951.99, 1951.105), Tiepleman (1951), VanStone ed. (1977:89), Wells and Kelly (1890:16), Woolfe (1893:151, 152).

229. F. Beechey (1831, I:393, 402, 406, 456, 458; II:305), Brower (ms:146–47), Dall (1866–67: entries for Oct. 12, 1866, through May 25, 1867), Kotzebue (1821, I:210, 223, 227), Wells and Kelly (1890:16), Weyer (1928).

230. F. Beechey (1831, I:361, 366), B. Foote (1992:152), Johnston and Pulu (1980:3), Murdoch (1892:385–88), Nelson (1998:347–57), Ostermann and Holtved (1952:108), Sunno (1951.70, 1951.104); VanStone (1976:35). See photo in Johnston (1976c:439).

231. L. Gallahorn (1969.2), Johnston (1976b:15), Ostermann and Holtved (1952:108), Ray and Blaker (1967:26–27, 32–33, plate 55), Sunno (1951.104). See photo in Johnston (1976c:441).

232. Q. Dives (1940:37), Jensen (1970.3), Murdoch (1892:367–70), Nelson (1899:393–415), Ostermann and Holtved (1952:60), D. Ray (1977: figs. 22a, 22b, 23, 34, 68, 69), Ray and Blaker (1967:11, 12–13, 15, 19, 32, 44, 47, 52, and plates 50–54), Sunno (1951.21, 1951.24, 1951.67, 1951.68, 1951.69), VanStone (1968–69; 1976:35–41; 1990:21). The masks collected by Knud Rasmussen and identified by Ostermann and Holtved (1952:131–36) as being from Point Hope were in fact from Nunivak Island (Sonne 1988:22–24), which is a considerable distance south of the region of interest in this volume.

233. Giddings (1961:163, fig. B), Murdoch (1892:365–66), Nelson (1899:415–16), Simpson (1875:243), Sunno (1951.69, 1951.113).

234. Oswalt (1967: plate 10), Rainey (1959:13), D. Ray (1967:13–14; 1977:84), VanStone (1990:21).

235. The word "charm" is often used to denote this type of object. However, the same word is also used to refer to a magical saying. Because of the resulting ambiguity, the term "amulet" is used here. My sources on amulets are cited in Chapter 6.

236. *Paipak* is obviously a loanword from English.

237. According to Lawrence Kaplan, the term *kuiŋiq* was a loanword from Chukchi.

238. Hooper (1884:103), Stoney (1900:844–45), VanStone (1976:43–44; 1980:65–67; 1990:22), Woolfe (1893:146).

239. Burch (2005), Campbell (1998:plate 37), Csonka (2000), Giddings (1961:124), Jensen (1970.5).

240. Burch (2005), D. Jenness (1928:74, 78), Jensen (1970.4), Nelson (1899: plate XCII), Simpson (1852–54: entry for April 5, 1854), Sauer (1802:247n), Stefansson (1914b:384, 386), Thornton (1931:42), Varjola (1990:39), Varjola et al. (1990:270–72).

241. L. Gallahorn (1970.1, 1970.3), C. and L. Jensen (1980), Mendenhall, Sampson, and Tennant (1989:65–71), Ostermann and Holtved (1952:67–68).

242. This definition avoids the issue of whether or not the activity yields a positive result for anyone. It thus encompasses acts that might be characterized as a disservice as well as a service in ordinary English usage. I do not know of an English word, other than effort, that would encompass both.

243. They consumed several sets of footgear every year, however.

244. Cantwell (1889b:84), Giddings (1956:34, 36), Simpson (1875:252), Thornton (1931:100), Trollope (1855:874), Wells and Kelly (1890:17), Woolfe (1893:135, 144).

245. Cantwell (1889b:81), Dall (1866–67), L. Gallahorn (1970.1), Giddings (1952:85; 1956:33–34; 1961:138), Hooper (1884:104), NANA Elders Conference (1979.3), Ostermann and Holtved (1952:125), Sunno (1915.44, 1951.46), Thornton (1931:213–14), N. Wood (1986), Woolfe (1893:145).

246. Avessuk (1983.6), F. Beechey (1831, I:355), Hooper (1881:24–25), Iviqsiq (1940:6), Jensen (1970.1), Keats (1970.2), Niġuwana (1940.1:14), Ostermann and Holtved (1952:123), Penn (1952.1), Quwana (1940.1:8).

247. The late-20th-century village was located still farther east.

248. This section relates very closely to my paper on "modes of exchange" (Burch 1988a). However, the perspective here is a bit different, and I have learned a few things since I wrote the original piece. I thank Barbara Bodenhorn and Ann Fienup-Riordan for comments on an early draft of this section.

249. Avessuk (1983.4), Coffin (1970), D. Foster (1970.1), J. Foster (1970), L. Gallahorn (1970.1), Giddings (1961:28, 52, 150), Glover (1970.1, 1970.5), Green (1969), A. Hawley (1965.11, 1967, 1973.3), Elwood Hunnicutt (1970), Jensen (1970.1, 1970.2, 1970.3, 1970.6), Keats (1970.2, 1970.8, 1970.9), Kialook (1970), C. Lee (1970), Lee, Sampson, Tennant, and Mendenhall (1990:165, 199), Olanna (1983), Sheidt (1969.1), C. Smith (1970), John Stalker (1970.1), Stone (1976), Stoney (1900:832, 836–37), Sun (1970), Martha Swan (1984.1), Thornton (1931:33, 46, 48, 69, 71–72, 79, 120, 121), Wright (1969.2).

250. A. Hawley (1965.2), Killigivuk (1960.7), Rasmussen (1925:534–35), Sunno (1951.106).

251. This custom was still followed in my time (1960s).

252. Aġviqsiiña (1940.1, 1940.3), Aldrich (1889:170), K. Burns (1960.2), Q. Dives (1940), L. Gallahorn (1970.6), M. Hawley (1965.1), Jensen (1970.2), Lee et al. (1990:165, 199), T. Mitchell (1969), NANA Elders Conference (1979.2), Northwest Iñupiat Elders Conference (1983g:1–4), Olanna (1983), Quwana (1940:10, 5–5a, 21–22), Sheidt (1969.1), C. Smith (1970), Stone (1976), Clinton Swan (1984.1), Martha Swan (1976), Vestal (1970).

253. A. Hawley (1965.5), Jensen (1970.6), Killigivuk (1940.2:3–4), Rainey (1947:241), Stoney (1900:833), Sunno (1951.57), Thornton (1931:107). Stoney's summary presents what seems to me to be an oversimplified and overformalized account of this subject. On the other hand, since many of the Iñupiat among whom he lived were descended from Athapaskans, he may have accurately described the local customs on the upper Kobuk. If so, their customs differed to some extent from the more general Iñupiaq pattern.

254. F. Beechey (1831, I:339, 391, 397, 408–9, 411; II:306), Bockstoce (1977:125–26), Bockstoce ed. (1988, I:97), Brower (ms:140, 244), Cantwell (1899a:71), J. Foster (1970), L. Gallahorn (1970.1), J. Grinnell (1901:67–68), A. Hawley (1965.9, 1973.3), Hooper (1884:39), Keats (1970.2, 1970.9), Kialook (1970), Kotzebue (1821, I:211, 222, 235), C. Lee (1970), Murdoch (1892:41), Nelson (1899:230–31), Rosse (1883:42), C. Smith (1970), Stefansson (1909:609), Martha Swan (1984.5), VanStone ed. (1973:84–85), Wolfe (ms:110).

255. F. Beechey (1831, I:287, 339, 343, 345, 347, 352, 359, 383–84, 390, 391–92, 394, 397, 408–9, 411, 423, 441; II:256–57, 263, 265, 283, 306), Brower (ms:140, 244), J. Grinnell (1901:67–68), Kotzebue (1821, I:211, 235), Nelson (1899:230–31), Stefansson (1909:609).

256. Aġviqsiiña (1940.1:60), E. Barr (1970.1), F. Beechey (1831, I:390–91, 441; II:306), H. Brown (1965), Cantwell (1887:25, 51; 1889a:70, 71, 72), A. Clark (1970, 1977), Clark and Clark (1976), Coffin (1970), S. Dives (1970), Eliyak (1931), *Explorer* (1885: entry for July 17), Foote and Williamson (1961:23–25, 30), D. Foster (1970.1), Giddings (1941:28; 1952:52; 1961:150), Glover (1970.1, 1970.5), Hadley and Sunno (1951), Healy (1887:13; 1889:16), Hickey (1979), Hooper (1881:28; 1884:39–40, 78, 102), Jensen (1970.1, 1970.2, 1970.4), Kingston (1996), Kisautaq and Kean (1981:619–21), Larsen and Rainey (1948:25), C. Lee (1970), McLenegan (1889:73, 74, 108), Nelson (1899:14, 229, 261–62), Rainey (1947:267–68), Schweitzer and Golovko (1995), Sheidt (1969.1), John Simpson (1875:235–36, 264–67, 269), John Stalker (1970.1), Stefansson (1914b:314–15), Stoney (1900:570–71, 813–14, 816–17, 836–37), Sun (1970), Thornton (1931:33, 46, 48, 120, 121), VanStone (1962a), Wells and Kelly (1890:13, 26), Woolfe (1893:137–38, 147), J. Wright (1969.2).

257. F. Beechey (1831, I:339, 391, 401; II:306), Bockstoce (1977:125–26), Hooper (1884:39), Kotzebue (1821, I:211, 222, 235), Murdoch (1892:41), Wolfe (ms:110).

258. I have described the trading partnership elsewhere in some detail Burch (1970a, 2005). Sources include Anderson (1974/75:68), Bockstoce ed. (1988, I:171), A. Clark (1970:20–21; 1974:232, 235; 1977), Clark and Clark (1976:196), J. Foster (1970), L. Gallahorn (1970.1), Giddings (1961:148–49), Green (1969), Gubser (1965:32, 133, 160–61, 179), A. Hawley (1965.11, 1967), E. Jones (1991), Keats (1970.2), Kialook (1970), C. Lee (1970), McKennan (1965:63), Osgood (1936:132), Pospisil (1964:408, 427), Rainey (1940.8), Solomon (1981:49), Spencer (1959:167–72 passim), Martha Swan (1984.1), VanStone (1962b:92–93).

259. Booth (1960.1, 1960.2), Burch (2005), Cantwell (1889a:71–73), Curtis (1930:195), Nelson (1899:261–62), C. Smith (1970).

260. If true in Stefansson's time, the situation had certainly changed by the early 1960s, a time when freeloaders were enthusiastically advised to get out when times got tough.

261. Unsigned report of the Government School at Point Hope for the year 1911–12.

262. I am grateful to Dr. Fortuine for his comments on a draft of this section.

263. Anderson et al. (1998:246–48, 290, 301–4), Beaver (1976.1, 1976.2), Call (1899:118, 120–25), Cantwell (1889b:83), A. Douglas (1976.6, 1976.7), Fortuine (1988a; 1989:33, 50, 51, 55, 69, 73–77, 80, 84, 85), L. Gallahorn (1970.3), Geary (1976), Giddings (1961:18), Gray (1976), B. Hawley (1989), S. and B. Hawley (1984), Hild (1983), Keats (1960.3), Kennedy (1965.3), Kirchner (1983), Lucier, VanStone, and Keats (1971), McClellan (1970.2), Northwest Iñupiat Elders Conference (1976d), Ongtowasruk (1999), Rosse (1883:23–24), B. Sheldon (1976), Stoney (1900:833, 874), Sunno (1951.71), Charlotte Swan (1965.1, 1965.2), V. Swan (1989), Thornton (1931:13, 21), G. Tocktoo (1984), M. Tocktoo (1983.6), Wells and Kelly (1890:21), Woolfe (1893:143).

264. Since medicines are goods, their manufacture constitutes the production of goods. However, it is more useful for present purposes to discuss them in the section on services. The information on traditional medicines in Anderson et al. (1998:246–48) was very helpful in preparing this discussion.

265. Fortuine (1985:30–31), Juul (1979:68–70), Kirchner (1983:102–3), Lucier, VanStone and Keats (1971:254).

266. Anderson et al. (1998:247), Beaver (1976.2), Brower (ms:672), Dixon and Kirchner (1982), Fortuine (1985:32, 34–35), L. Gallahorn (1970.3), J. Grinnell (1901:71), Juul (1979:69), Kirchner (1983:103–4), Nelson (1899:310), Sunno (1951.71), Wells and Kelly (1890:23).

267. I have been unable to determine just what the "core" of a boil is.

268. Aġviqsiiña (1940.1:17), Call (1899:121–22), Giddings (1961:18), Northwest Iñupiat Elders Conference (1983g:6), Simpson (1852–54: entry for April 28, 1854), Stoney (1900:833), Woolfe (1893:143).

269. K. Burns (1960.2), Cantwell (1887:51), L. Gallahorn (1969.2, 1970.1), Glover (1970.1), Hooper (1884:112), Kennedy (1965.2), Northwest Iñupiat Elders Conference (1976a, 1983a), Quwana (1940.1:27–28), Ralph (1951.1, 1951.2), Stefansson (1914b:126–27), Stoney (1900:833–34), Martha Swan (1965.2), Thornton (1931:102–3), Vestal (1969), Wells and Kelly (1890:22–23), Woolfe (1893:138–39).

270. Other terms for tabooed are *kiruġnaqtuaq* and *paquġaqtuaq*.

271. A similar, but shorter and less dramatic, account of a séance was published by Wells and Kelly (1890:22–23); see also Thornton (1931:102–3).

272. Anderson et al. (1998:128), E. Ballot in Lee et al. (1990:3), Brower (ms:178), K. Burns (1960.2), Cantwell (1889b:85), R. Cleveland (1965.7), Giddings (1961:144), T. Mitchell (1969), Northwest Iñupiat Elders Conference (1976e), Smith (1970), Martha Swan (1970), Thornton (1931:131).

273. Eliyak (1931), Murdoch (1892:357), Stoney (1900:564–65), Thornton (1931:154).

274. The only time I ever heard a husky bark was when a Noatak dog I brought to Pennsylvania confronted its first herd of cattle.

275. Anderson et al. (1998:235), F. Beechey (1831, I:362, 398), Giddings (1956:10), D. Keats (1970.4), T. Mitchell (1969), Stoney (1900:565), Sun (1985:59–60), Thornton (1931:155), VanStone (1980:63).

276. Brower (ms:146, 176), J. Grinnell (1901:48–49), Hooper (1884:107), Murdoch (1892:357), Thornton (1931:157).

277. Robert Lee (1960.2), Luther (1960.1), T. Morris (1970), S. Thomas (1970), Vestal (1970), Woolfe (1893:149).

278. This account was informed by my own experiences driving dogs in Northwest Alaska in the early 1960s, and by the following sources: Brower (ms:135, 148, 150, 160a, 161, 178), Cantwell (1889b:85), Eliyak (1931), Hobson (1855), Luther (1960.1), D. Naylor (1960.5), Quwana (1940.2), Stone (1976), Stoney (1900:567–78), and Trollope (1855).

279. E. Ballot in Lee et al. (1990:2), Cantwell (1889b:85), Dall (1870a:206), J. Konalook (1951.3), Stone (1976), Sun (1985:61), Sunno (1951.80), Sunno, Hadley, and Konalook (1951), Thornton (1931:131).

280. Brower (ms:135), L. Gallahorn (1970.3), Jensen (1970.5), T. Mitchell (1969), Paneak (1970), Stoney (1900:576–77, 812), Woolfe (1893:144).

281. Sometimes more temporary shelters were erected in winter (Stoney 1900:568–69), but rarely when whole families were traveling.

282. This account of *umiaq* travel is informed by the sources cited, and by my own experiences in the early 1960s traveling in *umiat* both in rivers and on the ocean.

283. E. Barr (1970), F. Beechey (1831, I:346, 358–59, 371, 389–90, 393, 404–5; II:301, 302), Belcher (ms:64), Hooper (1881:28–29; 1884:102), McClellan (1970.2), Muir (1917:147), Nelson (1899:231, 299), Thornton (1931:120–21, 125–26, 138), Tuckfield (1960), Wells and Kelly (1890:27), Woolfe (1893:149).

284. A. Hawley (1965.1), Keats (1970.3), Stoney (1900:818–19, 836–37), Towkshjea (1960.2).

285. Anderson et al. (1998:116), F. Beechey (1831, I:348), Brower (ms:129, 139), M. Curtis (1970), A. Douglas (1976.1), Foote and Williamson (1961:24), A. Hawley (1964.4), Hooper (1884:50), Keats (1970.5), Kennedy (1984), Kiana (1970), J. Killigivuk (1960.11), C. Lee (1970), E. Mills (1960.3, 1960.4), T. Mitchell (1970), Quwana (1940.2), John Stalker (1970.1), Stoney (1900:819), Sun (1989:33, 35), Sunno (1951.62), M. and M. Swan (1970), Milton Swan (1964.1), Walton (1965.1, 1965.2), C. Wood (1931), Woolfe (1893:131). For a sketch of foot travel, see Phebus (1972:87).

286. B. Foote (1992:115–16), Keats (1970.5), Rausch (1951:162), Sun (1985:62), Stoney (1900:819).

287. This actually happened in the winter of 1960–61.

Chapter Five

The Political Process

The political process is the distribution of power over and responsibility for the actions of the various members of a social system.[1] Power is the ability to control one's own actions and to influence the actions of others. Responsibility is the accountability of an individual(s) to another individual(s) or group(s) for his or her own acts and/or the acts of others. As is true generally of the definitions used in this volume, these are broader than most other social scientists' definitions of the same terms.

My analysis of the political process among the Iñupiat is phrased in terms of the various social and demographic contexts identified in Chapter 3. These are conjugal, domestic, and compound families; simple and complex settlements; and nations. The political aspect of international affairs is also discussed.

Sources of Power

There were several bases on which power was allocated in Iñupiaq nations, including at least the following: absolute age, seniority, generation, sex, knowledge, physical strength, solidarity, and wealth. The degree and scope of the power that accrued to an individual through these sources differed to some extent from one context to another, and the means whereby individuals could be held responsible for their wielding of power varied accordingly.

Absolute Age

A person's age, as such, was not a source of either power or responsibility. However, age was so closely correlated with other attributes that were sources of power that it is difficult to determine precisely where one ended and the other began. Thus, people who were in older age categories often belonged to an older generation, they were physically stronger (up to a point), and they were typically more knowledgeable than those in younger ones. These qualities gave adults considerable influence over subadults within the various family contexts, but little outside of them. Ideally, this power was wielded through instruction and persuasion, and it seems as though it usually was in fact.

As adults became elders (*utuqqanaat*), they gradually lost their physical superiority over people in lower age groups. However, their knowledge and wisdom continued to grow, and those were qualities the Iñupiat greatly respected. As Charles Lucier (1972) once wrote, Iñupiaq "leadership was a lot heavier on respect than force."

It is probably fair to say that the locus of the greatest institutionalized power in an Iñupiaq society resided in the elders, particularly male elders.[2] In complex settlements, this power accrued more to elders as a group than to specific individuals. The elders met informally in the qargi on almost a daily basis. There they were kept abreast of developments in the community, they formulated rules of conduct for people affiliated with that qargi—which meant everyone in simple settlements—they monitored people's behavior, and they chastised and sometimes disciplined troublemakers. An umialik had to be extremely brazen to go directly against the collective wishes of the elders, and suffered an enormous loss of esteem and support if he did so.

If a troublemaker refused to come for an interview or reprimand, younger men were sent to get him/her and bring him/her to the qargi, by force if necessary (Jensen 1970.6; Niguwana 1940.1). If lectures did not produce desired changes in a person's behavior, the elders eventually prescribed a remedy, which could range from a payment of food or furs to expulsion from the settlement. This task usually involved the use of force, hence was delegated to younger men to carry out. Female elders influenced these affairs primarily through their husbands. However, they also went through a roughly analogous process among themselves with respect to matters of concern primarily to women.

People in the oldest age category (anayuqaksraq for a male and aaquaksraq for a female) continued to wield authority in the community (Aġviqsiiña 1940.1:106; F. Beechey 1831, I:383–84; II:302; Q. Dives 1940:28). It was precisely these people—especially old women—who were thought to control the most powerful magic songs or sayings. These could be used to bring harm to those who offended them, and most people tried to treat elders well for this reason if for no other. When Rainey (1947) asked his Point Hope (Tikiġaġmiut) informants

> what they feared most in the old days, the Tikerarmiut almost invariably do not
> answer, starvation, the neighboring tribes, the spirits, ghosts, or evil angatkoks, but
> say that their greatest fear was the old people in the village (Rainey 1947:279).

Seniority

Seniority concerns the length of time a person has belonged to an organization relative to the length of time that the other members have belonged to it. The most pervasive form of seniority in Iñupiaq societies was based on relative age, with older people generally having authority over younger ones.

Families were essentially hierarchical systems based on the relative ages of their members (J. Simpson 1875:252). Older family members could and did tell younger ones what to do, even when the former were still young children. Until they reached adulthood, there was little juniors could do if seniors abused their power; complaints to parents usually failed to produce the desired result. As adults, people who were annoyed by the way they were treated could leave and either set off on their own or join another family. However, there was a very strong value attached to older people nurturing and protecting their younger siblings, beginning in early childhood. This ideal seems to have been realized in fact more often than not.

In the case of simple settlements, a single hierarchy based on relative age encompassed the entire unit, even where several households were involved. In complex settlements, where the members of several compound families resided, relative age was a significant source of power within families, but not between them.

Specific examples from the study period showing just how pervasive the relative age hierarchy was are not available. However, I observed dozens of examples in the early 1960s, and I was able to monitor many of them over a period of decades. One family in particular illustrated beautifully the pattern I was told had existed in the past. It involved five brothers who lived in a complex settlement. The one in the middle was a troublemaker who was forced by his siblings to leave town. The remaining four were all excellent hunters, but varied with regard to their other skills and leadership qualities. The one with the broadest array of talents happened to be the youngest. He was quiet and self-effacing as a young man, and he deferred to and helped support his older siblings. All four brothers originally belonged to the same (compound) family, whose dwellings were at one end of the village. However, when the youngest got married, he moved in with his wife's (compound) family, whose dwellings were located in a different part of the village. When her father died, he became the oldest male living in that unit. By persuading one of his wife's younger brothers to stay nearby when he married, and by having several children (who remained close at hand when they married), the youngest of the five brothers ultimately became head of a fairly substantial (compound) family.

The other context in which seniority-based power was important was in polygynous conjugal families. Ideally, and apparently to a large extent actually, the first wife (*nuliaqpak*) had power over subsequent wives, regardless of the actual or relative ages of the individuals involved, and regardless of the differences in the degree of affection with which the husband regarded them (Woolfe 1893:135).

Generation

Members of senior generations had authority over members of junior ones. In practice, this rule applied almost exclusively to the relationships between parents and children, secondarily to those between aunts and uncles, on the one hand, and nieces and nephews, on the other. Generation as a source of power was inextricably bound up with the various qualities discussed above in the contexts of absolute and relative age.

One thing that has not been discussed in this book is child abuse, which, in the present context, involves the abuse of power by a member of the parental or grandparental generation vis-à-vis a person of the child generation. In the dozens of interviews I conducted over the years about traditional family life, I rarely heard of serious mistreatment of children or about the rape of younger family women by older family men. (The incest taboo included parents and children, nepotics, and first cousins.) Early Western observers who spent the most time living among Iñupiat during the 19th century and who wrote about their experiences (e.g., Simpson 1875:249; Stoney 1900:832) generally speak highly about how parents treated their offspring. Kelly (Wells and Kelly 1890:21, 22), however, whose experience dated from the 1880s, claimed that there were "instances" of sexual relations between parent and child, and that sex between uncles and nieces was "quite common," even though forbidden by incest rules. Rainey (1947:243) said that incestuous relations were "not uncommon," particularly between father and daughter. Apparently the only means of dealing with such infractions was public ridicule (Aġviqsiiña 1940.1; Rainey 1947:243). It is impossible to know, at this remove in time, how much force was involved in incestuous affairs. It is also impossible to know if these statements apply accurately to the early 19th century; by the 1880s, alcohol may have been involved in many of these incidents.

By the time children became adults, there were definite limits on the extent to which parents could abuse their power. One possibility was for the children to leave home. Mistreatment could also lead to physical violence, particularly if fathers and sons were involved (Aġviqsiiña 1940.1; A. Hawley 1965.12). The father-son relationship was emotionally intense, even though the expression of sentiment was generally supposed to be muted. However, an argument could lead to a violent outburst of temper on the part of a mistreated son. That resulted either in the departure of the son, or else an easing of the tension.

Sex

Sex was a source of power in that males generally had authority over females, particularly in the context of the husband-wife relationship, secondarily in sibling and cousin relationships (Thornton 1931:63; Woolfe 1893:134). On the other hand, a woman wielded control over many of the raw materials, particularly food, that were produced by the members of her family, and that was not a trivial matter. Her decisions in this sphere probably could be countermanded by her husband, but that would have engendered considerable stress. Even in areas where a husband was clearly in command, such as in deciding whether to move the family from the settlement where it was living, he frequently sought his wife's opinion. If he did not, he usually heard it anyway. Where the wife was a shaman and her husband was not, it was she, not her husband, who ultimately was in charge.

When a woman disobeyed her husband, or if she was caught having an affair, her husband subjected her to a beating (Woolfe 1893:134). Depending on its severity, this procedure seems to have been considered normal and acceptable. In a few cases, women were strong enough to forestall, and even turn the tables on, their husbands (A. Hawley 1965.5). Repeated thrashings and other mistreatment by the husband usually led to one of two outcomes: divorce, or the active involvement of the wife's father and/or brothers.[3] If the man was a general troublemaker, several men might become involved. They might help the woman leave her husband, or, in extreme cases, they killed him. In complex settlements, flagrant promiscuity on the part of a woman sometimes resulted in her being gang-raped by the members of her husband's *qargi* (J. Killigivuk 1940.1). The only weapons at a woman's disposal for flagrant promiscuity on the part of her husband were scolding and divorce.

Physical Strength

Physical strength and toughness were highly valued by the Iñupiat, particularly in men. These qualities were developed over a lifetime of physical exertion, and honed through a wide range of athletic competitions, virtually all of which were carried out in public. These competitions, which were held several times a year, revealed who the strongest and most agile people were. Top athletes were admired for their strength and ability, and this gave them some special influence in the community. This influence was even greater when an athlete's physical prowess was accompanied by modesty and generally decorous behavior.

Physical strength intruded into the political process in other ways as well. In Iñupiaq settlements, which lacked police, courts, jails, and other types of formal restraint, a very strong man who was inclined to push people around was sometimes able to impose his will on others. In complex settlements, a bully could get away with only so much, however, because, sooner or later, he would be confronted by a large group of people determined to put a stop to his arrogant behavior (Jensen 1970.6; Elsie Weyiouanna 1983.1). The process usually began in the *qargi*, where the offender was lectured on his activities. If the lecture did not produce a satisfactory result and the person continued to cause trouble, he was killed, often by members of his own family so as to avoid a blood feud. In simple settlements, on the other hand, it was very difficult to offset the dominance of a bully. About the only recourse in extreme situations was for people to try to leave without him, or to kill him, neither of which was easily accomplished.

Within families, physical strength was an important element primarily in the husband-wife relationship. For one thing, a large number of first marriages were established when a man literally abducted a woman, sometimes with help, took her home, and virtually raped her.[4] The abduction was often carried out in full view of the community, including the woman's own relatives, so it was expected and approved; nevertheless, it was carried out through brute force. Force could also be involved when a man and woman *did* want to get married but their parents and other relatives disapproved. In extreme cases, the latter situation could result in bloodshed and a lingering feud (Giddings 1961:49–50). Applications of force were also fairly common after a marriage was established. If a woman disobeyed her husband or did not perform her chores properly, she was likely to get a thrashing; infidelity on her part virtually guaranteed one unless it had been approved in advance by her husband (Simpson 1875:253; Woolfe 1893:134). These beatings were rarely harsh enough to cause severe bodily harm to the wife, and they either decreased in frequency over time or the relationship was dissolved.

Also within families, force was at least a potential factor in the relationships between brothers, between male cousins, and between fathers and sons, in that order of relative frequency. Physical violence seems to have occurred during severe disagreements, when people lost their tempers and practically went berserk, hitting each other, trying to knock each other down, and beating each other with a stick or other object or resorting to the use of weapons (Jensen 1970.6). If such an encounter resulted in a draw, more peaceful negotiations might follow. However, if there was a clear-cut victor and loser, the latter might be left with a physical disability, and there would be lingering resentment.

The most common source of trouble between brothers, male cousins, and same-age males in general seems to have been the desire for the same woman. In the tiny settlements in which many Iñupiat lived, a man who desired a change in sexual partners would likely have only a sister, a mother, a daughter, a niece, or a sister-in-law to choose among. As noted above, incest certainly did occur, but the most desirable choice of the five alternatives—in principle, at least—was the sister-in-law. The potential for strife in having sexual relations with a sister-in-law is obvious. If the man desiring this woman was stronger and more brazen than her husband, he simply took her by force, and dared everyone else to do something about it. Of course, it wasn't always a man who initiated an illicit sexual relationship; women, too, sometimes sought sexual diversion, but the result was about the same. In compound families, and in complex settlements, alternative sexual partners were numerous and often less closely related, so there were more options. There were also a greater number of men to combine forces to keep a bully under control.

The most common source of stress between fathers and adult sons seems to have been tyrannical control and/or stinginess on the part of the father. This could be corrected only by one or the other leaving the family. However, as I have noted frequently, that was not always a satisfactory option. In addition, fathers sometimes developed a sexual interest in a daughter-in-law, which, if pursued to a conclusion, could lead to violence and bloodshed.

Physical violence between members of different families in complex settlements or in neighboring simple settlements seems to have been resorted to rather rarely, although it did occur (S. Dives 1970; Rainey 1940.10, 1947:242). In the large settlement of Point Hope, groups of youngsters or teenagers who belonged to different families sometimes formed gangs that fought each other for no apparent reason other than the fact that they belonged to different families (A. Hawley 1965.5). Another context in which interfamily violence occurred, apparently on a fairly regular basis, was during football games played by men only (Aġviqsiiña 1940.1:99; Kunuyaq 1940; Rainey 1947:242). (When women were involved, the objective was to have fun; when only men were involved, the objective was to win.) There were few rules of conduct, no referees, and no penalties for improper play. It seems as though fights were fairly common, and sometimes rather violent, leaving a bitterness among the participants that could escalate suddenly with only slight further provocation.

More generally, one of the most common causes of serious physical conflict was men from different families fighting over the same woman, followed in frequency by women fighting over the same man.[5] Usually this involved just the two or three people most directly affected, but on occasions entire families became involved (J. Killigivuk 1960.2). Still more serious altercations arose when people stole something from someone else's house or storage rack, or took animals or fish caught in someone else's snares or traps (Aġviqsiiña 1940.1:98–100; A. Hawley 1965.5).

In the more remote past, disputes between compound families making up the major factions in the complex settlements of Wales and Point Hope periodically erupted into virtual civil war, with weapons, bloodshed, and a legacy of mutual hostility.[6]

Solidarity

Solidarity-based power is that which derives from being involved in relationships with a relatively large number of people who are subordinates, regardless of the basis (e.g., generation, relative age) for their inferior status. For example, a man who headed a large compound family in which he had authority over all the other active members because he was older than they also held power in the community at large by virtue of the fact he had so many subordinates. The larger the family, the more power he had. The heads of the largest families were *umialgich*, or rich people. *Umialgich* were able to enhance their wealth and influence with the proceeds derived from partnerships (*niuvigiich*) with men of comparable stature in other societies, and sometimes through connections made through polygynous marriages.

Solidarity was an important factor in people's influence in complex settlements, since larger families had more control over community affairs than smaller ones simply by virtue of their size (Rainey 1947:242; S. Rock 1940:2). Everyone knew that if a dispute became serious enough to be settled by brute force, larger families probably would defeat smaller ones; people behaved accordingly.

The importance of solidarity as a source of power is also illustrated by its absence, that is, a lack of relationships with others. An orphan (*iḷiappak*), having no relatives, also had no influence. He/she generally had to act as a servant or slave to others in order to survive.[7] A frequent contrast made in conversation in my time was between an *umialik*, who had everything, and an *iḷiappak*, who had nothing, the two being considered polar opposites. A favorite theme in Iñupiaq folklore was the fantasy of an orphan boy somehow rising above the circumstances of his childhood to eventually become an *umialik* (A. Hawley 1965.5).

Wealth

It has been noted a number of times in this volume that the accumulation of wealth depended only partly on the hunting, trading, and management skills of a family head and his wife. Certainly they were important, but even more important was the pooling of resources that took place in compound families. The larger the family, the larger the size of the pool. Clever trading of raw materials and manufactured goods on the open market by the family head was particularly important because it increased the returns to the family at little or no extra cost.

Family heads and their wives could withdraw for their personal use the most and the best from the common stock as long as they retained the allegiance of their subordinates. The key to retaining that allegiance was to make sure that all the others felt that they received a return commensurate with their contribution. In effect, individuals were materially compensated for their efforts on behalf of the organization as a whole. The individuals who were most successful at persuading subordinates to do this became *umialgich*.

Umialgich

Early-19th-century Western visitors to Northwest Alaska frequently encountered men to whom they referred as "chiefs."[8] Although the Westerners had difficulty communicating with the Iñupiat, they could tell from the dignified way these individuals bore themselves, by their better clothing and more elegant personal adornment, and by the deference paid to them by others that they held a rank higher than that of most of their countrymen.

Froelich Rainey (1947), whose research was carried out in the complex coastal settlement of Point Hope, summarized the situation of the *umialik* as follows:

> Control of each extended family group rested with the fathers or the oldest men; among these the position of *umelik* [*umialik*], or boat captain, was paramount. He was normally the wealthiest man in the family, the captain of its whaling crew, and often an *angatkok* [*aŋatkuq*, or shaman] as well. His position was achieved through skill, intelligence, energy, and shrewdness rather than through inheritance of property or prestige. The *umelik* was, quite clearly, the central figure in the grouping of conjugal families. Invariably he attained his position by accumulating property which consisted of boats, hunting gear, household furnishings, clothing, etc. This kind of "wealth" among the Eskimo is simply a measure of a man's ability. It is a corollary of a clever *angatkok*, an energetic and intelligent hunter, a man of strong will, and one who is wise in council. It can never be inherited from a relative (Rainey 1947:241).

In this he echoed the observations of John Simpson (1875:273), made almost a century earlier, who wrote that "it cannot be doubted that their ume'liks have considerable influence, more especially over their numerous relations and family connections, and may use some art to maintain and extend it."

E. W. Nelson (1877–91) elaborated, albeit in rather cynical terms, in his journal:

> Certain men among the Malemuts gather large amount of goods (large for a native but only a few hundred dollars worth at most), but they can only retain them and their life by being open-handed with food among the less fortunate during winter, thus creating a body of parasites with whom each tyone or trading chief is surrounded, and by making frequent egruskas in which they are careful to give but a portion of their goods and as the natives understand that by allowing him to retain a certain amount he is enabled to continue his trading and thus continue his egruskas it is evidently in their interest to do so. Thus in nearly every large village of Malemuts and coast natives from Unalakleet to Cape Lisburne there is a head man who has more goods than the others by far and, in many places as Kotzebue Sound and the Bering Straits Islands this man has the say and often personally does the other men's trading. His authority is kept up only so long as he proves a public benefactor by his egruska and presents of food of which each of

these politicians are careful to collect a large stock every year to feed the indolent and needy wretches in winter.

> Frequently he has a double hold by combining the office of shaman with that of headman. The natives give him obedience as long as it is in their interest and the moment he ceases his favors or tries to secure his own comfort before that of the others he is doomed by universal envy and jealousy, either to be killed and his goods confiscated or he may be told authoritatively to make a large egruska and give all his goods. When he is given this chance he, of course, makes himself a beggar to save his life and then has to live like the meanest (Nelson 1877–81: entry for Sept. 5, 1880).

Nelson was based on Norton Sound, hence uses terms local to that area, such as *tyone* instead of *umialik*, and "*egruska*" instead of feast. However, this particular passage is specifically identified as pertaining to Malimiut ("Malemuts"), that is, people from the Kotzebue Sound region, many of whom had migrated to Norton Sound over the decades preceding Nelson's stay there.

The key point in the above passage is that *umialgich* were essentially self-made men. Perhaps more accurately, they were made wealthy through the efforts of their relatives, and their hold on the position depended on the continuing support of those relatives. As soon as, or to the extent that, support was withdrawn, their power declined. Finally, their institutionalized influence did not extend beyond the bounds of the compound family they headed.

Umialgich were not hereditary chiefs. However, the children of an *umialik* had some important advantages over their peers. They were probably better fed and clothed throughout their childhood, they had superior role models to guide and instruct them, and they were introduced to a wider range of both national and international contacts than other children. They also inherited a more substantial array of equipment—boats, sleds, tools, weapons, houses, household goods, and other items—when their father died. If the oldest son was the main beneficiary of an *umialik*'s estate, as he usually was, the position was his to lose.

Property

The wealth on which the *umialik* role was based consisted of property, and it is appropriate to digress a bit at this point to consider just what kinds of property existed in an Iñupiaq society, and, more precisely, what kinds of property would make a person be considered rich. These matters have already been discussed to some extent previously, particularly in the section on distribution in Chapter 4. However, a more focused treatment is required.

Property "consists in institutionally defined and regulated rights of persons (or other social units) in scarce values" (W. Moore 1943, quoted by Levy 1966:280). Property can be tangible (e.g., a boat) or intangible (e.g., a song), and empirical (e.g., a poke of seal oil) or nonempirical (e.g., a shaman's familiar spirit). Ownership can be either absolute or a matter of degree.

The most general form of property in early-19th-century Northwest Alaska was the land that constituted a nation's estate. Instead of saying that the members of the society owned the land, however, it is perhaps more appropriate to say that they exercised dominion over it. However, this control, by whatever name, was not total. The members of almost every nation had the right to travel across or otherwise use land belonging to one or more other nations at certain times of year and for certain purposes. For example, early every summer the majority of the Nuataaġmiut population of the upper Noatak River descended the river to its mouth, passing through the estate of the Napaaqtuġmiut and most of that of the Qikiqtaġruŋmiut. They stayed in the latter for about two months, during which time they made their clothing for the coming winter, hunted beluga, fished, and traded. Then, in August, they returned to their homeland.

The Nuataaġmiut, and apparently everyone else, considered their annual trip through the Napaaqtuġmiut estate and their stay in the Qikiqtaġruŋmiut estate to be a right, not a privilege. Any attempt to prevent them from making these movements would have been considered an act of war. However, if these same people traveled the same route by sled in winter without a specific invitation or without requesting permission to do so, such action would have been considered an act of war by the Napaaqtuġmiut and Qikiqtaġruŋmiut, and almost surely would have been intended as such by the Nuataaġmiut.

Similarly, for a certain period each summer, the members of almost every society had the right to travel by boat along coastlines that were part of the estates of other nations. Outside of that period, coastal travel in foreign territory was considered trespass. Since the right to use land belonging to others for certain purposes was based on traditional use dating from some ancient time, I consider it roughly equivalent to our notion of easement.

Within a nation's estate, land was generally considered to be the collective property of the members of the society (Sunno 1951.63; Vestal 1970). In general, people could live, hunt, and fish wherever they wanted. Families tended to prefer certain hunting and fishing areas, however, and they returned to these areas annually if they could (J. Killigivuk 1960.2). They might be annoyed if others intruded, but had no right to claim a locality as their own except, perhaps, in the northern part of the Seward Peninsula (D. Ray 1967:383–84). However, once the members of a family had built a house, it was considered their property as long as they lived in it or made it apparent that they intended to return to it. If they removed their goods and chattels and told everyone that they were abandoning it, then the members of another family were free to take it over. These same basic rules applied to storage pits and caches.

A *qargi* technically belonged to the man who organized its construction. In the great majority of cases, this was the head of the compound family whose members later used it the most. If the *qargi* continued to be used after the founder died, his descendants could claim primacy, although to a lesser degree with each passing generation. But the whole purpose of a *qargi* was to provide a place for many people to gather—to work, eat, trade, talk, and have fun. The other compound-family members, therefore, felt that they had a right to use the building. Thus they shared in its ownership, as well as in the obligation to help maintain it.

Tangible movable property entered the system as raw materials through the various means described in Chapter 4. Property rights over these items were established immediately upon their acquisition according to traditional rules for division into portions. The rules varied with the substance or species involved and the social context (e.g., crews vs. individuals) in which the goods were acquired. The details need not be repeated here.

In general, food and hides were pooled and placed under the control of the family head's wife to dispose of for the benefit of all family members. Raw materials destined to become tools or other kinds of equipment, or medicines, were generally considered to belong to the individuals who collected them. However, there were very few finished products amenable to being used by more than one person to which other family members could not assert some claim. Thus, clothing was usually owned and used exclusively by the person for whom it was made. Certain tools, such as skin scrapers and knives, were often made to fit a particular individual's hand, and thus constituted individual property. Jewelry, amulets, and many magic songs or sayings were individual property. Some rituals were collectively owned and used;

others were individually owned but had to be used for a collective benefit; still others were owned by all the members of the crew, *qargi*, or family. Items such as an adze, a mattock, or a boat, while nominally the property of their maker, were considered to belong to everyone. The person who made such an item had priority, but not the right of exclusive use.

The types of property that made a man wealthy, hence an *umialik*, were the full array of equipment described in Chapter 4, furs (for trade) and food in excess of family needs, and beads. The specific criterion used by some of my informants to differentiate between an *umialik* and an ordinary person was that an *umialik* usually had enough food on hand to last his family for more than a year, whereas an ordinary person did not. This surplus enabled the *umialik* and his wife to purchase luxury goods, such as spotted Siberian reindeer skins, tobacco, beads, and metal knives and pots. They kept what they wanted, shared some with other family members, and traded the rest. If they were clever negotiators, trade made them even wealthier.

Wealth enabled the *umialik* and his wife to be generous to family members, to feed and clothe widows and orphans, and to share what they had with others. As Brower (ms:161) said of the *umialik* at Qikiqtaġruq, near where Kotzebue now stands, he "kept his [influence] through his ability to supply his neighbors with things they needed during the winters, extending them credit when they were not in a position to pay."

Sharing of foodstuffs often made economic as well as political sense, since most of the goods making up an *umialik*'s wealth were perishable; it was better to give them away and incur a debt of gratitude than have them rot in a cache. The main exception was imported beads, particularly turquoise beads, which were cherished items during the early contact period (Brower ms:146–47, 161). They were also in very short supply. They might be sold during hard times, but usually were passed from father to son.

But of course the basic stock, the surplus, and the equipment required to get them had to be acquired through the collective efforts of *all* family members. Thus, an *umialik*'s entire establishment had to be more substantial than that of an ordinary person in order for him to have a significant food surplus. Only unusually capable people could manage their families in such a way as to maintain the necessary support year after year, through good times and bad.

Wealth, of course, is a matter of degree, and some *umialgich* were wealthier than others (Sheehan 1995:192). The wealthiest people in the entire study region were the leading whaling captains in Point Hope and Wales, whose assets derived primarily from the huge quantities of meat, blubber, and *maktaq* they received as their portion of every whale they took.

Rainey (1947:241) estimated that in Point Hope each *qargi* included four or five *umialgich* among its members. When there were seven *qargich* in the settlement in the early 19th century, that meant a total of between twenty-eight and thirty-five *umialgich* in Point Hope alone. If the ratio of *umialgich* to *qargich* was the same in Wales, where there were probably five *qargich*, there would have been between twenty and twenty-five. Together, these two settlements had more *umialgich* than all of the other nations in the study region combined.

In the whaling villages it was sometimes useful to distinguish between an *umialik* and an *umialiŋnaq*. The former was a wealthy person of the top rank, while the latter was a rich man of lesser degree. On ceremonial and other important occasions, the *umialgich* had special seats in the center of the *qargi*, the *umialiŋnat* (pl.) sat beside them, and ordinary men were still farther out.

Wealth was generally both more modest and more ephemeral outside the whaling villages than within them. Not only was it much more difficult to acquire quantities of food even remotely approaching that provided by a whale, it was more difficult to preserve for any length of time whatever wealth was acquired. Sometimes people living along the Kobuk and Selawik rivers did catch, dry, and safely store enough fish to provide their families with food for more than a year, but it was impossible to do this every year. Nevertheless, there were, outside of the whaling villages, people and families who were regularly much better off than their fellow countrymen. In the few complex inland settlements, these people were the functional equivalents of coastal *umialgich*, though relatively few were as affluent in absolute terms as a coastal *umialik* of the second rank.

In the 1880s, the richest people in nonwhaling settlements were men whose fall/winter houses were located in the upper reaches of the Iñupiaq sectors of the Kobuk and Selawik rivers, and who operated as middlemen in the fur trade between the interior-dwelling Athapaskans (who had access to lots of fur-bearing animals) and the coastal Iñupiat. The skins these traders acquired enabled them to buy valuable coastal products, such as seal oil and sealskin line, which they then sold at a substantial markup to people living in the interior. This trade likely developed gradually over the 18th century; by the beginning of the 19th, it may have been significant enough to make a few men wealthy even as judged by coastal standards.

Balancing Power and Responsibility

Nineteenth-century Western observers who commented on the subject were unanimous in their opinion that the span of control of an *umialik* did not extend beyond the limits of the compound family that he headed.[9] Furthermore, even within his own family, he could not compel obedience from anyone, except, perhaps, young children.

People who did not obey an *umialik*'s instructions were cut off from his largesse (Nelson 1899:305). In most instances, this reduced them to a lower material standard of living, which most people did not want. If they were unconcerned about their standard of living, or if they thought they could get along just as well living with or working for someone else, an *umialik* had no influence over them at all.

An *umialik* had considerable authority within his compound family. He decided such important matters as who could belong to the family and who could not; he decided when and where to move during the seasonal round; he conducted international trade and diplomacy; he mediated disputes within his own family and negotiated disputes with others; and he performed a number of important ceremonial and ritual functions. In all of these activities he was advised and assisted by his wife, and usually by other senior family members as well. A successful *umialik* listened more than he spoke. Simpson (1875:251) wrote of the Iñupiat, "As a people they are very communicative, those of most consideration being generally most silent; and wisdom is commonly imputed to those who talk least." But when an *umialik* did speak, people paid attention.

A major problem faced by an *umialik* was the fact that the Iñupiat were very jealous of anyone who accumulated much in the way of property or who attempted to place themselves ahead of the masses in any way.[10] This resentment was apparently felt more by the members of other families than the *umialik*'s own, since they were outside the daily redistribution network. Shamans were particularly upset by others' material wealth, since *umialgich* were the primary threats to their own power.

The primary way by which an *umialik* was held accountable for his actions was by withdrawal from the family (or the threat thereof) by subordinate members. Family members who disapproved of the way an *umialik* was acting generally or treating them personally simply moved out, or refused to join his whaling crew, or declined to help build a caribou drive fence for him. Since an *umialik* had no institutionalized means of physical coercion at his disposal, he was entirely dependent on the voluntary submission of others. Without the active support of family members, an *umialik* quickly ceased to be rich, and thus to be an *umialik*. Nelson (1877–81: entry for Sept. 5, 1880) put it even more strongly by saying that if the *umialik* "ceases his favors or tries to secure his own comfort before that of the others," he was doomed either to be killed or to have his possessions taken from him. The fact that some men were still considered *umialgich* when they were virtually in their dotage attests to the fact that support could continue beyond an *umialik*'s active years if he had commanded enough respect during them (Simpson 1850b: entry for Jan. 16–19, 1850).

In complex settlements, where the members of more than one compound family resided, matters were more complicated. In this context, an *umialik* had to attend to the affairs not only of his own family, but of others as well, especially in the *qargi*. It was in the public arena of a complex settlement that suitable demeanor was most important. As Thornton (1931:29) said of the wealthiest man in Wales in the early 1890s, his "every pose and movement and gesture is fraught with simple dignity and grace," this despite the fact that the man was known as a very hard-nosed trader. And it was in this arena that an *umialik* was subjected to the greatest test of both his wealth and his generosity, for he was expected to distribute food and other gifts not only to the members of his own family and *qargi*, but also to members of the general public (Nelson 1899:305). But if he carried this generosity too far, he would impoverish himself and his family, which meant he would lose not only his position as *umialik*, but also the support of the kinsmen who helped him achieve it.

Knowledge

Knowledge, both in the abstract and in the form of specific skills, was highly valued and respected by the Iñupiat. These qualities conveyed power through the general assent of the other people involved. As John Simpson (1875) stated,

> at the winter and summer festivals, when the people draw together for enjoyments, proficiency in music, with general knowledge of the customs and superstitions of their tribe, give to the most intelligent a further ascendancy over the multitude; and this sort of ascendancy once established, is retained without much effort (Simpson 1875:272–73).

In such small populations, ascertaining who knew most about what was fairly simple; it was demonstrated practically every day by what people said and did.

Knowledge conveyed power primarily within family units. In a few contexts, however, it was considerably broader in scope. In complex settlements, for example, where members of two or more different families belonged to each *qargi*, elders, as a group, wielded considerable influence over affairs in each of the families represented primarily because of their knowledge and experience. In another example, in the complex settlements of Point Hope and Wales, the division of a whale was carried out according to traditional rules that generally were well known to all the whaling captains. However, disputes did occur from time to time, particularly with regard to precisely where the lines between portions should be drawn.[11] If a wise and knowledgeable elder who had not been directly involved happened to be available, he might be called upon to adjudicate the matter. In a final illustration, the most knowledgeable beluga hunter among the Nuataaġmiut directed the coordinated beluga hunt carried out by practically all of his male countrymen.

Knowledge also conveyed power to a number of specialists. For example, a successful *iñuunniaqti* (tribal doctor) derived some influence from his/her knowledge of medicine and surgery. An *iḷisiiḷa* (clairvoyant) could see things happening far away and warn people of threats to their well-being. A *sivunniqsriqiri* (prophet) could see into the future and predict events before they happened, and a *quliaqtuaqti* (storyteller) was an expert on the historical chronicles and legends of his/her people. In each case, special knowledge conveyed the ability to influence the actions and opinions of others, sometimes to the point of being able to exact payment for their services. The greatest and most influential of the knowledge specialists, however, was the shaman (*aŋatkuq*).

Shamans

A shaman, or *aŋatkuq*, was a person who had an unusual ability to perceive, communicate with, and manipulate the spirit world. Those abilities enabled a shaman to heal the sick, divine the future, and perform a variety of other acts that relied heavily on magic for their success. In the eloquent and previously unpublished words of the late Don Charles Foote,

> It is difficult for us to believe the vast metaphysical powers the Eskimos had and which some still have. This group of human beings had developed methods by which man's will could invade and control realms of reality which, for us, remain still unbelievable and therefore, apparently, unattainable. For example, Eskimos could talk with animals. They could travel from Alaska to Siberia in seconds, visit the moon, disappear into the earth, walk on water, bring to life the dead, fly through the air, and communicate with friendly spirits.[12]

Some knowledge of how to do these things was fairly widespread among the Iñupiaq population. However, the individuals to whom the term *aŋatkuq* was applied could do more of them, and do them more effectively, than anyone else. Obviously, such people wielded considerable influence in the community. In 1884, Cantwell (1899b) reported that

> [t]he "shamans" whom we had occasion to deal with were observed to be more retiring and dignified in their bearing than what I was led to expect. . . . They were generally the last to make our acquaintance at a settlement and seldom remained long near our camp, which was a trait so unusual with the natives as to attract our attention at once (Cantwell 1889b:82).

The key to becoming an *aŋatkuq*, as noted in Chapter 2, was to acquire a "familiar" spirit (*qiḷa*).[13] A familiar was a spirit having a particularly close relationship with a person, and it was through the familiar that a shaman was able to relate to mystical phenomena in general and to other spirits in particular. Stefansson (1951) described how the system worked:

> A shaman among the Eskimos is in his own person no wiser than you or I. In every-day life he is quite as likely to do foolish things, quite as liable to be wrong; but when he goes into a trance his own spirit is superseded by the familiar spirit which enters his body, and it is the familiar spirit which talks through the mouth of the shaman. It is only then that his words become wisdom, on which you may rely unthinkingly (Stefansson 1951:412; see also Stoney 1900:835).

When a "spirit made his dwelling in a shaman, his chest was the spirit's 'house' and he had to speak the language of the spirit" (Ostermann and Holtved 1952:130). In order to understand what was involved here, it is helpful to have some understanding of the spirit world with which the Iñupiat were acquainted. What follows is a brief introduction to what I have called the "nonempirical environment" of northwestern Alaska (Burch 1971).

The Nonempirical Environment

Empirical phenomena are defined as "those phenomena about which data may be appre-hended directly through sensory perception (i.e., by one or more of the five following: taste, touch, sight, smell, or hearing), or indirectly inferred by the use of instruments in which a sensory chain of connection is clear or presumed to be clear" (Levy 1952:241). All other phenomena are nonempirical. Many people interpret these definitions to constitute a claim that nonempirical phenomena do not exist. That is not true at all. What they do imply is that one cannot *prove* that nonempirical phenomena do not exist. If a shaman claims to have communicated directly with his/her familiar spirit about a particular matter, there is no way to prove that he/she has not done so.

The empirical environment of northwestern Alaska consisted of the landscapes, climate, animals, vegetation, liquids, and minerals summarily described in Chapter 1, and alluded to throughout much of Chapter 4. Twenty-first-century Westerners and early-19th-century Iñupiat likely would have agreed on its basic structure and composition, even though per-ceiving and analyzing it somewhat differently. The nonempirical environment, on the other hand, although well known to the Iñupiat, was completely beyond the ken of Westerners. It is that environment that is of interest here.

The nonempirical environment of northwestern Alaska consisted of the souls of people and animals, and of a wide assortment of creatures and other phenomena generally outside the Western experience.[14] These included gigantic eagles, fish, shrews, and other animals; tiny humanlike creatures who had enormous speed and strength; weird babies with huge mouths; dragons; mermaids; trolls; and a broad array of phenomena generically called *tuuṅgat* (pl.). *Tuuṅgat* were usually invisible, although sometimes they manifested themselves as shadows, patches of light, or small fires. Some of them could move about; others could not. A few were simply disembodied voices. When possessed by their familiar spirits, shamans could see and communicate with such phenomena, but no one else could unless the particular entity involved chose to make itself visible. Even some features of the landscape were endowed with mystical power. If a person fell asleep in the wrong place, for example, or looked at a forbidden topographic feature, that person died.

All of these phenomena were believed to be sentient entities imbued with some kind of life force (*iñuułiq*). The great majority were hostile to humans and needed to be placated if people were to survive. Also in need of constant attention were the spirits of the animals on which the Iñupiat relied for sustenance (Ostermann and Holtved 1952:35). These were offended if the carcasses of the animals that permitted themselves to be killed were treated in a manner they deemed improper. Placating them involved obeying an enormous number of prohibitions, or taboos, and performing nearly as great a number of rituals.[15] Failure to comply with these requirements led inevitably to a calamity of some kind.

Taboos

A common misconception of the Iñupiat political process was expressed more than a century ago by John Cantwell (1889b:82), who wrote that "where there are no laws it follows that there is no necessity for rulers, and so it is with all these tribes." It is true that the Iñupiat lacked rulers, but they were subject to an enormous number of laws, in the form of taboos, and they were required to perform a large number of rituals. My oldest informants, who were born in the 1880s, often commented on the bewildering number and variety of rules they had had to obey as children, and how strict adults had been concerning them. As Robert

Cleveland (1970.2) put it, "There were lots of laws. They were worst before the white people came. There were *lots* of them! . . . The White people don't have many laws compared to those old people."

My general understanding of taboos was informed to a significant extent by both the general comments of Vilhjalmur Stefansson[16] and more specific information provided by many other sources.[17] According to Stefansson, there were probably no things, conditions, actions, locations, or relations that one could conceive of that were not potentially subject to being tabooed. Some taboos applied generally to the members of a society or settlement, others only to certain age groups or to members of one sex. Other variables included the time of year and the location.

The system of taboos was unbelievably complex. This is illustrated in the following example:

> In the mountains of Alaska, on the upper Kuvuk [Kobuk] and Noatak rivers, and on the headwaters of the Colville, the prohibitions which applied to the eating of the flesh of the mountain sheep alone were as extensive as the entire dietary section of the Mosaic law. A young girl, for instance, might eat only certain ribs; and when she was a little older she might eat certain other ribs; but when she was full grown she would for a time have to abstain from eating the ribs which had been allowed to her up to then. After a woman had had her first child, she might eat certain other ribs, after her second child still others, and only after having five children might she eat all the ribs; but even then she must not eat the membranes on the inside of the ribs. If her child was sick, she must not eat certain ribs, and if two of her children were sick, she might not eat certain other ribs. If her brother's child was sick, she might not eat certain portions; and if her brother's wife died, there were still different prohibitions. The taboos applying to the ribs of the sheep had relation to the health of her children and of her relatives. They also depended upon what animals her relatives or herself had killed recently, and on whether those animals were male or female.
>
> When all the compulsory taboos were remembered and complied with, there were still some optional ones. If she wanted her daughter to be a good seamstress, she would observe certain taboos with regard to the mountain sheep, and if her son was to be a good hunter, there was a different set of rules to be followed; when her son had killed his first game, there was still another variation, and so on (Stefansson 1951:410–11).

Taboo requirements applied equally to the wealthiest and the poorest members of a society. Stefansson (1914b) summarized how the system worked:

> In certain things a man may be aglirktok [under taboo] at birth and will have to remain so forever by reason of the tribe to which he belongs. . . . In other cases a man may become aglirktok automatically, as it were, by attaining a certain age or by having certain things that are in the nature of natural development happen to either himself or some relative or intimate associate. All these cases are fairly definite and are easily known and kept in mind with the result that offenses against the aglirktok condition are rare and the consequent misfortunes and punishments assigned to a breach of conduct are not likely to occur.
>
> Under certain conditions, however, a man may become aglirktok without knowing it. If, for instance, he lives in another community from that occupied by his relatives and were one of those relatives to die, certain articles of food and dress and certain lines of conduct would become prohibited and the violation of this prohibition would similarly become punishable but the man under the taboo would know nothing of it by reason of not knowing that his relative is dead. He

would then be likely or almost certain to break the taboo with attendant evil consequence to himself, his friends, and family and to the community at large. It is in connection with a misfortune that comes without assignable cause that the shamans go into seance and inquire who it is that is aglirktok and why. When they find out and tell the right man that he is aglirktok the misfortunes are likely to cease if the man acknowledges his fault and commences to observe the taboo (Stefansson 1914b:126–27).

In the passage just quoted, Stefansson identifies a number of key issues concerning the political consequences of taboos and rituals. The first is that an entire community could be negatively affected by just one person breaking a taboo or failing to perform a required ritual. This led people to monitor each other's behavior to make sure the rules were being followed. Second, when something went wrong, it was assumed at the outset that it was because someone had broken a taboo or failed to perform a required ritual. If a person fell and broke a leg, for example, while the break itself might be interpreted and initially treated in strictly empirical terms, the fact that the accident occurred in the first place would be attributed to some supernatural force having been annoyed. Third, it was the shaman's job to find out who had committed the infraction, and which taboo had been broken or which ritual had not been performed. This was a major source of shamanic influence, since ordinary people were not able to challenge a shaman's diagnosis.

Finally, there was the element of confession. Again quoting Stefansson (1914b):

> One of the most fundamental of the religious ideas of the Eskimo is this, that supernatural punishments come not so much on account of evil things as on account of their remaining unconfessed. If a famine occurs, for instance, a shaman will magically inquire from his familiar spirit why the food has become scarce and the answer is likely to be that some member of the tribe has done such and such a thing in secret. A woman may perhaps have eaten the meat from the wrong rib of a mountain sheep. When the spirit informs the medicineman that the woman has done this, he calls upon her to confess that she has done it. If she confesses the famine will end and all will be well, but if she brazenly asserts that she has done no such things as charged with, then the most serious misfortunes will continue to fall upon the people. A person who stubbornly refuses to confess is therefore a public enemy and will be treated accordingly. In extreme cases it may become necessary to kill a person who is incorrigible. This is rare, however, seeing that no punishment will fall upon one who has broken a taboo provided he confesses, it is obviously simpler and better to confess to a thing one has not done than to be punished for not confessing (Stefansson 1914b:128).

In some situations, one could avoid disaster by confessing promptly after the transgression occurred. Apparently, a proactive confession could be made to only a single individual (rather than to the public at large) and still be effective (A. Hawley 1965.7). However, in order for this to work, one had to be aware of one's mistake, which often was not the case.

Rituals

A subject not often singled out for attention in the literature on the Iñupiat is the myriad small rituals that had to be performed in order to appease the many malevolent spirits residing in the countryside of northwestern Alaska.[18] These rituals were not unlike taboos, and they are usually discussed under the heading of taboos; indeed, both fall within the Iñupiaq category of agliġnaq–. However, there is a useful analytic difference between them: taboos are rules *against* doing something, whereas rituals are prescriptions *for* doing something.

Rituals involved such things as offering a sea mammal carcass a drink of fresh water prior to butchering; failure to do so offended its spirit and resulted in a poor future harvest of that species. Just how complicated the system of rituals was is illustrated by those performed by the Akuniġmiut in the preparation for eating a brown bear.

> The skin is removed from the head and the head cut off. A native then takes it and standing astride the body with the head in both hands raises it high in the air and lowers it three times, touching the body each time just over the heart and muttering an incantation. After the third touch he throws the head with all his might so as to hit the same spot over the heart and utters a loud shout in which all the natives join. This ceremony is supposed to drive the bear's spirit to the mountains. After removing the skin the abdomen is opened with more superstitious observations; but never in the presence of a white man; and certain parts of the animal are left on the ground, for to remove them would drive the deer from the mountains. The ears are always cut off the skin (Stoney 1900:838–39).

A larger number of rituals were associated with the killing and processing of brown bears than with most other animals (Ostermann and Holtved 1952:117; Stefansson 1914b:347), but wolves and wolverines were not far behind (Ostermann and Holtved 1952:36–37, 118–20; Seveck 1951; Sunno 1951.107). The pursuit of no other animal, however, could compete with a bowhead whale hunt with respect to the number or complexity of associated rituals; even a partial catalogue of those associated with this activity has never been compiled. In addition to hunting, areas of life in which rituals played an important part were childbirth, various stages of childhood, menarche, death, and homicide.

Rituals under discussion here differed from a number of other ceremonies performed by the Iñupiat. Those of present concern were compulsory; failure to perform them, like the breaking of a taboo, automatically and inevitably led to trouble. Most of the other ceremonies were performed to increase the chances of success, not to prevent certain disaster. As with taboos, the shamans were the ones who first learned the necessary procedures. They were also the ones who discovered a lapse and prescribed a remedy.

Balancing Power and Responsibility

The influence shamans exercised over others derived from two primary sources. The first was their nearly exclusive ability to provide a number of services deemed critical to survival. These included healing the sick, warding off evil forces, mediating relations between people and both the empirical and nonempirical environments, predicting the future, locating lost people, and providing entertainment with demonstrations of their virtuosity. For all of these services except the last, shamans charged a fee.[19] This varied according to "the gravity of the case and the wealth of the patient" (Thornton 1931:101), and, at least in the case of male shamans, sometimes included sexual access to a particularly desirable woman (Northwest Iñupiat Elders Conference 1976e:9–10). According to Woolfe (1893:139), who observed them in the 1880s, shamans kept "the people poor by demanding their entire property for their work, and if the patient's family have nothing on hand that they desire exact promises to pay in whalebone, furs, or ivory." In support of this assertion, Woolfe (1839) claimed to know of:

> individuals who have been bereft of every article and piece of property to satisfy the demands of these thieves [i.e., the shamans]. In this manner they become the wealthiest of the tribe, according to their celebrity and number of cures effected or their luck in prognosticating events (Woolfe 1893:139; see also Call 1899:116; Ostermann and Holtved 1952:130–31).

In March of 1885, Kiḷagraq, the *umialik* at the settlement near where Kotzebue now stands, had a son who had a serious lung ailment. Kiḷagraq complained to Charles Brower (ms:162) that he had "tried all the An-et-kok's [*sic*] there were any where around, and they had done his son no good, but they were slowly getting considerable of his wealth." Charlie Sheldon (1973–74.3) described a shaman named Akiñaaluk who was "rich. He's got more than one cache filled up with all kinds of fur: lynx, beaver, land otter, wolverine, all kinds of valuable furs like marten and minks." By charging high fees, the most effective *aŋatkut* usually became *umialgich* as well, accruing even more power in the process.

The second source of shamanic influence was fear. How this worked was indicated by Stefansson (1951):

> When in a trance the shaman is the mouth-piece of a spirit, and at any time, by the use of the formulae by which the spirits are controlled, he can get them to do his bidding, be it good or ill. For that reason, the shaman is deferred to, irrespective of whether you like him personally or not, and without regard to what you may think of his character and natural abilities, except that the more you fear he may be disposed to evil actions, the more careful you are not to give him offense, and to comply with everything he commands or intimates, for (being evilly disposed) he may punish you harshly if you incur his displeasure (Stefansson 1951:412–13).

This assessment was echoed by Rasmussen (in Ostermann and Holtved 1952):

> [M]ankind was therefore threatened by bad, or evil angagkut, who because of their ambitions, vindictiveness, craving for power, or wickedness, struck people with sickness. The fact that people believed the shamans capable of controlling all sickness gave them extremely high power and influence (1952:130).

Thus, while shamans were often seen as being among the most valuable members of a settlement, they were also regarded as being among the most dangerous.[20] They were subject to the same array of base and noble sentiments as ordinary people, but were said to have been particularly resentful of the material success of others. This sometimes placed them in at least covert opposition to *umialgich*. When they were evilly inclined, they were sometimes willing, and often able, to bring considerable harm to other individuals, families, and even entire nations. Accidents, blizzards, and other calamities were just as likely to be caused by disgruntled shamans as they were by the breaking of a taboo or the failure to perform a ritual (Ostermann and Holtved 1952:131). One of the most famous examples of harm at the national level involved Samaruna, an *aŋatkuq* and *umialik* from Point Hope. Just before he was murdered, he put a curse on the Kivalliñiġmiut which precipitated the Great Famine of 1881–83 (Jensen 1970.4; see also Burch 1998a:47–50). So many people starved to death in that catastrophe that the Kivalliñiġmiut ceased to exist as an independent nation.[21]

It was very difficult to hold shamans effectively accountable for any disruptive activities they caused because of the extent to which their work involved nonempirical elements. Even a shaman who publicly appeared reasonable and helpful might secretly be working black magic. For this reason, otherwise inexplicable calamities were sometimes blamed on shamans (C. Sheldon 1973–74.20). Sometimes two shamans from either the same or different settlements struggled against one another through the medium of their respective familiars, a contest their companions did not even know about.[22] On the other hand, sometimes two shamans cooperated to produce generally favorable results (C. Sheldon 1973–74.2, 1973–74.18). The only certain way to bring an evil shaman's activities to a halt was to kill him/her, and then adhere to a number of taboos or perform a series of rituals to make sure that he/she stayed dead.[23]

Feuds

A feud (*akisaqłuk*) was a prolonged state of conflict between the members of two different (usually compound) families from the same nation. Feuds could be nonviolent, as when two or more families in a complex settlement competed in trying to dominate village affairs by strength of numbers, slander, arguments, and perhaps a few shoving matches (Jensen 1970.6; Rainey 1940.4). Since Iñupiaq societies lacked overriding institutions (such as courts) in terms of which interfamily disputes could be mediated in a structured way, however, these situations sometimes deteriorated into armed conflict.[24]

Rainey (1947) summarized the process as follows:

> The causes given by informants for the origin of feuds are often trivial: two men disagree over the ownership of a duck shot while hunting and one kills the other; a man beats his wife and she, seeking revenge, prevails upon one of her relatives to kill him; whaling captains disagree over the division of a whale, and so forth. Of course a killing always precipitated the feud which might develop from that point into a series of isolated, retaliatory murders, or into a pitched battle. At times, it is said, all the able-bodied men from one extended family met those from another group in front of their houses and fought until all the men in one group were killed. In such battles men wore armor made of bone plates and fought with lances or with bows. The outcome of such struggles might remain undecided for long periods, during which each house or house group posted sentries to avert a surprise attack and all the men went hunting as a well-armed party. Killings on the pack ice were not uncommon when a man became separated from his group (1947:242).

Much more common than these relatively large-scale encounters, which seem to have been limited to complex settlements and which were rare even there, was the "series of isolated, retaliatory murders" mentioned by Rainey (1947:242).[25] The sequence began when one person killed another. At that point, the oldest active close male relative of the deceased incurred the obligation to kill the murderer. When he had achieved that goal, the oldest male relative of the second victim incurred the obligation to retaliate. And so on. Theoretically, there was no end to the process.

Avengers operated by stealth, not through an open encounter. Most people killed in retaliation were shot in the back or while they were asleep, sometimes years and possibly even decades after the initial incident. It would be interesting to know what went through the mind of a murderer who lived for months or years in the same settlement as the person he knew had an obligation to kill him. Some murderers left town, but this was not always easy unless they had relatives living elsewhere who were willing to support them (Thornton 1931:41). More confident individuals simply girded themselves for battle and continued with their ordinary affairs, albeit presumably with increased watchfulness.

An example of a person who followed the second of the above alternatives was Samaruna, the Tikiġaġmiu who was mentioned above as the man who put the curse on the Kivalliñiġmiut leading to the Great Famine. In the summer of 1853, he and Aŋunisua, from Point Barrow, killed one of Samaruna's cousins in retaliation for his murder of Samaruna's brother and several others, and for threatening Aŋunisua (Bockstoce ed. 1988, I:303, 353, 357). The cousin was killed while sleeping. Subsequently, Samaruna went about his affairs while his enemies "shot numerous arrows at him many of which struck him but were turned by a coat of mail he wore under his coat" (Simpson 1852–54: entry for April 5, 1854; the "coat of mail" was probably ivory slat armor). Samaruna was estimated to have been about thirty-five at the time (Bockstoce ed. 1988, I:169), and he managed to live nearly another thirty years before he was assassinated by the Kivalliñiġmiut.

Bringing the cycle of retribution to a halt was not an easy matter. The only successful procedure I have heard of was for a murderer to present himself to his victim's relatives and offer to let them kill him. If they did, the cycle continued. If they declined, however, they were considered to have lost the right to perpetuate the feud. Offering oneself in this manner was a risky proposition, and probably was done only if the deceased had been such a troublemaker that the murderer had reason to believe that the relatives might approve of his action. In the case of extreme troublemakers, the relatives themselves carried out the execution, hence no feud would result from it.

A few examples will illustrate the above points. The first involves a man named Kupatquq, who caught a cousin stealing his caribou snares (A. Hawley 1965.5). When Kupatquq scolded him, the cousin told him that if he didn't like it, he should go ahead and kill him. So Kupatquq took out his bow and an arrow and shot, aiming low since he intended merely to frighten his cousin. However, the arrow ricocheted off the hard snow and hit his cousin in the chest, killing him instantly. Kupatquq was very ashamed of what he had done, and went immediately to see one of the dead man's brothers, who lived in another settlement. That brother forgave him. Kupatquq then went to his cousin's oldest brother, in still a third settlement. After hearing the story, this man told Kupatquq that his brother had received what he deserved for stealing the snares. And that is where the matter ended.

A second case involved a man named Iquluq, who heard that his sister's husband had killed one of his wives (Martha Swan 1965.1). Iquluq began to worry that the same fate might befall his sister (whose name had been forgotten by my source). So Iquluq and his father, Aqargiayuaq, went to the settlement where the sister and her husband lived, arriving while the latter was out hunting. They grabbed the woman and left, telling her husband's relatives to tell him not to follow. When they were partway home they saw her husband running after them; he was so angry that he had even forgotten to bring any weapons. Iquluq and Aqargiayuaq told the woman to keep going, then hid behind some driftwood. When the husband drew near, they stood up and shouted at him to turn around and go home. But he kept coming, so they shot him in the chest and the head, killing him. The next fall Aqargiayuaq returned to the settlement where the dead man had lived, defying the deceased's relatives to kill him. But they were afraid of him, and did nothing. Later, one of the dead man's brothers told Aqargiayuaq not to worry about it; the dead man had gotten what he deserved, and there were no hard feelings.

The final case involved a man named Apalliq, a known murderer who delighted in taking other men's wives.[26] Everyone was afraid to oppose him because he was a very powerful shaman. One day he decided to take Alalak as his wife, despite the fact that she had not yet reached puberty. Alalak's brother, Atchuġnaq, and father, Iñuŋniiḷaq, were adamantly opposed to the marriage because of her age and her suitor's notoriety, and they forbade it. Apalliq persisted, however, and finally Atchuġnaq and his father killed him. Iñuŋniiḷaq was subsequently murdered himself while seal hunting, but no one has been able to connect his death to the assassination of Apalliq.

Discussion

Power and responsibility were usually allocated among family members in a fairly subtle manner. This was feasible because Iñupiaq daily life was relatively simple and straightforward, and the number of individuals involved was very small. People went about their customary business one day pretty much as they had the day before, and as they would do again the next.

Adherence to taboos and the performance of required rituals was an ironclad rule for everyone, including chieftains and shamans. Beyond that, individuals, including even children, had considerable freedom of action in how they spent their time (Bodenhorn 1997:112). For example, if a youngster insisted on riding on a sled instead of walking beside it or helping push, he was not prevented from doing so. If a man did not feel like hunting or repairing a broken sled on a particular day, well, that was his choice. Even a whaling captain could never be absolutely certain who would appear to man the boat or share in the work, or how long crew members would stay as the whaling season neared conclusion.[27] Apparently, individuals sometimes did not participate in collective enterprises when expected to simply to assert their independence. On the other hand, everyone had to contribute at least something to the common good if the unit was to persist, and most people understood that. Past experience and general conversation in the home and in the *qargi* usually produced enough information for each individual to know what was expected of, or needed from, him or her, all day every day.

The problem was what to do with people who failed to produce what they were capable of producing, who were greedy or selfish, or who were cranky or otherwise difficult to get along with, on a prolonged basis. If a man chose *never* to go hunting, for example, but still drew food from the common stock, he was a parasite, and hence a troublemaker. A person who was always complaining, or who tried to take more than his/her share of meat, was also a troublemaker. Veiled hints about his/her behavior might be expressed from time to time by other members of the family. If veiled hints did not suffice, more focused suggestions, or even explicit instructions and orders might be issued by someone farther up the chain of command. In most cases, these sufficed.

A special relationship that held an interesting place in the political process was that of *iḷḷuġiik* (dual). This was the "joking cousin" relationship involving cross cousins (i.e., cousins who were the descendants of brothers and sisters). Albert Heinrich (1955a:101–3), who obtained more information on this relationship than I did, argued that it was a focal point of social control. Everything I learned about it is consistent with his findings. Joking cousins often commented critically and publicly on the negative aspects of one another's behavior. Although usually phrased in the form of sarcastic and even biting humor designed to evoke laughter from the audience, the remarks were also presented with a view to curbing some flaw in the activities of the person to whom they were directed. As Heinrich (1955a) said,

> the cajolery, admonishing, raibaldry [sic], ridicule and sarcasm that are permissible under the guise of this kinship form sometimes reach astonishing proportions, especially when we consider that it can obtain between sexes (1955a:102).

Unfortunately, at this remove in time, it is impossible to know just how pervasive and effective this type of activity was in reducing disruptive behavior during the study period, but it must have helped.

Another mechanism for holding troublemakers responsible for their actions may have been the song duel, a contest between two people who sang derisory songs about each other's behavior. This was done in front of an audience, the members of whom in effect formed a jury; the person who persuaded them to accept his or her version won the contest. Just how common this practice was in the study region is unclear. I did not hear about it myself, and I have seen only two references to it in other sources, one of which described it as a contest between men from different nations.[28]

In the absence of courts and judges, the only really acceptable way one could deal with an unsatisfactory marriage, family, *qargi*, or settlement was to withdraw. No one could stop a person, or a married couple and their children, from leaving. People who did not like the social context in which they lived were free to leave, although it was difficult to do this safely unless there were alternative families they could join. Similarly, a marriage could be broken off by either spouse if it became too stressful, although it was sometimes problematic when only one partner wanted the break.

Conversely, if a troublemaker refused to submit to the leaders of his family or *qargi* or to the general will of the other members, the next step at his companions' disposal was ostracism (D. Ray 1967:379–90). This was difficult to impose, since Iñupiat lived in such close quarters. It apparently involved people pretending that the troublemaker did not exist, even when he/she was in their midst. This would have made the culprit's life miserable, hence presumably would have produced a behavioral change most of the time. If it did not, the next step was banishment. This was the outright expulsion of the offending party from the dwelling, *qargi*, or settlement, by force if necessary. This amounted to a sentence of death if the person could not find other people with whom he or she could live. As John Kelly (Wells and Kelly 1890:24) so eloquently put it, "Outlawed by their tribe or relations, they become discouraged, hopeless, and gloomy, and literally 'go off and die.'" Presumably, most people threatened with this fate altered their behavior. In extreme cases, troublemakers, especially violent ones or people who repeatedly broke taboos, were killed by their own close relatives. This act, which did not initiate a blood feud, was the ultimate recourse in an Iñupiaq society.

Iñupiaq families were politically self-sufficient to a high degree. This does not mean that they were free of stress and strain; far from it. What it does mean is that they were generally able to contain the strains generated within them.

The level of political self-sufficiency was probably highest in large compound families whose members comprised the sole inhabitants of a settlement. With perhaps forty to sixty members, these units were sufficiently large to include enough men to prevent a bully from dominating the others, while small enough for the family head to provide effective leadership and guidance for the unit. As the only family in the settlement, the problem of interfamily relations did not exist. Families of this size were also large enough to mount an effective defense against enemy raiders, although not against a full-scale invasion.

In complex settlements, inter- (compound) family relations were a theoretical, and often an actual, source of stress. On the one hand, this was because there was competition between compound families for wealth, prestige, and influence. On the other, it was because there was neither an office nor an organization with a settlement-wide span of authority. Peace and harmony in such a settlement depended on the agreeable attitudes of the people, and on the strength of character, wisdom, and self-discipline of, and the degree of authority wielded by, the *umialgich* heading the different families. Most of the time people tended to their affairs without difficulty, but when trouble arose, it was difficult to contain. However, settlements of this size were the most capable of defending themselves against an attack by foreigners.

The least politically self-sufficient unit in an Iñupiaq nation was probably the domestic family of eight or so people whose members comprised an entire settlement. On the one hand, this would seem to be counterintuitive, since a unit with so few members was less likely to include a troublemaker than a unit with many; it was very self-contained. The problem was how so few people could deal with the rare person who did cause trouble. If a powerful bully raped his sister-in-law, then beat up his jealous wife and outraged brother in order to forestall retribution, who would hold him accountable? How would accountability be imposed? In a larger family or settlement, others could be called upon for help. In a small one, there was little recourse except to try to flee from or kill the tyrant, both highly problematic courses of action. Tiny settlements were also extremely vulnerable to attacks by raiders from another country.

The International Arena

An Iñupiaq nation did not exist in isolation, but was surrounded by other nations peopled by speakers of Eskimo, Chukchi, or Athapaskan languages and dialects. The members of these nations had to be dealt with on a yearly, seasonal, and sometimes more frequent basis. I have treated the issues involved here in considerable detail in another volume (Burch 2005), so only a general outline is presented here. The subjects discussed are defense, border maintenance, and alliances.

Defense

On the basis of his experiences in the summer of 1838, Kashevarov (VanStone ed. 1977:81) characterized the Iñupiat as "warlike." He had every reason to think so, for the members of his party were threatened time and again by hostile Iñupiat during his two-month trip along the coast, and his Native interpreter was frequently told that certain nations were enemies of one another (VanStone ed. 1977:26, 27, 36, 42, 43, 59–61). Kotzebue (1821, I:204–5, 225) was similarly threatened in 1816, while Vasil'ev in 1820 (D. Ray 1983c:34–37) and Beechey in 1827 (F. Beechey 1831, I:423–24, 426; II:283–87) were actually attacked.

The experiences of these early European explorers were consistent with the oral history of the region, which includes a substantial record of terrorist forays, raids, and battles (Burch 2005:259–73). In 1924, after listening to several of these accounts, Knud Rasmussen (1933) concluded that the Iñupiat

> appear to have been a warlike people, their young men being regularly trained for war, hardening themselves by all manner of athletic exercises, dieting themselves, and often obliged to fast in order to habituate themselves to great hardships, or making journeys on foot for many days in succession as a test of endurance (Rasmussen 1933:306).

In all of these respects, the Iñupiat were similar to their non-Iñupiaq neighbors.

Just why the people of northwestern Alaska were so warlike is the subject of some dispute. Glenn Sheehan (1995:190–91; 1997:202–3) contends that warfare was promoted by imbalances in international trade. He may be right on a very abstract level, although I do not think there is sufficient evidence to either support or challenge his conclusion in a definitive manner. I also do not think that imbalances in international trade were on the minds of the people who were actually involved. What was on their minds was revenge.[29] The members of one society attacked the members of another not for booty or slaves, which they did not seek, but in order to pay back some real or imagined grudge left over from some incident in the recent or remote past. Since the members of these nations had been in contact with one another for centuries, they could cite a whole catalogue of grievances against their neighbors if they had a mind to do so. All that was required to precipitate a raid or more general assault was a catalyst, such as an insulting remark or a fight during an international football game during the Sisualik fair.

Sometimes the issues involved were more substantial. For example, raiders usually tried to kill everyone in the target settlement, men, women, and children—except for one or two. These they intentionally let escape (J. Foster 1970; Jensen 1970.4, 1970.5, 1980.1). The same practice was followed after an open battle in which one side was clearly victorious. Allegedly, this was done so that the one or two survivors on the losing side could unambiguously identify for their countrymen the nation whose members had perpetrated the massacre. This information was intended to intimidate them, and thus subject them to further domination by the victorious side. However, one would have to assume that even if this was the initial result, a massacre would lead eventually to an attempt to even the score.

Given the circumstances just described, it may be understood that people had to proceed on the assumption that they could be attacked at any time. Eternal vigilance was the standard practice. To some extent this was accomplished through the daily forays of hunters scanning the landscape around their settlement for game. Any strangers in the vicinity would have been observed, reported, and probably attacked. Vigilance was also achieved by keeping weapons in good condition and close at hand at all times. The early historic literature supports the oral accounts on this point. When Kotzebue (1821) visited Northwest Alaska in 1816, for example, he found the Iñupiat armed to the teeth.

> Their arms consist of lances, bows, arrows, and a knife, two feet [60 cm] long, in
> a sheath; this military equipment, which they never lay aside, proves that they
> are in constant wars with other nations (Kotzebue 1821, I:211).

Similarly, in 1838, Kashevarov (VanStone ed. 1977:89) observed that "[t]he Eskimo devotes every spare moment to making or repairing his weapons. Wherever he goes he takes his bow and quiver of arrows with him." Men even took their weapons with them to the *qargi*, knowing that a favorite tactic of raiders was to trap everyone inside that building and annihilate them as they tried to escape (Burch 2005:99–100).

People employed other preventive measures in addition to vigilance. For example, the houses of small inland settlements were often built in willow thickets, both to hide their location and to make it difficult for strangers to approach them in silence. The houses of people living in small coastal settlements were sometimes located on the inland side of beach ridges in order to hide them from coastal raiders. The major Qikiqtaġruŋmiut settlement of Taksruq Saaŋa was located between the waters of Kotzebue Sound and those of a long narrow lagoon. Enemy raiders coming from interior districts had to cross the lagoon in order to attack the village, and when they did so, they could be easily seen from the settlement in both summer and winter (Elwood Hunnicutt 1970). Similarly, Qigiqtaq, the major settlement of the Tapqaġmiut, was situated on an island, at least in part for the same reason.

The most elaborate defense mechanism was employed at the large settlement of Point Hope, which was located at the end of a long spit. As noted in Chapter 3, the Tikiġaġmiut planted in the ground three rows of short, sharp bone and baleen stakes (sing. *sukisaq*) the whole way across the spit on the inland side of the houses, leaving only a few secret avenues local people could use to leave or enter the settlement (Jensen 1970.4, 1970.5, 1980.1).

On one occasion, raiders from the upper Colville River tried to cross this equivalent of a minefield and ended up with their boots and feet pierced by spikes. When the Point Hopers went out the next morning, they discovered their prospective assailants lying helplessly on the ground and leisurely killed them all (Jensen 1980.1). The only way nighttime raiders could approach without running the risk of having their boots and feet pierced by stakes was along the beaches, where stakes were quickly washed out by wave action. Even then, the stakes severely limited invaders' ability to maneuver, an important tactical element when attacking such a large settlement. Even if they managed to pass this barrier, a favorite tactic of the defenders was to drive the enemy back into the staked area, where they could be easily dispatched.

A final element in preventing or anticipating attacks was espionage. This was carried out in two very different contexts. One involved one, two, or perhaps three men from one nation paying a clandestine visit to the estate of another. Known as *iññuqutit* (pl.), these men prowled around the countryside, almost always in late summer (Burch 2005). They observed the size and location of enemy settlements, and often engaged in some kind of mischief, such as stealing fish or meat from a cache or drying rack, or even murdering someone. They did this to alert the local people to the fact that they had been there. I have never been able to learn what motivated *iññuqutit*. Whatever their intentions, the mischief had the effect of terrorizing the local population, and their survey provided intelligence on where enemy settlements were situated and how they could be approached.

The second context in which espionage took place was during peaceful international gatherings, of which there were two basic types: so-called "trade fairs," on the one hand, and messenger festivals, on the other. During these events, but particularly the fairs, people from two or more nations came together peacefully to trade, dance, hold athletic competitions, feast, and generally have a good time. During the course of these proceedings they learned a lot about recent and current events in other countries. If plans for an invasion were afoot, they were sometimes revealed, intentionally or otherwise. Given this information, those scheduled to be attacked could increase their vigilance and perhaps even make specific plans for defending themselves.

Border Maintenance

People in northwestern Alaska visited the estates of other nations in three different contexts. I have termed these easement, license, and trespass (Burch 2005:28–33). Easements were standing permits for people from one nation regularly to use or cross the estate of another for specific purposes and at specific times of year. They involved patterns developed at some ancient and unknown time, hence may be said to have been based on traditional use. These uses were so well established by the beginning of the study period that any attempt by the estate owners to stop them would have been considered an act of war.

License, in contrast, involved explicit permission granted by the members of one nation to those of another to cross, or to hunt or fish in, the estate of the latter. License was based on a specific request, and was granted on a one-time basis. A typical example was when people wanted to cross a foreign estate in order to participate in a messenger festival in a third country. License would have to have been granted by a nation's leading men, but I was unable to learn just how this would have been arranged among the widely dispersed settlements in most of the nations in the study region.

All other uses of a nation's estate by outsiders were considered trespass. National borders were sufficiently well defined and well known for there to be no doubt about precisely which type of encroachment was involved in any given case.

Many national borders in northwestern Alaska coincided with ecological thresholds, such as the divides of mountain ranges and the tree line (see Burch 1998a:310–12 for a discussion of border location). In other cases, the land along a border was either unproductive, or else much less productive than the core areas of adjacent nations' estates. In such cases, people sensibly preferred to live in the heartland rather than near the margin. It might be said that, wherever these factors were importantly involved, borders were maintained at least as much by environmental factors as by social ones. But there were other cases—particularly along the Selawik and Kobuk rivers, along the eastern and northern shore of Kotzebue Sound and the lower Noatak River, and along the northern coast of the Seward Peninsula—where borders had to have been maintained by social, demographic, or historical factors.

Trespass was considered an act of war, and was continually guarded against. However, the national estates of the study region were too large, and the national populations were too small, for people even to consider guarding their borders. Since the best places to live in the majority of cases were in the interior of a nation's estate rather than on the margin, it was the core, rather than the periphery, that was guarded in any meaningful sense. However, the entire estate was defended against any trespassers who were found in it. As Charlie Jensen (1970.6) put it, "they didn't want to see other man who belonged to the other country" in their own.

Trespassers were usually discovered accidentally by men hunting out in the country or on the frozen ocean. Inland, they sometimes found iññuqutit or perhaps small parties of caribou hunters who had overstepped their bounds in pursuit of their prey. Alternatively, they discovered men on the frozen ocean who had been hunting seals on the ice and drifted out to sea on the floating pack, only to come ashore in a foreign territory. In either case, if they were spotted, and if a sufficient number of men on the home side could be mustered in time, the intruders were captured and killed, often after being tortured. The certainty of this happening kept deliberate trespass by individuals or small parties to a minimum. Usually it involved desperate circumstances, such as a famine at home or the misfortune of a drifted seal hunter.

Trespass on a relatively large scale, involving, say, a dozen or more men, was deliberately undertaken with bloodshed in mind. Small war parties usually intended to make a surprise nighttime raid on a particular settlement (Burch 2005:99–104). They traveled at night, stayed out of heavily used localities as much as possible, and generally tried to maintain the element of surprise until the moment their attack was launched. Large parties, involving several dozen individuals or more, traveled openly. As they approached the enemy settlements, they put on headbands with one feather behind each ear, and brandished their weapons (Martha Swan 1965.1). Their objective was to provoke the intended victims into marshaling their own force to meet them in open battle somewhere on the way (Burch 2005:104–7).

It is a curious fact that the most frequent applications of international force in northwestern Alaska occurred between and among nations whose estates had borders that were ecologically constrained, while the least frequent applications were between those with little or nothing in the way of environmental barriers between them. Thus, the Akuniġmiut of the central Kobuk valley and the Nuataaġmiut of the upper Noatak valley had many brutal confrontations, yet the border between them followed the divide of the Baird Mountains, a significant environmental barrier. On the other hand, the Akuniġmiut seem to have gotten along quite well with the neighboring Kuuŋmiut of the Kobuk River delta despite the absence of any significant environmental threshold between them. In these cases I am forced to resort to an earlier conclusion:

> [T]he locations of the borders between their [estates] must have been the result of generations of give and take among the people concerned. People simply had to work out, through negotiation or force, just where the borders would be (Burch 1998a:312).

Unfortunately, I am not aware of any evidence revealing how this process worked.

The political map of northwestern Alaska was not entirely static during the study period. For example, there is evidence that the northeastern sector of the Tikiġaġmiut estate was forcefully taken over by the interior-dwelling Utuqqaġmiut in the late 18th or early 19th century (Burch 1981:12). However, this was very marginal fall and winter habitat for the Tikiġaġmiut. It was remote from the main population centers, and probably was very weakly defended, if it was defended at all. In summer, when it was important to the Tikiġaġmiut as a caribou hunting area, all the Utuqqaġmiut were either on the coast, or farther north in the interior.

There were several other changes in the political map of northwestern Alaska during the 19th century, but all of them stemmed from demographic changes brought about by famine or from disease following contact with Westerners. When a nation's population became so reduced by famine and disease that the survivors could not defend their estate, foreigners could move into it largely uncontested. In one interesting case apparently unrelated to Western contact, the Koyukon living in the upper Kobuk River valley became assimilated by the neighboring Iñupiat. Thus, they began the 19th century as Athapaskans and ended it as Eskimos. There seems to have been a slight readjustment of their border with the Akuniġmiut during the process (Burch et al. 1999).

The complete conquest of one nation by another is not recorded in either the oral or written history of northwestern Alaska. Except for the Tikiġaġmiut/Utuqqaġmiut case cited above, there is also no record of the territorial expansion of any nation within the study region. Given the small populations, the large estates, the locations of relatively unproductive areas along many national borders, the absence of centralized authority, and poor long-distance communication, significant territorial expansion or conquest would have been very difficult to sustain. In the few instances where nations seem to have tried, they were confronted by an international alliance and defeated.

Alliances

An alliance is a confederation of two or more nations. In early contact northwestern Alaska, it is impossible to distinguish between groups of nations whose members just happened to get along well together, and those whose leaders forged some kind of agreement to act in concert. This probably is not a particularly important issue, however, because relatively formal associations seem always to have been arranged between nations whose members got along well in the first place.

Alliances were arranged by *umialgich* in the nations involved, who were ofttimes already associated with one another individually in terms of trading partnerships (dual *niuvigiik*) or co-siblingship (*qataŋutigiik*). They used these personal bonds to establish the broader associations of an alliance, usually in reaction to a real or perceived collective threat. It was this general outside threat that prompted the several *umialgich* from a given nation to coordinate their policies, a necessity that was required before the leaders in one nation could approach their counterparts in another. Unfortunately, the evidence available to me does not contain any concrete information on how specific alliances were created.

But there is evidence that, somehow, alliances were formed. Dorothy Jean Ray lists a number of them in the Bering Strait area, including the southernmost portion of the region of interest here (D. Ray 1967:384–89). However, many of the ones she mentions consisted of easements and licenses, as I have used those terms here; alliances, as I have defined the term, were less common. They seem to have been based on the principle that, in the international arena, power was based on size; the larger a nation's population, the greater its potential for exercising hegemony over others. The only way small nations could contend with powerful outsiders was through alliances with similarly threatened neighbors.

The primary example within the study region proper was an alliance to counteract efforts being made by the Tikiġaġmiut to establish hegemony over the entire portion of the region lying north of Kotzebue Sound. With a population that may have approached 2,000, the Tikiġaġmiut were the only nation with enough people to even contemplate such a program. However, their efforts prompted the formation of an alliance that apparently included the Kivalliñiġmiut, Napaaqtuġmiut, and Nuataaġmiut, and probably also the Qikiqtaġruŋmiut. Sometime around 1800, forces from the two sides met in an epic battle near the Kivalliñiġmiut–Tikiġaġmiut border (Burch 1981:14; Ostermann and Holtved 1952:48; Wells and Kelly 1890:10). The allies were victorious, and hundreds of Tikiġaġmiut were killed. This disaster effectively ended the expansionist aspirations of the Tikiġaġmiut.

Notes to Chapter Five

1. This definition and those related to it are adapted from Levy (1952:468; 1966:290). Under his definition the political process is similar to what social scientists sometimes refer to as social control, except that it gives accountability equal billing with control.

2. Avessuk (1983.6), F. Beechey (1831, I:346, 390; II:302), Brown, Outwater, Sheldon et al. (1978:49), Cantwell (1889b:82), Jensen (1970.6), J. Killigivuk (1940.1), Rainey (1947:241), S. Rock (1940), Elsie Weyiouanna (1983.1).

3. Aġviqsiiña (1940.1), A. Hawley (1965.5, 1965.17), B. Hawley (1964.1), J. Killigivuk (1960.2), NANA Cultural Heritage Project (1975d), Walton (1965.3).

4. Giddings (1961:49), Rainey (1947:243), Simpson (1875:253), Walton (1965.3), Wells and Kelly (1890:10), C. Wood (1931), Woolfe (1893:135); cf. Giddings (1956:26).

5. R. Cleveland (1970.1), A. Hawley (1964.1, 1965.2, 1965.17), B. Hawley (1964.1), Jensen (1970.6), Keats (1970.9), J. Killigivuk (1960.10), NANA Cultural Heritage Project (1975d), Northwest Iñupiat Elders Conference (1976a:3), Rainey (1940.4), Samms (1899–1900: entry for Sept. 1, 1899), Simpson (1875:249–50), Stoney (1900:832), Martha Swan (1965.1), Thornton (1931:40), Woolfe (1893:134–35, 137). See also Spencer (1959:161).

6. H. Anungazuk (1999.1), E. Curtis (1930:136), J. Killigivuk (1960.2), Kunuyaq (1940), Rainey (1940.4; 1947:242).

7. A. Hawley (1965.14), B. and S. Hawley (1970), Keats (1970.8), T. Morris (1970), Elsie Weyiouanna (1983.1).

8. R. Cleveland (1970.3), L. Gallahorn (1970.1), Glover (1970.5), A. Hawley (1965.7), M. Hawley (1965.1), Jensen (1970.1, 1970.6), N. Knox (1965), T. Morris (1970), Nasugluk and Nasugruk (1940), J. Ningeulook (1981.2), S. Rock (1940:11), C. Smith (1970), Stoney (1900:832), Clinton Swan (1965.3), Martha Swan (1965.6), M. and M. Swan (1970), Vestal (1970).

9. Bertholf (1899a:24), Maguire (1857:438), McLenegan (1887:75), Nelson (1877–81: entry for Sept. 5, 1880), Seemann (1853, II:59–60), Simpson (1875:274), Thornton (1931:19).

10. K. Burns (1960.2:28), A. Hawley (1964.5, 1965.4), Jensen (1970.4), Nelson (1877–81: entry for Sept. 20, 1880; 1899:305).

11. Aġviqsiiña (1940.1), Hank (1959), J. Killigivuk (1960.7), S. Rock (1940).

12. This is an excerpt from a two-page undated (but probably 1961) and untitled set of musings on Iñupiaq metaphysics. I found it in the Foote Collection at the University of Alaska Archives, Fairbanks, in box 5, folder 6.

13. Aġviqsiiña (1940.1:79), Q. Dives (1940:26), Glover (1970.5, 1970.6), T. Morris (1970), Rainey (1947:275–76), Stefansson (1914b:368), Vestal (1969).

14. Aġviqsiiña (1940.1:100–1, 108), Beaver (1970.1), Brower (ms:878–81), Cantwell (1887:38), R. Cleveland (1970.1, 1970.2), M. Curtis (1970), Q. Dives (1940:8, 23, 25), D. Foster (1970.2), J. Foster (1970), L. Gallahorn (1970.3), Glover (1970.6), A. Hawley (1965.15, 1976.2, 1976.4), Elwood Hunnicutt (1970), D. Jenness (1953:8), Jensen (1970.3), Jensen and Jensen (1980), A. Karmun (1970), M. Karmun (1970), Keats (1969.1, 1970.5, 1970.7, 1970.9, 1970.10), J. Killigivuk (1959.2), Kingik (1980), Koutsky (1976), R. Marshall (1933:340–51), McClellan (1970.2), T. Mitchell (1970), T. Morris (1970), NANA Cultural Heritage Project (1975d), Paneak (1970), C. Sheldon (1973–74.8, 1973–74.9), Stefansson (1914b:202, 267, 321–22, 333, 342), Sun (1970), Martha Swan (1970), S. Thomas (1970), Thornton (1931:108), Vestal (1970), Wells and Kelly (1980:24), Woolfe (1893:139).

15. Other Iñupiaq terms for taboo are *kiruġnaqtuaq* and *paquġnaqtuaq*.

16. Stefansson on taboos: 1914b:126–28, 182, 196, 264, 273, 282, 284, 312, 316–17, 320, 334, 338, 347, 365; 1951:410–13.

17. Aġviqsiiña (1940.1:2, 20, 49, 60, 74, 82–83, 84, 93, 95, 108), Anderson et al. (1998:95), P. Atoruk in Lee et al. (1990:143, 145, 147), Avessuk (1983.2), E. Ballot in Lee et al. (1990:17, 19), W. Ballot (1970.2), Brower (ms:126, 185), K. Burns (1960.2:22), Cantwell (1889b:82), R. Cleveland (1966), E. Curtis (1930:163), Q. Dives (1940.2), B. Foote (1992:50), Glover (1970.6), J. Grinnell (1901:17, 23–24, 29, 39–40, 56, 70), M. Hawley (1965.1), Hooper (1881:24–25), Edna Hunnicutt (1960.3, 1970.1, 1970.2), Killigivuk (1960.9), T. Mitchell (1969, 1986, 1987), M. Naylor (1960.1), Niġuwana (1940.1, 1940.2), Ostermann (1942:36), Ostermann and Holtved (1952:36, 114, 117, 118, 120, 124, 125, 126), Penn (1952.1), Rainey (1947:274), Smith (1970), Stoney (1900:569–70, 814–15, 837–39), Sunno (1951.5, 1951.78, 1951.93, 1951.107), Thornton (1931:123), Tingook (1960.4), M. Tocktoo (1983.2), Wells and Kelly (1890:24), Ardith Weyiouanna (1983), Woolfe (1893:139, 140, 141, 147–48).

18. Aġviqsiiña (1940.1:82–83; 1940.2), Brower (ms:126), E. Curtis (1930:137–40, 148, 163–64, 165–66, 176, 209), Q. Dives (1940), Fair (1998:111), L. Gallahorn (1970.3), A. Hawley (1976.7), Hooper (1881:24–25), Elwood Hunnicutt (1970), Iviqsiq (1940), Jensen (1970.4), Keats (1970.10), Killigivuk (1959.2), Lowenstein (1993:51–172), J. Mitchell (1952.14), Mouse in Lee et al. (1990:219), Niġuwana (1940.1:6, 14; 1940.2), Ostermann and Holtved (1952:36–37, 117, 118–20, 122–23, 124, 125, 126–27), Quwana (1940.1:8, 43), Seveck (1951), Stefansson (1914b:316–17, 334–35, 338, 340, 347, 355, 389), Stoney (1900:838–39), Sunno (1951.1, 1951.107), Sunno and Hadley (1951), N. Swan (1984), Thornton (1931:165–67), Vestal (1970), Walton (1965.2), Wells and Kelly (1890:24), Ardith Weyiouanna (1983), Woolfe (1893:140, 141).

19. K. Burns (1960.2), Call (1899:116), L. Gallahorn (1969.2), Glover (1970.5), M. Hawley (1965.1), Keats (1970.8), C. Sheldon (1973–74.17), Vestal (1969).

20. Aġviqsiiña (1940.1), K. Burns (1960.2), Q. Dives (1940:22), J. Foster (1970), L. Gallahorn (1969.2), A. Hawley (1965.5, 1973.2), Jensen (1970.4), Ostermann and Holtved (1952:130), C. Sheldon (1973–74.1, 1973–74.3, 1973–74.7, 1973–74.19, 1973–74.20), Wells and Kelly (1890:24).

21. Several other nations also experienced famine at the same time as the Kivalliñiġmiut. Apparently Samaruna's curse was much more powerful than he intended it to be.

22. Aġviqsiiña (1940.1:3, 88), K. Burns (1960.2), J. Foster (1970), A. Hawley (1965.4, 1965.6), Quwana (1940:1–2), Rainey (1940.20), C. Sheldon (1973–74.7, 1973–74.18).

23. Aġviqsiiña (1940.1:3, 97), Q. Dives (1940:22), A. Hawley (1976.7), Ostermann and Holtved (1952:127).

24. Aġviqsiiña (1940.1:97), J. Killigivuk (1960.2), Kunuyaq (1940:1–2), S. Rock (1940), Sunno (19051.29).

25. Aġviqsiiña (1940.1:56, 97–100), A. Hawley (1965.5, 1965.17, 1976.5), B. Hawley (1964.1), Hooper (1881:62), Kunuyaq (1940), Quwana (1940:29–30), Simpson (1875:249–50, 251), Stoney (1900:832), Sunno (1951.29), Martha Swan (1965.1), Thornton (1931:40, 41), Weyer (1928), Woolfe (1893:134–35, 137).

26. A. Hawley (1964.7, 1965.17), B. Hawley (1964.1), Jensen (1970.6, 1970.7), NANA Cultural Heritage Project (1975d), Martha Swan (1965.1), Walton (1965.3).

27. This is one aspect of the oft-discussed individual autonomy of Eskimos. See, for example, Briggs (2001).

28. W. Anderson (1974/75), Sunno (1951.82). Anderson's article is the one describing the contest between men of different nations, but it was set so late in time that national boundaries had pretty well fallen apart by the time it happened.

29. R. Cleveland (1970.3), Eliyak (1931), J. Evok (1970), J. Ningeulook (1983.1), Martha Swan (1970), C. Wood (1931). See Burch (1988b:55–56).

Chapter Six

The Integration Process

Integration is the process whereby individuals make a positive adjustment to their life situation.[1] As Levy (1966:341) has pointed out, few if any activities are perfectly integrative. The concern here is with activities whose adaptive implications outweigh their maladaptive ones. The integration process has two primary aspects: information and motivation.

The Information Process

The information process is the one whereby knowledge is acquired and disseminated. For present purposes, I have divided it into three subcategories: communication, education, and research.

Communication

Communication is the process whereby one or more individuals infers from the behavior of another individual or group an idea, feeling, or state of affairs that the other individual(s) is trying to convey (Levy 1952:166). It is an enormously complex subject, one that would require several books to deal with with any degree of thoroughness. The present account is necessarily a brief summary.

Iñupiaq communication was what is generally referred to as face-to-face. In other words, for Iñupiat to communicate, they had to be able to see and hear one another directly.[2] This means that the media of communication consisted of speech, facial expression, gesture, and dress. The number of people in a position at any given time to receive a message or sign from a given initiator via these media ordinarily ranged from one to perhaps two dozen, most of them members of the speaker's own family or, in compound settlements, *qargi*. On special occasions, storytellers or *umialgich* might address as many as a hundred or more people, but occasions when they communicated with greater numbers than that at any one time must have been rare indeed.

Language

The primary medium of communication was the spoken language, known as Iñupiatun (or Iñupiaqtun).[3] As noted in Chapter 1, two dialect groups were represented in the study region, these being North Alaskan Iñupiaq and Seward Peninsula Iñupiaq. They are still represented there, but, since the interest here is in the early 19th century, the following discussion is phrased in the past tense.

The North Alaskan dialect group was divided into two dialects, Malimiut and North Slope. The Seward Peninsula group was likewise divided into two dialects, Qawiaraq and Bering Strait. The Qawiaraq dialect was the only one of the four that was not represented in the study region during the period of interest here.

The North Slope dialect was represented within the study region in the speech of the Tikiġaġmiut, and possibly the Kivalliñiġmiut, although the latter assignment is uncertain.[4] The Bering Strait dialect was represented in the speech of the Kiŋikmiut and the Tapqaġmiut. The members of all the other nations, possibly including the Kivalliñiġmiut, spoke a form of Malimiut. That is why almost all of the Iñupiaq terms presented in this book are in that dialect.

Iñupiaq dialects differed from one another in their phonology (sounds) and lexicon (vocabulary and suffixes). An example of phonological differences is the series of palatalized sounds—[ch], [ḷ], [l̡], and [ñ]—that occurred in the Malimiut dialect but not in the Bering Strait dialect. Examples of vocabulary differences are the term for broad whitefish (*Coregonus nasus*), which was *qausriḷuk* in Malimiut, but *pikuktuuq* on the North Slope. "Sun" was *masaq* in Seward Peninsula, but *siqiñiq* in Malimiut. Differences in suffixes are exemplified by *-niaq*, which indicated future time in Malimiut, whereas in Seward Peninsula that concept was expressed by *-ḷiuq*. These few examples were of course multiplied many times over in actual speech, and the speakers of different dialects required some practice before they could communicate effectively. However, along dialect and language borders, bilingualism and even multilingualism was common.

The members of each society spoke a subdialect that was distinctive enough for foreigners to identify a person's nationality after hearing him/her say just a few words in his/her own language (Stefansson 1933:314). Subdialects differed to some extent in the same features that distinguished dialects, but also in what might be called "speech styles." The latter included features such as intonation contours and the speed with which people talked, neither of which had any bearing on meaning in Iñupiatun.

The consonants in the Malimiut dialect are presented on page xiv. The language lacked the series of voiced stops b, d, and g familiar to English speakers; the symbol [g] in the table represents a voiced fricative, that is, a continuant in which the flow of air through the mouth is not stopped, as it is with English [g]. Iñupiatun also had some sounds that are made farther back in the mouth than most English sounds, represented by the symbols [q], [qh], and [ġ]. Other major differences included the voiceless laterals, and the two retroflex sounds, none of which occur in ordinary English. Unlike English, Iñupiatun had only three vowels, i, a, and u.

Both consonants and vowels appeared in short (e.g., [p], [i]) and long (e.g., [pp], [ii]) forms. The significance of length is shown by the following examples: *suvat* means "What are they doing?," whereas *suuvat* means "What are they?," the only difference between the two words being the length of the *u* (Kaplan 1984:21). Two different short vowels could be combined in diphthongs (e.g., [iu] and [ia]), and two different short consonants could be combined in clusters (e.g., [qp] and [nŋ]). However, there were some differences among both dialects and subdialects with respect to precisely which combinations occurred.

Perhaps the most notable characteristic of Iñupiatun from the viewpoint of English speakers is the fact that it was a polysynthetic language. This means that it was a language in which words were "composed of a stem or base which may be followed by derivational suffixes and an inflectional ending" (Kaplan 2000:3). An example of how this worked is demonstrated in Table 22. Here we see the rather simple base *tauqsiq–*, "buy," combined with a series of suffixes into progressively longer chains, each element adding meaning to the word.

Many Iñupiaq words carried the same informational load as an entire English sentence, since Iñupiatun expressed with suffixes many of the concepts that English expresses with separate words, particularly pronouns, adverbs, and adjectives. The last two entries in Table 22 illustrate this point. Iñupiaq words often carried so much information that their order in a sentence had no bearing on its meaning.

The specific example presented in Table 22 is a bit contrived, perhaps, since stores did not exist in early-contact Northwest Alaska. However, fluent speakers of Iñupiatun routinely use words as complicated as or even more complicated than this one (Kaplan 2003b); my older informants told me that their grandparents often talked with even longer and more complex words than my informants were able to themselves.

Further discussion of the details of Iñupiatun is beyond the scope of this volume. Suffice to say that linguistic research has demonstrated that the language was equal to English, Chinese, or any other language in its ability to convey complex information about ideas, feelings, or states of affairs from one person to another.

Other Media

Language as a medium of communication was augmented by gestures, facial expressions, and clothing. Unfortunately, the early-contact literature on northwestern Alaska contains almost no information on these subjects, and they are nearly impossible to investigate by means of interviews conducted 200 years later. Consequently, I do not have much to say about them.

Facial expressions readily convey information about one's emotional state, with frowns indicating displeasure, and smiles just the opposite. What cannot be determined now is the extent to which the early-contact Iñupiat employed these mechanisms deliberately to convey information, as opposed to spontaneously reacting to people or events. During my time (in the 1960s), a few facial expressions were often used instead of, or in addition to, words to convey information. For example, raised eyebrows indicated a positive reaction to something, or "yes" in response to a question; a wrinkled nose meant just the opposite. Curling the lips inward so that they could not be seen was a way of communicating surprise. Unfortunately, there is no way to know how old patterns such as these were, since the early European explorers did not mention them.

One can say with some certainty, however, that facial expressions were one of the primary means, in addition to touch, of communicating love and affection to infants. Both adults and older children smiled at, held, and oohed and aahed over babies a great deal; presumably babies were not very old before they learned to initiate exchanges with people older than they by smiling and making noises. However, as young people aged, the interaction with their elders became progressively more formal. Adherence to the societal norms, that is, formality, was probably an effective way to communicate respect and affection in these cases. I recall one of my good friends saying to me, "I had a wonderful mother-in-law. I couldn't look at her or say a word to her, and she never said anything to me." In other words, these two people communicated their respect and affection for one another by adhering as closely as they could to the behavioral ideal, which meant avoidance. I am told that is the way it was supposed to be long ago.

Gestures are also difficult to learn about as media of communication during the study period. During my time, Iñupiat did not "talk" conspicuously with their hands when compared to, say, Italians or even 21st-century Americans. The only early-19th-century gestures for which I have reasonably firm knowledge relate to when people from different places, and particularly different nations, encountered one another. The key issue here was to indicate peaceful or hostile intentions.[5] Peaceful intentions were indicated by raising the arms over the head, empty-handed, then lowering them to the sides. Another way to convey the same message was to hold the arms out to the side, with elbows bent and forearms raised, then lowering and raising the forearms in a kind of awkward waving motion. A third was to hold

Table 22. An Example of Polysynthesis*

Iñupiaq Word	Meaning & Construction
tauqsiq–	"buy"
tauqsigñiaq–	"will buy" *tauqsiq– + –niaq* buy + future
tauqsigñiaġvik	"store" *tauqsiq– + –niaq– + –vik* buy + future + place
tauqsigñiaġviŋmuk–	"go to the store" *tauqsiq– + –niaq– + –vik– + –muk* buy + future + place + go to
tauqsigñiaġviŋmuuti–	"take along to the store" *tauqsiq– + –niaq– + –vik– + –muk– + –uti* buy + future + place + go to + take along/do with
tauqsigñiaġviŋmuutiniaq–	"will take along to the store" *tauqsiq– + –niaq– + –vik– + –muk– + –uti– + –niaq* buy + future + place + go to + take along + future
tauqsigñiaġviŋmuutiniaŋit–	"will not take along to the store." *tauqsiq– + –niaq– + –vik– + –muk– + –uti– + –niaq– + –ŋit* buy + future + place + go to + take along + future + negative
tauqsigñiaġviŋmuutiniaŋitkai	"He won't take them to the store." *tauqsiq– + –niaq– + –vik– + –muk– + –uti– + –niaq– + –ŋit– + –kai* buy + future + place + go to + take along + future + negative + transitive verb ending (3rd. person sing. subject, 3rd. person pl. object)
tauqsigñiaġviŋmuutiniaŋitkaiguuq	"He reportedly won't take them to the store." *tauqsiq– + –niaq– + –vik– + –muk– + –uti– + –niaq– + –ŋit– + –kai + –guuq* buy + future + place + go to + take along + future + negative + transitive verb ending (3rd. person sing. subject, 3rd. person pl. object) + reportedly

* Source: Lawrence Kaplan (2003a). The n/ñ, q/ġ, k/g, and k/ŋ replacements are morphophonemic shifts.

one's arms up at an angle of 45 degrees, then to lower them, passing them over the chest and stomach. The way to convey a message of hostile intentions, on the other hand, was to approach shooting arrows ahead along one's intended line of travel. All of these gestures sent unequivocal messages that could be received at a distance of several hundred yards.

Clothing, in principle, can be used to send a variety of messages, such as one's economic status, perhaps, or one's adherence to or freedom from traditional standards of propriety. One might not expect Iñupiaq clothing to have conveyed much information of this sort, but at least some of it seems to have been designed specifically to convey a message. Figure 72 is a sketch of a man dressed and adorned in the same way as the man depicted in Kotzebue's (1821, I: frontispiece, right-hand figure) report on his 1816 voyage to northwestern Alaska. When I showed this sketch, separately, to Frieda Larsen, Albert McClellan, Levi Mills, Thomas Mitchell, and Evans Thomas, each of them immediately exclaimed, "*Umialik!*" As they explained it to me, the man wore two large ivory labrets, each with large stones or beads in the center; a broad walrus-hide headband with an appliqué in the front center, a row of beads around the bottom, and slivers of baleen projecting upward at angles from the top; and a large hairpiece under his chin made from the throat hair of a bull caribou. According to my informants, only an *umialik* could afford such extravagance.

The figure in the sketch appears to be dressed in winter clothing, despite the fact that it was summer when the sketch was made. However, it is unlikely that the artist invented all of these adornments, so they were likely part of his subject's regular paraphernalia. Either the subject put them on to have his portrait done, or he was wearing them when the expedition arrived. It would also seem clear that the man did not dress this way by accident. One must conclude that he *intended* to send the message that he was an important person; he was simply using clothing as the medium of communication.

In dances, about which more below, gestures were combined with facial expressions, body motions, and sometimes masks and headdresses in various ways to tell stories. These performances made use of well-known symbols to convey their messages without the performers having to speak and without the need for an explanatory monologue by a narrator.

Iñupiat may have also communicated through other media as well. Kelly (Wells and Kelly 1890:17), for example, reports that "there are instances where they have communicated with each other by means of pictures carved on wood or ivory." Unfortunately, he does not tell us what that means—beyond the fact that men carved images of real phenomena and events on wood or ivory. He also says (Wells and Kelly 1890:16) that "old men who have made a good record as whalemen tattoo their cheeks," which

FIGURE 72. An *umialik* from Kotzebue Sound, 1816.

presumably was intended to inform others of their success. Unfortunately, such interesting details will probably always remain beyond our reach.

Education

Education is the process whereby one learns from others and/or through experience. This general subject was discussed briefly in several earlier chapters. In Chapter 2, it was considered in the context of role differentiation on the basis of cognition. In Chapter 3, it was mentioned as being an important element in parent-child, nepotic, and grandparent-grandchild relationships. And, in Chapter 4, it was discussed under the heading of "services."

In the present chapter, the focus is on education as an element in how individuals adjusted to their life situation. More specifically, it concerns how people learned what they needed to know in order to get along in the social and material worlds of Northwest Alaska.

It is useful to divide the presentation into two parts. The first deals with socialization, the second with what I call "adult education."

Socialization

Socialization is the process whereby individuals learn to operate in a social system in which they are becoming or have become new members (Levy 1966:341). It includes the transfer of information about what a person needs to know, how a person should behave, and what a person should believe. The term "socialization" is usually employed only with reference to how infants—the most general category of "new members"—are raised to be adults in a given society; where relevant, I will refer to this as "primary socialization." However, as defined above, it also pertains to the process that a person must go through when, for example, marrying into another family, joining an organization such as a whaling crew for the first time, and emigrating to a new country. This is "secondary socialization." Unfortunately, information on secondary socialization is all but nonexistent for the study period.

Primary socialization began shortly after birth. An infant needed to learn how to become a human being, an Iñupiaq, and a functioning member of a particular family and nation. The process continued at least until a person was in his/her mid-teens.[6] Among the Kiŋikmiut, and probably among the Tikiġaġmiut, where men were usually in their twenties before they knew how to hunt safely on the moving sea ice, the process lasted a few years longer. In any case, the process was seamless. There were no day-care centers, schools, grades, or other thresholds, and there were no age classes requiring special training or initiation rites prior to entry.

Most of what a child learned about being an Iñupiaq was acquired within the family context.[7] Here it is important to recall that the typical Iñupiaq family was larger and more complex than what most of us today think of as being a family. Indeed, the great majority of settlements were inhabited by the members of a single (compound) family. In most cases there were at least as many adults as children, and often more, so adult role models and teachers usually equaled or exceeded children in number.

Infants were almost continually held by someone when they were awake, and often when they were not. They were talked to, smiled at, sung to, and generally made the center of attention by both men and women. Toddlers were clothed and permitted to walk around or play, inside the house or outside, depending on the weather, but always under the supervision of an older sibling, cousin, or adult relative. Physical punishment, such as spanking, was rarely inflicted on children of any age, although it was not unknown.

A youngster was taught the names of his/her relatives and the ways in which he/she was related to each one at an early age. As part of the learning process, children were quizzed on these subjects from time to time as they grew older. Subsequently, through observation and instruction, trial and error, children learned the behavior appropriate to each of the relationships, and to each of the *types* of relationship to which they belonged.

Iñupiaq children learned a great deal by watching and listening. It helped that most adult activities and conversation occurred in their presence, virtually from birth on. It also helped that every adult had to perform the same basic duties as every other adult of the same general age and the same sex, so a youngster could observe almost anyone and learn something about what he/she needed to know. The only exceptions to this generalization were some of the knowledge specialist roles, about which more later.

The Iñupiat also set great store on learning by doing.[8] For example, a little girl who had spent her first few years of life watching her mother, aunts, and grandmothers sewing, setting snares, feeding the dogs, and butchering and storing meat and other foodstuffs, day in and day out, eventually wanted to try to do some of those things herself. When she expressed an interest in doing so she was given the necessary tools or other equipment, often made in miniature just for her, and she set to work. Older girls and women offered advice and instruction from time to time, but otherwise let the youngster forge ahead on her own. Similarly, a young girl learned the care of babies, first with dolls or puppies, then with younger siblings or cousins.

Boys learned to be men by following procedures analogous to those girls followed to become women, except that their role models (fathers, grandfathers, uncles) spent much of their time in hunting, outside the settlement. Thus, adult males could not be observed by boys too young to accompany them. However, if a boy expressed an interest, a father or other older male relative made him a small bow and a set of miniature arrows and showed him how to use them. Boys practiced doing what they had been told by stalking and attempting to kill shorebirds (on the coast) or sparrows or other small birds (inland) during the spring and summer, and pretended to do the same thing with targets in winter. The results provided instant feedback on their success or failure in mastering their lessons. When they grew a little older they were given a small kayak, which they learned to paddle under the watchful eyes of a parent. As they approached puberty, boys were provided with more adult-size weapons, and began to accompany their fathers or uncles on big-game hunts. As Thomas Johnston (1976a:249–50) pointed out, the Iñupiaq method of learning by doing included a lot of "positive reinforcement: a feast for the boy's first kill, but nothing said about the one that got way."

Learning by doing involved much practice, and was by no means restricted to material pursuits such as sewing or hunting. I have read only one early account of such things from the study region (see below), but John Murdoch (1892) included one in his volume on Barrow in the early 1880s:

> One night I saw a party of children having quite an elaborate performance near our station. The snow at the time was drifted up close under the eaves of the house. On the edge of the roof sat three little boys, each beating vigorously on an empty tomato can [in lieu of a drum] and singing at the top of his lungs, while another boy and a little girl were dancing on the snow waving their arms and singing as usual, and at the same time trying to avoid another girl about thirteen years old, who represented a demon. She was stooping forward, and moving slowly round in time with the music, turning from side to side and rolling her eyes fiercely, while she licked the blade of an open clasp knife, drawing it slowly across her lips. They

seemed intensely in earnest, and were enjoying themselves hugely. After dancing
a while at the station they went over to the village, and as they told me the next
day spent the whole night singing in a vacant snow house (Murdoch 1892:384).

A second instructive example was provided by H. R. Thornton (1931), from Wales, in
the early 1890s:

> In spring the children play at numerous sports in imitation of the graver pursuits of
> their elders. One will stand by a small chasm in the ice; and, pretending that the
> part of the ice, on which his companions are, is moving away, call to them to hurry
> across before they are carried off. Some form an imitation flock of ducks, simulating
> the cries of the birds, while others throw their mittens at them as they rush past.
> Others get up a mock walrus hunt. Still others pretend to harpoon a whale, the
> animal under attack being made of walrus hide (Thornton 1931:123).

I do not think it too far-fetched to presume that early-19th-century youngsters in the study
region would have engaged in the same kind of activity.

Speaking harshly to children was definitely frowned upon, as was perpetually forbidding
them to do something they wanted to do (Stefansson 1914b:207, 282). However, explicit
instruction was also an important part of a child's education.[9] In fact, the Iñupiat had a
concept, algaqsruun, which means "teaching by exhortation."

Most instruction seems to have taken place in two contexts. One was when males were
in the qargi, and females were congregated in one or more dwellings (which were analogous
settings with regard to their educational significance). These were the occasions when the
elders, men in one case and women in the other, held forth on what was considered appropriate behavior and what was not. (Not surprisingly, one of the primary values conveyed
during these proceedings was respect for elders.) These were also occasions for a great deal
of conversation and storytelling, both of which served important educational functions for
any youngsters within earshot. On a more mundane level, they were also contexts where
quite a bit of work was done: women scraping and sewing skins in the house, for example,
and men making tools or weapons in the qargi. Youngsters in their late preteen years in
particular benefited from watching their seniors perform these tasks.

The second context in which instruction and exhortation took place was when a youngster
and one parent (or surrogate, such as an aunt or uncle), usually of the same sex, were alone
together. For males, this was usually when hunting; for females, it could be while gathering
berries or other vegetable products, setting snares, or perhaps fishing through holes chopped
in the ice. It was apparently during these semi-private interludes that parents were most likely
to instruct their children on the standards underlying appropriate behavior in general, the
principles of finding their way around the country and surviving in it, and the procedures
for carrying out the specific activity in which they were engaged.

There were other ways in which young people learned as well. One of them was through
learning how to do cat's cradles, many of which related to legends from the remote past.
More important were stories told while traveling, in the qargi, or in the home. As Chuck
Greene (2003) states in the foreword to Wanni Anderson and Ruthie Sampson's collection
of relatively brief folktales,

> most of them emphasize or reveal the importance of human values and . . . pass
> on the knowledge associated with animal behavior, weather, strength, wisdom,
> common sense, the will to live, death, sharing, adapting, forgiving, laughter, family
> ties, loneliness, the sun, the moon, the stars, the light, darkness, the northern

> lights, winter, spring, summer, fall, hunger, competition, cooperation, animals, birds and survival, just to name a few (Greene 2003:v).

Still another way to learn about the history and traditions of their nation was to learn the place-names of the district in which they lived (Fair 2004:233–34; O. Swan 1984). Many Iñupiaq place-names were descriptions of the physical characteristics of the particular landform concerned, but most referred to specific individuals or events connected to the place concerned. Learning the place-names and the stories associated with them yielded a considerable amount of information on a wide variety of subjects.

The education of knowledge specialists differed to some extent from the pattern just described. Knowledge specialists, as outlined in Chapter 2, included the following: *iḷisiiḷat*, or clairvoyants; *sivunniqsriqirit*, or prophets; *iñuunniaqtit*, or tribal doctors; *quliaqtuaqtit*, or storytellers; and *aŋatkut*, or shamans.[10]

Clairvoyants and prophets did not acquire their special abilities through instruction or practice.[11] Indeed, they did not seek their role at all. It was simply thrust upon them, as it were, by some unknown force. However, viewed from the perspective of this book, it must be assumed that the individuals to whom this happened acquired a general knowledge of what the roles entailed through observation and listening to stories when they were youngsters.

Storytellers definitely acquired their special knowledge as they were growing up. Diamond Jenness (1924) described the process:

> In Alaska story-telling is one of the most favourite pastimes wherever three or four natives are gathered together, especially in the long evenings of winter. The old tales and traditions are repeated again and again in semi-stereotyped forms to never-wearying audiences, until they become almost as familiar to the young men of twenty as they are to the old men of fifty and sixty years. There are special "raconteurs," men who are famous for their knowledge of the old tales and traditions... (D. Jenness 1924:1; see also Lowenstein 1992:xxxv–xl; Ostermann 1942:163; and Rainey 1947:269).

The difference between *quliaqtuaqtit* and everyone else was not special training or different exposure to the basic information, but a better memory and perhaps a greater gift of eloquence. "Story-telling [was] regarded as an art and cultivated as such" (Ostermann 1942:163).

Iñuunniaqtit, or tribal doctors, acquired their special knowledge through one or a combination of procedures.[12] One was simply to watch experienced doctors going about their tasks and to listen to patients talk about the experience. Probably everyone acquired some knowledge of organ manipulation and bloodletting this way, but few became experts. Those who were particularly interested in learning how to do this type of work, in the absence of a mentor, could learn through trial and error if they had willing subjects. Most settlements were too small for them all to have *iñuunniaqtit* among their members, so many people must have tried simple medical procedures because they had no alternative. The final method was to serve as an apprentice to an acknowledged expert in the field, but this falls more under the heading of adult education than it does primary socialization. However, the acquisition of a general knowledge of what *iñuunniaqtit* did and how they did it had to have been part of everyone's primary socialization.

The final role in the knowledge specialist category is that of *aŋatkuq*, or shaman.[13] As noted in Chapters 2, 4, and 5, one needed to be associated with a familiar spirit (*qiḷa*) in order to be a shaman. There were several ways in which this could be done, including spontaneous possession by a familiar; purchase, inheritance, or solicitation of a familiar; and apprenticeship under an experienced practitioner.[14] The specialized knowledge required of shamans was rarely acquired as part of one's primary socialization. However, learning in a general way what shamans did, and to at least some extent how they did it, was part of the basic learning process.

Adult Education

Education does not cease when primary socialization is completed. Adults and near adults must also exchange information with one another, at least from time to time. In the absence of a better label, I call such exchanges "adult education."

In Northwest Alaska, the shift from primary socialization to adult education occurred gradually during the transition from the *nutaat* (teenager) to the *iñuguŋaruq* (adult) stages of life. In our terms, this would have been during people's early to late teens, probably a bit earlier for women than for men. Unfortunately, adult education in early-19th-century Northwest Alaska is a poorly researched subject. The account that follows, therefore, is necessarily brief, and based as much on speculation as on evidence.

The key to understanding adult education in Northwest Alaska lies in the fact that, as Simpson (1875:251) noted, the Iñupiat were, in general, very communicative people. They talked to each other a lot, whether in idle gossip or in more structured ways, such as story-telling sessions (Woolfe 1893:143, 144, 148). At certain times of year, particularly in winter, they devoted a great deal of time to conversation.

Trollope (1855) described a scene that must have been typical of most households. In January 1854, he was staying in Wales at the home of two brothers who had been out hunting seals, separately, most of the day.

> After dinner a very animated conversation took place between them, which we
> by their motions, and a word here and there recognized, were quite able to follow
> as being a description of the sport they had had, and their success with the seal
> (Trollope 1855:874).

It is not unreasonable to suppose that, during the course of this conversation, they discussed ice conditions, the weather, observations of bear or fox tracks, other hunters they had seen, and any unusual incidents that may have occurred. In the process, they would have provided useful information both to one another and to any other people who were listening. If similar scenes were being played out that night in all or most of the other fifty-nine households of Wales, it may be understood that a tremendous amount of important information was being exchanged. Since women were by no means house-bound, but ventured forth to snare ptarmigan, fetch firewood, hook for fish, and perhaps retrieve their husband's harvest of the day, similar exchanges must have occurred among them as well. Exchanges of information like these must have taken place almost every day.

The Iñupiat differentiated between men's and women's normal activities, but there was no prohibition (in general) against men doing women's work and vice versa. However, men probably tended to exchange certain types of information more with other men than they did with women, particularly when they were gathered together in a *qargi*. Similarly, women exchanged more information with other women than they did with men. The overall flow of information probably favored women, because they were often present but quiet when men were conversing and thus could hear what was being said. When women were conversing, men were often either somewhere else or, if present, ignoring the discussion. Casual conversations around the village, or more concentrated ones in the *qargi* or someone's house, would have facilitated the spread of information throughout the settlement.

Geographic information, which was very important to people who traveled so extensively, was widely exchanged. When the matter was not too complex, this was done verbally. Place-names for major topographic features, many of which were descriptive (e.g., "razorback ridge"), were very helpful in this regard. In more complicated situations, the Iñupiat created maps—in snow, mud, or gravel.[15] The best documented case of this was recorded in August 1826. F. W. Beechey was exploring and mapping the coast of northwestern Alaska, and happened to visit a camp of Iñupiat who were apparently returning home to Wales from the trade fair at Sisualik. Natives and Englishmen could not understand each other's language and there was no interpreter present, but the former understood that the latter wished to acquire some knowledge of the country. So, the Iñupiat produced a map on the beach for the Englishmen.

> The coast line was first marked out with a stick, and the distances regulated by the days' journeys. The hills and ranges of mountains were next shown by elevations of sand or stone, and the islands represented by heaps of pebbles, their proportions being duly attended to. As the work proceeded, some of the bystanders occasionally suggested alterations. . . . When the mountains and islands were erected, the villages and fishing stations were marked by a number of sticks placed upright, in imitation of those which are put up on the coast wherever these people fix their abode. In time we had a complete topographical plan of the coast from Point Darby to Cape Krusenstern [a coastline some 500 miles/800 km long] (F. Beechey 1831, I:399).

The Iñupiat's proficiency in producing this display indicates that it was probably not their first time. Exercises of this kind must have been particularly common at international gatherings, such as the Sisualik fair or messenger festivals. By such means people could learn the basic physical characteristics of other countries without visiting them; Beechey learned about the existence of an important harbor which he had missed, and which was not on any Western map of the country.

The sharing of information was by no means limited to families and settlements. Men, in particular, ventured some distance from their homes in their search for game and must have encountered men from neighboring settlements from time to time. When meeting, it is hard to believe that they would not have stopped to chat. At certain times of year, entire families moved about the country, and in doing so would cross paths with relatives and friends from time to time. In addition, people often visited relatives in other settlements. When these small contacts are added together over an entire yearly cycle, it is clear that an Iñupiaq nation was a major information network.

One context in which information seems *not* to have been exchanged was when a teenage or adult male or female was engaged in a project and was making or was about to make a mistake. No matter how many people were observing, and no matter how many of them knew that the worker was headed the wrong way, they would not bring it to the worker's attention—unless, perhaps, the error would have been fatal. Learning by doing included making mistakes.

Research

Regardless of how much information is passed from one generation to the next, there is always a need to add to or update it from time to time. New information can be discovered by accident, of course, but at least some must be acquired deliberately. The most appropriate term I can think of to label this process is "research," which I define as the deliberate search for information that is new to the investigator. Unfortunately, this is another poorly investigated subject in northwestern Alaska about which relatively little can be said.

I begin with two examples of what I consider to be research, both from the late 19th century. The first involved the Nuataaġmiut, of the upper Noatak basin.[16] In the late 1870s and early 1880s, the Nuataaġmiut sensed that caribou were becoming progressively less numerous in their estate, and they learned by talking to people from other nations at the Sisualik fair that caribou numbers were rapidly diminishing in estates farther south. As the people most dependent on caribou in the entire study region, the Nuataaġmiut envisioned themselves as being headed for disaster. They had heard that caribou were abundant in a largely uninhabited district in northeastern Alaska, but they wanted to have the rumor confirmed.[17] So, before breakup one spring, a small party of Nuataaġmiut crossed to the north side of the Brooks Range, traveled down the Colville River, and reconnoitered the country to the east to see if what they had heard was true. It was, so they returned home and reported their findings. The following winter, a large percentage of the Nuataaġmiut abandoned their homeland and moved to the North Slope. While this example dates from about thirty years after the study period, I think it reasonable to suppose that it represents an approach to acquiring information which had ancient roots.

The second example probably dates from the late 1890s. By this time, some people from the Kivalina, lower Noatak, central Kobuk, and Kotzebue Sound districts were making annual spring visits to Jabbertown, near Point Hope, to work for American shore whalers based there (Jensen 1970.3). Late one winter some Kivalina people were making preparations for the trip, but were worried about illness, which often struck Point Hope and other coastal settlements during the summer months. So, they hired a shaman named Aiviṇuaq to investigate. Aiviṇuaq brought out a little wooden doll, dressed it in a miniature rain parka made from oogruk intestine, and placed it with a miniature lamp inside a tiny tent in the middle of a house floor. Then he beat his drum, danced, and sang a mysterious song. In due course, the doll stood up inside the tent, lit the lamp, and began to sing and dance also; the observers could infer what it was doing from the play of light and shadow on the tent wall, and of course they could hear its song. Then the shaman and the doll, or, more accurately, the spirits that now possessed them, held a conversation in some incomprehensible language that my informant concluded many years later must have been Japanese. After more drumming, the light went out in the little tent, the doll lay down, and silence reigned. After a pause, the shaman reported to the assembled multitude that the doll's familiar spirit had told his own that the whalers would be successful in the spring, and that no sickness would come to them during the summer. Accordingly, the Kivalina people went to Jabbertown, and both predictions proved correct. Again, although this event occurred more than two generations after the end of the study period, I think it fair to assume that it represented an ancient form of investigation.

These two examples represent fundamentally different ways of conducting research. The first was based entirely on empirical procedures and phenomena, while the second was based to a significant extent on magic, involving nonempirical elements, hence was unverifiable by a nonbeliever. Oversimplifying to some extent, one might characterize the first process as predominantly rational research, and the second as predominantly nonrational research, but both were thoroughly Iñupiaq.

It is impossible to know for certain at this remove in time the basis on which a particular approach was selected. It would appear as though the Iñupiat emphasized predominantly rational research in certain spheres of life, and predominantly nonrational research in others. For example, their tools, weapons, means of transport, clothing, dwellings—practically everything discussed in Chapter 4 under the heading of manufactured goods—must have been developed over the generations through research that was predominantly rational. It was probably conducted in the form of trial and error, which, if carried out self-consciously, is definitely a form of research. The question of whether or not game was present in a given area seems to have been subject to predominantly rational research. Mysterious phenomena, such as disease—the primary concern in the second story—were more likely to be investigated through predominantly nonrational research.

Whether these two modes of research were employed during the study period is a fair question, but one I cannot answer. Simpson (1875:251) said that, although exhibiting the usual individual variation with respect to intelligence, the Iñupiat generally possessed "great curiosity," a trait that would lend itself to creative investigation. Similarly, Thornton (1931:44) claimed that Iñupiat seemed to "possess a remarkable desire for learning for its own sake and an equally remarkable appreciation of its value." In contrast, Stefansson (1951:62–63, 146–49) claimed that Iñupiat were not interested in visiting country they had never seen before unless the district in which they were living had run out of game. "They do not go over the mountain for the sake of finding out what there may be on the other side" (Stefansson 1951:152).

Research into the relationship between broken taboos and calamities, which definitely took place during and after the study period, had a substantial nonrational component because it depended on the relationship between shamans and their familiar spirits. It was not totally nonrational, however. After watching several people die (from hypervitaminosis A) after eating polar bear liver, for example, a shaman's determination that it was a tabooed substance had a solid basis in empirical fact. Most taboos and rituals probably were not so well grounded.

Most research conducted by Iñupiat was more mundane than the above examples imply, and it was also more frequent, being carried out nearly every day. Examples of regular research included the hunters' daily study of weather conditions, examination of animal and human tracks around the settlement, and frequent scanning of the countryside for game.

Iñupiat also conducted research at the international level, or at least *umialgich* did. The main foci of trade fairs and messenger festivals were trade and having fun, but a secondary focus was finding out what was going on in other countries. Through this process, at least the leaders in each nation acquired some knowledge of the landscapes of countries beyond the borders of their own estate that they themselves had never seen, and also updated themselves on the general situation existing beyond their own borders (F. Beechey 1831, I:399; Murdoch 1892:43–46; Simpson 1852–54: entry for Jan. 11, 1853). At all international gatherings, but particularly at the fairs, they also attempted to discover if raids were being planned against them so that they could make preparations for dealing with them. *Iññuqutit*, the prowlers who plagued almost every district each summer, may have been deliberately reconnoitering the country in advance of a raid. Unfortunately, I have been unable to acquire specific information on this point.

The Motivation Process

Motivation is the process whereby people acquire and maintain purpose (cf. Levy 1952:509). Whereas the information process has to do with the "what" of social and material life, the motivation process is concerned with the "why." It encompasses a number of subcategories, including the following: religion, integration to certainty situations, integration to uncertainty situations, affective expression, and artistic expression.

Religion

Religion consists of those aspects of action directly oriented to ultimate ends (Levy 1952:511). As I noted in Chapter 2 (under the heading of role differentiation on the basis of religion), the ultimate goals of early-19th-century Iñupiat seem to have been two in number: physical survival, and loyalty to blood kin (Simpson 1852–54:entries for Sept. 21, 1853, and Feb. 12, 1854; 1875:247, 249, 275; Stoney 1900:831–32, 834).

Family solidarity seems to have ranked ahead of physical survival as a goal in Iñupiaq life since failure in the former seems to have led to greater stress than failure in the latter. The goal of physical survival motivated Iñupiat to endure hunger, cold, and pain without giving up, and they often managed to sustain themselves through extreme hardship and carry on. Failure in the social sphere, however, frequently resulted in a less positive outcome. Harsh treatment by a spouse or parent, for example, sometimes led a person to commit suicide. The most commonly reported mechanism was hanging.[18] Technically, this must have been rather difficult north of the tree line, and indeed, some attempts failed. However, all of the successes of which I am aware were from districts in the tundra (Northwest Iñupiaq Elders Conference 1976a; Walton 1965.3). Another mechanism was reported by Brower (ms:483): badly mistreated by her husband, a Tikiġaġmiu woman drove her dogs several miles down the beach, fastened the towline around her neck, and started the dogs for home. She was dead by the time they got there. When the social failure was more general and a troublemaker was shunned by his or her relatives collectively, the rejected person frequently became "discouraged, hopeless, and gloomy," and literally went off and died (Wells and Kelly 1890:24).

The Iñupiat lacked a notion of an otherworldly afterlife for humans. Instead, after a period in limbo, the souls of the deceased were reincarnated in the bodies of newborn human infants. The Iñupiat did have a notion of a supreme being, which they called *siḷam iñua*, but they did not worship it; it was simply the most abstract of the many entities constituting the nonempirical sector of their world (T. Morris 1970; Ostermann and Holtved 1952:128).

For the Iñupiat, even ultimate goals related quite directly to concrete affairs of this worldly life: those involving survival and family. Intermediate and immediate goals reflected these orientations. These conclusions are consistent with Nelson's (1887–81) general observation on what motivated people in western Alaska:

> There appears to be a perfect lack of any feeling of conscience or moral duty among the Innuits—that which the experience of ages has taught them as best they do—guided by superstitious customs and usages the reason for which are, in many cases, unknown. I do not know of a case in which they do not look upon that most conducive to their own ends as the most "normal," if the word may be thus used.
>
> If asked why they do so and so, they answer, "We have always done so," considering this an unanswerable explanation (Nelson 1887–81:journal 11, first entry).[19]

In other words, the Iñupiat were guided more by tradition and by practical concerns than by lofty religious or philosophical ideals.

Integration to Certainty Situations

One circumstance that Iñupiat frequently had to deal with was boredom. While certain seasons, such as spring and early summer, were necessarily times of enormous activity, others, such as the short days of early winter, were not. In January 1854, Trollope (1855:873) reported that "certainly these people are a lounging race with many idle hours on their hands."[20] Kashevarov (VanStone ed. 1977:91) said that the life of the Iñupiat proceeded "regularly, monotonously, like a wound-up machine"; Thornton (1931:44) also commented on "the monotony of their existence." In addition, at any given time of year, a certain percentage of the population was prevented by taboo restrictions from doing much, if any, work. The present section describes how the Iñupiat dealt with boredom or, more importantly, how they prevented it from developing.

One subject that is *not* discussed here is gambling, which is a classic way of dealing with certainty situations (Levy 1952:526). During the second half of the 19th century, playing cards were brought to Northwest Alaska, and the Iñupiat quickly learned to use them. By the mid-1880s, Stoney (1900:836) could report that "card playing takes precedence of all games. These people are natural gamblers, and never let an opportunity pass of gratifying their passion." However, I have no information on card-playing or any other kind of gambling during the period of interest here.

Games

The Iñupiat had a large repertoire of games.[21] These ranged from innocent children's games to almost brutal athletic contests between highly competitive young men to games played by practically everyone just for fun. It is useful to divide them into two groups, indoor games and outdoor games.

Indoor games consisted primarily of athletic competitions between men designed to test the participants' strength, agility, courage, endurance, and ability to tolerate pain.[22] All of them could be performed in the confined space of a *qargi*, which meant that they could proceed regardless of the weather.

A brief sample of the types of activities involved in these competitions is presented in Table 23. I divide the events into two groups, open and closed. Closed events were structured as a series of two-person competitions, each of which may be said to constitute one "round" in a given event. In the finger pull, for example, two people from opposing teams went onto the floor, positioned themselves, locked fingers, and pulled; whoever's finger straightened first lost. The loser was immediately replaced by another member of his team, while the victor remained on the floor. This process of competing and replacing the vanquished continued until all members of both teams who wanted to try had competed and been defeated, and only one person was left. Anyone could then challenge that person. If there was no further challenge, or no one could beat him, he, and thus his team, was declared the winner of the event. Then they moved on to another finger and repeated the process.

In open events, only one competitor was on the floor at any given time. In the two-foot high kick, for example, a person made one or more attempts to hit with both feet simultaneously a mark suspended from the ceiling. Members of the opposing teams took alternate turns; everyone who hit the mark remained in the competition, everyone who missed was

Table 23. A Sample of Indoor Competitions

CLOSED EVENTS

finger pulls: The competitors sat on the floor facing each other, positioned so that one leg crossed over the opposite leg of the opponent. Then each hooked the middle finger of one hand around the other's and, at a signal, pulled. Whoever's finger straightened first lost. The next event was a third finger pull, followed by the fourth (little) and finally the index finger, respectively.

lip press: In this event the two competitors got down on their hands and knees facing each other. Then a stick about six inches long and sharpened at both ends was placed against each of their upper lips. They pushed forward, each trying to cause his opponent to yield because of the pain.

head pull: Two competitors sat on the floor facing each other with their legs interlocked; a single strap was placed around both of their heads. At a signal, each pulled his or her head back, trying to make his or her opponent bend forward. When one did bend forward or give up, he or she lost.

nose squash: This was similar to the head pull except that it was more of a pain tolerance contest. The opponents sat back to back, with the strap across the bridges of their respective noses, and pulled forward with their bodies, pushing with their hands on the floor. Whoever gave up lost.

OPEN EVENTS

Alaskan high kick: The contestant sat on the floor and with one hand grabbed the opposite foot. With the other hand remaining on the floor, he sprang up and kicked with the free foot a suspended mark hanging from the ceiling. Then he had to land on that same foot before any other part of his body touched the floor.

two-foot high kick: The competitor stood on the floor, feet together, and, keeping them together, jumped up and tried to touch with both feet simultaneously a mark suspended from the ceiling or a pole. Both feet had to land back on the floor simultaneously, still pressed together, without the contestant losing balance. As the competition advanced, the mark was raised to progressively higher levels until a winner emerged.

two-foot back kick: This was like the two-legged high kick except that the mark was suspended behind the person's back.

uyamiutaq: A short loop of sealskin line was attached to a short stick. The competitor held the stick in his hand and looped the cord around his neck. Then he tried to put his feet through the loop as far as possible.

out. After everyone had had a turn, the mark was raised to a higher level. Eventually the mark was raised to a point where only a few people could reach it, and finally only one person could. That person, and thus his team, was declared the winner.

Where simple settlements are concerned, competitions were usually between the members of one settlement (the hosts, or home team) and the members of another (the guests, or visiting team). In complex settlements, most competitions involved members of different *qargich*. A third alternative was for people from one end of a (complex) settlement to compete against those from the other. *Qargi* contests were dual affairs in which the members of one *qargi* invited those of another to visit them and compete. Just to indicate the intensity of such events, the games were sometimes continued without a break for as much as five days and nights before the members of one team would concede defeat.

Qargi games included a number of difficult events. They were not things that most people could do well without a fair amount of practice, and probably some coaching. The larger the settlement, the greater the opportunity for practice against a variety of opponents. Organized games were also more frequent in large settlements because the members of different *qargich* were very competitive. Thus, in general, the most accomplished athletes in these particular events tended to come from the larger settlements, particularly Point Hope, the largest settlement of all. At the Sisualik fair, Tikiġaġmiut athletes frequently outperformed the physically larger and more robust inlanders in many events, to the perpetual frustration of the latter.

There was no set schedule or sequence of events. The members of the home team selected the first event. The team whose representative won that event selected the second, and the winner of that event selected the third, and so on. They probably progressed from events that were less challenging to those that were more so, although I may be mistakenly imposing recent patterns on the past when I say that.

A favorite tactic was to invent and secretly practice an event that no one on the opposing side had seen before. At some appropriate point in the proceedings—usually fairly well along in the competition—the inventor walked out on the floor, performed it, and challenged the members of the opposition to do likewise.[23] These special events tended to be either rather humorous or extremely difficult. An example of the latter involved Frank Aġviqsiiña's (1940.1:44) older brother, who brought a walrus tusk sharpened like a knife along one edge. He lay facedown on the ground, his hands behind his back, and the tusk across and beneath his face, just above the bridge of his nose. Then two men grasped the ends of the tusk and used it to lift him to a standing position. He bled profusely. (It must be presumed that he did not practice this beforehand.) The other team was then challenged to equal or surpass his achievement. Someone from the other *qargi* brought out a knife and said, "Here, this would be good for your trick." To that, Frank's brother responded, "If any of you will try the knife, I will try it after you." No one took up the challenge, so Frank's brother, hence his team, won the event.

More peaceful indoor games included cat's cradles, dart games, and a trading game. There were probably others as well.

The art of making cat's cradles (*ayahaaq-*), or string figures, was highly developed. There were too many string figures for me to attempt a description here. Fortunately, Diamond Jenness (1924, Part B) has published an extensive illustrated account of the subject, which the interested reader is advised to consult. String games were played only during certain times of day or night, the specific time varying from one district to another. They were often accompanied by games, stories, or songs.

There were at least two kinds of dart game.[24] One, known as *napaatchaq–*, used pointed wooden darts about 5 inches (13 cm) long, each with a feather at the rounded end, and a wooden tube about a foot (30 cm) long. The tube was placed upright on the floor. A dart was held across the open palm of the contestant's hand with the pointed end under a thumb and the feathered tail projecting beyond the medial edge of the hand, palm up. The contestant flipped the dart upward with a quick thumb movement, causing it to sail in a looping arc and, ideally, fall down into the tube. The second dart game, called *nauligauraq–*, required different equipment. This dart also was made of wood, but was about 3 inches (7.5 cm) long, and was tipped with a sharpened antler point having a rear shoulder and a projecting smaller-diameter cylindrical tang that fitted onto the wooden shaft. A tail of feathers about 6 inches (15 cm) long was affixed to the other end. The object of this game was to throw the dart from behind a baseline at a target about 15 feet (4.5 m) away, the target being a circle about one and a half inches (3.8 cm) in diameter painted on the wall with soot.

The final example of indoor game was a trading game whose Iñupiaq name was not recorded.[25] Should a man or woman become restless one evening, he/she selected a suitable trade item and walked to the home of a friend or relative. Once there, he/she climbed onto the roof, opened the skylight, and lowered the article through it by means of a cord. The transaction was concluded with an exchange of greetings between the friends, and the game's initiator returned home. An hour or so later, if motivated to do so, the recipient reciprocated, following the same procedure. Such exchanges could continue into the early-morning hours of the following day. Whoever ran out of tradable goods first lost the game.

Outdoor games included a variety of athletic contests and other activities, many of which were or could be performed by men or women, and some of which could be performed by both simultaneously.[26] Virtually all of the indoor games discussed above could be conducted outside and sometimes were, but none of the outdoor games could be conducted satisfactorily inside.

Most of the outdoor games and contests of the Iñupiat are readily understood by the modern reader. They included, but were not limited to, foot races (sometimes sprints, but often runs of eight to ten miles [13–16 km]), standing long jump, kayak races, spear-throwing contests, archery contests, slingshot contests, keep away, playing catch with balls, keeping a ball in the air with the feet, juggling, tag, wrestling, blindman's buff, tug of war, carrying heavy weights (in the form of rocks), and a number of children's games. Four others require more detailed comment.

A game that I never observed or heard about was referred to by both Thornton (1931:122) (at Wales) and Stoney (1900:835) (in the central Kobuk valley) as "shinney" or "bandy." It apparently resembled what we know as field hockey, except there were no goals; it was like keep away played with sticks. The equipment consisted of "a small ball of ivory, leather, or wood, and a stick curved at the lower end" (Nelson 1899:337). The players—always men and boys—divided into two teams. Presumably the game continued until the members of one team conceded. It was played primarily in the fall.

Eskimo football (*aqsrautraq–*) was a favorite game in Northwest Alaska (A. Hawley 1973.2; S. Jenness 1991:28). It was sometimes played just by men, sometimes just by women, and frequently by members of both sexes and all age groups. The most intense and roughest games involved men only.

The ball (*aġraurraun*) was round, about 6 inches (15 cm) in diameter, and variously made of sealskin (stuffed with baleen shaves), caribou hide (stuffed with hair or moss), or rolled-up bark peeled from willows. The ball was moved by being kicked. One could catch the ball (then drop it) or stop it with the body, but one was not allowed to run with it. It was like a game of keep-away soccer. As with most Iñupiaq games, this one involved two teams. These variously represented different *qargich*, different settlements, people from one end of town vs. those from the other end, saltwater people vs. inlanders, different nations (at the summer trade fair), or, in pick-up games, two ad hoc teams selected on the spot by people chosen as captains. There were no goals, so a team won only when the opposing team gave up. There were also no boundaries to the playing field, so a prolonged game could wander all over a settlement, the smoother sections of the surrounding countryside, and, often, the frozen surface of a nearby river or lake. The more closely matched the teams, the smaller the size of the playing area tended to be, since the members of each team could prevent their opponents from escaping with the ball.

Football was a favorite activity during the short days of early winter, when it often involved everyone in the community who was physically able to participate. Because starlight and moonlight reflected off the snow in the clear skies of northern Alaska, the game could be played at night as well as during the brief period of daylight. It was also played during national gatherings in early summer after the spring hunt had been completed, and during trade fairs.

Another special outdoor game was *nalukataq*, the so-called "blanket toss."[27] The "blanket" was made from two walrus hides sewn together and cut in a circular or oval shape. Holes for grips were cut all around the edge so that many people could hold it. Sometimes the edge of the blanket was attached to the tops of four tripods placed at equal intervals around it for added support. A performer (or contestant) stood in the middle of the blanket and was lifted off the ground, often to the accompaniment of drumming and singing. After three partial lifts to get a rhythm established, the members of the crew holding the blanket pulled back in unison as hard as they could, shooting the performer six or seven or more feet (1.8–2 m) into the air.[28] The performer's minimal objective was to land back on his/her feet. A more advanced objective was to move the legs as though walking while in the air. Experts, the best of whom seem to have been young women, did back flips, front flips, and a variety of other aerial maneuvers. The activity resembled bouncing on a trampoline, except that the walrus hide lacked a trampoline's resilience, so jumps had to be done one at a time.

Nalukataq was such an important feature of a whaling feast that the term is often thought to refer specifically to that festival. However, the blanket toss was also performed at summer fairs, at national gatherings, and early each summer at settlements along the Kobuk and Selawik rivers when the upriver traders went through on their way to Sisualik. In fact, it could be done any time or place where there happened to be a blanket and enough people to man it.

John Simpson (1852–54: entry for June 23, 1854), who observed the *nalukataq* at the whaling feast at Point Barrow in the spring of 1854, reported that accidents often attended this activity, apparently through either poor tosses or faulty execution by the performer. Similarly, but much later, Rasmussen (Ostermann and Holtved 1952:28) said that the blanket toss "not infrequently ends with broken limbs."

The final special outdoor game was baseball (*anauraġaq-*). This was not mentioned in any of the 19th-century sources, and it never occurred to me to ask my informants about its antiquity. It may have been a late-19th- or early-20th-century import, but it differs in many respects from American baseball. In the summer of 1968, I saw Inuit playing the identical game at Arviat, on the west coast of Hudson Bay, which suggests to me that it must have ancient roots in Inuit culture. Other investigators may resolve this issue.

As with the great majority of Iñupiaq games, baseball was played by two teams. The team in the field had a pitcher, a catcher, and several outfielders. The equipment consisted of a stick (for a bat), and a small ball (the composition of which I did not learn). The batter stood behind a line and tried to hit a (slowly) pitched ball. Only one attempt was allowed. Even if he/she did not hit the ball, the batter could run; but if he/she did hit it, the batter had to run. The single base was another line some distance way from the first. The outfielders tried to hit the runner with the ball as he/she ran through them. If they succeeded, the batter was out. Should the batter miss, or not swing at all, and the catcher dropped the ball, the batter's entire team tried to run to the base without anyone being hit. If a hit ball was caught in midair, the "inning" was over and the teams switched positions. This game was popular evening recreation during the long days of early summer, and was played by girls and women, by boys and men, and by mixed age and sex groups. As far as I could tell, this game was played primarily for fun and was accompanied by lots of laughter. When the players were all young men, however, it could be more serious.

Dancing

On August 5, 1826, the Beechey expedition arrived at Point Hope, the largest settlement in Northwest Alaska. It was largely abandoned, as it was every summer, the only inhabitants being a few elders, a couple of physically disabled people, and some children left behind to look after them. The Englishmen were invited into the settlement, seated upon some skins, and offered food (which they declined). Then,

> an old man produced a tambourine, and seating himself upon the roof of one of the miserable hovels, threw his legs across, and commenced a song, accompanying it with the tambourine, with as much apparent happiness as if fortune had imparted to him every luxury of life. The vivacity and humour of the musician inspired two of the old hags, who joined chorus, and threw themselves into a variety of attitudes, twisting their bodies, snapping their fingers, and smirking from behind their seal-skin hoods, with as much shrewd meaning as if they had been half a century younger. Several little chubby girls, roused by the music, came blinking at the daylight through the greasy roofs of the subterranean abodes, and joined the performance; and we had the satisfaction of seeing a set of people happy who did not appear to possess a single comfort upon earth (F. Beechey 1831, I:366).

This and Beechey's other experiences were consistent with Kashevarov's (VanStone ed. 1977:90) report that "the Eskimos love songs and dancing," and Stoney's (1900:836) claim that "dancing is the greatest pleasure of men, women and children." The Iñupiat danced in ceremonies and rituals, as a means of getting in touch with familiar spirits, as a way to greet guests, and to have fun.[29] Only the last two are purposes of particular relevance here, but this is a useful place to discuss the subject in general.

The little scene Beechey described illustrates several important points about Iñupiaq dancing. The first is the pleasure that it gave the participants. The second is that the musical accompaniment for the dance was produced by drumming and singing. Third, there seemed to be no age restrictions on who could participate. Fourth, dancing was a friendly way to greet strangers.[30] And finally, a dance could be produced and enjoyed by a very small number of people, in this case three adults and a few children (see Giddings 1956:20). This last point is particularly important, since the great majority of Iñupiaq settlements were inhabited by the members of fewer than five households. Much of the following describes dancing in complex settlements, particularly in the large coastal villages. However, it should be understood that the same general procedures were followed in other settlements, but with adjustment for their smaller populations.

The simplest types of dance must have been those employed by shamans to contact their familiar spirits. Unfortunately for the present work, the missionaries who Christianized the Kotzebue Sound area at the end of the 19th century taught people that dancing in general was evil, and that shamanic dancing was particularly so (Burch 1994a; Johnston 1975c:54–55; 1976a:247–48; 1977:65–68; 1978a:48). Therefore, it was very difficult for me to obtain information about it. All I learned was that shamans used relatively small tambourine-type drums, which they beat with thin sticks while singing magical songs and dancing. Only one shaman performed at a time. Presumably each used his or her own unique song(s) and dance step(s), but I have no evidence to support these statements.

Another simple dance was witnessed by Beechey (1831) at a camp of Tikiġaġmiut seal hunters near Cape Thompson:

> An old man then braced a skin upon a tambourine frame, and striking it with a
> bone gave the signal for a dance, which was immediately performed to a chorus
> of Angna aya! angna aya! the tambourine marking time by being flourished and
> twirled about against a short stick instead of being struck. The musician, who was
> also the principal dancer, jumped into the ring, and threw his body into different
> attitudes until quite exhausted, and then resigned his office to another, from whom
> it passed to a lad who occasioned more merriment by his grimaces and ludicrous
> behavior than any of his predecessors (F. Beechey 1831, I:361–62).

Up to this point this dance was much more like Inuit dancing in the central Canadian Arctic than what is typical in Northwest Alaska in that there was just a single drummer who was also the only dancer.[31] However, the performance became more complex when the young man was

> joined by the young women, who until then had been mute and almost motionless,
> but who now acquitted themselves with equal spirit with their leader, twisting
> their bodies, twirling their arms about, and violently rubbing their sides with
> their garments, which, from some ridiculous associations no doubt, occasioned
> considerable merriment (F. Beechey 1831, I:362).

As the above examples suggest, the predominant pattern in northern Alaska was for drummers and singers to provide the music, while one or more people danced. In complex settlements, the drummers were usually four to six older men who sang as they beat the drums, while a chorus of older women sang in unison with them (Johnston 1975a:6–7; 1978a:49–50; 1988a). Dancers, who could range in number from one to more than a dozen, generally were young and middle-aged men and/or women, depending on the occasion. In general, "the dancers at the side always face[d] the audience, but the dancers in the center sometimes turn[ed] and face[d] the drummers" (Johnston 1975a:6–7). Positioning was generally linear across the dance floor except in rare cases when the specific story being told by the dance required an alternative arrangement (Johnston 1975a:7). Most dances were performances in which onlookers outnumbered the orchestra and dancers combined.

In summer, dancing was done outdoors. The usual arrangement was for the drummers to sit in a row on the ground beside the dance floor (L. Gallahorn 1970.2). One or two rows of female singers sat or stood behind them, and sometimes a few male singers stood behind the women. In windy weather, the orchestra and dancers were usually protected by a windbreak made of *umiat* turned on their sides with the bottoms facing into the wind. The audience sat or stood around the performance area.

An example of an outdoor performance is a dance Beechey witnessed at a camp, apparently of traveling Kaṇiġmiut, on the shore of Eschscholtz Bay. He said it was the best one he saw.

> A double ring was formed in front of us by men seated upon the grass [each of whom had a drum], and by women and children in the background, who composed the orchestra. . . . The leader of the party, a strong athletic man, jumped into the ring and threw himself into various attitudes, which would have better become a pugilist than a performer on the light fantastic toe! As his motions became violent, he manifested his inspiration by loud exclamations of Ah! Ah! until he became exhausted and withdrew amidst shouts of approbation from all present, and the signal was given for new performers. Five younger men then leaped into the area, and again exhibited feats of activity, which, considering the heavy clothing that encumbered their limbs, were very fair. A simple little girl about eight years of age, dressed for the occasion, joined the jumpers, but did not imitate their actions. Her part consisted in waving her arms and inclining her body from side to side. The poor little thing was so abashed that she did not even lift her head or open her eyes during the whole of her performance . . . (F. Beechey 1831, I:395–96).

What Beechey did not realize was that the little girl was not being shy, but was dancing in the female style, which was very different from that of males (see below).

During the winter, dancing was done indoors, in the *qargi*. In this context, the singers sat in a row on the floor beside the dance floor, and the drummers sat on a bench behind them (L. Gallahorn 1970.2). The audience sat on benches around the other three sides of the room. A detachment from the Western Union Telegraph Expedition observed such an event at Wales in late November 1866:

> The [*qargi*] was about twenty feet [6 m] square . . .; around the walls were placed seats or shelves for the spectators, one side of which was occupied by the musicians; two raised platforms at the side served as galleries for the youth, who laid on all fours, and thus looked at the performance. . . . After some delay the show commenced, the crowd in the meantime flocking in; men, women and children, until there must have been no less than 150 [people] present. . . . The music, vocal and instrumental, soon got the dancers excited, and stripped to the waist, with their fancy knee-breeches and decorated boots, their heads set off with beads and feathers, they pow-wowed in a frantic manner. At one time we counted 14 stalwart men on the floor, twisting their bodies in all conceivable shapes, and deafening ears with their demoniac screeching (*The Esquimaux* 1866, 1(3):15; see also Thornton 1931:111–12).

The crowd and the lamps combined produced considerable heat and foul air inside the *qargi*; the Iñupiat apparently enjoyed this, but the visiting Westerners did not (*The Esquimaux* 1886, 1(3):15; see also Johnston 1975a:1, 8; 1976a:50–51). Twenty-five years after the Western Union expedition, Thornton (1931:113), also in Wales, reported that kerosene lamps brought to help light the scene and placed up high in the *qargi* went out in less than an hour from lack of oxygen.

Much Iñupiaq dancing was mimetic, emphasizing "humor, drama and play" (Johnston 1978a:54; see also Woolfe 1893:141–42). The gestures, facial expressions, and motions symbolizing different activities or sentiments were sufficiently standardized for people who had never seen a particular dance before to grasp the basic message it was designed to convey even without hearing the words of the accompanying song (for examples, see Johnston 1978a:57–61; and Pulu, Johnston, Sampson, and Newlin 1979:9–31). As Thomas Johnston (1978a:52) put it, "dance movements each possess[ed] a special significance known to all, and in new dances the vocabulary of motions [was] re-arranged to form intelligible pictorializations and representations of events." Dances could reflect daily activities, such as boat building and hunting for men, and sewing and butchering for women, or more extraordinary activities, such as warfare, animal behavior, and stories taken from folklore (Johnston 1975a:4, 7; 1976a:247; 1976b:7; 1978a:50, 52). Sexual innuendos were common, as were humorous representations of such things as scratching and defecating (F. Beechey 1831, I:396; Johnston 1975a:4; 1978a:51–52; Wells and Kelly 1890:22). Still other dances had magical import, such as increasing the returns from hunting, improving the weather, celebrating a successful caribou hunt, or generally placating the hostile spirits that abounded in the Iñupiaq universe (Johnston 1975a:4; 1976a:249; 1976c:439).

Meaning was also conveyed by special clothing. This was often enhanced by accoutrements or facial paint, usually worn by men.[32] Accoutrements included masks, headdresses, headbands with feathers inserted in them, antlers, raven skins, loon heads, and feathers held in the hand. Long, stiff gauntlet gloves made from sealskin were decorated with sticks or bones attached by strings; when shaken in time to the music, they served as large rattles. Both males and females wore gloves when dancing.

Most dances were divided into two phases (Johnston 1975a:9; Johnston and Pulu 1980; Pulu, Johnston, Sampson, and Newlin 1979:6–8). In the preliminary phase, the drummers tapped lightly on their instruments and sang vocables in a relatively soft voice, while the dancers went through a few desultory movements on the floor. In the second phase, the volume and speed of both the singing and the drumming suddenly increased dramatically, vocables were replaced by real words, and the dancers' movements became more vigorous.

There were two major sets of distinctions in Iñupiaq dance styles. The first was between males and females (Johnston 1975a:7; 1978a:50). Knud Rasmussen (Ostermann and Holtved 1952) described the difference:

> The men radiate strength; in all their movements they are supposed to make an attractive and harmonious display of the suppleness of their bodies; and whenever the chorus joins in, and as often as the words of the song occasion it, they put sappy humour into their arm gestures and body writhings.
>
> The men moved about constantly, whereas the female dancers scarcely moved from where they stood, swaying at the hips, now on their toes, now on their heels, their arms keeping time with the rhythm of the music. Their object is to represent charm, beauty, and femininity; and truly, with their half-closed veiled eyes and their light, graceful movements they captivated the onlookers and made an extremely effective foil to the wanton muscle-play of the men (Ostermann and Holtved 1952:28; see also Johnston 1975a:7; 1978a:50; Woolfe 1893:141–42).

One specific dance, *taliq-*, was performed only by women while seated on a bench (L. Gallahorn 1970.2; A. Hawley 1973.5; Johnston 1975a:1).

The second basic distinction in Iñupiaq dance styles depended on whether or not the motions of the several dancers were fixed and synchronized (*sayuun*), or improvised (*atuutipiaq*).[33] During *atuutipiaq* dances, anyone and everyone could go onto the floor and dance in a fashion of his or her own choosing. These dances were relatively slow, and marked by men yodeling while they danced. In contrast, *sayuun* dances, the musical accompaniment to them, and the clothing and other regalia to be worn by the dancers were deliberately created, taught to a specific group of dancers and musicians, and practiced intensively before being publicly performed (Johnston 1975a:4; Sunno 1951.88). *Sayuun* dances tended to be much more sophisticated than their *atuutipiaq* counterparts, and, when imaginatively choreographed and successfully performed, conveyed considerable prestige on both the choreographer and the participants.

There were also, in addition to the foregoing, several special dances.[34] Almost every ceremony and festival had a special dance associated with it. There was also a giving dance (*maġlak-*) in which people gave each other gifts, attempting to outdo one another in their generosity. The *uuliavik-* dance involved one woman and two men, where one man pretended to take the woman from his counterpart. Another dance was performed by a dummy sitting on a stool whose jointed limbs were manipulated by a person hidden by a screen. There was also the whaler's spinning-top dance, the whaler's puppet dance, the whaler's masquerade dance, the northern lights dance, and the box-drum dance.[35] The most impressive of all was the *qirgiq*, or wolf dance, which is discussed below in the section on festivals.

Singing

In an oft-quoted passage, Knud Rasmussen reported that an Iñupiaq man told him, "How many songs I own, I cannot say. I have not kept count of them. I merely know I have many, and that everything in me is song. I sing as I draw breath" (Ostermann and Holtved 1952:137). In a less poetic but equally compelling remark, Hawkes (1913:3) was told by a man at Unalakleet that "to stop the Eskimo singing and dancing was like cutting the tongue out of a bird."

Dancing, as noted in the previous section, was invariably accompanied by singing and drumming. But Iñupiat also sang with or without drum accompaniment to pass the time and to express joy or sorrow.[36] Songs were integral components of ceremonies and festivals. They punctuated many stories, and they accompanied several games, such as juggling or doing string figures. Some songs also had magical power; these are discussed below in the section on magic.

Songs were composed by individuals for their own use, but if they were sung in public, others often appropriated them. Stoney (1900) reported that

> whenever a native from a different locality comes among them and sings a new song they gather about, listening until they catch the tune, when they take it up and sing it for hours (Stoney 1900:836).

Songs were composed by males or females to accompany dances; to celebrate major occasions, such as a victory in battle or a successful hunt; to depict scenes from folklore or history; to ridicule a cross cousin (*iḷḷuq*); to greet a new day; to entertain themselves while doing a boring job; or to express a simple thought.[37] Most of the songs sung in rituals or ceremonies probably originated in the distant past, but new ones could be composed at any time. Many songs were quite brief, the equivalent of only one or two English sentences, but they were repeated over and over, sometimes with different tempos and sometimes with words alternating with vocables. Some songs depicted scenes from visions, or were taught to humans by spirits, most of these being of magical significance.

To early Western visitors, Iñupiaq songs sounded monotonous, nasal, and "destitute of melody" (Stoney 1900:836; see also Woolfe 1893:141–42). More sophisticated 20th-century observers said that they were characterized by nasal timber, glottal pulsation, asymmetrical pulse, shrillness, and lack of vertical harmony.[38] Where more than one singer was involved, singing was in unison or, if both men and women were included, in unison at the octave. Melody was based on a scale possessing five main tones (DEGAC ascending), with microtonal inflections. Some six-tone and seven-tone scales also occurred within the study area. Melodic shapes in songs sung to accompany dances contained

> almost equal amounts of ascent and descent, a common melodic contour being an initial large leap followed by gradual [five-tone stepwise] descent, then a rise of a whole tone during the prolonged ending phrase (Johnston 1978b:109).

Average "song length was thirty measures of music, each measure containing five fast pulses at a tempo of 260 pulses per minute" (Johnston 1978b:109). Songs that were sung for purposes other than dance accompaniment were often shorter and simpler in structure.

Festivals

"Festival" is defined in my *Webster's New Collegiate Dictionary* as "a time of celebration marked by special observances" (G. and C. Merriam Co. 1977). It is a useful term to identify certain events in early-19th-century Northwest Alaska that are commonly referred to in English as "feasts." My objection to the latter term is that these events were always much more than just binges of eating—although they certainly included plenty of eating. "Ceremony" does not appear suitable either, given its definition in the same dictionary as "a formal act or series of acts prescribed by ritual, protocol, or convention," although they often included those as well. The events that I am going to describe in this section ordinarily took place just at the end of particularly productive times of year, and they are most accurately thought of as having been celebrations. "Festival" seems like the most appropriate word.[39]

All of the events included here under the heading of "festival" had several features in common. These included elaborate feasts in which guests seated in rows were served by women circulating among them, dancing and singing, and athletic contests and games of various kinds. Many dances and songs were prepared especially for these events. Summer festivals were held outside and virtually always included the blanket toss. Winter festivals were held in a *qargi*, often just a temporary building erected for the occasion; although some ceremonies and athletic events were held outside in winter, I have never heard of the blanket toss being among them. Most festivals lasted several days and nights. They varied in the amount of ceremonialism involved, and in the extent to which trading was a focus of activity, although both seem always to have been involved to some extent.

Festivals could be held on an ad hoc basis any time something truly exciting happened, such as an exceptional caribou kill, a victory in battle, or the surprise arrival of guests from another settlement. Examples of more or less regularly scheduled festivals include the whaling festival that took place at Point Hope in early June at the end of each successful whaling season; the celebration of the Tikiġaġmiut when they returned from their summer dispersal; the whale-tail festival of the Tikiġaġmiut in March before the beginning of the whaling season; the gatherings of the Kivalliñiġmiut at the end of spring seal-hunting season, and again before their fall dispersal; the late-summer gathering of the Qikiqtaġruŋmiut; the early-summer gathering of the Kiitaaġmiut; the early-winter gathering of the Pittaġmiut; and the October "housewarming" of the Kiŋikmiut.[40] In addition, there were several gatherings of people from two or more settlements in every society during the short days of December and early January, the general holiday season of the Iñupiat. In any given year, some of these events were messenger festivals, which ordinarily were international affairs. The final one on the list was the annual trading festival that took place at Sisualik in late July and early August. Of these, only the whaling festival, messenger festivals, and trading festivals require some special comment.

The Point Hope whaling festival is usually referred to nowadays as *nalukataq*, which in fact refers more specifically to one of its central events, the blanket toss.[41] It is more accurately identified as *qagruġvik*, which means "place or time of the whaling festival." This festival included all of the activities noted above—feasting, dancing, blanket toss, etc.—but it also had more ceremonial interludes than most. In each, *umialgich* and their wives played prominent roles, while the *qargich* served as organizational and physical foci of the various events.

The proceedings began with a race among the whaling crews to bring their boats from the lead back to the village.[42] The boats were then hauled out and drawn up in front of their owner's *qargi*. During the second day there was a fluke feast during which *umialgich*, wearing special clothing and facial paint, gave away pieces of tail fluke to anyone wanting some. Gifts of food were made to relatives, friends, and others who had been helpful. Substantial quantities of meat were eaten, either raw or raw and fermented, on this occasion. The morning of the third day was given over to mourning for people who had died during the preceding winter. Mourning turned to celebration during the afternoon with singing, dancing, athletic contests, blanket tossing, and the consumption of vast quantities of cooked or sour meat.

Detailed information about the Point Hope whaling festival dates from the late 19th century, by which point there were only two *qargich* left. Rainey (1947:263) reported that several generations earlier, when there were seven *qargich*, the feasting and games continued for several days. It seems likely that the festival began at one *qargi* and moved during successive days to the others, which is known to have occurred at Point Barrow in the early 1850s (Simpson 1852–54: entry for June 25, 1853). Such being the case, the overall festival would actually have been a series of smaller festivals, and it would have continued for at least a week.

Messenger festivals, more commonly referred to as "messenger feasts" or "inviting-in feasts," were affairs that usually involved people from different nations.[43] However, they could also take place between settlements within the same nation, or, in complex settlements, between different *qargich* within the same settlement. Within the study region they are generally known as *aqpatat* (pl.), a term that refers more specifically to the runners who played a central role in the event.

There was considerable variation in the details of messenger festivals. All had certain elements in common, however.[44] First, the *umialik* (or several *umialgich*) who was initiating the event sent out two men (the "messengers") to carry invitations, represented by marks on sticks to their partner (sing. *niuvik*) or partners.[45] The latter would have been located in another settlement (sometimes *qargich*), often several tens or even hundreds of miles away. When they arrived among the prospective guests, the messengers publicly issued the invitations, and informed each prospective guest of a food gift the host wanted to receive from him. The latter accepted the invitation or not, then informed the messengers of gifts they wanted to receive in return from the hosts. Then the messengers returned home. Some weeks later, when the guests arrived in the vicinity of the host settlement, young men from the settlement went to meet them, and young men from both contingents held a foot race back to the settlement. Considerable prestige accrued to the winner. The next day the full body of guests arrived at the host settlement, where they were greeted by people dancing and singing in front of the houses. There followed days of feasting, dancing, games and athletic contests, and a great deal of gift exchanging between partners. On the first night, a very important and special event, the wolf ceremony, was held.

The wolf ceremony, more commonly known as the wolf dance, was probably the most elaborate ceremony performed in Northwest Alaska during the study period. Unfortunately, it was also one of the first to be stamped out by the missionaries in the Kotzebue Sound region, and was very difficult to learn about in most of the villages where I worked.[46] Within the study region, it has been attested only among the Kiŋikmiut (E. Curtis 1930:174), Pittaġmiut (M. Morris 1951.1), Qikiqtaġruŋmiut (Green 1959:56; Koranda 1964:18–19), and Napaaqtuġmiut (R. Gallahorn 1952.19). However, a series of sketches of a particularly elegant version of the ceremony was made by an unidentified artist who is now thought to have been from Shishmaref (Tapqaġmiut).[47] One version or another of the ceremony was probably celebrated in all of the nations having estates bordering the coast, with somewhat less elaborate versions enacted in the interior.

The most detailed descriptions I have of the wolf ceremony in the study region were obtained by Charles Lucier from Ralph Gallahorn (1952.19, 1952.20) and Mary Howard (1952), both concerning the event as performed among the Napaaqtuġmiut. The following summary is based on these accounts.

The scene was set in the *qargi*. The time was after the race had been run, the guests had been greeted, and some eating and dancing had been completed. A low screen with four holes representing a wolf den was placed in front of the rear platform. Each hole was covered with fancy strips of gut decorated with the skin of a baby seal. Four featured male dancers wore carved wooden wolf-head masks with eyes made of large blue beads, long gauntlet gloves made of dried sealskin with pieces of wood attached, and headbands with white and brown feathers sticking up in front. The orchestra, consisting of at least one tambourine drummer, at least one box drummer, and a number of singers, must have been off to the side. The featured performers did four dances, miming the actions of wolves, and shaking their glove rattles in time to the music. At the end of the fourth dance, each jumped backwards through one of the holes in the screen.

The dancers relaxed for awhile behind the screen while the music continued in the main arena. At a designated point, each thrust his gloved arms through the holes and shook them, one at a time, in time to the music. After this was done four times, the dancers thrust their masked faces partway through the holes, acting as though they wanted to leave the "den." When the drum was hit particularly hard, it frightened the wolves, who pulled their heads back through the holes. This sequence was repeated several times, with the wolves' faces emerging a bit farther each time. Finally they ceased trying to emerge, and the wolf ceremony was ended.

The performance, as described, was unusual in that masks were made of wood rather than real wolf skins,[48] the jump backwards through the screen did not end the performance, and the entire proceeding, as described, was not particularly elaborate. Koranda (1964:19), also citing Lucier's field notes but without identifying his source, described the Kotzebue (Qikiqtaġruŋmiut) version of the ceremony as having a different sequence of events. Here the dancers, four or six in number, and wearing wolf-skin masks, started behind the screen.

As the performance began, skin curtains were rolled up, exposing only the flexed right arm and shoulder of the four men. Assisted by unseen helpers, the dancers executed some contortions before they emerged as "wolves." The wolves danced and carried presents in their mouths to guests in the audience, as directed by the donors. When this was done, the dancers leaped backward in unison through the small holes from which each had emerged. The holes were so small that the mittens and headskin masks were peeled from the dancers' bodies and fell in a heap as the dancers vanished.

The Shishmaref sketches mentioned above suggest an even more elaborate performance, having several episodes, each with different actors or actresses wearing special costumes. These examples suggest that there was a fair amount of variation in the ceremony from one nation to another, and there may have been variation from one year to the next even within a single country.

The final festival requiring special comment is the *katŋut*, or international trading festival, which is known more generally in English as a "trade fair."[49] The term *katŋut* indicates a large gathering of people. Another Iñupiaq term for this festival is *niuviġiaq*, which means (roughly) a large gathering of trading partners (Keats 1970.2). The only such event taking place within the study region during the relevant time period was held at Sisualik, an excellent beluga and salmon fishing station on the northeastern corner of Kotzebue Sound. Every summer, in late July and early August, some 1,500 to 2,000 people from every nation within the study region and a few from beyond converged there for a week or two of international trading, dancing, feasting, storytelling, athletic competitions, and general socializing (Burch 2005:180–92). Representatives of the several nations encamped some distance apart, but mingled to locate their trading partners, play games, dance, feast, and generally socialize. I am not certain, but I believe that the many dances and athletic competitions held during this festival were organized between two nations at a time, although all could come around to observe the proceedings.

Shamanic Demonstrations

Shamans were importantly involved in dealing magically with illness, famine, and other misfortunes. Most of the time, the people who witnessed such performances were tense because much depended on a successful outcome; there was nothing recreational about them. Such events are discussed at other places in this book. The shamanic activities that are relevant here are those that basically served as entertainment for the onlookers. They were not intended to solve problems, but to serve as demonstrations of a shaman's skill. From the shaman's point of view, they were risky ventures in advertising: if they were daring and successful, he/she could raise his/her fees and generally increase his/her influence; if they were boring or failed, they had exactly the opposite effect. From the audience's perspective, however, they were a fascinating form of entertainment regardless of the outcome. (It should be noted that shamans sometimes were suddenly possessed by evil spirits, which caused them to perform in ways that were terrifying to the onlookers.)[50]

There are many accounts of incredible feats performed by *aŋatkut*.[51] However, my purpose is merely to illustrate the relevant phenomena, not provide an exhaustive record. I begin with some brief examples.

- A shaman took some charcoal from a burned log, rubbed it between the palms of his hands, and blew on it; the most beautiful butterfly flew out (T. Morris 1970).
- In broad daylight, a shaman turned a stone pot inside out and back without breaking it (Stefansson 1914b:312).
- A shaman took a woman's murre-skin parka and held it over his drum, which was lying on the floor, singing some unintelligible song as he did so. A murre egg fell out of the

parka onto the drum without breaking. The shaman carried it around on the drum for all to see, then swallowed the (very large) egg (Aġviqsiiña 1940.1:3).

- Shamans "have allowed themselves to be drawn up to great heights by means of sealskin ropes around their necks and then suddenly dropped without being hurt. They have permitted themselves to be sunk through holes in the ice . . . and have reappeared hale and hearty after the lapse of several months. They have suffered themselves to be burnt, speared, or knifed without sustaining any injury" (Thornton 1931:102).
- Shamanic "tricks of legerdemain" included "driving a knife into the body without marking the skin; bending a long, narrow piece of nephrite; swallowing a bead and later on recovering it from another's ear or eye; and tricks with twine cut into lengths, chewing the pieces, amid heaving of the chest and violent contortions, and drawing the twine out entire" (Woolfe 1893:139).
- A shaman, his arms tied "apparently hard and fast," suddenly gets loose, "and performs many other simple feats of legerdemain; he spits fire; he pulls birds from his mouth; and he does tricks of jugglery" (Stoney 1900:834).

Almost anyone would find the above demonstrations entertaining.

Some shamanic performances were more complex. An example is provided by a Qikiqtaġruŋmiut shaman named Ikiñiq (L. Gallahorn 1969.2; Northwest Iñupiat Elders Conference 1976e:5; 1983e:2–3). One night, during the short days of early winter, he danced for awhile, then sat on the floor, sang and drummed some more, then became still. His body remained motionless for some time, but eventually began to stir. He stood up and gave the following report. He—or, more accurately, his *iñuułiq* (animating force)—had been on the moon, he said, and, while there, had met the *iñuułiq* of a shaman named Asatchaq, who hailed from Point Hope. Then he proceeded to tell his audience the latest news from Point Hope. At the Sisualik trade festival the following summer, a Qikiqtaġruŋmiut *umialik* named Nasuk invited some Tikiġaġmiut, including Asatchaq, to eat with him. During the conversation following the meal, it emerged that Asatchaq had indeed been to the moon, and that he had met Ikiñiq while he was up there.

A spirit flight (*iḷimmaq-*),[52] often, but not necessarily, to the moon, was one of the more common displays shamans performed for the edification of an audience. One even brought back a moon rock. Another frequent type of performance was doing all kinds of things while tied up. For example, a shaman named Qaagra, from somewhere on the lower Kobuk River, once lit his pipe, and told six of the strongest young men in the settlement to tie a rope around his neck and hold on to both ends. Despite the restraint, Qaagra moved around, and one could hear the rope vibrating from the great tension placed on it. His neck eventually broke, but the skin held his head loosely attached to his body. The young men then took him into the storm shed and covered him with a tarpaulin. As soon as they did, Qaagra stood up, his neck fully restored. He kept his pipe in his mouth the whole time (Northwest Iñupiat Elders Conference 1976f:1–2).

The final example featured a Kaŋiġmiut shaman.

> He took a length of rawhide line, made a loop at one end and threw it out into the doorway. The line started to go out like somebody was pulling it. The [shaman] asked a very strong man to come and take hold of the line. . . . The man pulled with all his strength, but something stronger was pulling against him and he had to give ground. Finally he managed to make some progress in pulling in the line as whatever was pulling at the other end gave way. With a big yank the man pulled into the room a whole tree, roots and all (Sunno 1951.12, 1951.91).

This feat becomes especially interesting when it is realized that the nearest tree may have been as much as 100 miles (160 km) away.

Tobacco Consumption

Tobacco first came to Northwest Alaska from Asia, brought from Chukotka by Yupik Eskimo and Chukchi traders. It probably arrived in the mid- to late 18th century, and a substantial trade featuring tobacco from the Asiatic side and furs from the Alaskan side quickly developed (D. Ray 1975b:97–102). By the time Kotzebue (1821, I:209, 239) arrived in the region in the summer of 1816, Iñupiat were extremely fond of tobacco, if not already addicted to it, and they chewed, snuffed, and smoked it.

Ten years later, Beechey (1831) witnessed a "smoking party" in which men, women, and children all took part:

> The pipe used on this occasion was small, and would contain no more tobacco than could be consumed at a whiff. To these instruments there were attached a pricker and a strip of dog's skin, from the last of which they tore off a few hairs, and placed them at the bottom of the bowl of the pipe to prevent the tobacco, which was chopped up very fine, being drawn into the mouth with the smoke. The tobacco which they used had pieces of wood cut up fine with it, a custom which is no doubt derived from the Tschutschi, who use the bark of the birch-tree in this manner, and imagine it improves the quality of the herb. The pipe being charged with about a pinch of this material, the senior person present took his whiff and passed the empty pipe to the next, who replenished it and passed it on, each person in his turn inflating himself to the fullest extent, and gradually dissipating the fumes through the nostrils. The pungency of the smoke, and the time necessary to hold the breath, occasioned considerable coughing with some of the party, but they nevertheless appeared greatly to enjoy the feast (Beechey 1831:I:411–12).

The following summer, he found people having contests in which they endeavored "to excel each other in exhausting the contents of the bowl at one breath" (F. Beechey 1831, II:304).

Other than the fact that tobacco continued to be in great demand in Northwest Alaska through mid-century,[53] virtually no more information on its consumption is available until the 1880s. In contrast to the situation existing in the mid-1820s, by the 1880s practically every adult seems to have had a pipe, and the population was "universally addicted to the use of tobacco" (Cantwell 1889b:88; see also Grinnell 1901:29). Stoney (1900) reported that tobacco was

> taken as snuff; chewed, and the juice swallowed, and is smoked. . . . The smoke is taken into the lungs and kept there some time, producing exhaustive attacks of coughing resulting frequently in complete prostration. This is not objected to and is repeated about every hour of the day and often during the night. The stronger the tobacco, the more it is relished. One of the first instructions to children is how to smoke and chew. It is customary for the mother to take her babe from the breast and put her pipe or quid of tobacco in its mouth (Stoney 1900:844–45).

Other observers reported essentially the same pattern of behavior (J. Grinnell 1901:29; Hooper 1881:60, 1884:104–5; Thornton 1931:216; Woolfe 1893:146).

Since there was rather little difference between what Beechey witnessed in the 1820s and what Stoney and others saw in the 1880s, it seems reasonable to assume that this pattern remained unchanged during the intervening years. On this basis, one may conclude that, throughout most if not all of the study period, Iñupiat generally were addicted to nicotine.

Tobacco consumption was probably the nearest thing the Iñupiat had to escapist recreation (Levy 1952:520–33) until alcohol arrived in the region around mid-century.

Storytelling

The importance of storytelling in the lives of the Iñupiat has been mentioned many times in this volume.[54] One may presume that its recreational aspect was appreciated more by the audience than by the speaker, but that does not militate against discussing the subject here.

Stories could be and probably were told in a variety of contexts, such as when an *umiaq* was being slowly tracked along the beach, when an old battleground or other important site was visited, when the members of a household were preparing to retire at night, or when a few men were relaxing in the *qargi* on an ordinary afternoon.[55] There were also many children's stories, which were short, and which could be told almost any time (Vestal 1970). However, the main storytelling sessions took place in the evening in the *qargi* during the long nights of November, December, and January. Men, women, and children were all present on these occasions. Unlike the recent elders conferences, where each participant was given just a few minutes to speak, the older storytelling sessions apparently featured one person, the *quliaqtuaqti*, and that person was allotted as much time as the story or stories required.

The speaker of the evening sat in the place of honor in the center of the bench across from the entrance to the *qargi* or in the middle of the *qargi* floor, depending on the type of building. Even though everyone knew perfectly well who the speaker was, he or she typically introduced himself or herself with a few, somewhat self-deprecatory phrases, and also cited the source of the story or information he or she was about to tell. For example: "I am Nasruk, an old man from Qalugraitchiaq. My father was Kukik, an Akuniġmiu, and my mother was Qapuġiña, who came from the Kuuŋmiut. I did not see, myself, the things about which I am going to speak, but I heard about them from my father's father, whose name was Kunuk." (Acknowledgment of the person from whom the speaker learned the story was apparently standard, at either the beginning or the end of the story.) The speaker then proceeded to tell the story. The audience, seated around the sides of the room, listened intently, and frequently interrupted with comments, questions, and exclamations of approval.

As noted earlier, the Iñupiat recognized two basic types of story: historical chronicles (*uqaluktuat*) and legends (*unipkaat*) (D. Jenness 1924:1; Ostermann 1942:163; Rainey 1947:269). The former dealt with exciting or disastrous events, such as accidents, battles, or particularly wonderful messenger festivals, all situated in the relatively recent past. The latter concerned an enormous variety of creatures and events from the more remote past; some were realistic in tone, but many were fantastic. As far as I know, there were no restrictions on which type could be told on any given occasion.

In my own experience, either kind of story took thirty minutes to an hour to tell, and ofttimes more, even when it was made clear that I was getting an abbreviated version. The old storytellers apparently included in their accounts details that might be of interest to their audience—for example, the precise location where each event happened, perhaps some information about what the weather conditions were, descriptions of special clothing, genealogical data about the protagonists (if human), and so on. Many accounts had songs and even short dances interspersed among narrative segments, and speakers also employed gestures and facial expressions to help them tell the story. The longest story of all was the legend of Qayaqtuaġiŋnaqtuuq, which reportedly took every evening for a month to tell in its entirety.[56]

It is beyond the scope of this work to attempt even a summary analysis of Iñupiaq stories. Readers who are interested in pursuing the matter are advised to consult the sources listed in endnote 57, which include stories told either in or just outside of the study region. Some of these materials have been published, but many have not. However, I believe that most are publicly accessible in Kotzebue, in Nome, or at the Rasmuson Library at the University of Alaska Fairbanks.[57]

Integration to Uncertainty Situations

Many activities were repeated day after day, week after week, and so grew to be boring. At certain seasons there was little to do in any case, and that, too, was boring. On the other hand, many fundamental elements in life were not so assured. Will the sea ice open up enough to make the seal-hunting and whaling seasons successful this spring? Why is my husband so late coming home from hunting tonight? Will so much rain fall this summer that fishing will be impossible? Where will the caribou migration take the animals this year? When will the storm abate so that men can hunt? What was the shadow that followed me yesterday while I checked my snares? The answers to questions like these would become known in time, but people wanted to try to do something to increase the odds of a positive outcome. The Iñupiat employed the same means as most other peoples to do this: magic.[58]

The Iñupiat employed magic in an effort to prevent calamities arising from unknown (and usually empirically unknowable) causes. This magic can be divided into two broad types: preventive and applied. Preventive magic, as the name suggests, was designed to prevent disaster from happening. Applied magic was employed to halt or ameliorate a disaster already in progress.

Preventive Magic

Preventive magic took four main forms: adherence to taboos, the performance of rituals, the use of amulets, and the performance of ceremonies. Taboos and rituals were discussed in Chapter 5, so only a brief review of those subjects is necessary at this point. A taboo, it may be recalled, is a prohibition against doing something, such as eating the meat of a hare before all the caribou-hide clothing had been made in the fall. If everyone obeyed the prescibed taboos and performed the requisite rituals, then the spirits of the animals would be pleased and allow more of their number to be taken by human hunters. If, on the other hand, someone broke a taboo or failed to perform a crucial ritual, trouble of some kind would ensue.

Amulets, it may be recalled, were objects imbued with magical properties.[59] Their most common purpose was protecting the owner from harm, although many were employed to produce a particular outcome. Examples of the latter include the following: an object worn by a pregnant woman to ensure her child would be of the sex she preferred; one placed in the bow of a boat to ensure success in whaling; and one attached to a float to keep a struck whale from sinking.

Amulets could take almost any form: an ermine skin, an effigy of an animal or spirit, a dried raven skin, a dried eagle skin, a small piece of rock, a bone, a small piece of wood, a bead, a dried bumblebee, a feather, an ivory or wood carving, a piece of dried polar bear nose, or a piece of wolf hide, just to name a few examples. Almost any object would do as long as it was imbued with the necessary power. However, there seems to have been an emphasis on using dried parts of those animals (including birds) thought to have special mystical powers, such as ravens, birds of prey, wolves, wolverines, and ermines.

Amulets were variously sewn to the outside of a person's clothing, attached to one's belt, fastened to a strap running across one's chest inside the parka, hung from the ceiling of a *qargi* or dwelling, or affixed to or made an integral part of a weapon or boat. They were placed wherever their particular power would be most effective. The Tikiġaġmiut distinguished between two types of amulet, a *tupitkaq*, which was worn on a person's body or clothing, and an *aanġuaq*, which was kept in a special place, such as the bow of a boat (Rainey 1947:272). If that distinction was made in other districts, the information has been lost. *Aanġuaq* is the term generally used in the study region today to refer to an amulet.

In 1924, when there were still lots of old-timers around, Knud Rasmussen (Ostermann and Holtved 1952) inquired about an amulet's power.

> In my talks with these Eskimos I always began with the question of whether it is the object *itself* that possesses magic power, or it is the *spirit* of the object that acts. For example in the case of the owl claw: is it the owl claw itself that helps the wearer, like a lucky half-penny helps anyone who may happen to have it in his purse, or is it the spirit of the owl that stands in a certain mystic relationship to the owner?
>
> The answer was the same everywhere: it is the *spirit of the owl* that helps: the claw is merely a characteristic symbol (Ostermann and Holtved 1952:129; italics in the original).

A key aspect of the use of amulets is that they could be used at the discretion of the owner, not a group of people, and not under the direction of a shaman.

The next question is, how did the power come to reside in the object in the first place? There seem to have been two ways. One was for a shaman to put it there, usually for a fee, and usually after performing a ritual of some kind. Alternatively, it happened spontaneously. As noted above, many of the animals whose skins or parts were commonly used as amulets were thought to have magical properties, ermines and ravens being perhaps the most common examples. Other objects had power as well, so the problem was to learn which ones had it and what the power did. It appears this was usually discovered by accident. For example, if a crew made an unusually successful harvest of oogruks in a short period of time, and if the captain subsequently discovered a piece of ivory, bone, or wood in the bottom of the boat, he would suspect that it might have been a factor in their success. He would take it along again in the boat, and if a similar outcome resulted, the object was quickly elevated to amulet status.

Amulets could be acquired by various means. One was to be fortunate in discovering one by accident. Another was to hire a shaman to produce one. Amulets could also be inherited or purchased, although their power was sometimes weakened in the process, particularly through purchase. They could also be stolen, although thieves ran the risk of having the amulet's power turn against them. If a woman secretly cut off a piece of clothing belonging to an outstanding hunter and used it as an amulet for her son, it took that man's skill and conveyed it to her son. When that man discovered that a piece had been cut from his clothing, he had to discard it. Otherwise, his skill would leave him and pass to the woman's child (Ostermann and Holtved 1952:125).

There was no limit to the number of amulets a given individual could own, and most people probably owned several. However, most people had one special amulet that gave them a mystical relationship with a certain species of animal. In addition to providing protection, the power in the amulet enabled its owner to turn into that kind of animal under certain conditions.

Among the Tikiġaġmiut, children were placed by their spiritual guardians or parents into one of two amulet classes.[60] The people in one of them, known as *quŋuqtuqtuq–*, received power from things relating to death. The people in the other, known as *iġniruaqtuqtuq–*, received power from things relating to birth.[61] The amulets were activated or strengthened by contact with agents relating to their class. For example,

> a person who is *irniroaktuktuk* may cure his own wound, broken arm, or any sickness by rubbing his body with a woman's menstrual pad or with something used by a woman during childbirth. . . . Similarly, a person who is *qongoakktuktuk* may use something taken from a grave or anything that had been made or used by a dead person (Rainey 1947:272).

Objects associated with one amulet class were taboo to people in the other one, greatly compounding the complications caused by taboos in general. However, there was a way to defend against this.

> Before a child received his charms [amulets] and after it had been decided to which class he should belong, his mother ate something which was kiruk [taboo] to people of that class, and this, acting in the manner of a vaccine serum, made him immune to the *kiruk* [tabooed] objects of his *anagoak's* [amulet's] class (Rainey 1947:273).

I have not heard of amulet classes existing in any other part of the study region.

Ceremonies, many of which were really an array of concatenated rituals, were the final form of preventive magic employed by the Iñupiat. Of particular interest here were those intended to ensure hunting success, bring good weather, and, more generally, prevent disaster. While other ceremonies were held to celebrate past success, usually their ultimate purpose was to lay the groundwork for future success in the same activity. In this respect, they anticipated future events as much as they recognized those past.

A few ceremonies consisted of procedures that could be performed by a single individual in just a few moments. Somewhat more complex were singing ceremonies in which several people joined their voices to sing magic songs intended to bring luck in a beluga or caribou hunt, in battle, or in fishing (Elwood Hunnicutt 1970; Jensen 1970.5). Still more elaborate ceremonies were embedded in festivals as distinct episodes in the larger celebrations, but others were discrete events. The most complex ceremonies involved entire settlements and took hours to complete.

The most elaborate and the most numerous ceremonies seem to have been held in the major whaling center of Point Hope. A considerable amount of information on these ceremonies is available thanks to Froelich Rainey (1947).[62] As his monograph shows, the annual cycle there featured one ceremony after another, practically all year long. The only break came in July and August, when the settlement was largely abandoned. Wales probably was not far behind Point Hope in ceremonial elaboration, but the documentation there is not nearly as complete (E. Curtis 1930:137–42; Thornton 1931:165–71). Most of the major ceremonies in both settlements were directly or indirectly related to success in bowhead whaling.

Ceremonies were concerned with many important aspects of Iñupiaq life.[63] They were performed at critical points in the processing and consumption of many animals, but particularly bowhead whales, beluga, bears, and wolves and wolverines. Increasing the supply of game was a common focus of ceremonies held during difficult times. Also important on the ceremonial agenda were pregnancy, birth, name-giving, a child's first kill or other harvest, menarche, and death. Particularly important ceremonies typically required special clothing and ornaments (often including masks), and they frequently incorporated episodes of dancing and feasting.

To give the reader some idea of what relatively complex Iñupiaq ceremonies were like, I present summary descriptions of two of them. These are the Kaŋiġmiut game increase ceremony and the feast of the dead.

The Kaŋiġmiut game increase ceremony was held on an ad hoc basis, whenever food was scarce and hard times were at hand.[64] Under a shaman's direction, hunters hoping for success carved effigies of the desired game.

> The figures were about six inches [15 cm] long and showed in fine detail the form of the species depicted. Eye holes were inlaid with baleen . . . or filled with greasy soot. A hole was drilled through the back of each carving for reception of a sinew suspension cord. When a hunter had completed his carvings, they were hung from a horizontal pole fastened to the interior rear wall of the [*qargi*] (Sunno 1951.117).

The village residents then gathered in the *qargi*, and a shaman began to beat his drum, sing, and dance. Eventually a spirit entered the carvings and animated them, causing them to swing.

The shaman then called each of the participating hunters one by one. When his name was called, the hunter stepped forward and seated himself on the floor near the center of the room and facing the rear wall of the *qargi*.

> The [shaman] then placed in the man's hands an imaginary model bow and arrow.[65] Carefully now he aimed at a vital spot on one of his carvings. The [shaman] asked him, "Do you really recognize it? Are you ready? Do you kill it?" At this moment the hunter released the invisible arrow. If the man had sincerely concentrated upon his objective the arrow found its mark and the [effigy] began to bleed profusely. Sea mammals were killed in the same manner, but a small imaginary dart was thrown (Sunno 1951.117).

Sea mammal and fish carvings were disposed of by dropping them into deep water through a hole chopped in the ice. Land mammal and bird carvings were burned in an open fire a hundred yards (90 m) or so from the *qargi*. The rationale for these procedures is presently unknown.

A feast of the dead of some kind was apparently held throughout the study region, although it has been attested only for the Wales (E. Curtis 1930:149), Point Hope (Rainey 1947:26, based on information obtained from Quwana 1940), Buckland (Sunno 1951.17, 1951.50), lower (?) Selawik (E. Curtis 1930:227), and central Kobuk districts (Giddings 1961:22–24, his source being Charlie Piġliġiaq Custer).[66] I say *a* feast instead of *the* feast because there seems to have been considerable variation in when it was held and how it was conducted.[67] It is more appropriately thought of as a ceremony than as a feast, because eating was only one part of it. In Point Hope, it was held on the morning of the third day of the whaling festival (at a time when the settlement had only two *qargich*), and everyone who had died in the preceding year was mourned and honored at the same time. In other districts, a separate ceremony was held for each person who had died a year (sometimes more) earlier. Since the Point Hope and Kobuk versions of this event have been described in print, and since very little has been recorded of the event in Wales and Selawik, I summarize below the Buckland (Kaŋiġmiut) version, which has not been published, but for which, thanks to Charles Lucier, there is a fairly complete account.

The Kaŋiġmiut mourning ceremony was held a year or more after a person's demise, depending on how long it took his or her family to acquire the wherewithal to produce it (Sunno 1951.17). When enough supplies were on hand, a messenger was sent by the deceased's family to invite three special guests: someone having the same name and sex as the deceased, and two others who had helped place the body on the grave. When the messenger arrived with the guests, who usually brought several relatives with them, they were greeted with a display of food. The hosts asked what presents they would like to receive. The guests usually asked for something the dead person was especially fond of. Then the hosts turned to preparing the gifts, which sometimes required an intense effort spanning several days.

The ceremony itself took place in the *qargi*, and involved the relatives of the deceased, the three special guests, and various others as well. The deceased's namesake was dressed in a new outfit of fine clothing made for him or her by the honored dead's family. When everyone was seated, three large bowls of "Eskimo ice cream" (*akutuq*) were brought in and set on the floor in front of the three honored guests. They proceeded to portion it out to all who wanted some. After the feasting, the requested gifts were presented to the three honored guests, who responded with gifts of their own. Gifts were also made to others who had assisted with the burial of the honored dead. The gift exchange was followed by joyous dancing and singing, during the first part of which small bits of food and drops of water were thrown up toward the skylight as offerings to the deceased. The dancing continued all night.

Applied Magic

What I am referring to as "applied" as opposed to "preventive" magic is magic employed to deal with some kind of unfortunate situation that was either at hand or in progress. There were two basic forms: magic songs and shamanic procedures.

Most magic songs were, like amulets, owned and used by individuals for their particular purposes.[68] These purposes were usually fairly specific. They included such things as bringing down a wounded animal that was on the verge of escaping, breaking the bow of an enemy who was about to release an arrow, flushing out terrorists who were thought to be hiding in the willows, driving away an evil shadow that was following one around, and causing a troublesome wind to die down. A song that worked in one context did not necessarily work in another, although some seem to have been multipurpose. I was told that these songs could be acquired by purchase or inheritance, and I presume that shamans could invent new ones. Many people apparently did not own any, and only a few people owned more than one or two.

These songs were unusual in that they almost never consisted of more than three or four short words, and in that they were expressed in some mysterious language other than Iñupiaq. They were used only in times of extreme duress, perhaps just three or four times in the owner's entire lifetime, perhaps never. But the owner would be reassured knowing that the songs were there if needed.

The other general type of applied magic was shamanic procedures.[69] These were initiated when someone was sick, or missing, say, and a shaman was hired to solve the problem. Or, they could be provided without fee when the entire group or settlement to which the *aŋatkuq* belonged was afflicted in some way. Iñupiaq shamans seem to have employed a wide variety of procedures to solve the many problems they were asked to deal with. Their general approach is perhaps best indicated through some specific examples.

The first case involved a group of Tikiġaġmiut who used to net beluga together (Aġviqsiiña 1940.1:61–62; Q. Dives 1940:26–27). Eight of them happened to be shamans, presumably with differing degrees of expertise. On one occasion the rope holding the outer edge of the net broke loose, so the net became ineffective. One of the men, who was not a shaman, challenged the shamans to solve the problem. So they made a little tent. Two of the older men got their drums and started to beat them and sing. Two of the younger men, one with an eagle amulet and the other with that of a raven, walked round and round the tent until their familiar spirits had taken over their bodies. Then they were stripped, tied up with long lines having nooses on the end, and placed in the tent. The other men continued singing and drumming. After awhile an eagle feather and a raven feather—that is, the two young men in different forms—flew out of a hole at the top of the tent and went to Cape Thompson, which was quite some distance away. There they tied their ropes to a big rock, and flew back, bringing the rock with them. One of them fell into the sea before he reached the others, but his companion made it and the rock was attached to the line holding the net. Soon a walrus crawled out on the beach and turned into the missing man. That night another walrus got caught in the net and was killed. From then on the net was successful in capturing beluga.

The second example involved some Kaŋiġmiut (Sunno 1951.89). The people were at their beluga-hunting stations on Eschscholtz Bay, but the hunting was poor. Three shamans, two women and a man, decided to do something about it. So, dressed in fine new clothes,

> they walked together from the beach out onto the mud flats that the low tide had laid bare. They kept walking until the water came to their waists and then to their necks and then over their heads. The three people, these shamans, they disappeared completely from the sight of people who were watching from the beach.
>
> The tide rose to high, slacked, and turned to ebb. Then, the three shamans came from the water and their clothing was completely dry, as dry as when they went into [the] water (Sunno 1951.89).

Apparently, the three had gone well out into Kotzebue Sound, located the beluga, and driven them toward Eschscholtz Bay. After they emerged, the water became calm, and then a large number of belugas appeared just offshore. The hunt that followed was very successful.

The third example purportedly took place in the Qikiqtaġruŋmiut area (Fletcher Gregg, in Northwest Iñupiat Elders Conference 1983c:3). A channel had become blocked so that fish could not run through it. A shaman named Kunannaagruk had some men bind his ankles with a long rope, the other end of which was loose. Then the shaman removed his head and gave it to another man. His body was thrown into the water, and his head was taken into the *qargi*. When the rope became taut, several men held onto it with all their strength. Eventually they managed to pull it from the water and into the *qargi*, feet first. When they finished pulling, the person who had possession of the head placed it back on the body. With that, Kunannaagruk announced, "Your river is clean now," and it was. Kunannaagruk reportedly performed this feat on a number of occasions.

The final example is a more recent one, probably from around the beginning of the 20th century (Vestal 1970). It happened near Deering, in former Pittaġmiut territory. One evening a young man with a pain in his back so severe that he could not walk was being hauled on a sled by the members of his family. They brought him into the little settlement and offered to pay a shaman named Uluġaak some strips of wolverine skin (parka trim) to help them. After dinner, they put the stricken man into a tent, and the shaman told everyone to be quiet and not walk around outdoors. Uluġaak began to drum and sing to call his familiar spirit.

The familiar arrived in due course. It stayed on the tent's ceiling, but talked to the shaman. After a brief conversation, the shaman put the drum on the floor, took the drumstick, and walked over to the sick man. He asked him, "Where's your pain?" After the man showed him, Uluġaak sniffed around for a few moments, then placed one end of the drumstick on the man's back and sucked on the other. After doing this a few times, he walked over to his drum and spit out a bullet. It turned out that the patient had been shot some time before, but he had not informed Uluġaak of that fact.

One must concede that shamans who could do the kinds of things described in these stories could solve monumental problems. Unfortunately, the stories deal only with successes. There are no accounts of failure, which one must assume was fairly common. Knud Rasmussen (1925) wrote that he

> heard of several cases where the conjuror himself was so sure of his supernatural powers that these demonstrations resulted in [his/her] death. This fact answers the question as to the genuineness of the conjuror's art. Many are conscious fakers, but there are others who take it in profound earnest (Rasmussen 1925:532).

Regardless of occasional or even frequent failure, the expectation and hope that shamans had at least the potential to perform what most of us would call miracles had to have been a positive motivating factor for people facing the many uncertainties of Iñupiaq life.

Affective Expression

Affective expression is the process whereby individuals exhibit their feelings (cf. Levy 1952:505). This is a singularly difficult subject to investigate at a distance of more than 150 years from the relevant time period, but some information on the subject is available.

I begin with Simpson's (1875:246) statement that "in disposition [the Iñupiat] are good-humoured and cheerful, seemingly burdened by no care. Their feelings are lively but not lasting, and the temper frequently quick, but placable." He also said (Simpson 1875:239) that "the expression of the countenance is one of habitual good-humour in the great majority of both sexes." One may question whether this was so among themselves, or just when meeting with Westerners with whom they were familiar. Most of the 19th-century sources (e.g., F. Beechey 1831, II:303; Maguire 1857:416–32; VanStone ed. 1977:81) did not characterize Iñupiaq demeanor in such positive terms; some of my informants volunteered the information that important people used to wear a "sad" expression when they were out and about in the settlement. A few elders in Kotzebue were mentioned as examples, and they certainly did walk around with dour expressions.

Grief was expressed by women with loud crying and moaning, whereas among men there was a tendency to express it through violent or otherwise disruptive behavior, such as breaking things, attacking people, and generally causing trouble (Simpson 1875:247, 250; Stoney 1900:830–31; Woolfe 1893:135). Anger was apparently exhibited by both men and women through sullen facial expressions, although angry middle-aged women sometimes unburdened themselves with lengthy tirades as well (Woolfe 1893:135). According to Simpson (1875),

> as a general rule, they are particularly careful not to say anything displeasing in each other's presence. If a man gets angry or out of temper, the others, even his nearest friends, keep out of his way, trusting to his recovery in a short time (Simpson 1875:250).

Thornton (1931) reported that affection was expressed by people "putting (not rubbing!) their noses together," a practice known as *kuniktuq*.

> Among males the *koniktuk* is hardly ever practiced—except perhaps between a father and his infant children. Mothers *koniktuk* their little ones, lovers their sweethearts, and husbands their wives (Thornton 1931:61).

However,

> in other relations they are inclined to be stoically undemonstrative. Under most circumstances no caresses are either given or received. Even when the members of the same family meet after having been separated for several months there is not even a shake of the hand—hardly a lighting up of the eye (Thornton 1931:61).

Thornton (1931) also found that stoicism had some benefits.

> It often happens that they are reduced almost to the verge of starvation by unfavorable weather that prevents them from hunting. In like manner, their trading voyages may be seriously hindered by adverse winds. Under such circumstances the complaints and curses of the average Caucasian hunter or sailor would be both loud and deep; but the Kinik-Mete [Kiŋikmiut], so far as we can ascertain, accept all such dispensations of Providence without a murmur. In other words, with a wonderfully philosophical patience they resign themselves to the inevitable (Thornton 1931:62; see Woolfe 1893:135 for a similar observation).

Another context in which stoicism was exhibited was in athletic competitions, especially of the one-on-one variety. Even though each competitor was using all the strength he could muster, each tried to wear an impassive expression in order to intimidate his opponent.

One form of expression almost all of the early observers commented on was the Iñupiaq sense of humor. It featured mimicry, irony, sarcasm, plays on words, and "a strong sense of the ludicrous," all of which evoked enthusiastic laughter.[70] A man participating in the blanket toss, for example, was greeted with "shrieks of derision" if he lost his balance (Ostermann and Holtved 1952:28; see also Stoney 1900:835), as was a smoker who was "thrown into a fit of coughing by the smoke getting into his lungs" (F. Beechey 1831, II:304). Iñupiaq humor could also be pretty raunchy, much to the disgust of early Western arbiters of good taste (F. Beechey 1831, I:396; Wells and Kelly 1890:22; Woolfe 1893:141–42).

A general sense of Iñupiaq humor can be conveyed with a few examples. The first was observed by Kotzebue (1821) in 1816. An *umiaq* with eight people aboard approached the ship for purposes of trade.

> [B]ut the Americans [i.e., Iñupiat] treated us very contemptuously, offering us little rags of rats' and dogs' skins in exchange [for our goods]; but when they observed that we laughed at their goods, they also joined heartily in the laugh, talking much to each other, and at last advised us to put the rags in our noses and ears (Kotzebue 1821, I:222).

The second example was observed by the members of Beechey's expedition, in 1826. The ship was off the Tapqaġmiut coast and was visited by several boatloads of people who wanted to trade. Among the things desired by the British were labrets.

> They readily disengaged these from their lips, and sold them, without minding the inconvenience of the saliva that flowed through the badly cicatriced orifice over the chin; but on the contrary derided us when we betrayed disgust at the

spectacle, by thrusting their tongues through the hole and winking their eyes
(F. Beechey 1831, I:343).

The next example was witnessed in 1826 by the members of a barge party detached from
Beechey's expedition. Several *umiat* were trying to get close to the barge. One of them tipped
over, and its occupants were thrown into the water.

> An Esquimaux dress is very ill adapted to aquatic exercises, and persons acquainted
> with it would think there was considerable danger in being plunged into the sea
> thus habited; but the natives in the other baidars [*umiat*] did not seem to reflect
> on these consequences, and laughed most immoderately at the accident; they,
> however, went to the assistance of their friends, and rescued them all. It must have
> been a cold dip for these people, as the rigging and masts were partially covered
> with ice (F. Beechey 1831, I:418).

The final example occurred in June of 1886. Ensign W. L. Howard, of Stoney's expedition,
was accompanying a large party of Natives heading to Barrow to trade.

> The ice began breaking and the river rising. The high water forced everybody
> to leave the quarters on the spit and move into the interior. . . . The shamans
> gathered at the bank and would stick their knives at the water's edge to prevent
> any rising beyond it. Each failure was greeted with derisive laughter as the
> discomfited medicine men stepped back and picked up their submerged knives
> (Stoney 1900:818).

Infants and children could express their sentiments more openly than teenagers or adults.
Young adults, particularly women, were supposed to be reticent, at least in public; middle-
aged and old ladies could express almost any sentiment they wanted through gesture, facial
expression, and speech; and adult men, and particularly older men, were supposed to act
dignified most of the time. But much depended on the social context of the interaction. A
man, for example, could coo and smile and talk in an animated way to his infant daughter,
but was not supposed to look at or talk to his mother-in-law (even if she lived in the same
house). Cross cousins (*iḷḷuġiik*) could express both joy and anger to one another in ways that
were inappropriate for people in almost every other kind of relationship. A group of old men
in the *qargi* could express dismay at a young man's misbehavior, but the same individuals
could not do so anywhere else. Unfortunately, complexities such as these elude us for the
most part as far as the early 19th century is concerned.

Artistic Expression

Artistic expression is the process whereby skill and creative imagination are used in the
production of aesthetic texts, sounds, movements, or objects (cf. Levy 1952:535). Iñupiaq
storytellers were producers of aesthetic texts, since, in addition to factual accuracy and
completeness, eloquence was a major criterion in terms of which their performances were
appraised even if they were not the creators of the story. (But, of course, someone, sometime, had to create each story.) Creators of Iñupiaq dances and songs (which often went
together) were producers of aesthetic sounds and movements. Storytellers and creators of
songs and dances have been discussed. The creation of aesthetic objects, however, has not
been considered.

Beechey (1831, I:344, 345, 409; II:302, 307, 310) was amazed at the variety and quality of
the ivory and bone carvings that he found among the Iñupiat. He quickly discovered that
he could learn a lot about the Iñupiaq way of life simply by looking at such objects.

On the outside of this and other instruments there were etched a variety of figures of men, beasts, and birds, andc., with a truth and character which showed the art to be common among them. The reindeer were generally in herds: in one picture they were pursued by a man in a stooping posture in snow-shoes; in another, he had approached nearer to his game, and was in the act of drawing his bow. A third represented the manner of taking seals with an inflated skin of the same animal as a decoy; it was placed upon the ice, and not far from it a man was lying upon his belly with a harpoon ready to strike the animal when it should make its appearance. Another was dragging a seal home upon a small sledge; and several baidars [*umiat*] were employed harpooning whales which had been previously shot with arrows; and thus by comparing one device with another a little history was obtained which gave us a better insight into their habits than could be elicited from any signs and intimations (F. Beechey 1831, I:344–45).[71]

There is no hint of the specific carvings described by Beechey being imbued with magical properties, but they might have been present in others. Components of whaling harpoons, for example, which were frequently carved in the likeness of a whale, probably had magical power. Wooden masks, which were often (usually?) created under the direction of a shaman, definitely did have magical power.

At least some carving seems to have been done primarily for the purpose of demonstrating the skill of the workman. Once again, I turn to Beechey (1831):

Of all their manufactures, that of ivory chains is the most ingenious. These are cut of solid pieces of ivory, each link being separately relieved, and are sometimes twenty-six inches [66 cm] in length. For what purpose they are used I know not; but part of the last link is frequently left solid, and formed in imitation of a whale; and these chains being strong, they may in some way or other be appropriated to the capture of that animal (F. Beechey 1831, II:310).[72]

If chains were involved in the capture of whales, it was through magic rather than by means of a mechanical process.

There is a considerable literature on Eskimo art, including some excellent work on that produced in Northwest Alaska (e.g., D. Ray 1961:13–26, 154–56; 1977:9–36; Ray and Blaker 1967). Most of this literature focuses on the objects themselves rather than on the motivation of the artists, which is the concern here. To the extent the literature does deal with the motivation, it inevitably emphasizes recent periods rather than the era of interest here.

Iñupiaq men made objects from wood, bone, antler, and ivory by carving, while women made objects from hide, bark, and grass by cutting, sewing, and weaving. Many of the items were made for practical use, yet the majority were created with an elegance and style that far surpassed the requirements of their utilitarian purposes. Line splicers, for example, were made in the shape of a seal or some other animal; harpoon heads were carved in the shape of a seal or a whale; fancy clothes were made of a mosaic of skins, enhanced with trim made from the furs of a variety of different animals. The question is, did people make these things the way they did just to pass the time of day, or did they do it to create something beautiful? The true answer to that question may never be known, but my own suspicion is that they did it for both reasons.

E. W. Nelson (1899) concluded that they did this work primarily as a way to pass the time.

In places where ivory is plentiful the men appeared to delight in occupying their leisure time in making carvings from that material or from bone, sometimes for use, but frequently merely for pastime, and many little images are made as toys

for children. The articles thus produced are not regarded by them as having any
particular value, and I was often amused at the delight with which they sold
specimens of their work for one or two needles, a brass button, or some similar
trifle (Nelson 1899:196–97).

In other words, Nelson is saying that what he regarded as art objects were viewed by the
Natives themselves as being the equivalent of our doodles. Presumably the same things could
have been said about at least some of women's work in hides, bark, and grass. If Nelson's
view is correct, then this discussion should have been presented in the section dealing with
adaptation to certainty situations instead of here.

It is difficult to believe that the Iñupiat would have created such handsome work just to
pass the time of day. However, it is also hard to argue with Nelson's informed observation,
despite the fact that it was probably based primarily on what he saw somewhat to the south
of the study region. The artists certainly could not have done such work if they had not
had free time, for these objects were not hurriedly created. Furthermore, they were made by
ordinary people, not members of an artisan class. Until further evidence is acquired, then,
one may conclude that the Iñupiat lavished special care on the things they made *both* to
while away the time *and* for the satisfaction it gave them to produce attractive work.

Notes to Chapter Six

1. The approach taken here is adapted from Levy's (1952:504–41; 1966:341–74) "structure of integration and expression." However, I do not employ his very convoluted but technically more precise definitions of key concepts. I also regard it as axiomatic that emotional expression is an essential part of integration as he defines those terms, although neither Levy nor I have demonstrated that to be the case.

2. This does not mean that deaf and blind people could not survive, but they needed the help of people who could see and hear.

3. This section is based partly on my personal knowledge, but primarily on the work of Lawrence Kaplan (1981, 1984, 1990, 2000). The reader interested in greater detail is urged to consult Kaplan's work. I thank Professor Kaplan for his comments on a draft of this section.

4. According to Jimmy Killigivuk (1960.5) there was a "dialect difference in language" between the Tikiġaġmiut and the Kivalliñiġmiut, but he could have been speaking merely of subdialect differences. My own informants made distinctions at the subdialect level, but couldn't aggregate subdialects into larger linguistic units.

5. F. Beechey (1831, I:343, 425), Gough (1973:148), Hooper (1881:62), Nelson (1899:302), D. Ray (1983c:38), Sours (1987).

6. Aġviqsiiña (1940.1), Avessuk (1983.5), Brown, Outwater, Sheldon, et al. (1978), Eutuk (1983), A. Hawley (1964.3), B. Hawley (1982), Lee et al. (1990:43, 53, 55, 109, 111), H. Ningeulook (1983.2), C. Okpowruk (1983.3), Sunno (1951.96), Martha Swan (1965.4), M. Tocktoo (1983.4, 1983.6), Elsie Weyiouanna (1981), Essau Weyiouanna (1983.2).

7. C. and R. Adams (1965), Cantwell (1889b:89), A. Hawley (1964.3, 1965.16, 1965.17), Hooper (1881:109), Simpson (1875:249–50), Stoney (1900:831–32), Clinton Swan (1965.5), Woolfe (1893:134–35, 137).

8. Cantwell (1889b:89), Clinton Swan in Lee et al. (1990:55), O. Swan (1965), Sun (1985:22–23, 30), Tingook (1960.4).

9. B. Hawley (1965), L. Jensen in Lee et al. (1990:43), Northwest Iñupiat Elders Conference (1976a, 1976c, 1983d), Sunno (1951.18).

10. Most of the sources of information on these roles are cited in Chapter 2.

11. E. Ballot in Lee et al. (1990:5, 7), A. Douglas (1976.6), J. Foster (1970), Glover (1970.5), Jensen (1970.3), Keats (1970.9) T. Morris (1970), Northwest Iñupiat Elders Conference (1976.a:4; 1976d:8), C. Sheldon (1973–74.3, 1973–74.5, 1973–74.6, 1973–74.7, 1973–74.17).

12. Beaver (1984), Dixon and Kirchner (1982), Keats (1976), Kennedy (1965.2), Lucier, VanStone, and Keats (1971:253–54), Martha Swan (1984.4), Wells and Kelly (1890:23).

13. Aġviqsiiña (1940.1:63–65, 79), Beaver (1984), K. Burns (1960.2), Q. Dives (1940:37), J. Foster (1970), L. Gallahorn (1969.2), Glover (1970.5, 1970.6), A. Hawley (1965.8. 1976.2), B. Hawley (1965, 1989), Jensen (1970.3), Keats (1970.7), Kennedy (1965.2), Northwest Iñupiat Elders Conference (1976.d:10–11), Sheldon (1973–74.1, 1973–74.2, 1973–74.3, 1973–74.7, 1973–74.10, 1973–74.14, 1973–74.16, 1973–74.17), Stoney (1900:834–35), Sunno (1951.14, 1951.114), Martha Swan (1965.2), Wells and Kelly (1890:22–23), Vestal (1969, 1970).

14. The sources are cited in Chapter 2.

15. F. Beechey (1831, II:255), Collinson (1889:139), Hooper (1884:111), Sunno (1951.66). See also Cantwell (1889a:61), Spencer (1956).

16. This is recapitulated from Burch (1998a:373–74).

17. Actually, it was not uninhabited, but was part of the summer range of Athapaskans living in the eastern part of Alaska. However, their numbers had been so reduced by disease at this point that the Iñupiat regarded the country as being uninhabited.

18. The use of firearms in suicides came later (Thornton 1931:140).

19. Most of Nelson's experience was south of the study region, but he was in frequent contact with emigrants from it.

20. In late May he would have come to a very different conclusion.

21. E. Atoruk (1989), Brower (ms:484–85), K. Burns (1960.2), R. Cleveland (1965.7), Q. Dives (1940:33–36), B. Foote (1992:164–66), Grinnell (1901:35), D. Jenness (1953:11–13), Johnston (1978a:47–48), Lowenstein (1993:96–99), Rainey (1940.1), Stoney (1900:835), Sunno (1951.54), Thornton (1931:122–24), M. Tocktoo (1983.3), Wells and Kelly (1890:28), Woolfe (1893:141).

22. Aġviqsiiña (1941.1:44–45), *Alaska Native News* (1985), R. Cleveland (1965.1, 1965.7), Q. Dives (1940:33–36), S. Dives (1970), B. Foote (1992:164–66), Keats (1970.5, 1970.10), Sunno (1951.6), VanStone (1962b:115). Many of these contests are still enjoyed in Iñupiaq villages during Christmas week, and at the World Eskimo-Indian Olympics in Fairbanks each summer. For photographs of some of these events at the latter, see Kelly and Lund (1986:102–13).

23. Events number 3, 5, 10, 11, 17, and 20 in Berit Foote's (1992) list appear to have been of this type.

24. This account is taken almost verbatim from Lucier's record of an interview with Andrew Sunno (1951.53).

25. This account is taken almost verbatim from Lucier's record of an interview with Andrew Sunno (1951.92).

26. F. Beechey (1831, II:308), Cantwell (1889b:89), R. Cleveland (1965.9), Q. Dives (1940.33), B. Foote (1992:170–72), L. Gallahorn (1970.1), Glover (1970.5), A. Hawley (1973.2), Elwood Hunnicutt (1970), Jensen (1970.4, 1970.6), Kialook (1964), T. Mitchell (1970), Niġuwana (1940.1:8), C. Okpowruk (1983.4), C. Smith (1970), Stoney (1900:835), Wells and Kelly (1890:25), Woolfe (1893:141).

27. R. Cleveland (1965.7), Glover (1970.5), Rainey (1947:262), Sunno (1951.30). For photographs of the blanket toss, see Kelly and Lund (1986:98, 99, 100–1).

28. See photo in Van Valin (1944:97).

29. Aġviqsiiña (1940), A. Hawley (1973.5), J. Killigivuk (1960.2), Rainey (1940.1, 1947:252), Ray and Blaker (1967:45–46), Seemann (1853, II:63–64), VanStone (1962b:121), Vestal (1970), Woolfe (1893:141–42).

30. If the number of people in residence had been much larger, Beechey and his men might not have been greeted in such a friendly manner.

31. This dance may have been referred to by the term *mumaaqqiq–* (verb stem).

32. Aġviqsiiña (1940.1:33), A. Hawley (1973.5), Johnston (1975a:7), S. Rock (1940).

33. L. Gallahorn (1970.2), A. Hawley (1973.5), Johnston (1975a:1; 1975b:223), Pulu, Johnston, Sampson, and Newlin (1979:1–4).

34. In this paragraph I used Iñupiaq verb stems as English nouns.

35. Aġviqsiiña (1941.1:69), B. Foote (1992:166–70), Johnston (1975a:2–4), Killigivuk (1961.2), Kunuyaq (1940:8), Pulu, Johnston, Sampson, and Newlin (1979), Rainey (1947:150–51).

36. K. and F. Burns (1960), Glover (1970.4, 1970.6), Grinnell (1901:51), Koranda (1972), Stoney (1900:836), Thornton (1931:78), Wells and Kelly (1890:22), Woolfe (1893:141–42).

37. Aġviqsiiña (1940.1:64), K. Burns (1960.1), R. Cleveland (1966, 1970.3), J. Hadley (1951.1), A. Hawley (1976.6), Jensen (1970.4), Johnston (1974a; 1974b; 1974c; 1976b:12–13; 1976c:439; 1988b; 1990), Killigivuk (1959.1), Koranda (1964, 1972), Ostermann and Holtved (1952:28), Pulu, Johnston, Sampson, and Newlin (1979), Sunno (1951.20, 1951.82, 1951.83, 1951.84, 1951.85, 1951.86, 1951.100), Thornton (1931:78), Woolfe (1893:141–42).

38. This paragraph is based entirely on the work of Thomas Johnston (particularly 1975b, but also 1975c, 1976a, 1976b, 1978b) and Lorraine Koranda (1964, 1972).

39. I regret having applied the term "festival" to the bone-smashing sessions of the Kivalliñiġmiut, and to the bone-smashing and sewing sessions of the Nuataaġmiut (Burch 1998a:45, 104, 106). Those were very different types of occasion from the ones discussed here.

40. Eliyak (1931), Elwood Hunnicutt (1970), Jensen (1970.1, 1970.2), C. Smith (1970), Thornton (1931:226), Vestal (1970).

41. The other major whaling center, Wales, apparently did not have a festival comparable to the whaling festival at Point Hope. At Wales they seem to have had a smaller, ceremony-filled festival after each whale that was taken (E. Curtis 1930:140–42; Fair 2003; Thornton 1931:167–70).

42. This account is based primarily on Rainey (1947:262–63), who got his information in 1940 from Frank Aġviqsiiña, Ququk Dives, Iviqsiq, Peter Kunuyaq, Nasugluk and Nasugruk, Niġuwana, Quwana, and Sam Uyaġaq Rock. See also Brower (ms:188), Larson (2003), Woolfe (1893:141).

43. Alġaqsruutit (1983), Attla and Attla (1991), Booth (1960.4:45–49), F. Burns (1952), R. Cleveland (1970.2), E. Curtis (1930:146–47, 173–77, 213–14), M. Curtis (1970), Eliyak (1931), Fair (2001), D. Foster (1970.2), L. Gallahorn (1969.2), R. Gallahorn (1952.19, 1952.20), Giddings (1956:37–38, 43–46; 1961:24–28, 52–60, 151–53), F. Glover (1970.5), Hall (1975:18–19, 259–62, 356–57, 370–71), Hawkes (1913, 1914), M. Howard (1952), Edna Hunnicutt (1960.3:33–36), J. Killigivuk (1961.3), Lucier (1952), Luther (1960.2), Monroe (1960), Oquilluk (1973:149–66), Ostermann and Holtved (1952:103–12), Ray and Blaker (1967:34–36, 45–46), C. Smith (1970), Stefansson (1951:87–89), Stoney (1900:844), Sun (1985:80–81), Sunno (1951.6, 1951.7, 1951.62, 1951.113), Vestal (1970), Walton (1965.2), Woolfe (1893:140–41).

44. For a summary, see Burch (1998b:170–79).

45. A photograph of a man with two of these sticks is accessible online in the Digital Archive of the Alaska State Library, record group P320 (Reverend Samuel Spriggs photographs), photo 22.

46. The most detailed study of the wolf dance was made by Deanna Kingston (1999), but that was from King Island, south of the region of interest here.

47. The sketches were published by Phebus (1972:109–14). Regarding the artist's possible place of origin, see Kingston (1999:73, no. 6).

48. Ostermann and Holtved (1952:111) have published a photograph of a real wolf's head apparently used during this dance, and Koranda (1964:19) also refers to wolf-skin head masks.

49. F. Beechey (1831, I:390–91, 441), Cantwell (1887:25, 51; 1889a:70, 71, 72), A. Clark (1970; 1977; 1995:31), Clark and Clark (1976), Eliyak (1931), J. Foster (1970), L. Gallahorn (1969.2, 1970.3), Healy (1887:13, 16), Hooper (1881:25–26, 39, 44; 1884:39–40, 78, 102), Elwood Hunnicutt (1970), Jensen (1970.4), Keats (1970.2, 1970.5), Kiana (1970), Kingston (1996), Kisautaq and Kean (1981:619–21), C. Lee (1970), McClellan (1970.2), McLenegan (1887:73, 74), McElwaine (1901:108), T. Mitchell (1970), Nelson (1877–81: entry for July 17, 1881; 1899:14, 229, 231, 261–62), Northwest Iñupiat Elders Conference (1976d:16), Rainey (1947:267–68), Samms (1897–98, 1899–1900, 1901–2), Simpson (1875:236), C. Smith (1970), Stefansson (1914a; 1914b:314–15), Stoney (ms:160), VanStone ed. (1977:58–59), White (1889: entry for Aug. 22, 1889), Woolfe (1893:137).

50. See, for example, Anderson et al. (1998:98).

51. Aġviqsiiña (1940.6–12), E. Ballott in Lee et al. (1990:7, 9), Brower (ms:168–68, 260, 273–74), Glover (1970.1), B. Hawley (1982), M. Hawley (1965.1), H. Hunnicutt (1970), D. Jenness (1953:5–6), Keats (1970.7), T. Morris (1970), Northwest Iñupiat Elders Conference (1976a, 1976f), Sunno (1951.8, 1951.12, 1951.13, 1951.91).

52. This is a verb stem.

53. Collinson (1889:137), Hooper (1881:60; 1994:104–5), Jensen (1970.3), Simpson (1850b, 1850c), J. Stalker (1965.1).

54. To my knowledge, no Westerner ever observed a storytelling session in the study region during the first half of the 19th century, nor did any of my Iñupiaq informants. However, I think it reasonable to suppose that the storytelling customs my oldest informants saw and heard in the 1880s and 1890s must have been pretty close to those existing fifty years earlier. I believe that the level of generalization of the present account admits of its application to the early 19th century.

55. This account of stories and storytelling is based on brief conversations with Robert Cleveland and Simon Paneak in 1970, extensive conversations over many years with Amos Hawley, and the following documentary sources: Bergsland (1987), Giddings (1956:34–36), Hall (1975), D. Jenness (1924:1–2; 1957:62–63), Kisautaq and Kean (1981), Lowenstein (1992:xxv–xl), Ostermann (1942:164), Ostermann and Holtved (1952:52, 150), Rasmussen (1932:v–vl; 1933:295–96), Sokonik (1918), Stefansson (1914b:207), Wells and Kelly (1890:22).

56. E. Brown (1981a), Giddings (1961:94–98), Lee, Sampson, and Tennant (1991), Ostermann and Holtved (1952:52, 68–71, 229–53), Rasmussen (1932), Stefansson (1914b:207).

57. The number of entries listed below may serve as a crude indicator of the substantial volume of material contained in Iñupiaq folktales and historical narratives. There is some, but not a great deal of, overlap between the different collections. However, the entire set must be only a small sample of the repertoire available to Iñupiaq raconteurs in the early 19th century. Furthermore, I suspect, although I cannot demonstrate, that many or most of the stories presented in these sources are relatively brief, and often extremely brief, summaries of the stories that Iñupiat would have heard from a master storyteller 200 years ago.

    Anderson (2005), Anderson and Sampson (2003), Aġviqsiiña (1940.1:54–56, 74–75, 98–100, 108–10), Beaver (1970.3), Bergsland, ed. (1987), Boas (1894), E. I. Brown (1959, 1981a, 1981b, 1987), M. Brown (1976), K. Burns (1960.1, 1960.2), Campbell, ed. (2004:1–21). R. Cleveland (1965.3, 1965.6, 1965.7, 1965.8, 1965.9, 1965.10, 1965.11, 1965.12, 1966, 1980), E. Curtis (1930:150–60, 168–92, 197–206, 214–24, 228–40, 254–63), M. Curtis (1970), A. Douglas (1976.2, 1976.4), W. Downey (1976), J. Foster (1970), R. Gallahorn (1952.1, 1952.2, 1952.3, 1952.4, 1952.5, 1952.6, 1952.7, 1952.8, 1952.9, 1952.10, 1952.11, 1952.12, 1952.13, 1952.14, 1952.15, 1952.16, 1952.17, 1952.18, 1952.19), Garber (1975), Giddings (1961:65–122), Glover (1952.3), Gubser (1965:39–43), Hall (1975), Harris (1952.1, 1952.2, 1952.3, 1952.4, 1952.5, 1952.6, 1952.7), A. Hawley (1965.4, 1965.5, 1965.15), Edna Hunnicutt (1960.1, 1960.2, 1970.1, 1970.2), D. Jenness (1924:44–47, 53–59, 60–65, 66–67, 68–70), Keats (1970.6), Keithan (1958), J. Killigivuk (1959.2, 1960.2, 1960.3, 1960.6, 1960.12, [1982]), S. Killigivuk (1960), Kingik (1978), Koranda (1972), Kunuyaq (1940:2–5), Lee, Sampson and Tennant (1991, 1992), Lee, Sampson, Tennant and Mendenhall (1990), Lowenstein (1983, 1992, 1993), Lucier (1954, 1958), Mendenhall, Sampson and Tennant (1989), J. Mitchell (1952.2, 1952.3, 1952.4, 1952.5, 1952.6, 1952.7, 1952.8, 1952.9, 1952.10, 1952.11, 1952.12, 1952.13, 1952.16, 1952.17, 1952.18, 1952.19, 1952.20), M. Mitchell (1951, 1952.1, 1952.2, 1952.3, 1952.4), Monroe (1960), T. Morris (1970), National Bilingual Materials Development Center (1980a), H. Ningeulook (1983.3, 1983.4), J. Ningeulook (1983.1), Northwest Iñupiat Elders Conference (1976b), C. Okpowruk (1983.1, 1983.2), Oman (1975), Oquilluk (1973), Ostermann (1942:61–68), Ostermann and Holtved (1952:67–71, 179–254), Paneak (1971a, 1971b, 1971c, 1971d), F. Penn (1952.2), Pulu and Ramoth-Sampson (1981), Pulu, Ramoth-Sampson, and Newlin (1980), J. Ralph (1951.1, 1951.2, 1951.3), Ramoth-Sampson and Newlin, compilers (1981), Sun (1985:77–79, 85–92, 113–25), Ransom (1980), Rasmussen (1925; 1932:56–67, 121–32, 136–49), Sokonik (1918), J. Stalker (1976), Sun (1985), Sunno (1951.23, 1951.24, 1951.35, 1951.36, 1951.54, 1951.58, 1951.59, 1951.67, 1951.87, 1951.94, 1951.100, 1951.102, 1951.118), Tingook (1960.1, 1960.2), Tingook and Killigivuk (1961), M. Tocktoo (1983.1, 1983.3, 1983.4, 1983.6), Towkshjea (ms), Vestal (1969, 1970), Elsie Weyiouanna (1983.1), Essau Weyiouanna (1983.1).

58. Magic is defined as "action in which the ends of the actor are empirical, but the means are nonempirical, at least in part" (Levy 1952:243).

59. Aġviqsiiña (1940.1:44, 88–89), Brower (ms:176, 188, 673), E. Curtis (1930:165), Glover (1970.6), A. Hawley (1964.5), Jensen (1970.3), Keats (1970.7), Murdoch (1892:434–41), Nelson (1899:434–41), Northwest Iñupiat Elders Conference (1983g:6), Niġuwana (1940.1:14–16), Ostermann and Holtved (1952:125), Rainey (1947:272–73), D. Ray (1977:16–18, 92, 85), Ray and Blaker (1967:13), C. Sheldon (1973–74.4), Stefansson (1914b:336, 387, 390), Sunno (1951.10, 1951.11, 1951.26), Thornton (1931:165), VanStone (1967; 1976:35), Vestal (1970), Wells and Kelly (1890:24), Woolfe (1893:148). What I refer to as amulets are often referred to as charms, e.g., by Rainey (1947:272).

60. Aġviqsiiña (1940.1:20), Q. Dives (1940:17), Rainey (1947:272–73). Lowenstein's (1993:75–76) account conflicts to some extent with that of Aġviqsiiña, Dives, and Rainey. I have no independent information on this subject myself.

61. According to Lawrence Kaplan, these are verbs meaning "he is of the amulet class dealing with birth/death."

62. Rainey's primary informants on ceremonies included Aġviqsiiña, Ququk Dives, Kunuyaq, Niġuwana, Quwana, and Sam Uyaġaq Rock. See also Lowenstein (1993:39–41 passim).

63. Aġviqsiiña (1940.1), E. Curtis (1930:148, 163–66, 176, 209, 213), Q. Dives (1940), A. Hawley (1976.7), Hooper (1881:24–25), L. Gallahorn (1970.3), Giddings (1961:22–24), Elwood Hunnicutt (1970), Iviqsiq (1940), Jensen (1970.4), Keats (1970.10), Niġuwana (1940.1), Ostermann and Holtved (1952:36–37, 117–20, 124–27), Quwana (1940:43), Rainey (1947), Seveck (1951), Stoney (1900:838–39), Stefansson (1914b:316–17, 334–35, 338, 347, 355), Sunno (1951.1, 1951.17, 1951.19, 1951.37, 1951.107, 1951.117), Sunno and Hadley (1951), Thornton (1931:111–13), Vestal (1950, 1970), Walton (1965.2), Ardith Weyiouanna (1983), Woolfe (1893:140, 141).

64. The information for this summary was provided to Charles Lucier by Andrew Sunno (1951.19, 1951.37, 1951.117). Lucier kindly gave me permission to use this material.

65. Lucier's notations are inconsistent here. In Sunno (1951.19), he says these were miniature weapons, not imaginary ones.

66. See also E. Curtis (1930:210) and C. Wood (1931).

67. Rasmussen's account (Ostermann and Holtved 1952:136–37) of a five-day festival for the dead was probably recorded south of the study region.

68. Aġviqsiiña (1940.1:80), Q. Dives (1940:29), Glover (1970.6), A. Hawley (1965.5, 1965.11), M. Hawley (1965.1), Jensen (1970.1, 1970.2, 1970.5), Lee et al. (1990:37), NANA Cultural Heritage Project (1976d), Northwest Iñupiat Elders Conference (1976f:4).

69. Aġviqsiiña (1940.1:72–73, 101), M. Cleveland (1989), R. Cleveland (1970.1), Q. Dives (1940:26), J. Foster (1970), A. Hawley (1965.8), B. Hawley (1982), Jensen (1970.3), Keats (1970.9), J. Mitchell (1952.10, 1952.20), J. and M. Ningeulook (1983), Northwest Iñupiat Elders Conference (1976f:3–4), Rainey (1947:274–79), C. Sheldon (1973–74:13, 14, 19, 20), Stefansson (1914b:337, 368–69), Stoney (1900:834–35), Sunno (1951.12, 1951.13, 1951.20, 1951.24), G. Tocktoo (1984), Wells and Kelly (1890:22–23), Woolfe (1893:138–39).

70. F. Beechey (1831, I:343; II:257), Kotzebue (1821, I:211, 222, 230), Simpson (1875:251–52), Stoney (1900:570), Thornton (1931:74), Wolfe (1893:137). The quote is from Simpson.

71. Photographs of some of the objects collected by Beechey have been published by Bockstoce (1977:82–86). See also VanStone (1990:35, 38, 39, 40 passim).

72. For a photograph of a chain collected by Beechey, see Bockstoce (1977:fig. 69).

Epilogue

The ethnographic reconstruction of several nations of hunter-gatherers after an interval of more than 150 years might appear at first glance to be an exercise in self-deception.[1] Skepticism on this issue is not unwarranted, but it fails to take into account the number and quality of the sources on which this reconstruction is based.

The purpose of this brief chapter is to address the issue of temporal reliability in a general way by listing and briefly characterizing the major sources available to me when writing the book. The material is presented in a sequence intended to make a prima facie case that the data are adequate to permit a reconstruction of both continuity and change in the study region over a 200-year period—at the broad level of generalization employed in this volume. The discussion recapitulates to some extent material presented in Chapter 1, but it is presented here from a different perspective.

1800–1855

The foundation of the reconstruction consists of the eyewitness observations of Otto von Kotzebue, Frederick William Beechey, Aleksandr Kashevarov, Berthold Seemann, John Simpson, and Henry Trollope, which have been cited throughout the book. Without their accounts I could not have been so specific in asserting that various customs were practiced during the early-contact period.

Kotzebue

Otto von Kotzebue is generally recognized as the first Westerner to visit the study region, arriving off Cape Prince of Wales on July 30, 1816.[2] Within the study region, he explored what is now known as Kotzebue Sound, and the northern coast of the Seward Peninsula. He departed the region on August 17, 1816.

During their time in Northwest Alaska, the expedition's members had frequent contacts with local Iñupiat; these were sometimes friendly, sometimes not. They observed the large settlement of Wales from afar, but visited and explored the main settlement of the Tapqaġmiut; unfortunately, its inhabitants were either elsewhere or in hiding at the time.

Kotzebue (1821, I:198–241) wrote graphic descriptions of Iñupiaq demeanor and material possessions. The naturalist on the expedition, Adelbert von Chamisso

(1986), wrote a brief account of his observations, and Ludovik Choris (1822; VanStone 1960) prepared a number of sketches of the people he saw and of the equipment they used. While not as voluminous as one might wish, their reports help connect the oral accounts of 20th-century Iñupiat elders to the early-19th-century situation.

Beechey

The expedition under the command of Frederick William Beechey spent several months during the summers of 1826 and 1827 exploring the coastline of northern Alaska, from the southern Seward Peninsula to Point Barrow. During this period Beechey and his men had extensive and diverse contacts with Iñupiat in many areas. These contacts ranged from feasting and trade at one extreme, to armed confrontation at the other.

Beechey had spent the winter of 1819–20 in the Canadian Arctic under the command of William Edward Parry in the *Hecla*. This experience heightened his powers of observation in Alaska because of the differences between the Inuit-speaking inhabitants of the two regions. He recorded his observations of many aspects of Iñupiaq life in his two-volume account of the expedition (Beechey 1831, I:338–464; II:270–318). Some of Beechey's officers also kept journals of the voyage, one of which has been published (Gough 1973), others of which are accessible in archives.[3] In addition, John Bockstoce (1977) published a volume describing collections of artifacts acquired on the expedition, and he included in it informative excerpts from both the published and unpublished accounts.

Kashevarov

Aleksandr F. Kashevarov led an expedition to explore the northwestern coast of Alaska in the summer of 1838. The men were taken in the ship *Polifem* to Cape Lisburne, at the northern edge of the study region, where they disembarked to explore the coastline beyond. The party reached a point a short distance beyond Point Barrow, then returned south along the coast well past their starting point to Kotzebue Sound, where they rejoined the *Polifem*. Kashevarov kept a journal of his travels and wrote a separate set of notes on the people he encountered; both were translated and published in an annotated volume edited by James VanStone (1977).

Because they traveled along the shore in small boats, the members of this expedition were in frequent contact with Iñupiat. In most cases they were initially taken to be other Iñupiat, so they were treated differently than the Westerners who traveled by ship. They also had an interpreter with them, which enabled Kashevarov to learn many important facts about Iñupiaq life which had eluded his predecessors. Of particular significance for the present work was Kashevarov's identification of the several nations whose estates he visited.

Franklin Search Expeditions

In 1845, an expedition under the command of Sir John Franklin set out to locate the Northwest Passage, entering the Canadian Arctic from the east. Nothing was heard from any one of them again. A massive search for the missing explorers was mounted, lasting twelve years and involving nearly three dozen major expeditions. Several of the expeditions visited the area of interest in this book (see Bockstoce 1985 for a summary).

Many of the Franklin search vessels visited Kotzebue Sound during the late 1840s and early 1850s, most for brief periods during the summer. However, HMS *Plover* overwintered (1849–50) near Chamisso Island, at the head of Kotzebue Sound, and the crew was in frequent, perhaps even constant, contact with Iñupiaq visitors while there.[4] In addition, detachments were sent to explore surrounding areas from time to time, often traveling with Iñupiat and staying in Native dwellings.

The most important of the Franklin search reports for the present volume were those of John Simpson, whose work is summarized below. Of secondary value, although still very useful, was the account of Berthold Seemann, the naturalist on HMS *Herald* in 1848–50. Seemann (1853, II:50–67, 99–101, 118–21, 130–48, 176) described many aspects of Iñupiaq life, and reported on what he learned of events on the *Plover* while it was overwintering at Chamisso Island. Other contributions were made in 1853–54, when two detachments from HMS *Rattlesnake*, overwintering at Grantley Harbor (near the western end of the Seward Peninsula), visited the study region. The first detachment was a party led by Henry Trollope (1855), which made a winter visit to Wales; his report is quoted frequently in this volume. The other detachment was led by William Hobson (1855), who traveled overland from Grantley Harbor to Chamisso Island, also in winter. Unfortunately, Hobson encountered very few people once he reached the area of interest here.

John Simpson, the surgeon aboard HMS *Plover* during the Franklin search, wrote one of the best ethnographic reports on any Eskimo population for the entire 19th century. It was originally published in 1855, and republished in 1875 and 1988.[5]

Simpson states (1875:233, 267) that he got most of his information from informants at Point Barrow, particularly from a man named "Erk-sin'-ra." His unpublished journal (Simpson 1852–54) confirms these statements, which means that most of his account is ostensibly based on information obtained in the region just to the north of the one of concern in this volume. However, I believe his account was based on more than that.

Simpson spent five years in the Arctic, all of them aboard the *Plover*. During the first year (1848–49), the ship was in Providenia Bay, in southeastern Chukotka; during the second (1849–50), it was at Chamisso Island, at the head of Kotzebue Sound; and in the following year (1850–51), it was at Grantley Harbor, on the Seward Peninsula. Throughout that time, the ship was under the command of T.E.L. Moore. For most of the period 1849–51, Simpson was in close contact with Iñupiat in or near the study region.

Simpson left the *Plover* at least three times while it was based at Chamisso Island. The first trip was to Spafarief Bay, on the northern Seward Peninsula (Simpson 1850a); the second was to a village on the eastern shore of Baldwin Peninsula (Simpson 1850b); and the third was to the entrance to Selawik Lake (Simpson 1850c, 1852a, 1852b). During each of these expeditions he stayed in Iñupiaq dwellings. That he already had a special interest in Iñupiaq life at this time is demonstrated by his collection of at least five word lists from Iñupiat living in the region covered by the present study (Simpson ms.b, ms.c, ms.d, ms.e, 1851). It is on this basis, combined with frequent comments scattered in his unpublished journal from Point Barrow and in his published ethnographic report, that I contend that the latter was informed in part by his observations in and near the study region.

Simpson took a year's sabbatical in England (1851–52), but returned north to spend the years 1852–54 under the *Plover*'s new commander, Rochefort Maguire. The ship wintered near Point Barrow both winters. During this period Simpson was in almost daily contact with Iñupiat. Judging from the increasingly abstract nature of the topics he was able to discuss with them, he acquired considerable fluency in their language. He maintained a daily journal, much of which was devoted to his contacts with Natives and to his observations of Iñupiaq life (Simpson 1852–54). The journal reveals both how he acquired the information summarized subsequently in his ethnographic report, and, in many cases, the identity of the person or people from whom it came. Much of the ethnographic information contained in Maguire's published journal (Bockstoce ed. 1988) is taken directly from Simpson's unpublished account.

1855–1880

The period 1855–80 was a tumultuous time in northwestern Alaska. American whalers decimated the bowhead whale and walrus stocks, and both whalers and shipborne traders brought epidemic diseases to the region on an almost annual basis. The fur trade rapidly increased in importance, leading to a decline in the number of fur-bearing animals in the region. After Russia sold Alaska to the United States in 1867, firearms began to be imported in increasingly large numbers, which led to important changes in Native hunting techniques. In the 1870s, the Seward Peninsula and Nulato Hills caribou herds began significant declines.[6]

Documentary material is rather sparse for this period, consisting primarily of observations made by members of the Western Union Telegraph Expedition. This expedition was sent in 1865 to survey a route for, and to construct, a telegraph line through Alaska by way of the Yukon River and Seward Peninsula, and across Bering Strait.[7] Several crews were sent to western Alaska for this purpose, establishing camps on the eastern end of Norton Sound, and near the western end of the Seward Peninsula. The project was abandoned in 1867.

Except for a few brief visits of some men to Wales, the activities of the members of this expedition were to the south and southeast of the region of concern here. However, by the mid-1860s, several Iñupiaq families from the study region had moved to Norton Sound, where they were clearly identified by both local Natives and the members of the expedition as "Mahlemut" (or something similar) (D. Ray 1975b:121–39). Consequently, the voluminous records of the expedition contain quite a bit of information relevant to this study, all of it from a period in which no other documents are available.[8]

The naturalist on the Western Union Telegraph Expedition was William Healy Dall. He returned to Alaska several times after the project terminated, and published a number of documents describing his experiences, the people he met, and the country he visited. However, his unpublished notebook from the period October 12, 1866, to May 25, 1867 (Dall 1866–67) contains the most comprehensive summary of the "Mahlemut" way of life of any of the documents from this era.

The first Native sources who contributed information directly to this book were born during this period. Ira S. Purkeypile's informants Eliyak and Charley Uluġaaġruk Wood, and Charles Lucier's informants Andrew Sunno and Mark Misigaq Mitchell, were born in the 1850s or early 1860s. Knud Rasmussen's informants Apaakak and Isaac Nasuk Lincoln, interviewed in 1924, were probably born in the 1850s or earlier. Edward Curtis did not identify the people he interviewed in 1927, but his photograph (reproduced in Burch 1998a:167) of the same Charley Uluġaaġruk Wood interviewed later by Purkeypile suggests that Wood was among them. No doubt several of Curtis's informants were born in the 1850s and 1860s. J. L. Giddings's informants Charlie Piġliġiaq Custer and Charlie Nayuk Johnson were born in the 1860s. Froelich Rainey's sources Frank Aġviqsiiña, Ququk Dives, Iviqsiq, Peter Kunuyaq, Nasugluk, Niġuwana, Quwana, and Sam Uyaġaq Rock were all born during, if not before, the 1870s, as were Lucier's informants Mary Howard and Jenny Aluniq Mitchell, and Giddings's informants Stonewall Ullaaq Jackson, Kobuk Mary Nunaġiaq, and Kobuk Mike

Qaqiq. Vilhjalmur Stefansson's Nuataaġmiut informant Iḷaviñiq also was born in the late 1860s or early 1870s. All of these individuals would have been raised in the company of, if not directly by, individuals who grew to adulthood before 1850.

1880–1910

Famine and disease continued to take their toll of the human population between 1880 and 1910, and hundreds of people moved to the north and east trying to find better places to make a living. These factors combined to destroy the demographic basis of most of the traditional nations. A gold rush brought several hundred miners to the region in 1898, and shore-based Western whalers established stations along the coast south of Point Hope. At least some Westerners have been based permanently in northwestern Alaska ever since.

By 1910, the Seward Peninsula and Nulato Hills caribou herds had virtually ceased to exist, and the Western Arctic caribou herd was drastically reduced in size. Domesticated reindeer were imported from Asia to fill the need for meat and hides, and Native-owned herds were soon established in many districts. Schools and Christian missions were established at Point Hope and Wales in 1890, at Kotzebue in 1897, and at most of what became the other modern settlements by 1910. Control of disruptive behavior and foreign affairs came under the purview of the United States government.

Several important documentary accounts exist from this period. Those of Charles Brower, John Kelly, E. W. Nelson, George Stoney, the International Polar Year Expedition to Barrow, Vilhjalmur Stefansson, Harrison R. Thornton, the U.S. Revenue Marine, and Henry D. Woolfe stand out as sources of ethnographic information.

Edward William Nelson

Nelson spent three years (1879–81) as a U.S. Signal Officer based at St. Michael, on the south coast of Norton Sound. During that period he made a number of forays from that base, exploring and gathering information on the people and country around Norton Sound and the Yukon-Kuskokwim Delta. He also collected a huge number of artifacts.

Nelson, like his predecessors on the Western Union Telegraph Expedition, had frequent encounters with "Mahlemute" (Malimiut) emigrants or visitors from Kotzebue Sound. On his way out of the country, in the summer of 1881, he served as the naturalist on the U.S. Revenue Cutter *Corwin*, which visited a number of coastal points within the study region.

The results of Nelson's ethnographic investigations were published in a massive monograph (Nelson 1899).[9] Most of the book concerns regions south of the area of interest here, but information specifically on Malimiut is scattered throughout both the book and in Nelson's unpublished diary (Nelson 1877–81). The details of his 1881 trip along the coast of the study region are recorded in Journals 12 and 13 of the diary.

Revenue Marine Cruises

In 1879, the U.S. Revenue Marine, precursor of the U.S. Coast Guard, began making regular summer cruises to Alaska for the purposes of showing the American flag, keeping an eye on whaling ships, and stopping the illegal trade in whisky and firearms with the Natives. The reports of four of the early cruises are of particular interest.

The cruises of 1880 and 1881 were rather narrowly focused on coastal areas, although the published reports (Hooper 1881, 1884; Rosse 1883) do contain valuable observations on

Iñupiaq life. In 1884 and 1885, detachments from the coastal patrol were sent to explore the Kobuk, Noatak, and Selawik river drainages. These were the first known visits by Westerners to the interior of the study region.[10] Altogether, these reports contain enough information to permit the compilation of a comprehensive picture of Iñupiaq life during the early 1880s.

International Polar Year Expedition

The International Polar Year Expedition was based a few miles southwest of Point Barrow from July 18, 1881, to October 15, 1883. Its members kept meteorological and magnetic observations, and recorded observations on the country and Native life throughout their time in the field; an enormous amount of ethnographic material was collected. Most of it was published in a monograph by John Murdoch (1892), but Patrick Henry Ray's (1885:35–88) summary of the expedition as a whole included an ethnographic sketch of the Natives.

Murdoch's monograph was recently republished in a volume that also contains Ray's report and several other related documents (Murdoch 1988). Most of these reports describe Iñupiaq life on the North Slope, which did not differ greatly from Native life in the study region. Murdoch's volume was particularly useful to me for its descriptions of manufacturing processes.

Charles Brower

Brower went to Alaska in the fall of 1884 to work with a group of men who were exploring coal-mining possibilities north of Point Hope. Not having much to do at the mine during the winter, Brower traveled widely over the country, visiting Iñupiaq settlements scattered along the entire coast between Barrow and Kotzebue. He made a number of remarkable observations of Iñupiaq life in the study region during the winter and spring of 1885, and recorded hundreds of observations and experiences from the North Slope over the ensuing decades. These are described in an abbreviated published journal (Brower 1994), and a much more detailed unpublished journal (Brower ms). The latter has been cited frequently in this book.

George M. Stoney

Stone was a U.S. Navy Lieutenant who explored the lower Kobuk River in 1883, and he conducted a more extensive exploration of that river and Selawik Lake in 1884. In 1885–86 he led an expedition that explored much of the interior of the country from his base in the central Kobuk district. During these expeditions he and his colleagues traveled and lived with Iñupiat. His reports (Stoney ms, 1883, 1900) on these expeditions—particularly the last—were full of important ethnographic data.

John W. Kelly

Kelly was a prospector turned whaler who apparently first visited northern Alaska in 1883, and who spent parts of the next seven years there, including three winters. During his time in the region he traveled widely, and seems to have been in close contact with Iñupiat much of the time. In 1889, while serving as the interpreter for the captain of the USS *Thetis*, he wrote an important ethnographic summary of Iñupiaq life based on his observations and experiences in northern Alaska. It was published in a report allegedly coauthored by Ensign Roger Wells, who, in fact, obtained most of his information from Kelly (Wells and Kelly 1890).

Henry D. Woolfe

Woolfe was an adventurer and correspondent for the *New York Herald* who joined forces with Johan Adrian Jacobsen in the summer of 1882. This brought him to the study region for the first time. His next trip was in 1884, when he joined the coal-mining expedition in which Charles Brower also participated. By the time Woolfe wrote the chapter on the Arctic District for the 1890 census, he claimed to have spent five winters in the region over the course of the previous ten years. Woolfe (1890, 1893, 1894) did get to know Iñupiat very well, and his census report is a valuable ethnographic summary. Unfortunately, his reputation as an ethnographer is slightly tainted by the fact that he plagiarized parts of his report with uncited quotations from Kelly's.

Harrison Robertson Thornton

Thornton was a teacher and missionary who spent the winters of 1890–91 and 1892–93 at Wales. He was assassinated there on August 19, 1893 (Thornton 1931:xxi). Before he died, he wrote a book about Native life that was eventually published in 1931.

Thornton's book is important because it is about Wales, which was rarely visited by early explorers, and because of its broad scope. The book has sixty-five chapters, each of which deals with a separate topic. Further, Thornton wrote about Iñupiaq life in a generally objective manner, one that was rare among missionaries of his era.

Vilhjalmur Stefansson

Stefansson was a well-known explorer and anthropologist, most of whose work was done in northern Canada. However, he spent the winter of 1908–9 on the North Slope of Alaska, by which time he already could speak some Iñupiatun. During that year he was accompanied by a man named Ilaviñiq, who Stefansson variously described as being either a Nuataaġmiu or Qikiqtaġruŋmiu, born about 1870. He also said that Ilaviñiq "possessed . . . a vast store of the lore and religions of his people" (Stefansson 1951:353), and that he had a very good memory (Stefansson 1951:327). Through Ilaviñiq particularly, but through a few others as well, Stefansson was able to obtain useful information about Iñupiaq life in the study region even though he never visited it himself.

Stefansson's work (Pálsson 2001; Stefansson 1909, 1914a, 1914b, 1944, 1951) was important to the present study partly for the tidbits of ethnographic information concerning northwestern Alaska that were scattered through it, but even more because of his insights into the Eskimo system of taboos and rituals. More than any other single writer, he was able to observe this system in operation, and to ascertain the general principles under which it operated (see Stefansson 1951:37–39, 89–100, 390–407, 410–12).

Discussion

After schools and missions were established in the early years of the 20th century, the Native population moved in to be near them. However, in order to make a living as trappers and reindeer herders, families had to spend the winter in widely scattered camps some distance away from the villages. This led to a kind of tug-of-war between the villages and the camps, with people spending parts of the year in one, and other parts in the other. Children who managed to get a second- or third-grade education during this period often took four or five years to do it. In summer, when school was not in session, coast dwellers were spread out in seal-hunting camps, and inlanders were spread out in fishing camps. Conversation in camps was entirely in Iñupiatun.

Camp life was extremely important to the preservation and communication of traditional knowledge during the early 20th century because it kept people out on the land where their ancestors had lived, and thus in touch with the old place-names and the stories associated with them. Furthermore, youngsters in the camps discovered the remains of old settlements, battlegrounds, and other residue of earlier times, and they inquired about these things from knowledgeable grown-ups. Camp life in winter was doubly informative because elders were often brought out from the mission-school villages to provide entertainment in the form of storytelling sessions during the long nights.

Of the oral sources born after 1879 who contributed to this volume, eighteen were born during the 1880s and twenty-one during the 1890s. An additional forty-four were born during the first decade, and thirty-four during the second, of the 20th century. All of these people were questioned by their interviewers about how people lived before, as well as during, their own lifetimes; those who did not know about earlier times did not contribute to this book, hence are not included in the above numbers.

Each passing generation of elders was further removed from the study period than its predecessors, and less able to discuss it in detail. However, I do not think that the people who the Iñupiat themselves recognized as historians in these later generations were any less capable of describing early-contact Native life than were their ancestors; they just did not know as many details.

My task in writing this book was to combine the information provided by the documentary and oral sources into a coherent whole.[11] In general, wherever the two types of data concerned the same subjects, they were mutually reinforcing. Thus, oral sources described their ancestors as being warlike, and so did early Western observers; oral sources said their ancestors had a raunchy sense of humor, and so did early Western observers; oral sources said that their ancestors successfully hunted the huge bowhead whale, and so did early Western observers. Oral sources also said that things began to change about the time Muuġa (T.E.L. Moore) overwintered near Chamisso Island, in 1849–50: whales became scarce, epidemic diseases began to strike each summer, and foreign traders began to visit the Sisualik trade festival. On these and many other changes, early Western observers and later Iñupiaq elders agreed.

There are many information gaps, of course, and some discrepancies among sources concerning details; but there are scarcely any disagreements on general patterns. It is also true that there are many subjects discussed by oral sources that are not mentioned at all in the early written accounts. With respect to this issue, it is my view that the extent of congruence between the oral and written accounts, wherever they can be checked against one another, is so high that the burden of proof is on those who would challenge the accuracy of the oral accounts.

The only glaring anomaly in the entire body of information I examined for this book is the alleged use of firearms by the Kaṇiġmiut against the members of the Vasil'ev-Shishmarev expedition, in 1820 (D. Ray 1975a; 1983a:55–66; 1983b; 1983c). When Kotzebue was in the region four years earlier, the Iñupiat he encountered had no idea what firearms were. Beechey's men were in an armed confrontation with people from the same nation seven years after the Vasil'ev-Shishmarev expedition, yet not a single firearm was observed on the Iñupiaq side. In other words, the reported Native use of firearms in 1820 does not fit with any other information from before or since; if it really did occur, it was of only momentary and local significance.

Richard A. Pierce (1983:iii) once observed that "ethnohistory reflects no esoteric doctrine, but instead the commonsense view that whatever [evidence] can help [solve] a problem should be used, and that several disciplines may take a researcher farther than one." I adopted this approach in the present study by integrating information from both documentary and oral sources. I also took advantage of the excellent research and generosity of several Native organizations and professional colleagues. The Kawerak Eskimo Heritage Program, the NANA Elders Council, and the Iñupiaq History, Language and Culture Commission of the North Slope Borough are prominent among the former; Laurel Bland, John Bockstoce, Charles Lucier, Don Charles Foote, and Froelich Rainey stand out among the latter. Finally, I have benefited from a number of more specialized studies, such as those of Thomas Johnston on music, Robert Fortuine on health care, Lawrence Kaplan on language, Albert Heinrich on kinship, Anore Jones on plant use, and Douglas Anderson et al., Berit Foote, J. L. Giddings, John Murdoch, Edward W. Nelson, and James VanStone on material culture. I hope that the resulting synthesis will be useful and informative to students of hunter-gatherer societies, and to future generations of Northwest Alaskans.

Notes to Epilogue

1. I thank Igor Krupnik for his critique of an earlier version of this chapter.
2. According to Lydia Black (1998), the Russian-American Company sent trading expeditions to Eschscholtz Bay prior to 1816. See also Black (2004:13, 199).
3. Bechervaise (1839), R. Beechey (ms.a, ms.b), Belcher (ms), J. Wolfe (ms).
4. See T.E.L. Moore (1851) for a summary. There was so much sexual contact between the English and the Iñupiat near Chamisso Island during the summer that Miertsching (1967:37) predicted that "here one will soon have an Anglo-Eskimo colony."
5. Simpson (1855, 1875), Bockstoce ed. (1988, II:501–50).
6. The changes that occurred in northwestern Alaska after 1850 are summarized in Burch (1975:26–34) and Burch (1998a).
7. See Neering (1989) for a comprehensive summary of the Western Union Telegraph Expedition.
8. G. Adams (ms, 1982), Bulkley (ms), Dall (1866–67, 1870a, 1870b, 1877, 1881, 1885, 1898), Taggart (1954, 1956), Whymper (1868, 1869a, 1869b). The members of the expedition also published a newspaper, called *The Esquimaux*, which contains quite a bit of useful ethnographic information.
9. The monograph was republished, with an introduction by William Fitzhugh, in 1983.
10. Cantwell (1887, 1889a, 1889b), Healy (1887, 1889), McLenegan (1887, 1889), Townsend (1887). It gets confusing because the reports on the 1884 cruise were published in 1889, two years *after* the reports of the 1885 cruise appeared.
11. The method used to conduct the analysis is described in Burch (1998a:17–19).

Glossary

Note: Nouns in Iñupiatun may be singular, dual, or plural (pl.).[1] All those in this list are singular unless otherwise indicated. Words followed by a hyphen are verb stems that would ordinarily be accompanied by one or more suffixes when spoken. Many terms can be turned into either nouns or verbs depending on the suffixes that are attached to them. The vast majority of the words in this list are in the Malimiut dialect. Terms presented only in tables are not included in the list. I thank Lawrence Kaplan for reviewing the glossary.

aagruuk (dual), the paired stars Altair and Tarazed

aaka, mother

aakiaq, older sister

aakiyaaq, older sister

aalġuvik, menarche hut

aana, grandmother

aanġuaq, amulet

aapa, father

aapiaq, older brother.

aapiyaq, older brother

aaquaksraq, very old woman

agliġnaq– to be under taboo

aguupmak, grass basket

aġnaq, female

aġnaqatigiik (dual), matrilateral parallel cousins

aġraurraun, the ball used in Eskimo football

aġviq, bowhead whale

aippaġiik (dual), co-wives

aiviq, walrus

aiyakpak, simple bow

akiḷiq–, to pay

akiqsruq–, to buy or sell on credit

akisaqłuk, a feud

akłaq, brown bear

akutuq, "Eskimo ice cream"

alluiyaq, platter

alugvik, a kind of white rock, salt lick

amaułuk, great-grandparent

amilġaqtuayaat, very large family

anaqasaaġiaq, late afternoon

anauraġaq–, Eskimo baseball

aniġniq, life (breath)

aniqatigiich, conjugal family

aniqqamiaq, newborn infant

aniyutyaq, snow house

aŋak, uncle

aŋatkuq, shaman

aŋayunġuq, senior co-in-law

aŋayuqaak (dual), parents

aŋayuqaksraq, very old man

aŋmaaq, chert

aŋuaqtit (pl.), paddlers in a whaling boat

aŋun, male

aŋutiqatigiik (dual), patrilateral parallel cousins

aŋuyakti, soldier

aññaġiik (dual), two female friends

aqaluŋniaġvik, fish camp

aqargiq, willow ptarmigan

aqsrautraq–, to play Eskimo football

aquti, helmsman

argaat (pl.), *masru* roots dug up by people

argaun, ice scratcher used in seal hunting

ataata, grandfather

ataniq, boss, work leader

atchak, aunt

atiq, name, namesake

atiqatigiik (dual), namesakes

atuutipiaq, dance with improvised motions

avaatchiqiq, birch fungus

avalġusiq, stockade

avilaisuqatigiik (dual), a friendship

avilaitqatigiik (dual), two friends

ayahaaq–, to make cat's cradles

igavaun, bucket

iggiaq, funnel-shaped opening of a fish trap

igluġruaq, semisubterranean house

igniqaġvik, hearth

iġñiq, son

iġñiruaqtuqtuq–, to be in the amulet class relating to birth things

iġñivik, parturition hut

iitaaq, rock used to make black pigment

ikiġġaq, open platform cache

ikniñ, pyrite

iḷitqusriq, personality

iḷagiiksit (pl.), affines

iḷapiat (pl.), consanguines

iḷiappak, orphan

iḷimmaq–, to make a spirit flight (shaman)

iḷiḷgaaq, child

iḷiḷgauraq, infant

iḷisiḷa, clairvoyant

iḷḷuġiik (dual), cross cousins

iḷuliaġun, great grandchild

iḷuvġich (pl.), graves, graveyard

imaq, unpotable water

imigluktaaq, bull roarer

imiq, fresh water

iññuqun, prowler, terrorist

iññuqutit, (pl.), prowlers, terrorists

iñugialiŋmiut, very large family

iñuguŋaruq, adult

iñuksuk, "scarecrow"

Iñupiatun, Iñupiaq-Eskimo language

iñuuḷiq, life force, animating force

iñuunniaqti, "tribal doctor"

iñuuraq, doll

iñuusriq, soul

ipiġaksraq, type of moss

ipiksaun, whetstone

ipniaq, Dall sheep

iraqsraun, tobacco pouch

irigaak (dual), goggles

isiŋnaq, nephrite (jade)

isivruġaq, wolf killer

itchalik, building covered with a caribou-hide tarp

itqutaq, breakfast

ituqtuuq, ruffed grouse

ivisaaq, hematite

ivrauraq, reindeer moss

ivrulik, moss-covered building

ivruq, sphagnum moss

kakiat (pl.), three-pronged fish spear

kaḷukaq, box drum

kannuyaq, copper(?)

kanuŋŋiq, diamondleaf willow

kapi–, to pierce for bloodletting

kapun, bodkin

kapuqqaun, one-pointed fish spear

kapuqti, harpooner

katirut, large gathering of people from one nation

katittut, large gathering of people from one nation

katŋut, large gathering of people from several nations, "trade fair"

kautaq, maul

kavraġmiutaq, tump line

kayuḷuk, pumice

kigilġutaq, wooden tongs

kiiñaġuq, wooden mask

kikituk, "shaman's helper"

kikmiññaq, cranberry

kiŋmiaq, mouthpiece of a bow drill

kiŋuvaannaq–, to inherit

kitik, soft, easily ground rock

kuiŋiq, woman's pipe

kuniktuq–, to touch noses in a gesture of affection

kuvraq, gill net

kuvriñ, net gauge

magluqsaq, snare for small game

maġlak–, to give a gift in connection with a dance

maksruksaq, ground squirrel snare

maktaaq, beluga whale skin with blubber attached

maktak, bowhead whale skin with blubber attached

malimiut, Yup'ik name for people from the Kotzebue Sound region

mamaiḷaq, mineral spring

mamaqtaq, muddy substance

manigraq, playing field

maniq, tussock moss

mannisaq, plate armor, movable defensive wall

manusiññak (dual), two white shoulder strips on a parka

masru, Eskimo potato

mikigaq, fermented whale meat

mitlik, curved knife

nalukataq, "blanket toss"

naniġiapiat (pl.), deadfall traps

naniq, oil lamp

nanuq, polar bear

napaaqtum aqargiq, spruce grouse

natchiġñiaġvik, seal-hunting camp

natchiq, ringed seal

natchiqsiun, net for catching ringed seals

natmaktuq–, to carry things forward in relays

nuligauraq–, to play a dart game

nayak, younger sister

niaquun, headband

nigaq, snare for big game

nigatchiaq, ptarmigan snare

nigrat (pl.), tassels

nikivġautaq, three-legged stool used in breathing hole hunting

niksaaktuŋiq, rock ptarmigan

niksik, hook

ninŋuq, balsam poplar (cottonwood)

niŋau, in-marrying male

niqaaq, reindeer lichen

niqailaq, famine

niuviġiaq, large gathering of trading partners, trade fair

niuviġiik (dual), two "trading" partners

niuvik, "trading" partner

niviaqsialugruaq, little girl

niviaqsiaq, young woman

nivit (pl.), *masru* roots dug up and cached by voles

nuġġiġvik, a soft white clay

nukaġaq, second (or subsequent) wife

nukatchiaq, younger sibling

nukatpialugruaq, little boy

nukatpiaq, young man

nukaunġuq, junior co-in-law

nuliaq, wife

nuliaqatigiik (dual), co-husbands

nuliaqpak, first wife (of two or more)

napataatchak–, to play a dart game

nuliiraq, co-wife

nullautaq, dinner

nulliq, co-parent-in-law

nunaaqqiq, village

nunaŋiaq, American green alder

nunaqatigiich, nation

nutaġaaluk, teenager

nuviḷḷaun, net shuttle

paiṗak, smoking pipe

panik, daughter

pattaq, drill

pattaqtuun, the bow of a bow drill

pauŋŋaak (dual), sealskin waders

piksrun, shovel

piktaliq, cooking pot

piñiaġvik, a camp

pisiksi, complex bow

pisiktaġvik, archery range

puggutauraq, dish

putyugiaq, short snowshoe

puuġu, net for catching foxes or wolves

puuġuaq, net for catching ptarmigan

puuq, bag made of a whole sealskin

qaaktuun, seine

qaglu, fishing hole in a stream or river

qagruġvik, place or time of the whaling festival

qaġruqsaq, set (fishing) line, wolf killer

qallivik, birchbark basket

qalluiññaq, complex bow

qalu, long-handled dip net

qalutaq, berry-picking instrument

qaluuġvik, dome-shaped building

qaiḷiñiq, old ivory

qamun, flat sled

qanniq–, to place an order (for something)

qargi, community hall

qargich (pl.), community halls

qasigiaq, spotted seal

qataŋun, co-sibling

qataŋutigiik (dual), co-siblings

qatiġniñ, bleached sealskin

qatqitchuaq, person in the prime of life

quagrulik, triangular-shaped needle

qaukḷiq, family head

qaukḷiich (pl.), family heads

qaummaḷuk, quartzite

qauqtaq, old ivory

qaviaq, sand

qayaġiaq, undecked canoe

qayaq, kayak, decked canoe

qayuŋnilik, hard crystalline rock

qayuq, blood soup
qayuttaq, wooden spoon
qiku, pottery clay
qila, "familiar" spirit
qilaun, tambourine drum
qilamitaun, a bolas
qiŋaġun, nose ornament
qirgiq, wolf ceremony
qiruk, driftwood
qisiqsiutit (pl.), spruce needles
qitiqłiaġun, finger ring
qituŋaġiich (pl.), conjugal family
qituŋat (pl.), children
quaq, raw fish or meat
quliaqtuaqti, storyteller
quŋuqtuqtuq–, to be in the amulet class relating to death things
quŋusiġun, necklace
quppiġñiq, part in the hair
saiyut, semisubterranean log cache
sakiġaq, spouse's relative
salliñ, obsidian (volcanic glass)
sapun, weir
sargiq, common wormwood ("stinkweed")
savaktaaġruk, servant
savik, man's (straight) knife
sayuun, dance with predetermined movements
siaquya, a type of clay
siġluaq, storehouse, storage pit, ice cellar
sikłaq, pick
siku, shank of a bow drill
sisuaq, beluga whale
sisuaqsiun, beluga net
siuġaq, sandstone
sivunniksriqiri, prophet
suġliaq, spruce sap
suġruk, raider
sukisaġnaq, kind of rock
sura, young willow leaf
suunaaġiik (dual), two friends
taglu, snowshoe
taglupiaq, long snowshoe
taġiuq, salt, salt water, sea, ocean
taliq–, do a woman's dance while seated
taluyaq, fish trap
tanuġak, dusk
taquupik, ear ornament
tatirgaq, lesser sandhill crane
taugaaqqipiaq, leaf tobacco
tauqsiq–, to buy

tavluġun, tattoo
tayaq, bracelet
tiglik–, to steal
tiguaq, adopted child
tigutaaluk, slave
tilaaqqiuq, Labrador tea
timi, body
tinaakatiisruuk, a slate-like rock
tininniq, sponge moss
tugliġun, leather strip used in hair decoration
tugliq, knot of fat behind the neck of a Dall sheep ram
tulugaq, raven
tulukkam asriaq, common juniper
tuni–, to sell
tupiq, conical tent
tutitchiaq, grandchild
tuttunniaġvik, caribou-hunting camp
tuuŋat (pl.), evil spirits
tuuq, ice chisel, ice pick
tuutaq, labret
tuvaaqan, spouse
ugruk, bearded seal
ui, husband
uiluaqtaq, young woman who refuses to marry
uiŋuraq, co-husband
ukiaq, fall (autumn)
ukiaqsrivik, fall camp
ukiivik, winter house, winter camp
ukiuq, winter
ukuaq, in-marrying female
ulimaun, adze, mattock
ulu, semilunar woman's knife
ulugraq, slate
umiagiiraq, undecked canoe
umiaġluk, raft
umiaġriatchiaq, undecked canoe
umialgich (pl.), chieftains, wealthy people
umialik, chieftain, wealthy person
umialiŋnaq, rich man of lesser rank
umiaq, large open boat
unaaq, ice pick
uniapiaq, railed sled
unipkaat (pl.), legends
unnuaq, night
unnuk, evening
uŋaluuraq, covered platform cache
upiŋaaq, summer
upiŋaksraq, spring
upiŋaksrivik, spring camp

upiṅġivik, summer camp, summer house
uqaluktuaq, historical chronicle
uqaluktuat (pl.), historical chronicles
uqpik, feltleaf willow
uqsruq, seal oil
urgiiḷiq, paper birch
utuqqanaaq, elder

uumaq, standing timber
uunaqtuat, hot spring
uvlaaq, morning
uvluq, day
uyamik, needle case
uyamitquaq, necklace
uyuġu, nephew, niece

References

This list includes (1) published documentary sources, (2) unpublished documentary sources, (3) transcripts of or notes on interviews currently available to the general public in archives, and (4) transcripts of or notes on interviews that are not available to the general public at the present time but that eventually will be. In a few cases, references to material obtained from a particular individual fall into two or more of these categories. The citation format varies to some extent from one category to another, but the general pattern of alphabetical and chronological order is followed throughout. The year in parentheses behind an oral source's name is the year that person was born or thought to have been born.

Adams, Caleb Saqqan (1926), and Ruth Naŋaqtuaq Adams (1923)
1965   Personal communication to E. S. Burch, Jr., Kivalina, Alaska, July 29, 1965.
1984   Personal communication to E. S. Burch, Jr., Kivalina, Alaska, April 30, 1984.

Adams, David Iñuqtaq (1907)
1960.1   Notes from an interview by Don Foote, Noatak, Alaska, February 11, 1960. Don Charles Foote Papers, box 3, folder 5, Alaska and Polar Regions Department, University of Alaska Fairbanks.
1960.2   Notes from an interview by Don Foote, Noatak, Alaska, August 1, 1960. Don Charles Foote Papers, box 3, folder 1, Alaska and Polar Regions Department, University of Alaska Fairbanks.
1986   Personal communication to E. S. Burch, Jr., Noatak, Alaska, February 25, 1986.

Adams, Enoch, and Lucy Adams
1984   Personal communication to E. S. Burch, Jr., Kivalina, Alaska, April 30, 1984.

Adams, George R.
ms   Diaries dated 26 September 1865 to 23 March 1866, and 1 October 1866 to 8 October 1867. In E. S. Hubbell Collection, University of Washington Library, Seattle, Washington.
1982   *Life on the Yukon, 1865–1867*. Kingston, ON: Limestone Press. (Alaska History, no. 22.)

Adams, Ruth Naŋaqtuaq (1923)
1965   Personal communication to Deanne M. Burch, Kivalina, Alaska, September 9, 1965.
1984   Personal communication to E. S. Burch, Jr., Kivalina, Alaska, April 29, 1984.

Adams, Victor (1912)
1964   Personal communication to E. S. Burch, Jr., Kivalina, Alaska, June 10, 1964.

Agnabooguk, Clara Niiviaq (1918)
1999   Personal communication to E. S. Burch, Jr., Anchorage, Alaska, March 24, 1999.

Aġviqsiiña, Frank (1875)
1940.1   Frank's story, as told to Froelich G. Rainey, Point Hope, Alaska. Typed and indexed transcript in author's possession. [Other versions are in the Rainey Collection, box 3, folders 44 and 45, Archives, Alaska and Polar Regions Department, University of Alaska Fairbanks.]

1940.2   Qalgi ceremonies, as told to Froelich G. Rainey, Point Hope, Alaska. Handwritten notes in author's possession.

1940.3   Family groups, as told to Froelich G. Rainey, Point Hope, Alaska. Handwritten notes in author's possession.

Ahgook, Bob
1970   Personal communication to E. S. Burch, Jr., Anaktuvuk Pass, Alaska, April 29, 1970.

Alaska Geographic Society
1996   Mammals of Alaska. Anchorage: The Alaska Geographic Society.

Alaska Native News
1985   Guide to the Games. Alaska Native News 3(9).

Aldrich, Herbert L.
1889   Arctic Alaska and Siberia, or, Eight Months with the Arctic Whalemen. Chicago: Rand McNally and Company.

Alg̓aqsruutit
1983   Messenger Feast. Alg̓aqsruutit. Words of Wisdom from Your Elders, September, 1983. Kotzebue, Alaska: Mauneluk.

Allen, Clarence Talik (1925)
1960   Notes from an interview by Don Foote, Noatak, Alaska, February 18, 1960. Don Charles Foote Papers, box 3, folder 1, Alaska and Polar Regions Department, University of Alaska Fairbanks.

Ammitsbøll, T., S. Ry Andersen, H. P. Andersson, et al.
1991   The People. In Jens Peder Hart Hansen, Jørgen Meldgaard, and Jørgen Nordqvist, eds., The Greenland Mummies, pp. 64–101. Washington, DC: Smithsonian Institution Press.

Anderson, Douglas D.
1974/75   Trade Networks among the Selawik Eskimos, Northwestern Alaska, During the Late 19th and Early 20th Centuries. Folk 16–17:63–72.

1988a   Onion Portage: The Archaeology of a Stratified Site from the Kobuk River, Northwest Alaska. Anthropological Papers of the University of Alaska 22(1–2):1–163.

1988b   Personal oral communication to E. S. Burch, Jr., October 8, 1988.

Anderson, Douglas D., and Wanni W. Anderson
1982   Selawik Inupiat (Eskimo) Archeological Settlements, Resources and Subsistence Lifeways, Northwestern Alaska: Final Report (revised). Unpublished manuscript. Department of Anthropology, Brown University, Providence, Rhode Island.

Anderson, Douglas D., Wanni W. Anderson, Ray Bane, Richard K. Nelson, and Nita Sheldon Towarak
1998   Kuuvaŋmiit Subsistence: Traditional Eskimo Life in the Latter Twentieth Century. Washington, DC: U.S. National Park Service.

Anderson, Eskil
1945   Asbestos and Jade Occurrences in the Kobuk River Region, Alaska. Juneau: Alaska Department of Mines. Pamphlet No. 3-R.

Anderson, J. P.
1939   Plants Used by the Eskimo of the Northern Bering Sea and Arctic Regions of Alaska. American Journal of Botany 26:714–16.

Anderson, Patricia M.
1982   List of Plant Species for the Selawik River Valley. In Appendix 3 in Douglas D. Anderson and Wanni W. Anderson, Selawik Inupiat (Eskimo) Archeological Settlements, Resources and Subsistence Lifeways, Northwestern Alaska: Final Report (revised). Unpublished manuscript. Department of Anthropology, Brown University, Providence, Rhode Island.

Anderson, Wanni Wibulswasdi
1974/75   Song Duel of the Kobuk River Eskimo. Folk 16–17:73–81.

2005   The Dall Sheep Dinner Guest: Iñupiaq Narratives of Northwest Alaska. Fairbanks, AK: University of Alaska Press.

Anderson, Wanni W., and Ruthie Tatqaviñ Sampson
2003   *Folktales of the Riverine and Coastal Iñupiat.* Kotzebue: Northwest Arctic Borough and the National Endowment for the Humanities.

Andrews, Clarence L.
1939   *The Eskimo and His Reindeer in Alaska.* Caldwell, ID: The Caxton Printers Ltd.

Anungazuk, Herbert Aġayaġaq (1945)
1995   Whaling: A Ritual of Life. In Allen P. McCartney, ed., *Hunting the Largest Animals: Native Whaling in the Western Arctic and Subarctic*, pp. 339–45. Edmonton: The Canadian Circumpolar Institute, University of Alberta. (Studies in Whaling, no. 3; occasional publication no. 36.)
1999.1   Personal oral communication to E. S. Burch, Jr., Anchorage, Alaska, February 23, 1999.
1999.2   Personal oral communication to E. S. Burch, Jr., Nome, Alaska, February 25, 1999.
1999.3   Personal oral communication to E. S. Burch, Jr., Wales, Alaska, February 28, 1999.
1999.4   Personal oral communication to E. S. Burch, Jr., Wales, Alaska, March 2, 1999.
1999.5   Personal written communication to E. S. Burch, Jr., December 21, 1999.
1999.6   Personal written communication to E. S. Burch, Jr., December 27, 1999.
1999.7   Personal written communication to E. S. Burch, Jr., December 28, 1999.
2000.1   Division of walrus. Personal written communication to E. S. Burch, Jr., September 11, 2000.
2000.2   Personal written communication to E. S. Burch, Jr., September 13, 2000.
2000.3   Personal written communication to E. S. Burch, Jr., November 16, 2000.
2000.4   Personal written communication to E. S. Burch, Jr., November 28, 2000.
2000.5   Personal oral communication to E. S. Burch, Jr., November 29, 2000.
2001   Prehistoric waste disposal in Kiŋiġen [*sic*]. Written personal communication to E. S. Burch, Jr., September 5, 2001.
2002.1   Personal written communication to E. S. Burch, Jr., May 2, 2002.
2002.2   Personal written communication to E. S. Burch, Jr., May 15, 2002.

Anungazuk, Toby Maŋnak (1913)
1991   Personal communication to E. S. Burch, Jr., Wales, Alaska, July 8, 1991.

Armstrong, Connell Aaġayuk (1907)
1970   Personal communication to E. S. Burch, Jr., Deering, Alaska, April 16, 1970.

Ashby, Wilson Titqiaq (1893)
1970   Personal communication to E. S. Burch, Jr., Kotzebue, Alaska, May 19, 1970.

Atoruk, Effie Taapsuk (1902)
1989   Personal communication to E. S. Burch, Jr., Kiana, Alaska, March 1, 1989.

Atoruk, Peter Aaquuraq (1903), and Effie Taapsuk Atoruk (1902)
1989   Personal communication to E. S. Burch, Jr., Kiana, Alaska, February 28, 1989.

Attla, Catherine Nodoyedee'onh (1927), and Stephen Denaa'ek' oogheeɬtune' Attla (1924)
1991   Personal communication to E. S. Burch, Jr., Fairbanks, Alaska, March 16, 1991.

Attungana, Eva Usak (1908), and Patrick Kimmiałuk Attungana (1909)
1980   Personal communication to E. S. Burch, Jr., Point Hope, Alaska, October 18, 1980.

Attungana, Patrick Kimmiałuk (1909)
1959   Notes from an interview by Don Foote, Noatak, Alaska, September 15, 1959. Don Charles Foote Papers, box 4, folder 13, Alaska and Polar Regions Department, University of Alaska Fairbanks.
1980   Personal communication to E. S. Burch, Jr., Point Hope, Alaska, October 17, 1980.

Avessuk, Lola Naaksaak (Mizuknaat) (1921)
1983.1   Food customs. Interview by Georgianna Ahgupuk, Shishmaref, Alaska, May 9, 1983. Transcribed and translated by Georgianna Ahgupuk. Kawerak Eskimo Heritage Program transcript no. SHH.83.033, Nome, Alaska.
1983.2   Pregnancy rules. Interview with Georgianna Ahgupuk, Shishmaref, Alaska, August 10, 1983. Translated and transcribed by Georgianna Ahgupuk. Kawerak Eskimo Heritage Program transcript no. SHH.83.040, Nome, Alaska.

1983.3   Naming traditions. Interview with Gertrude Analaak, Shishmaref, Alaska, September 28, 1983. Translated and transcribed by Georgianna Ahgupuk. Kawerak Eskimo Heritage Program transcript no. SHH.83.041, Nome, Alaska.

1983.4   Making clothes. Interview with Edgar Ningeulook, Shishmaref, Alaska, May 20, 1983. Translated and transcribed by Edgar Ningeulook. Kawerak Eskimo Heritage Program transcript no. SHH.83.061, Nome, Alaska.

1983.5   Traditional life. Interview with Georgianna Ahgupuk, Shishmaref, Alaska, May 24, 1983. Translated and transcribed by Georgianna Ahgupuk. Kawerak Eskimo Heritage Program transcript no. SHH.83.062, Nome, Alaska.

1983.6   Traditional life. Interview with Georgianna Ahgupuk, Shishmaref, Alaska, May 24, 1983. Translated and transcribed by Georgianna Ahgupuk. Kawerak Eskimo Heritage Program transcript no. SHH.83.036, Nome, Alaska.

Ballot, Elmer Imġusriq
1990   Ways that are no more. In Linda Lee, Ruthie Sampson, Ed Tennant, and Hannah Mendenhall, eds., *Lore of the Iñupiat: The elders speak / Utuqqanaat uqaaqtuaqtut uqaaqtuaŋich Iñupiat.* Kotzebue, AK: Northwest Arctic Borough School District.

Ballot, Paul Iyaġun (1903)
1970   Personal communication to E. S. Burch, Jr., Selawik, Alaska, March 10, 1970.

Ballot, Walter Mannik (1900)
1970.1   Personal communication to E. S. Burch, Jr., Selawik, Alaska, March 9, 1970.
1970.2   Personal communication to E. S. Burch, Jr., Selawik, Alaska, March 11, 1970.

Barr, Emily Qimmikpiauraq (1889)
1970   Personal communication to E. S. Burch, Jr., Kotzebue, Alaska, April 23, 1970.

Barr, Gideon Qałłuk (1917)
1982.1   War with Siberians. Interview by Albert Ningeulook, Shishmaref, Alaska, February 3, 1982. Transcribed and translated by Georgianna Ahgupuk. Kawerak Eskimo Heritage Program transcripts no. SHH.82.004 and SHH.82.005, Nome, Alaska.
1982.2   Snares, hunting. Interview by Albert Ningeulook, Shishmaref, Alaska, February 3, 1982. Transcribed and translated by Georgianna Ahgupuk. Kawerak Eskimo Heritage Program transcript no. SHH.82.006, Nome, Alaska.
1987   Bering Land Bridge cultural resources inventory. Transcript of an interview by Jeanne Schaaf, May 15–16, 1987, Nome, Alaska. Transcribed by Herbert O. Anungazuk. On file in the Cultural Resources Library, U.S. National Park Service, Alaska Region, Anchorage, Alaska.
1991   Personal communication to E. S. Burch, Jr., Shishmaref, Alaska, July 11, 1991.

Barr, Gilford Piŋu (1923)
1987   Personal communication to E. S. Burch, Jr., Deering, Alaska, March 5, 1986.

Bates, Robert L., and Julia A. Jackson, eds.
1980   *Glossary of Geology.* 2nd ed. Falls Church, VA: American Geological Institute.

Beaglehole, John Cawte, ed.
1967   *The Journals of Captain James Cook on His Voyages of Discovery.* Vol. 3, *The Voyage of the Resolution and Discovery, 1776–1780.* Cambridge: Cambridge University Press for the Hakluyt Society.

Beaver, Mamie Naaġaayiq (1907)
1967   Personal communication to E. S. Burch. Jr., Kotzebue, Alaska, November 25, 1967.
1970.1   Personal communication to E. S. Burch, Jr., Kotzebue, Alaska, February 21, 1970.
1970.2   Personal communication to E. S. Burch, Jr., Kotzebue, Alaska, March 4, 1970.
1973   Personal communication to E. S. Burch, Jr., Kotzebue, Alaska, June 10, 1973.
1976.1   On Medicine. Typescript. NANA Elders Council Collection, Kotzebue, Alaska (H88–2A-1).
1976.2   To Remember. In Minnie Gray, Bertha Sheldon, Arthur Douglas, Sr., Mamie Beaver, and Lulu Geary, *Timimun Mamirrutit* ["Eskimo folk medicine"]. Kotzebue: The Mauneluk Cultural Heritage Program.
1984   Personal communication to E. S. Burch, Jr., Kotzebue, Alaska, April 27, 1984.

[Bechervaise, John]
 1839   *Thirty-Six Years of a Seafaring Life*. London: Woodward.

Beechey, Frederick William
 1831   *Narrative of a Voyage to the Pacific and Bering's Strait to Co-operate with the Polar Expeditions; Performed in His Majesty's Ship "Blossom" . . . in the Years 1825, 26, 27, 28*. 2 vols. London: Colburn and Bently.

Beechey, Richard
 ms.a   Remarks on a Voyage of Discovery to the Pacific and Bhering's Straits on Board H.M.S. *Blossom* by Rich. Beechey Midn., Aged 15. 2 vols. Public Record Office of Northern Ireland, Belfast, T.2479/2&3.
 ms.b   24 Drawings of the *Blossom*'s Voyage. Public Record Office of Northern Ireland, Belfast, T.2479.4.

Belcher, Edward
 ms   Private Journal, Remarks, Etc., *HM Ship Blossom* on Discovery During the Years 1825, 6, 7, . . . and Continuation of Private Journal. Typescript copy in University of British Columbia Library, Special Collections Division, Vancouver. Photocopy in the Scott Polar Research Institute Archives, Cambridge, England. (Manuscript no. 1044/.1.)

Bergsland, Knut, ed.
 1987   *Nunamiut unipkaaŋich* [Nunamiut Stories]. Collected 1949–50 by Helge Ingstad with the help of Homer Mekiana; edited and translated by Knut Bergsland with the help of Ronald W. Senungetuk and Justus Mekiana. Barrow: The North Slope Borough Commission on Iñupiat History, Language and Culture.

Berkh, Vasilii N.
 1983   Captain-Lieutenants Vasil'ev and Shishmarev, 1819. Translated by Rhea Josephson, edited by Dorothy Jean Ray. In Dorothy Jean Ray, *Ethnohistory in the Arctic: The Bering Strait Eskimo*, pp. 15–24. Kingston, ON: Limestone Press. (Alaska History, no. 23.)

Bernhardt, Tony
 1970   Personal communication to E. S. Burch, Jr., Kobuk, Alaska, February 26, 1970.

Berrie, Peter, Jeanette Earnest, and Bob Stephenson
 1994   Lynx. In *Wildlife Notebook Series*. Juneau: Alaska Department of Fish and Game.

Bertholf, Ellsworth Price
 1899a   Report of Second Lieut. E. P. Bertholf, R. C. S., Point Hope, Alaska, July 15, 1898. In *U.S. Treasury Department, Report of the Cruise of the U.S. Revenue Cutter "Bear" and the Overland Expedition for the Relief of the Whalers in the Arctic Ocean from November 27, 1897, to September 13, 1898*, pp. 18–27. Washington, DC: Government Printing Office.
 1899b   Report of Second Lieut. E. P. Bertholf, R. C. S., Point Hope, Alaska, September 1, 1898. In *U.S. Treasury Department, Report of the Cruise of the U.S. Revenue Cutter "Bear" and the Overland Expedition for the Relief of the Whalers in the Arctic Ocean from November 27, 1897, to September 13, 1898*, pp. 103–14. Washington, DC: Government Printing Office.

Best, Troy L., and Travis Hill Henry
 1994   *Lepus othus. Mammalian Species* 458:1–5.

Black, Lydia
 1998   Personal written communication to E. S. Burch, Jr., regarding Russian-American Company expeditions to Eschscholtz Bay prior to 1816.
 2004   *Russians in Alaska 1732–1867*. Fairbanks: University of Alaska Press.

Bliss, Lawrence C., and Karen M. Gustafson
 1981   Proposed Ecological Natural Landmarks in the Brooks Range, Alaska. Report to the U.S. Department of the Interior, Division of Natural Landmarks, Heritage Conservation and Recreation Service. (Copy seen in the Alaska and Polar Regions Department, University of Alaska Fairbanks.)

Boas, Franz
 1894   Notes on the Eskimo of Point Clarence, Alaska. *Journal of American Folklore* 7:205–8.
 1899   Property Marks of Alaskan Eskimo. *American Anthropologist* n.s. 1(4):601–13.

Bockstoce, John R.

1977   *Eskimos of Northwest Alaska in the Early Nineteenth Century, Based on the Beechey and Belcher Collections and Records Compiled During the Voyage of H.M.S. "Blossom" to Northwest Alaska in 1826 and 1827.* Oxford: University of Oxford. (Pitt Rivers Museum monograph series, no. 1.)

1980   A Preliminary Estimate of the Reduction of the Western Arctic Bowhead Whale Population by the Pelagic Whaling Industry: 1848–1915. *Marine Fisheries Review* 42(9–10):20–27.

1984   From Davis Strait to Bering Strait: The Arrival of the Commercial Whaling Fleet in North America's Western Arctic. *Arctic* 37(4):528–32.

1985   The Search for Sir John Franklin in Alaska. In Patricia D. Sutherland, ed., *The Franklin Era in Canadian Arctic History, 1845–1859*, pp. 93–113. Ottawa: National Museum of Man. (Archaeological Survey of Canada Paper no. 131.)

1986   *Whales, Ice and Men: The History of Whaling in the Western Arctic.* Seattle: University of Washington Press.

1993   Froelich Gladstone Rainey (1907–1992). *Arctic* 46(1):88–89.

2002   Personal written communication to E. S. Burch, Jr., November 4, 2002.

Bockstoce, John R., ed.

1988   *The Journal of Rochfort Maguire, 1852–1854: Two Years at Point Barrow, Alaska, Aboard HMS Plover in the Search for Sir John Franklin.* 2 vols. London: The Hakluyt Society. (2nd series, nos. 169 & 170.)

Bockstoce, John R., and Daniel B. Botkin

1982   The Harvest of Pacific Walruses by the Pelagic Whaling Industry, 1848 to 1914. *Arctic and Alpine Research* 14(3):183–88.

1983   The Historical Status and Reduction of the Western Arctic Bowhead Whale (*Balaena mysticetus*) Population by the Pelagic Whaling Industry, 1848–1914. *Scientific Reports of the International Whaling Commission, Special Issue* 5:107–41.

Bockstoce, John R., and John J. Burns

1993   Commercial Whaling in the North Pacific Sector. In John J. Burns, J. Jerome Montague, and Cleveland J. Cowles, eds., *The Bowhead Whale*, pp. 563–77. Lawrence, KS: The Society for Marine Mammalogy. (Special publication, no. 2.)

Bodenhorn, Barbara

1997   Person, Place, and Parentage: Ecology, Identity, and Social Relations on the North Slope of Alaska. In S. A. Mousalimas, ed., *Arctic Ecology and Identity*, pp. 102–32. Budapest: Akadémiai Kiadó; Los Angeles: International Society for Trans-Oceanic Research.

2000   'He Used to Be My Relative': Exploring the Bases of Relatedness Among Iñupiat of Northern Alaska. In Janet Carsten, ed., *Cultures of Relatedness: New Approaches to the Study of Kinship*, pp. 128–48. Cambridge: Cambridge University Press.

Booth, Ezra Kumak (1887)

1960.1 Notes from an interview by Don Foote, Noatak, Alaska, February 11, 1960. Don Charles Foote Papers, box 3, folder 1, Alaska and Polar Regions Department, University of Alaska Fairbanks.

1960.2 Notes from an interview by Don Foote, Noatak, Alaska, February 12, 1960. Don Charles Foote Papers, box 3, folder 2, Alaska and Polar Regions Department, University of Alaska Fairbanks.

1960.3 Notes from an interview by Don Foote, Noatak, Alaska, February 16, 1960. Don Charles Foote Papers, box 3, folder 1, Alaska and Polar Regions Department, University of Alaska Fairbanks.

1960.4 Notes from an interview by Don Foote, Noatak, Alaska, February 19, 1960. Don Charles Foote Papers, box 3, folder 1, Alaska and Polar Regions Department, University of Alaska Fairbanks.

1961   Notes from an interview by Tony Williamson, Noatak, Alaska, April 26, 1961. Don Charles Foote Papers, box 3, folder 1, Alaska and Polar Regions Department, University of Alaska Fairbanks.

Booth, Ezra Kumak (1887), Robert Iñauluk Lee (1901), and Julian Towkshjea
1960   Notes from an interview by Don Foote, Noatak, Alaska, February 16, 1960. Don Charles Foote Papers, box 3, folder 1, Alaska and Polar Regions Department, University of Alaska Fairbanks.

Bowling, Sue Ann
1985   Climatological Summary, Kobuk, Alaska. Means and Extremes, 1953–1979. Unpublished data from the Alaska Climate Center, Arctic Environmental Information and Data Center, University of Alaska Anchorage.

Briggs, Jean L.
2001   "Qallunaat Run on Rails; Inuit Do What They Want to Do." 'Autonomies' in Camp and Town. *Études/Inuit/Studies* 25(1–2):229–47.

Bromley, Dennis, and Tim Osborne
1994   Porcupine. In *Wildlife Notebook Series*. Juneau: Alaska Department of Fish and Game.

Brower, Charles David
ms   The Northernmost American: An Autobiography. Unpublished manuscript. Stefansson Collection. Dartmouth College Library, Hanover, New Hampshire.
1899   Sinew Working at Pt. Barrow. *American Anthropologist* n.s. 1:597.

Brower, Charles D., in collaboration with Philip J. Farrelly and Lyman Anson
1994   *Fifty Years Below Zero: A Lifetime of Adventure in the Far North.* Fairbanks: University of Alaska Press. (Classic reprint series, no. 3.) [Originally published by Dodd, Mead and Company, 1942.]

Brower, William A., Jr., Harold W. Searby, James L. Wise, Henry F. Diaz, and Anton S. Brechtel
1977   *Climatic Atlas of the Outer Continental Shelf Waters and Coastal Regions of Alaska.* Vol. III, *Chukchi-Beaufort Sea*. University of Alaska, Arctic Environmental Information and Data Center (Anchorage) and U.S. National Climatic Center (Asheville, NC).

Brown, A. R.
1918   Notes on the Social Organization of Australian Tribes. *Journal of the Royal Anthropological Institute* 48:222–53.

Brown, Emily Ivanoff
1959   *Eskimo Legend of Kotzebue.* College, AK: Privately printed.
1981a   *The Longest Story Ever Told. Qayaq: The Magical Man*. Anchorage: Alaska Pacific University Press.
1981b   *The Roots of Ticasuk: An Eskimo Woman's Family Story.* Rev. ed. Anchorage: Alaska Northwest Publishing Company.
1987   *Tales of Ticasuk: Eskimo Legends and Stories.* Fairbanks: University of Alaska Press.

Brown, Harry (ca. 1876)
1965   Notes from an interview by Don Foote, Kobuk, Alaska, August 25, 1965. Don Charles Foote Papers, box 8, folder 101A, Alaska and Polar Regions Department, University of Alaska Fairbanks.

Brown, Mabel
1976   Story. In Northwest Inupiat Elders Conference, March 4, 1976. Transcribed by Hannah Paniyavluk Loon, translated by Lorena Kapniaq Williams. Transcript 76–06, pg. 3. Copy in possession of the author.

Brown, Mabel, Grace Outwater, Charlie Sheldon, and others
1978   Juvenile Delinquency. Typescript. Kotzebue: NANA Elders Council Collection (H88-2C-12).

Bulkley, Charles L.
ms   Journal, Russo-American Telegraph Expedition, 1865–67. Manuscript journal at the Portland (OR) Library Association. Microfilm at the University of Washington Library, Seattle.

Burch, Ernest S., Jr.
1970a   The Eskimo Trading Partnership in North Alaska: A Study in Balanced Reciprocity. *Anthropological Papers of the University of Alaska* 15(1):49–80.

1970b   Marriage and Divorce Among the North Alaskan Eskimos. In Paul Bohannan, ed., *Divorce and After: An Analysis of the Emotional and Social Problems of Divorce*, pp. 152–81. Garden City, NY: Doubleday & Co.

1971   The Nonempirical Environment of the Arctic Alaskan Eskimos. *Southwestern Journal of Anthropology* 27(2):148–65.

1972   The Caribou/Wild Reindeer as a Human Resource. *American Antiquity* 37(3):339–68.

1975a   *Eskimo Kinsmen: Changing Family Relationships in Northwest Alaska.* St. Paul, MN: West Publishing Company. (American Ethnological Society monograph, no. 59.)

1975b   Inter-Regional Transportation in Traditional Northwest Alaska. *Anthropological Papers of the University of Alaska* 17(2):1–11.

1980   Traditional Eskimo Societies in Northwest Alaska. *Senri Ethnological Studies* 4:253–304.

1981   *The Traditional Eskimo Hunters of Point Hope, Alaska: 1800–1875.* Barrow: North Slope Borough.

1983   Sociodemographic Correlates of House Structures in Three Beringian Populations: An Exploratory Study. In Henry N. Michael and James W. VanStone, eds., *Cultures of the Bering Sea Region: Papers from an International Symposium*, pp. 112–39. Published for the American Council of Learned Societies and the Academy of Sciences of the USSR by the International Research and Exchanges Board, New York.

1984   Kotzebue Sound Eskimo. In William C. Sturtevant, general ed., *Handbook of North American Indians*. Vol. 5, *Arctic*, David Damas, ed., pp. 303–19. Washington, DC: Smithsonian Institution Press.

1988a   Modes of Exchange in North-West Alaska. In Tim Ingold, David Riches, and James Woodburn, eds., *Hunters and Gatherers 2: Property, Power and Ideology*, pp. 95–109. Oxford: Berg Publishers Ltd.

1988b   War and Trade. In William W. Fitzhugh and Aron Crowell, eds., *Crossroads of Continents: Cultures of Siberia and Alaska*, pp. 227–40. Washington, DC: Smithsonian Institution.

1991   From Skeptic to Believer: The Making of an Oral Historian. *Alaska History* 6(1):1–16.

1994a   The Iñupiat and the Christianization of Arctic Alaska. *Études/Inuit/Studies* 18(1–2):81–108.

1994b   Rationality and Resource Use Among Hunters. In Takashi Irimoto and Takako Yamada, eds., *Circumpolar Religion and Ecology: An Anthropology of the North*, pp. 163–85. Tokyo: University of Tokyo Press.

1998a   *The Iñupiaq Eskimo Nations of Northwest Alaska.* Fairbanks: University of Alaska Press.

1998b   Boundaries and Borders in Early Contact North-Central Alaska. *Arctic Anthropology* 35(2):19–48.

2005   *Alliance and Conflict: The World System of the Iñupiaq Eskimos.* Lincoln: University of Nebraska Press.

Burch, Ernest S., Jr., Eliza Jones, Hannah P. Loon, and Lawrence D. Kaplan
1999   The Ethnogenesis of the *Kuuvaum Kaŋiaġmiut*. *Ethnohistory* 46(2):291–327.

Burch, Ernest S., Jr., and Craig W. Mishler
1995   The Di'haii Gwich'in: Mystery People of Northern Alaska. *Arctic Anthropology* 32(1):147–72.

Burns, Frank
1952   Napaaktomyut messenger feast. Personal communication to Charles Lucier, June 1952. In Charles Lucier Collection, box 3, folder 15, Archives, Alaska and Polar Regions Department, University of Alaska Fairbanks.

Burns, John J.
1994a   Bearded Seal. In *Wildlife Notebook Series*. Juneau: Alaska Department of Fish and Game.
1994b   Spotted Seal. In *Wildlife Notebook Series*. Juneau: Alaska Department of Fish and Game.
1994c   Walrus. In *Wildlife Notebook Series*. Juneau: Alaska Department of Fish and Game.
1994d   Mink. In *Wildlife Notebook Series*. Juneau: Alaska Department of Fish and Game.

Burns, Kate Qagauraq (1891)
1960.1   Kate Burns's stories, recorded by Don Foote, Noatak, Alaska, July 28, 1960. Don Charles Foote Papers, box 3, folder 2, Alaska and Polar Regions Department, University of Alaska Fairbanks.

1960.2   Kate Burns's stories, recorded by Don Foote, Noatak, Alaska, July 30, 1960. Don Charles Foote Papers, box 3, folder 2, Alaska and Polar Regions Department, University of Alaska Fairbanks.

Burns, Kate Qagauraq (1891), and Frank Burns
1960   Songs. Recorded by Don Foote, Noatak, Alaska, July 28, 1960. Don Charles Foote Papers, box 3, folder 1, Alaska and Polar Regions Department, University of Alaska Fairbanks.

Call, S. J.
1899   Report of Surgeon S. J. Call, R.C.S., September 1, 1898. In U.S. Treasury Department, *Report of the Cruise of the U.S. Revenue Steamer "Bear" and the Overland Expedition for the Relief of the Whalers in the Arctic Ocean from November 27, 1897, to September 13, 1898*, pp. 114–27. Washington, DC: Government Printing Office.

Campbell, John Martin
1978   Aboriginal Overkill of Game Populations: Examples from Interior North Alaska. In R. C. Dunnell and E. S. Hall, Jr., eds., *Archaeological Essays in Honor of Irving B. Rouse*, pp. 179–208. The Hague: Mouton Publishers.
1998   *North Alaska Chronicle: Notes from the End of Time*. Santa Fe: Museum of New Mexico Press.

Campbell, John Martin, ed.
2004   *In a Hungry Country: Essays by Simon Paneak*. Fairbanks: University of Alaska Press.

Cantwell, John C.
1887   A Narrative Account of the Exploration of the Kowak River, Alaska, Under the Direction of Captain Michael A. Healy. In M. A. Healy, *Report of the Cruise of the Revenue Marine Steamer 'Corwin' in the Arctic Ocean in the Year 1885*, pp. 21–52. Washington, DC: Government Printing Office.
1889a   A Narrative Account of the Exploration of the Kowak River, Alaska. In M. A. Healy, *Report of the Cruise of the Revenue Marine Steamer 'Corwin' in the Arctic Ocean in the Year 1884*, pp. 47–74. Washington, DC: Government Printing Office.
1889b   Exploration of the Kowak River, Alaska, 1884: Ethnological Notes. In M. A. Healy, *Report of the Cruise of the Revenue Marine Steamer 'Corwin' in the Arctic Ocean in the Year 1884*, pp. 75–98. Washington, DC: Government Printing Office.

Carroll, Geoffrey
1994   Bowhead Whale. In *Wildlife Notebook Series*. Juneau: Alaska Department of Fish and Game.

Carter, Tommy Sagluaq (1902)
1986   Personal communication to E. S. Burch, Jr., Buckland, Alaska, February 19, 1986.

Chamisso, Adelbert von
1986   *The Alaska Diary of Adelbert von Chamisso, Naturalist on the Kotzebue Voyage, 1815–1818*. Translated from the German, with an introduction and notes, by Robert Fortuine. Anchorage: Cook Inlet Historical Society.

Chaussonnet, Valérie
1988   Needles and Animals: Women's Magic. In William W. Fitzhugh and Aron Crowell, eds., *Crossroads of Continents: Cultures of Siberia and Alaska*, pp. 209–26. Washington, DC: Smithsonian Institution.

Chernenko, M. B.
1957   The Voyages of Ivan Kobelev, Kazak Sotnik, to Chukotka Land and Sea Voyage to Alaska in 1779 and 1789–91. *Letopis' Severa* 2:121–41.

Choris, Ludovik
1822   *Voyage pittoresque autour du monde, avec des portraits de sauvages d'Amérique, d'Asie, d'Afrique, et des îles du Grand Océan; des paysages, des vues maritimes, et pleusiers objets d'histoire naturelle; accompagné de descriptions par M. Le Baron Cuvier, et M. A. de Chamisso, et d'observations sur les crânes humains par M. le Docteur Gall*. Paris: Firmin Didot.

Christensen, Jill
1989   Nutrition. In Ed Hall, ed., *People and Caribou in the Northwest Territories*, pp. 43–49. Yellowknife: Government of the Northwest Territories, Department of Renewable Resources.

Christy, Kathy
1982   Stinky Flippers Were Nutritious. *Alaska Magazine*, January 1982, pp. 20–23, 73.

Clark, Annette McFadyen
1970   The Athabaskan-Eskimo Interface. *Canadian Archaeological Association Bulletin* 2:13–23.
1974   *Koyukuk River Culture.* Ottawa: National Museums of Canada. (Canadian Ethnology Service paper, no. 18.)
1977   Trade at the Cross Roads. In J. W. Helmer, S. Van Dyke, and F. J. Kense, eds., *Problems in the Prehistory of the North American Subarctic: The Athapaskan Question*, pp. 130–34. Calgary: University of Calgary Archaeological Association.
1995   *Who Lived in This House? A Study of Koyukuk River Semisubterranean Houses.* Hull, QC: Canadian Museum of Civilization. (Archaeological Survey of Canada Paper, no. 153.)

Clark, Annette McFadyen, and Donald W. Clark
1976   Koyukuk Indian–Kobuk Eskimo Interaction. In Edwin S. Hall, Jr., ed., *Contributions to Anthropology: The Interior Peoples of Northern Alaska*, pp. 193–220. Ottawa: National Museum of Man. (Archaeological Survey of Canada Paper, no. 49.)

Clark, Donald W.
1972   Archaeology of the Batza Tena Obsidian Source, West-Central Alaska. *Anthropological Papers of the University of Alaska* 15(2):1–21.

Cleveland, George Aumałuk (1917)
1965   Notes from an interview by Don Foote, Bornite, Alaska, July 8, 1965. Don Charles Foote Papers, box 8, folder 99, Alaska and Polar Regions Department, University of Alaska Fairbanks.

Cleveland, Mark Uluatchiaq (1911)
1989   Personal communication to E. S. Burch, Jr.. Ambler, Alaska, February 23, 1989.

Cleveland, Robert Nasruk (1883)
1965.1   Notes from an undated interview by Don Foote, Kobuk River, Alaska. Don Charles Foote Papers, box 8, folder box 1, spiral notebook, Alaska and Polar Regions Department, University of Alaska Fairbanks.
1965.2   The early days. Recorded by Don Charles Foote. Typescript. Kotzebue: NANA Elders Council Collection (H88–2D-1).
1965.3   *Tumitchiałuk.* Recorded by Don Charles Foote. Typescript. Kotzebue: NANA Elders Council Collection (H88–2D-1).
1965.4   Notes from an interview by Don Foote, Black River, Alaska, July 10, 1965. Don Charles Foote Papers, box 8, folders 99, 101A, Alaska and Polar Regions Department, University of Alaska Fairbanks
1965.5   Notes from an interview by Don Foote, Shungnak, Alaska, July 22, 1965. Don Charles Foote Papers, box 8, folders 99, 101A, Alaska and Polar Regions Department, University of Alaska Fairbanks.
1965.6   Notes from an interview by Don Foote, Black River, Alaska, July 24, 1965. Don Charles Foote Papers, box 8, folder 101A, Alaska and Polar Regions Department, University of Alaska Fairbanks.
1965.7   Notes from an interview by Don Foote, Black River, Alaska, July 25, 1965. Don Charles Foote Papers, box 8, folder 101A, Alaska and Polar Regions Department, University of Alaska Fairbanks.
1965.8   Notes from an interview by Don Foote, Black River, Alaska, July 29, 1965. Don Charles Foote Papers, box 8, folder 101A, Alaska and Polar Regions Department, University of Alaska Fairbanks.
1965.9   Notes from an interview by Don Foote, Black River, Alaska, July 31, 1965. Don Charles Foote Papers, box 8, folder 101A, Alaska and Polar Regions Department, University of Alaska Fairbanks.
1965.10   Notes from an interview by Don Foote, Shungnak, Alaska, August 17, 1965. Don Charles Foote Papers, box 8, folder 101A, Alaska and Polar Regions Department, University of Alaska Fairbanks.

1965.11 Notes from an interview by Don Foote, Shungnak, Alaska, August 20, 1965. Don Charles Foote Papers, box 8, folder 101A, Alaska and Polar Regions Department, University of Alaska Fairbanks.

1965.12 Notes from an interview by Don Foote, Shungnak, Alaska, August 22, 1965. Don Charles Foote Papers, box 8, folder 101A, Alaska and Polar Regions Department, University of Alaska Fairbanks.

1966   Account of Traditional Eskimo Life. Don Charles Foote, Human Geographical Studies in Northwestern Alaska: The Point Hope and Upper Kobuk River Projects, 1965. Appendix C, Eskimo Stories and Songs of the Upper Kobuk River. Story 1. Unpublished manuscript. Montréal. (Copy in the Don Charles Foote Papers, Alaska and Polar Regions Department, University of Alaska Fairbanks.)

1970.1   Personal communication to E. S. Burch, Jr., Shungnak, Alaska, January 28, 1970.

1970.2   Personal communication to E. S. Burch, Jr., Shungnak, Alaska, January 29, 1970.

1970.3   Personal communication to E. S. Burch, Jr., Shungnak, Alaska, January 30, 1970.

1980   Stories of the Black River people [*Unipchaaŋich Imaġluktuġmiut*]. Recorded by Don Charles Foote, transcribed by Minnie Aliitchak Gray, translated and proofread by Ruth Tatqaviñ Ramoth-Sampson and Angeline Ipiiḷik Newlin. Kotzebue: NANA Elders Council Collection.

Cleveland, Sophie

1965   Personal communication to Don Foote, Bornite, Alaska, July 10, 1965. Don Charles Foote Papers, box 8, folder 101A, Alaska and Polar Regions Department, University of Alaska Fairbanks.

Coady, John W.

1980   History of Moose in Northern Alaska and Adjacent Regions. *Canadian Field-Naturalist* 94(1):61–68.

Coffin, Issack Irauraq (1884)

1970   Personal communication to E. S. Burch Jr., Noorvik, Alaska, April 1, 1970.

Collins, Henry Bascom

1937a   Archaeology of St. Lawrence Island, Alaska. *Smithsonian Miscellaneous Collections* 96(1).

1937b   Archaeological Investigations at Bering Strait. *Explorations and Field-Work of the Smithsonian Institution in 1936*, pp. 63–68.

Collinson, Richard

1889   *Journal of H.M.S. "Enterprise" on the Expedition in Search of Sir John Franklin's Ships by Bering Strait, 1850–55*. London: Sampson, Low, Marsten, Searle and Rivington.

Crowell, Aron

1988   Dwellings, Settlements, and Domestic Life. In William W. Fitzhugh and Aron Crowell, eds., *Crossroads of Continents: Cultures of Siberia and Alaska*, pp. 194–208. Washington, DC: Smithsonian Institution.

Csonka, Yvon

2000   Ekven, a Prehistoric Whale Hunters' Settlement on the Asian Shore of Bering Strait. Paper presented at the annual meeting of the Alaska Anthropological Association, Fairbanks, March 22, 2000.

Curby, Catherine

1994   Marmot. In *Wildlife Notebook Series*. Juneau: Alaska Department of Fish and Game.

Curtis, Edward C.

1930   *The North American Indian*, vol. 20. New York: Privately printed.

Curtis, Mary Aullaqsruaq (1889)

1969   Personal communication to E. S. Burch, Jr., Kotzebue, Alaska, November 20, 1969.

1970   Personal communication to E. S. Burch, Jr., Kotzebue, Alaska, April 24, 1970.

Dall, William Healy

1866–67 Field notebook, October 12, 1866–May 25, 1867. William Healy Dall Papers, 1865–1927, record unit 7073, Western Union Telegraph Expedition Notebooks 1865–1868, collection division 7, box 23. Smithsonian Archives, Washington, DC.

1870a   *Alaska and Its Resources*. Boston: Lee and Shepard.

1870b On the Distribution of the Native Tribes of Alaska. *Proceedings of the American Association for the Advancement of Science* 18:263–73.

1877 On the Distribution and Nomenclature of the Native Tribes of Alaska and the Adjacent Territory. In *Contributions to North American Ethnology*. Vol. 1, part I, *Tribes of the Extreme Northwest*, pp. 7–40. U.S. Geographical and Geological Survey of the Rocky Mountain Region. Washington, DC: Government Printing Office.

1881 Notes on Alaska and the Vicinity of Bering Strait. *The American Journal of Science*, whole no. 121, 3rd series, vol. 21, pp. 104–11.

1885 On Masks, Labrets, and Certain Aboriginal Customs, with an Inquiry into the Bearing of Their Geographical Distribution. In *Bureau of American Ethnology Third Annual Report, 1881–82*, pp. 67–202. Washington, DC: Government Printing Office.

1898 Travels on the Yukon and in the Yukon Territory. In *The Yukon Territory*, pp. 1–242. London: Downey and Company.

Dives, Ququk (1873)
1940 Dives's story, as told to Froelich G. Rainey, Point Hope, Alaska. Typed and indexed transcript in author's possession. [Another version is in the Froelich Rainey Collection, box 2, folder 44, Archives, Alaska and Polar Regions Department, University of Alaska Fairbanks.]

Dives, Samuel Paalauran (1912)
1970 Personal communication to E. S. Burch, Jr., Kotzebue, Alaska, May 7, 1970.

Dixon, Mim, and Scott Kirchner
1982 Poking: An Eskimo Medical Practice in Northwest Alaska. *Études/Inuit/Studies* 6(2):109–25.

Dolman, Claude E.
1960 Type E Botulism: A Hazard of the North. *Arctic* 13(4):230–56.

Douglas, Arthur Siḷaigaq, Sr. (1925)
1976.1 Old way of traveling. Translated by Art Douglas. Typescript. Kotzebue: NANA Elders Council Collection H88–2A-10, side A).
1976.2 Short stories. Translated by Art Douglas. Typescript. Kotzebue: NANA Elders Council Collection (H88–2A-6).
1976.3 The way people lived. Translated by Art Douglas. Typescript. Kotzebue: NANA Elders Council Collection (H88–2A-10).
1976.4 Kobuk River Eskimo myths about wild animals. Typescript. Kotzebue: NANA Elders Council Collection (H88–2A-6).
1976.5 Different ways of fishing. Typescript, April 1976. Kotzebue: NANA Elders Council Collection (H88–2A-8).
1976.6 Upper Kobuk medicinal cures. In Minnie Gray, Bertha Sheldon, Arthur Douglas, Sr., Mamie Beaver, and Lulu Geary, *Timimun Mamirrutit* ["Eskimo folk medicine"]. Kotzebue: The Mauneluk Cultural Heritage Program.
1976.7 Upper Kobuk Eskimo cures for ailments. Kotzebue: NANA Elders Council Collection (H88–2A-7).
1989.1 Personal communication to E. S. Burch, Jr., Ambler, Alaska, February 23, 1989.
1989.2 Personal communication to E. S. Burch, Jr., Ambler, Alaska, February 24, 1989.
1989.3 Personal communication to E. S. Burch, Jr., Ambler, Alaska, February 25, 1989.

Douglas, Tommy Paaniikaliaq (1925)
1986 Personal communication to E. S. Burch, Jr., Kivalina, Alaska, February 23, 1986.

Downey, Harold Iḷaippak (1892), John Pamiiqtaq Stalker (1910), and Kenneth Ashby (1914)
1987 Transcript of an interview by Robert Drozda and Brian Hoffman, Noatak, Alaska, August 10, 1987. Bill Bailey, interpreter. File no. 87NAN43, Bureau of Indian Affairs, ANCSA Office, Anchorage, Alaska.

Downey, Walter (1904)
1976 Kayayaktoelook. Kotzebue: NANA Elders Council Collection (H88–2A-38).

Draper, Harold H.
1977 The Aboriginal Eskimo Diet in Modern Perspective. *American Anthropologist* 79(2):309–16.

1978   Nutrition Studies: The Aboriginal Eskimo Diet—a Modern Perspective. In Paul L. Jamison, Stephen L. Zegura, and Frederick A. Milan, eds., *Eskimos of Northwestern Alaska: A Biological Perspective*, pp. 139–44. Stroudsburg, PA: Dowden, Hutchinson & Ross, Inc.

Driggs, John B.
1905   *Short Sketches from Oldest America*. Philadelphia: George W. Jacobs and Co.

Dumond, Don E.
2000   *Henry B. Collins at Wales, Alaska, 1936: A Partial Description of Collections*. Eugene: University of Oregon Department of Anthropology and Museum of Natural History. (University of Oregon Anthropological Papers, no. 56).

Edson, E. H.
1895   News of the Point Hope Mission. *The Spirit of Missions*, November 1895, pp. 470–72.

Egeland, Grace M., Lori A. Feyk, and John P. Middaugh
1998   *Use of Traditional Foods in a Healthy Diet in Alaska: Risks in Perspective*. Anchorage: Alaska Department of Health and Social Sciences, Division of Public Health. State of Alaska Epidemiology Bulletin 2(1).

Eide, Sterling, Sterling Miller, and Harry Reynolds
1994   Brown Bear. In *Wildlife Notebook Series*. Juneau: Alaska Department of Fish and Game.

Eisler, David
1978   Subsistence Activities of Shishmaref, Brevig Mission, Teller, Wales, and Deering. Unpublished manuscript. On file in the Cultural Resources Library, U.S. National Park Service, Alaska Region, Anchorage, Alaska.

Eley, Thomas J.
1994   Ringed Seal. In *Wildlife Notebook Series*. Juneau: Alaska Department of Fish and Game.

Eliyak (ca. 1854)
1931   The Oppownie (old) Eskimo and his customs, as told by Eliyak (Pechuk) and Oolooaharuk (Charley Wood), as told to Ira S. Purkeypile, Selawik, Alaska. Typed transcript appended to Bulletin of the N.W. District, U.S. Department of the Interior, Office of Indian Affairs, Alaska Division, October 28, 1931 [Kotzebue, Alaska]. Bland Collection, box 30, folder 38, Alaska and Polar Regions Department, University of Alaska Fairbanks.

Ellison, Lawrence N.
1994   Grouse. In *Wildlife Notebook Series*. Juneau: Alaska Department of Fish and Game.

The Eskimo Bulletin
1902   *The Eskimo Bulletin*. Published at Wales, Alaska. Copy viewed in the Rare Books Department, Rasmuson Library, University of Alaska Fairbanks.

The Esquimaux
1866–67 Newspaper published at Port Clarence, Russian America, and Plover Bay, Siberia. Copy viewed in the Archives, Alaska and Polar Regions Department, University of Alaska Fairbanks.

Explorer
1885   Log Book of the U.S. Steam Launch *Explorer*, from July 17, 1885, U.S. National Archives, R.G. 24. Records of the Bureau of U.S. Naval Personnel, Washington, DC.

Eutuk, Verne Wituana (1912)
1983   Hunting, shamans. Interview by Lucy Obruk, Shishmaref, Alaska, May 20, 1983. Transcribed and translated by Lucy Obruk. Kawerak Eskimo Heritage Program transcript no. SHH.83.052, Nome, Alaska.

Evok, John Ivaaq (1910)
1970   Personal communication to E. S. Burch, Jr., Kotzebue, Alaska, April 7, 1970.

Evok, Sarah
1987   Personal communication to E. S. Burch, Jr., Kotzebue, Alaska, March 1, 1987.

Fair, Susan W.
1998   Documentation of Toponyms and Site Information Along the Saniq Coast and in Bering Land Bridge National Preserve. Final Report to the Department of the Interior, National

Park Service, and the Shishmaref I.R.A. Village Council. Copy in possession of the author.

2001   The Inupiaq Eskimo Messenger Feast: Celebration, Demise, and Possibility. *Journal of American Folklore* 113(450):464–94.

2003   'Story of a Whale Hunt': Suzanne Rognon Bernardi's Photographs and Observations of Iñupiaq Whaling, Wales, Alaska, 1901–2. In Allen P. McCartney, ed., *Indigenous Ways to the Present: Native Whaling in the Western Arctic*, pp. 25–67. Edmonton: Canadian Circumpolar Institute Press; Salt Lake City: University of Utah Press.

2004   Names of Places, Other Times. In Igor Krupnik, Rachel Mason, and Tonia Horton, eds., *Northern Ethnographic Landscapes: Perspectives from Circumpolar Nations*, pp. 230–54. Washington, DC: Arctic Studies Center, National Museum of Natural History, Smithsonian Institution, in collaboration with the National Park Service.

Fallers, Lloyd A.
1965   The Range of Variation in Actual Family Size: A Critique of Marion Levy, Jr.'s Argument. In Ansley J. Coale, L. A. Fallers, M. J. Levy, Jr., D. M. Schneider, and Silvan S. Tomkins, *Aspects of the Analysis of Family Structure*, pp. 70–82. Princeton, NJ: Princeton University Press.

Fenton, William N.
1962   Ethnohistory and Its Problems. *Ethnohistory* 9(1):1–23.

Foote, Berit Arnestad
1992   *The Tigara Eskimos and Their Environment*. Point Hope, AK: North Slope Borough Commission on Iñupiat History, Language and Culture.

Foote, Don Charles
ms.a   Whaling, former. Brief notes on information obtained from various sources, apparently while whaling in April and May, but year not specified. Don Charles Foote Papers, box 53, folder 5, Archives, Alaska and Polar Regions Department, University of Alaska Fairbanks.

ms.b   Whaling traditions. Brief notes on information obtained from various sources, apparently while whaling in April and May, but year not specified. Don Charles Foote Papers, box 53, folder 5, Archives, Alaska and Polar Regions Department, University of Alaska Fairbanks.

1965a   Exploration and Resource Utilization in Northwestern Arctic Alaska Before 1855. 2 vols. Unpublished Ph.D. thesis, Department of Geography, McGill University.

1965b   Field notes from Shungnak, Alaska. Don Charles Foote Collection, box 8, Archives, Alaska and Polar Regions Department, University of Alaska Fairbanks.

Foote, Don Charles, and H. Anthony Williamson
1961   A Human Geographical Study in Northwest Alaska: Final Report of the Human Geographical Studies Program, U.S. Atomic Energy Commission, Project Chariot. Typescript. Cambridge, Massachusetts.

1966   A Human Geographical Study. In Norman J. Wilimovsky and John N. Wolfe, eds., *Environment of the Cape Thompson Region, Alaska*, pp. 1041–1111. Oak Ridge, TN: U.S. Atomic Energy Commission.

Fortuine, Robert
1975   Health Care and the Alaska Native: Some Historical Perspectives. *Polar Notes* XIV:1–42.
1984   Traditional Surgery of the Alaska Natives. *Alaska Medicine* 26(1):22–25.
1985   Lancets of Stone: Traditional Methods of Surgery Among the Alaska Natives. *Arctic Anthropology* 22(1):23–45.
1986/87 Early Evidence of Infections Among Alaskan Natives. *Alaska History* 2(1):39–56.
1988a   Empirical Healing Among the Alaska Natives: A Historical Perspective. In Hakan Linderhold, Christer Backman, Noel Broadbent, and Ingemar Joelsson, eds., *Circumpolar Health 87: Proceedings of the 7th International Congress on Circumpolar Health, Umeå, Sweden, June 8–12, 1987*, pp. 296–302. Oulu: Nordic Council for Arctic Medical Research. (Arctic Medical Research 47, Supplement 1.)
1988b   The Use of Medicinal Plants by the Alaska Natives. *Alaska Medicine* 30(6):185–226.
1989   *Chills and Fever: Health and Disease in the Early History of Alaska*. Fairbanks: University of Alaska Press.

1990 Health of Alaskan Natives Around the Time of European Contact. *Caduceus* 6(1):1–30.

Foster, Daniel Kunaŋnaaluk (1894)
1970.1 Personal communication to E. S. Burch, Jr., Noorvik, Alaska, March 30, 1970.
1970.2 Personal communication to E. S. Burch, Jr., Noorvik, Alaska, March 31, 1970.

Foster, Johnnie Tuuyuq (1903)
1970 Personal communication to E. S. Burch, Jr., Selawik, Alaska, March 11, 1970.
1986.1 Personal communication to E. S. Burch, Jr., Selawik, Alaska, February 26, 1986.
1986.2 Personal communication to E. S. Burch, Jr., Selawik, Alaska, February 27, 1986.

Foster, Johnnie Tuuyuq (1903), and Fay Uyuġaq Foster (1911)
1986 Personal communication to E. S. Burch, Jr., Selawik, Alaska, February 26, 1986.

Frankson, Andrew (1910)
1940 Marriage, as told to Froelich G. Rainey, Point Hope, Alaska. Unpublished field notes in possession of the author.

Frankson, David Umigluk (1900)
1980 Personal communication to E. S. Burch, Jr., Point Hope, Alaska, October 16, 1980.

Frankson, Dinah Aviq (1908)
1980 Personal communication to E. S. Burch, Jr., Point Hope, Alaska, October 16, 1980.

Frost, Kathy
1994 Gray Whale. In *Wildlife Notebook Series*. Juneau: Alaska Department of Fish and Game.

Gadsby, Patricia
2004 The Inuit Paradox. *Discover* 25(10):48–55.

Gallahorn, Lester Qaluraq (1892)
1969.1 Personal communication to E. S. Burch, Jr., Kotzebue, Alaska, December 5, 1969.
1969.2 Personal communication to E. S. Burch, Jr., Kotzebue, Alaska, December 29, 1969.
1970.1 Personal communication to E. S. Burch, Jr., Kotzebue, Alaska, January 8, 1970.
1970.2 Personal communication to E. S. Burch, Jr., Kotzebue, Alaska, January 22, 1970.
1970.3 Personal communication to E. S. Burch, Jr., Kotzebue, Alaska, April 21, 1970.

Gallahorn, Ralph Aŋnuyaq (1883)
1952.1 He made clothes from leaves and grass. Personal communication to Charles Lucier, Sheshalik, Alaska. In Charles Lucier Collection, box 3, folder 14, Archives, Alaska and Polar Regions Department, University of Alaska Fairbanks.
1952.2 *Tayangnirluk* (Big Wrist), a Napaktomyut story. Personal communication to Charles Lucier, Sheshalik, Alaska, July 2, 1952. In Charles Lucier Collection, box 3, folder 14, Archives, Alaska and Polar Regions Department, University of Alaska Fairbanks.
1952.3 Wives for three men. Personal communication to Charles Lucier, Sheshalik, Alaska, July 9, 1952. In Charles Lucier Collection, box 3, folder 14, Archives, Alaska and Polar Regions Department, University of Alaska Fairbanks.
1952.4 Raven catches a magic seal. Personal communication to Charles Lucier, Sheshalik, Alaska, July 11, 1952. In Charles Lucier Collection, box 3, folder 14, Archives, Alaska and Polar Regions Department, University of Alaska Fairbanks.
1952.5 Raven and the woman in the water. Personal communication to Charles Lucier, Sheshalik, Alaska, July 11, 1952. In Charles Lucier Collection, box 3, folder 14, Archives, Alaska and Polar Regions Department, University of Alaska Fairbanks.
1952.6 Starving. Personal communication to Charles Lucier, Sheshalik, Alaska, July 11, 1952. In Charles Lucier Collection, box 3, folder 14, Archives, Alaska and Polar Regions Department, University of Alaska Fairbanks.
1952.7 The cottonwood tree that became a man. Personal communication to Charles Lucier, Sheshalik, Alaska, July 25, 1952. In Charles Lucier Collection, box 3, folder 14, Archives, Alaska and Polar Regions Department, University of Alaska Fairbanks.
1952.8 The girl who married her own grandfather. Personal communication to Charles Lucier, Sheshalik, Alaska, July 25, 1952. In Charles Lucier Collection, box 3, folder 14, Archives, Alaska and Polar Regions Department, University of Alaska Fairbanks.

1952.9 The spotted wolverine skin. Personal communication to Charles Lucier, Sheshalik, Alaska, July 25, 1952. In Charles Lucier Collection, box 3, folder 14, Archives, Alaska and Polar Regions Department, University of Alaska Fairbanks.

1952.10 Boy takes Innyokakneluk's wife. Personal communication to Charles Lucier, Sheshalik, Alaska, July 26, 1952. In Charles Lucier Collection, box 3, folder 14, Archives, Alaska and Polar Regions Department, University of Alaska Fairbanks.

1952.11 The boy whose amulet was *atmaq*. Personal communication to Charles Lucier, Sheshalik, Alaska, August 5, 1952. In Charles Lucier Collection, box 3, folder 14, Archives, Alaska and Polar Regions Department, University of Alaska Fairbanks.

1952.12 The two brothers and the man-killer. Personal communication to Charles Lucier, Sheshalik, Alaska, August 6, 1952. In Charles Lucier Collection, box 3, folder 14, Archives, Alaska and Polar Regions Department, University of Alaska Fairbanks.

1952.13 The little boy and the man-killers. Personal communication to Charles Lucier, Sheshalik, Alaska, August 7, 1952. In Charles Lucier Collection, box 3, folder 14, Archives, Alaska and Polar Regions Department, University of Alaska Fairbanks.

1952.14 Naming a baby. Personal communication to Charles Lucier, Sheshalik, Alaska, August 7, 1952. In Charles Lucier Collection, box 3, folder 14, Archives, Alaska and Polar Regions Department, University of Alaska Fairbanks.

1952.15 Raven gets fooled. Personal communication to Charles Lucier, Sheshalik, Alaska, August 7, 1952. In Charles Lucier Collection, box 3, folder 14, Archives, Alaska and Polar Regions Department, University of Alaska Fairbanks.

1952.16 Raven sees who has the stronger teeth. Personal communication to Charles Lucier, Sheshalik, Alaska, August 7, 1952. In Charles Lucier Collection, box 3, folder 14, Archives, Alaska and Polar Regions Department, University of Alaska Fairbanks.

1952.17 Raven and his partner. Personal communication to Charles Lucier, Sheshalik, Alaska, August 7, 1952. In Charles Lucier Collection, box 3, folder 14, Archives, Alaska and Polar Regions Department, University of Alaska Fairbanks.

1952.18 Raven and the mother squirrel. Personal communication to Charles Lucier, Sheshalik, Alaska, August 7, 1952. In Charles Lucier Collection box 3, folder 14, Archives, Alaska and Polar Regions Department, University of Alaska Fairbanks.

1952.19 Napaaqtuġmiut (and Kotzebue?) inviting-in feast or "eagle-wolf dance." From Charles Lucier's consolidated field notes, N. Kotzebue Sound, 1950–52. In Charles Lucier's personal collection.

1952.20 Messenger feast, Napaktomiut. Undated personal communication to Charles Lucier. In Charles Lucier Collection box 3, folder 14, Archives, Alaska and Polar Regions Department, University of Alaska Fairbanks.

Garber, Clark McKinley
1975 *Stories and Legends of the Bering Strait Eskimos*. New York: AMS Press. [Originally published by Christopher Publishing House, 1940.]

Geary, Lulu Tuttugruk
ms History of Buckland. Typed transcript in English. Kotzebue: NANA Elders Council Collection (H88-2A-12).
1976 Before Modern Medicine. In Minnie Gray, Bertha Sheldon, Arthur Douglas, Sr., Mamie Beaver, and Lulu Geary, *Timimun Mamirrutit* ["Eskimo folk medicine"]. Kotzebue: The Mauneluk Cultural Heritage Program.

Geraci, Joseph, and Thomas G. Smith
1979 Vitamin C in the Diet of Inuit Hunters from Holman, Northwest Territories. *Arctic* 32(2):135–39.

Gibbs, George S.
1906 Transportation Methods in Alaska. *National Geographic Magazine* 17(1):69–82.

Giddings, James Louis, Jr.
1941 Ethnographic Notes, Kobuk River Region, Alaska. *Kiva* 6(7):25–28.
1952 *The Arctic Woodland Culture of the Kobuk River*. Philadelphia: University of Pennsylvania Museum monographs.

1956   Forest Eskimos: An Ethnographic Sketch of Kobuk River People in the 1880s. *University Museum Bulletin* 20(2):1–55.

1961   *Kobuk River People.* College: University of Alaska Press. (Studies of Northern Peoples, no. 1.)

1967   *Ancient Men of the Arctic.* New York: Alfred A. Knopf.

Giddings, James L., and Douglas D. Anderson

1986   *Beach Ridge Archeology of Cape Krusenstern. Eskimo and Pre-Eskimo Settlements Around Kotzebue Sound, Alaska.* Washington, DC: U.S. Department of the Interior, National Park Service. (Publications in Archeology, no. 20.)

Glover, Frank Kutvak (1886)

1952.1   Word list, archery. Personal communication to Charles Lucier, Sheshalik, Alaska, August 1, 1952. In Charles Lucier Collection, box 3, folder 11, Archives, Alaska and Polar Regions Department, University of Alaska Fairbanks.

1952.2   Words (list, birch bark bucket). Personal communication to Charles Lucier, Sheshalik, Alaska, August 1, 1952. In Charles Lucier Collection, box 3, folder 11, Archives, Alaska and Polar Regions Department, University of Alaska Fairbanks.

1952.3   A boy who could defend himself. Personal communication to Charles Lucier, Sheshalik, Alaska, August 1, 1952. In Charles Lucier Collection, box 3, folder 11, Archives, Alaska and Polar Regions Department, University of Alaska Fairbanks.

1952.4   Drill nomenclature. Personal communication to Charles Lucier, Sheshalik, Alaska, August 1, 1952. In Charles Lucier Collection, box 3, folder 11, Archives, Alaska and Polar Regions Department, University of Alaska Fairbanks.

1952.5   *Tuguluk* type snowshoes. Personal communication to Charles Lucier, Sheshalik, Alaska, August 1, 1952. In Charles Lucier Collection, box 3, folder 11, Archives, Alaska and Polar Regions Department, University of Alaska Fairbanks.

1970.1   Personal communication to E. S. Burch, Jr., Kotzebue, Alaska, January 9, 1970.

1970.2   Personal communication to E. S. Burch, Jr., Kotzebue, Alaska, January 22, 1970.

1970.3   Personal communication to E. S. Burch, Jr., Kotzebue, Alaska, February 16, 1970.

1970.4   Personal communication to E. S. Burch, Jr., Kotzebue, Alaska, March 2, 1970.

1970.5   Personal communication to E. S. Burch, Jr., Kotzebue, Alaska, April 6, 1970.

1970.6   Personal communication to E. S. Burch, Jr., Kotzebue, Alaska, April 20, 1970.

Golder, Frank Alfred

1960   *Russian Expansion on the Pacific, 1641–1859.* Gloucester, MA: Peter Smith. (Reprint of 1914 volume.)

Goodwin, Freda Anniviaq (1887)

1970   Personal communication to E. S. Burch, Jr., Kotzebue, Alaska, January 7, 1970.

Gould, Julius, and William L. Kolb, eds.

1964   *A Dictionary of the Social Sciences.* New York: Free Press.

Gough, Barry M., ed.

1973   *To the Pacific and Arctic with Beechey: The Journal of Lieutenant George Peard of H.M.S. 'Blossom,' 1825–1828.* Cambridge: Cambridge University Press.

Gray, Minnie Aliitchak (1924)

1976   Body healers. In Minnie Gray, Bertha Sheldon, Arthur Douglas, Sr., Mamie Beaver, and Lulu Geary, *Timimun Mamirrutit* ["Eskimo folk medicine"]. Kotzebue: The Mauneluk Cultural Heritage Program.

Gray, Minnie Aliitchak (1924), Mark Uluatchiaq Cleveland (1911), and Clara Paaniikaaluk Lee (1922)

1987   Transcript of an interview by Robert Drozda and David Staley, Ambler, Alaska, July 11, 1987. File no. 87NAN31, Bureau of Indian Affairs, ANCSA Office, Anchorage, Alaska.

Gray, Minnie Aliitchak, Tupou L. Pulu, Angeline Ipiiḷik Newlin, and Ruth Tatqaviñ Ramoth-Sampson

1981a   *Birch Bark Basket Making/Aimmiḷik Qiaġumik.* Anchorage: University of Alaska, Rural Education, National Bilingual Materials Development Center.

1981b   Old beliefs [*Taimaknaqtat*]. Kotzebue: NANA Elders Council Collection.

Gray, Minnie Aliitchak (1924), Bertha Kitik Sheldon, Arthur Siḷaigaq Douglas, Sr. (1925), Mamie Naagaayiq Beaver (1907), and Lulu Tuttugruk Geary (1903)
1976   *Timimun Mamirrutit* ["Eskimo folk medicine"]. Kotzebue: The Mauneluk Cultural Heritage Program.

Green, Paul Aġniq (1901)
1959   *I Am Eskimo, Aknik My Name.* Juneau: Alaska-Northwest Publishing Company.
1969   Personal oral communication to E. S. Burch, Jr., Kotzebue, Alaska, December 18, 1969.
1970   Personal oral communication to E. S. Burch, Jr., Kotzebue, Alaska, January 20, 1970.

Greene, Chuck
2003   Foreword. In Wanni W. Anderson and Ruthie Tatqaviñ Sampson, *Folktales of the Riverine and Coastal Iñupiat,* pp. iv–vi. Kotzebue: Northwest Arctic Borough and the National Endowment for the Humanities.

Greist, Henry W.
ms   Seventeen Years with the Eskimo. Incomplete manuscript in the Stefansson Collection, Dartmouth College Library, Hanover, New Hampshire.

Greist, Levi Qaġġauluk (1906)
1970   Personal communication to E. S. Burch, Jr., Barrow, Alaska, May 12, 1970.

Grinnell, Joseph
1901   *Gold Hunting in Alaska.* Edited by Elizabeth Grinnell. Chicago: David Cook Publishing Company.

Grybeck, Donald
1977   Known Mineral Deposits of the Brooks Range, Alaska. U.S. Geological Survey. Open-File Report 77–166C.

Gubser, Nicholas J.
1965   *The Nunamiut Eskimos: Hunters of Caribou.* New Haven, CT: Yale University Press.

Guthrie, R. Dale, and J. V. Matthews
1978   The Cape Deceit Fauna—Early Pleistocene Mammalian Assemblage from the Alaskan Arctic. *Quaternary Research* 1:474–510.

Hadley, John Aulaġiaq (ca. 1880)
1951   Morning song. Undated personal communication to Charles Lucier. In Charles Lucier Collection, box 3, folder 14, Archives, Alaska and Polar Regions Department, University of Alaska Fairbanks.

Hadley, John Aulaġiaq (ca. 1880), and Andrew Sannu Sunno (ca. 1857)
1951   Buckland Eskimo–Koyukuk Indian relations. Undated personal communication to Charles Lucier. In Charles Lucier's personal collection [JH, AS-KAN-9].

Hadley, Paul Masuana (1910)
1986   Personal communication to E. S. Burch, Jr., Buckland, Alaska, February 19, 1986.

Hall, Edwin S., Jr.
1975   *The Eskimo Storyteller: Folktales from Noatak, Alaska.* Knoxville: University of Tennessee Press.
1988a   Personal written communication to E. S. Burch, Jr., November 15, 1988.
1988b   Personal oral communication to E. S. Burch, Jr., December 20, 1988.

Hall, Edwin S., Jr., and Charles G. Mull
1976   An Aboriginal Chert Quarry in Northwestern Alaska. *Anthropological Papers of the University of Alaska* 19(1):11–15.

Hamilton, Lawrence C., Carole L. Seyfrit, and C. Bellinger
1997   Environment and Sex Ratios Among Alaska Natives: A Historical Perspective. *Population and Environment* 18(3):283–99.

Hamilton, T. M.
1970   The Eskimo Bow and the Asiatic Composite. *Arctic Anthropology* 6(2):43–52.

Hank, Nicholas
1959   Notes from an interview by Don Foote, Point Hope, Alaska, September 15, 1959. Don Charles Foote Papers, box 105, folder 6, Alaska and Polar Regions Department, University of Alaska Fairbanks.

Harris, Albert Yaiyuk (1880)

1952.1   War at Segoruitch: A spirit kills a hunter. Personal communication to Charles Lucier, Sheshalik, Alaska, July 28, 1952. In Charles Lucier Collection, box 3, folder 14, Archives, Alaska and Polar Regions Department, University of Alaska Fairbanks.

1952.2   A spirit kills a hunter. Personal communication to Charles Lucier, Sheshalik, Alaska, July 29, 1952. In Charles Lucier Collection, box 3, folder 14, Archives, Alaska and Polar Regions Department, University of Alaska Fairbanks.

1952.3   Noiyuk and Upkik. Personal communication to Charles Lucier, Sheshalik, Alaska, July 30, 1952. In Charles Lucier Collection, box 3, folder 14, Archives, Alaska and Polar Regions Department, University of Alaska Fairbanks.

1952.4   The baby puffin that wanted an inviting-in feast. Personal communication to Charles Lucier, Sheshalik, Alaska, July 30, 1952. In Charles Lucier Collection, box 3, folder 14, Archives, Alaska and Polar Regions Department, University of Alaska Fairbanks.

1952.5   Mink and raven. Personal communication to Charles Lucier, Sheshalik, Alaska, July 30, 1952. In Charles Lucier Collection, box 3, folder 14, Archives, Alaska and Polar Regions Department, University of Alaska Fairbanks.

1952.6   The poor boy and the wild man. Personal communication to Charles Lucier, Sheshalik, Alaska, July 31, 1952. In Charles Lucier Collection, box 3, folder 14, Archives, Alaska and Polar Regions Department, University of Alaska Fairbanks.

1952.7   Raven and the seal. Personal communication to Charles Lucier, Sheshalik, Alaska, July 31, 1952. In Charles Lucier Collection, box 3, folder 14, Archives, Alaska and Polar Regions Department, University of Alaska Fairbanks.

Harritt, Roger K.

2003a   A Preliminary Reevaluation of the Punuk-Thule Interface at Wales, Alaska. Paper presented at the 30th annual meeting of the Alaska Anthropological Association, Fairbanks, Alaska, March 28, 2003.

2003b   Re-Examining Wales' Role in Bering Strait Prehistory: Some Preliminary Results of Recent Work. In Allen P. McCartney, ed., *Indigenous Ways to the Present: Native Whaling in the Western Arctic*, pp. 25–67. Edmonton: Canadian Circumpolar Institute Press; Salt Lake City: University of Utah Press.

2004   A Preliminary Reevaluation of the Punuk-Thule Interface at Wales, Alaska. *Arctic Anthropology* 41(2):163–76.

Hartman, Charles W., and Philip R. Johnson

1984   *Environmental Atlas of Alaska*. 2nd ed., revised. Fairbanks: University of Alaska, Institute of Water Resources/Engineering Experiment Station.

Hawkes, Ernest William

1913   *The "Inviting-In" Feast of the Alaskan Eskimo*. Ottawa: Government Printing Bureau. (Canada Department of Mines, Geological Survey Memoir 45, Anthropological Series no. 3.)

1914   The Dance Festivals of the Alaskan Eskimo. *University of Pennsylvania Anthropological Publications* 6(2):3–41.

Hawley, Amos Apuġiña (1913)

1964.1   Personal communication to E. S. Burch, Jr., Kivalina, Alaska, July 3, 1964.

1964.2   Personal communication to E. S. Burch, Jr., Kivalina, Alaska, July 22, 1964.

1964.3   Personal communication to E. S. Burch, Jr., Kivalina, Alaska, August 17, 1964.

1964.4   Personal communication to E. S. Burch, Jr., Kivalina, Alaska, August 27, 1964.

1964.5   Personal communication to E. S. Burch, Jr., Kivalina, Alaska, October 31, 1964.

1964.6   Personal communication to E. S. Burch, Jr., Kivalina, Alaska, September 19, 1964.

1964.7   Personal communication to E. S. Burch, Jr., Kivalina, Alaska, September 10, 1964.

1965.1   Personal communication to E. S. Burch, Jr., Kivalina, Alaska, May 15, 1965.

1965.2   Personal communication to E. S. Burch, Jr., Kivalina, Alaska, May 26, 1965.

1965.3   Personal communication to E. S. Burch, Jr., Kivalina, Alaska, June 8, 1965.

1965.4   Personal communication to E. S. Burch, Jr., Kivalina, Alaska, June 9, 1965.

1965.5   Personal communication to E. S. Burch, Jr., Kivalina, Alaska, June 10, 1965.

1965.6   Personal communication to E. S. Burch, Jr., Kivalina, Alaska, June 15, 1965.

1965.7   Personal communication to E. S. Burch, Jr., Kivalina, Alaska, June 22, 1965.

1965.8   Personal communication to E. S. Burch, Jr., Kivalina, Alaska, July 4, 1965.
1965.9   Personal communication to E. S. Burch, Jr., Kivalina, Alaska, July 6, 1965.
1965.10 Personal communication to E. S. Burch, Jr., Kivalina, Alaska, July 22, 1965.
1965.11 Personal communication to E. S. Burch, Jr., Kivalina, Alaska, July 26, 1965.
1965.12 Personal communication to E. S. Burch, Jr., Kivalina, Alaska, July 31, 1965.
1965.13 Personal communication to E. S. Burch, Jr., Kivalina, Alaska, August 2, 1965.
1965.14 Personal communication to E. S. Burch, Jr., Kivalina, Alaska, August 5, 1965.
1965.15 Personal communication to E. S. Burch, Jr., Kivalina, Alaska, August 11, 1965.
1965.16 Personal communication to E. S. Burch, Jr., Kivalina, Alaska, August 30, 1965.
1965.17 Personal communication to E. S. Burch, Jr., Kivalina, Alaska, September 10, 1965.
1965.18 Personal communication to E. S. Burch, Jr., Kivalina, Alaska, September 17, 1965.
1966   Personal communication to E. S. Burch, Jr., Kivalina, Alaska, February 7, 1966.
1967   Personal written communication to E. S. Burch, Jr., Kivalina, Alaska, November 24, 1967.
1970.1   Personal communication to E. S. Burch, Jr., Kivalina, Alaska, February 11, 1970.
1970.2   Personal communication to E. S. Burch, Jr., Kivalina, Alaska, February 12, 1970.
1973.1   Personal communication to E. S. Burch, Jr., Kivalina, Alaska, June 3, 1973.
1973.2   Personal communication to E. S. Burch, Jr., Kivalina, Alaska, June 6, 1973.
1973.3   Personal communication to E. S. Burch, Jr., Kivalina, Alaska, June 7, 1973.
1973.4   Personal communication to E. S. Burch, Jr., Kivalina, Alaska, June 8, 1973.
1973.5   Personal communication to E. S. Burch, Jr., Kivalina, Alaska, June 9, 1973.
1976.1   Personal communication to E. S. Burch, Jr., Kivalina, Alaska, April 2, 1976.
1976.2   Personal communication to E. S. Burch, Jr., Kivalina, Alaska, April 5, 1976.
1976.3   Personal communication to E. S. Burch, Jr., Kivalina, Alaska, April 7, 1976.
1976.4   Personal communication to E. S. Burch, Jr., Kivalina, Alaska, April 8, 1976.
1976.5   Personal communication to E. S. Burch, Jr., Kivalina, Alaska, April 9, 1976.
1976.6   Personal communication to E. S. Burch, Jr., Kivalina, Alaska, April 10, 1976.
1976.7   Personal communication to E. S. Burch, Jr., Kivalina, Alaska, August 26, 1976.
1980   Personal communication to E. S. Burch, Jr., Kivalina, Alaska, October 12, 1980.
1982   Personal communication to E. S. Burch, Jr., Kivalina, Alaska, October 22, 1982.

Hawley, Bob Tuvaaksraq, Sr. (1930)
1964.1   Personal communication to E. S. Burch, Jr., Kivalina, Alaska, August 31, 1964.
1964.2   Personal communication to E. S. Burch, Jr., Kivalina, Alaska, October 16, 1964.
1965   Personal communication to E. S. Burch, Jr., Kivalina, Alaska. August 16, 1965.
1970   Personal communication to E. S. Burch, Jr., Kivalina, Alaska, February 11, 1970.
1982   Personal communication to E. S. Burch, Jr., Kivalina, Alaska, October 21, 1982.
1984   Personal communication to E. S. Burch, Jr., Kivalina, Alaska, March 5, 1984.
1989   Personal communication to E. S. Burch, Jr., Kivalina, Alaska, February 18, 1989.

Hawley, Bob, and Sarah Hawley
1970   Personal communication to E. S. Burch, Jr., Kivalina, Alaska, February 12, 1970.
1984   Personal communication to E. S. Burch, Jr., Kivalina, Alaska, April 30, 1984.

Hawley, James Asaqpan, Sr. (1917)
1976   Personal communication to E. S. Burch, Jr., Kivalina, Alaska, April 1, 1976.
1984   Personal communication to E. S. Burch, Jr., Kivalina, Alaska, March 11, 1984.

Hawley, Myra Akurruaq (1888)
1965.1   Personal communication to E. S. Burch, Jr., Kivalina, Alaska, August 25, 1965.
1965.2   Personal communication to E. S. Burch, Jr., Kivalina, Alaska, September 7, 1965.

Hawley, Sarah Nigiaġvik (1928)
1984   Personal communication to E. S. Burch, Jr., Kivalina, Alaska, May 7, 1983.

Healy, Michael A.
1887   Report of the Cruise of the Steamer 'Corwin'. In M. A. Healy, *Report of the Cruise of the Revenue Steamer* 'Corwin' *in the Arctic Ocean, 1885*, pp. 5–20. Washington, DC: Government Printing Office.
1889   *Report of the Cruise of the Revenue Steamer* 'Corwin' *in the Arctic Ocean in the Year 1884.* Washington, DC: Government Printing Office.

Heimer, Wayne E., and Ken Whitten
1994   Dall Sheep. In *Wildlife Notebook Series*. Juneau: Alaska Department of Fish and Game.

Heinrich, Albert
ms   Field notes on kinship in the Bering Straits area. Albert Heinrich Collection (MS 169), box 1, folder 4, Alaska and Polar Regions Department, University of Alaska Fairbanks.
1955a   An Outline of the Kinship System of the Bering Straits Eskimos. Unpublished M.A. thesis, Department of Education, University of Alaska.
1955b   A Survey of Kinship Forms and Terminologies Found Among the Inupiaq-Speaking Peoples of Alaska. Unpublished manuscript in the Albert Heinrich Collection, Alaska and Polar Regions Department, University of Alaska Fairbanks.
1960   Structural Features of Northwestern Alaskan Eskimo Kinship. *Southwestern Journal of Anthropology* 16(1):110–26.
1963a   Eskimo-Type Kinship and Eskimo Kinship: An Evaluation and a Provisional Model for Presenting the Evidence Pertaining to Inupiaq Kinship Systems. Ann Arbor, MI: University Microfilms International.
1963b   *Personal Names, Social Structure, and Functional Integration*. Missoula: Montana State University, Department of Sociology, Anthropology and Social Welfare. (Anthropology & Sociology Papers, no. 27.)
1972   Divorce as an Alliance Mechanism Among Eskimos. In D. L. Guemple, ed., *Alliance in Eskimo Society: Proceedings of the American Ethnological Society, 1971*, Supplement, pp. 79–88. Seattle: University of Washington Press.

Heinrich, Albert C., and R. Anderson
1968   Co-Affinal Siblingship as a Structural Feature Among Some Northern North American Peoples. *Ethnology* 7(3):290–95.

Helm, June
1965   Bilaterality in the Socio-Territorial Organization of the Arctic Drainage Dene. *Ethnology* 4(4):361–85.
1968   The Nature of Dogrib Socio-Territorial Groups. In Richard B. Lee and Irven DeVore, eds., *Man the Hunter*, pp. 118–25. Chicago: Aldine Publishing Company.

Hemming, James E.
1971   *The Distribution and Movement Patterns of Caribou in Alaska*. Juneau: Alaska Department of Fish and Game. (Technical Bulletin no. 1.)
1994   Caribou. In *Wildlife Notebook Series*. Juneau: Alaska Department of Fish and Game.

Hickey, Clifford G.
1968   The Kayak Site: An Analysis of the Spatial Aspects of Culture as an Aid to Archaeological Inference. M.A. thesis, Brown University, Providence, Rhode Island.
1979   The Historic Beringian Trade Network: Its Nature and Origins. In Allen P. McCartney, ed., *Thule Eskimo Culture: An Anthropological Retrospective*, pp. 411–34. Ottawa: National Museum of Man. (Archaeological Survey of Canada Paper, no. 88.)

Hild, Vicki
1983   Traditional Inuit Health Methods Reviewed. *Tundra Times*, June 15, 1983, p. 11.

Hillsen, Karl K.
1983   A Voyage of the Sloop "*Blagonamerennyi*" to Explore the Asiatic and American Coasts of Bering Strait, 1819 to 1822. Translated by Rhea Josephson. Edited by Dorothy Jean Ray. In Dorothy Jean Ray, *Ethnohistory in the Arctic: The Bering Strait Eskimo*, pp. 25–54. Kingston, ON: Limestone Press. (Alaska History, no. 23.)

Hobson, W. R.
1855   Journal of the Proceedings of Mr. W. R. Hobson (Mate) and Party Under His Charge, Whilst Travelling from Port Clarence to Chamisso Island, and Returning to the Ship, Between February 9 and March 27, 1854 (inclusive). In House of Commons, United Kingdom. *Sessional Papers, 1854–55, Accounts and Papers*, vol. 35, no. 1898, pp. 884–98.

Hoffecker, John F., Scott A. Elias, Georgeanne L. Reynolds, Owen K. Mason, Diane K. Hanson, Jana Harcharek, Chris Savok, and Karlene Leeper
2000   Uivvaq: Archaeology and Paleoclimatology of an Arctic Coastal Midden: Preliminary Report to Point Hope Elders and the National Science Foundation. Typescript. Boulder: University of Colorado, Institute of Arctic and Alpine Research.

Hooper, Calvin Leighton
1881   *Report of the Cruise of the U.S. Revenue Steamer "Corwin" in the Arctic Ocean . . . 1880.* Washington, DC: Government Printing Office.
1884   *Report of the Cruise of the U.S. Revenue Steamer "Thomas Corwin" in the Arctic Ocean, 1881.* Washington, DC: Government Printing Office.

Hopkins, David M., Thor N. V. Karlstrom, and others
1955   Permafrost and Ground Water in Alaska. *U.S. Geological Survey Professional Paper* 264-F, pp. 113–46.

Hopkins, David M., and R. S. Sigafoos
1951   Frost Action and Vegetation Patterns on Seward Peninsula, Alaska. *U.S. Geological Survey Bulletin* 974-C, pp. C51–C101.

Hopson, Flossie, ed.
1978   North Slope Elders Conference (May 22–26, 1978). Typescript. Barrow, AK: Commission on History & Culture, North Slope Borough.

Howard, Mary Akuliaq (1878)
1952   Napaktoktuok messenger feast, circa 1893. Personal communication to Charles Lucier, Sheshalik, Alaska, July 2, 1952. In Charles Lucier Collection, box 3, folder 14, Archives, Alaska and Polar Regions Department, University of Alaska Fairbanks.

Hrdlička, Aleš
1930   Anthropological Survey of Alaska. In *Bureau of American Ethnology 46th Annual Report, 1928–1929,* pp. 19–374. Washington, DC: Government Printing Office.

Hunnicutt, Edna Iragauraq (1880)
1960.1 Notes from an interview by Don Foote, Noatak, Alaska, February 9, 1960. Don Charles Foote Papers, box 3, folder 2, Alaska and Polar Regions Department, University of Alaska Fairbanks.
1960.2 Notes from an interview by Don Foote, Noatak, Alaska, February 10, 1960. Don Charles Foote Papers, box 3, folder 2, Alaska and Polar Regions Department, University of Alaska Fairbanks.
1960.3 Notes from an interview by Don Foote, Noatak, Alaska, February 12, 1960. Don Charles Foote Papers, box 3, folder 2, Alaska and Polar Regions Department, University of Alaska Fairbanks.
1970.1 Personal communication to E. S. Burch, Jr., Kivalina, Alaska, February 10, 1970.
1970.2 Personal communication to E. S. Burch, Jr., Kivalina, Alaska, February 11, 1970.

Hunnicutt, Elwood Uyaan (1904)
1970   Personal communication to E. S. Burch, Jr., Kotzebue, Alaska, March 26, 1970.
1984   Personal communication to E. S. Burch, Jr., Kotzebue, Alaska, March 13, 1984.

Issenman, Betty Kobayashi
1997   *Sinews of Survival: The Living Legacy of Inuit Clothing.* Vancouver: UBC Press.

Iviqsiq (1872)
1940   Iviqsiq's story, as told to Froelich G. Rainey, Point Hope, Alaska. Typed and indexed transcript in author's possession. [Another version is in the Froelich Rainey Collection, box 3, folder 45, Archives, Alaska and Polar Regions Department, University of Alaska Fairbanks.]

Jackson, Percy Uula (1926)
1989   Personal communication to E. S. Burch, Jr., Kiana, Alaska, March 1, 1989.

Jacobsen, Johan Adrian
1977   *Alaskan Voyage, 1881–1883: An Expedition to the Northwest Coast of America, from the German Text of Adrian Woldt.* Translated by Erna Gunther. Chicago: University of Chicago Press.

Jarvis, D. H.
1899   Report of First Lieut. D. H. Jarvis, July 10, 1898. In U.S. Treasury Department, *Report of the Cruise of the U.S. Revenue Steamer "Bear" and the Overland Expedition for the Relief of the Whalers in the Arctic Ocean from November 27, 1897, to September 13, 1898*, pp. 29–103. Washington, DC: Government Printing Office.

Jenness, Diamond
1924   Eskimo Folk-Lore. Part A. Myths and Traditions from Northern Alaska, the Mackenzie Delta, and Coronation Gulf. Part B. Eskimo String Figures. *Report of the Canadian Arctic Expedition, 1913–18*, vol. XIII. Ottawa: King's Printer.
1928   Archaeological Investigations in Bering Strait, 1926. In Annual Report for 1926, pp. 71–80. *National Museum of Canada Bulletin* no. 50.
1953   Stray Notes on the Eskimo of Arctic Alaska. *Anthropological Papers of the University of Alaska* 1(2):5–13.
1957   *Dawn in Arctic Alaska.* Minneapolis: University of Minnesota Press.

Jenness, Stuart E., ed.
1991   *Arctic Odyssey: The Diary of Diamond Jenness, Ethnologist with the Canadian Arctic Expedition, in Northern Alaska and Canada, 1913–1916.* Hull, QC: Canadian Museum of Civilization.

Jennings, Larry
1994   Red Fox. In *Wildlife Notebook Series.* Juneau: Alaska Department of Fish and Game.

Jensen, Charlie Saġġaaluraq (1893)
1970.1   Personal communication to E. S. Burch, Jr., Kotzebue, Alaska, February 19, 1970.
1970.2   Personal communication to E. S. Burch, Jr., Kotzebue, Alaska, March 5, 1970.
1970.3   Personal communication to E. S. Burch, Jr., Kotzebue, Alaska, March 22, 1970.
1970.4   Personal communication to E. S. Burch, Jr., Kotzebue, Alaska, April 9, 1970.
1970.5   Personal communication to E. S. Burch, Jr., Kotzebue, Alaska, May 20, 1970.
1970.6   Personal communication to E. S. Burch, Jr., Kotzebue, Alaska, May 22, 1970.
1970.7   Personal communication to E. S. Burch, Jr., Kotzebue, Alaska, May 28, 1970.
1976   Personal communication to E. S. Burch, Jr., Kotzebue, Alaska, April 11, 1976.
1980.1   Personal communication to E. S. Burch, Jr., Kotzebue, Alaska, October 8, 1980.
1980.2   Personal communication to E. S. Burch, Jr., Kotzebue, Alaska, October 19, 1980.
1984.1   Personal communication to E. S. Burch, Jr., Kotzebue, Alaska, March 2, 1984.
1984.2   Personal communication to E. S. Burch, Jr., Kotzebue, Alaska, May 8, 1984.

Jensen, Charlie Saġġaaluraq (1893), and Lucy Ayagiaq Jensen (1897)
1980   Personal communication to E. S. Burch, Jr., Kotzebue, Alaska, October 8, 1980.

Johnson, Loyal
1994   Black Bear. In *Wildlife Notebook Series.* Juneau: Alaska Department of Fish and Game.

Johnston, Thomas F.
1974a   Eight North Alaskan Eskimo Dance Songs. *Tennessee Folklore Society Bulletin* 40(4):123–36.
1974b   A Historical Perspective on Alaskan Eskimo Music. *Indian Historian* 7(4):17–26.
1974c   A Juggling-Game Song from Point Hope. *Tennessee Folklore Society Bulletin* 40(1):11–16.
1975a   Alaskan Eskimo Dance in Cultural Context. *Dance Research Journal* 7(2):1–11.
1975b   Eskimo Music: A Comparative Survey. *Anthropologica* n.s. 7(2):217–32.
1975c   Eskimo Music of the Northern Interior, Alaska. *Polar Notes* 14:54–62.
1976a   Alaskan Eskimo Musical Revitalization. *Acts of the 42nd International Congress of Americanists*, Paris, September 2–9, 1976, vol. V:247–54.
1976b   The Eskimo Songs of Northwestern Alaska. *Arctic* 29(1):7–19.
1976c   The Social Background of Eskimo Music in Northwest Alaska. *Journal of American Folklore* 89(354):438–48.
1977   Differential Cultural Persistence in Inuit Musical Behavior, and Its Geographic Distribution. *Études/Inuit/Studies* 1(2):57–72.
1978a   Humor, Drama, and Play in Alaskan Eskimo Mimetic Dance. *Western Canadian Journal of Anthropology* 8(1):47–64.
1978b   Musical Characteristics Common to Different Alaskan Eskimo Areas. *Ethnologische Zeitschrift* 1:107–15.
1988a   Drum Rhythms of the Alaskan Eskimo. *Anthropologie* 26(1):75–82.

1988b   Community History and Environment as Wellspring of Inupiaq Eskimo Songtexts. *Anthropos* 83:161–71.

1990   Context, Meaning, and Function in Inupiaq Dance. In Lynnette Y. Overby and James H. Humphrey, eds., *Dance: Current Selected Research 2*, pp. 193–266. New York: AMS Press.

Johnston, Thomas F., and Tupou L. Pulu

1980   *Learning Eskimo Drumming.* Anchorage: University of Alaska, Rural Education, National Bilingual Materials Development Center.

Jones, Anore

1983   *Nauriat Niġiñaqtuat: Plants That We Eat.* Kotzebue, AK: Maniiḷaq Association.

Jones, Eliza Neełteloyeenełno (1938)

1991   Personal communication to E. S. Burch, Jr., Fairbanks, Alaska, March 12, 1991.

Juul, Sandra

1979   Portrait of an Eskimo Tribal Health Doctor. *Alaska Medicine* 21(6):66–71.

Kaplan, Lawrence D.

1981   *Phonological Issues in North Alaskan Inupiaq.* Fairbanks: Alaska Native Language Center, University of Alaska Fairbanks. (Research Paper no. 6.)

1984   *Inupiaq and the Schools: A Handbook for Teachers.* Juneau: Alaska Department of Education, Bilingual/Bicultural Education Programs.

1990   The Language of the Alaskan Inuit. In Dirmid R. F. Collis, ed., *Arctic Languages: An Awakening*, pp. 131–58. Paris: UNESCO.

2000   L'Inupiaq et Les Contacts Linguistiques en Alaska. In Nicole Tersis and Michèle Therrien, eds., *Les Langues Eskaleoutes: Siberie, Alaska, Canada, Greenland*, pp. 91–108. Paris: CNRS Éditions.

2001   Inupiaq Identity and Inupiaq Language: Does One Entail the Other? *Études/Inuit/Studies* 25(1–2):249–57.

2003a   Personal written communication to E. S. Burch, Jr., March 6, 2003.

2003b   Personal written communication to E. S. Burch, Jr., July 8, 2003.

Karl, Susan

1990   Personal written communication to E. S. Burch, Jr., concerning the composition of *kitik*.

Karmun, Alfred Qaaġraq (1910)

1970   Personal communication to E. S. Burch, Jr., Deering, Alaska, April 16, 1970.

Karmun, Mamie Ataŋan (1914)

1970   Personal communication to E. S. Burch, Jr., Deering, Alaska, April 16, 1970.

Keats, Della Puyuk (1907)

1960.1   Notes from an interview by Don Foote, Noatak, Alaska, February 19, 1960. Don Charles Foote Papers, box 3, folder 1, Alaska and Polar Regions Department, University of Alaska Fairbanks.

1960.2   Notes from an interview by Don Foote, Noatak, Alaska, February 20, 1960. Don Charles Foote Papers, box 3, folder 1, Alaska and Polar Regions Department, University of Alaska Fairbanks.

1960.3   Notes from an interview by Don Foote, Noatak, Alaska, February 23, 1960. Don Charles Foote Papers, box 3, folder 1, Alaska and Polar Regions Department, University of Alaska Fairbanks.

1969.1   Personal communication to E. S. Burch, Jr., Kotzebue, Alaska, December 3, 1969.

1969.2   Personal communication to E. S. Burch, Jr., Kotzebue, Alaska, December 10, 1969.

1970.1   Personal oral communication to E. S. Burch, Jr., Kotzebue, Alaska, January 2, 1970.

1970.2   Personal communication to E. S. Burch, Jr., Kotzebue, Alaska, January 7, 1970.

1970.3   Personal communication to E. S. Burch, Jr., Kotzebue, Alaska, January 14, 1970.

1970.4   Personal communication to E. S. Burch, Jr., Kotzebue, Alaska, January 21, 1970.

1970.5   Personal communication to E. S. Burch, Jr., Kotzebue, Alaska, February 6, 1970.

1970.6   Personal communication to E. S. Burch, Jr., Kotzebue, Alaska, March 4, 1970.

1970.7   Personal communication to E. S. Burch, Jr., Kotzebue, Alaska, March 25, 1970.

1970.8   Personal communication to E. S. Burch, Jr., Kotzebue, Alaska, April 8, 1970.

1970.9   Personal communication to E. S. Burch, Jr., Kotzebue, Alaska, April 22, 1970.

1970.10 Personal communication to E. S. Burch, Jr., Kotzebue, Alaska, May 6, 1970.
1976 Personal communication to E. S. Burch, Jr., Kotzebue, Alaska, March 30, 1976.

Keithan, Edward L.
1958 *Alaskan Igloo Tales.* Seattle: Craftsman Press.

Kellett, Henry
1850 Narrative of the Proceedings of Captain Kellett, of Her Majesty's Ship "*Herald,*" and Commander Moore and Lieutenant Pullen, of Her Majesty's Ship "*Plover,*" Through Behring's Straits, and Towards the Mouth of the Mackenzie River. In House of Commons, United Kingdom. *Sessional Papers, 1850, Accounts and Papers,* vol. 35, no. 107, pp. 9–44.

Kelly, Mark, and Annabel Lund
1986 *Heartbeat: World Eskimo Indian Olympics.* Juneau: Fairweather Press.

Kennedy, Edith Puptaun (1893)
1964 Personal communication to Deanne M. Burch, Kivalina, Alaska, July 7, 1964. Transcript in possession of the author.
1965.1 Personal communication to E. S. Burch, Jr., Kivalina, Alaska, July 12, 1965.
1965.2 Personal communication to E. S. Burch, Jr., Kivalina, Alaska, July 14, 1965.
1965.3 Personal communication to Deanne M. Burch, Kivalina, Alaska, August 20, 1965.
1973 Personal communication to E. S. Burch, Jr., Kivalina, Alaska, June 7, 1973.
1976 Personal communication to E. S. Burch, Jr., Kivalina, Alaska, April 5, 1976.
1984 Personal communication to E. S. Burch, Jr., Kivalina, Alaska, May 1, 1984.

Kialook, Frank Qitchaun (1923)
1964 Personal communication to E. S. Burch, Jr., Chicago, Illinois, January 27, 1964.
1970 Personal communication to E. S. Burch, Jr., Deering, Alaska, April 15, 1970.

Kiana, Charlie Qaġmak (1926)
1969 Personal communication to E.. S. Burch, Jr., Kotzebue, Alaska, December 31, 1969.
1970 Personal communication to E. S. Burch, Jr., Kotzebue, Alaska, January 17, 1970.

Kignak, Ernest
1976 The life of Ernest Kignak. Personal communication to Robert and Alice Glenn, Barrow, Alaska, June 28, 1976. Copy in possession of the author.

Killigivuk, Jimmy Asatchaq (1890)
1940.1 Control, old style. Personal communication to Froelich G. Rainey, Point Hope, Alaska. Copy in possession of the author.
1940.2 Marriage. Personal communication to Froelich G. Rainey, Point Hope, Alaska. Typed and indexed transcript in possession of the author. [Another version is in the Froelich Rainey Collection, box 2, folder 44, Archives, Alaska and Polar Regions Department, University of Alaska Fairbanks.]
1959.1 Notes from an interview by Don Foote, Point Hope, Alaska, December 11, 1959. Don Charles Foote Papers, box 5, folder 6, Alaska and Polar Regions Department, University of Alaska Fairbanks.
1959.2 Notes from an interview by Don Foote, Point Hope, Alaska, December 21, 1959. Don Charles Foote Papers, box 5, folder 3, Alaska and Polar Regions Department, University of Alaska Fairbanks.
1960.1 Notes from an interview by Don Foote, Point Hope, Alaska, January 4, 1960. Don Charles Foote Papers, box 5, folder 6, Alaska and Polar Regions Department, University of Alaska Fairbanks.
1960.2 Notes from an interview by Don Foote, Point Hope, Alaska, January 6, 1960. Don Charles Foote Papers, box 5, folder 6, Alaska and Polar Regions Department, University of Alaska Fairbanks.
1960.3 Notes from an interview by Don Foote, Point Hope, Alaska, January 18, 1960. Don Charles Foote Papers, box 5, folder 6, Alaska and Polar Regions Department, University of Alaska Fairbanks.
1960.4 Notes from an interview by Don Foote, Point Hope, Alaska, January 19, 1960. Don Charles Foote Papers, box 5, folder 6, Alaska and Polar Regions Department, University of Alaska Fairbanks.

1960.5   Notes from an interview by Don Foote, Point Hope, Alaska, January 23, 1960. Don Charles Foote Papers, box 5, folder 6, Alaska and Polar Regions Department, University of Alaska Fairbanks.

1960.6   Notes from an interview by Don Foote, Point Hope, Alaska, January 27, 1960. Don Charles Foote Papers, box 5, folder 7, Alaska and Polar Regions Department, University of Alaska Fairbanks.

1960.7   Notes from an interview by Don Foote, Point Hope, Alaska, February 29, 1960. Don Charles Foote Papers, box 5, folder 6, Alaska and Polar Regions Department, University of Alaska Fairbanks.

1960.8   Notes from an interview by Don Foote, Point Hope, Alaska, May 15, 1960. Don Charles Foote Papers, box 47, folder 13, Alaska and Polar Regions Department, University of Alaska Fairbanks.

1960.9   Jimmy Killigivuk's life. Notes from an interview by Don Foote, Point Hope, Alaska, November 2, 1960. Don Charles Foote Papers, box 5, folder 6, Alaska and Polar Regions Department, University of Alaska Fairbanks.

1960.10   Notes from an interview by Don Foote, Point Hope, Alaska, December 16, 1960. Don Charles Foote Papers, box 5, folder 6, Alaska and Polar Regions Department, University of Alaska Fairbanks.

1960.11   Notes from an interview by Don Foote, Point Hope, Alaska, December 18, 1960. Don Charles Foote Papers, box 5, folder 6, Alaska and Polar Regions Department, University of Alaska Fairbanks.

1960.12   Notes from an interview by Don Foote, Point Hope, Alaska, December 31, 1960. Don Charles Foote Papers, box 5, folder 6, Alaska and Polar Regions Department, University of Alaska Fairbanks.

1961.1   Old Point Hope settlements. Notes from an interview by Don Foote, Point Hope, Alaska, January 7, 1961. Don Charles Foote Papers, box 4, folder 12, Alaska and Polar Regions Department, University of Alaska Fairbanks.

1961.2   Notes from an interview by Don Foote, Point Hope, Alaska, January 9, 1961. Don Charles Foote Papers, box 5, folder 6, Alaska and Polar Regions Department, University of Alaska Fairbanks.

1967   Terms of relationship. Provided to Don Charles Foote, Point Hope, Alaska, May 20, 1967, at the request of E. S. Burch, Jr. In possession of the author.

1982   *The Shaman Aningatchaq: An Eskimo Story from Tikiraq, Alaska.* Translated by Tukummiq Carol Omnik and Tom Lowenstein. London: Many Press.

Killigivuk, Solomon Piquq

1960   Story. Notes from an interview by Don Foote, Point Hope, Alaska, December 18, 1960. Don Charles Foote Papers, box 5, folder 6 Alaska and Polar Regions Department, University of Alaska Fairbanks.

Killiguvuk, Jimmy. See Killigivuk, Jimmy Asatchaq (1980).

Kingik, Laurie Uyaġaaluk (1909)

1978   Stories of the Tulugak and the First Tikigaqmiut. In Flossie Hopson, ed., North Hope Elders Conference, May 22–26, 1978, Barrow, Alaska, pp. 18–19. Typescript. Barrow: North Slope Borough, Commission on History and Culture.

1980   Personal communication to E. S. Burch, Jr., Point Hope, Alaska, October 15, 1980.

Kingston, Deanna M.

1996   Ugiuvangmiut—Middle-Men in the Bering Strait Trade Network. Unpublished typescript report in possession of the author.

1999   Returning: Twentieth Century Performances of the King Island Wolf Dance. Ann Arbor, MI: UMI Dissertation Services (#9939800).

Kirchner, Scott

1983   Andrew Skin, Sr.: Eskimo Doctor. *Alaska Medicine* 24(6):101–5.

Kisautaq (Leona Okakok) and Gary Kean, eds.

1981   *Puiguitkaat: The 1978 Elder's Conference.* Barrow: The North Slope Borough Commission on History and Culture.

Kishigami, Nobuhiro
2004   A New Typology of Food-Sharing Practices Among Hunter-Gatherers, with a Special Focus on Inuit Examples. *Journal of Anthropological Research* 60:341–58.

Kiyutelluk, Morris
1976   Statements of Significance for 14(h)(1) Historic and Cemetery Sites in the Shishmaref Area. Unpublished manuscript submitted to the Bering Straits Native Corporation, Shishmaref, Alaska. Copy viewed in the Kathryn Koutsky Cohen Collection, box 1, folder 8, Alaska and Polar Regions Department, University of Alaska Fairbanks.

Klengenberg, Christian
1932   *Klengenberg of the Arctic, An Autobiography.* London: J. Cape.

Knapp, Edward J.
1904   Point Hope Happenings. II. Looking Forward. *The Spirit of Missions*, October, pp. 726–28.

Knox, Nellie Kuyuurak (1922)
1965   Personal communication to Deanne M. Burch, Kivalina, Alaska, July 30, 1965.

Knox, Oran Siigwana (1939)
1984   Personal communication to E. S. Burch, Jr., Kivalina, Alaska, March 5, 1984.

Knox, Ralph Iɲutaq (1911)
1965   Personal communication to E. S. Burch, Jr., Kivalina, Alaska, July 1, 1965.

Koenig, Joy (1924)
1984   Personal communication to E. S. Burch, Jr., Kivalina, Alaska, May 1, 1984.

Kolenda, Pauline M.
1968   Religion, Caste, and Family Structure: A Comparative Study of the Indian "Joint" Family. In Milton Singer and Bernard S. Cohn, eds., *Structure and Change in Indian Society*, pp. 339–96. New York: Wenner-Gren Foundation for Anthropological Research.

Konalook, John Kaunaaluk (1882)
1951.1   Selawik dip net. Undated personal communication to Charles Lucier (JKN-SEL-5), Elephant Point, Alaska. In Charles Lucier's personal collection.
1951.2   Selawik Eskimo lamps. Undated personal communication to Charles Lucier (JKN-SEL-2), Elephant Point, Alaska. In Charles Lucier's personal collection.
1951.3   Buckland and Selawik sleds and dog traction. Undated personal communication to Charles Lucier (AS-KAN-8), Elephant Point, Alaska. In Charles Lucier's personal collection.

Konalook, John, and May Konalook
1951.1   Grass baskets, Selawik. Undated personal communication to Charles Lucier (MJKN-SEL-7), Elephant Point, Alaska. In Charles Lucier's personal collection.
1951.2   Fire making, Selawik. Undated personal communication to Charles Lucier (MJKN-SEL-8), Elephant Point, Alaska. In Charles Lucier's personal collection.

Konalook, May
1951   Notes on girl's puberty observances: Selawik Eskimo. Undated personal communication to Charles Lucier, Kotzebue, Alaska. In Charles Lucier Collection, box 3, folder 19, Archives, Alaska and Polar Regions Department, University of Alaska Fairbanks.

Koranda, Lorraine D.
1964   Some Traditional Songs of the Alaskan Eskimos. *Anthropological Papers of the University of Alaska* 12(1):17–32.
1972   *Alaskan Eskimo Songs and Stories.* Seattle: University of Washington Press.

Kotzebue, Otto von
1821   *A Voyage of Discovery into the South Sea and Beering's Straits, for the Purpose of Exploring a North-East Passage, Undertaken in the Years 1815–18.* 3 vols. London: Longman, Hurst, Reese, Orme and Brown. [Reprinted by N. Israel, Amsterdam, New York, 1967.]

Koutsky, Kathryn
ms.a   Wales Region—Word List. Typewritten notes in the Kathryn Koutsky Cohen Collection, box 1, folder 10, Alaska and Polar Regions Department, University of Alaska Fairbanks.
ms.b   Handwritten notes on D2 lands from Shishmaref in the Kathryn Koutsky Cohen Collection, box 1, folder 8, Alaska and Polar Regions Department, University of Alaska Fairbanks.

1975a   Typewritten notes from a meeting with "the Corporation members," Shishmaref, October 15, 1975. In the Kathryn Koutsky Cohen Collection, box 1, folder 8, Alaska and Polar Regions Department, University of Alaska Fairbanks.

1975b   Shishmaref, October 15–17, 1975. Handwritten notes in the Kathryn Koutsky Cohen Collection, box 1, folder 8, Alaska and Polar Regions Department, University of Alaska Fairbanks.

1975c   Typed summary of sites from Shishmaref, October 15–17, 1975. In the Kathryn Koutsky Cohen Collection, box 1, folder 8, Alaska and Polar Regions Department, University of Alaska Fairbanks.

1976   Handwritten notes from Wales, June 4, 1976. In the Kathryn Koutsky Cohen Collection, box 1, folder 10, Alaska and Polar Regions Department, University of Alaska Fairbanks.

1981a   *Early Days on Norton Sound and Bering Strait: An Overview of Historic Sites in the BSNC Region.* Vol. I, *The Shishmaref Area.* Fairbanks: University of Alaska, Anthropology and Historic Preservation Cooperative Park Studies Unit. (Occasional Paper no. 29.)

1981b   *Early Days on Norton Sound and Bering Strait: An Overview of Historic Sites in the BSNC Region.* Vol. II, *The Wales Area.* Fairbanks: University of Alaska, Anthropology and Historic Preservation Cooperative Park Studies Unit. (Occasional Paper no. 29.)

Kowunna, Walter Sigliuna (1910)

1970   Personal communication to E. S. Burch, Jr., Kotzebue, Alaska, March 24, 1970.

1980   Personal communication to E. S. Burch, Jr., Kotzebue, Alaska, October 9, 1980.

Kunuyaq, Peter (1879)

1940   Peter's story, as told to Froelich G. Rainey, Point Hope, Alaska. Typed and indexed transcript in the Rainey Collection, box 2, folder 46, Archives, Alaska and Polar Regions Department, University of Alaska Fairbanks.

Kuzuguk, Mildred Amŋaġuna (1953)

1983   Naming traditions. Interview by Ennis Apatiki, Shishmaref, Alaska, September 28, 1983. Transcribed and translated by Edgar Ningeulook. Kawerak Eskimo Heritage Program transcript no. SHH.83.012, Nome, Alaska.

Larsen, Frieda Paukana (1914)

1999   Personal communication to E. S. Burch, Jr., Nome, Alaska, February 26, 1999.

Larsen, Helge, and Froelich Rainey

1948   Ipiutak and the Arctic Whale Hunting Culture. *Anthropological Papers of the American Museum of Natural History* 42:44–50.

Larson, Mary Ann

1995   And Then There Were None: The "Disappearance" of the *Qargi* in Northern Alaska. In Allen P. McCartney, ed., *Hunting the Largest Animals: Native Whaling in the Western Arctic and Subarctic,* pp. 207–20. Edmonton: Canadian Circumpolar Institute, University of Alberta. (Occasional Publication no. 36, Studies in Whaling no. 3.)

2003   Festival and Tradition: The Whaling Festival at Point Hope. In Allen P. McCartney, ed., *Indigenous Ways to the Present: Native Whaling in the Western Arctic,* pp. 341–55. Edmonton: Canadian Circumpolar Institute Press; Salt Lake City: University of Utah Press.

Lee, Charlie Qiñuġan (1901)

ms   Snow Shoe Making. Kotzebue: NANA Elders Council Collection (H88-2F-1).

1970   Personal communication to E. S. Burch, Jr., Shungnak, Alaska, January 29, 1970.

Lee, Linda Piquk, Ruthie Tatqaviñ Sampson, and Edward Tennant, eds.

1991   *Qayaqtuagiŋuaqtuaq: Qayaq, the Magical Traveler.* Kotzebue: Northwest Arctic Borough School District.

1992   *Lore of the Inupiat: The Elders Speak. Utuqqanaat uqaaqtuaqtut. Uqaaqtuaŋich iñupiat.* Vol. III. Kotzebue: Northwest Arctic Borough School District.

Lee, Linda Piquk, Ruthie Tatqaviñ Sampson, Edward Tennant, and Hannah Mendenhall, eds.

1990   *Lore of the Inupiat: The Elders Speak. Utuqqanaat uqaaqtuaqtut.* Vol. II. Kotzebue: Northwest Arctic Borough School District.

Lee, Molly, and Gregory A. Reinhardt

2003   *Eskimo Architecture: Dwelling and Structure in the Early Historic Period.* Fairbanks: University of Alaska Press.

Lee, Richard B.

1972   The !Kung Bushmen of Botswana. In Marco G. Bicchieri, ed., *Hunters and Gatherers Today,* pp. 327–68. New York: Holt, Rinehart and Winston.

1988   Reflections on Primitive Communism. In Tim Ingold, David Riches, and James Woodburn, eds., *Hunters and Gatherers 1: History, Evolution, and Social Change,* pp. 252–68. Oxford: Berg Publishers Ltd.

Lee, Robert Iñauluk (1901)

1960.1 Notes from an interview by Don Foote, Noatak, Alaska, February 12, 1960. Don Charles Foote Papers, box 3, folder 1, Alaska and Polar Regions Department, University of Alaska Fairbanks.

1960.2 Notes from an interview by Don Foote, Noatak, Alaska, February 16, 1960. Don Charles Foote Papers, box 3, folder 1, Alaska and Polar Regions Department, University of Alaska Fairbanks.

Lentfer, Jack, and Lloyd Lowry

1994   Polar Bear. In *Wildlife Notebook Series.* Juneau: Alaska Department of Fish and Game.

Levy, Marion J., Jr.

1952   *The Structure of Society.* Princeton, NJ: Princeton University Press.

1966   *Modernization and the Structure of Societies: A Setting for International Affairs.* Princeton, NJ: Princeton University Press.

Lieb, Jim

1994   Weasels. In *Wildlife Notebook Series.* Juneau: Alaska Department of Fish and Game.

Lisburne, Daniel

1959   Notes from an interview by Don Foote, Point Hope, Alaska, September 15, 1959. Don Charles Foote Papers, box 4, folder 13, Alaska and Polar Regions Department, University of Alaska Fairbanks.

Loney, Robert A., and Glen R. Himmelberg

1985   Ophiolitic Ultramafic Rocks of the Jade Mountains–Cosmos Hills Area, Southwestern Brooks Range. In Susan Bartsch-Winkler, ed., United States Geological Survey in Alaska: Accomplishments During 1984, pp. 13–15. *U.S. Geological Survey Circular* 967.

Loon, Hannah Paniyavluk

1990   Thank the Industrious Mouse for Masru. *Tundra Times,* September 10, 1990, p. 17.

Lowenstein, Tom

1983   Eskimo Narratives. In Daniel Weissbort, ed., *Modern Poetry in Translation,* 1983, pp. 88–101. London: MPT/Carcanet.

1992   *The Things That Were Said of Them: Shaman Stories and Oral Histories of the Tikiġaq People.* Translated from the Iñupiaq by Tukummiq and Tom Lowenstein; told by Asatchaq. Berkeley: University of California Press.

1993   *Ancient Land, Sacred Whale: The Inuit Hunt and Its Rituals.* New York: Farrar, Straus and Giroux.

Lowry, Lloyd

1994   Beluga Whale. In *Wildlife Notebook Series.* Juneau: Alaska Department of Fish and Game.

Lucier, Charles V.

1951   Selawik Eskimo pottery. Fragmentary notes. Personal communication from an unidentified informant, Elephant Point, Alaska, April 19, 1951. In Charles Lucier's personal collection.

1952   Nuataaġmiut messenger feast. Consolidated notes from interviews with Jenny Aluniq Mitchell and Mark Misigaq Mitchell. In Charles Lucier's personal collection.

1954   Buckland Eskimo Myths. *Anthropological Papers of the University of Alaska* 2(2):215–33.

1958   Noatagmiut Eskimo Myths. *Anthropological Papers of the University of Alaska* 6(2):89–117.

1969   Personal oral communication to E. S. Burch, Jr., Kotzebue, Alaska, November 16, 1969.

1972   Written personal communication to E. S. Burch, Jr., June 8, 1972.

1989   Written personal communication to E. S. Burch, Jr., January 30, 1989.

1990   Undated written personal communication to E. S. Burch, Jr. concerning iron oxide.

2000a   A Qikiqtaġruŋmiu shaman's burials and reburials. Written personal communication to E. S. Burch, Jr., October 24, 2000.

2000b   Written personal communication to E. S. Burch, Jr., November 2, 2000.

Lucier, Charles V., and James W. VanStone

1991a   The Traditional Oil Lamp Among Kangigmiut and Neighboring Iñupiat of Kotzebue Sound, Alaska. *Arctic Anthropology* 28(2):1–14.

1991b   Winter and Spring Fast Ice Seal Hunting by Kangigmiut and Other Iñupiat of Kotzebue Sound, Alaska. *Études/Inuit/Studies* 15(1):29–49.

1992   Historic Pottery of the Kotzebue Sound Iñupiat. *Fieldiana: Anthropology* n.s. 18.

1995   Traditional Beluga Drives of the Iñupiat of Kotzebue Sound, Alaska. *Fieldiana: Anthropology* n.s. 25.

Lucier, Charles V., James W. VanStone, and Della Keats

1971   Medical Practices and Human Anatomical Knowledge Among the Noatak Eskimos. *Ethnology* 10(3):251–64.

Luther, Carl Avigauraq (1891)

1960.1   Notes from an interview by Don Foote, Noatak, Alaska, February 16, 1960. Don Charles Foote Papers, box 3, folder 1, Alaska and Polar Regions Department, University of Alaska Fairbanks.

1960.2   Notes from an interview by Don Foote, Noatak, Alaska, February 18, 1960. Don Charles Foote Papers, box 3, folder 2, Alaska and Polar Regions Department, University of Alaska Fairbanks.

1976   Autobiography. Typescript. Kotzebue: NANA Elders Council Collection (H88–2A-34a).

MacDonald, John

1998   *The Arctic Sky: Inuit Astronomy, Star Lore, and Legend.* Toronto: Royal Ontario Museum; Iqaluit, Nunavut: The Nunavut Research Institute.

Maguire, Rochefort

1854   Report of the Proceedings of Her Majesty's Discovery Ship *"Plover,"* Commander Rochefort Maguire. In House of Commons, United Kingdom. *Sessional Papers, 1854, Accounts and Papers,* vol. 42, no. 1725, part XIII, pp. 160–86.

1857   Narrative of Captain Maguire, Wintering at Point Barrow. In Sherard Osborn, ed., *The Discovery of the North-West Passage by H.M.S. "Investigator" . . . Appendix II,* pp. 409–63. 2nd ed. London: Longman, Brown, Green, Longmans and Roberts.

Majors, Harry M.

1983   Early Russian Knowledge of Alaska, 1701–1730. *Northwest Discovery* 4(2):84–152.

Mala, Ted

1984   Native Foods Offer All That Is Needed. *Tundra Times,* March 7, 1984, pp. 6, 23.

Marshall, Robert

1933   *Arctic Village.* New York: The Literary Guild. (Reprinted by University of Alaska Press, Fairbanks, 1991.)

Masterson, James R., and Helen Brower

1948   *Bering's Successors, 1745–1780: Contributions of Peter Simon Pallas to the History of Russian Exploration Toward Alaska.* Seattle: University of Washington Press.

McClellan, Albert Nalikkaɬuk (1901)

1970.1   Personal communication to E. S. Burch, Jr., Kotzebue, Alaska, April 9, 1970.

1970.2   Personal communication to E. S. Burch, Jr., Kotzebue, Alaska, April 10, 1970.

1986   Personal communication to E. S. Burch, Jr., Kotzebue, Alaska, March 3, 1986.

1987   Personal communication to E. S. Burch, Jr., Kotzebue, Alaska, February 28, 1987.

McElwaine, Eugene

1901   *The Truth About Alaska, the Golden Land of the Midnight Sun.* Chicago: Regan Printing House.

McKennan, Robert A.
1965   *The Chandalar Kutchin*. Montreal: Arctic Institute of North America. (Technical Paper no. 17.)

McLenegan, S. B.
1887   Exploration of the Noatak River, Alaska. In M. A. Healy, *Report of the Cruise of the Revenue Marine Steamer "Corwin" in the Arctic Ocean, 1885*, pp. 53–80. Washington, DC: Government Printing Office.
1889   Exploration of the Kowak River, Alaska: Notes on the Natural History and Resources, 1884. In M. A. Healy, *Report of the Cruise of the Revenue Marine Steamer "Corwin" in the Arctic Ocean in the Year 1884*, pp. 99–108. Washington, DC: Government Printing Office.

Mendenhall, Hannah, Ruthie Sampson, and Edward Tennant, eds.
1989   *Lore of the Iñupiat: The Elders Speak. Utuqqanaat uqaaqtuaqtut / Uqaaqtuaŋich iñupiat*. Vol. I. Kotzebue: Northwest Arctic Borough School District.

Merck, Carl Heinrich
1980   *Siberia and Northwestern America 1788–1792: The Journal of Carl Heinrich Merck, Naturalist with the Russian Scientific Expedition Led by Captains Joseph Billings and Gavril Sarychev*. Edited by Richard A. Pierce. Kingston, ON: Limestone Press. (Materials for the Study of Alaska History, no. 17.)

Merriam, G. & C., Co.
1977   *Webster's New Collegiate Dictionary*. Springfield, MA: G. & C. Merriam Company.

Miertsching, Johann August
1967   *Frozen Ships: The Arctic Diary of Johann Miertsching, 1850–1854*. Translated and with an introduction and notes by L. H. Neatby. New York: St. Martin's Press.

Mills, Ethel Niiqsik
1960.1 Notes from an interview by Don Foote, Noatak, Alaska, February 16, 1960. Don Charles Foote Papers, box 3, folder 1, Alaska and Polar Regions Department, University of Alaska Fairbanks.
1960.2 Notes from an interview by Don Foote, Noatak, Alaska, February 17, 1960. Don Charles Foote Papers, box 3, folder 1, Alaska and Polar Regions Department, University of Alaska Fairbanks.
1960.3 Notes from an interview by Don Foote, Noatak, Alaska, February 18, 1960. Don Charles Foote Papers, box 3, folder 1, Alaska and Polar Regions Department, University of Alaska Fairbanks.
1960.4 Notes from an interview by Don Foote, Noatak, Alaska, February 19, 1960. Don Charles Foote Papers, box 3, folder 1, Alaska and Polar Regions Department, University of Alaska Fairbanks.

Mills, Kenneth Aqukkasuk (1908)
1989   Personal communication to E. S. Burch, Jr., Kotzebue, Alaska, February 21, 1989.

Mills, Kenneth Aqukkasuk (1908), and Ethel Niiqsik Mills
1960   Notes from an interview by Don Foote, Noatak, Alaska, February 23, 1960. Don Charles Foote Papers, box 3, folder 1, Alaska and Polar Regions Department, University of Alaska Fairbanks.

Mills, Levi Alasuk, Sr. (1903)
1986   Personal communication to E. S. Burch, Jr., Kotzebue, Alaska, February 18, 1986.
1987   Personal communication to E. S. Burch, Jr., Kotzebue, Alaska, March 2, 1987.
1989   Personal communication to E. S. Burch, Jr., Kotzebue, Alaska, February 20, 1989.
1991   Personal communication to E. S. Burch, Jr., Kotzebue, Alaska, March 25, 1991.

Mitchell, Jenny Aluniq (1875)
1952.1 Boy's first-kill observances, upper Noatak. Personal communication to Charles Lucier. In Charles Lucier Collection, box 3, folder 16, Archives, Alaska and Polar Regions Department, University of Alaska Fairbanks.
1952.2 Kunungnakak. Personal communication to Charles Lucier. In Charles Lucier Collection, box 3, folder 17, Archives, Alaska and Polar Regions Department, University of Alaska Fairbanks.

1952.3   Men with ivory eyes. Personal communication to Charles Lucier. In Charles Lucier Collection, box 3, folder 16, Archives, Alaska and Polar Regions Department, University of Alaska Fairbanks.

1952.4   Qupiliroilhuq' [Kopil'raɬhuk]. Personal communication to Charles Lucier. In Charles Lucier Collection, box 3, folder 17, Archives, Alaska and Polar Regions Department, University of Alaska Fairbanks. [Also as Kobil'raɬhuk. Sheshalik, Alaska, July 31, 1952. In Charles Lucier Collection, box 3, folder 16, Archives, Alaska and Polar Regions Department, University of Alaska Fairbanks.]

1952.5   Stones that move. Personal communication to Charles Lucier. In Charles Lucier Collection, box 3, folder 17, Archives, Alaska and Polar Regions Department, University of Alaska Fairbanks.

1952.6   Walrus dog. Personal communication to Charles Lucier. In Charles Lucier Collection, box 3, folder 17, Archives, Alaska and Polar Regions Department, University of Alaska Fairbanks.

1952.7   Feigned death, Utorqagmiut old story. Personal communication to Charles Lucier, Sheshalik, Alaska, June 1952. In Charles Lucier Collection, box 3, folder 16, Archives, Alaska and Polar Regions Department, University of Alaska Fairbanks.

1952.8   A corpse in the river. Personal communication to Charles Lucier, Sheshalik, Alaska, July 7, 1952. In Charles Lucier Collection, box 3, folder 16, Archives, Alaska and Polar Regions Department, University of Alaska Fairbanks.

1952.9   A giant bird's nest. Personal communication to Charles Lucier, Sheshalik, Alaska, July 7, 1952. In Charles Lucier Collection, box 3, folder 16, Archives, Alaska and Polar Regions Department, University of Alaska Fairbanks.

1952.10 Innyoɬuruk. Personal communication to Charles Lucier, Sheshalik, Alaska, July 7, 1952. In Charles Lucier Collection, box 3, folder 16, Archives, Alaska and Polar Regions Department, University of Alaska Fairbanks.

1952.11 A Lapp story. Personal communication to Charles Lucier, Sheshalik, Alaska, July 7, 1952. In Charles Lucier Collection, box 3, folder 16, Archives, Alaska and Polar Regions Department, University of Alaska Fairbanks.

1952.12 Kusupqwak. Personal communication to Charles Lucier, Sheshalik, Alaska, July 9, 1952. In Charles Lucier Collection, box 3, folder 16, Archives, Alaska and Polar Regions Department, University of Alaska Fairbanks.

1952.13 Raven and King Loon color one another. Personal communication to Charles Lucier, Sheshalik, Alaska, July 11, 1952. In Charles Lucier Collection, box 3, folder 16, Archives, Alaska and Polar Regions Department, University of Alaska Fairbanks.

1952.14 Girl's puberty observances, Noatak. Personal communication to Charles Lucier, Sheshalik, Alaska, July 15, 1952. In Charles Lucier Collection, box 3, folder 16, Archives, Alaska and Polar Regions Department, University of Alaska Fairbanks.

1952.15 Girl's puberty observances, upper Kobuk. Personal communication to Charles Lucier, Sheshalik, Alaska, July 15, 1952. In Charles Lucier Collection, box 3, folder 12, Archives, Alaska and Polar Regions Department, University of Alaska Fairbanks.

1952.16 Yoɬiɬik. Personal communication to Charles Lucier, Sheshalik, Alaska, July 15, 1952. In Charles Lucier Collection, box 3, folder 16, Archives, Alaska and Polar Regions Department, University of Alaska Fairbanks.

1952.17 Young man who choked on mosquitoes in the winter. Personal communication to Charles Lucier, Sheshalik, Alaska, July 15, 1952. In Charles Lucier Collection, box 3, folder 16, Archives, Alaska and Polar Regions Department, University of Alaska Fairbanks.

1952.18 A cave. Personal communication to Charles Lucier, Sheshalik, Alaska, August 7, 1952. In Charles Lucier Collection, box 3, folder 16, Archives, Alaska and Polar Regions Department, University of Alaska Fairbanks.

1952.19 The abused brother. Personal communication to Charles Lucier, Sheshalik, Alaska, August 7, 1952. In Charles Lucier Collection, box 3, folder 16, Archives, Alaska and Polar Regions Department, University of Alaska Fairbanks.

1952.20 An *angatkok*'s performance. Personal communication to Charles Lucier, Sheshalik, Alaska, August 7, 1952. In Charles Lucier Collection, box 3, folder 16, Archives, Alaska and Polar Regions Department, University of Alaska Fairbanks.

Mitchell, Jenny Aluniq (1875), and Della Puyuk Keats (1907)

1952   Lower and upper Noatak burials. Personal communication to Charles Lucier, Sheshalik, Alaska, July 7, 1952. In Charles Lucier Collection, box 3, folder 16, Archives, Alaska and Polar Regions Department, University of Alaska Fairbanks.

Mitchell, Mark Misigaq (1865)

1951   Small people. Personal communication to Charles Lucier, Sheshalik, Alaska, August 25, 1951. In Charles Lucier Collection, box 3, folder 17, Archives, Alaska and Polar Regions Department, University of Alaska Fairbanks.

1952.1   Animals come from wood shavings. Personal communication to Charles Lucier, Sheshalik, Alaska, July 3, 1952. In Charles Lucier Collection, box 3, folder 16, Archives, Alaska and Polar Regions Department, University of Alaska Fairbanks.

1952.2   My father's travels. Personal communication to Charles Lucier, Sheshalik, Alaska, July 3, 1952. In Charles Lucier Collection, box 3, folder 16, Archives, Alaska and Polar Regions Department, University of Alaska Fairbanks.

1952.3   Ulului, an upper Noatak story. Personal communication to Charles Lucier, Sheshalik, Alaska, July 3, 1952. In Charles Lucier Collection, box 3, folder 16 Archives, Alaska and Polar Regions Department, University of Alaska Fairbanks.

1952.4   Pularook, eclipse of the moon. Personal communication to Charles Lucier, Sheshalik, Alaska, July 15, 1952. In Charles Lucier Collection, box 3, folder 16, Archives, Alaska and Polar Regions Department, University of Alaska Fairbanks.

Mitchell, Thomas Uqsruġaaluk (1904)

1969   Personal oral communication to E. S. Burch, Jr., Kotzebue, Alaska, December 20, 1969.

1970   Personal oral communication to E. S. Burch, Jr., Kotzebue, Alaska, May 5, 1970.

1976   Personal oral communication to E. S. Burch, Jr., Kotzebue, Alaska, April 2, 1976.

1986   Personal communication to E. S. Burch, Jr., Kotzebue, Alaska, March 3, 1986.

1987   Personal communication to E. S. Burch, Jr., Kotzebue, Alaska, February 27, 1987.

Monroe, Paul Palaŋan (1890)

1960   Notes from an interview by Don Foote, Noatak, Alaska, February 18, 1960. Don Charles Foote Papers, box 3, folder 1, Alaska and Polar Regions Department, University of Alaska Fairbanks.

Moore, Sharon D., and Sophie M. Johnson

1986   Lena Sours. Suuyuk. In *The Artists Behind the Work*, pp. 99–122. Fairbanks: University of Alaska Museum.

Moore, T. E. L.

1851   Narrative of the Proceedings of Commander T. E. L. Moore, of Her Majesty's Ship *"Plover,"* from September 1849 to September 1850. In House of Commons, United Kingdom, *Sessional Papers, 1851, Accounts and Papers*, vol. 33, no. 97, part 4(B), pp. 19–44.

Moore, Wilbert E.

1943   The Emergence of New Property Conceptions in America. *Journal of Legal and Political Sociology* 1(3–4):34–58.

Moritz, Richard E., Cecilia M. Bitz, and Eric J. Steig

2002   Dynamics of Recent Climate Change in the Arctic. *Science* 297:1497–1502.

Morris, Mary Ayatchiaq (1879)

1951.1   Some miscellaneous comments. Personal communication to Charles Lucier, Deering, Alaska, January 11, 1951. In the Charles Lucier Collection, box 3, folder 4, Archives, Alaska and Polar Regions Department, University of Alaska Fairbanks.

1951.2   Additional notes on tattooing, applicable to Kotzebue Sound. Personal communication to Charles Lucier, January 11, 1951. In the Charles Lucier Collection, box 3, folder 4, Archives, Alaska and Polar Regions Department, University of Alaska Fairbanks.

Morris, Thomas Aniqsuaq (1904)

1970   Personal communication to E. S. Burch, Jr., Deering, Alaska, April 17, 1970.

Morseth, C. Michele

1997   Twentieth-Century Changes in Beluga Whale Hunting and Butchering by the Kaŋiġmiut of Buckland, Alaska. *Arctic* 50(3):241–66.

Muir, John
 1917 *The Cruise of the* Corwin. Boston and New York: Houghton Mifflin Co.

Murdoch, John
 1885a The Sinew-Backed Bow of the Eskimo. *Transactions of the Anthropological Society of Washington* 3:168–71.
 1885b A Study of Eskimo Bows in the U.S. National Museum. *Annual Report of the U.S. National Museum, 1884.* Washington, DC: U.S. Government Printing Office.
 1892 *Ethnological Results of the Point Barrow Expedition.* Ninth annual report of the Bureau of Ethnology, 1887–88. Washington, DC: Government Printing Office.
 1988 *Ethnological Results of the Point Barrow Expedition.* Washington, DC: Smithsonian Institution Press. (Smithsonian Classics of Anthropology Series reprint, no. 6.)

Nagozruk, Arthur Nagaaq, Sr. (1890)
 1928 Personal communication to Edward Weyer. In Weyer Field Notes, p. 82. Department of Anthropology Archives, American Museum of Natural History, New York.
 1970 Personal communication to E. S. Burch, Jr., Anchorage, Alaska, February 25, 1970.
 1971 Personal communication to Charles Lucier, February 16, 1971. In Charles Lucier's personal collection [AN-W-2].

NANA Cultural Heritage Project
 1975a Ambler cemetery sites and historical places. Draft report. Copy in possession of the author.
 1975b Buckland cemetery sites and historical places. Draft report. Copy in possession of the author.
 1975c Deering. Draft report. Copy in possession of the author.
 1975d Kivalina. Draft report. Copy in possession of the author.
 1975e Kotzebue. Draft report. Copy in possession of the author.
 1975f Noorvik. Draft report. Copy in possession of the author.
 1975g Selawik. Draft report. Copy in possession of the author.

NANA Elders Conference (several participants)
 1976.1 Subsistence living. Conference held in unspecified location, March 3, 1976. Typescript. Kotzebue: NANA Elders Council Collection (H88–2C-2).
 1976.2 Sod houses and war stories. Conference held in unspecified location, March 6, 1976. Typescript. Kotzebue: NANA Elders Council Collection (H88-2G-6A).
 1979.1 Clothing manufacturing. Conferences held in Shungnak, Ambler, and Kobuk, January 18, 1979. Typescript. Kotzebue: NANA Elders Council Collection (H88-2B-5B).
 1979.2 Hunter and starvation. Conferences held in Shungnak, Ambler, and Kobuk, January 19, 1979. Typescript. Kotzebue: NANA Elders Council Collection (H88–2B-7).
 1979.3 Food preparation and preservation of meat. Conferences held in Shungnak, Ambler, and Kobuk, January 22, 1979. Typescript. Kotzebue: NANA Elders Council Collection (H88–2B-8a, 8b).

Nasugluk (1870) and Nasugruk (1880)
 1940 Nasugluk and Nasugruk in the form of a duet, as told to Froelich G. Rainey, Point Hope, Alaska. Typed and indexed transcript in author's possession. [Other versions are in the Rainey Collection, box 2, folders 44 and 45, Archives, Alaska and Polar Regions Department, University of Alaska Fairbanks.]

National Bilingual Materials Development Center
 1980a *Unipchaallu Uqaaqtuallu II / Legends and Stories II.* Anchorage: University of Alaska, Rural Education, National Bilingual Materials Development Center.
 1980b *Unipchaaŋich Imaġluktuġmiut / Stories of the Black River People.* Anchorage: University of Alaska, Rural Education, National Bilingual Materials Development Center.

National Climatic Data Center
 1984 Local Climatological Data: Annual Summary with Comparative Data, 1983, revised. Kotzebue, Alaska. Asheville, NC: U.S. Department of Commerce, National Oceanic and Atmospheric Administration, National Climatic Data Center.

Naylor, Dana Kukusaan (1903)

1960.1 Notes from an interview by Don Foote, Noatak, Alaska, February 8, 1960. Don Charles Foote Papers, box 3, folder 1, Alaska and Polar Regions Department, University of Alaska Fairbanks.

1960.2 Notes from an interview by Don Foote, Noatak, Alaska, February 11, 1960. Don Charles Foote Papers, box 3, folder 1, Alaska and Polar Regions Department, University of Alaska Fairbanks.

1960.3 Notes from an interview by Don Foote, Noatak, Alaska, February 15, 1960. Don Charles Foote Papers, box 3, folder 1, Alaska and Polar Regions Department, University of Alaska Fairbanks.

1960.4 Notes from an interview by Don Foote, Noatak, Alaska, February 17, 1960. Don Charles Foote Papers, box 3, folder 1, Alaska and Polar Regions Department, University of Alaska Fairbanks.

1960.5 Notes from an interview by Don Foote, Noatak, Alaska, February 19, 1960. Don Charles Foote Papers, box 3, folder 1, Alaska and Polar Regions Department, University of Alaska Fairbanks.

Naylor, Minnie Arigiatchaaq (1907)

1960.1 Notes from an interview by Don Foote, Noatak, Alaska, February 12, 1960. Don Charles Foote Papers, box 3, folder 1, Alaska and Polar Regions Department, University of Alaska Fairbanks.

1960.2 Notes from an interview by Don Foote, Noatak, Alaska, February 14, 1960. Don Charles Foote Papers, box 3, folder 1, Alaska and Polar Regions Department, University of Alaska Fairbanks.

Naylor, Minnie Arigiatchaaq (1907), and Dana Kukusaan Naylor (1903)

1960 Notes from an interview by Don Foote, Noatak, Alaska, February 10, 1960. Don Charles Foote Papers, box 3, folder 1, Alaska and Polar Regions Department, University of Alaska Fairbanks.

Nayokpuk, Walter (1919)

1991 Personal communication to E. S. Burch, Jr., Shishmaref, Alaska, July 12, 1991.

1999 Personal communication to E. S. Burch, Jr., Shishmaref, Alaska, March 4, 1999.

Neering, Rosemary

1989 *Continental Dash: The Russian-American Telegraph.* Ganges, BC: Horsdal and Schubart Publishers, Ltd.

Nelson, Edward William

1877–81 Alaska Journals, April 12, 1877, to October 20, 1881. Archives of the U.S. National Museum, Smithsonian Institution.

1898 Notes on the Wild Fowl and Game Animals of Alaska. *National Geographic Magazine* 9(4):121–32.

1899 The Eskimo About Bering Strait. *Eighteenth Annual Report of the Bureau of American Ethnology, 1896–97,* part 1, pp. 3–518. Washington, DC: Government Printing Office. (Republished in 1983 by the Smithsonian Institution.)

Nelson, Edward William, and F. W. True

1887 Mammals of Northern Alaska. In E. W. Nelson, *Report Upon Natural History Collections Made in Alaska Between the Years 1877 and 1881,* pp. 227–93. Washington, DC: U.S. Army Signal Service.

Newell, Raymond R.

1985 A Report to the North Slope Borough Commission on Iñupiat History, Language and Culture on the Works and Results of the University of Groningen/State University of New York Binghamton Point Hope Ethnology Project, 1984. Groningen, the Netherlands: Biologisch Archaeologisch Instituut, Rijksuniversiteit Groningen; Binghamton: Department of Anthropology, State University of New York Binghamton.

Niġuwana (1875)

1940.1 Nirowana's story, as told to Froelich G. Rainey, Point Hope, Alaska. Typed and indexed transcript in the Rainey Collection, box 2, folder 45, Archives, Alaska and Polar Regions Department, University of Alaska Fairbanks.

1940.2 Taboos, rules. Typed notes in the Rainey Collection, Archives, Alaska and Polar Regions Department, University of Alaska Fairbanks.

Ningeulook, Hattie Ivviłiq/Aapaałuq (1926)

1983.1 Customs and food. Interview by Ennis Apatiki, Shishmaref, Alaska, September 30, 1983. Transcribed and translated by Edgar Ningeulook. Kawerak Eskimo Heritage Program transcript no. SHH.83.011, Nome, Alaska.

1983.2 Respect for elders. Interview by Edgar Ningeulook, Shishmaref, Alaska, May 23, 1983. Transcribed and translated by Edgar Ningeulook. Kawerak Eskimo Heritage Program transcript no. SHH.83.015, Nome, Alaska.

1983.3 Hunting. Interview by Edgar Ningeulook, Shishmaref, Alaska, June 15, 1983. Transcribed and translated by Edgar Ningeulook. Kawerak Eskimo Heritage Program transcript no. SHH.83.019, Nome, Alaska.

1983.4 Stories. Interview by Edgar Ningeulook, Shishmaref, Alaska, July 26, 1983. Transcribed and translated by Edgar Ningeulook. Kawerak Eskimo Heritage Program transcript no. SHH.83.022, Nome, Alaska.

Ningeulook, Jack Ulugumaaq (1903)

1981.1 Hunting/clothing. Interview by Albert Ningeulook, Shishmaref, Alaska, October 27, 1981. Transcribed by Lucy Obruk, translated by Jack Ningeulook. Kawerak Eskimo Heritage Program transcript no. SHH.81.001, Nome, Alaska.

1981.2 Housing, sodhouses. Interview by Albert Ningeulook, Shishmaref, Alaska, January 1, 1981. Transcribed and translated by Albert Ningeulook. Kawerak Eskimo Heritage Program transcript no. SHH.81.002, Nome, Alaska.

1983.1 The blown-away people. Taped interview translated and transcribed by Edgar Ningeulook. Shishmaref, Alaska. Kawerak Eskimo Heritage Project, SH/EN-83–006-T4, Nome, Alaska.

1983.2 History. Interview by Edgar Ningeulook, Shishmaref, Alaska, May 25, 1983. Transcribed and translated by Edgar Ningeulook. Kawerak Eskimo Heritage Program transcript no. SHH.83.017, Nome, Alaska.

1983.3 Child raising. Interview by Harriet Penayah, Shishmaref, Alaska, September 30, 1983. Transcribed and translated by Edgar Ningeulook. Kawerak Eskimo Heritage Program transcript no. SHH.83.046, Nome, Alaska.

Ningeulook, Jack Ulugumaaq (1903), and Marie Aaġiaq Ningeulook

1983 Respect for elders. Interview by Edgar Ningeulook, Shishmaref, Alaska, May 20, 1983. Transcribed and translated by Edgar Ningeulook. Kawerak Eskimo Heritage Program transcript no. SHH.83.014, Nome, Alaska.

Northwest Iñupiat Elders Conference

1976a Northwest Iñupiat Elders Conference, March 4, 1976 (Mabel Brown, Cora Cleveland, Louie Commack, Sr., Charlie Jensen, Lucy Jensen, Billy Neal, Nora Norton, Chester Seveck, Charlie Sheldon, Lena Sours, Joe Sun). Transcribed by Hannah Loon, translated by Lorena Williams. Transcript 76–05. Copy in possession of the author.

1976b Northwest Iñupiat Elders Conference, March 4, 1976 (Grant Ballot, Mabel Brown, Joe Carter, Lila Gregg, Charlie Jensen, Lucy Jensen, Clara Lee, Nora Norton, Chester Seveck, Lena Sours, Herman Tickett). Transcribed by Hannah Loon, translated by Lorena Williams. Transcript 76–06. Copy in possession of the author.

1976c Northwest Iñupiat Elders Conference, March 4, 1976 (Grant Ballot, Mabel Brown, Joe Fields, Elwood Hunnicutt, Chester Seveck, Charlie Sheldon, Lena Sours, Wilson Ticket, Sr). Transcribed by Hannah Loon, translated by Lorena Williams. Transcript 76–07. Copy in possession of the author.

1976d Northwest Iñupiat Elders Conference, March 5, 1976 (Louie Commack, Sr., Joe Field, Fletcher Gregg, Elwood Hunnicutt, Charlie Jensen, Charlie Lee, Chester Seveck, Charlie Sheldon, Clinton Swan, Joe Sun). Transcribed by Hannah Loon, translated by Lorena Williams. Transcript 76–08. Copy in possession of the author.

1976e Northwest Iñupiat Elders Conference, March 5, 1976 (Joe Carter, Paul Green, Elwood Hunnicutt, Tommy Lee, Chester Seveck, Charlie Sheldon, Joe Sun). Transcribed by

Hannah Loon, translated by Lorena Williams. Transcript 76–09. Copy in possession of the author.

1976f   Northwest Iñupiat Elders Conference, March 5, 1976 (Paul Ballott, Joe Carter, Paul Green, Fletcher Gregg, Charlie Sheldon). Transcribed by Hannah Loon, translated by Lorena Williams. Transcript 76–10. Copy in possession of the author.

1983a   Northwest Iñupiat Elders Conference, Deering, Alaska, April 6, 1983 (speakers not identified). Transcript 83–05. Copy in possession of the author.

1983b   Kotzebue History. Northwest Iñupiat Elders Conference, Kotzebue, Alaska, April 20, 1983 (Fletcher Gregg, Lila Gregg, Elwood Hunnicutt, Lena Sours). Transcribed by Janet Barr. Transcript 83–30. Copy in possession of the author.

1983c   Kotzebue History, continued. Northwest Iñupiat Elders Conference, Kotzebue, Alaska, April 20, 1983 (Fletcher Gregg, Elwood Hunnicutt, Amy Jones, Lena Sours). Transcribed by Janet Barr. Transcript 83–31. Copy in possession of the author.

1983d   Kotzebue History, continued. Northwest Iñupiat Elders Conference, Kotzebue, Alaska, April 20, 1983 (Fletcher Gregg, Elwood Hunnicutt, Amy Jones, Lena Sours). Transcribed by Janet Barr. Transcript 83–32. Copy in possession of the author.

1983e   Kotzebue History, continued. Northwest Iñupiat Elders Conference, Kotzebue, Alaska, April 20, 1983 (Fletcher Gregg, Elwood Hunnicutt, Amy Jones, Lena Sours). Transcribed by Janet Barr. Transcript 83–33. Copy in possession of the author.

1983f   Kotzebue History, continued. Northwest Iñupiat Elders Conference, Kotzebue, Alaska, April 20, 1983 (Fletcher Gregg, Elwood Hunnicutt, Amy Jones, Lena Sours). Transcribed by Janet Barr. Transcript 83–34. Copy in possession of the author.

1983g   Kotzebue History, continued. Northwest Iñupiat Elders Conference, Kotzebue, Alaska, April 20, 1983 (Fletcher Gregg, Lila Gregg, Amy Jones, Lena Sours). Transcript 83–35. Copy in possession of the author.

1983h   Kotzebue History, continued. Northwest Iñupiat Elders Conference, Kotzebue, Alaska, April 21, 1983. Transcript 83–36. Copy in possession of the author.

Norton, Daniel (1909)
1965   Personal communication to E. S. Burch, Jr., Kivalina, Alaska, June 5, 1965.

Norton, Emma Nuŋuluk (1887)
1969   Personal communication to E. S. Burch, Jr., Kotzebue, Alaska, November 24, 1969.

Oakes, Jill, and Rick Riewe
1995   *Our Boots: An Inuit Women's Art*. Vancouver: Douglas and McIntyre.

Obruk, Esther Qinugina (1917)
1981   Food preparation. Interview by Lucy Obruk, Shishmaref, Alaska, May 9, 1983. Kawerak Eskimo Heritage Program transcript no. SHH.81.047, Nome, Alaska.

Obruk, Serge Avzraq (1912)
1981   Weather forecasting. Interview by Albert Ningeulook, Shishmaref, Alaska, December 12, 1981. Transcribed and translated by Sophie Weyiouanna. Kawerak Eskimo Heritage Program transcript no. SHH.81.003, Nome, Alaska.

Obruk, Serge Avzraq (1912), and Esther Qinugina Obruk (1917)
1983.1   Customs. Interview by Dorothy Waghiyi, Shishmaref, Alaska, September 28, 1983. Transcribed and translated by Edgar Ningeulook. Kawerak Eskimo Heritage Program transcript no. SHH.83.009, Nome, Alaska.

1983.2   Family relationships. Interview by Dorothy Waghiyi and Georgianna Ahgupuk, Shishmaref, Alaska, September 27, 1983. Kawerak Eskimo Heritage Program transcript no. SHH.83.010, Nome, Alaska.

Okpowruk, Charlie Tiyuasiaq (1925)
1983.1   Legends. Interview by Edgar Ningeulook, Shishmaref, Alaska, August 2, 1983. Kawerak Eskimo Heritage Program transcript no. SHH.83.023, Nome, Alaska.

1983.2   Boy who grew up by the river. Interview by Edgar Ningeulook, Shishmaref, Alaska, August 10, 1983. Transcribed and translated by Edgar Ningeulook. Kawerak Eskimo Heritage Program transcript no. SHH.83.025, Nome, Alaska.

1983.3   History. Interview by Georgianna Ahgupuk, Shishmaref, Alaska, May 10, 1983. Transcribed and translated by Georgianna Ahgupuk. Kawerak Eskimo Heritage Program transcript no. SHH.83.034, Nome, Alaska.

1983.4   History. Interview by Georgianna Ahgupuk, Shishmaref, Alaska, May 24, 1983. Transcribed and translated by Georgianna Ahgupuk. Kawerak Eskimo Heritage Program transcript no. SHH.83.037, Nome, Alaska.

Oktalik, Donald Qiliġniq (1907)
1970   Personal communication to E. S. Burch, Jr., Point Hope, Alaska, May 27, 1970.
1980   Personal communication to E. S. Burch, Jr., Point Hope, Alaska, October 18, 1980.

Oktalik, Lilly
1980   Personal communication to E. S. Burch, Jr., Point Hope, Alaska, October 18, 1980.

Olanna, Arnold Iliugutaq (1911)
1983   Encounter with a polar bear. Interview by Johnson Eningowuk, Shishmaref, Alaska, February 17, 1983. Transcribed and translated by Edgar Ningeulook. Kawerak Eskimo Heritage Program transcript no. SHH.83.048, Nome, Alaska.

Oman, Lela Kiana
1975   *Eskimo Legends.* 2nd ed. Anchorage: Alaska Methodist University Press.

Onalik, Herbert Ipaaluk (1916)
1986   Personal communication to E. S. Burch, Jr., Noatak, Alaska, February 25, 1986.

Ongtowasruk, Faye Ikkana (1920)
1999   Personal communication to E. S. Burch, Jr., Wales, Alaska, March 1, 1999.

Opler, Morris E.
1955   An Outline of Chiricahua Apache Social Organization. In Fred Eggan, ed., *Social Anthropology of North American Tribes,* Enlarged Edition, pp. 171–239. Chicago: University of Chicago Press.

Oquilluk, William A.
1973   *People of Kauwerak: Legends of the Northern Eskimo.* Anchorage: Alaska Methodist University Press.

Osgood, Cornelius
1936   Contributions to the Ethnography of the Kutchin. *Yale University Publications in Anthropology* no. 14.

Ostermann, Hother, ed.
1942   The Mackenzie Eskimos, After Knud Rasmussen's Posthumous Notes. *Report of the Fifth Thule Expedition 1921–24,* vol. X, no. 2. Copenhagen: Gyldendal.

Ostermann, Hother, and Erik Holtved, eds.
1952   The Alaska Eskimos, as Described in the Posthumous Notes of Dr. Knud Rasmussen. *Report of the Fifth Thule Expedition 1921–24,* vol. X, no. 3. Copenhagen: Gyldendal.

Oswalt, Wendell H.
1967   *Alaskan Eskimos.* San Francisco: Chandler Publishing Co.

Owens, Raymond
1971   Industrialization and the Indian Joint Family. *Ethnology* 10(2):223–50.

Oxereok, Ernest Inausiaq (1923)
1991   Personal communication to E. S. Burch, Jr., Wales, Alaska, July 8, 1991.
1999.1   Personal communication to E. S. Burch, Jr., Wales, Alaska, March 1, 1999.
1999.2   Interview with Herbert Anungazuk, Wales, Alaska, June 20, 1999. Transcript in possession of E. S. Burch, Jr.
1999.3   Interview with Herbert Anungazuk, Wales, Alaska, June 21, 1999. Transcript in possession of E. S. Burch, Jr.
1999.4   Interview with Herbert Anungazuk, Wales, Alaska, June 22, 1999. Transcript in possession of E. S. Burch, Jr.

Oxereok, Ernest, and Betty Oxereok
1998   Interviews with Alaska Native experts. Interview in the home of Ernest and Betty Oxereok of Wales, Alaska, on August 9, 1899, by Herbert O. Anungazuk. Transcript on file at the U.S. National Park Service, Anchorage, Alaska.

Pálsson, Gísli, ed.
2001   *Writing on Ice: The Ethnographic Notebooks of Vilhjalmur Stefansson.* Hanover, NH: University Press of New England.

Paneak, Simon Panniaq (1900)
1970   Personal communication to E. S. Burch, Jr., Anaktuvuk Pass, Alaska, April 28, 1970.
1971a   Indian and Kobuk disputes; hunting trips. Doris Duke Foundation Oral History Archive 314, tape 842, University of New Mexico, General Library, Albuquerque.
1971b   Oral narratives. Doris Duke Foundation Oral History Archive 314, tape 842, University of New Mexico, General Library, Albuquerque.
1971c   Oral narratives. Doris Duke Foundation Oral History Archive 314, tape 843, University of New Mexico, General Library, Albuquerque.
1971d   Oral narratives. Doris Duke Foundation Oral History Archive 314, tape 844, University of New Mexico, General Library, Albuquerque.

Patten, Sam, and Dan Rosenberg
1994   Harlequin Duck. In *Wildlife Notebook Series.* Juneau: Alaska Department of Fish and Game.

Patton, William W., Jr., and Thomas P. Miller
1970   A Possible Bedrock Source for Obsidian Found in Archaeological Sites in Northwestern Alaska. *Science* 169(3947):760–61.

Paul, Tom, and William Lehnhausen
1994   Puffins. In *Wildlife Notebook Series.* Juneau: Alaska Department of Fish and Game.

Paul, Tom, Dan Rosenberg, and Tom Rothe
1994   Sandhill Crane. In *Wildlife Notebook Series.* Juneau: Alaska Department of Fish and Game.

Paul, Tom, and Nancy Tankersley
1994   Loons. In *Wildlife Notebook Series.* Juneau: Alaska Department of Fish and Game.

Penn, Flora Aquġluq/Aviŋŋaq (1914)
1952.1 Practices and beliefs associated with beluga hunting. Personal communication to Charles Lucier, Sheshalik, Alaska, July 7, 1952. In Charles Lucier Collection, box 3, folder 15, Archives, Alaska and Polar Regions Department, University of Alaska Fairbanks.
1952.2 Innuakotlikgoruk. Personal communication to Charles Lucier, Sheshalik, Alaska, July 7, 1952. In Charles Lucier Collection, box 3, folder 14, Archives, Alaska and Polar Regions Department, University of Alaska Fairbanks.

Peterson, Nicolas
1993   Demand Sharing: Reciprocity and the Pressure for Generosity Among Foragers. *American Anthropologist* 95(4):860–74.

Phebus, George, Jr.
1972   *Alaskan Eskimo Life in the 1890s as Sketched by Native Artists.* Washington, DC: Smithsonian Institution Press. (Reprinted by University of Alaska Press, Fairbanks, 1995.)

Pierce, Richard A.
1983   Preface. In Dorothy Jean Ray, *Ethnohistory in the Arctic: The Bering Strait Eskimo,* pp. iii–iv. Kingston, ON: Limestone Press.

Pospisil, Leopold
1964   Law and Societal Structure Among the Nunamiut Eskimo. In Ward H. Goodenough, ed., *Explorations in Cultural Anthropology: Essays in Honor of George Peter Murdock,* pp. 395–431. New York: McGraw-Hill Book Company.

Pulu, Tupou L., Minnie Aliitchak Gray, Angeline Ipiiḷik Newlin, and Ruth Tatqaviñ Ramoth-Sampson
1981   *Net Making/Kuvriñiaḷiq.* Anchorage: University of Alaska, Rural Education, National Bilingual Materials Development Center.

Pulu, Tupou L., Thomas F. Johnston, Ruth Tatqaviñ Ramoth-Sampson, and Angeline Ipiiḷik Newlin
1979   *Iñupiat Aġġisit Atuutinich: Iñupiat Dance Songs.* Book and tape from information provided by David Frankson and Dinah Frankson. Anchorage: University of Alaska, Rural Education, National Bilingual Materials Development Center.

Pulu, Tupou L. (Qipuk), and Ruth Tatqaviñ Ramoth-Sampson, eds.
1981   *Maniiḷaq.* Kotzebue: Northwest Arctic School District.

Pulu, Tupou L. (Qipuk), Ruth Tatqaviñ Ramoth-Sampson, and Angeline Ipiiḷik Newlin
1980   *Whaling: A Way of Life/Aġvigich Iglauniŋat Niġinmun.* Anchorage: University of Alaska, Rural Education, National Bilingual Materials Development Center.

Pungalik, Jack Qitchaq, Sr. (1896)
1970   Personal communication to E. S. Burch, Jr., Noorvik, Alaska, March 31, 1970.

Quwana (1875)
1940.1   Quwana's story, as told to Froelich G. Rainey, Point Hope, Alaska. Typed and indexed transcript in author's possession. [Other versions are in the Rainey Collection, box 2, folders 44 and 45, Archives, Alaska and Polar Regions Department, University of Alaska Fairbanks.]
1940.2   Hunting, as told to Froelich G. Rainey, Point Hope, Alaska. Transcript in possession of the author.

Raboff, Adeline Peter
2001   *Iñuksuk: Northern Koyukon, Gwich'in and Lower Tanana, 1800–1901.* Fairbanks: Alaska Native Knowledge Network.

Rainey, Froelich
ms   An Ancient Culture at Point Hope, Alaska. Unpublished manuscript. In Rainey Collection, box 1, folder 36, Archives, Alaska and Polar Regions Department, University of Alaska Fairbanks.
1940.1   Amusements. Unpublished field notes, Point Hope, Alaska. Copy in possession of the author.
1940.2   Childbirth. Unpublished field notes, Point Hope, Alaska. Copy in possession of the author.
1940.3   Fishing—crabs. Unpublished field notes, February 26, 1940, Point Hope, Alaska. Copy in possession of the author.
1940.4   Family groups. Unpublished field notes, Point Hope, Alaska. Copy in possession of the author.
1940.5   Genealogies. Unpublished field notes, Point Hope, Alaska. Copy in possession of the author.
1940.6   Kinship terms. Unpublished field notes, Point Hope, Alaska. Copy in possession of the author.
1940.7   Naming. Unpublished field notes, Point Hope, Alaska. Copy in possession of the author.
1940.8   Partners. Unpublished field notes, Point Hope, Alaska. Copy in possession of the author.
1940.9   Personal names. Unpublished field notes, Point Hope, Alaska. Copy in possession of the author.
1940.10   Quarrels and rivalries. Unpublished field notes, Point Hope, Alaska. Copy in possession of the author.
1940.11   Sexual life. Unpublished field notes, Point Hope, Alaska. Copy in possession of the author.
1940.12   Technology sketches. Unpublished field notes, Point Hope, Alaska. Copy in possession of the author.
1940.13   Archaeological specimens. Unpublished field notes, Point Hope, Alaska. Copy in possession of the author.
1940.14   Whalers. Unpublished field notes, Point Hope, Alaska. Copy in possession of the author.
1940.15   Eskimo Method of Capturing Bowhead Whales. *Journal of Mammalogy* 21(3):362.
1940.16   Winter Fishing. Unpublished field notes, Point Hope, Alaska. Copy in possession of the author.
1940.17   Fishing. June 13, 1940. Unpublished field notes, Point Hope, Alaska. Copy in possession of the author.
1940.18   Marriage. Unpublished field notes, Point Hope, Alaska. Copy in possession of the author.

1940.19   Wife exchange. Unpublished field notes, Point Hope, Alaska. Copy in possession of the author.

1940.20   Angatkok. Unpublished field notes, Point Hope, Alaska. Copy in possession of the author.

1941a   Culture Changes on the Arctic Coast. *Transactions of the New York Academy of Sciences,* series 2, vol. 3, pp. 172–76.

1941b   Native Economy and Survival in Arctic Alaska. *Applied Anthropology* 1(1):9–14.

1947   The Whale Hunters of Tigara. *Anthropological Papers of the American Museum of Natural History,* vol. 41, part II.

1959   The Vanishing Art of the Arctic. *Expedition* 1(2):3–13.

Ralph, Jessie Yiasrik (1898)

1951.1   An *angatkok* stops bad bleeding, Selawik Eskimo. Personal communication to Charles Lucier, place and date not indicated. In Charles Lucier Collection, box 3, folder 19, Archives, Alaska and Polar Regions Department, University of Alaska Fairbanks.

1951.2   Shaman stops severe bleeding. Personal communication to Charles Lucier. In Charles Lucier's personal collection [JR-SEL-10].

1951.3   *Iaḷiṅġaak*: Spirits of places. Personal communication to Charles Lucier. In Charles Lucier's personal collection [JR-KAN-69].

Ramoth, Ralph Ayataŋaq, Sr. (1932)

1970   Personal communication to E. S. Burch, Jr., Selawik, Alaska, March 9, 1970.

1986   Personal communication to E. S. Burch, Jr., Selawik, Alaska, February 27, 1986.

Ramoth-Sampson, Ruth Tatqaviñ

1987   Personal communication to E. S. Burch, Jr., Kotzebue, Alaska, February 27, 1987.

Ransom, Velez Hayes

1980   Transitions Between Traditional and Modern Life as Shown Through Alaskan Northwest Arctic Folklore and Legends. Ph.D. thesis, United States International University. Ann Arbor, MI: University Microfilms.

Rasmussen, Knud Johan Victor

1925   Folklore. In the Danish Ethnographic and Geographic Expedition to Arctic America. Preliminary Report of the Fifth Thule Expedition. *The Geographical Review* 15(4):525–35.

1932   *The Eagle's Gift: Alaska Eskimo Tales.* Translated by Isobel Hutchinson. Illustrated by Ernst Hansen. Garden City, NY: Doubleday, Doran and Company.

1933   *Across Arctic America: Narrative of the Fifth Thule Expedition.* London: G. P. Putnam's Sons. (Reprinted by University of Alaska Press, Fairbanks, 1999.)

Rausch, Robert

1951   Notes on the Nunamiut Eskimo and Mammals of the Anaktuvuk Pass Region, Brooks Range, Alaska. *Arctic* 4(3):146–95.

1970   Trichinosis in the Arctic. In S. E. Gould, ed., *Trichinosis in Man and Animals,* pp. 348–73. Springfield, IL: C. C. Thomas.

Ray, Dorothy Jean

1961   *Artists of the Tundra and the Sea.* Seattle: University of Washington Press.

1964   Nineteenth-Century Settlements and Settlement Patterns in Bering Strait. *Arctic Anthropology* 2(2):61–94.

1967   Land Tenure and Polity of the Bering Strait Eskimos. *Journal of the West* 6(3):371–94.

1975a   Early Maritime Trade with the Eskimo of Bering Strait and the Introduction of Firearms. *Arctic Anthropology* 12(1):1–9.

1975b   *The Eskimos of Bering Strait, 1650–1898.* Seattle: University of Washington Press.

1977   *Eskimo Art: Tradition and Innovation in North Alaska.* Seattle: University of Washington Press.

1983a   *Ethnohistory in the Arctic: The Bering Strait Eskimo.* Edited by R. A. Pierce. Kingston, ON: Limestone Press. (Alaska History, no. 23.)

1983b   The Vasil'ev-Shishmarev Expedition to the Arctic, 1819–1822. In Dorothy Jean Ray, *Ethnohistory in the Arctic: The Bering Strait Eskimo,* pp. 1–14. Kingston, ON: Limestone Press. (Alaska History, no. 23.)

1983c   A Voyage on the Sloop "*Blagonamerennyi*" to Explore the Asiatic and American Coasts of Bering Strait, 1819 to 1822. In Dorothy Jean Ray, *Ethnohistory in the Arctic: The Bering Strait Eskimo*, pp. 25–54. Kingston, ON: Limestone Press. (Alaska History, no. 23.)

1984   Bering Strait Eskimo. In David Damas, ed., *Handbook of North American Indians*. Vol. 5, *Arctic*, pp. 285–302. Washington, DC: Smithsonian Institution Press.

Ray, Dorothy Jean, and Alfred A. Blaker
1967   *Eskimo Masks: Art and Ceremony*. Seattle: University of Washington Press.

Ray, Patrick Henry
1885   *Report of the International Polar Expedition to Point Barrow, Alaska*. Washington, DC: Government Printing Office.

1988   Narrative. Appendix 5 in John Murdoch, *Ethnological Results of the Point Barrow Expedition*, pp. lxix–cxxiv. Washington, DC: Smithsonian Institution Press.

Redfield, Robert
1941   *The Folk Culture of Yucatan*. Chicago: University of Chicago Press.

Redmond, Elsa M.
1998   The Dynamics of Chieftaincy and the Development of Chiefdoms. In Elsa M. Redmond, ed., *Chiefdoms and Chieftaincy in the Americas*, pp. 1–17. Gainsville: University Press of Florida.

Reynolds, Georgeanne Lewis
2001   Archaeological Deposits at the Uivvaq Site (Cape Lisburne) in a Regional Perspective. Paper presented at the annual meeting of the Alaska Anthropological Association, Fairbanks, March 21–23, 2001.

Roberts, Arthur O.
1978   *Tomorrow Is Growing Old: Stories of the Quakers in Alaska*. Newberg, OR: Barclay Press.

Rock, Eebrulik
1980   Personal communication to E. S. Burch, Jr., Point Hope, Alaska, October 18, 1980.

Rock, Sam Uyaġaq (1874)
1940   Sam's story, as told to Froelich G. Rainey, Point Hope, Alaska. Typed and indexed transcript in the author's possession. [Another version is in the Rainey Collection, box 2, folder 46, Archives, Alaska and Polar Regions Department, University of Alaska Fairbanks.]

Rogers, Edward S.
1965   Leadership Among the Indians of Eastern Subarctic Canada. *Anthropologica* n.s.(2):263–84.

1969   Band Organization Among the Indians of Eastern Subarctic Canada. In David Damas, ed., *Contributions to Anthropology: Band Societies*, pp. 21–50. National Museum of Canada Bulletin 228.

Rosenberg, Dan, and Tim Rothe
1994   Swans. In *Wildlife Notebook Series*. Juneau: Alaska Department of Fish and Game.

Rosse, Irving C.
1883   Medical and Anthropological Notes on Alaska. In U.S. Revenue Service, *Cruise of the Revenue-Steamer Corwin in Alaska and the N.W. Arctic Ocean in 1881*, pp. 5–53. Washington, DC: James Anglim & Co.

Rothe, Tom
1994a   Canada Geese. In *Wildlife Notebook Series*. Juneau: Alaska Department of Fish and Game.
1994b   Geese. In *Wildlife Notebook Series*. Juneau: Alaska Department of Fish and Game.

Rothe, Tom, and Sue Matthews
1994   Eiders. In *Wildlife Notebook Series*. Juneau: Alaska Department of Fish and Game.

Rowe, Peter T.
1904   In the Land of the Midnight Sun. *The Spirit of Missions*, January 1904, pp. 46–49.

Saario, Doris J., and Brina Kessel
1966   Human Ecological Investigations at Kivalina. In Norman J. Wilimovsky and John N. Wolfe, eds., *Environment of the Cape Thompson Region, Alaska*, pp. 969–1039. Oak Ridge, TN: U.S. Atomic Energy Commission, Division of Technical Information.

Sage, Lena (1942)
1964.1   Personal communication to E. S. Burch, Jr., Kivalina, Alaska, July 25, 1964.
1964.2   Personal communication to E. S. Burch, Jr., Kivalina, Alaska, July 27, 1964.

Sage, Lowell, Sr. (1938)
1984   Personal communication to E. S. Burch, Jr., Kivalina, Alaska, March 7, 1984.

Sage, Mildred Kaguna (1916)
1965   Personal communication to E. S. Burch, Jr., Kivalina, Alaska, June 28, 1965.

Sage, Tommy Aġnagauraq (1893)
1965.1   Personal communication to E. S. Burch, Jr., Kivalina, Alaska, June 26, 1965.
1965.2   Personal communication to E. S. Burch, Jr., Kivalina, Alaska, July 13, 1965.

Sahlins, Marshall
1963   Poor Man, Rich Man, Big Man, Chief: Political Types in Melanesia and Polynesia. *Comparative Studies in Society and History* 5(3):285–303.

Saladin d'Anglure, Bernard
1986   Du Foetus au Chamane: La Construction d'un "Troisième Sexe" Inuit. *Études/Inuit/Studies* 10(1–2):25–113.

Samms, Carrie
1897–98   Journal of Carrie Samms, June 9, 1887, through June 30, 1898. California Yearly Meeting of Friends Church Archives, Whittier, California.
1899–1900   Friends Mission diary kept by Carrie Samms, July 1, 1899, through July 1, 1900. California Yearly Meeting of Friends Church Archives, Whittier, California.
1900–1   Journal of Friends Mission in Kotzebue, Alaska, from July 1, 1900, to June 30, 1901. California Yearly Meeting of Friends Archives, Whittier, California.
1901–2   Diary of Friends Mission from July 1, 1901, to July 3, 1902. California Yearly Meeting of Friends Archives, Whittier, California.

Sampson, Joe Pukuluk (1909)
1970   Personal communication to E. S. Burch, Jr., Noorvik, Alaska, March 31, 1970.

Sarychev, Gavril A.
1806–7   *Account of a Voyage of Discovery to the Northeast of Siberia, the Frozen Ocean and the Northeast Sea.* 2 vols. London: Richard Phillips.

Sauer, Martin
1802   *An Account of a Geographical and Astronomical Expedition to the Northern Parts of Russia . . . in the Years 1785 etc. to 1794.* London: T. Cadell.

Savelle, James M.
2000   Bowhead Whale and Gray Whale Selection by Prehistoric and Early Historic Alaskan Whaling Societies. Paper presented at the symposium on Native Whaling in the Western Arctic: Development, Spread, and Responses to Changing Environment. Anchorage, March 22, 2000.

Savelle, James M., and Allen P. McCartney
2003   Prehistoric Bowhead Whaling in the Bering Strait and Chukchi Sea Regions of Alaska: A Zooarchaeological Assessment. In Allen P. McCartney, ed., *Indigenous Ways to the Present: Native Whaling in the Western Arctic*, pp. 167–84. Edmonton: Canadian Circumpolar Institute Press; Salt Lake City: University of Utah Press.

Savok, James Putuuqti, Sr. (1911)
1986   Personal communication to E. S. Burch, Jr., Buckland, Alaska. February 19, 1986.

Schoephorster, Dale B., and Charles D. Bowen
1965   Soils of the Kobuk Area, Alaska. U.S. Department of Agriculture, Soil Conservation Service. [Typescript.] Copy seen at Arctic Environmental Information and Data Center, Anchorage, Alaska.

Schwan, Mark
1994   Raven. In *Wildlife Notebook Series*. Juneau: Alaska Department of Fish and Game.

Schweitzer, Peter P., and Evgeny Golovko

1995   Contacts Across Bering Strait, as Seen from Nevuqaq. In *Traveling Between Continents, Phase One*. Report prepared for the U.S. National Park Service, Alaska Regional Office.

Scott, G. Richard

1991   Dental Anthropology. *Encyclopedia of Human Biology*, vol. 2, pp. 789–804. San Diego: Academic Press.

Seemann, Berthold Carl

1853   *Narrative of the Voyage of H.M.S. "Herald" During the Years 1845–51 . . . in Search of Sir John Franklin*. 2 vols. London: Reeve and Company.

Selkregg, Lidia L., coordinator

1976a   *Alaska Regional Profiles*. Vol. II, *Arctic Region*. Anchorage: University of Alaska, Arctic Environmental Information and Data Center.

1976b   *Alaska Regional Profiles*. Vol. V, *Northwest Region*. Anchorage: University of Alaska, Arctic Environmental Information and Data Center.

Sereadlook, Pete (1930)

1999   Personal oral communication to E. S. Burch, Jr., Wales, Alaska, February 28, 1999.

Service, Elman

1975   *Origins of the State and Civilization: The Process of Cultural Evolution*. New York: W. W. Norton.

Seveck, Chester Sivviq (1890)

1951   Wolf kill observances. Personal communication to Charles Lucier, Kotzebue, Alaska, August 1951. In Charles Lucier Collection, box 3, folder 14, Archives, Alaska and Polar Regions Department, University of Alaska Fairbanks.

1973   *Longest Reindeer Herder*. Anchorage: Arctic Circle Enterprises.

Sheehan, Glenn W.

1995   Whaling Surplus, Trade, War, and the Integration of Prehistoric Northern and Northwestern Alaska Economies, A.D. 1200–1826. In Allen P. McCartney, ed., *Hunting the Largest Animals: Native Whaling in the Western Arctic and Subarctic*, pp. 185–206. Edmonton: Canadian Circumpolar Institute, University of Alberta. (Studies in Whaling, no. 3, Occasional Publication no. 36.)

1997   *In the Belly of the Whale: Trade and War in Eskimo Society*. Anchorage: Alaska Anthropological Association. (Aurora: Alaska Anthropological Association Monograph Series VI.)

Sheidt, Dolly Narvaq

1969.1   Personal communication to E. S. Burch, Jr., Kotzebue, Alaska, November 16, 1969.

1969.2   Personal communication to E. S. Burch, Jr., Kotzebue, Alaska, December 24, 1969.

Sheldon, Bertha

1976   Toothache. In Minnie Gray, Bertha Sheldon, Arthur Douglas, Sr., Mamie Beaver, and Lulu Geary, *Timimun Mamirrutit* ["Eskimo folk medicine"]. Kotzebue: The Mauneluk Cultural Heritage Program.

Sheldon, Charles Aqpaliq (1908)

1973–74.1   Misaq the shaman. Personal taped communication to Laurel Bland. Story #2. Original in possession of the author.

1973–74.2   The shaman from Point Hope. Personal taped communication to Laurel Bland. Story #3. Original in possession of the author.

1973–74.3   Akiñaaluk the shaman. Personal taped communication to Laurel Bland. Story #4. Original in possession of the author.

1973–74.4   The weasel. Personal taped communication to Laurel Bland. Story #5. Original in possession of the author.

1973–74.5   The vision. Personal taped communication to Laurel Bland. Story #6. Original in possession of the author.

1973–74.6   The phantom. Personal taped communication to Laurel Bland. Story #7. Original in possession of the author.

1973–74.7   Sautiłana the shaman. Personal taped communication to Laurel Bland. Story #8. Original in possession of the author.

1973–74.8 The giant shrew. Personal taped communication to Laurel Bland. Story #10. Original in possession of the author.

1973–74.9 The giant eagle. Personal taped communication to Laurel Bland. Story #11. Original in possession of the author.

1973–74.10 Iñuġun the shaman. Personal taped communication to Laurel Bland. Story #13. Original in possession of the author.

1973–74.11 The rafting accident. Personal taped communication to Laurel Bland. Story #14. Original in possession of the author.

1973–74.12 An accident. Personal taped communication to Laurel Bland. Story #15. Original in possession of the author.

1973–74.13 The little drum. Personal taped communication to Laurel Bland. Story #17. Original in possession of the author.

1973–74.14 My daddy, the shaman. Personal taped communication to Laurel Bland. Story #18. Original in possession of the author.

1973–74.15 A vision of caribou. Personal taped communication to Laurel Bland. Story #19. Original in possession of the author.

1973–74.16 Uyaan Island. Personal taped communication to Laurel Bland. Story #21. Original in possession of the author.

1973–74.17 Kituq the shaman. Personal taped communication to Laurel Bland. Story #23. Original in possession of the author.

1973–74.18 Łaakki and Old Man Mountain. Personal taped communication to Laurel Bland. Story #24. Original in possession of the author.

1973–74.19 Shamans. Personal taped communication to Laurel Bland. Story #25. Original in possession of the author.

1973–74.20 Qipmiałuk the shaman. Personal taped communication to Laurel Bland. Story #26. Original in possession of the author.

Shepherd, Peter
1994   Beaver. In *Wildlife Notebook Series*. Juneau: Alaska Department of Fish and Game.

Shepherd, Peter, and Herb Melchior
1994   Marten. In *Wildlife Notebook Series*. Juneau: Alaska Department of Fish and Game.

Shinkwin, Anne, and the North Slope Borough Planning Department
1978   *A Preservation Plan for Tigara Village*. Barrow: North Slope Borough Commission on History and Culture.

Simpson, John
ms.a   Sketch of a dancing hut at Hotham Inlet, and comments on same. John Simpson Papers, Rare Book, Manuscript, and Special Collections Library, Duke University, box 2; Eskimo files. Writings by Simpson, August 1853–54 & n.d.

ms.b   Undated and untitled word list, apparently from Hotham Inlet. John Simpson Papers, Rare Book, Manuscript, and Special Collections Library, Duke University, box 2; Eskimo files. Language notes, 1852–53 & n.d.

ms.c   Hotham's Inlet word list. John Simpson Papers, Rare Book, Manuscript, and Special Collections Library, Duke University, box 2; Eskimo files. Language notes, 1852–53 & n.d.

ms.d   Kotzebue Sound word list. John Simpson Papers, Rare Book, Manuscript, and Special Collections Library, Duke University, box 2; Eskimo files. Language notes, 1852–53 & n.d.

ms.e   List of seasons and moons, apparently from Hotham Inlet. John Simpson Papers, Rare Book, Manuscript, and Special Collections Library, Duke University, box 2; Eskimo files. Language notes, 1852–53 & n.d.

ms.f   Undated and untitled paper concerning childbirth. John Simpson Papers. Rare Book, Manuscript, and Special Collections Library, Duke University, box 2; Eskimo files. Writings by Simpson, August 1853 to May 1854 & n.d.

1850a   Journal of a journey from Chamisso Island to Spafarief Bay, January 9–12, 1850. John Simpson Papers, Rare Book, Manuscript, and Special Collections Library, Duke University, box 3; Eskimo files. Accounts of voyages, general, September 1849 to March 1854.

1850b   Journal of a journey from Chamisso Island to Hothams Inlet, January 15–25, 1850. John Simpson Papers, Rare Book, Manuscript, and Special Collections Library, Duke University, box 3; Eskimo files. Accounts of voyages, general, September 1849 to March 1854.

1850c   Journal of a detached party from Chamisso Island to the eastern head of Hotham's Inlet, Kotzebue Sound, in May, 1850. (A revised version of this was published in 1852.)

1851   List of moons obtained from "a native of King-a-gian" Cape Prince of Wales, February 5, 1851. John Simpson Papers, Rare Book, Manuscript, and Special Collections Library, Duke University, box 2; Eskimo files. Language notes, 1852–53 & nd.

1852a   Journal of Mr. John Simpson, surgeon of Her Majesty's Ship "*Plover*," in command of a detached party to the eastern head of Hotham's Inlet, Kotzebue Sound, in May, 1850. John Simpson Papers, Rare Book, Manuscript, and Special Collections Library, Duke University, box 3. Accounts of voyages, general, September 1849–54.

1852b   Journal of Mr. John Simpson, surgeon of Her Majesty's Ship "*Plover*," in command of a detached party to the eastern head of Hotham's Inlet, Kotzebue Sound, in May, 1850. In United Kingdom, House of Commons. *Sessional Papers, Accounts and Papers, 1852*, vol. 50, no. 1449, part VIII, pp. 91–93.

1852–54 Point Barrow Journal, 1852–1854. John Simpson Papers, Rare Book, Manuscript, and Special Collections Library, Duke University, box 5. Accounts of voyages, oversized, 1851–54.

1855   Observations on the Western Esquimaux and the Country They Inhabit; from Notes Taken During Two Years at Point Barrow, by Mr. John Simpson, Surgeon, R.N, Her Majesty's Discovery Ship "*Plover*." In House of Commons, United Kingdom. *Sessional Papers, 1854–55, Accounts and Papers*, vol. 35, no. 1898, pp. 917–42.

1875   Observations on the Western Eskimo and the Country They Inhabit. Reprint of 1855 report. In *A Selection of Papers on Arctic Geography and Ethnology, Reprinted and Presented to the Arctic Expedition of 1875*, pp. 233–75. London: Royal Geographical Society.

Skin, Arthur
1970   Personal communication to E. S. Burch, Jr., Selawik, Alaska, March 10, 1970.

Skin, Ray
1970   Personal oral communication to E. S. Burch, Jr., Selawik, Alaska, March 10, 1970.

Skoog, Ronald O.
1968   Ecology of the Caribou (*Rangifer tarandus granti*) in Alaska. Ph.D. thesis, University of California, Berkeley.

Smith, Agnes Utigruaq (1916)
1989   Personal communication to E. S. Burch, Jr., Kiana, Alaska, February 28, 1989.

Smith, Charlie Nalikkałuk (1898)
1970   Personal communication to E. S. Burch, Jr., Selawik, Alaska, March 10, 1970.

Smith, Elijah Everett
1873   Malimoot (Malemute) language, Kotzebue Sound, Alaska, comparative vocabulary. Summer, 1873. National Anthropological Archives, MS 319. Washington, DC: National Museum of Natural History, Smithsonian Institution.

Smith, Ella Putruq (1885)
1970   Personal communication to E. S. Burch, Jr., Kotzebue, Alaska, June 2, 1970.
1976   Personal communication to E. S. Burch, Jr., Kivalina, Alaska, April 8, 1976.

Smith, Kathleen Lopp, and Verbeck Smith, eds.
2001   *Ice Window: Letters from a Bering Strait Village 1892–1902*. Fairbanks: University of Alaska Press.

Snaith, Skip
1997   *Umiak: An Illustrated Guide*. Eastsound, WA: Walrose & Hyde.

Sokonik, Joe
1918   The Story of Kai-ya-yuh-tua-look. *The Eskimo* 2(5).

Solf, J. D., and Howard Golden
1994   River Otter. In *Wildlife Notebook Series*. Juneau: Alaska Department of Fish and Game.

Solomon, Madeline
1981   *Madeline Solomon—Koyukuk: A Biography*. Blaine, WA: Hancock House.

Sonne, Birgitte

1988 *Agayut. Nunivak Eskimo Masks and Drawings from the Fifth Thule Expedition, 1921–24, Collected by Knud Rasmussen.* Copenhagen: Gyldendal.

Sours, Lena Suuyuk (1892)

1984 Personal communication to E. S. Burch, Jr., Kotzebue, Alaska, April 28, 1984

1987 Personal communication to E. S. Burch, Jr., Kotzebue, Alaska, February 26, 1987.

Sowls, Arthur L., Scott A. Hatch, and Calvin J. Lensink

1978 *Catalog of Alaska Seabird Colonies.* Washington, DC: U.S. Department of the Interior, Fish and Wildlife Service, Office of Biological Services.

Spencer, Robert F.

1956 Map Making of the North Alaskan Eskimo. *Proceedings of the Minnesota Academy of Science* 23:46–50.

1959 *The North Alaskan Eskimo: A Study in Ecology and Society.* Washington, DC: Government Printing Office. (Bureau of American Ethnology Bulletin, 171.)

Speth, John D., and Katherine A. Spielmann

1983 Energy Source, Protein Metabolism, and Hunter-Gatherer Subsistence Strategies. *Journal of Anthropological Archaeology* 2(1):1–31.

Sprott, Julie E.

1998 *Raising Young Children in an Alaskan Iñupiaq Village: The Family, Cultural, and Village Environment of Rearing.* Final Report to the National Science Foundation and the Northwest Arctic Borough. Anchorage, Alaska.

1999 Institutionalizing Love: The *Nuniaq*-ing Custom among Alaskan Iñupiat. *Arctic* 52(2):152–59.

Stalker, Jacob Aakitchiaq (1924)

1970 Personal communication to E. S. Burch, Jr., Kotzebue, Alaska, April 6. 1970.

Stalker, John Pamiiqtaq (1910)

1965.1 Personal communication to E. S. Burch, Jr., Kivalina, Alaska, May 21, 1965.

1965.2 Personal communication to E. S. Burch, Jr., Kivalina, Alaska, June 5, 1965.

1965.3 Personal communication to E. S. Burch, Jr., Kivalina, Alaska, September 13, 1965.

1970.1 Personal communication to E. S. Burch, Jr., Shungnak, Alaska, January 27, 1970.

1970.2 Personal communication to E. S. Burch, Jr., Shungnak, Alaska, January 28, 1970.

1970.3 Personal communication to E. S. Burch, Jr., Shungnak, Alaska, January 30, 1970.

1976 Ilaganniq. Taped and translated by Art Douglas, Sr., April 21, 1976. Kotzebue: NANA Elders Council Collection (H88–2G-13).

1986 Personal communication to E. S. Burch, Jr., Noatak, Alaska, February 25, 1986.

Stanner, W. E. H.

1965 Aboriginal Territorial Organization: Estate, Range, Domain, and Regime. *Oceania* 36(1):1–26.

Stefansson, Vilhjalmur

1909 Northern Alaska in Winter. *Bulletin of the American Geographical Society* 41(10):601–10.

1914a Prehistoric and Present Commerce Among the Arctic Coast Eskimo. *Geological Survey of Canada Museum Bulletin* 6. (Anthropological Series, no. 3.)

1914b The Stefansson-Anderson Arctic Expedition of the American Museum: Preliminary Ethnological Report. *Anthropological Papers of the American Museum of Natural History,* vol. 14, pt. 1.

1933 Introduction, to the Anthropometry of the Western and Copper Eskimos, Based on Data of Vilhjalmur Stefansson by Carl C. Seltzer. *Human Biology* 5(3):313–70.

1944 *The Friendly Arctic: The Story of Five Years in the Polar Regions.* New edition, with new material. New York: MacMillan Co.

1951 *My Life with the Eskimo.* New York: MacMillan Co. (Republication of 1913 work.)

1955 Clothes Make the Eskimo. *Natural History* 64(1):32–41.

1956 Causes of Eskimo Birth-Rate Increase. *Nature* 178(4542):1132.

1958 Eskimo Longevity in Northern Alaska. *Science* 127(3288):16–19.

Stephenson, Bob
1994a   Arctic Fox. In *Wildlife Notebook Series*. Juneau: Alaska Department of Fish and Game.
1994b   Wolf. In *Wildlife Notebook Series*. Juneau: Alaska Department of Fish and Game.

Steward, Julian H.
1942   The Direct Historical Approach to Archaeology. *American Antiquity* 7(4):337–43.

Stone, Alfred Taapsuk (1907)
1976   Old Ways of Travel. Typescript. Kotzebue: NANA Elders Council Collection (H88–2A-33).

Stoney, George Morse
ms   Report of the "Northern Alaska Exploring Expedition, April 13, 1884–November 9, 1886." National Anthropological Archives, ms. no. 2925. Washington, DC: Smithsonian Institution.
1883   Survey of Hotham Inlet and the Kobuk Delta. Letters Received by the Revenue Cutter Service, 1867–1914. H37, vol. 40, 1883. Records of the Coast Guard, Record Group 26, National Archives, Washington, DC. (Also on Microcopy 641, roll 1, frames 640–641.)
1900   Naval Explorations in Alaska. *U.S. Naval Institute Proceedings, September and December, 1899*, 91:533–84, 92:799–849.

Stuck, Hudson
1920   *A Winter Circuit of Our Arctic Coast*. New York: Charles Scribner's Sons.

Sun, Joe Immałuuraq (1900)
1970   Personal communication to E. S. Burch, Jr., Shungnak, Alaska, January 28, 1970.
1985   *My Life and Other Stories*. Translated from the original Iñupiaq language by Susie Sun, and compiled from the English translations by David Libbey. Kotzebue: NANA Museum of the Arctic.
1989   Hunting on the North Slope. In Hannah Mendenhall, Ruthie Sampson, and Edward Tennant, eds., *Lore of the Inupiat: The Elders Speak. Utuqqanaat uqaaqtuaqtut. Uqaaqtuaŋich iñupiat.* Vol. I, pp. 31–46. Kotzebue: Northwest Arctic School District.

Sunno, Andrew Sannu (ca. 1857)
1951.1   First kill observances, Buckland Eskimo. Elephant Point, Alaska, April 25, 1951. In Charles Lucier Collection, box 3, folder 4, Archives, Alaska and Polar Regions Department, University of Alaska Fairbanks.
1951.2   Door covering for Buckland tupek (moss-covered house). Elephant Point, Alaska, May 8, 1951. In Charles Lucier Collection, box 3, folder 4, Archives, Alaska and Polar Regions Department, University of Alaska Fairbanks.
1951.3   Buckland Eskimo bird darts. Elephant Point, Alaska, May 8, 1951. In Charles Lucier Collection, box 3, folder 4, Archives, Alaska and Polar Regions Department, University of Alaska Fairbanks.
1951.4   Dog whip, Buckland Eskimo. Elephant Point, Alaska, April 15, 1951. In Charles Lucier Collection, box 3, folder 4, Archives, Alaska and Polar Regions Department, University of Alaska Fairbanks.
1951.5   Land-sea mammal taboo, Buckland Eskimo. Elephant Point, Alaska, April 19, 1951. In Charles Lucier Collection, box 3, folder 4, Archives, Alaska and Polar Regions Department, University of Alaska Fairbanks.
1951.6   A cycle of games and contests following the gift exchange at the messenger feast, Buckland. Account in Charles Lucier Collection, box 3, folder 4, Archives, Alaska and Polar Regions Department, University of Alaska Fairbanks.
1951.7   Before the Buckland messenger feast. Account in Charles Lucier Collection, box 3, folder 4, Archives, Alaska and Polar Regions Department, University of Alaska Fairbanks.
1951.8   Shaman's performance, fragmentary notes. Account in Charles Lucier Collection, box 3, folder 4, Archives, Alaska and Polar Regions Department, University of Alaska Fairbanks.
1951.9   Buckland fish weir (*saputit*). Account in Charles Lucier Collection, box 3, folder 4, Archives, Alaska and Polar Regions Department, University of Alaska Fairbanks.
1951.10   An amulet against wounds. Personal communication to Charles Lucier. In Charles Lucier Collection, box 3, folder 4, Archives, Alaska and Polar Regions Department, University of Alaska Fairbanks.

1951.11 Hunting amulets, Buckland Eskimo. Personal communication to Charles Lucier. In Charles Lucier Collection, box 3, folder 4, Archives, Alaska and Polar Regions Department, University of Alaska Fairbanks.

1951.12 An *angatkok* shows his power. Personal communication to Charles Lucier. In Charles Lucier Collection, box 3, folder 4, Archives, Alaska and Polar Regions Department, University of Alaska Fairbanks.

1951.13 The burning alive of the *angatkok* Sululikh. Personal communication to Charles Lucier. In Charles Lucier Collection, box 3, folder 4, Archives, Alaska and Polar Regions Department, University of Alaska Fairbanks.

1951.14 *Angatkok*ing with a buzz. Personal communication to Charles Lucier. In Charles Lucier Collection, box 3, folder 4, Archives, Alaska and Polar Regions Department, University of Alaska Fairbanks.

1951.15 Offering to the dead at the burial place. Personal communication to Charles Lucier. In Charles Lucier Collection, box 3, folder 4, Archives, Alaska and Polar Regions Department, University of Alaska Fairbanks.

1951.16 Caribou hunting. Personal communication to Charles Lucier. In Charles Lucier Collection, box 3, folder 4, Archives, Alaska and Polar Regions Department, University of Alaska Fairbanks.

1951.17 Feast for the dead, *Kungyikirok*. Personal communication to Charles Lucier. In Charles Lucier Collection, box 3, folder 4, Archives, Alaska and Polar Regions Department, University of Alaska Fairbanks.

1951.18 Pure and impure hunters. Personal communication to Charles Lucier. In Charles Lucier Collection, box 3, folder 4, Archives, Alaska and Polar Regions Department, University of Alaska Fairbanks.

1951.19 A hunting ceremony employing carved animal figures. Personal communication to Charles Lucier. In Charles Lucier Collection, box 3, folder 4, Archives, Alaska and Polar Regions Department, University of Alaska Fairbanks.

1951.20 Shaman's songs. Personal communication to Charles Lucier. In Charles Lucier Collection, box 3, folder 4, Archives, Alaska and Polar Regions Department, University of Alaska Fairbanks.

1951.21 Buckland shaman's masks. Personal communication to Charles Lucier. In Charles Lucier Collection, box 3, folder 4, Archives, Alaska and Polar Regions Department, University of Alaska Fairbanks.

1951.22 Cremation of a shaman. Personal communication to Charles Lucier. In Charles Lucier Collection, box 3, folder 4, Archives, Alaska and Polar Regions Department, University of Alaska Fairbanks.

1951.23 Spirit in the fire. Personal communication to Charles Lucier. In Charles Lucier Collection, box 3, folder 4, Archives, Alaska and Polar Regions Department, University of Alaska Fairbanks.

1951.24 About Tuqoa. Personal communication to Charles Lucier. In Charles Lucier Collection, box 3, folder 4, Archives, Alaska and Polar Regions Department, University of Alaska Fairbanks.

1951.25 Animals that weren't eaten at Buckland. Personal communication to Charles Lucier. In Charles Lucier's personal collection [AS-KAN-42].

1951.26 Buckland amulets and amulet body strap. Personal communication to Charles Lucier. In Charles Lucier's personal collection [AS-KAN-27].

1951.27 Buckland adze. Personal communication to Charles Lucier. In Charles Lucier's personal collection [AS-KAN-41].

1951.28 Boat building. Personal communication to Charles Lucier. In Charles Lucier's personal collection [AS-KAN-96].

1951.29 Blood revenge (*akisaakluq*). Personal communication to Charles Lucier. In Charles Lucier's personal collection [AS-KAN-23A].

1951.30 Buckland skin blanket toss. Personal communication to Charles Lucier. In Charles Lucier's personal collection [AS-KAN-50].

1951.31 Bird darts and bird arrows. Personal communication to Charles Lucier. In Charles Lucier's personal collection [AS-KAN-19b].

1951.32 Kanguirmiut [sic] beluga hunting harpoon head. Personal communication to Charles Lucier. In Charles Lucier's personal collection [AS-KAN-88].

1951.33 Bull roarer [imigilutaak]. Personal communication to Charles Lucier. In Charles Lucier Collection, box 3, folder 4, Archives, Alaska and Polar Regions Department, University of Alaska Fairbanks.

1951.34 Hare skin blankets. Personal communication to Charles Lucier. In Charles Lucier's personal collection [AS-KAN-97].

1951.35 Origin of Chamisso Island. Personal communication to Charles Lucier. In Charles Lucier's personal collection [AS-KAN-82].

1951.36 Caribou rewards man. Personal communication to Charles Lucier. In Charles Lucier's personal collection [AS-KAN-52].

1951.37 Ceremony with carved figures to better think success. Personal communication to Charles Lucier. In Charles Lucier's personal collection [AS-KAN-35B].

1951.38 Cooking with hot rocks. Personal communication to Charles Lucier. In Charles Lucier's personal collection [AS-KAN-28B].

1951.39 Patataktuutik: clapping to control animals. Personal communication to Charles Lucier. In Charles Lucier's personal collection [AS-KAN-70].

1951.40 Wooden dolls. Personal communication to Charles Lucier. In Charles Lucier's personal collection [AS-KAN-65].

1951.41 Death and burial customs at Buckland and Selawik. Personal communication to Charles Lucier. In Charles Lucier's personal collection [AS-KAN-49B].

1951.42 Death and burial customs: closing the corpse's eyes. Personal communication to Charles Lucier. In Charles Lucier's personal collection [AS-KAN-49A].

1951.43 Death and burial customs: a dead shaman is buried at St. Michael. Personal communication to Charles Lucier. In Charles Lucier's personal collection [AS-KAN-49C].

1951.44 Buckland food and fluids. Personal communication to Charles Lucier. In Charles Lucier's personal collection [AS-KAN-28A].

1951.45 Food gathering and storage. Personal communication to Charles Lucier. In Charles Lucier's personal collection [AS-KAN-10].

1951.46 Steam roasting food. Personal communication to Charles Lucier. In Charles Lucier's personal collection [AS-KAN-29].

1951.47 Netting a fox. Personal communication to Charles Lucier. In Charles Lucier's personal collection [AS-KAN-19].

1951.48 Buckland fish spears and harpoons. Personal communication to Charles Lucier. In Charles Lucier's personal collection [AS-KAN-38].

1951.49 Antler tubes: fish hook container. Personal communication to Charles Lucier. In Charles Lucier's personal collection [AS-KAN-43].

1951.50 Kuŋyikiǥuk: feast for dead. Personal communication to Charles Lucier. In Charles Lucier's personal collection [AS-KAN-24].

1951.51 River ice fish cache. Personal communication to Charles Lucier. In Charles Lucier's personal collection [AS-KAN-10].

1951.52 First animal kill observances. Personal communication to Charles Lucier. In Charles Lucier's personal collection [AS-KAN-13A].

1951.53 Two dart games. Personal communication to Charles Lucier. In Charles Lucier's personal collection [AS-KAN-80].

1951.54 Human/animal people. Personal communication to Charles Lucier. In Charles Lucier's personal collection [AS-KAN-54].

1951.55 "Pure" hunters. Personal communication to Charles Lucier. In Charles Lucier's personal collection [AS-KAN-57].

1951.56 Fall and winter houses. Personal communication to Charles Lucier. In Charles Lucier's personal collection [AS-KAN-7A].

1951.57 Inheritence [sic]. Personal communication to Charles Lucier. In Charles Lucier's personal collection [AS-KAN-26].

1951.58 Iñuktat: place of the dead. Personal communication to Charles Lucier. In Charles Lucier's personal collection [AS-KAN-61].

1951.59 *IlyaGanik* and his brothers: a Deering story. Personal communication to Charles Lucier. In Charles Lucier's personal collection [AS-KAN-91].

1951.60 Buckland ice creepers. Personal communication to Charles Lucier. In Charles Lucier's personal collection [AS-KAN-86].

1951.61 Man's composite knife. Personal communication to Charles Lucier. In Charles Lucier's personal collection [AS-KAN-64].

1951.62 *Kivyiksuat*: messenger feast at Buckland. Personal communication to Charles Lucier. In Charles Lucier's personal collection [AS-KAN-11].

1951.63 Were hunting and fishing places owned? Personal communication to Charles Lucier. In Charles Lucier's personal collection [AS-KAN-61].

1951.64 Buckland lamps. Personal communication to Charles Lucier. In Charles Lucier's personal collection [AS-KAN-17].

1951.65 Leather preparation and tanning. Personal communication to Charles Lucier. In Charles Lucier's personal collection [AS-KAN-30].

1951.66 Maps. Personal communication to Charles Lucier. In Charles Lucier's personal collection [AS-KAN-32].

1951.67 Tuqua: owner spirit. Personal communication to Charles Lucier. In Charles Lucier's personal collection [AS-KAN-68].

1951.68 Buckland shaman's masks. Personal communication to Charles Lucier. In Charles Lucier's personal collection [AS-KAN-27A].

1951.69 Buckland skin and leather [. . . ?] and wooden dance masks. Personal communication to Charles Lucier. In Charles Lucier's personal collection [AS-KAN-27B].

1951.70 Musical devices and instruments. Personal communication to Charles Lucier. In Charles Lucier's personal collection [AS-KAN-103].

1951.71 Buckland medicine. Personal communication to Charles Lucier. In Charles Lucier's personal collection [AS-KAN-48].

1951.72 Needles and needlecases. Personal communication to Charles Lucier. In Charles Lucier's personal collection [AS-KAN-55].

1951.73 Wound or skin plug for floating seal. Personal communication to Charles Lucier. In Charles Lucier's personal collection [AS-KAN-87].

1951.74 Buckland mineral pigments, uses and trade. Personal communication to Charles Lucier. In Charles Lucier's personal collection [AS-KAN-16A].

1951.75 Buckland Eskimo fired clay pot manufacture. Personal communication to Charles Lucier. In Charles Lucier's personal collection [AS-KAN-16].

1951.76 Hunting ptarmigan. Personal communication to Charles Lucier. In Charles Lucier's personal collection [AS-KAN-19A].

1951.77 Buckland girls' puberty observances. Personal communication to Charles Lucier. In Charles Lucier's personal collection [AS-KAN-84].

1951.78 Rules concerning animals and the killing of them. Personal communication to Charles Lucier. In Charles Lucier's personal collection [AS-KAN-13].

1951.79 Raven wins a wife and loses her. Personal communication to Charles Lucier. In Charles Lucier's personal collection [AS-KAN-53].

1951.80 Buckland and Selawik sleds and dog traction. Undated personal communication to Charles Lucier, Elephant Point. In Charles Lucier's personal collection [AS-KAN-8].

1951.81 Spirits of the dead. Personal communication to Charles Lucier. In Charles Lucier's personal collection [AS-KAN-31].

1951.82 Songs of derision. Personal communication to Charles Lucier. In Charles Lucier's personal collection [AS-KAN-100].

1951.83 Trading songs. Personal communication to Charles Lucier. In Charles Lucier's personal collection [AS-KAN-77].

1951.84 Behind a blanket toss song. Personal communication to Charles Lucier. In Charles Lucier's personal collection [AS-KAN-76].

1951.85 Song to a joking partner. Personal communication to Charles Lucier. In Charles Lucier's personal collection [AS-KAN-79].

1951.86 Koyukuk Indian Aliiniuktuk (song). Personal communication to Charles Lucier. In Charles Lucier's personal collection [AS-KAN-78].

1951.87 People flee a dead woman's spirit. Personal communication to Charles Lucier. In Charles Lucier's personal collection [AS-KAN-62].

1951.88 What shamans did: they taught dancing. Personal communication to Charles Lucier. In Charles Lucier's personal collection [AS-KAN-35A].

1951.89 What shamans did: they found belugas. Personal communication to Charles Lucier. In Charles Lucier's personal collection [AS- KAN-35C].

1951.90 Amateur shaman. Personal communication to Charles Lucier. In Charles Lucier's personal collection [AS-KAN-95].

1951.91 What shamans did: they showed their powers. Personal communication to Charles Lucier. In Charles Lucier's personal collection [AS-KAN-35].

1951.92 *Kaŋyirmiut* trading game. Personal communication to Charles Lucier. In Charles Lucier's personal collection [AS-KAN-89].

1951.93 Buckland taboos. Personal communication to Charles Lucier. In Charles Lucier's personal collection [AS-KAN-36].

1951.94 *TiGicak*: giant worm. Personal communication to Charles Lucier. In Charles Lucier's personal collection [AS-KAN-51].

1951.95 Buckland stone and metal tools and projectile points. Personal communication to Charles Lucier. In Charles Lucier's personal collection [AS-KAN-33].

1951.96 Training a boy to hunt. Personal communication to Charles Lucier. In Charles Lucier's personal collection [AS-KAN-67].

1951.97 Man's tool box. Personal communication to Charles Lucier. In Charles Lucier's personal collection [AS-KAN-74].

1951.98 *Itcalik*: domed tent. Personal communication to Charles Lucier. In Charles Lucier's personal collection [AS-KAN-7B].

1951.99 Men's and women's tatoos [sic]. Personal communication to Charles Lucier. In Charles Lucier's personal collection [AS-KAN-105].

1951.100 War's revenge and *Ayauhruaq*'s song. Personal communication to Charles Lucier. In Charles Lucier's personal collection [AS- KAN-75].

1951.101 Buckland yearly round, middle and late 19th century. Personal communication to Charles Lucier. In Charles Lucier's personal collection [AS-KAN-4].

1951.102 *Aŋuiaktuq*: war. Personal communication to Charles Lucier. In Charles Lucier's personal collection [AS-KAN-23].

1951.103 Wolf killer. Personal communication to Charles Lucier. In Charles Lucier's personal collection [AS-KAN-55].

1951.104 Some musical instruments and musical toys used by the Buckland Eskimo. Personal communication to Charles Lucier, Elephant Point, Alaska, February 2, 1951. In Charles Lucier Collection, box 3, folder 4, Archives, Alaska and Polar Regions Department, University of Alaska Fairbanks.

1951.105 Some remarks about facial tatooing [sic]. Personal communication to Charles Lucier, Elephant Point, Alaska, February 2, 1951. In Charles Lucier Collection, box 3, folder 4, Archives, Alaska and Polar Regions Department, University of Alaska Fairbanks.

1951.106 Information on owner's marks for the Buckland Eskimo. Personal communication to Charles Lucier, February 3, 1951. In Charles Lucier Collection, box 3, folder 4, Archives, Alaska and Polar Regions Department, University of Alaska Fairbanks

1951.107 Some animal kill observances among the Buckland Eskimo. Personal communication to Charles Lucier, February 3, 1951. In Charles Lucier Collection, box 3, folder 4, Archives, Alaska and Polar Regions Department, University of Alaska Fairbanks.

1951.108 Buckland Eskimo catch a fox in a net. Personal communication to Charles Lucier, Elephant Point, Alaska, April 13, 1951. In Charles Lucier Collection, box 3, folder 4, Archives, Alaska and Polar Regions Department, University of Alaska Fairbanks.

1951.109 Face covering for the dead, Buckland Eskimo. Personal communication to Charles Lucier, Elephant Point, Alaska, April 13, 1951. In Charles Lucier Collection, box 3, folder 4, Archives, Alaska and Polar Regions Department, University of Alaska Fairbanks.

1951.110 Buckland Eskimo lamp drip-pan. Personal communication to Charles Lucier, Elephant Point, Alaska, April 21, 1951. In Charles Lucier Collection, box 3, folder 4, Archives, Alaska and Polar Regions Department, University of Alaska Fairbanks.

1951.111 Flint working, fragmentary notes. Personal communication to Charles Lucier, Elephant Point, Alaska, April 21, 1951. In Charles Lucier Collection, box 3, folder 4, Archives, Alaska and Polar Regions Department, University of Alaska Fairbanks.

1951.112 Soapstone (?), use of by Kiwalik Eskimo. Personal communication to Charles Lucier, Elephant Point, Alaska, April 21, 1951. In Charles Lucier Collection, box 3, folder 4, Archives, Alaska and Polar Regions Department, University of Alaska Fairbanks.

1951.113 Feather "diadem," Buckland Eskimo. Personal communication to Charles Lucier, Elephant Point, Alaska, April 25, 1951. In Charles Lucier Collection, box 3, folder 4, Archives, Alaska and Polar Regions Department, University of Alaska Fairbanks.

1951.114 A boy becomes *angatkok*. Personal communication to Charles Lucier, April 28, 1951. In Charles Lucier Collection, box 3, folder 4, Archives, Alaska and Polar Regions Department, University of Alaska Fairbanks.

1951.115 Ghost of the dead, Buckland Eskimo. Personal communication to Charles Lucier, April 28, 1951. In Charles Lucier Collection, box 3, folder 4, Archives, Alaska and Polar Regions Department, University of Alaska Fairbanks.

1951.116 No child marriage (?), Buckland Eskimo. Personal communication to Charles Lucier, Elephant Point, Alaska, May 8, 1951. In Charles Lucier Collection, box 3, folder 4, Archives, Alaska and Polar Regions Department, University of Alaska Fairbanks.

1951.117 Buckland game increase ceremony. Personal communication to Charles Lucier, undated; no location given. In Charles Lucier Collection, box 3, folder 4, Archives, Alaska and Polar Regions Department, University of Alaska Fairbanks.

1951.118 Tiŋmakpak and [?]. Giant eagle and giant albatross. In Charles Lucier's personal collection [AS-KAN-63].

Sunno, Andrew Sannu (ca. 1857), and John Aulaġiaq Hadley (ca. 1880)

1951   Beliefs relating to caribou bones. Undated personal communication to Charles Lucier. In Charles Lucier Collection, box 3, folder 4, Archives, Alaska and Polar Regions Department, University of Alaska Fairbanks.

Sunno, Andrew Sannu (ca. 1857), John Aulaġiaq Hadley (ca. 1880), and John Kaunaaluk Konalook (1882)

1951   Buckland Eskimo swivels. Personal communication to Charles Lucier, Elephant Point, Alaska, April 13, 1951. In Charles Lucier Collection, box 3, folder 4, Archives, Alaska and Polar Regions Department, University of Alaska Fairbanks.

Swan, Alice

1983   Personal communication to E. S. Burch, Jr., Kivalina, Alaska, June 22, 1983.

Swan, Charlotte Saviugan (1913)

1964   Personal communication to E. S. Burch, Jr., Kivalina, Alaska, October 8, 1964.

1965.1   Personal communication to E. S. Burch, Jr., Kivalina, Alaska, May 16, 1965.

1965.2   Personal communication to Deanne M. Burch, Kivalina, Alaska, May 25, 1965.

1965.3   Personal communication to E. S. Burch, Jr., Kivalina, Alaska, May 28, 1965.

1965.4   Personal communication to Deanne M. Burch, Kivalina, Alaska, July 2, 1965.

Swan, Clinton Iŋnitchiaq (1913)

1964   Personal communication to E. S. Burch, Jr., Kivalina, Alaska, July 23, 1964.

1965.1   Personal communication to E. S. Burch, Jr., Kivalina, Alaska, May 28, 1965.

1965.2   Personal communication to E. S. Burch, Jr., Kivalina, Alaska, June 16, 1965.

1965.3   Personal communication to E. S. Burch, Jr., Kivalina, Alaska, August 14, 1965.

1965.4   Personal communication to E. S. Burch, Jr., Kivalina, Alaska, August 15, 1965.

1965.5   Personal communication to E. S. Burch, Jr., Kivalina, Alaska, August 24, 1965.

1967   Personal communication to E. S. Burch, Jr., Kivalina, Alaska, November 25, 1967.

1984.1   Personal communication to E. S. Burch, Jr., Kivalina, Alaska, March 7, 1984.

1984.2   Personal communication to E. S. Burch, Jr., Kivalina, Alaska, May 7, 1984.

Swan, Louis Aŋaiñ (b. 1891)

1965   Personal communication to E. S. Burch, Jr., Kivalina, Alaska, July 29, 1965.

Swan, Martha Nunamiu (1907)

1964   Personal communication to E. S. Burch, Jr., Kivalina, Alaska, August 18, 1964.

1965.1   Personal communication to E. S. Burch, Jr., Kivalina, Alaska, June 5, 1965.

1965.2   Personal communication to E. S. Burch, Jr., Kivalina, Alaska, June 18, 1965.
1965.3   Personal communication to E. S. Burch, Jr., Kivalina, Alaska, August 14, 1965.
1965.4   Personal communication to E. S. Burch, Jr., Kivalina, Alaska, August 18, 1965.
1965.5   Personal communication to E. S. Burch, Jr., Kivalina, Alaska, August 27, 1965.
1965.6   Personal communication to E. S. Burch, Jr., Kivalina, Alaska, September 18, 1965.
1965.7   Personal communication to Deanne M. Burch, Kivalina, Alaska, July 27, 1965.
1970   Personal communication to E. S. Burch, Jr., Kivalina, Alaska, February 10, 1970.
1976   Personal communication to E. S. Burch, Jr., Kivalina, Alaska, April 5, 1976.
1984.1   Personal communication to E. S. Burch, Jr., Kivalina, Alaska, March 5, 1984.
1984.2   Personal communication to E. S. Burch, Jr., Kivalina, Alaska, March 7, 1984.
1984.3   Personal communication to E. S. Burch, Jr., Kivalina, Alaska, March 12, 1984.
1984.4   Personal communication to E. S. Burch, Jr., Kivalina, Alaska, May 1, 1984.
1984.5   Personal communication to E. S. Burch, Jr., Kivalina, Alaska, May 5, 1984.

Swan, Martha Nunamiu (1907), and Milton Niaqualuk Swan (1904)
1964.1   Personal communication to E. S. Burch, Jr., Kivalina, Alaska, June 3, 1964.
1964.2   Personal communication to E. S. Burch, Jr., Kivalina, Alaska, June 4, 1964.
1964.3   Personal communication to E. S. Burch, Jr., Kivalina, Alaska, July 7, 1964.
1970   Personal communication to E. S. Burch, Jr., Kivalina, Alaska, February 10, 1970.
1976   Personal communication to E. S. Burch, Jr., Kivalina, Alaska, April 5, 1976.

Swan, Milton Niaqualuk (1904)
1964.1   Personal communication to E. S. Burch, Jr., Kivalina, Alaska, June 3, 1964.
1964.2   Personal communication to E. S. Burch, Jr., Kivalina, Alaska, July 23, 1964.

Swan, Nellie Kuyuurak (1922)
1984   Personal communication to E. S. Burch, Jr., Kivalina, Alaska, May 5, 1984.

Swan, Oscar Kiñugana (1923)
1965   Personal communication to E. S. Burch, Jr., Kivalina, Alaska, August 27, 1965.
1984   Personal communication to E. S. Burch, Jr., Kivalina, Alaska, May 2, 1984.

Swan, Victor (1932)
1989   Personal communication to E. S. Burch, Jr., Kivalina, Alaska, February 18, 1989.

Taggart, Harold F.
1954   Journal of William H. Ennis, Member, Russian-American Telegraph Exploring Expedition. *California Historical Society Quarterly* 33(1):1–11; 33(2):147–68.
1956   Journal of George Russell Adams. *California Historical Society Quarterly* 35(4):291–307.

Taylor, Ken
1994   Wolverine. *Wildlife Notebook Series.* Juneau: Alaska Department of Fish and Game.

Teben'kov, M. D.
1981   *Atlas of the Northwest Coasts of America, from Bering Strait to Cape Corrientes . . . Compiled by Captain 1st. Rank M. D. Teben'kov . . . 1852.* Translated and edited by Richard A. Pierce. Kingston, ON: Limestone Press.

Thomas, Austin (1899)
1965   Personal communication to E. S. Burch, Jr., Kivalina, Alaska, July 20, 1965.

Thomas, Evans Avli (1918)
1986   Personal communication to E. S. Burch, Jr., Buckland, Alaska, February 19, 1986.
1987   Personal communication to E. S. Burch, Jr., Buckland, Alaska, March 4, 1987.

Thomas, Mabel Ulugluk (1906)
1964   Personal communication to E. S. Burch, Jr., Kivalina, Alaska, June 27, 1964.

Thomas, Susie Siqvaun (1890)
1970   Personal communication to E. S. Burch, Jr., Deering, Alaska, April 15, 1970.

Thornton, Harrison R.
1931   *Among the Eskimos of Wales, Alaska, 1890–93.* Edited by Neda S. Thornton and William M. Thornton. Baltimore: Johns Hopkins Press.

Tickett, Herman Aumaałuuraq (1901)
1970.1   Personal communication to E. S. Burch, Jr., Kotzebue, Alaska, January 5, 1970.
1970.2   Personal communication to E. S. Burch, Jr., Kotzebue, Alaska, May 8, 1970.

Tiepleman, Ina Nagruk (1890)

1951   Some notes on tattooing as practiced at Topqok (Cape Espenberg). Personal communication to Charles Lucier, Alaska, January 2, 1951. In Charles Lucier Collection, box 3, folder 4, Archives, Alaska and Polar Regions Department, University of Alaska Fairbanks.

Till, Alison

1990   Written personal communication to Charles Lucier, March 10, 1990. Copy in possession of the author.

Till, Alison B., Julie A. Dumoulin, Bruce M. Gamble, Darrell S. Kaufman, and Paul I. Carroll

1986   Preliminary Geologic Map and Fossil Data, Solomon, Bendeleben, and Southern Kotzebue Quadrangles, Seward Peninsula, Alaska. U.S. Geological Survey Open-File Report 86–276.

Tingook, Christopher Tiŋuk (1881?)

n.d.   Undated handwritten notes from an interview with Christopher Tingook. Don Charles Foote Papers, box 4, folder 11, Alaska and Polar Regions Department, University of Alaska Fairbanks.

1960.1 Notes from an interview by Don Foote, Point Hope, Alaska, January 21, 1960. Don Charles Foote Papers, box 5, folder 6, Alaska and Polar Regions Department, University of Alaska Fairbanks.

1960.2 Notes from an interview by Don Foote, Point Hope, Alaska, January 29, 1960. Don Charles Foote Papers, box 5, folder 6, Alaska and Polar Regions Department, University of Alaska Fairbanks.

1960.3 Notes from an interview by Don Foote, Point Hope, Alaska, February 1, 1960. Don Charles Foote Papers, box 5, folder 6, Alaska and Polar Regions Department, University of Alaska Fairbanks.

1960.4 Life of Tingook. Notes from an interview by Don Foote, Point Hope, Alaska, February 9, 1960. Don Charles Foote Papers, box 4, folder 11, Alaska and Polar Regions Department, University of Alaska Fairbanks.

1961   Notes from an interview by Don Foote, Point Hope, Alaska, February 3, 1961. Don Charles Foote Papers, box 4, folder 12, Alaska and Polar Regions Department, University of Alaska Fairbanks.

1965   Notes from an interview by Don Foote, Point Hope, Alaska, July 26, 1965. Don Charles Foote Papers, box 4, folder 13, Alaska and Polar Regions Department, University of Alaska Fairbanks.

Tingook, Christopher Tiŋuk, and Jimmy Asatchaq Killiguvuk

1961   Stories and notes from an interview by Don Foote, Point Hope, Alaska, January 30, 1961. Don Charles Foote Papers, box 4, folder 12, Alaska and Polar Regions Department, University of Alaska Fairbanks.

Tocktoo, Eddie

1983   Subsistence activities. Interview by Gertrude Ningeulook, translated by Edgar Ningeulook. Kawerak Eskimo Heritage Program transcript no. SHH.83.044, Nome, Alaska.

Tocktoo, Grace Maniq (1914)

1984   Serpentine Hot Springs. Interview by Edgar Ningeulook, Shishmaref, Alaska. Undated. [Transcribed and translated by Edgar Ningeulook?] Kawerak Eskimo Heritage Program transcript no. SHH.84.031, Nome, Alaska.

Tocktoo, Molly Annigiina (1925)

1983.1 Two stories. Interview with Edgar Ningeulook, Shishmaref, Alaska, August 12, 1983. Translated and transcribed by Edgar Ningeulook. Kawerak Eskimo Heritage Program transcript no. SHH.83.026, Nome, Alaska.

1983.2 Pregnancy rules. Interview with Edgar Ningeulook, Shishmaref, Alaska, August 12, 1983. Translated and transcribed by Edgar Ningeulook. Kawerak Eskimo Heritage Program transcript no. SHH.83.029, Nome, Alaska.

1983.3 Stories. Interview with Georgiana Ahgupuk, Shishmaref, Alaska, May 20, 1983. Translated and transcribed by Georgiana Ahgupuk. Kawerak Eskimo Heritage Program transcript no. SHH.83.035, Nome, Alaska.

1983.4   History. Interview with Lucy Obruk, Shishmaref, Alaska, February 1, 1983. Kawerak Eskimo Heritage Program transcript SHH.83.050, Nome, Alaska.

1983.5   Naming. Interview with Mary Koutchak, Shishmaref, Alaska, September 28, 1983. Transcribed and translated by Edgar Ningeulook. Kawerak Eskimo Heritage Program transcript SHH.83.053, Nome, Alaska.

1983.6   Stories. Interview with Stella Weyiouanna, Shishmaref, Alaska, September 28, 1983. Transcribed and translated by Stella Weyiouanna. Kawerak Eskimo Heritage Program transcript SHH.83.064, Nome, Alaska.

Tocktoo, Molly Anigiina (1925), and Vincent Kiiziktaq Tocktoo (1925)

1999.1   Personal communication to E. S. Burch, Jr., Shishmaref, Alaska, March 3, 1999.

1999.2   Personal communication to E. S. Burch, Jr., Shishmaref, Alaska, March 4, 1999.

Tocktoo, Vincent Kiiziktaq (1925)

1983   Serpentine area. Interview with Edgar Ningeulook, Shishmaref, Alaska, May 19, 1983. Translated and transcribed by Edgar Ningeulook. Kawerak Eskimo Heritage Program transcript no. SHH.83.013, Nome, Alaska.

Townsend, Charles H.

1887   Notes on the Natural History and Ethnology of Northern Alaska. In M. A. Healy, *Report of the Cruise of the Revenue Marine Steamer 'Corwin' in the Arctic Ocean in the Year 1885*, pp. 81–102. Washington, DC: Government Printing Office.

Towkshjea, Julian

ms   Undated transcript of a story told to Don Foote, Noatak, Alaska. Don Charles Foote Papers, box 3, folder 1, pp. 97–109. Alaska and Polar Regions Department, University of Alaska Fairbanks.

1960.1   Notes from an interview by Don Foote, Noatak, Alaska, February 15, 1960. Don Charles Foote Papers, box 3, folder 1, Alaska and Polar Regions Department, University of Alaska Fairbanks.

1960.2   Notes from an interview by Don Foote, Noatak, Alaska, February 17, 1960. Don Charles Foote Papers, box 3, folder 1, Alaska and Polar Regions Department, University of Alaska Fairbanks.

1960.3   Notes from an interview by Don Foote, Noatak, Alaska, February 22, 1960. Don Charles Foote Papers, box 3, folder 1, Alaska and Polar Regions Department, University of Alaska Fairbanks.

Trollope, Henry

1855   Journal Kept by Commander Henry Trollope During a Trip from H. M. Sloop *Rattlesnake* in Port Clarence to King-A-Ghee, a Village Four or Five Miles Round Cape Prince of Wales, January 9, 1854–January 27, 1854. In House of Commons, United Kingdom. *Sessional Papers, 1854–55, Accounts and Papers*, vol. 35, no. 1898, pp. 868–79.

Tuckfield, Bob Qipmiuraq (1890)

1960   Notes from an interview by Don Foote, Point Hope, Alaska, January 27, 1960. Don Charles Foote Papers, box 5, folder 7, Alaska and Polar Regions Department, University of Alaska Fairbanks.

Tuckfield, Bob Qipmiuraq (1890), and Christopher Tiŋuk Tingook (1881?)

1960.1   Notes from an interview by Don Foote, Point Hope, Alaska, February 1, 1960. Don Charles Foote Papers, box 5, folder 6, Alaska and Polar Regions Department, University of Alaska Fairbanks.

1960.2   Notes from an interview by Don Foote, Point Hope, Alaska, February 4, 1960. Don Charles Foote Papers, box 5, folder 6, Alaska and Polar Regions Department, University of Alaska Fairbanks.

1960.3   Notes from an interview by Don Foote, Point Hope, Alaska, February 6, 1960. Don Charles Foote Papers, box 5, folder 6, Alaska and Polar Regions Department, University of Alaska Fairbanks.

Tundra Times

1969   Dr. Don Foote Dies of Cardiac Arrest After Car Wreck Injuries. *Tundra Times* 6(165):1, 6.

United States Department of the Interior, Alaska Planning Group
1974a   Proposed Cape Krusenstern National Monument: Final Environmental Impact Statement. Washington, DC: Government Printing Office.
1974b   Proposed Chukchi–Imuruk National Reserve: Final Environmental Impact Statement. Washington, DC: Government Printing Office.
1974c   Proposed Gates of the Arctic National Park: Final Environmental Impact Statement. Washington, DC: Government Printing Office.
1974d   Proposed Kobuk Valley National Monument: Final Environmental Impact Statement. Washington, DC: Government Printing Office.
1974e   Proposed Noatak National Arctic Range: Final Environmental Impact Statement. Washington, DC: Government Printing Office.
1974f   Proposed Selawik National Wildlife Refuge, Alaska: Final Environmental Impact Statement. Washington, DC: Government Printing Office.

Utqiaġvigmiut Aġviqsiuqtit Aġnaɲich
2000   *Piḷġallasiñiq Ivalupianik.* Learning to Braid 'Real' Thread. Iḷisaġvik College, Barrow, Alaska.

VanStone, James W.
1960   An Early Nineteenth Century Artist in Alaska: Louis Choris and the First Kotzebue Expedition. *Pacific Northwest Quarterly* 51(4):145–58.
1962a   Notes on Nineteenth Century Trade in the Kotzebue Sound Area, Alaska. *Arctic Anthropology* 1(1):126–28.
1962b   *Point Hope: An Eskimo Village in Transition.* Seattle: University of Washington Press.
1967   Eskimo Whaling Charms. *Field Museum Bulletin* 38(11):6–8.
1968/69   Masks of the Point Hope Eskimo. *Anthropos* 63/64:828–40.
1976   The Bruce Collection of Eskimo Material Culture from Port Clarence, Alaska. Chicago: Field Museum of Natural History. *Fieldiana: Anthropology* 67.
1980   The Bruce Collection of Eskimo Material Culture from Kotzebue Sound, Alaska. *Fieldiana: Anthropology* n.s. 1.
1990   The Nordenskiöld Collection of Eskimo Material Culture from Port Clarence, Alaska. *Fieldiana: Anthropology* n.s. 14.

VanStone, James W., ed.
1973   V. S. Khromchenko's Coastal Explorations in Southwestern Alaska, 1822. Translated by David H. Kraus. *Fieldiana: Anthropology* 64.
1977   A. F. Kashevarov's Coastal Explorations in Northwest Alaska, 1838. Translated by David H. Kraus. *Fieldiana: Anthropology* 69.

Van Valin, William B.
1944   *Eskimoland Speaks.* Caldwell, ID: Caxton Printers.

Varjola, Pirjo
1990   *Alaska: Venäjän Amerikka/Russian America.* Helsinki: Museovirasto/National Board of Antiquities [of Finland].

Varjola, Pirjo, with contributions by Julia P. Averkieva and Roza G. Liapunova
1990   *The Etholén Collection: The Ethnographic Alaskan Collection of Adolf Etholén and His Contemporaries in the National Museum of Finland.* Helsinki: National Board of Antiquities [of Finland].

Vestal, Leonard Putuuraq (1892)
1969   Personal oral communication to E. S. Burch, Jr., Kotzebue, Alaska, December 31, 1969.
1970   Personal oral communication to E. S. Burch, Jr., Kotzebue, Alaska, May 4, 1970.

Viereck, Eleanor G.
1987   *Alaska's Wilderness Medicines: Healthful Plants of the Far North.* Edmonds, WA: Alaska Northwest Publishing Company.

Viereck, L. A., C. T. Dyrness, A. R. Batten, and K. J. Wenzlick
1992   *The Alaska Vegetation Classification.* U.S. Department of Agriculture, Forest Service, Pacific Northwest Research Station. (General technical report PNW-GTR-286.)

Walker, Nelson
1986   Personal communication to E. S. Burch, Jr., Kotzebue, Alaska, February 21, 1986.

Walton, Regina Qiaġan (1885)
1965.1   Personal communication to E. S. Burch, Jr., Kivalina, Alaska, August 4, 1965.
1965.2   Personal communication to E. S. Burch, Jr., Kivalina, Alaska, August 12, 1965.
1965.3   Personal communication to E. S. Burch, Jr., Kivalina, Alaska, August 28, 1965.

Weeden, Robert B.
1994   Ptarmigan. In *Wildlife Notebook Series*. Juneau: Alaska Department of Fish and Game.

Wells, James K.
1974   *Ipani Eskimos: A Cycle of Life in Nature*. Anchorage: Alaska Methodist University Press.

Wells, Roger, and John W. Kelly
1890   *English-Eskimo and Eskimo-English Vocabularies, Preceded by Ethnographical Memoranda Concerning the Arctic Eskimos in Alaska and Siberia*. Washington, DC: Government Printing Office. (Bureau of Education Circular of Information, no. 2.)

Wesley, Floyd Maasak (1921)
1986   Personal communication to E. S. Burch, Jr., Noatak, Alaska, February 25, 1986.

Weyapuk, Winton Uyaapak (1908)
1991.1   Personal communication to E. S. Burch, Jr., Wales, Alaska, July 8, 1991.
1991.2   Personal communication to E. S. Burch, Jr., Wales, Alaska, July 8, 1991.

Weyer, Edward M., Jr.
1928   Field notes of the Stoll-McCracken expedition. Department of Anthropology Archives, American Museum of Natural History, New York.

Weyiouanna, Alex Nuusi (1918)
1983   Interview with Edgar Ningeulook, July 14, 1983, Shishmaref, Alaska. Kawerak Eskimo Heritage Program transcript no. SH/EN.83.020-T1, Nome, Alaska.
1999   Personal communication to E. S. Burch, Jr., Shishmaref, Alaska, March 5, 1999.

Weyiouanna, Alex Nuusi (1918), and Elsie Aapaagłuq Weyiouanna (1920)
1999   Personal communication to E. S. Burch, Jr., Shishmaref, Alaska, March 3, 1999.

Weyiouanna, Ardith Sukiniq (1947)
1983   Childbirth. Interview with Dorothy Waghiyi, Shishmaref, Alaska, September 30, 1983. Translated and transcribed by Edgar Ningeulook. Kawerak Eskimo Heritage Program transcript no. SHH.83.008, Nome, Alaska.

Weyiouanna, Elsie Aapaagłuq (1920)
1981   Native life style. Interview with Lucy Obruk, Shishmaref, Alaska, November 20, 1981. Translated and transcribed by Lucy Obruk. Kawerak Eskimo Heritage Program transcript no. SHH.83.049, Nome, Alaska.
1983.1   Short stories. Interview with Edgar Ningeulook, Shishmaref, Alaska, August 22, 1983. Translated and transcribed by Edgar Ningeulook. Kawerak Eskimo Heritage Program transcript no. SHH.83.027, Nome, Alaska.
1983.2   Adoption. Interview with Mary Koutchuk, Shishmaref, Alaska, September 20, 1983. Translated and transcribed by Georgianna Ahgupuk. Kawerak Eskimo Heritage Program transcript no. SHH.83.054, Nome, Alaska.

Weyiouanna, Essau Kaġikłuiłak (1925)
1983.1   Childrearing stories. Interview by Edgar Ningeulook, Shishmaref, Alaska, August 2, 1983. [Transcribed and translated by Edgar Ningeulook?] Kawerak Eskimo Heritage Program transcript no. SHH.83.024, Nome, Alaska.
1983.2   Subsistence, weather. Interview by Sophie Weyiouanna, Shishmaref, Alaska, May 10, 1983. Transcribed and translated by Sophie Weyiouanna. Kawerak Eskimo Heritage Program transcript no. SHH.83.055, Nome, Alaska.
1983.3   Seasonal hunting. Interview by Sophie Weyiouanna, Shishmaref, Alaska, June 21, 1983. Transcribed and translated by Sophie Weyiouanna. Kawerak Eskimo Heritage Program transcript no. SHH.83.056, Nome, Alaska.

1983.4   Animal migrations, hunting. Interview by Sophie Weyiouanna, Shishmaref, Alaska, August 19, 1983. Transcribed by Sophie Weyiouanna, translated by Georgianna Ahgupuk. Kawerak Eskimo Heritage Program transcript no. SHH.83.057, Nome, Alaska.

1987   Hunting, yearly cycle. Interview by Stella Weyiouanna, Shishmaref, Alaska, March 19, 1987. Transcribed and translated by Stella Weyiouanna. Kawerak Eskimo Heritage Program transcript no. SHH.87.065, Nome, Alaska.

White, James Taylor

1889   Diary, *"Bear"* Cruise, 1889. Transcribed from the original by Gary Stein. James T. White Papers, University of Alaska Archives, Anchorage.

Whitridge, Peter

1999   The Construction of Social Difference in a Prehistoric Inuit Whaling Community. Ph.D. thesis, Arizona State University. Ann Arbor, MI: University Microfilms International.

Whymper, Frederick

1868   A Journey from Norton Sound, Bering Sea, to Fort Yukon. *Journal of the Royal Geographical Society* 38:219–37.

1869a   Russian America, or 'Alaska': The Natives of the Youkon River and Adjacent Country. *Transactions of the Ethnological Society of London* 7:167–85.

1869b   *Travel and Adventure in the Territory of Alaska.* New York: Harper and Bros.

Willner, Gale R., George A. Feldhamer, Elizabeth E. Zucker, and Joseph A. Chapman

1980   *Ondatra zibethicus. Mammalian Species* 141:1–8.

Wood, Charley Uluġaaġruk (ca. 1852)

1931   The Oppownie (old) Eskimo and his customs, as told by Eliyak (Pechuk) and Oolooaharuk (Charley Wood), as told to Ira S. Purkeypile, Selawik, Alaska. Typed transcript appended to Bulletin of the N.W. District, U.S. Department of the Interior, Office of Indian Affairs, Alaska Division, October 28, 1931 [Kotzebue, Alaska]. Bland Collection, box 30, folder 38, Alaska and Polar Regions Department, University of Alaska Fairbanks.

Wood, Nellie Nakauraq (1908)

1986   Personal communication to E. S. Burch, Jr., Noatak, Alaska, February 25, 1986.

Woodburn, James

1982   Egalitarian Societies. *Man* 17(3):431–51.

Wolfe, James

ms   *Journal of a Voyage on Discovery in the Pacific and Beering's Straits on Board H.M.S. Blossom, Capt. F. W. Beechey.* Yale University, Beinecke Rare Book and Manuscript Library, New Haven, Connecticut.

Woolfe, Henry D.

1890   Letter to Sheldon Jackson dated December 18, 1890. Published by Sheldon Jackson in *Report on Educational Affairs in Alaska: Report of the Commissioner of Education for 1892–93,* whole no. 218, vol. 2, pp. 1726–27.

1893   The Seventh or Arctic District. In Robert P. Porter, *Report on the Population and Resources of Alaska: Eleventh Census of the United States, 1890,* pp. 129–52. Washington, DC: Government Printing Office.

1894   Names of the Native Tribes of Northwest Alaska, Their Villages and Approximate Geographical Positions. In Sheldon Jackson, *Report on Introduction of Domesticated Reindeer into Alaska. [Third report.] Report of the U.S. Bureau of Education,* whole no. 215, pp. 181–83. Washington, DC: Government Printing Office.

Worl, Rosita

1980   The North Slope Inupiat Whaling Complex. *Senri Ethnological Studies* 4:305–20.

Wright, John Qaniqsiruaq (1885)

1969.1   Personal communication to E. S. Burch, Jr., Kotzebue, Alaska, December 1, 1969.

1969.2   Personal communication to E. S. Burch, Jr., Kotzebue, Alaska, December 10, 1969.

Young, Christopher

2002   Late Western Thule House Construction in Northwest Alaska: The "Kobuk-Type" House. In Don E. Dumond and Richard L. Bland, eds., *Archaeology in the Bering Strait Region:*

Research on Two Continents, pp. 207–26. Eugene: University of Oregon. (Anthropological Papers, no. 59).

Young, Steven B., ed.
1974   *The Environment of the Noatak River Basin, Alaska. Results of the Center for Northern Studies Biological Survey of the Noatak River Valley, 1973.* (Contributions from the Center for Northern Studies, no. 1). Wolcott, VT: The Center for Northern Studies.

Zimmerly, David W.
2000   *Qayaq: Kayaks of Alaska and Siberia.* Fairbanks: University of Alaska Press.

Zimmerman, Michael R., and Arthur C. Aufderheide
1984   The Frozen Family of Utqiagvik: The Autopsy Findings. *Arctic Anthropology* 21(1):53–64.

Zimmerman, Michael R., Anne M. Jensen, and Glenn W. Sheehan
2000   Agnaiyaaq: The Autopsy of a Frozen Thule Mummy. *Arctic Anthropology* 37(2):52–59.

Index

Page numbers in *italics* refer to illustrations.

drills and drilling, 203, 204, 207,
    226, 242, 260, 262, 263
  of amber, 192
  bow, 205, 226
  of ivory, 201, 203
  of stones, 196, 202, 204, 238
  of wood, 210, 248, 253, 259
drive fences, 134–136, *135*, 196
drives, 111
  of beluga, 164, 266
  of caribou, 134–136, 137–138,
    296n8; leadership and, 68,
    266; shrubs used in, 187; use
    of snow houses during, 219
  of hares, 174
  of ptarmigan, 181
  of waterfowl, 111, 179
drumming, 356–359, 360, 363
  by shamans, 69, 73, 281–282,
    348, 371, 373
drums, 169, 186, 357, 358, 364
  box (*kalukaq*), 258, 360, 363
  shaman's, 291, 364–365, 374
  tambourine (*qilaun*), 258, 357,
    363
ducks, 178–179
  capturing, 240–241, 247
  for clothing, 208, 210, 262
  and pottery temper, 227
  See also waterfowl
dwelling units, 97, 118, 119, 120,
    122, 123. *See also* houses;
    huts; shelters
dye, 65, 187, 208, 258

E

eagles, 27, 183, 210, 257, 260, 368
easements, 165, 315, 331, 334
economic allocation: and role
    differentiation, 53, 64, 65,
    66–71, 314, 315
economic process, 10, 133–106
  definition of, 133, 296n1
education: adult, 346–347
  of children, 92
  process of, 72, 85, 263–264,
    342–348
eggs: bird, 27, 36, 179, 180, 182,
    184, 212, 213, 291
  fish, 36, 146, 213
elders (sing. *utuqqanaaq*), 60, 63,
    92, 102, 125, 256, 307–308
  abandonment of, 86
  care of, 86, 92, 272, 286, 308
  contributions of, 61, 144, 180,
    184, 308
  grandchildren and, 92, 339

information provided by, xiii, 5,
    13–15, 384, 390; on fish, 27;
    on settlements, 103
  learning from, 72, 74, 103, 344
  power of, 308, 318
  qargich and, 105, 110
  in summer settlements, 36, 38,
    40, 102, 105, 143, 292, 356
entertainment, 54, 61, 74, 262,
    264, 323, 364. *See also* feasts
    and feasting; festivals
environment, 114, 126, 266, 294,
    295, 332
  nonempirical, 258, 320, 323, 350
environmental thresholds, 22,
    332, 333
epidemics, 2, 3, 333, 386, 387, 390
equipment, 292–293, 314
  capital stock of, 67, 316
  as fee for service, 110
  fire-making, 207, 226, 229
  fishing, 27, 52, 229, 234,
    247–249, 283
  for games, 354, 356
  hunting, 232–247
  inheritance of, 314
  maintenance of, 263
  manufacture of, 54, 81, 106
  military, 261–262, 330
  net-making, 246
  ownership of, 315, 316; and
    property marks, 271,
    274–275
  repair of, 54, 64, 288
  sewing, 208, 224, 229, 230
  stored in *qargi*, 221, 330
  tools, 201–207
  for transportation, 249–254
  utensils, 230–231
  weapons, 232–237, 261–262,
    267, 330
ermines, 25, 175, 257, 260, 368,
    369
Eschscholtz Bay, 19, 26, *43*, 43,
    44, 45, 48, 68, 161, 164, 373
"Eskimo ice cream" (*akutuq*), 188,
    213, 272
Espenberg Peninsula, *18*, 24, 178
estates: national, 331–332, 349
  Akuniġmiut, 38, 39
  coastal, 53, 165, 171, 276, 363
  and conflict, 267–268, 349
  defined, 7, 8
  inland, 165
  Kaŋiġmiut, 43, 57
  Kiitaaġmiut, 41, 88, 105
  Kiŋikmiut, 45, 48
  Kivalliñiġmiut, 33, 35, 57, 105
  Kuuŋmiut, 41

Napaaqtuġmiut, 33, 35, 38, 39,
    57, 314, 315
  Nuataaġmiut, 38, 39, 40, 41,
    137, 165, 348
  Qikiqtaġruŋmiut, 39, 45, 57,
    165, 314, 315
  Pittaġmiut, *47*, *49*, *50*, 105
  and property rights, 314–315
  Siilviim Kaŋianiġmiut, 41,
    88, 105
  solidarity of, 126–128
  Tapqaġmiut, 45, 48, 57
  Tikiġaġmiut, 33, 333
  *See also under specific districts
    and nations*
evening activities, 54–55, 56, 80,
    98, 264, 367
expeditions, 12, 383
  Beechey, 4, 12, 122, 329, 347,
    356, 375, 376, 384, 390
  Billings, 12
  Franklin search, 2, 12, 384–386
  International Polar Year, 388
  Kashevarov, 12, 384
  Kotzebue, 12, 383–384
  Revenue Marine, 12, 387–388
  Stefansson, 389
  Stoney, 376, 388
  Vasil'ev-Shishmarev, 390
  Western Union Telegraph, 221,
    358, 386, 387
explorers, 65, 383–386, 388
  See also specific explorers
expression: affective, 81, 310,
    374–376
  artistic, 376–378
expressions: facial, 339, 341, 358,
    367, 374–376
expulsion, 308, 328

F

factions, 108, 119–120, 124, 312
fall (*ukiaq*), 32, 52, 97, 229
  animal movements in, 25, 26,
    41, 148, 156, 165, 167, 169
  camps in, 41, 290, 347
  caribou hunting in, 25, 32, 33,
    38, 41, 43, 53, 135, 136
  ceremonies in, 267
  daily cycle in, 53–55, 56
  dwellings in, 41, 96–97, 104
  fishing in, 33, 34, 38, 41, 42,
    43, 53, 65, 143
  food gathering in, 184
  food preservation in, 138, 139,
    147, 170
  freezeup and, 25, 34, 38, 52,
    103, 148, 151, 214, 287
  game playing in, 354

settlements (*continued*)
  simple, 33, 41, 48, 56, 63,
    102–103, 105, 106, 108,
    353, 383; examples of, *107*,
    101, *102*, 220–221; isolation
    of, 80, 103, 105, 126, 266,
    273; names of, 101; political
    process in, 308, 310–311,
    329; *qargich* in, 54, 106,
    308; recreation in, 356–357;
    residents of, 106, 273, 275,
    276–277; vulnerability of,
    283, 319. *See also* camps
  spring, *35*, *44*, *49*
  summer, *36*, *40*, *46*, *50*, 105,
    218
  See also camps; settlement
    location; villages
Seward Peninsula, 5, 17, *18*, 19,
  23, 24, 27, 172, 198
  caribou herd, 24, 386, 387
  exploration of, 12, 383, 384,
    385, 386
sewing equipment. *See* bodkins;
  needles; scrapers; thimbles;
  thread
sex and role differentiation, 15,
  31, 59, 64–65, 80, 81, 85
sexual intercourse, 79, 80, 115,
  309, 311, 323
sexual partners. *See* partners,
  sexual
shamans (sing. *aŋatkuq*), 68–69,
  73, 319
  amulets and, 260, 369
  dancing and, 357, 371
  as doctors, 110–111, 199, 279
  equipment of, 175, 257, 258,
    260
  failure of, 376
  feats of, 130*n*45, 364–366,
    373–374
  gender/sex of, 65, 81, 310, 323
  hiring, 274, 279, 323
  and integration process, 348–
    349, 364–366, 371, 374
  killing of, 326
  masks and, 258–259, 374, 281,
    377
  performance of rituals by, 266,
    323, 371
  power of, 317, 323–324
  ravens and, 184
  recruitment of, 68–69, 319,
    345–346
  research by, 348–349
  role of, 66, 68–69, 73
  and spirits, 295, 348, 371
  taboos and, 322
  use of dolls by, 348

use of magic by, 281–282,
  372–373
weasels and, 175
whaling and, 112, 163
shares of harvest, 28, 145, 153,
  171, 179, 181, 316, 327
  of bowhead whales, 112, 158,
    160, 162–163, 239
  See also distribution; division of
    harvest; pooling; portions;
    sharing; trade
sharing, 86, 91, 94, 153, 271–272,
  276–277, 316, 347, 356
  dwellings, 66, 89, 97, 117, 119
  food, 316, 356
  See also distribution; division of
    harvest; pooling; portions;
    trade
sheefish, 26, 43, 48, 145, 219
sheep. *See* Dall sheep
shelters, 219–220, 288, 293
  boats as, 55, 106, 220
  for dogs, 284
  during festivals, 106
  on sea ice, 158, 219
  while traveling, 55, 211, 219,
    288
  use of bark in, 186
  use of grass in, 191
  See also huts
Sheshalik Spit. *See* Sisualik
Shishmaref (village), 14, *20*, 21,
  45, 197, 268, 269, 275, 284,
  363, 364
Shishmaref district, 1, 7, 26, 69,
  179, 195, 198, 200. *See also*
  Tapqaġmiut (nation)
shorebirds, 181–182, 343
shovels (sing. *piksrun*), 186, 190,
  194, 206, 216, 219, 222, 223
shrubs, 19, 23, 56, 170, 174, 181,
  185, 187, 188, 284, 287, 290
  uses of, 134, 135, 140, 187, 285
  See also alders; willows
siblings. *See* relationships, sibling
Siiḷviim Kaŋianiġmiut (nation),
  60, 190, 191, 216
  estate of, 7, 8, 88
  population of, 7
  settlements of, 41, *42*, 43, *44*,
    45, *46*
  yearly cycle of, 41–45
  See also Upper Selawik district
Simpson, John, 4, 5, 12, 51, 203,
  220, 222, 254, 313, 318,
  355, 385–386
  on families, 72, 83, 88, 277
  on houses, 98, 100, 216, 217
sinew, 165, 174, 175, 181, 228,
  242, 243, 261, 371

caribou, 138, 139, 140, 205,
  208, 230, 235, 252, 281
  uses of, 58, 61, 64, 140, 176,
    232, 233, 234, 240, 246,
    254, 258
singing. *See* songs and singing
sinkers, 140, 142, 143, 169, 196,
  201, 247, 249
sisters, 62, 63, 87, 88, 95, 102,
  129*n*5, 326
  See also relationships, sibling
Sisualik, 21, 39, 48, *50*, 218, 347
  beluga hunt at, 161, 164, 165,
    364
  Kuuŋmiut at, 43, 45
  Napaaqtuġmiut at, 39, 40
  Qikiqtaġruŋmiut at, 48, 51, 127
Sisualik trade fair, 36, 37, 51,
  75*n*19, 274, 276, 353, 390
  description of, 364
  information gathering at, 331,
    348
  skill, 112, 167, 204, 242, 250,
    273, 312, 313, 318, 364,
    369, 376
  variations in, 73, 116, 169, 266,
    274, 293–294, 309, 377
skylights, 169, 217, 221, 226, 270,
  295, 354, 372
slate, 192, 195, 201, 202, 204,
  205, 207, 235, 236, 262, 280
slaves (sing. *tigutaaluq*), 65, 71,
  312, 329
sleds, 22, 41, 52, 67, 124, 272,
  285–288, 291, 314
  maintenance of, 106, 119, 176,
    223, 263
  manufacture of, 187, 207, 243,
    253, 269
  propulsion of, 22, 65, 84, 253,
    283
  travel with, 55, 56, 218, 253,
    254, 269, 276, 327
  types of, 153, *252*, *253*
slingshots, 5, 180, 182, 321, 352
smelt, 26, 141, 145, 146
snares, 181, 240–241, 243, 245,
  312, 343, 344
  bear, 170, 171, 240
  bird, 179, 182, 183, 184
  caribou, 135–137, 144, 236,
    240, 292, 295, 326
  Dall sheep, 177, 239
  fox, 175
  ground squirrel, 173, 292
  hare, 174, 292
  marmot, 172
  mustelid, 175
  ptarmigan, 175, 181, 292, 346
  See also traps